Daryl Siedentop

Jacqueline Herkowitz

Ohio State University

Judith Rink

University of South Carolina

Elementary Physical Education Methods

PRENTICE-HALL, INC., ENGLEWOOD CLIFFS, NEW JERSEY 07632

Library of Congress Cataloging in Publication Data

SIEDENTOP, DARYL.
 Elementary physical education methods.

 Bibliography: p.
 Includes index.
 1. Physical education for children—Study and teach-
ing. I. Herkowitz, Jacqueline. II. Rink, Judith.
III. Title.
GV363.S525   1984   372.8'6044   83-4585
ISBN 0-13-259382-3

Editorial/production supervision: *Edith Riker*
Interior design: *Edith Riker*
Manufacturing buyer: *Harry Baisley*
Cover design: *Diane Saxe*
Cover illustration: *Jody Fulks*

Printed in the United States of America

10 9 8 7 6 5 4 3 2 1

ISBN 0-13-259382-3

Prentice-Hall International, Inc., *London*
Prentice-Hall of Australia Pty. Limited, *Sydney*
Editora Prentice-Hall do Brasil, Ltda., *Rio de Janiero*
Prentice-Hall Canada Inc., *Toronto*
Prentice-Hall of India Private Limited, *New Delhi*
Prentice-Hall of Japan, Inc., *Tokyo*
Prentice-Hall of Southeast Asia Pte. Ltd., *Singapore*
Whitehall Books Limited, *Wellington, New Zealand*

contents

Part One
UNDERSTANDING CHILDREN

1
the role of play and movement in childhood

1

2
learning motor skills
10

3
affective development and physical activity
19

4
efficiency of movement
30

5
growth and physical activity

46

6
physical fitness

64

7
perceptual-motor development
81

Part Two
TEACHING CHILDREN

8
planning for effective learning
94

9
current concepts of teaching
111

TEACHER ROLES AND
EFFECTIVENESS, *111*

The Many Roles of the Teacher, *111*
Characteristics of Effective Teaching, *112*
A Question of Style, *114*
A Note on Direct Instruction, *115*

MODELS FOR INSTRUCTION IN
PHYSICAL EDUCATION, *115*

Mosston's Spectrum of Styles, *115*
The Environment as Teacher, *118*

CURRENT INNOVATIONS IN
ORGANIZING FOR
INSTRUCTION, *118*

Contracting, *119*
Programmed Learning Units, *119*
The Open Gymnasium, *120*
Stations, *121*
Task Cards and Task Teaching, *121*
Teaching Aides, *122*

IMPROVING OUTCOMES, *122*

Enhancing Cognitive Outcomes, *122*
Enhancing Affective Outcomes, *123*

10
developing a climate for personal growth
125

PERSONAL GROWTH AND STUDENT-
TEACHER INTERACTIONS, *125*

Factors in Personal Growth, *125*
Student-Teacher Interactions, *126*
Building Positive Interaction Skills, *127*
A Word about Punishment, *128*
Believability, Sincerity, and Positive
  Teaching, *128*
The Personal Touch, *129*
Growth through Enthusiasm, *130*
Student-Student Interactions, *130*

COMMUNICATION SKILLS, *130*

Intrapersonal Communication Skills, *130*
Interpersonal Communication Skills, *131*
Roadblocks to Communication, *133*

COPING MECHANISMS USED BY
  CHILDREN, *134*
THE HELPING RELATIONSHIP, *135*

11
managing groups of children
136

12
the exceptional child in physical education
153

13
developmentally engineered equipment and playgrounds
172

DEVELOPMENTALLY ENGINEERED EQUIPMENT, *172*

Accommodating Physical Growth of Young Children, *172*

Equipment that Provides Knowledge of Results (KR), *177*

Facilitating the Acquisition of Ballistic Skills, *179*

Facilitating the Acquisition of Receipt Skills, *181*

Encouraging Normal Posture and Physical Fitness, *182*

Providing for Children's Safety, *182*

DEVELOPMENTALLY ENGINEERED PLAYGROUNDS, *184*

Encouraging Motor Activity, *184*

Provide for All Forms of Motor Play, *186*

Part Three
MOVEMENT EDUCATION

14
movement education
188

DISTINGUISHING CHARACTERISTICS, *188*
CONTENT, *191*
THE MOVEMENT FRAMEWORK OF RUDOLPH LABAN, *191*

What the Body Is Doing, *191*

The Use of Space, *193*

The Effort Aspect, *194*

The Relationship Aspect, *195*

USING MOVEMENT ANALYSIS TO DEFINE AND DEVELOP CONTENT, *195*

DESIGNING MOVEMENT EXPERIENCES, *197*

Helping Children Move with Skill and Versatility, *198*

Different Experiential Levels of Students, *198*

Providing Maximum Active Participation, *198*

Involving Students Affectively, Cognitively, and Motorically, *198*

15
developing games skills
200

16
educational gymnastics
231

17
educational dance
254

Part Four
ACTIVITIES FOR CHILDREN

18
games
294

19
introductory games
302

20
classroom and playground games
315

21
major sports
328

22
gymnastics and aquatics
397

23
traditional dance
430

24
adventure activities

455

25
special programs and events

468

preface

We believe that the physical education of children is a matter of utmost importance, both for the children themselves and for the vitality of the society in which they will someday live as adults, citizens, parents, and workers. It is especially important now to take the physical education of children seriously, since there are forces at work which have created a dilemma in this field. Indeed, these forces may soon bring into question the continued existence of physical education as a school subject.

We are entering an era that many believe will be characterized by the use of computers; an era that in many respects is a technological extension of the television era. Television and computers contribute much to our lives, but for the most part they require little more than passive attention or intellectual involvement. Neither is conducive to vigorous activity, the development of motor skills, or physical fitness.

We also find now that people are living longer, a situation that creates entirely new problems for a society. Many years of people's lives will typically be spent in some version of retirement, a time when physical activity is crucially important for health reasons and when participation in sport, games, and dance provides a meaningful form of leisure.

Still another force that has been with us for several generations is the growing incidence of cardiovascular disease and trauma, or what most medical personnel have for some time described as the cardiovascular plague. A healthy, active lifestyle with the benefits of fitness activities and recreational pursuits is clearly the single best way to combat this modern version of the plague.

In recent years society has grown increasingly sensitive to the depersonalizing forces present in business and industry. The factory worker, the middle-level management person, the "data coolie"—all are fixed in positions which provide little intrinsic reward, little job satisfaction, and high degrees of boredom and stress. While the work place must respond to this situation, it is clear that people will increasingly seek the meaning in their leisure existence that they lack in their vocational lives.

Taken together, these forces describe a situation in which physical education for children is clearly important. We know that fitness habits, play skills, and recreational interests develop early in life and are harder to modify as people reach adulthood. Men and women who have learned good fitness habits, who have acquired a repertoire of sport and dance skills, and who have developed positive attitudes toward activity will be better able to live productive lives than those who lack this knowledge. They will contribute more to society and cost society less in terms of mental and physical health care and social problems. Elementary school is the most important place to teach these habits, skills, and attitudes.

While the need for physical education is crucial, we have entered an era of tightened school budgets and an increasing resistance among taxpayers to fund schools adequately. Specialists in physical education are not normally found in American elementary schools. However, even where they have been employed, their jobs are currently under scrutiny because as budgets tighten, specialists are typically the first to be released.

The classroom teacher is under great pressure to emphasize basic skills in literacy and numeracy and to teach many other subjects which have crept into the elementary-school curriculum over the years. Unfortunately, classroom teachers seldom have the training, inclination, time, or energy to plan and conduct a quality physical education program for their children.

Thus, it appears that the future of physical education will rest on which way the dilemma is settled. At a time when physical education ought to receive greater emphasis, it is difficult to hold the line, let alone upgrade programs. Nevertheless, there are certain hopeful signs that give us confidence. First, we believe that the importance of physical education for children will be increasingly recognized and appreciated—by parents, by school administrators, and by all who value the relationship between the education of the current generation of children and the vitality of society in the future.

Another ray of hope is seen in an emerging model for elementary education that is growing slowly in several parts of the world, a model in which the physical education needs of children are given appropriate attention. The "1/3 P.E." model was originally developed in France in the now famous Vanves experiment. The model is quite simple and straightforward. Approximately one third of the school curriculum and available school time is devoted to activities which traditionally have been referred to as physical education, such as games, fitness, sport skill education, dance, outdoor pursuits, and aquatics. More specialists in physical education are employed. Further, classroom teachers receive a more thorough background in physical education.

The results of 1/3 P.E. school programs have, thus far, been very positive: Children are absent less often; they are ill less often; they score higher on measures of fitness; and they acquire more motor skills. Further, children in such programs perform as well or better on academic exercises as do children in control schools who experience a more typical curriculum.

The 1/3 P.E. model is being employed in many elementary schools in South Australia. Also, it is being studied in parts of Canada, and it continues to be used extensively in France. As this model is adopted in other places, it will come under closer scrutiny. If the early results are confirmed, it can be expected that the model will become even more widely adopted.

The authors have undertaken this project because we feel strongly about the value of elementary-school physical education and because there is at present no single source which treats that topic completely. Our aim has been to take the best of what can be found in diverse areas of research, blend it carefully with what is known about effective teaching and classroom management, and combine it with what we have learned from experienced, successful practitioners.

The physical education of children is important. It deserves to be treated seriously and thoroughly. It has been our view that such treatment must include knowledge from scientific areas, strategies from teaching research, the practical results of movement theory, and an overview of important activity areas.

This text consists of four parts, each of which is devoted to one major area of concern. Part One focuses on research and theory in a number of scientific areas that are particularly relevant to planning and conducting elementary-school physical education programs. The section also presents a rationale for the program and explains how to interpret it for the public and for other professionals.

Part Two emphasizes pedagogical techniques, derived from research and theory, which can help teachers to manage more efficiently and teach more effectively. It also contains information on children with special needs and on the crucial role that equipment can play if it is developmentally appropriate in design and function.

Part Three defines and presents the body of theory and technique in movement education, clearly the most important programmatic and pedagogical trend in elementary-school physical education. The section provides a rationale for movement education and includes specific guidelines for educational games, educational dance, and educational gymnastics.

Part Four focuses on the culture of games and activities. From football to rappelling, from hurdling to swimming, and from four square to volleyball, the activities are presented in ways that are helpful to teachers.

The four parts of the book are interwoven into a meaningful pattern of information so that the physical education of children can be all that it should be. The text is intended to be scientific and practical, readable and useful.

DS, JH, JR

acknowledgments

No text of this scope could be compiled without a great deal of help from people who possess the extraordinary ranges of expertise that fall under the elementary-school physical education umbrella. We are also indebted to a number of competent and talented elementary-school physical education specialists who have shown us, through their teaching and program development, the best of what exists in the field. In particular, we are indebted to Dr. Virginia Caruso for her initial draft of Chapter 24, Adventure Activities and to Garry Moore for his suggestions regarding the climbing activities.

We would like to express our gratitude to Connie Montgomery, of the Dublin, Ohio schools and to Garry Moore of the Worthington, Ohio public schools for their contribution to the gymnastics section of Chapter 22 and for the very good elementary gymnastics programs they conduct.

We are grateful to Bobbie Siedentop, Elementary Physical Education specialist, Bexler, Ohio for her help and advice with several parts of the text and specifically *The Sports Page* in Chapter 25.

Thom McKenzie, Assistant Professor San Diego State University contributed descriptions of the Relay Playday, Centennial Day, and Klondike Day events used by him at Parkside Elementary School in Summerside P.E.I., Canada. Dolly Lambdin and Thom McKenzie suggested the Lee Olympics, including the letters, that Ms. Lambdin used at the Robert E. Lee Elementary School in Austin, Texas.

We would also like to acknowledge the contributions of our text illustrator Jody Fulks and our text photographer Tracey Sieklicki.

1

the role
of play and movement
in childhood

Students of physical education are often asked why physical education should be in the school curriculum. Often the question is asked as part of an academic exercise and the adequacy of the answer is judged by academic criteria. On other occasions the question is asked rhetorically as part of a public relations campaign; the answer is judged on the basis of how many benefits can be claimed as a result of physical education. Physical education has been naively described from time to time as a cure-all for ills ranging from poor reading to race relations. Somehow, in our profession we have built a mythology that implies, "If we can just get them actively involved on a team, then everything will be O.K."

For the elementary-school physical education specialist the answer to the question "Why should physical education be in the schools?" is considerably more serious than the difference between a B or an A grade in a class on physical education principles. In the past several decades the answer to that question has too often not been sufficiently convincing to avoid the firing of physical education teachers. The physical education of children is then entrusted to the already overburdened classroom teachers, who,

even though they may really care about the physical education of their children, may not be well prepared to do anything about it. Even if well prepared, classroom teachers seldom have the energy necessary to do this task as well as the many other tasks required when entrusted with twenty to thirty-five children each day.

We may be approaching a time when our society is more ready to consider the many reasons why physical education is important for children. Thus, it is imperative that professionals in the field fully explain the role of play and movement in childhood. If we do not, physical education may not survive in the struggle for resources and curriculum time that surely lies ahead. Also, instructors in physical education must recognize that increasingly there is competition from other sectors of society to provide services in this area. Consider the following ideas of an unhappy and seemingly overburdened taxpayer.

I've had it with taxes for schools! Teachers seem to care more about their unions than they do about my children. There are too many frills in the school and the curriculum. It's no wonder the kids don't read and write as well as they used to. I'm sorry if the art, music, and

P.E. teachers can't be rehired for next year, but it's the only way we can save the money we need to meet the increased costs of higher salaries and things like heating costs. Sure, I guess I'd like my kids to have regular P.E. class, but they get enough exercise after school. Besides, my wife and I are spending good money to have Cheryl take gymnastics lessons. And, Bobby plays on the pee-wee football team in the autumn and swims at the rec center all winter. In the summer, they are both active in sports. On top of that, I'm considering buying a family membership at that new "sports club" they are building north of town. So, P.E. may be one thing we can do without in the school curriculum.

How would you answer this taxpayer? All the complaints about government, taxes, and the schools are erroneously focused on the issue of rehiring an elementary-school physical education specialist. Yet, could you present a case that would help convince this taxpayer that physical education should not only stay in the curriculum, but that the specialist should be rehired? We believe that in different ways and perhaps with slightly differing arguments, this scene is being repeated far too often each year and that far too often professional educators cannot argue strongly enough for physical education. Therefore, we do not take this chapter lightly. Hopefully, neither will you.

CHILDHOOD AND PLAY

It is 10:15 AM. As you drive down Front Street you see a large group of children in the space adjacent to the school. Some are involved with a large, wooden apparatus that looks quite unlike the swing, slide, or metal climbing apparatus you used in school. The children are climbing, swinging, hanging, and balancing on various parts of the apparatus. Other children are involved in a simple circle game that, upon reflection, you remember as one of your favorites. Other children are hitting a ball against a wall. At one end of the playground you see several youngsters playing hopscotch. There is much noise, almost all of it joyful. What could be more natural than a group of children at play. Right? Wrong!

In terms of Western civilization, what you are viewing is a phenomenon of quite recent origin. On the whole, in the development of Western culture the thought of children playing gleefully has been tolerated, grudgingly supported as a respite from work, or even permitted in some limited way because of some perceived educational benefits. Nevertheless, play itself was never *promoted* as a phenomenon that is both natural to childhood and of immense positive benefit in terms of physical, social, emotional, cognitive, and cultural growth and development. Of course children played—children everywhere have always played. However, throughout the history of Western culture play was not considered to be a totally legitimate enterprise.

HISTORICAL DEVELOPMENT

When we think about the term *children*, certain concepts and images are brought to mind. Generally, we think of youngsters who are beyond infancy but not yet into adolescence. Because they are *in childhood*, we expect different things from them, treat them somewhat differently, and generally respect this developmental stage. It was not always so.

> Although the classical Greek civilization (and those it influenced directly) had distinguished children socially from babes and adults if only as objects of aesthetic appreciation, children did not emerge as social entities in the subsequent history of Western civilization until the early seventeenth century. Prior to the seventeenth century there were babes and adults in Western civilization, but no in-betweens. Babes were swaddled; adults attired; children were, in fact, *homunculi*. There was no distinctive dress to differentiate them, and expectations directed toward them were not age-specific. (Stone, 1965, p. 23)

With the emergence of childhood as a recognizable developmental stage came the recognition of play. Writers and educationists began to moralize about children's play. For example, it was quite common to justify it as a preparation for later military service to the state and thus cloak it with the growing sense of nationalism in Europe.

At the same time that childhood was emerging as a recognizably separate developmental stage, free enterprise capitalism was emerging in Western culture, especially in the Protestant nations of Europe. Reformation theology was never very kind to the notion of play. According to this doctrine, it was through work that good Christian citizens showed themselves to be worthy. Clergy often spoke against the supposed evils of play, warning that if children were allowed to play, they would be inclined to continue to play as adults—the implication being that play among adults was downright sinful. In England and in early America it was common for towns to pass legislation which prohibited children from playing (Stone, 1965).

The little amount of play that was tolerated was considered necessary in order to refresh people for a return to productive work. Much play was hidden in the form of work, such as in quilting parties and barn-raisings (Green, 1956) in early America. Work was the central theme in life; play was peripheral. Indeed, too much play was harmful. It was from this background that terms such as *frivolous* and *nonserious* came to be used in attempts to define the concept of play.

During the Industrial Revolution and the period that witnessed the rise of capitalism, children worked. The religious and social philosophies of the day accommodated that fact. Children did not have much time to play. Time that might have been allotted to play was devoted to work. This was true for the child in a factory in England and also for the child on a frontier farm in America. Echoes can be heard of serious parents or stern clergy lecturing children on the evils of play and the potential ruination of their souls should they succumb to these evils. Many of us share that legacy.

The Renaissance of the Concept of Play

In ancient philosophy and literature play was considered to be central to a meaningful existence. In fact, it was considered a fundamentally important form of human behavior. However, beginning with the Socratic philosophers in Greece, this view of play gradually disappeared for almost twenty-five centuries (Miller, 1970). It was during this time that play became associated with evil and sinfulness and began to be described as frivolous and nonserious. The best description that play could muster during its dark ages was what David Miller (1970) has called the "coca-cola" view of play—that is, a pause that refreshes.

During the nineteenth century philosophers, psychologists, and educationists began to recapture the view that play is central to meaningful living. Scholars of great stature, such as Nietzsche, Schiller, and Dewey, began to promote play as a valuable human experience at the center of life rather than at its periphery.

At the same time the excesses of laissez-faire capitalism produced a countermovement among both laboring classes and intellectuals. Part of this movement dealt with increased benefits and rights for workers. Another part focused primarily on children and child-labor laws. Hand in hand with these movements grew the notion of compulsory, free education and the growth of schools. Together these forces began to create a climate of opinion and law within which children's play became more fully legitimized.

In 1938 Johann Huizinga, a Dutch historian, published a book entitled *Homo Ludens* (Man the Player). The book was a study of the influence of play on the development of culture. In the book Huizinga developed the first comprehensive definition of play. He examined how cultural practices in law, economics, and politics had developed from earlier forms of play. This view of cultural evolution as based on play provided an important framework within which scholars could begin to more fully understand the importance of play, both in the life of the individual and of the society.

Today concepts of play pervade everyday life. The developmental role of play in childhood is fully accepted. Its potential as a vehicle for social and physical growth in adolescence is understood. Even its fundamental role in a full adult life is better appreciated. To be sure, the Protestant ethic is still an important part of our culture. However, the importance of play is no longer seen as opposed to the importance of work. Many have come to understand better that a full and complete life can be achieved only through meaningful work *and* meaningful play—one complementing the other.

It should be understood that among the general public, opinions about the value of play are still quite diverse. Many still believe that work and play are opposite states. The period within which we now live is probably a transitional one. While we expect that more and more people will come to understand and value the role of play in good living, we know that cultures change slowly. Old misconceptions are difficult to change. Many will still need to be convinced about the role of play in human life.

PLAY AND PHYSICAL EDUCATION

The definition and meaning of physical education is not unchanging. Rather, it is highly contextual. In the final analysis, physical education is what goes on in the schools, YMCAs, recreation programs, youth agencies, and many other places; that is, physical education is what we *do*. At another level, physical education is what we say it is; that is, whatever activity or endeavor we are willing to label as physical education.

There was a time when physical education in America consisted mostly of physical conditioning and was the province of the medical and health professions. During the early part of this century physical education began to include the teaching of sports and games. Further, social/emotional objectives attained the same status as physical goals.

It seems that professors of *physical education* like to debate the meaning of that term. Advocates of the several major positions on the subject have always shown strong allegiances to their theories. Physical education in schools is largely unaffected by these debates, although from time to time a theory becomes so strong that it can be said to have changed the process and content of physical education. We would very much like to avoid a theoretical debate in this text, since we view such a debate as counterproductive at this point in time: It places people who care about children and who are working hard to improve the physical education of children in competing camps. As a result, these people tend to be combative rather than supportive of each other's efforts. Most importantly, the "real enemy" gets less attention from each group.

The real enemies are those who don't care about the physical education of children—those who still treat children as mini-adults. The real enemies are those who don't value the physical education of children highly enough to provide time and space and teachers so that children may learn and grow and prosper in that part of their young lives. The real enemies are all the physical educators and classroom teachers who have stopped trying.

What is important in physical education today is that we increase the number of people who are skilled in working with children in a loving, caring environment and in helping them to learn in physical education. If two people care about children, are skilled in working with them, and work hard at their jobs as teachers, it matters little whether their approach is a movement approach or a games approach. At least, it matters very little when compared to the differences between those two people and others who don't care, who aren't skilled, or who don't really work at their jobs.

We believe that physical education includes any program that teaches children how *to play* competitive and expressive forms of motor activity (Siedentop, 1980). We are not trying to be exclusive nor do we mean to suggest that this is the one right view of physical education. What is important is that you think seriously about physical education and that you eventually develop your own view.

Play Defined

There is no totally satisfactory way to define play. An activity can be *played* on one occasion; yet, the same activity engaged in by the same person can, at another time, be considerably less than playful. One problem in defining play is that it is a psychological state that cannot be observed directly. Another problem is that we have not come to any conclusion about what to call an activity that is not play. Traditionally, play has been set against work, yet we know that we can engage in our *work* playfully and sometimes our *play* can be sheer work.

The best current thinking (Ellis, 1973, 1976) supports the theory that play is a physiologically based drive within the individual to maintain an optimal range of arousal which results in a pleasurable operating state. This is accomplished by seeking constant variation in the environment by manipulating and investigating new events and/or combinations of events. However, this theory focuses primarily on mechanisms within the individual and is, therefore, only indirectly observable or verifiable through an examination of overt behavior.

The most widely used definition of play is that first developed by Huizinga (1962) and later refined by Caillois (1961). In this definition an attempt is made to define play by citing its characteristics.

Play is activity that is:

1. Free: It is voluntarily entered into.
2. Separate: The time and space limits are defined and fixed in advance.
3. Uncertain: The results and course of action are not predetermined.
4. Economically unproductive: Neither goods nor wealth is produced.
5. Regulated: It has laws of its own established for that purpose alone; or
6. Fictive: It is accompanied by a make-believe state. (Caillois, 1961, pp. 9–10)

Play, then, is activity that is voluntary, separate, uncertain, economically unproductive, and either regulated by special rules or by make-believe. It is inappropriate to think about play behavior as being either totally playful or totally nonplayful. It is far better to view each of the characteristics of play as if it represented a continuum with the play characteristic at one end and its opposite at the other. For instance, a game might have all the characteristics of play, yet the opponents are so unevenly matched that the outcome is fairly certain. It is our experience that such an encounter is less playful than encounters where participants are very evenly matched and where the outcome is therefore uncertain. Likewise, many of the characteristics of play might be present in a situation, but if one is *forced* into engaging in the activity, it can be less playful than if one voluntarily engages in it.

Play Delimited

Play is the lifeblood of childhood. The play element in culture sustains individuals throughout life. Certain forms of play are institutionalized within our culture. Together they form what people increasingly refer to as the *ludic arts*. The ludic arts include music, art, drama, dance, and sport. Each springs from the play element in culture. They are so important that our culture has institutionalized them and passes them on to each succeeding generation through formal and informal education. Those forms of play that are primarily gross motor forms are the province of physical education. We may refer to them as dance activities, gymnastics, aquatic activities, wilderness activities, games, sport, or movement activities—yet, they share two things in common. First, they are playful; second, they involve some gross motor skills.

Thus, when we talk about physical education, we are talking about educational programs where children learn playful movement forms. The latter may include forms that are institutionalized in our culture as games and also those forms which we call sport forms. Children may also learn to create new forms of moving and new ways of relating through playful movement, as in expressive dance and in the creation of new games.

There are many good reasons why physical education belongs in school curricula, in preschool curricula, in the implementation of day-care center programs, in recreational programs, and in a host of other programs which affect the lives of children. The reasons you cite will reflect your feelings and your program emphasis.

JUSTIFYING PHYSICAL EDUCATION

We would like to alert you to several ways in which physical education can be justified. We do not promote these viewpoints out of any sense of defensiveness about our subject matter. We believe fully that a good physical education program is as important to the life of the child as any other subject matter. However, there is no doubt that the physical education specialist or the classroom teacher will more often have to justify time and money spent on physical education than on reading or mathematics: That is a fact of life for the professional educator. We would like you to be able to defend your subject matter in a positive, forceful manner. Thus, we offer several lines of argument that can be used singly or in combination.

The Physical Development Function

Most of the child's waking hours are spent in physically active play. It is obvious that motor play has a significant function in total growth and development. There is also a time during infancy and early childhood when physical development through motor play is intimately related to all other forms of development, including cognitive development and socioemotional development. (See Chapters 2–7 for a fuller explanation of the importance of motor play in growth and development.)

A primary reason why physical education is needed is that in modern society children require help and direction in order to secure sound physical development. For example, American children are consistently below international norms on tests of upper body muscular strength. There is little in the life of the modern child which requires strenuous exercise of the upper body. Carrying, climbing, chopping, pushing, and pulling are no longer activities that all children do as part of growing up in their natural environment. Thus, physical education plays an in-

creasingly important role in our modern, urbanized, mechanized society.

The Cognitive Development Function

Cognitive development is extremely difficult to study because it is not directly observable; rather, it must be inferred from observations of overt behavior. Likewise, it is extremely difficult to isolate the contribution of a factor such as motor play to such a complex process. However, it is clear that during infancy motor play contributes a great deal to cognitive development, simply because it is through motor play that the infant explores his or her world.

There has been a tendency to suggest direct relationships between motor activity and intellectual performance among children. For example, Hackett and Jenson (1966) suggest that "the quick, alert potential athlete is most often a child qualified for reaching a high academic standing. As one's physical abilities increase, he is better able to attain higher classroom standards." (p. 74) This is a lesson in overkill. There is *no* experimental evidence to suggest such a direct relationship between physical development and intellectual functioning.

Physical educators have been even guiltier in claiming strong relationships as regards the less-than-gifted child. While perceptual-motor training programs are of value (see Chapter 7), we must be very careful about the claims we make, as suggested by Bryant Cratty (1974), one of the leading physical educators in the area of perceptual-motor development of children.

> The physical educator who claims to improve cognitive ability by exposing children with perceptual-motor problems to movement experiences is naive and is likely to produce a backlash from his more sophisticated colleagues. (p. 38)

Part of the problem has been that physical educators focus on the role of movement or motor activities without insisting that they be *playful* movement activities. The relationship between movement and cognition is much more readily defensible when examined within the context of play. Many important contemporary theorists, including Berlyne (1971) and Piaget (1962), have built theories which elaborate on the specific and diverse exploration of children through play. Play, in these theories, is activity in which children stimulate themselves (maintain an optimum level of arousal) through exploration of their environment in its physical, social, and emotional contexts. Play can then be seen as a problem-solving mechanism in which the child continually introduces variability into a setting and manipulates events within the setting in a variety of ways. That such activity contributes to cognitive development is clear. What must be remembered, however, is that these benefits are attributes of *playful* behavior. Thus, we have continually insisted here that a basic understanding of physical education for children must rest on the concept of play and its function in human behavior.

The Socializing/Moralizing Function

It has long been understood by scholars and researchers that a primary function of play is to socialize the child into appropriate role behaviors. Children imitate adults and peers. They "try on" different role behaviors in the play setting. They learn to interact in play settings, where the rules and boundaries for behavior are much clearer than in the real world. Brian Sutton-Smith and his colleagues (Herron and Sutton-Smith, 1971) have demonstrated very clearly that the kinds of games that are played within a society are a real clue to the kinds of role behaviors that the society values in adult behavior; that is, the games emphasize certain values (winning by cunning as opposed to winning by physical skill) that are embodied within the culture or subculture within which the child's game is popular.

Play contributes not only to socialization but also to the moral growth of the child. Piaget (1948) in particular has stressed the moralizing function of play in children. The child is self-centered as an infant. Moral development hinges on an increasing sensitivity to "others," to interactional roles, and to cooperative behavior. Play provides struc-

ture and rules that are appropriate to the developmental stages. As children develop, play becomes increasingly complex with boundaries and rules that are increasingly fixed and increasingly communal. If children want to engage in play, they must, of necessity, learn to modify and control their own gratification so as to remain within the interpersonal limits of the play setting (Barnett, 1976). As children grow older, this early socialization through play becomes much more highly specialized in terms of role behaviors appropriate to institutionalized forms of play such as those found in sport.

The Emotional Development Function

Sensitive observers of children at play long ago recognized that children tend to recreate in play settings situations and relationships that occur in the real world. By "playing through" the situation and/or relationship in a playful setting, children learn to cope with potentially difficult situations and/or relationships that occur in their lives.

A main effect of play in this sense is the child's growing sense of mastery over situations, objects, and relationships. It is this sense of mastery that lies at the heart of the psychoanalytic theory of play first suggested by Freud (1908, 1926) and later refined both by Anna Freud (1936) and Erik Erikson (1963). Erikson has said: "I propose the theory that the child's play is the infantile form of the human ability to deal with experience by creating model situations and to master reality by experiment and planning." (1950, p. 195)

One reason why children are able to profit from playful encounters is that the consequences generated by behavior in play settings are not as serious as their counterparts in the real world. Losing a doll or a ball or a play partner may be momentarily difficult, but it is not the same as losing a parent, a relative, or a real friend. Thus, the social and emotional development of the child is not permanently marred by either fortunate or unfortunate playful consequences. They are thus allowed to grow and mature in this "protected" kind of setting. Rules broken in play may be momentarily serious, but they are soon forgotten. Rules broken in real life may produce more serious, long-term consequences.

The Cultural Transmission Function

When one recalls that until quite recently play was considered necessary only as it allowed one to get back to the more important work-related aspects of life, it is no wonder that physical educators have been hesitant to suggest that their primary function is to teach youngsters how to play. For a profession and a subject matter that was struggling for a legitimate place in education, we had to create all kinds of serious-sounding and highly intellectual defenses of what we do. Thus, the major program theories of physical education in this century have spoken directly to the physical, social, emotional, and moral development issues described briefly above. Recently, however, physically active play has become somewhat more liberated. In fact, it is clear that we are now in the first stages of what may well be known as the "era of sport" in our cultural history: Sport dominates television, interschool sport has grown tremendously; private age-group sport opportunities abound; and professional sport is very successful. Further, cross-country skiing, wilderness sport, running, tennis, boating, and many other individual pursuits are booming. Few things are as important as physically active play in our culture.

Therefore, the argument that physical education is justified because it functions as an agent of cultural transmission is much more important than it has ever been. It is also clear that physical educators are much more willing to talk about physical education in those terms (Siedentop, 1980). At a national physical education conference Lawrence Locke (1977) spoke out very forthrightly:

> It is assumed here that the central role of the physical educator is to help students learn how to play and to love physically active games, to dance, and to exercise. The principal 'valuable' that we have to give our client is motor skill. The principal target for our service is youth.

The principal locale for our operation is the public school, and the main reason our role exists is because society so values active play that it arranges to pass the subject matter on to the next generation. We are designated agents of cultural transmission. (p. 35)

There are many in physical education who react adversely to having *physical education for children* explained in terms of physically active play and especially in terms of sport. They react this way because they have seen highly competitive mini-sport programs forced on children in the name of physical education. They are vigorously opposed to highly competitive and highly specialized sport programs for youngsters because they see them as developmentally inappropriate and harmful. We agree. There will be no attempt in this text to describe a mini-sport model for the physical education curriculum.

Nevertheless, as agents of cultural transmission we value sport and the meaning it has in our society. Condemning sport because of some of its excesses is like condemning literature because we have pornography in our society. Good literature is part of our heritage. Knowledge of literature, love of literature, and literary skills should be passed on to our children in a manner that respects their developmental status and fosters within them a continuing love for good literature. The same is true for physically active play, especially for sport.

PLAYING TO LEARN OR LEARNING TO PLAY

Physical educators must decide whether they are using play to help children learn or whether they are more directly helping children learn how to play. Traditionally, physical educators have justified their contributions not on the grounds that the subject matter itself is worth learning, but that through learning the subject matter, the child would grow socially, physically, cognitively, and emotionally. One is never sure whether this tradition derived from a sense of inferiority about the inherent value of physically active play or whether it was simply a strategy used by earlier physical educators to protect their place in education at a time when the culture was still basically hostile to the role of play in human life.

We have no quarrel with the suggestion that children learn through play. Indeed, we have just presented several lines of argument that can be used to defend physical education for those very reasons. However, our predisposition is to forcefully advocate the notion that the subject matter of physical education (physically active play, games, sport, exercise, and dance) is inherently meaningful both at the personal and cultural level. The danger, of course, is that in *using* the subject matter to reach other goals, one might lose the essence of the subject matter itself.

> We do not have to *use* our activities. There is no doubt that they can be used, and often for quite legitimate, even noble purposes. But those other purposes are of a different order than play education. In play education we can let our subject matter be just what it is—institutionalized forms of play that are of fundamental importance to the culture within which we live and grow. Art therapy has become a legitimate method for helping mentally and emotionally disturbed people to gain skills in living, but that fact does not mean that painting should be taught in schools because it promotes psychological growth. Painting should be taught because art is a valuable part of our culture. Should the violin or French horn be taught because playing in an orchestra promotes discipline and good citizenship? No! Like art and music, physical education activities can be used to reach other goals, but this does not mean that they should so be used in school programs of physical education. And there is always the danger that in using the activities for other purposes, a person might never come to know what we know—the joy, frustration, and wholeness of being a player. (Siedentop, 1976, p. 238)

With declining enrollments in our nation's schools and with financial crisis a way of life in the educational world, it is important that all who work with children be able to explain why physical education must continue to be a fundamental part of the curriculum for children. We have heard a great deal in recent years about the "back-to-basics" movement. We are told that schools need to reemphasize fundamental skills such as reading and writing. We hope that we have shown in this chapter that nothing is more fundamental to the life of the child than physically active play.

We all value the role of play in the life of the child. We all need a greater appreciation for the role of play in the life of the adult. Learning how to play and learning to love to play is as valuable a set of skills and attitudes as can be fostered in children.

2

learning
motor skills

We teach because we want children to learn: One of the saddest of all educational situations takes place when teachers teach but children do not learn. This may occur because teachers do not understand how children learn. This chapter is devoted to a discussion of that topic.

HOW CHILDREN LEARN

Major Factors Which Affect Learning

It is not uncommon for texts on teaching to have a chapter on learning and several sections on "learning theories." These sections are usually reviews of what one might have found in a standard educational psychology text book of 20 years ago. Typically, one might find sections on S-R bond theory, a Gestalt view, and several other theories. The era of overarching theories of learning has been over for some time. While theoretical work in learning is not dormant, most psychologists have found the search for *one* complete theory to be fruitless. It has proven far more useful to research factors which affect learning. These are numerous, especially in complex real-world settings such as the gymnasium, as opposed to more rigorously controlled settings such as the laboratory. We shall now look at the major learning factors and then suggest other factors which, while of lesser import, are particularly related to teaching motor skills to children.

Understanding what is to be learned. It is clear that children acquire skills more quickly when goals are thoroughly clarified for them. In learning "jargon" this situation is referred to as "clarifying the stimulus field" or "setting the regulatory stimulus subset"; in the teaching literature it appears in sections on *writing clear objectives* or on *clarity* as a characteristic of effective teaching. While it sounds quite simple, it is amazing the degree to which this basic learning principle is violated in day-to-day teaching. On one hand, teachers sometimes give so few instructions and clarify the learning task so imprecisely that children hardly know what to do in their early attempts at a skill. Gradually, as they get corrective feedback, the children come to better understand what they are to do and learning proceeds much more quickly. On the other hand, teachers may analyze a skill so thoroughly that children are overloaded with information and, therefore, can't respond appropriately to the central learning goal.

Verbal instructions, demonstrations, and teaching aids such as pictures are all used to clarify learning goals. Generally speaking, children learn best when they are given a good description and/or demonstration which emphasizes only the major features of the skill to be learned or the goal to be achieved, what Lawther (1968) has referred to as the "gross framework idea" of the skill. This means that the children should *see* the entire skill and then have the major aspects of the skill emphasized before they attempt to begin to master it.

Opportunity to respond. As research on school learning advances, it becomes more and more clear that opportunity to respond is a dominant factor affecting the degree to which learning will occur. In other words, a learner must make a legitimate motivated attempt to reach a learning goal and get some feedback about his or her efforts. It is useful to refer to this kind of attempt as a "quality" response. Obviously, children sometimes make many responses during a learning period which are not "quality" responses. It is clear from Nixon and Locke's (1973) massive review of teaching research in physical education that the sheer quantity of practice may be the single most important determinant of how much children learn in the gymnasium.

Many studies that focus on practice schedules, ways of organizing children within the learning environment, class size, and learning devices get significant results because the experimental groups *get more practice per unit of time*. Many argue that the major contribution of the recent movement education trend in physical education for children is that children get more practice. Traditionally, physical educators have used a "drill" approach, where children stand in line awaiting a turn. In movement education children are active all the time. This increases the quantity of practice tremendously and should account for much more learning, if children are making quality responses.

Feedback. It has been known for some time that feedback is necessary for learning;

without it, no learning occurs. If we ask you to draw a line 17 inches long, you make an attempt to do so, and we call that attempt trial number 1. If we then ask you to try again, you might make a line equal to, shorter than, or longer than the line you drew on trial number 1. You can draw lines forever without getting any closer to the 17-inch goal. However, as soon as we give you some feedback, you will improve immediately and within one or two more trials will achieve the goal. How quickly you achieve the goal will depend on the kind of feedback you are given. If we simply say "no," you will need many, many trials to achieve the goal. If we say "that's closer," you will achieve it more quickly. If we say "too short" or "too long," you will achieve it still more quickly. If we tell you that your line is 2½ inches too long, you will achieve the goal almost immediately. The different feedback messages are examples of different levels of *precision*, or different *amounts of information*. As a general rule, the more precise the information in feedback, the more quickly we learn.

Fortunately, motor skills are rich in feedback; most skills taught in physical education have a goal, and students' responses produce immediate information about goal achievement. If children are asked to throw a ball at a target, they know whether or not they hit the target and, if not, how close they came. This feedback is *intrinsic* to the task itself and gives *knowledge of results* (KR). KR is abundant in most physical education skills and is the main reason why people can learn sport skills on their own. Weekend tennis or golf players can get some idea of the goal of both games by watching someone else play. They can then go out and try it for themselves and get immediate KR on how well they are doing. If sufficiently motivated to stick with it, such learners can progress to a fairly high skill level simply by relying on the KR intrinsic to the task.

While knowledge of results (KR) is usually abundant in motor activities, knowledge of the physical form of the performance (KP) is harder to determine. We seldom have a good idea about how we executed a particular skill attempt. Responses themselves do not pro-

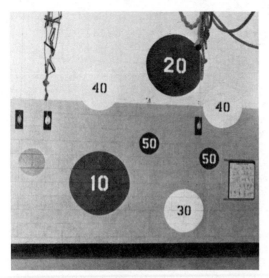

FIGURE 2.1. Wall targets provide goals and help children interpret feedback.

duce much *knowledge of performance* (KP). Usually we must depend on outside sources to provide us with this. Feedback from sources that are not intrinsic to the task are referred to as *augmented,* or *artificial,* feedback. Good KP is almost always augmented. The teacher provides some helpful comments. Dancers observe themselves in a mirror. Basketball players watch video tapes. These are all examples of augmented KP.

Physical educators must learn to be expert deliverers of feedback. This requires the ability to analyze performance, to pick out strong and weak points, and to give precise and concise feedback to learners based on that analysis.

Most physical educators rely almost exclusively on corrective feedback in that they watch for errors in performance and give feedback to correct those errors (Quarterman, 1978; Stewart, 1977). However, preservice physical educators can also be taught to deliver positive feedback emphasizing the correct elements of skill attempts.

Reinforcement. Theoreticians have had a hard time sorting out the difference between reinforcement and feedback. Reinforcement is generally defined as any event which follows a behavior and increases the chances that the behavior will recur. Feedback is information following a response. When a teacher says, "Nice going, Billy, you kept your head tucked that time," the statement obviously has some feedback qualities and some reinforcing qualities. Thus, for the teacher the theoretical distinctions are not always so important.

It is important to recognize that reinforcement, as a basic factor in learning, encompasses the motivational aspects of motor skill acquisition. Reinforcement comes in many shapes and forms: a kind word from a teacher, acknowledgement from peers, winning a game, getting better at a skill, receiving a star beside your name, getting to sign a "top of the rope" poster, attention from parents, and many other sources.

We all need to be motivated in order to learn. When a teacher works with highly motivated children, teaching becomes much easier; when children are unmotivated, the reverse is true. The chapters in this text on managing groups of children, building a climate for personal growth, and modern concepts of teaching all have specific suggestions for how reinforcement can be used to improve school learning.

Other Factors Which Affect Learning

While opportunity to respond, feedback, and reinforcement are the major factors affecting learning, there are several other variables worthy of mention. Attention to these factors can also enhance learning.

Learning meaningful wholes. For many years physical educators broke skills down into their component parts and experimented with part-whole and progressive-part learning techniques. Research in this area is inconclusive, and it thus seems that children learn best when they are presented with tasks that are meaningful wholes in themselves. This probably has much to do with motivation. A meaningful whole carries with it a source of intrinsic reinforcement; improvement and success in the task will be reinforcing to the extent that the task is meaningful to the learner. This does not mean that skills can never be broken down into component parts, but it does mean that if they are broken down, they must be made into meaningful wholes on their own.

Progression in skill learning. The cycle described above (task understanding, response, and feedback/reinforcement) has to be repeated for each series of skills learned, or more precisely, for each stage of learning within a skill. Children don't learn to "set" a volleyball all at once. They learn best if presented with a careful progression of skills in which achievement of one level of skill leads naturally into a higher, more complex level of skill. In behavioral psychology this phenomenon is referred to as *successive approximation,* which means that one gradually reinforces closer and closer approximations of the final goal. The chapter on planning for instruction is especially concerned with planning appropriate skill progressions.

Prompting appropriate responses. A time-honored and well-researched area of learning concerns *guiding* the learner through learning progressions by prompting. A teacher trying to help children learn a schottische step in a folk dance unit might say "step, step, step, hop" over and over again so that the children will move rhythmically. Gradually the teacher's verbal guidance is removed and the children's behavior is prompted by the cues in the music. This is an example of *verbal prompting.*

Another teacher might help a child through a beginning gymnastics movement by physically guiding the child's body until the child has the proper idea of what is to be done. This is referred to as *manual guidance.* At other times teachers may prompt correct performance by *physically restricting* the occurrence of errors. Floats for beginning swimmers or a harness for those practicing gymnastics activities are two examples of prompting through physical restriction.

Prompting is intervention by the teacher to help children move along more quickly, to help them get the idea of a skill more easily, or to prevent unnecessary errors from impeding progress.

Mental practice. Research supports the contention that *thinking* about a skill helps people learn it more quickly. Many coaches of high-level athletic teams help their athletes rehearse their performances mentally. Such practice usually involves mentally going through the entire skilled performance, seeing yourself as being successful. In practical terms, working with a gymnasium full of children, mental practice is unlikely to be of great importance. However, one could argue that children who are generally well motivated and who are kept on-task through a successful managerial style (see Chapter 11) are more likely to think about what they are doing than children who are unmotivated or more frequently off-task. Thus, the well-managed, highly motivated physical education class is likely to benefit from whatever good accrues from general mental involvement with the learning task. While mental practice is never as good as physical practice, it may be helpful during "wait" times.

WHAT CHILDREN LEARN

Categories of Learned Behavior

One of the most helpful movements within instructional design theory over the past several decades has been to provide categories of learned behavior. Each category represents a certain type of learning outcome. The conditions necessary to bring about that outcome differ from category to category. By understanding the learning outcome categories, we can place in proper perspective learning tasks that may appear to be quite diverse. Kicking a stationary soccer ball may appear to be a quite different skill than striking a ball from a batting tee with a bat; in fact, the learned behavior in each of those activities falls into the same category. Once a learning outcome is categorized, we can sort out quickly the conditions necessary to bring about such learning.

A further benefit of the learning category approach is that each category is related. To learn at one level requires that you have already mastered the behaviors at lower levels. Thus, if a teacher wants children to learn a skill in a particular level, the category system can help the teacher know what advance skills must first be mastered in order to bring the children to the point where they can learn the skill at the desired level. The various levels within this hierarchical system may be presented as follows:

Level one:	Emotional learning
Level two:	Simple response learning
Level three;	Discriminated response learning
Level four:	Multiple discriminated response learning
Level five:	Motor concept formation
Level six:	Motor chains
Level seven:	Complex skill learning

(Merrill, 1971)

It should be noted that the levels of learning cited above are for psychomotor behavior rather than for cognitive behavior. There are cognitive equivalents for each of the psychomotor levels. The emphasis here is on motor skill acquisition. We are not suggesting that cognitive learnings do not occur in physical education, nor are we suggesting that cognitive skills are unimportant. Once the hierarchy is understood, the cognitive equivalents are easily recognizable.

Emotional learning. Children react emotionally to learning situations. The observable behaviors from which their emotional responses can be inferred are approach and avoidance behaviors. Positive emotional responses (approach behaviors) enhance learning. When children have negative emotional responses to a learning situation, they are much less likely to achieve. The only fair test of emotional learning is to judge the children's approach or avoidance tendencies when they have an unrestrained choice as to their participation in a learning setting.

Simple response learning. This stage of motor skill acquisition focuses on learning simple motor responses. Examples are hopping, swinging a bat, overarm throwing patterns, or jumping. Notice that we did not say hitting a ball but instead talked only of swinging a bat. Nor did we talk about throwing a

ball at a target but rather emphasized only the overarm throwing motion. Such behavior can be said to be learned when it occurs rapidly and automatically in a fairly smooth fashion without aid from a teacher. Simple responses need to be *shaped* in the sense that the appropriate physical form of the response is acquired gradually.

Discriminated response learning. This level of learning requires that a simple response be executed properly in relationship to a specific stimulus situation. Examples are hitting a ball off a tee, kicking a ball that is stationary, hopping on the fourth note of a 4/4 rhythm, or mounting a high bar. Achievement at this level is measured by judging the skill proficiency in the presence of the relevant cue or stimulus situation and without the use of external prompts or aids.

Multiple discriminated response learning. This level, which is among the most common learning situations in physical education, focuses on the child making appropriate responses to each of a set of stimulus cues. Here the child must have learned a number of responses and must also know how to choose which response to use in which situation. Examples are hitting a thrown ball, kicking a moving ball, dodging a thrown ball, or moving to an appropriate cue in a musical selection. Each slight change in the stimulus situation requires a corresponding change in the response. Learning at this level requires many trials in which all relevant stimulus situations are presented many times so that appropriate responses can be reinforced. This implies a rich and varied learning environment with many opportunities to respond to constantly changing settings. It also implies that teachers must help children identify the relevant cues and the appropriate responses to each cue.

Motor concept formation. It is obvious that we do not learn *specific* discrete responses to each new stimulus setting we encounter; that is, a child learning how to bat does not actually learn a separate, new swing for every ball pitched to her. Rather, we learn *classes* of responses called concepts. A child learns that a slightly different swinging pattern is needed to hit a high ball than is needed to hit a low ball. All the individual responses within a class are generalized while the child learns concurrently how to discriminate between responses needed to hit a high ball and those needed for a low ball (just as a child learns to generalize the concept of car to stimuli as different as Cadillacs and MG's and also how to discriminate between members of the class of responses called car and a similar class of responses called truck). In other words, there is generalization within a concept and discrimination between concepts. Once they learn a concept, children can apply it successfully in new situations.

Movement education relies heavily on teaching movement concepts such as level, path, and focus. Once children have acquired these concepts and can discriminate between concepts, they have a rich and varied movement repertoire consisting of a large number of motor concepts that can then be applied to solve motor problems.

Motor chains. A chain is a series of simple motor responses that are executed smoothly and rapidly in the presence of a set of specific cues. Jumping over a bar, as in a high jump, is a good example of a motor chain. It includes an approach, a gathering moment, the jump itself, and the landing. The chain is held together by a set of cues, so that the skilled jumper knows where to take off in relation to the obstacle, when to move so as to clear the obstacle, and when to begin the descent. It is obvious that one must perform all parts of a motor chain smoothly in order to achieve the terminal goal of the chain. Folk dance steps such as the schottische, which involves a step, step, step, and hop, each done to a cue in the music, are another good example of motor chains.

The cues to which a learner responds in a motor chain can be self-paced or externally paced. An example of a self-paced motor chain would be a skill such as the high jump or long jump. The learner decides when to initiate the chain and succeeding cues are produced by the earlier parts of the chain. An example of an externally paced chain would be a folk dance step in which the order of the chain is fixed in advance, but the cues to move from one part to the other are in the music and therefore not under the control of the learner. Achievement at the motor chain level is shown when the chain is completed smoothly and in synchronization with the cues without the aid of prompts.

Complex skills. Complex skills demand that children be able to sequentially execute combinations of motor chains, each initiated by a specific cue that is discriminated from among a group of other cues present in a dynamic learning/performance setting. In basketball a child dribbles the ball and, on cue, picks it up to pass to a teammate who is open. In volleyball-type games a child positions himself to receive a pass from a teammate and then passes to another teammate. In soccer-type games a child dodges an opponent and cuts toward a goal to receive a pass from a teammate. In each case several motor chains are combined to produce the desired effect. In each case the skill is executed in a dynamic situation in which the relevant cues must be distinguished and acted upon with great speed and precision. It is no wonder that complex skills take many years to develop.

In the physical education literature complex skills are often referred to as "open" skills, since the learner must constantly respond to a changing set of cues. Very little of the child's behavior is fixed in advance. In a "closed" skill the environmental demands are much more predictable. Closed skills are analagous to motor chains. A self-paced motor chain would be at one end of the closed-open continuum. An externally paced motor chain would be somewhat more open. Complex motor skills are even more open.

Complex skills are evaluated by judging the degree to which children can perform smoothly and appropriately, without external prompting, in unfamiliar performance settings. In other words, they must be skilled enough to respond quickly and effectively to each new situation they encounter.

Complex skill performance is highly analagous to problem solving in the cognitive domain. In problem solving, children select relevant principles and structure them into an effective solution strategy to solve an unfamiliar problem (Merrill, 1971). This is almost identical to our definition of complex skill behavior in that motor chains are effectively sequenced to perform appropriately in the presence of a dynamic cue setting. The major difference is that complex skill learning requires a movement solution, while problem solving calls for a verbal or written solution.

Understanding the Learning Hierarchy

There are several features of the learning hierarchy approach that warrant further explanation. First, it must be understood that *it is a hierarchy:* Each level of learning is built upon the previous level. It is difficult to teach even simple motor responses to children who have strong avoidance behaviors to the learning setting. Children can't be taught to respond to a specific cue unless they first have the ability to execute the response. A child has to be able to swing a bat before that child can learn to hit a ball off a tee.

Motor concept formation and multiple discrimination usually occur together. It is almost impossible to teach one without contributing to the other. Both require that simple discrimination learning has previously occurred. The concept of path cannot be learned without discriminating it from the concept of direction. The motor concept of catching a ball above the waist cannot be learned without discriminating it from the concept of catching a ball below the waist.

Motor chains cannot be taught to children unless the students have a wealth of motor concepts and have made the appropriate discriminations. Likewise, complex skills won't be learned until the component chains are well mastered. Otherwise, the result will be a clumsy, uncoordinated effort in which the child is doomed to failure and frustration.

The value of the hierarchical approach is that a teacher can make decisions about which level of learning is required at the start of a learning sequence and then proceed logically through the hierarchy. This helps to ensure success for the children because it increases the likelihood that they will have the necessary skilled behavior to participate successfully in each succeeding level of the hierarchy.

Motor behavior is evaluated by having the child respond to an appropriate set of cues without external prompts or aid. Tests of complex skill are best accomplished by placing the child in a relatively new configuration of cue settings and judging the smoothness and effectiveness of the manner in which the child responds to the dynamics of the setting.

Motor concept formation and multiple discrimination are usually crucial steps on the way to skilled performance. Two problems are inherent in this kind of learning. One problem is called *undergeneralization.* This results when children have failed to generalize their behavior to the total class of responses that should be included. Undergeneralization is detected when students do not make the appropriate class response to a relevant cue. In ball games we expect children to learn to strike at a ball that is within a strike zone. When they undergeneralize, they swing only at balls that are in the center of the strike zone and do not swing at balls that are on the periphery of the strike zone.

The companion concept to undergeneralization is *overgeneralization.* Here, the children have failed to make the necessary discriminations and are likely to swing at any ball, whether or not it is in the strike zone. The children have not learned sufficiently to distinguish between instances and noninstances of the concept class.

There are two major rules for using the hierarchy. First, teachers must ensure that children have already learned that which is necessary to participate successfully at a particular learning level. Second, teachers need to pay attention to the kind (level) of learning involved in any lesson so that they can arrange the instructional setting properly. If the lesson involves multiple discrimination, then many relevant cues must be presented. These should be highlighted at the outset with prompts from the teacher or by simplifying the stimulus setting. Gradually the prompts should be removed and the setting allowed to move toward its natural complexity. The children need to make many, many responses; they must receive accurate feedback for each effort and reinforcement for their successful efforts. Thus, the major factors of learning, cited earlier in this chapter, reappear as the basic elements in utilizing the learning hierarchy.

VERIFYING LEARNING IN PHYSICAL EDUCATION

While it is extremely important for physical education teachers to understand basic factors which affect learning in physical education settings, it is also important that they take time to verify the degree to which learning has taken place. There are two approaches to the verification of learning in physical education—the product, or outcome, approach and the process approach.

The Product Approach

The product, or outcome, approach measures the actual change in behavior of students in physical education. Can they run faster? Throw more accurately? Play games

more skillfully? Know rules and apply them more appropriately? Behave in a socially approved manner during competition? Move more creatively? Many of these outcomes are difficult to measure reliably. For all of them it takes a long time to see real development. Many physical educators keep records on their students so that they may accurately gauge their progress in learning across a 5- to 7-year period. This is an admirable practice and one that needs to become more widespread.

The physical educator does not have the convenient ways to measure progress that are possessed by the classroom teacher. We don't really have any equivalents to standardized achievement tests. We can't chart skill development as easily as reading development. Students in physical education seldom produce permanent products such as math papers, reading papers, or writing samples. Nonetheless, physical educators can keep individual and group records on learning progress in a number of areas (see pages 108–109 for examples).

The Process Approach

A second approach can be used at any time to estimate the degree to which children

FIGURE 2.2. Children learn best when they are actively engaged.

in a physical education setting are learning. This approach, which is derived from the process of learning, is referred to as Academic Learning Time-Physical Education (ALT-PE). (Siedentop, Metzler, & Birdwell, 1979). A child is considered to be in ALT-PE when she is engaged in physical education content tasks at a high level of success (low error rates). The number of such children in a given class provides a total estimate of learning on a class basis.

Our research has shown that many physical education classes operate so as to produce very low rates of ALT-PE (Metzler, 1979). While teachers may allocate a large amount of time to practice and instruction, this allocation does not affect all students in the same way. Even though physical education content is assumed to be the focus of the immediate moment, our data show that there is a substantial amount of time lost in transitions, waiting, interim activity, and classroom management activities. Further, children are often engaged in physical education content, but with too low a success rate to have it count as ALT-PE. Engaged time at medium or high error rates has been shown to be unrelated to achievement (Berliner, 1979). Thus, even though a teacher may plan for and assume that as much as 85 percent of class time is devoted to learning, the actual amount of ALT-PE that accrues to any given child is more typically in the area of 20 percent of class time. Part Two of this text details techniques which can help improve this percentage dramatically through better planning and better management.

3

affective development and physical activity

Socialization is the process by which society trains children to behave as adults. Through this process children learn that society has certain values or ideas about what is right and wrong. They learn patterns of behavior common in our society, or what we call norms. Further, they come to realize that our society has a social structure in which people are assigned different roles and statuses. A role is the behavior expected of a person who occupies a particular status, and status is a position of relative esteem in the social structure. Each child assumes certain statuses and roles within the social structure and quickly becomes aware of the privileges and responsibilities of each.

The goal of society, to be realized through the socialization process, is the creation of socially competent people. Competence in this sense means the ability to socially and physically interact with one's environment in ways that are in keeping with society's expectations. In order to possess such an ability, people must acquire many skills and a good deal of knowledge. The keys to the acquisition of these skills and this knowledge are social learning and maturation. Social learning is learning about a society's culture through the processes of modeling, social reinforcement, and social comparison. Matu-

ration is a process by which the potentialities of an organism demonstrate themselves more or less automatically. Maturation, to a large extent, determines when and to what extent social learning will occur.

The culture of a society encompasses all the beliefs, institutions, art forms, socially transmitted behavior patterns, and other societal products that are passed from one generation to the next. Culture provides people with a social reality that lends coherence to their outlooks and approaches to life. Influenced by cultural forces such as race, social class, and ethnic and religious differences, agencies such as the family, peer group, community, and school transmit and teach our culture through their agents. These socialization agents include all members of society, but for children the primary agents are parents, teachers, siblings, and peers.

A frequent misconception about the socialization process is that it is concerned only with developing interpersonal skills. The socialization process is concerned not only with interpersonal skills but also with many other skills and areas of knowledge, all of which help make a person a socially competent member of society. It is important to distinguish between interpersonal competence and social competence. Interpersonal competence refers to certain attitudes and interpersonal skills that facilitate relations between two or more persons. However, a great many other skills and a good deal of additional knowledge must also be acquired by a person in order to be socially competent. Motor skills, writing skills, and speaking skills facilitate effective functioning in society.

These two facets of the socialization process are interdependent. For example, many young children who are poor climbers, throwers, and runners have difficulty developing the interpersonal skills that normally arise through peer group interaction. This is because many peer group interaction opportunities occur within gross motor play situations which unskilled children avoid. Conversely, children may be skilled in running, throwing, and climbing, but their lack of interpersonal competencies may cause them to be rejected by their peer groups.

The primary socialization function of physical education (as an agency of society) is to teach knowledge and skills involving movement, games, sport, and physical fitness. A secondary socialization function of physical education is to develop interpersonal skills and competence.

SOCIAL PROCESSES AND PHYSICAL EDUCATION

Social processes and variables influence the manner in which children obtain knowledge and skills having to do with physical activity and sport. In this chapter three social processes and several social variables will be examined with regard to their relationship to motor behavior. The social processes include modeling, social reinforcement, and social comparison. The social variables include cultural forces (that is, social class, race, ethnic and religious differences), agencies, and agents of society.

Modeling

Modeling is a very potent social learning process that occurs when an individual patterns his or her behavior after that of another person or model in order to learn that behavior. The young child watches his brother mount and ride a bicycle and tries to do the same thing. A teacher demonstrates an underhand volleyball serve in a fifth-grade physical education class and asks her children to "do it this way." It is through the modeling process that children learn to speak, gesture, and perform a large variety of specialized sport skills. It is not by accident that physical educators rely heavily on modeling rather than verbally oriented instructional techniques. The nomenclature of movement is relatively undeveloped and imprecise. Demonstrations frequently provide a more economical means of sharing information. Models may be chosen from a variety of sources. The family is an early primary source. Age-mates, relatives, teachers, coaches, athletes, and television and film stars provide rich sources later on in life.

How does observational learning occur? There are four processes involved in modeling. A person must: (1) attend to the other person's behavior; (2) remember it; (3) have the capability to perform it; and (4) be motivated to do so. The first two processes influence the learning of a response and the last two influence the actual performance of the learned response. The acquisition of imitative behaviors is a function of the fact that the observer is exposed to a model's behavior. The actual performance of a learned response depends on the performer's ability to perform what was previously observed and his or her inclination to perform. Modeling could occur in the following manner. Sue is watching Tracy Austin perform during a major national tennis tournament on television. Several days later Sue decides to play tennis with a friend of hers. As she is playing, she remembers the manner in which Tracy served the ball. Sue decides to try to duplicate Tracy's serve. She remembers what the serve looked like, and with this thought in mind she attempts the serve. To the extent that Sue closely attended to Tracy's serve, remembers it, has the ability to perform it, and wishes to do so, she will duplicate the serve. To the extent that any of the four processes are interfered with, she will not be able to duplicate the serve.

Before modeling can occur, the observer must attend to the modeled response. Beginners tend to focus on more general characteristics of a modeled performance, while more highly skilled children focus on details. Beginners benefit most from several initial demonstrations, followed by additional demonstrations spaced throughout the skill learning process. Nonessential features of modeled performances, such as an extra wind-up prior to a pitch, draw attention away from more essential features, such as force production and the oppositional stepping pattern of the pitch. The end products of modeled performances, such as whether a target was hit by a pitched ball, also draw attention away from more essential features of performance.

Verbal guidance, such as "step forward on the foot opposite to the hand that is throwing," helps focus the observer's attention on the most important information in the modeled performance. Coupling verbal cues, such as "step-throw," with a demonstration helps an observer develop symbolic representations of the modeled event and speeds the motor skill learning process.

The second component of modeling—remembering—involves information storage in imaginal forms and symbolic codes. Retention of a modeled motor skill is facilitated by such symbolic coding. The careful selection of word cues by an instructor during instruction can serve to provide the observer with meaningful symbols representing portions of the motor skill being learned. Opportunities to physically practice a skill are particularly important in the remembering process, providing opportunities for the observer to code and organize patterns of motor behavior into integrated units. Mental practice, passively thinking through the movements involved in the skilled performance, facilitates retention. Retention is better when modeled cues are presented in small numbers and at spaced intervals.

The third component of modeling, motor reproduction, is facilitated when the skills to be imitated require that the observer synthe-size previously acquired motor components. Many complex motor skills are really a series of simpler subunits. The use of the whole-part-whole method of instruction acknowledges this concept. It requires that a model first demonstrate the entire motor skill; then demonstrate the motor skill's first natural subunit until it is acquired; next demonstrate the motor skill's second natural subunit, allowing the observer to practice it until it is acquired; and so on for all subunits, concluding by modeling the integration of all the subunits and allowing the observer to practice the integration as well.

Incentives, the fourth component, influence all the other components. Even after an observer attends to a modeled performance, retains the modeled performance, and becomes capable of performing the modeled behavior, the modeled behavior will not be demonstrated if positive incentives do not motivate the observer.

Reinforcement given to a model increases imitation of the model by the observer. The implication of this is that observers more frequently imitate models who are successful, who have high status, who control resources valued by the observer, and who are perceived as competent. The more frequently a model's responses are rewarded, the more the observer tends to imitate those responses. A model influences to a great extent the self-reinforcement behavior of an observer. If a child is exposed to an inferior model, that child will tend to adopt relatively low standards. Conversely, if a child is exposed to a more competent model, the child will establish relatively high standards of performance for self-reinforcement. Therefore, it is important that those who model motor skills be skilled. It is effective to make use of skilled peer models in physical skills learning settings.

Observers more readily imitate nurturant, supportive models who control resources valued by the observer. Teachers with these characteristics can effectively employ modeling techniques.

Both incorrect and correct behaviors can be modeled in learning situations. Incorrect models are a great impediment to the learner unless they are used to show incorrect performance features. It is essential that models demonstrate accurately. To the extent that teachers are highly skilled and can model many skills effectively, they are more effective teachers.

A teacher models all the time he or she is with a class. Not only are specific skills fair game for the observer, but the teacher's general behavior is also influential. Teachers who demonstrate rational control of their behavior, respect for others, interest in students as individuals, good listening and communication skills, emotional control, logical thinking and problem-solving behavior, and curiosity and interest in learning for its own sake encourage those behaviors in children who observe them.

Social Reinforcement

Social reinforcements include both nonverbal and verbal messages sent by an individual to a child that increase the tendency of the child to behave in a certain manner. Praise and censure, smiles and sneers, and friendly and hostile gestures are some forms that social reinforcement often take. The young child making her first attempt to ice skate looks up to see her father smiling approvingly at her. Or, a coach may chastise a Little Leaguer who strikes out.

A number of factors mediate the influence of social reinforcement on social and verbal behaviors and on very simple motor tasks. One of the most consistent findings in the social reinforcement literature is the cross-sex effect—the finding that females who act as social reinforcers have more influence on male subjects and vice versa. This is not true with children under 5 years of age, however. Both girls and boys in this age group are consistently most influenced by social reinforcements delivered by females.

Another interesting difference is that younger children are more affected by social reinforcement than are older children. The period of childhood during which verbal encouragement and various other kinds of social reinforcers appear to affect performance most is roughly between 6 and 10 years of age. After this age children, although still motivated by social reinforcers, become more sensitive to the intrinsic interest and difficulty of the task itself.

Still other interesting differences have been found in the manner in which social reinforcement influences behavior: For example, more intelligent children are more affected by social reinforcement; praise is less effective with middle-class children than with lower-class children; unfamiliar adults are more effective reinforcers than are familiar adults, and praise from a disliked peer is more effective in influencing a child's behavior than is praise by a liked peer. Additionally, when teachers provide children with social reinforcement that the children do not perceive to be contingent upon their own behavior, the influence of the social reinforcement is less than when the children do perceive the reinforcement as directly related to their own behavior.

Social reinforcers have been shown to improve performance when other forms of feedback are unavailable. The more specific the information pertaining to a response, the more it facilitates learning. General praise or reproof (for example, "Great, Sam!" or "Fantastic!") provides the learner with little in the way of specific information that can be used to improve performance. Specific information about the performance appears far more helpful (for example, "You did step forward on the foot opposite to the hand that is grasping the ball that time!"). However, once a motor task has been learned, social reinforcement may act as an incentive, encouraging those who are not motivated to perform well at this stage of performance.

Social reinforcements are important in motor skill learning situations. Extensive use of positive social reinforcement contributes to the development and maintenance of positive interpersonal relations between the learner and the teacher. Combining positive social reinforcements with specific feedback about performance seems the most effective manner in which to proceed in most instructional settings (for example, "Great Sam! You did step forward on the opposite foot when you threw the ball to the target.").

Social Comparison

The key component of social comparison is social evaluation. Social comparison involves the appraisal of a child's ability through receiving information from other persons. Developing children have little past experience upon which to draw and consequently are very dependent on others for information about reality and the adequacy of their abilities to deal with this reality. There are three separate processes involved in social comparison of ability: comparative appraisal, reflected appraisal, and consultation.

Comparative appraisal is the process of comparing oneself with others to determine one's own relative standing in some ability. Comparative appraisal occurs when the comparison standard is another individual's performance rather than a past or idealized performance standard. Developmental literature indicates that the comparative appraisal process becomes extremely important to children at about 4 or 5 years of age and intensifies as children progress through the elementary-school years.

Very young children do not compare themselves with others. They spend their time autonomously accruing considerable information about their own personal abilities through solitary play, exploration, mastery attempts, and by striving to attain autonomous achievement goals. Eventually, however, children must place personal ability into a larger relative framework in order to achieve an accurate assessment of ability. It appears that children begin to engage in the process of comparative appraisal at about 4 or 5 years of age. Comparing behavior increases with age throughout the elementary-school years with a peak reached around grades four, five, or six. It is during this period that many children engage in competitive sport activities, and it is in this arena that much comparative appraisal occurs. Further, since the appraisal concerns motor ability and since excelling in physical skills is often an esteemed attribute among children, comparative appraisal involves a potentially very potent group of outcomes.

The second social comparison process that can occur is reflected appraisal. This is the process by which the child derives an impression of his position with regard to some attribute through the behavior of another person toward him. For example, a coach might unintentionally transmit reflected appraisal cues to a child after the child has lost a tennis match or missed a fly ball. A good deal of reflected appraisal exists in competitive situations. Since competitive situations are public, numerous persons can potentially provide reflected appraisal. These include coaches, parents, teammates, opponents, and spectators. Among these, coaches, parents, and peers seem to be the most important. Many evaluative cues may be unintentionally emitted but easily detected by the child: for example, parental cues of pride and approval after scoring a goal in soccer or of embarrassment and disapproval after missing a pass.

A third social comparison process is consultation. Here the child directly asks another person for an ability appraisal or directly receives an evaluation without having asked for one. The consultation process which occurs usually involves evaluation from parents, coaches, or peers. For example, parents frequently provide children with information about how well they are throwing a ball, batting, or performing a gymnastics stunt. Coaches have the job of evaluating ability and providing extensive information during practices that indicates the strengths, weaknesses, and progress of a child. Also, the coach often must make overt evaluations that indicate his or her appraisal of a player's ability as compared to other players. Examples include selecting who makes a team and who does not and choosing starters and substitutes.

Cultural Forces

Social class. Social class is often divided into upper, middle, and lower class, based on family income, occupational level, educational level, or location of residence. Social class is important because class differences influence the socialization of children. The types of learning experiences to which children are exposed, children's self-concepts, the manner in which personality dispositions and attitudes are developed, and the goal-setting behavior of children differ from one social class to another.

Unfortunately, little is known about the relationship between social class and physical activity. It may be that social class interacts with other variables to influence physical activity. For example, social approval has been found to facilitate the performance of boys from lower socio-economic status families and disapproval impairs their performance more than it affects that of boys from middle socio-economic status families. It may well be that different social classes use different forms of social reinforcement, and it is this fact that directly influences motor skill acquisition. Many questions regarding the relationship between differences in social class and motor behavior need to be asked. Is the amount of physical activity engaged in by children of a particular social class associated with encouragement by adult members of that social class? Do differing social classes value different motor skills? Are peer groups in different social classes important sources of encouragement as regards skill acquisition in child members? Do the families of different social classes provide more or less opportunity to participate in certain physical activities? At the moment, few answers are available.

Ethnic factors. Ethnic differences influence the socialization process because members of ethnic groups possess unique knowledge, skills, attitudes, and perspectives that are associated with that subcultural group. Frequently the unique cultural differences associated with an ethnic group are in conflict with the values and norms of the larger society. When this occurs, the ethnic group is generally assigned inferior status and roles in the social structure of society and subjected to unequal treatment. Minority groups are often denied equal access to the material goods of society as well as many cultural opportunities and experiences. Such

material and social deprivation generally restricts minority groups' opportunities to learn the norms and values of the larger society and influences minority members' self-concepts, attitudes, and personalities. Not only are the members of ethnic and minority groups socialized in a culturally distinct group, but they are discriminated against for their differences by other socialization agents of society who should be helping these people fit into the larger society.

Are ethnic differences and corresponding differences in socialization patterns related to differences in minority members' physical skillfulness or fitness? Most available evidence has been gained by studying blacks. It appears that black infants develop more rapidly than white infants. Black elementary-school children seem to perform physical skills slightly better than white elementary-school children. However, there are relatively few differences between whites and blacks in physical performance at all other ages. Unequal access to various sport equipment, the effect of black athletes appearing on television frequently, and possible differences in child-rearing practices may, to some extent, explain whatever differences do exist.

Agents and agencies. Agencies such as the family, peer group, and school and agents such as parents, siblings, peers, and teachers influence motor skill learning. The family is the first and most important socialization agency. Parents attempt to socialize their children to reflect what the parents believe the child ought to be like. Their efforts, in turn, are influenced by the social settings in which the family operates.

The child's development of physical skillfulness and acquisition of knowledge and attitudes regarding physical performance are enormously influenced by the family. The amount of physical control exerted by parents appears influential in the acquisition of motor skills by children between the ages of 2 and 6 years. The amount of physical mobility permitted by parents varies markedly. Some parents restrict children of 5 and 6 years to their immediate neighborhood, others restrict their children to the yard, while still others impose no geographical restrictions on their children's play areas. While some parents do not permit children to jump from furniture or engage in other vigorous activity within the home, others permit their children to move in the home in a moderate fashion within certain restricted areas.

The family also plays a potent role in defining gender-appropriate movement behavior for young children. Girls are generally socialized to be more dependent than boys, to show less exploratory play behavior, to demonstrate quieter play behaviors, and to demonstrate less interest in force-productive activities. Boys are generally socialized to play with toys that require more gross motor activity and to be more vigorous in their play. Parent's sex-labeling of toys, games, and sports as inappropriate, appropriate, or neutral for a certain sex child influences the amount of physical performance and preference that the child demonstrates.

The peer group plays an increasingly important role in socialization as the child grows older. It provides the child with the opportunity to learn about "taboo" subjects, to expand social horizons, to establish self-concept, to participate in egalitarian types of relationships, and to participate in situations involving group expression. The peer group has its own norms and values. Acceptance in and rejection from peer groups are largely determined by a child's ability to learn these norms and accept these values.

The school is a formal institution of society designed to socialize its members. Its basic function is to transmit basic skills and knowledge to children. In addition to reading, writing, and arithmetic, many less obvious skills and areas of knowledge are intended to be transmitted by the school. As the agent of the school, the teacher obviously serves as an important model and reinforcer of a wide range of skills and knowledge. Physical education is a unit of the school whose primary socialization function is the transmission of skills and knowledge about physical fitness and movement.

SOCIAL COMPETENCE THROUGH PHYSICAL ACTIVITY AND SPORT

Physical educators have frequently claimed that physical activity and sport are among the most effective means of socializing the children of our society. By this they usually mean that participation in physical activities helps develop social competence. In the development of socially competent people, physical educators have been particularly interested in four social variables: attitudes, self-concept, aggression, and interpersonal competence.

Attitudes

An attitude is an emotional idea that predisposes the child to perform certain actions in response to a particular class of social situations. It implies a readiness to respond to a situation. Attitudes are capable of change, but at the same time, they are relatively stable. Attitudes are learned rather than innate.

Many people believe that there is a strong relationship between the attitudes a child holds and the behavior the child demonstrates. To understand how attitudes relate to behavior, three interrelated components of attitudes must be distinguished. The first is cognitive. It is a person's beliefs, ideas, or factual knowledge about some object or person. The second is affective. It is a person's evaluation of, liking of, or emotional response to some object or person. The third is behavioral and consists of a person's intention to behave toward an object or person in a certain manner. If a young girl indicates that she is aware of the importance of physical exercise for maintaining a desirable health level (cognitive component), that a desirable health level is something she wishes to have (affective component), and that she intends to participate daily in a physical exercise program (behavioral component), what assurance do we have that she will exercise daily? If all we know is her attitude, as defined above, our assurance is very weak. The relationship between attitude and behavior is relatively weak. Behavior is determined not only by what children would like to do but also by what they think they should do (social norms), by what they have usually done (habits), and by the expected consequences of behavior.

Attitudes can be changed by modifying any of the three components discussed above. There is a tendency for the components to be consistent. Therefore, a change in one is usually reflected in changes in the other components. The cognitive component can be changed by providing new information; the affective component can be changed by pleasant or unpleasant experiences; and the behavior component can be adjusted by changes in norms (such as those associated with the relatively recent values placed on jogging programs) or by various pieces of legislation (such as that associated with girls and women in sport programs in the public schools).

Self-Concept

The self-concept of a child is a system of images that a child has about himself. In part, it is an attitude that a child has about himself. Like all other attitudes, self-concept has a cognitive, affective, and behavioral component. The cognitive portion of the self-attitude encompasses all the categories a child uses to describe himself (for example, fast, strong, skilled). The affective component encompasses the child's self-regard and how the child generally feels about himself (for example, I like the fact that I can run fast). The behavioral component encompasses a child's tendency to act in various ways toward himself (for example, seeks opportunities to demonstrate how fast he can run). Like all other attitudes, those regarding the self are learned and can be changed by providing opportunities to change any or all three attitude aspects.

It is doubtful whether merely involving a child in physical activity and sport programs will result in improving the child's self-esteem. Physical education programs that are fitness-oriented or remedial in nature are potentially more effective modifiers of self-esteem than are other types of physical ac-

tivity programs. Physical activity programs which require aggressiveness and courage are also more effective in modifying self-concept than are other types of physical activity programs—hence, perhaps, the touted success of adventure programs emphasizing physical and psychological risk.

A child's attitude about herself is perhaps the most significant idea in her constellation of attitudes. Self-attitude influences a child's goals and behavior in attaining those goals. It is also important because a large body of evidence indicates that negative self-attitudes predispose one negatively toward others. Fortunately, self-attitude can be influenced by participation in physical activity and sport programs. To the extent that physical education teachers are able to predict how their students view themselves, their subject, and the world, these teachers are in a more favorable position to nurture the development of positive self-concepts.

Aggression

Teachers, parents, and school administrators have always been concerned with the maintenance of classroom order. Today, however, they are preoccupied not only with classroom order but also with the physical and psychological abuse that plagues both teachers and students in the classroom. It has been estimated that as many as 70,000 public-school teachers are physically assaulted each school year (this figure does not include assaults on students).

Many view physical activity and sports participation as socially acceptable outlets for expressing aggressions which arise from daily frustration. Yet, the very sports and activities which are supposed to provide outlets for aggressive tendencies often produce enormous amounts of frustration, tension, and anxiety for those who participate in them. Additionally, the rules governing how one should behave within various sports and physical activities are frequently more restrictive than rules in many other social situations.

Aggression is behavior that inflicts pain or harm on another person. It is best considered in two broad categories. Instrumental aggression is concerned with aggressive behavior whose purpose is to achieve some goal, and in which harm to another person occurs only because it is the most efficient way of achieving the desired goal. Reactive aggression has as its purpose injury or harm to another person. Here both perception of the other person as a threat and the emotion of anger are necessary concomitants.

Instrumental aggression is concerned solely with reward. One is aggressive in a football game in order to win the game. The primary goal is not to injure one's opponent, even though this may be necessary in achieving an objective; the infliction of injury and pain are incidental. Cool objectivity rather than emotional anger is the essence of this type of aggression. Competitive athletics are generally the domain of instrumental aggression, which is not a response to frustration and does not involve anger.

Anger can be thought of as a physiological arousal state which occurs in concert with fantasied or intended acts that culminate in harm being done to another person. However, anger may occur without a person committing an act of aggression, and a person may aggress without being angry.

Perhaps the most plausible view of aggression suggests that each person is born with an innate need and ability to be aggressive, which is mediated by continuous and complex learning opportunities. The first aggressive responses of indiscriminate anger seen in newborn babies are probably due to discomfort and restraint. As children grow older, however, they learn to focus their anger in order to remove sources of discomfort and restraint (instrumental aggression). In essence, they learn that aggressiveness helps them achieve desirable goals. Young children pass through critical periods having to do with feeding, toilet training, cleanliness, and control of emotions; during this time they experience increased frustration. These periods represent real conflicts between the children's desires and those of their parents. Frequently children respond aggressively in such conflict situations. The major source of frustration for growing children appears to be a basic conflict between their desires and those of the society, culture, and family of which they are a part. It is probably in this context that children acquire most of their aggressiveness.

As children learn to attack those things which are frustrating, they also learn that punishment usually accompanies aggression directed toward parents. They also learn about the consequences of aggression in dealings with peers. A child's aggressive experiences are usually a matter of chance in that no two situations are ever identical. Children grow up in different environments and respond differently to variable situations. Aggressiveness, influenced by variables such as socioeconomic background, sex, number of siblings, age, and personality characteristics of parents and peers, becomes a very individual matter.

The growing child learns to repeat rewarded responses and not to repeat those responses which result in punishment. Children prefer to engage in behaviors that lead to gratification of desires. Once this is learned, they begin to become adept at using their knowledge to control and manipulate others aggressively. If the child is fairly successful, he or she will become an aggressive person. If unsuccessful, the child will employ nonaggressive behaviors to achieve various ends.

During the preschool and early elementary-school years, children experience a rapid increase in social awareness, often engaging in friendly, cooperative play. Aggression usually appears in peer group interactions. The child who interacts with other children probably learns to be more aggressive than the child who interacts with other children only infrequently.

Finally, the athlete who is highly aggressive is probably one who has had a past history of being successful in instrumental aggression; that is, this person has been continually successful in achieving various goals by being aggressive.

Many have placed considerable emphasis on the cathartic effect of physical activity, explaining that people need to purge themselves of aggressive tendencies through vigorous participation in sport. However, there is little, if any, scientific support for this point of view. There is even some evidence to indicate that increased physical activity makes individuals even more susceptible to aggression when they are confronted with aggressive stimuli, and further, that the observation of violence, rather than having a cathartic effect, increases the likelihood of aggression.

Physical activity is not a mysterious panacea that reduces aggressive tendencies. Aggression is the result of pain, frustration, and learned responses. The occurrence of aggression can be fairly accurately predicted if one knows something about the aggressor, the victim, and the immediate situation. The occurrence of aggression can be fairly effectively managed if one selects appropriate instructional strategies designed to motivate and involve students.

It is also clear that competitive sports have inherent qualities that make them potentially frustrating and, hence, a potential source of aggression. However, children can learn nonaggressive responses to aggressive situations. Learning occurs largely by observing others and by being reinforced positively for appropriate responses and negatively for inappropriate responses. Persons who observe violence and are reinforced for violence when participating in physical activity are likely to continue such violent behavior. When individuals observe and are reinforced for nonviolent behavior, they are likely to continue behaving in this manner.

Interpersonal Competence

Interpersonal competence refers to one's ability to effectively interact with others. Participation in physical activity, including games, play, and sport, provides children with the opportunity to engage in considerable social interaction in a wide variety of settings. What may be learned in such situations may be both desirable and undesirable.

Between 1 and 3 years of age, physical prowess is usually not an important factor in gaining leadership, because the social organization of children at those ages is not complex. Children in this age group usually imitate and engage in parallel play, perhaps with one other individual. Forming groups and deciding upon a leader does not occur until about age 4. As the child reaches 5 or 6 years of age, play units grow larger. At that time leadership and social recognition are often gained through effective physical performance. Social recognition during the elementary-school years is closely related to the ability to distinguish oneself from peers. Children who demonstrate high levels of physical skillfulness are able to distinguish themselves. Because of this, they are often able to capture and maintain leadership and high status positions.

When examining the relationship of maturity, leadership, status, and physical activity, one must differentiate between the concept of dominance and group-conferred leadership. Young children tend to dominate one another. Genuine leadership of a group is seldom evident among children younger than 10 years of age. Young children who dominate others are often taller and heavier than their peers. These children are perceived as having a greater capacity for action by the children they dominate.

As adolescence is reached and boys engage in sports within codified rules, leadership may be bestowed for different reasons than were apparent during early, middle, and late childhood. Physically accelerated boys are frequently more accepted and are treated more favorably by both peers and adults. Their status leads to positions of leadership which often persist into adulthood. As boys progress beyond the elementary-school years, their social status frequently increases as a function of athletic ability, although the effects of athletic ability on social status may be diminished as boys begin to look for less obvious personality qualities on which to base their friendships.

As girls grow older, less emphasis is placed on excellence in physical activity. Differentiation based on sex role occurs regarding the acquisition of leadership through physical prowess. This sex difference becomes most pronounced as adolescence is reached. Girls between the ages of 12 and 15 who possess athletic skillfulness frequently gain little prestige and at times are looked upon with disfavor.

The relationship between physical activity and interpersonal competence may be a circular, spiraling relationship. Those children who are emotionally healthy and socially better-adjusted engage in a good deal of physical activity and social interaction because they have higher levels of physical skillfulness. Because of their higher levels of physical skillfulness, they receive favorable evaluation by their peers. Poorly adjusted children probably elect to engage in more individualized, less demanding physical activities or in fewer physical activities. They are therefore in a less favorable position to obtain desirable evaluation by their peers.

4

efficiency
of movement

Popular sports and physical activities require the performance of throwing, climbing, running, jumping, kicking, striking, and catching skills. Teaching efficient performance of each of these tasks is a goal of all physical education programs. Those who expect to effectively design, carry out, and evaluate movement experience programs for children need competency in: (a) assessing the degree to which each of these tasks is performed efficiently, (b) making appropriate decisions as to when intervention is necessary to facilitate the development of increasing efficiency, and (c) administering appropriate interventions (for example, provision of equipment, games and drills, verbal directions, demonstrations) that will result in more efficient performance.

EVALUATING THE EFFICIENCY OF PERFORMANCE

People can be taught to accurately observe movement in throwing, climbing, running, jumping, kicking, striking, and catching tasks. Beginners often find that they need to spend a considerable amount of time watching a child perform a given task before they feel they can evaluate accurately. While watching, observers should direct their attention to each of a series of components ordered in terms of how much they contribute to total task performance efficiency. These components include factors such as leg action, pelvic-spinal rotation, arm action, and foot positioning.

The following pages contain charts for the major movement tasks. Each chart identifies performance at low, intermediate, and high levels. Directions for setting up the movement tasks so that observations can be made are included with each task. The observer must determine which level of each component is most characteristic of the child being observed. These observations will then be used to make decisions regarding interventions to improve the performances.

It may be necessary for the observer to watch a child perform many times on several different occasions. No attempt to intervene or influence the child's performance should be made during this initial evaluation. If a child becomes tired or disinclined to move, evaluation should be postponed; any observations made then will not represent the child's characteristic performance. Children's performances will undoubtedly vary.

CHART 4.1 Overhand throw

DIRECTIONS: The child will stand behind a tape mark 10′ away from a hoop target, 3′ in diameter, which is attached to a wall so that it is no closer than 4′ from the floor. The child will repeatedly throw a yarn ball, 3″ in diameter, at the target. The observer will stand in front of and to the side of the child. Directions given to the child by the observer should be to *throw as hard as possible.*

EQUIPMENT: yarn ball, 3″ in diameter; hoop, 3′ in diameter; masking tape; tape measure.

COMPONENTS TO BE ASSESSED:	Efficiency Levels			
	LOW	INTERMEDIATE		HIGH
1. Foot position	Feet parallel, no step forward	Step forward on same side as throwing arm		Step forward on foot opposite throwing arm
2. Pelvic-spinal rotation on backswing	No rotation, trunk may extend backward	Shoulder rotates backward while hips are stationary	Shoulders and hips rotate as a unit (block rotation)	Shoulders rotate backward followed by hips
3. Pelvic-spinal rotation on forward swing	No rotation, trunk may flex forward	Shoulder rotates forward while hips are stationary	Shoulders and hips rotate as a unit (block rotation)	Hips rotate forward followed by shoulders
4. Hand position at end of backswing	Hand above shoulder, well over head level	Hand out to side, far away from body		Hand next to or just behind ear
5. Elbow position at end of backswing	Little if any elbow flexion; elbow is held well above or away from the side of the body	Elbow is flexed and held in front of and above the shoulder		Elbow is flexed and held away from the side and slightly behind the shoulder
6. Arm action during forward swing	Downward	Downward and across body		Elbow swings horizontally forward followed by forearm extension
7. Wrist position at end of backswing	Flexed	Natural or normal		Extended
8. Position of fingers	Fingers spread, ball is touching palm			Fingers spread, ball does not touch palm
9. Flexion of the wrist at ball release	Wrist snap absent			Wrist snap completes the throw

CHART 4.2 Ladder climb

DIRECTIONS: The observer should stand to the side of the child and encourage the child to *climb to the top of the ladder and down to the bottom as quickly as possible.*

EQUIPMENT: 12′ ladder, rungs 1′ apart, 16″ wide, inclined at a 30-degree angle.

COMPONENTS TO BE ASSESSED:	Efficiency Levels		
	LOW	INTERMEDIATE	HIGH
1. Leg action upward	Marking time pattern		Alternating foot pattern
2. Leg action downward	Marking time pattern		Alternating foot pattern
3. Arm-leg action upward	Hands move up ladder, legs follow	Homolateral (right hand, right foot move together)	Contralateral (right hand, left foot move together)
4. Arm-leg action downward	Legs move downward, arms follow	Homolateral (right hand, right foot move together)	Contralateral (right hand, left foot move together)

CHART 4.3 Run

DIRECTIONS: Clearly mark off a 20' distance. Make certain that the child to be observed is wearing nonslip shoes and nonrestrictive clothing. Ask the child to run the distance *as quickly as possible.* Should the child become fatigued or disinterested, discontinue assessment until the child has recovered. View components 1–10 from the side, 11–13 from the rear, and 14–15 from the front.

EQUIPMENT: a well-marked starting and stopping line separated by a 20' distance. Ground should be level and firm.

COMPONENTS TO BE ASSESSED:	Efficiency Levels		
	LOW	INTERMEDIATE	HIGH
1. *Length of stride*	Very short	Average	Long
2. *Amount of time spent in nonsupport phase*	No period of nonsupport	Short period of nonsupport	Long period of nonsupport
3. *Relative amount of upward movement of the body*	Bouncy run, with much up and down motion	Moderate amount of up & down motion	Very little up and down motion
4. *Extension of the propulsive leg*	Minimal extension of hip, knee, and ankle	Moderate extension of hip, knee, and ankle	Great extension of hip, knee, and ankle
5. *Contact of propulsive foot with the ground*	Entire foot contacts surface at one time		Heel-to-toe contact; or toe contact only
6. *Closeness of heel to buttock on forward swing of the recovery leg*	Heel far from buttock	Heel is lifted halfway to the buttock	Heel close to buttock
7. *Height of the knee at the end of the forward leg swing*	Thigh is lifted to a 30° angle or less from the vertical	Thigh is lifted to a 45° angle from the vertical	Thigh is almost parallel to the ground (90° angle from the vertical)
8. *Elbow bend and arm position*	Elbows extended; arms carried high and far from the sides of the body for balance	Elbows slightly bent; arms carried high and far from the body	Elbows bent at 45°–90° angle; arms carried close to the sides of the body
9. *Distance forward foot is ahead of center of gravity when it makes contact with ground*	Child upright, center of gravity behind forward contact foot	Slight forward lean; center of gravity over forward contact foot	Well-defined forward lean, center of gravity ahead of the forward contact foot
10. *Arms swing through an arc in a forward and backward direction in opposition to leg movements*	No arm swing	Slight arm swing	Extensive arm swing
11. *Outward swing of the knee of the recovery leg*	Great amount	Slight	None; total motion is in a forward-backward plane
12. *"Toeing-out" of the foot during recovery of leg*	Foot points sideward to a large extent	Foot points sideward slightly	Absent; toes point forward
13. *"Toeing-In" of the foot during recovery of leg*	Great amount	Foot points inward slightly	Absent; toes point forward
14. *Arms hook toward the midline of the trunk on the forward swing*	Arms swing across the midline of the body	Arms swing toward, but do not cross, the midline of the body	Arms do not swing toward midline of the body
15. *Arms loop outward on the backswing*	Arm held in front and away from body, moves outward (sideward) and backward	Arm held slightly in front and away from body, moves slightly outward (sideward) and backward	Arm does not move outward and backward

CHART 4.4 Standing long jump

DIRECTIONS: Mark an open area with two sections of tape, each 36″ in length. One piece shall designate the take-off line and the other (placed 8′ away and parallel to the first line) shall represent the line toward which the child will jump. Instruct the child to stand with toes behind the take-off line. Ask the child to *jump as far as possible*. Observe the child from the side, approximately 5′ away. The first three observations focus on the preparatory phase of the jump. The fourth through sixth observations focus on the take-off phase. The sixth and seventh observations focus on the flight phase. The eighth through tenth observations focus on the landing phase.

EQUIPMENT: 1″-wide masking tape; a measuring tape.

COMPONENTS TO BE ASSESSED:	*Efficiency Levels*		
	LOW	INTERMEDIATE	HIGH
1. *Preparatory crouch*	No crouch; knees, ankles, and hips not bent	Moderate crouch; knees, ankles, and hips slightly bent	Deep crouch; knees, ankles, and hips well bent
2. *Preparatory forward trunk lean*	Trunk is close to the vertical	Trunk close to 70° angle in forward lean	Trunk close to 45° angle in forward lean
3. *Preparatory backward arm swing*	Arms held down or out to sides of the body, but not behind body	Arms move from in front of body to a position slightly behind the back	Arms move from in front of body to a position well behind the back
4. *Take-off body extension*	Arms, hips, knees, and ankles slightly extended	Arms, hips, knees, and ankles moderately extended	Arms, hips, knees, and ankles fully extended
5. *Angle of the body at take-off*	Body almost vertical	Body inclined forward slightly	Body inclined forward at a 45° angle
6. *Swing of the arms during take-off and flight*	Arms are held at the sides or at shoulder height for balance	Arms swing forward and upward, but then are retracted backward	Arms swing forward and upward
7. *Hip action during flight*	Minimal hip flexion	Moderate hip flexion	Well-defined hip flexion
8. *Leg-hip action on landing*	Landing occurs with jolt due to nearly straight hips	Some bend in hips, knees, and ankles upon landing	Deep crouch; force of landing is well absorbed
9. *Angle of the legs at landing*	Almost perpendicular to ground; 90° angle	Greater than 45° angle, but less than 90° angle	45° angle or less
10. *Position of arms during landing*	Arms behind and/or far from sides of body	Arms slightly forward and far from sides of body	Arms well forward of body

It is not unusual to see a child demonstrate two contiguous levels of any single component on successive trials. When evident, such variability should be acknowledged in the evaluation.

As an observer becomes more skilled, he or she may assess a performance component for an entire group of children. For example, the foot position component of the overhand throw could be assessed by roughly evaluating what proportion of children in a given instructional group demonstrate each of the three levels of that component.

MAKING DECISIONS ABOUT INTERVENTION

If the child being observed demonstrates intermediate or high efficiency levels on the first component of a task, the observer should examine the second component. If the child is performing at a relatively low efficiency level on the second component, it should become the focus for the first intervention. If the second component is also at an intermediate level, then the observer should study the third. Once intervention is

CHART 4.5 Place kick

DIRECTIONS   Place two 6"-long masking tape marks on the floor parallel to one another and 4' apart. Make a circle, 4" in diameter, of sash cord by connecting the ends of a length of sash cord together with masking tape. Place the rope coil on one of the 6" marks and place a plastic or foam ball, 8"–10" in diameter, on the coil. Ask the child to stand on the tape line opposite the ball. Direct the child, when ready, to *kick the ball hard.* Observe the child's performance from the side, approximatley 5' away.

EQUIPMENT: Masking tape; tape measure; one plastic or foam ball, 8"–10" in diameter; circular coil of sash cord, 4" in diameter.

COMPONENTS TO BE ASSESSED:	Efficiency Levels		
	LOW	INTERMEDIATE	HIGH
1. *Steps taken prior to ball contact*	Child is still; child walks up to ball, stops, then kicks from a parallel foot position	Child takes a single step; walks up to ball, stops, then takes a single step prior to contact	Child takes several steps prior to contacting the ball
2. *Arm action throughout the kick*	Arms held loosely near sides of body, hands near thighs	Arms held away from sides of body, symmetrically	Arms move in opposition to the legs
3. *Knee during preparatory backswing*	Knee is fully extended	Minimal knee flexion	Knee is fully flexed
4. *Hip during preparatory backswing*	Thigh remains perpendicular to ground or hip is flexed	Minimal hip extension	Hip fully extended
5. *Knee action during forward swing*	No action	Minimal extension over a short range of motion	Great extension over a long range of motion
6. *Hip action during forward swing*	Minimal flexion over a short range of motion	Moderate flexion over an intermediate range of motion	Great flexion over a long range of motion
7. *Trunk action after ball contact*	No backward trunk lean		Backward trunk lean
8. *Leg action after ball contact*	Leg stops moving immediately	Leg is retracted	Leg follows through

completed and a child is performing all components at an intermediate level, the process of assessing each component in order can begin once again and intervention decisions can be made which reflect a desire to help the child move toward increasing efficiency in appropriate components.

Much the same process should be used in making decisions regarding whether and where to intervene with a group of children. If a sizeable proportion of a class demonstrates intermediate or high efficiency levels on the first component of a task, the observer should examine the second component and proceed as discussed above.

In determining whether intervention is economical or effective for children at different ages and developmental levels, we must note that there are "ripe" periods for

acquiring increasingly more mature and efficient motor skills. These are times when a child's neurological, physiological, and anatomical maturation and psychological set are such that the child can most economically acquire skills. Many of these ripe times occur during the preschool and elementary-school years.

Children usually develop efficient motor skills when rich environments are continuously provided—filled with appropriately weighted and sized equipment—and when parents, teachers, and other nurturing adults provide and encourage positive and successful experiences. However, when modern urban environments limit motor opportunities, when parents' and teachers' attitudes and commitments result in the restriction of motor experiences, and when appropriately sized and weighted equipment is not provided, many children do not realize their mature and efficient skill potential. Unfortunately, it is all too common to see a high school girl throw, stepping forward on the foot which is on the same side of the body as the throwing hand, and turn her head to the side in fear when catching. These are inefficient and immature behaviors that most children normally leave behind when they enter elementary school. Unless efficient skills are developed by the time a child reaches 6 or 7 years of age, later attempts to learn these skills will tend to be less economical. Once a ripe period has passed, it may be possible for children to learn, but the energy which must be devoted to such learning will be greater than that needed earlier.

All children are capable of improvement (some movement to the right) in each skill continuum. While maturational factors may limit the skill acquisition of some children more than others, this factor is generally less significant than situational variables. All children can benefit from intervention, whatever their age or level of development.

INTERVENTION

Wherever a child may be on a skill continuum, intervention strategies should be directed at developing the most efficient movement possible. It is inappropriate to ask a child to perform intermediate behaviors that are not totally efficient, even though he

CHART 4.6 Sidearm strike

DIRECTIONS: Suspend a foam ball, 8″ in diameter, from a 6′ length of sash cord at the child's waist level. Instruct the child to pick up the bat and hit the stationary ball with the bat *as hard as possible.*

EQUIPMENT: plastic bat, 30″–36″ long, with a head 2″–2½″ in diameter; 6′ sash cord; foam ball, 8″ in diameter; plastic tape.

COMPONENTS TO BE ASSESSED:	Efficiency Levels		
	LOW	INTERMEDIATE	HIGH
1. *Weight shift*	No transfer of weight from one foot to the other; weight distributed equally on both feet	Definite transfer of weight from one foot to the other; neither foot shifts position	Definite transfer of weight from one foot to the other; leading foot moves in the direction of the ball
2. *Pelvic rotation on backswing and forward swing*	No rotation	Block rotation; pelvis and shoulders rotate simultaneously	Shoulder rotation followed by pelvic rotation on backswing; pelvic rotation followed by shoulder rotation on forward swing
3. *Hand position on bat*	Grips bat with one hand	Grips bat with hands apart; uses a reverse grip	Grips bat with one hand immediately above the other; preferred hand on top
4. *Sequential movement of body parts in the forward swing*	Arms initiate movement, followed by the wrists	Arms initiate movement, followed by the wrists and trunk, in that order	Foot initiates movement, followed by the pelvis, spine and shoulder, arms and wrists, in that order
5. *Arm action after ball contact*	Arms stop moving immediately	Arms are retracted	Arms follow through
6. *Striking pattern employed*	Overhand pattern; child strikes down upon the ball in a vertical plane	Diagonal pattern; child strikes down upon and across the ball in a diagonal plane	Sidearm pattern; child strikes across the ball in a horizontal plane

CHART 4.7 Catch

DIRECTIONS: The observer suspends a foam ball, 8½" in diameter, from a 6' length of sash cord so that the bottom of the ball at rest is between the knee and waist level of the child. The observer then places two 6"-long pieces of masking tape on the floor 12' apart so that the center of the resting ball lies directly over the middle of an imaginary line connecting the two pieces of masking tape. The observer asks the child to stand on one tape mark, and then positions himself on the other, holding the ball in his hands between his chest and head level with the sash cord fully extended but not stretched. Should the observer find it necessary to adjust his distance slightly behind or ahead of the floor mark, he may do so. The observer should tell the child that he will release the ball and that the task of the child will be to catch the ball. The observer should not give impetus to the ball in any way but should simply release the ball and allow gravity to cause the ball to travel toward the child.

EQUIPMENT: foam ball, 8½" in diameter, suspended from a 6'–8' length of sash cord so that the bottom of the ball rests between the knee and waist level of the child; masking tape; tape measure.

COMPONENTS TO BE ASSESSED:	Efficiency Levels			
	LOW	INTERMEDIATE		HIGH
1. *Movement just prior to receiving ball*	No movement toward the ball	Minimal arm movement toward the ball		Step(s) toward the ball
2. *Arm position just prior to receiving ball*	Arms fully extended in front of body			Arms bent; hands held in front of body; elbows point toward the ground
3. *Evidence of fear reaction at ball contact*	Evidence of fear reaction; turning head to side to avert the eyes, or slight backward bend of trunk away from oncoming ball, or closing eyes			No evidence of fear reaction; head and eyes directed forward; trunk upright or bent forward; eyes open
4. *Hand and arm action at ball contact*	Ball does not contact child's hands or arms; ball simply strikes the child's chest and falls to ground; child's arms remain extended in front of body with palms facing upward or inward	Ball initially hits the child's chest and is then trapped against child's body by arms or arms and hands	Ball initially touches child's hands and is then trapped against child's chest by hands or hands and arms	Ball is caught entirely in the child's hands; ball does not touch child's chest; arms flex to absorb the force of the oncoming ball
5. *Force absorption occurring after ball contact*	No force absorption; ball bounces off hands, arms, or body; feet are parallel			Force absorption; elbows are flexed and/ or feet are in a forward-backward stance, so that weight is shifted from the front to the rear foot

or she may be demonstrating behaviors that indicate the child's position is at the far left of a continuum.

Motor tasks may be thought of as either predominantly *closed* or *open* in nature. Tasks which are predominantly closed involve striking, throwing, and kicking stationary balls at stationary targets, climbing, running races, and jumping toward stationary targets. These tasks are considered closed in the sense that they allow the performer to make decisions about when to initiate and terminate movements. Open tasks, on the other hand, require that the performer respond to others' movements or to the movements of an oncoming projectile. Tasks such as catching, striking, and kicking moving balls, throwing at a moving target, attempting to tag a moving runner, and jumping upward to tap a tossed ball are open skills. Both categories of tasks make unique demands on learners. Teachers often find this knowledge useful when selecting and employing intervention strategies.

The effectiveness of intervention in closed skill tasks depends on the teacher's ability to acknowledge, emphasize, encourage, and facilitate effective force production. On the other hand, successful intervention strategy for open skill tasks requires that the teacher acknowledge the unique visual demands of the task and also the force productive character of the task. It is not by accident that children acquire open skills more slowly than closed skills. The requirements of open skills are far more rigorous than those for closed skills. Generally, the intervention strategy employed in teaching open skills is to treat them initially as if they were closed skills, attempting to keep the projectile stationary in initial stages of learning. Primary concentration is on the development of mechanical efficiency. Afterward, the child is exposed to increasingly complex practice situations in which factors such as speed of the ball, complexity of the ball's trajectory, performer locomotor spatial adjustments, and performer nonlocomotor spatial adjustments are manipulated until the behavior evolves from a closed skill performance context into an open skill performance context.

Open or closed skills really represent two ends of a continuum. It is the position of a skill on the continuum that in large part colors the intervention strategy employed by teachers.

In general, most throwing, climbing, running, jumping, kicking, and striking tasks are dealt with as closed skills in the preschool. Little attention is given to the development of catching skills, which are, by their very nature, open. In the primary school attention centers on the continued practice of

these tasks as closed skills, although by the end of the primary-school years children are generally expected to have experienced these skills in a large variety of contexts and, to some extent, as partially open skills. More attention is paid to catching tasks toward the end of the primary-school years, and in the intermediate grades they become more specialized in sport-form contexts. It is in the intermediate grades that children are generally moved from a closed to an open skill orientation.

In the following pages we will discuss specific selected intervention suggestions particularly relevant to the mechanical demands of closed skills. Additionally, selected intervention strategies are suggested for open skills, though a more thorough analysis is left for Chapter 7. Intervention suggestions are presented in the form of suggestions for equipment, games, and verbal and visual guidance.

Overhand Throw

Initially targets should be large, located at the thrower's head level, nonmoving, and located far enough away from the thrower so that they communicate the need to throw forcefully. Later, as the child becomes increasingly efficient, targets may become smaller, slow-to-fast moving, and increasingly farther from the thrower.

FIGURE 4.1. Neat Feet, Cookie Monster Windowshade Target, and cone barrier.

FIGURE 4.2. Flower Target, rope barrier, and pressure sensitive mat connected to lightbulb.

Initially balls should be small enough so that they can be easily grasped in one hand. Larger balls restrict the range of motion because they encourage bilateral throwing action. Balls should be of moderate weight. If they are so light that wind resistance interferes with their trajectory, or so heavy that they are difficult to manipulate, they are undesirable.

Footprints painted on black rubber floor matting can facilitate the development of the oppositional foot pattern, spinal rotation, and an increasing range of motion in the throw (Figures 4.1 and 4.2).

An inclined plastic rope, 3/8″ in diameter, fixed to a basketball hoop on one end and a floor plate on the other end, encourages the development of the oppositional foot pattern, spinal rotation, and an increasing range of motion in the throw (Figure 4.3). Children must attempt to sling a 1-foot-long plastic pipe, 2″ in diameter, up the rope toward a cymbal and colored tape markers.

Distance barriers that require the child to throw from specified distances from targets encourage effective force production. These may be made from traffic cone markers and elastic cords (Figures 4.1 and 4.2).

Keep-Off is an excellent game for evaluating and encouraging efficient overhand throwing. It is played by dividing a large, marked-off rectangular area into two halves by means of a net approximately 3 feet high. Yarn balls, sponge balls, or sock balls are scattered on both sides of the net. Children are divided into two teams. Children on each team share the space on their side of the net. On the signal children on each side of the net attempt to keep balls off their side of the net by throwing them overhand, one at a time, across the net. The team on the side of the net with the least number of balls after the stop signal is given is considered the winner. While this game is played, it is possible for a teacher to evaluate throwing efficiency or provide instruction for individuals or the total group.

Snap is an effective drill which encourages the development of efficient spinal rotation. The child is asked to stand holding a yarn ball against his or her ear, with the oppositional foot in front of a hoop, and the nonoppositional foot inside the hoop. The child is asked to turn and face the teacher, who is standing behind the child. When the teacher

FIGURE 4.3. Inclined plastic throwing rope.

says "Snap," the child turns and throws the ball toward the target in front.

Demonstrations are effective instructional techniques. It is best to have children view the demonstrations from several angles. This may be accomplished by allowing the children to move as you demonstrate. Perhaps the best single viewing angle for the overhand throw is in front and slightly to the side of the demonstrator's favored arm. The demonstrator should perform the throw many times at normal speed. If the demonstration is shown only once, many children will not be able to obtain enough useful information. If the demonstrator attempts to slow the demonstration rather than perform it at normal speed, the essential force production information in the demonstration will be lost to observers. Verbally calling the children's attention to a single component of the throw (for example, oppositional stepping behavior) will help them attend to important information. Do not ask beginners to attend to more than one component at a time.

Word cues and other verbal guidance are also quite effective in helping children attain increasing overhand throwing efficiency. Call children's attention to only that single component of performance which is focal. Do not provide detailed discussions and descriptions for beginners. Try to combine your verbal guidance with a demonstration. Repeat word cues and key phrases over and over until they are retained in children's memories. Directions such as "throw hard" and "step-throw" are often helpful.

Run

Children should be encouraged to run in straight lines on firm, level surfaces while wearing nonslip shoes before they are asked to run on uneven, unfirm surfaces, or to run after other children and things, or to run in complex pathways. Care should be taken that obstacles and walls are a safe distance from running areas.

Running to and through crepe paper finish lines, balloon walls (a series of balloons suspended from string), and paper barriers

FIGURE 4.4. Birdseed Timer.

encourages efficient force production. Timing devices such as a birdseed-filled hourglass device made from plastic pop containers (Figure 4.4), a large clock which starts and stops when children step on pressure mats, and stopwatches provide information which children can use to improve their running efficiency. Equipment configurations which stress accuracy of performance rather than effective force production should be avoided. Attempting to improve running efficiency by having children run over spaced hoops or taped lines causes children to attend only to the accuracy of their foot placement. Practice opportunities such as these do not have much value in helping children achieve running efficiency.

Demonstrations are also effective in helping to improve the running efficiency of children. It is imperative that children be directed to view running demonstrations from the side, front, or rear, depending on the component of the run which is being attended to in the demonstrations. As with demonstrations of the overarm throw, running demonstrations should proceed at normal speed (unless loop films or videotapes are being employed), should emphasize correct rather than incorrect features of performance, should be free from distracting mannerisms, should focus on one component of performance at a time, and should be repeated several times. Word cues should be selected carefully and should emphasize the force productive nature of the task (for example, "Run as fast as possible").

FIGURE 4.5. Long jump mat.

Standing Long Jump

Initially beginners should be encouraged to jump on firm, level surfaces, across empty space, wearing nonslip shoes. Later, as children demonstrate increasing efficiency in the long jump, increasingly unstable surfaces and obstacles may be introduced. Jumping mats with distances delineated effectively encourage efficient long jumps (Figure 4.5). A *Jump-the-Stream* mat (Figure 4.6) and colored floor mat squares that may be located at different distances from one another (Figure 4.7) are also effective. Body extension at take-off and in flight can be encouraged by

asking a child to jump from a position in which both feet are side-by-side over a pair of painted footprints painted on a rubber floor mat so that the child's hands strike a tin can filled with pebbles which is suspended from a piece of sash cord that can be adjusted for height. The can is placed at a 45-degree angle from the child, approximately 2 to 3 feet above the child's head (Figure 4.8).

Elastic ropes can also be manipulated to encourage efficient body extension in take-off and flight. If a child is asked to stand in front of two ropes—one placed in front of the other, the farthest rope elevated to a higher level than the closest rope—and then asked to jump over both ropes, more efficient take-off and flight extension is seen.

As with the overhand throw and the run, demonstrations and verbal guidance can help children with the long jump. Verbal cues such as "Jump as far as possible" should emphasize force production.

Place Kick

You can encourage children to perform efficient place kicks by presenting them with large, lightweight stationary balls, resting on the ground. A coiled rope serves as an excel-

FIGURE 4.6. Jump-the-Stream mat.

FIGURE 4.7. Graded-size jumping squares.

FIGURE 4.9. Sound Curtain and coiled rope ball support.

lent ball holder (Figure 4.9). In early stages of skill development kicking targets should be very large, extending from ground level to well above head level. Later, as the child demonstrates increasing efficiency, smaller, heavier, and increasingly faster moving balls may be introduced; the trajectories of oncoming balls may become increasingly complex; targets may become smaller and take on movement characteristics; and the child may be called upon to make greater locomotor and nonlocomotor spatial adjustments prior to the kick.

Targets should encourage efficient force production. A series of aluminum pipes sus-

pended from a dowel make a good deal of noise when kicked forcefully (Figure 4.9). Muslin targets placed one behind the other, with a hole in each, also encourage force production (Figure 4.10). So do Indian club or plastic-pin targets, the *Dr. Seuss Space Ship* (Figure 4.11), and a three-tiered muslin target strung on sash cord (Figure 4.12).

FIGURE 4.10. Muslin Mouth Targets.

FIGURE 4.8. Long jump apparatus.

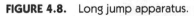

FIGURE 4.11. Dr. Seuss Space Ship Target.

The game of *Keep-Off* can be used with place kicking skills, allowing the teacher the opportunity to monitor general class or individual child kicking efficiency.

Demonstrations are best viewed from in front and to the favored side of the demonstrator. Verbal guidance is best directed to the force-productive aspects of the kick (for example, "Kick as forcefully as possible!").

Sidearm Strike

Initially balls should be large, lightweight, nonmoving, and placed at the striker's waist level on the striker's favored side. Targets should be large and nonmoving to encourage forceful striking behaviors. Bats, paddles, and racquets should be lightweight and

FIGURE 4.12. Three-Tiered Kicking Target.

FIGURE 4.13. Neat Feet, Batting tee of adjustable height, Sheet Metal Target, plastic ball, and plastic bats.

short, and provide large striking surfaces. Later balls may be smaller, heavier, faster moving, placed on the child's nonfavored side, and they may travel toward the child in increasingly complex trajectories. Targets

FIGURE 4.14. Whiffle ball suspended from an inverted hangman's noose, Monster Bat, and Mouth Target.

FIGURE 4.15. Neat Feet, Mouth Target, Striking Machine, foam balls, and plastic bat.

FIGURE 4.16. Plastic ball placed in a mesh bag and supported from an inverted hangman's noose, Neat Feet, and plastic bats.

may become smaller and increasingly faster moving. Bats may become longer and heavier. Paddles and racquets may become longer, heavier, and smaller in striking-surface area.

Footprints painted on black rubber floor matting may be used to encourage a step into the strike (Figure 4.13). Batting tees of adjustable height (Figure 4.13), balls suspended on inverted hangman's nooses made from sash cord which detach from Velcro fasteners when struck (Figure 4.14), and air jets from vacuum cleaners (Figure 4.15) ensure that the normal trajectory of a ball will not be interfered with once it has been struck.

A plastic ball placed in a mesh bag and supported from an inverted hangman's noose made from sash cord can be used to help children develop effective force production in the sidearm strike. If the child's task is to strike the ball forcefully enough to make it spin as many times as possible around a line of sash cord placed slightly

above head level, force production is encouraged (Figure 4.16).

Demonstrations should be viewed from the front. Verbal guidance should stress

FIGURE 4.17. Plexiglass Screen.

FIGURE 4.18. Catching Ramp, foam balls.

Catch

Initially beginners should work with large, lightweight balls such as foam balls, plastic balls, and beach balls, which travel slowly and in fairly predictable trajectories (for example, rolling along the ground, rolling down a ramp). Later smaller, heavier, and faster-moving balls may be introduced,

FIGURE 4.19. Foam balls suspended on inverted hangman's nooses.

force production (for example, "Strike as forcefully as possible").

with less predictable trajectories (for example, pendular trajectory, aerial balls). These require increasingly greater locomotor and nonlocomotor spatial adjustments prior to the catch.

A plexiglass shield encourages children to make effective decisions regarding necessary spatial adjustments prior to the catch and attenuates the possibility of children demonstrating a "fear reaction" in response to moving projectiles. The task of the child is to anticipate where on a large plexiglass sheet placed perpendicular to the floor a beanbag or ball will land that has been sent by a thrower. The child indicates a decision by placing a hand on the opposite side of the plexiglass sheet where the beanbag or ball will hit (Figure 4.17).

Catching ramps made of muslin that are capable of being adjusted to different inclines effectively control the speed with which objects travel (Figure 4.18).

Some control over speed and the complexity of ball trajectory can be obtained if balls suspended on inverted hangman's nooses are employed. Such balls can be adjusted upward or downward (Figure 4.19).

The game of *Move Back* is also helpful in developing skill in catching. Two children stand facing one another approximately 10 feet apart. They throw a ball back and forth, attempting to catch each throw. If both partners are able to catch the ball in sequence at the initial distance, they both step back 1 foot and attempt the task again. If at any point the ball is not caught, they must move 1 foot toward one another and try again. The goal is to move apart as far as possible and still catch the ball.

Demonstrations are helpful in teaching children how to catch. It is best not to throw the ball against a wall yourself prior to catching it in a demonstration. The attention of the children who observe you may be drawn to the throwing, rather than the catching, aspect of the demonstration. It would be best to use a videotaped or filmed demonstration to avoid distracting demonstration elements (for example, verbal exchange prior to demonstration, throw prior to catch).

5

growth
and
physical activity

Whatever our age or sex, our performance in sport and physical activity is influenced by, and to some extent influences, our physical growth. We differ from one another in height and weight, body proportions, physique, posture, distribution of various body tissues, and the speed with which the various tissues grow—factors that help explain why we perform as we do in sport and physical activity. Stresses to bones, joints, and muscles during rigorous exercise programs influence bone growth, joint flexibility, muscle growth, the development of strength, and the relative proportions of fat, muscle, and bone tissue in our bodies.

Examining the relationship between growth and physical activity and sport can (a) help explain vast differences in physical performance, (b) provide insight which may influence the selection of program objectives, content, instructional tactics, and evaluative procedures, (c) provide more realistic expectations for the physical performances of people at various ages, of various races, and of both sexes, and (d) suggest coaching strategies and training procedures appropriate for use with children in competitive sport situations.

GROWTH

Growth is an increase in the size of a living thing or any of its parts. Today the terms *growth, development, maturation, heredity,* and *environment* are frequently used together: Here *growth* means anatomical changes and differentiation within structures; *development* means the emergence and expansion of capabilities of the individual to provide progressively greater facility in functioning; *maturation* means change in the complexity of structure which makes it possible for a structure to begin functioning or to function at higher levels; *heredity* means the genetic inheritance of an individual; and *environment* means habits and circumstances of living.

The Nature of Growth

Growth processes are not capricious. They are the lawful and predictable product of a dynamic relationship between heredity and environment:

1. Growth is continuous and orderly. Increases in size occur with such regularity that it is possible to predict the stature a child will have upon reaching adulthood. Each growth pattern and process is closely related to later growth developments.

2. *Growth sequences do not proceed at a steady pace.* There are periods of accelerated growth and periods of decelerated growth. During infancy growth moves swiftly, while the growth rate slows during the preschool and elementary-school years. When adolescence is reached, certain phases of growth become accelerated before they taper off to the adult level.

3. *Not all aspects of growth proceed at the same rate or at the same time.* For example, the nervous system grows rapidly in the earlier years, while the most rapid growth of the genital system occurs during adolescence.

4. *The rate and pattern of growth can be influenced by numerous variables.* Although patterns of growth are fairly well defined for all children by heredity, both rate and exact pattern can be modified by a variety of factors including mutations, interference with fetal development, brain damage, or environmental influences after birth. Nutrition, activity, rest, hormonal activity, socioeconomic class, disease, climate, emotion, and exercise are other factors which can influence growth.

5. *The growth of each individual is unique.* Children differ in their rate of growth, going through predictable sequential steps at slower or faster rates. Some children may be slow starters. Others may fail to keep up their early growth rate. There are also definite differences between boys and girls.

Methods of Studying Growth

In the past researchers have employed two major methods of studying growth: the *cross-sectional* method and the *longitudinal* method. The cross-sectional method involves measuring or testing different groups of children at different ages. In such studies large groups are often tested and the results expressed as averages for those groups. Many of the norms now used, such as those for height and weight, were collected in this way.

The longitudinal method, which involves measuring the same children over a number of years, is a more reliable method of determining growth trends. This method can also be used to study individual patterns of growth and speed of growth. The cross-sectional method cannot be used in this way.

Growth is often represented graphically in two ways: by distance curves and by velocity curves. Measurements taken for a single individual or group of individuals at intervals can be plotted against time to show progress (for example, Figure 5.1). A graph of this kind is called a distance curve, since any point on it indicates the distance the body has traveled along the road to maturity.

Another way of presenting the same data is shown in Figure 5.2, in which increments in growth, within specified time intervals, are plotted against time. Such a curve shows variation in the rate of growth with time. It is therefore known as a velocity curve.

FIGURE 5.1. Typical individual distance curves for height. (From Tanner, J. M., Whitehouse, R. H., and Takaishi, M. *Archives of Diseases in Childhood* 41[1966]: 467.)

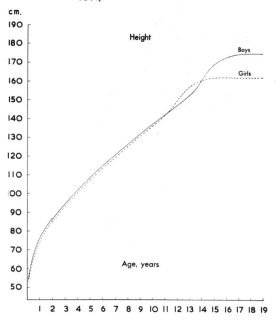

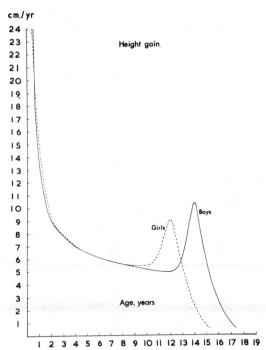

cm./yr

Height gain

Boys

Girls

Age, years

FIGURE 5.2. Typical individual velocity curves for height. (From Tanner, J. M., Whitehouse, R. H., and Takaishi, M. *Archives of Diseases in Childhood* 41[1966]: 466.)

GROWTH: IMPLICATIONS FOR PHYSICAL EDUCATION

Height and Weight

There exist significant differences in growth in height and weight that are attributable to age, sex, and individual variations. This situation causes several implications for the design of physical education programs and sport opportunities.

Velocity curves. The growth patterns for height and weight are characterized by alternating periods of faster and slower growth (Figures 5.2 and 5.3). The first period of fast growth occurs in infancy; the second period, known as the adolescent spurt, occurs in early adolescence. Following this second spurt, growth slows down and, especially in height, ceases at maturity. Upon reaching elementary school, the child is al-

ready in the middle period of slower growth. The early elementary-school years are characterized by decelerating growth in height (Figure 5.2). At approximately 9 years of age, girls begin their adolescent growth spurt, which reaches a peak in the twelfth or thirteenth year. Boys begin their growth spurt at around 11 years of age and reach their maximum gains, which are greater than those of girls, in the fourteenth or fifteenth year.

In weight (Figure 5.3) the school-age child increases in momentum slowly each year until girls reach a peak at about age 12 and boys at about age 14. The peak in weight tends to lag behind that of height by 6 months or more. Thus, many children have a brief filling-out period after their rapid growth in height. Growth in height generally ceases somewhere between 16 years of age and the early 20s. Growth in weight for the average adolescent probably stops in the early 20s.

Changes in height and weight as discussed above carry with them several implications for physical education. The steadiness of the height-and-weight growth period of the first four elementary-school years probably encourages children to steadily acquire physical skills and gradually develop accurate conceptions of their performance capabilities. However, the adolescent growth spurt represents a volatile, rapid period of growth during which children frequently demonstrate difficulty in maintaining steady progress in skill acquisition and in accurately conceptualizing their ability to perform physical skills. Performance abilities change as children grow taller and heavier, but the accuracy of children's perceptions often cannot keep up with these changes. Those who design activity programs for adolescents should not be surprised to see awkward physical performance or frustrated learning attempts at this stage.

Distance curves. From birth to 12 years of age, boys tend to be slightly taller than girls. Between 12 and 14 years of age, girls tend to be taller than boys. Between 14 and 18 years of age boys become increasingly taller than girls. Eventually boys assume their

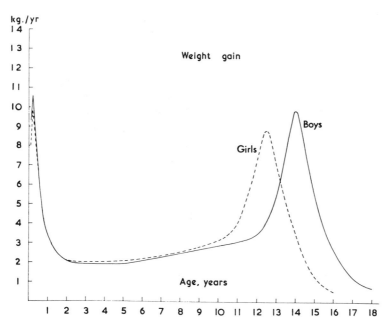

FIGURE 5.3. Typical individual velocity curves for weight. (From Tanner, J. M., Whitehouse, R. H., and Takaishi, M. *Archives of Diseases in Childhood* 41[1966]:466.)

adult height advantage. This can be examined graphically in Figure 5.1. Between 2 and 4 years of age, boys tend to be slightly heavier than girls. Between 4 and 11 years of age, there is no discernable difference in weight between the sexes. Between the ages of 11 and 15, girls are frequently heavier than boys. Between the ages of 15 and 18, this relationship reverses, moving toward the characteristically greater weight of boys (Figure 5.4).

Boys grow in height from about 18½ to 21 inches at birth to about 66 to 74 inches at 18 years of age; in weight they range from 6½ to 9½ pounds at birth to about 120 to 169 pounds at 18 years of age. Girls grow from approximately 18½ to 21 inches and 6½ to 9 pounds at birth to about 62 to 67 inches and 104 to 160 pounds at 18 years of age. These figures are taken from National Center for Health Statistics (NCHS) Growth Charts (1976), using as the range the tenth to ninetieth percentiles.

These differences in stature and weight carry with them several implications for physical education. There are many advan-

tages and disadvantages to being very large or very small in a variety of physical performance and sport situations. Large people have a greater inertia and momentum than smaller people. This may be a decided advantage in a blocking situation in football. However, when agility is necessary, as may be the case in soccer, a large person is at a disadvantage.

The few differences that exist between the sexes in height and weight before 10 years of age would seem to suggest the appropriateness of combining boys and girls for instruction in physical education and sport situations through the third or fourth grade. However, after this age differences between the sexes in stature and weight call into question the common practice of homogeneous age-sex groups. Between 10 and 13 years of age girls are heavier and taller than boys. Our culture does not reward girls for outperforming boys in sport settings. Competitive situations which pit boy against girl at this time may result in girls refusing to participate freely or energetically and/or in some boys having self-doubts about their

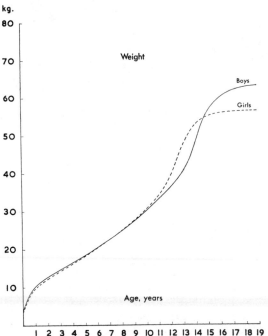

FIGURE 5.4. Typical individual distance curves for weight. (From Tanner, J. M., Whitehouse, R. H., and Takaishi, M. *Archives of Diseases in Childhood* 41[1966]: 467.)

cent years, when growth is tapering off, individual differences can be expected to be less than during the late elementary-school and early high-school years.

A child's individual pattern of growth tends to become well established between the ages of 2 and 4 and to become regular during the years of steady growth in middle childhood. During the early adolescent years the pattern may change for some children. Some are tall from a very early age and remain tall. These children will be tall adults and achieve their mature height 2 or 3 years before most of their peers. Some children are small throughout their growing years, mature

FIGURE 5.5. Girls' stature by age percentiles: ages 2 to 18 years. The central line represents the mean, or 50th centile. The two lines above and below it represent the 75th and 25th centiles (i.e., 25 percent of the cross-sectional sample fell below the lower line and 25 percent above the upper line). Other centile lines are also provided. (From National Center for Health Statistics, U.S. Department of Health, Education and Welfare, HRA 25, 3 June 22, 1976 and David L. Gallahue, *Understanding Motor Development in Children,* New York: John Wiley & Sons, Inc., 1982.)

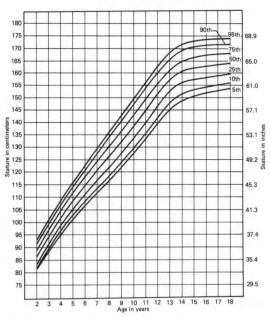

masculinity. After 14 years of age, boys hold the height and weight advantage.

Individual differences. Individual differences in height and weight are apparent at birth and continue throughout the years of growth. The considerable spread in the height figures for a given age is indicated by the percentile lines on the charts in Figures 5.5 and 5.6. These show the percentages of children whose heights lay on or below the labeled line. Thus, 25 percent of the group had heights which lay on or below the labeled twenty-fifth centile line. The same may be said for differences among individuals in weight (Figures 5.7 and 5.8).

The degree of variability in height and weight changes from time to time. Individual differences in size tend to be greater as children grow older and especially during periods of more rapid growth. During the elementary-school years, when growth is slower, and during the college or late adoles

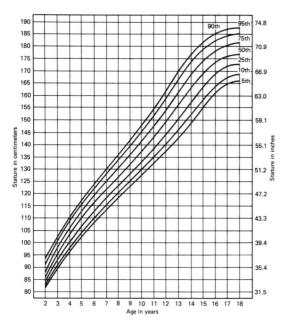

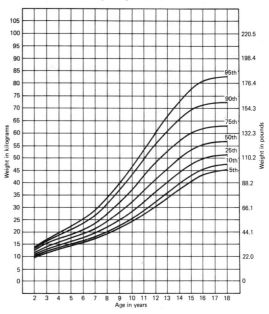

FIGURE 5.6. Boys' stature by age percentiles: ages 2 to 18 years. Centiles as in Figure 5.5. (From National Center for Health Statistics, U.S. Department of Health, Education and Welfare, HRA 25, 3 June 22, 1976 and David L. Gallahue, *Understanding Motor Development in Children,* New York: John Wiley & Sons, Inc., 1982.)

FIGURE 5.7. Girls' weight by age percentiles: ages 2 to 18 years. Centiles as in Figure 5.5. (From National Center for Health Statistics, U.S. Department of Health, Education and Welfare, HRA 25, 3 June 22, 1976 and David L. Gallahue, *Understanding Motor Development in Children,* New York: John Wiley & Sons, Inc., 1982.)

dren, on the other hand, tend to begin later and grow more slowly. They are not necessarily shorter at maturity. In fact, some are taller than those who mature early. Thus, later-maturing children may catch up eventually with their faster-developing peers.

The growth of an individual child is dependent upon the interaction of heredity and environment. Heredity sets the potential for growth; health and environment, including nutrition, determine the degree to which that potential is achieved.

Tremendous variability and individual differences in height and weight exist within homogeneous age and sex groups. This fact strongly suggests that we need to individualize instruction, physical skills goals, and evaluation processes for children—particularly during adolescence, when individual variability is at its greatest. Competition against oneself should probably take precedence

slowly, and reach small adult stature usually after age 18 for girls and age 20 for boys. Some, however, who are tall or short, may emerge from the adolescent growth spurt taller or shorter than might have been expected. This is because they are slow or fast maturers and not necessarily constitutionally large or small.

There are extensive differences in the timing and length of the adolescent spurt for boys. It can last anywhere from 2 to 4 years. Some boys have an early beginning, some are late; some have a short period, some a long one. The picture of fifth-grade boys enrolled in a typical physical education class helps illustrate this situation (Figure 5.9).

However, the majority of children who begin their adolescent spurt early tend to grow faster and complete their growth early. At maturity they may not be taller than late-maturing children. The late-maturing chil-

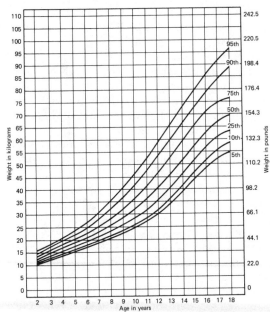

FIGURE 5.8. Boys' weight by age percentiles: ages 2 to 18 years. Centiles as in Figure 5.5. (From National Center for Health Statistics, U.S. Department of Health, Education and Welfare, HRA 25, 3 June 22, 1976 and David L. Gallahue, *Understanding Motor Development in Children*, New York: John Wiley & Sons, Inc., 1982.)

over competition with others. Physical education and sport experiences which allow height and weight to be decisive factors in successful performance are probably not as desirable as experiences in which skillfulness is the major factor influencing performance.

Measuring and evaluating height and weight. Since height and weight—and changes within them—carry many implications for designing and carrying out programs of movement experience for children, it is often useful to assess this aspect of growth. The only pieces of equipment necessary for measuring height are a flat surface against which the child can stand, a measuring tape calibrated in centimeters and/or quarter-inches, and an object to place on the child's head that forms a right angle to the flat surface. Children should be measured without shoes, standing with their backs

against a support to encourage them to stretch to their full height. The chin should be tucked in slightly and the head held erect. The object used to form a right angle to the flat surface should be pressed firmly onto the child's head. Care should be taken that the upper surface is horizontal and not tilted and also that this pressure does not cause the child to slump or alter position.

A child's height and weight can be compared against the measurements of an extremely large and representative sample of United States children of like sex and age. The most recently constructed growth charts for United States infants and children are those published in 1976 by the National Center for Health Statistics. Among these are charts for children 2 to 18 years of age which include body weight by age and stature by age (separate charts for boys and girls). These are included in Figures 5.5 through 5.8.

Trends over the decades. For the last two centuries children have become increasingly taller as a result of improved nutrition and better control of disease (see Figure 5.10). However, this trend has leveled off and it appears that the average American has probably reached the maximum stature that personal genetic endowment permits.

Growth Curves

Most body tissues follow approximately the growth curve described for height. Most of the skeleton and musculature grows in this manner, as do internal organs such as the liver, spleen, and kidneys. However, there are some exceptions: the brain and skull; the reproductive tissues; the lymphoid tissue of the tonsils, adenoids, and intestines; and subcutaneous fat.

These differences are shown in Figure 5.11 using the size attained by various tissues as a percentage of the birth-to-maturity increment. Height follows the general curve. The reproductive organs, internal and external, have a slow prepubescent growth, followed by a very large adolescent spurt. The brain, together with the skull covering it and the eyes and ears, develops earlier than any

FIGURE 5.9. Varied growth status of fifth-grade boys enrolled in a physical education class.

other part of the body and thus has a unique curve.

The eye probably has a slight adolescent spurt, although present data are not accurate enough to be certain. It is probably this that is responsible for the increase in frequency of shortsightedness in children during adolescence.

Implications can be drawn from growth curves for different tissues and parts of the body, which may be useful to those interested in sport and physical activity: (a) The general leveling off of growth curves for muscle, the skeleton, and height during the elementary-school years probably helps to explain the steady progress in the attainment of physical skills that characterizes this growth period; and (b) The rapid rise in growth curves for muscle, bone, height, and especially the reproductive system in adolescence represents tremendous growth changes. To some extent they help to explain adolescent unevenness in skill acquisition and suggest the inappropriateness of demanding high levels of skill from children during this period. They also suggest the need for individualized instruction and for

allowing children to select from a broad range of movement opportunities.

Bone

Those interested in children's participation in sport and physical activity have questioned the effects of such activity on the development of the immature skeleton.

A good deal is known about bone growth. In the embryo long bones are formed of cartilage. Ossification (hardening) of these bones begins at primary ossification centers located in the midportion of the bone. Usually at birth ossification has occurred to include the entire bone shaft. Cartilaginous epiphyseal centers develop at the end of the long bones. Secondary ossification centers appear in the epiphyseal areas. Between the secondary ossification center and the remainder of the bone shaft is a growth plate. Bone growth occurs in this area. When full growth has been completed, the epiphysis fuses to the rest of the bone shaft and the growth plate disappears. Disturbances of bone growth generally involve the growth plate.

LEVELING OFF

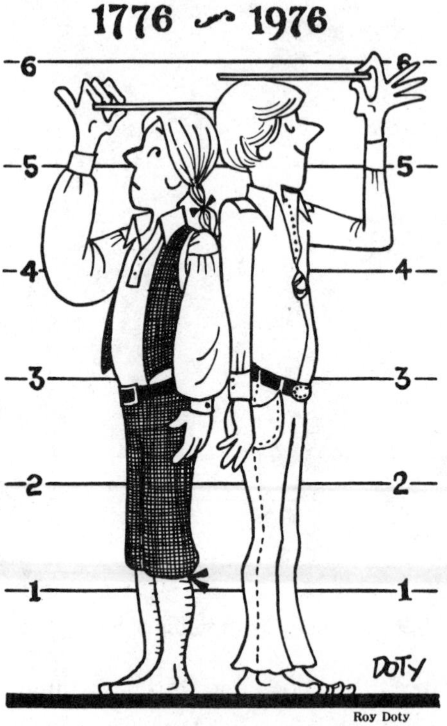

1776 ~ 1976

For as far back as anyone can remember, American children have been noticeably taller than their parents. And most mothers and fathers have expected their offspring to continue to scale new heights. But now the century-old national trend toward taller children seems to have leveled off, and experts say the average American has probably reached the maximum stature that his own genetic endowment permits him to attain.

The National Center for Health Statistics bases this conclusion on studies of more than 20,000 children over the past fifteen years. The data show that the height of the average teen-age boy and girl has not increased since the 1960s. The center drew upon much older records as its basis of comparison. These showed that the average height of a recruit during the Revolutionary War was almost 5 feet 6 inches, and there was little change between 1776 and 1876. But starting about 1876, there began a steady decade-by-decade increase in the growth rate. Today, the average 18-year-old boy stands at nearly 5 feet 9½, and girls of the same age at 5 feet 4¼. The boys weigh more than 150 pounds, and the girls 123.

Scientists at the NCHS attribute the rise in stature to a number of factors, such as the steady improvement in diet and hygiene that began in the mid-nineteenth century, and to the development of drugs and vaccines against the major childhood illnesses. The NCHS figures also show that girls tend to reach their maximum height at 15 or 16, while boys continue to grow for several years more.

FIGURE 5.10. Trends in height and weight over the decades. (From "Leveling Off." *Newsweek*, June 21, 1976, p. 58.)

Can participation in sport and physical activity over long periods of time influence skeletal development? Professor Ivanitsky, Director of the Central Pedagogical Institute of Physical Culture of the Soviet Union, believes that it can. He cites the following examples from his studies:

1. The femur of soccer players who have competed for years is often larger than that of nonathletes.
2. The radius of tennis players was larger than that of swimmers or gymnasts in a study of young athletes 11 to 13 years of age.
3. The pelvis of female gymnasts of the same height was smaller in girls who started gymnastics before the age of 14 than was the case for women who started gymnastics later in life.
4. The marrow cavity of the tibia of runners active over 5 years was enlarged.

It has long been acknowledged that bone will adapt to the strains and stresses placed upon it. What is not predictable, however, are the unique bone adaptations of individuals to various long-term exercise and sport-training regimens. Professor Ivanitsky's findings are interesting. However, at the present time it is difficult to say with certainty exactly how bone growth is influenced by physical activity regimens engaged in for long periods of time. It appears that mild degrees of stress act as stimulants and are absolutely necessary for normal bone growth, while severe degrees of stress result in bone inflammation and destruction.

Fat

The growth of the subcutaneous fat layer has a unique growth curve of its own, which is slightly more complicated than the curves previously presented. The thickness of the fat layer can be measured at certain sites in the body by picking up a fold of skin and fat between the thumb and forefinger and measuring its thickness with a special, constant-pressure caliper. Figure 5.12 shows the distance curves of skinfolds taken halfway down the back of the arm (triceps) and at the back of the chest, just below the shoulder blade (subscapular). The triceps measures represent limb fat. The subscapular measures represent body fat.

The fat content of the body increases considerably between birth and the age of 6

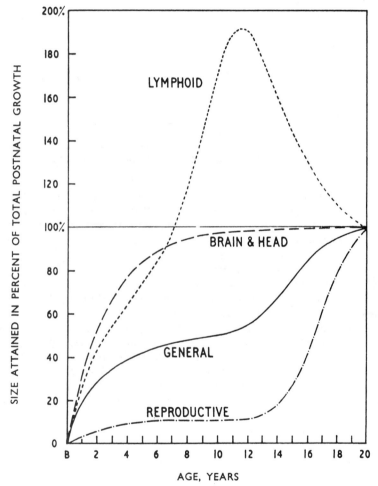

FIGURE 5.11. Growth curves for different tissues and parts of the body, showing the four chief types. All the curves are of size attained and are plotted as percent of total gain from birth to 20 years, so that size at age 20 is 100 on the vertical scale. (From Tanner, J. M. *Growth at Adolescence.* Springfield, Ill.: Chas. C. Thomas, 1962, 11.)

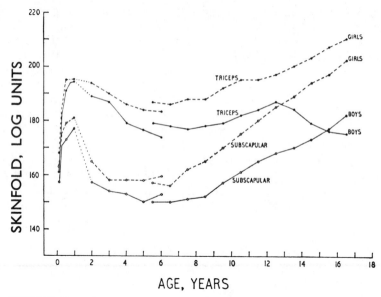

FIGURE 5.12. Distance curve of subcutaneous fat tissue measured by skinfold calipers over triceps and under scapula. Logarithmic transformation units. (From Tanner, J. M. *Growth at Adolescence.* Springfield, Ill.: Chas. C. Thomas, 1962, 22.)

months, but the rate of increase rapidly falls off in the last 6 months of the first year. After this the fat content actually decreases until the age of 6 or 8 years, by which time the thickness of the subcutaneous tissue is approximately half of what it was at the age of 1 year. The decrease is less in girls than in boys, so that after 1 year of age, girls are fatter than boys of the same age. Subsequently the body fat begins to increase again, and many children put on excess fat just before the adolescent spurt. During the male spurt the fat on the limbs decreases and is not gained back until the late 20s. In girls there is no such decrease, though there may be a temporary interruption of the increase. In both sexes fat on the trunk continues to increase fairly steadily, but in girls additional fat is laid down in keeping with secondary sex characteristics (hips, thighs, breasts, upper arms).

The discrepancy between the sexes in the laying down of fat tissue not only contributes to the characteristic differences in body contour that differentiate the sexes, but it is probably responsible, in conjunction with muscle tissue growth, for many of the performance differences seen between boys and girls in adolescence.

Muscle and Strength

From birth to maturity muscle weight increases forty times. At birth muscles make up one-fifth to one-fourth of the body weight; in early adolescence, about one-third; and in early maturity, about two-fifths.

After birth muscles grow in size by increasing the length, breadth, and thickness of their component fibers. Muscles do not grow by increasing the number of fibers. Muscles change in composition with age and become more firmly attached to bones. They also gradually come under increased voluntary control. This is reflected in the change from awkward and inefficient to graceful and efficient movement in preschool and elementary-school children.

Boys are generally more muscular than girls, but there is wide variation within a given age and sex group. Considerable muscle growth occurs during the school years.

Muscle growth lags behind growth in size but catches up later. Therefore, adolescents who may have attained their adult stature and sexual characteristics may not necessarily be fully grown in terms of their musculature.

Although boys are somewhat stronger than girls (the greatest discrepancy being in the upper extremities), there is fairly even progress in strength development for both sexes until about 11 years of age. After puberty the rate of increase for boys greatly exceeds that for girls (Figure 5.13).

For boys the beginning of the growth spurt in strength comes at about the time boys reach a skeletal age of 14 years and generally lags behind the spurt in height and weight. The peak of the spurt of growth in strength comes about 1½ years after that in height and 1 year after that in weight. Growth in strength continues into the third decade for boys. The discrepancy between the spurts in height and weight and strength imply that an adolescent boy may grow taller and heavier before he grows stronger. This may influence his ability to perform in sport and physical activity.

Girls generally experience their spurt of growth in strength in the year preceding menarche. By age 13 their growth in strength slows down very appreciably. By 16 years of age practically all boys are superior in strength to the average girl. As in other phases of growth, girls mature earlier than boys, and thus at the same chronological age, girls are farther advanced toward their terminal strength than boys. For example, at 13 years of age boys have reached approximately 45 percent of their terminal strength in pull and thrust; girls have reached 75 percent in pull and 90 percent in thrust. It is undoubtedly true that these differences in strength have a biological basis. However, cultural expectations probably operate to increase motivation and practice in boys and diminish it in girls.

When body weight is considered, the strength differences between boys and girls appear even more exaggerated after puberty (Figure 5.13). When corrected for body weight, there is typically no increase in strength for girls after puberty. However,

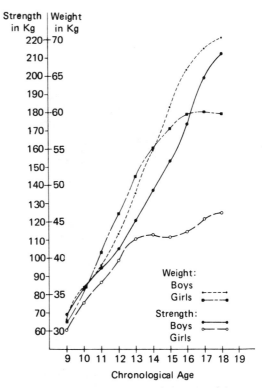

FIGURE 5.13 Strength and weight in 9 through 18-year-old boys and girls. (From R. D. Tuddenham and M. M. Snyder. Physical Growth of California Boys and Girls from Birth to Eighteen Years, *Child ChildeDevelopment* 1:2 University of California Press, 1954, 364. By permission of Wm. C. Brown.)

relative strength increases dramatically after puberty for boys.

During the adolescent growth period early-maturing individuals are generally superior in strength to the later maturers. This is most marked in boys around 14½ years of age and girls at 13 years of age. The superiority of early-maturing boys continues into later adolescence; this does not hold for girls. Early-maturing girls tend to drop below the average-maturing group. The lag in the puberal spurt of strength behind that of other physical measurements is more noticeable for the early than for the late maturers. While the later-maturing boys, with their slower pattern of growth, may have a more closely synchronized physical development

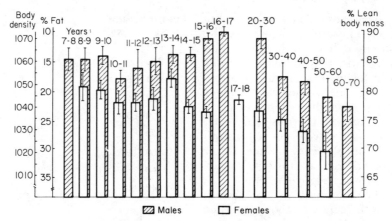

FIGURE 5.14. The development of body composition (percent of lean body mass, fat, body density) during growth and aging in males and females. (From Parizkova, J. "Body composition and exercise." In *Physical Activity,* ed. G. L. Rarick. New York: Academic Press, 1973, 98.)

and thus escape some of the strains incident to rapid growth, the early-maturing boys, with their rapid and in some ways less well-integrated growth, often gain an early advantage in athletic competition and in associated prestige.

Exercise can influence the size of muscles by causing muscle fibers to increase in breadth, length, and thickness beyond that which would be expected simply by growth. Increase in muscle mass and strength results either from high resistance overload training with very few repetitions or from highly repetitive and low resistance exercise.

Body Composition

Body composition refers to the proportion of total body mass which is lean and the proportion of total body mass which is fat. The relative proportions of these components are different for males and females through much of the life span (Figure 5.14). The proportion of lean body mass is highest and the proportion of fat lowest at approximately 16 to 17 years of age for males and 13 to 14 years of age for females. At all ages males have a higher lean body mass than do females. The differences between the sexes are less pronounced before age 13 and after

age 30. The differences between the sexes are most pronounced at about 15 or 16 years of age.

Exercise can have a profound impact on body composition during growth periods, as in all other periods of life. Physical activity is associated with the development of lean body mass at the expense of fat in both boys and girls. The extent of change depends on the intensity and duration of the exercise. After interruption of training there is gener-

TABLE 5.1 Obesity standards for Caucasian American children

Age (Years)	Minimum Triceps Skin-fold Thickness Indicating Obesity (Millimeters)	
	MALES	FEMALES
5	12	14
6	12	15
7	13	16
8	14	17
9	15	18
10	16	20
11	17	21
12	18	22
13	18	23

From C. C. Seltzer and J. Mayer, "A Simple Criterion of Obesity." *Postgraduate Medicine,* 38(1965):101.

ally an increase in body weight, largely fat, which is not caused solely by increase in caloric intake but also by metabolic adaptations in fat and muscular tissues. During training there is an increased ability to use fat as a fuel for muscular work. When energy output is suddenly decreased, fat is laid down.

Often one wishes to employ a screening device to locate children who are obese. The most direct, simple, and accurate method is to measure the thickness of the triceps skinfold, using constant-tension calipers, comparing the child's skinfold measurement in millimeters to the obesity standards defined by Seltzer and Mayer (1965) which are presented in Table 5.1.

Body Proportions

Differences in degree and timing in the growth of different segments of the body produce changes in body proportions with age for both sexes (Figure 5.15). After birth the rate with which the head grows steadily diminishes. The legs grow longer until about 15 years of age in boys and about 13 years of age in girls. After that, trunk-length increases are larger than leg length changes. The head changes from one-fourth of the total length at birth to about one-sixth at 6 years and about one-eighth at maturity. Legs change from about three-eighths of total length at birth to about half the total length at adulthood. Legs increase in length almost five times from birth to maturity; the head, twice; and the trunk, three times. As this occurs the center of gravity of the body drops, resulting in increased body stability.

During the early elementary-school years girls begin to evidence a characteristic proportional sex difference in width of shoulders and hips (they increase hip width relatively more than shoulder width). Boys, on the other hand, do not show any increase in relative shoulder width until age 10. From approximately 10 years of age on, however, these sex differences consistently appear; girls develop proportionally broader hips and boys develop proportionally broader shoulders. During the adolescent spurt growth in hip width is as great for males as

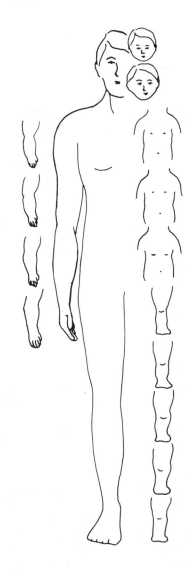

FIGURE 5.15. During a child's growth, the head doubles in size, the arms become four times as long, the legs five times as long, and the trunk three times as long. (Photograph used with permission of Wm. C. Brown Publishers. From J. Herkowitz, "Physical growth," in *A Textbook of Motor Development,* ed. C. B. Corbin. Dubuque, Iowa: Wm. C. Brown Publishers, 1980, 12.)

for females. However, males have greater adolescent spurts in shoulder width.

Those interested in sport and physical activity should note the following: (a) As body proportions change, the center of gravity of the body descends, resulting in better balance and greater stability. This probably encourages the development of increased skillfulness, particularly in activities that call for a good deal of balance. (b) Since leg length contributions to total stature during the growth spurt are greater for males than for females of the same stature, females' lower centers of gravity may give them performance advantages in activities that require a good deal of stability and balance. (c) The differences between the sexes in lateral growth of the hips and shoulders would seem to give men the performance advantage in activities which involve considerable arm action or running agility. (d) The fact that limbs grow proportionally more than other body parts, for both sexes, may imply that children should be exposed to frequent opportunities to participate in sport and physical activity so that they may learn to use their increased limb lengths effectively.

Physique

Body proportions and the amounts and distribution of fat, muscle, and bone contribute to an overall body form, build, or physique, which is a vital and fairly stable part of an individual's uniqueness. Body form may be designated in various ways. For example, individuals may be classified as slender to stocky or they may be classified by somatotype—as having soft-roundness (endomorphs), muscular solidity (mesomorphs), or linearity-delicacy (ectomorphs) in varying degrees and proportions (Figure 5.16). Differences in physique may be recognized at a fairly early age. Physique consistency tends to be low in infancy. However, it increases throughout the school years.

Body build seems to have some relation to growth and maturation. Endomorphic children tend to be heavier, shorter, reach their peak in the puberal growth spurt in height and weight earlier, and grow faster than ec-

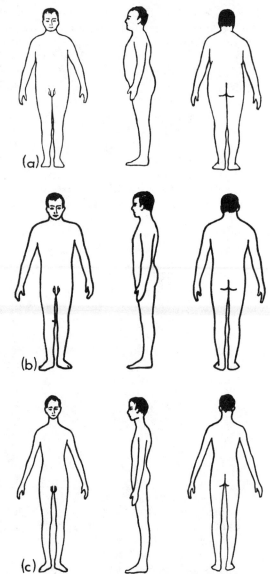

FIGURE 5.16. Somatotypes: (a) Endomorph, (b) Mesomorph, and (c) Ectomorph. (Adapted from photographs in Sheldon, W. H., and Stevens, S. S. *The Varieties of Temperament.* New York: Hafner Publishers, 1942.)

tomorphs. Endomorphy is associated with early biological maturity in women. Mesomorphy seems to bear no significant relationship to maturation rate.

Although there seems to be little relationship between physique and strength in childhood, a clearly defined relationship exists in adolescence, especially for males. While we might assume that heavily boned children should be stronger than children of ectomorphic build, when strength per unit of body mass is examined, the difference in strength between the heavily boned and light boned child is not well defined.

It is clearly evident, however, that strength, muscularity, and mesomorphy are closely associated in males throughout the preadolescent and adolescent years. Mesomorphs appear substantially stronger than ectomorphs or endomorphs. Ectomorphs appear weakest of all three somatotype categories. The strength superiority of the mesomorph increases with advancing age. In terms of strength per pound of body weight, the mesomorphs are, as a group, stronger on the average than ectomorphs and endomorphs at 11 years of age and older. Only limited study has been made of the relationship between the physique and strength of adolescent girls.

Performance of motor skills during the elementary-school ages is largely unaffected by body build, except at the extremes of the physique continuum. Many factors, either related or unrelated to physique, appear to affect motor performance during these formative years. Although agility seems positively related to mesomorphy, negatively related to endomorphy, and not related to ectomorphy in elementary-school-aged boys, in general, relationships between somatotype and motor variables are low.

In adolescence, as in childhood, high relationships between physique and gross motor performance have not been found. Body build has little influence on average performance. However, it does seem an important factor in exceptional achievement. High-performing boys tend to have a medium physique with relatively short legs and narrow hips as compared to low performers who have a stocky build, wide hips, and relatively long legs. High-performing girls are generally characterized by slender physiques and short legs in contrast to the broad and heavy build of poor-performing girls. It appears

that in both sexes high endomorphy is related to poor motor performance during adolescence.

It would also seem that certain physiques are predisposed to certain types of physical activity pursuits and habits during the years of active growth as well as in adulthood. Both experience and the observation that athletes tend to gravitate to sports suited to their body build reinforces this point of view.

At present there is no definitive answer as to whether exercise regimens and sports participation can change physique. However, from what evidence exists, it would seem that exercise does not significantly influence physique, either in childhood, in adolescence, or during the early adult years.

It would seem logical that physical activity should be influential in encouraging mesomorphy and reducing fatness and possibly endomorphic ratings. Short-term training studies, however, indicate that training-induced changes are not sufficient to alter somatotype ratings.

An examination of the relationship between physique, strength, and physical performance provides some useful insights. In general, most children, adolescents, and

FIGURE 5.17. Changes in the spinal curvatures with growth (a) Infant—two primary curvatures (b) 6 months—the secondary cervical curvature has appeared (c) Adult—two primary and two secondary curvatures (d) Old age—the two secondary curvatures, dependent on the discs and the postural muscles, are becoming obliterated (e) Final stage—corresponding to the condition in the infant (From Sinclair, D. *Human Growth after Birth.* London: Oxford University Press, 1973, 116.)

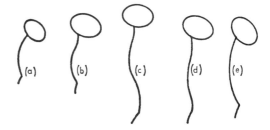

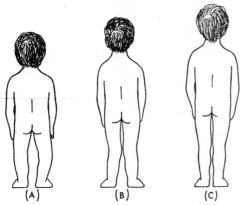

tive adults provide programs of movement experiences that deemphasize competition among peers and emphasize individual progress, individual choice, and individualized instruction. It is also likely that the adolescent mesomorphic boy and adolescent ecto-mesomorphic girl may feel a lack of challenge if special provisions are not made for them. Their high levels of strength and performance capabilities need the challenge of interschool competition.

adults do not represent extreme physique types. In their case physique is not extremely influential in determining strength or ability to perform in physical education or sport settings. Extreme adolescent endomorphs and mesomorphs, however, should be treated with considerable care in such activities. It is unlikely that the endomorphic girl or boy will have the same strength or ability to perform as his or her peers. It is likely that extremely endomorphic children may learn to avoid physical activity and sport unless sensi-

Posture

Significant changes occur over time in the spinal curves, leg and foot position, prominence of the abdomen and shoulder blades, and appearance of the thorax. Curves in the spine appear concurrently with progress in motor development (Figure 5.17). The first curve in the neck region appears when children hold their heads erect; the lumbar curve in the lower part of the back gradually develops with standing and walking. Every baby has bowing of the legs, which, all other factors being equal, straighten in due time after the child begins to walk (Figure 5.18). The toddler has knock-knees and some degree of pronation, a prominent abdomen and, in proportion to the prominence of the abdomen, an exaggerated lumbar curve (Figure 5.19). The prominent abdomen and lumbar curve can be expected to continue through the preschool and primary-school

FIGURE 5.19. The posture of a child from 1 year, 7 months to 16 years, 3 months, showing changes in body balance accompanying growth. (From Breckenridge, M. E., and Vincent, E. L. *Child Development*. Philadelphia: Saunders, 1965, 219.)

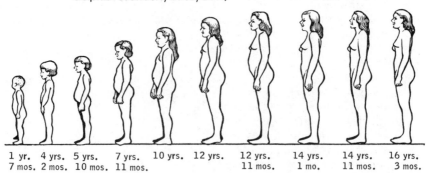

| 1 yr.
7 mos. | 4 yrs.
2 mos. | 5 yrs.
10 mos. | 7 yrs.
11 mos. | 10 yrs. | 12 yrs. | 12 yrs.
11 mos. | 14 yrs.
1 mo. | 14 yrs.
11 mos. | 16 yrs.
3 mos. |

years. Knock-knees and pronation gradually decrease. The condition of the knees and feet improves by age 6 or 7; the protrusion of the abdomen changes noticeably at about age 10 or 12. The normal prominence of the shoulder blades and the barrel-chested appearance of the infant, preschool, and elementary-school child gradually disappear.

In the adolescent period postural tendencies which have begun earlier tend to become fixed and thus the characteristics of adult posture appear. The abdomen flattens, the typical dorsal and lumbar curves emerge, and the pelvis tilts slightly upward in front and downward in the back. These changes are illustrated in Figure 5.19.

The following implications may be drawn from the above: (a) Activity can contribute to the strength-building necessary for developing and maintaining efficient upright posture. Therefore, activity programs in elementary, junior high, and high schools should be soundly supported. (b) The lack of balance shown by children in preschools and primary schools is, in part, caused by normal postural development. Teachers should not expect efficient running performances from children until the legs become straight, the abdomen becomes less prominent, the exaggerated lumbar lordosis disappears, and the shoulder blades become less prominent. (c) Early recognition of poor postural habits in late elementary school and junior high school can generally lead to fairly easy correction of these conditions due to the plasticity of the bones. Perhaps postural screening for exaggeration of postures typical of earlier developmental stages (for example, pronation, protruding abdomen, prominent shoulder blades, prominent knock-knees, bowed legs) as well as other deviations should be undertaken at these times. Programs could then be carried out to encourage good posture, and referrals could be made to physicians where there were severe problems. One means of evaluating posture is included in the New York State Physical Fitness Test. This assessment is described in Chapter 12.

6

physical fitness

American adults generally are concerned about physical fitness and are reasonably convinced that regular exercise is essential to living a healthy, vigorous life. This is particularly true of the young, the well-educated, and the more affluent members of our society. Most of them believe that exercise is "good for you," and they are making some attempt to get or keep themselves in shape. Except for a dedicated minority, however, their efforts are too irregular and too feeble to bring much success. For example, of the 6.5 million adults who jog, one-third do so only once or twice a week, and about the same number jog no more than 10 minutes per outing.

There appears to be a widespread belief that the need for exercise recedes as the years advance, and even that vigorous activity beyond a certain age may be dangerous. For example, a sizeable majority of men and women don't exercise at all—yet nearly three-fourths of them say they are getting all the exercise they need.

The above findings are the highlights of the National Adult Physical Fitness Survey conducted late in 1972 by Opinion Research Corporation of Princeton, New Jersey, for the President's Council on Physical Fitness

and Sports. The following are some more specific findings.

1. Forty-five percent of all adult Americans (roughly 49 million of the 109 million total) do not engage in physical activity for the purpose of exercise.
2. Only 55 percent of American men and women do any exercise at all. However, 50 percent believe that they get enough exercise.
3. Persons who don't exercise are more inclined to say that they get enough exercise than are those who do exercise. Sixty-three percent of the nonexercisers say they get enough exercise, while only 53 percent of the exercisers believe that they are as physically active as they should be.
4. Of the 60 million American men and women who engage in various forms of exercise, nearly 44 million walk for exercise. More than 18 million ride bicycles for exercise (as opposed to recreation), 14 million swim for exercise, and 14 million do calisthenics.

Taken together, these facts provide a sad commentary on the effectiveness of educators in giving children the knowledge, skills, and attitudes that lead to lifelong physical fitness.

Physical fitness is the ability to carry out daily tasks with vigor and alertness, without undue fatigue, and with ample energy to enjoy leisure-time pursuits and to meet unforeseen emergencies. It is the ability to last, to bear up, to withstand stress, and to persevere under difficult circumstances where an unfit person would quit. It is the opposite of becoming fatigued from ordinary efforts, of lacking energy to enter zestfully into life's activities, and of becoming exhausted from unexpected, demanding physical exertion. This definition implies that fitness is more than "not being sick" or merely "being well."

Perhaps the complexity of physical fitness can best be understood in terms of its four components: circulatory-respiratory fitness, muscular strength and endurance fitness, flexibility fitness, and body-weight fitness. In the following pages we shall define each component, describe its normal course of development in children, note methods of evaluation, and discuss procedures for improvement.

CIRCULATORY-RESPIRATORY (CR) FITNESS

CR fitness is a measure of the capacity of the heart, lungs, and circulatory system to deliver oxygen to and remove wastes from the working cells of the body. It is an observable and predictable benefit of training. It is a state of body efficiency that enables a person to exercise vigorously for a long period of time without fatigue and to respond to sudden physical and emotional demands with an economy of heartbeats and only a modest rise in blood pressure. The CR fit child has endurance or stamina and is able to supply more energy to the muscles—so that they can work harder and longer, with less effort—than the child who is not CR fit. Thus, when fit, children put less strain on the cardiovascular system. They generally sleep better, feel better, have improved digestion and disposition, and are less subject to cardiovascular disease as they grow older.

How is CR Fitness Evaluated?

CR fitness is most accurately measured in a laboratory by determining the maximum amount of oxygen one utilizes when performing a vigorous large muscle activity (usually running on a motor-driven treadmill or pedaling a bicycle ergometer). However, it is more reasonably—and still accurately—evaluated in school settings by (a) recording one's recovery heart rate following a standardized amount of work, such as controlled bench stepping, (b) observing the total distance covered during a 9- or 12-minute run/walk, or (c) observing the total amount of time it takes to run 1 or 1½ miles.

A modified Harvard step test is recommended for use with children 10 years of age and older. Children dressed in gymnasium shoes and light clothing are asked to step on and off an 8-inch bench for 3 minutes at a rate of twenty-four steps per minute. At the signal "up," the child places one foot on the platform, steps up placing both feet fully on the platform, straightens legs and back and immediately steps down again, one foot at a time. The pace is counted by the teacher, generally assisted by a metronome: "Up-2-3-4, up-2-3-4," the command "up" coming every 2 seconds. It is easier for the child to "lead off" with the same foot each time rather than to try to alternate the feet, but this can be done two or three times during the test if one leg gets tired. After stopping, the child sits down. The teacher notes the number of beats of the heart (carotid pulse) from 1 minute to 1 minute 10 seconds after exercise and multiplies that by 6 to get the number of beats per minute. This data is compared to that collected by Montoye, Willis, Cunningham, and Keller (1969) on persons 10 years of age and older to see how the child's recovery heart rate compares with that of other boys and girls in the same age group (see Table 6.1).

The 1-mile or 9-minute run/walk is recommended for 10- through 18-year-old children, although the 1½-mile or 12-minute run/walk may be used with children 13 years of age and older. A track or well-marked area (see Figure 6.1) and a stopwatch are necessary for administering distance runs. Pupils are generally asked to begin with a standing start on the signal "Ready? Go!" Though running may be interspersed with

TABLE 6.1 Modified Harvard Step Test percentile ranks for 1-minute post-exercise heart rates*

PERCENTILE	10–11		12–13	
	M	F	M	F
95	67	71	67	74
90	72	77	70	78
85	75	80	72	80
80	77	83	74	83
75	78	85	75	86
70	80	88	77	88
65	82	91	79	89
60	85	93	80	92
55	87	95	82	94
50	89	98	85	97
45	90	100	86	99
40	92	102	88	100
35	95	105	91	103
30	96	108	94	106
25	100	113	95	108
20	104	115	97	112
15	107	119	102	118
10	114	122	106	122
5	120	126	115	126
N	192	160	166	163
Mean	90	99	86	98
SD	16	18	15	16

*Data are presented as beats per minute.

From H. J. Montoye, P. W. Willis, D. A. Cunningham, and I. B. Keller. "Heart Rate Response to a Modified Harvard Step Test: Males and Females, Age 10–69." *Research Quarterly* 40(1969):160.

walking, the object is to cover the stipulated distance in the shortest amount of time or to cover as much distance as possible in a stipulated period of time. Two procedures are recommended for the 9-minute run/walk for distance. One requires a 440-yard track marked in eight 55-yard increments. The score is recorded as the number of yards run to the last yard. The second procedure requires a 110-yard field (straight-away) marked at 5- or 10-yard intervals. Children start at one end of the field and run around the marker at the opposite end and back as many times as possible in 9 minutes. Distance is marked by counting the number of laps run and adding the additional yardage covered beyond the last starting point that is passed. Distance is paced back from the stopping point to the last 5- or 10-yard marker passed. The scorer calls out the elapsed time each time the student passes the starting line. The score is the number of yards run to the last yard. The 1-mile run/walk for time requires that the scorer call out the elapsed time each time the student passes the starting line. *The American Alliance for Health, Physical Education, Recreation and Dance Health Related Physical Fitness Test Manual* (1980) provides data to which individual pupil performances may be compared (see Tables 6.2 and 6.3).

Normal Development of CR Fitness

Absolute maximal oxygen intake values during maximal exercise effort, generally regarded as the most accurate assessments of CR fitness, are lower for children than for adults. However, when children are equated with adults for body weight and maximal oxygen intake per kilogram of body weight is examined, children have scores equal to or higher than adults (except for extremely young children who do not appear willing to perform the maximal work efforts necessary). Maximal oxygen intake increases are fairly gradual to age 13 for both sexes. After that age the scores of males increase more rapidly than those of females, indicating that boys generally demonstrate better CR fitness than girls.

Children are capable of working at maximal heart rates which exceed those of adults. Young children can and do achieve high heart rates in maximal work situations. Maxi-

FIGURE 6.1. Areas suitable for distance-run tests.

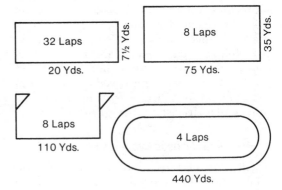

TABLE 6.2 One-mile run percentile norms for ages 5 to 13*

PERCENTILE					Age				
	5	6	7	8	9	10	11	12	13
BOYS									
95	9:02	9:06	8:06	7:58	7:17	6:56	6:50	6:27	6:11
75	11:32	10:55	9:37	9:14	8:36	8:10	8:00	7:24	6:52
50	13:46	12:29	11:25	11:00	9:56	9:19	9:06	8:20	7:27
25	16:05	15:10	14:02	13:29	12:00	11:05	11:31	10:00	8:35
5	18:25	17:38	17:17	16:19	15:44	14:28	15:25	13:41	10:23
GIRLS									
95	9:45	9:18	8:48	8:45	8:24	7:59	7:46	7:26	7:10
75	13:09	11:24	10:55	10:35	9:58	9:30	9:12	8:36	8:18
50	15:08	13:48	12:30	12:00	11:12	11:06	10:27	9:47	9:27
25	17:59	15:27	14:30	14:16	13:18	12:54	12:10	11:35	10:56
5	19:00	18:50	17:44	16:58	16:42	17:00	16:56	14:46	14:55

*Data are presented in minutes and seconds.
From American Alliance for Health, Physical Education, Recreation and Dance. *AAHPERD Health Related Physical Fitness Test Manual.* Reston, Va.: AAHPERD, 1980, pp. 23–24.

mal heart rates tend to decrease with age, as do resting heart rates. There appears to be little difference in the maximal heart rates of boys and girls. The high heart rates normally achieved by children engaged in strenuous activity are in no way injurious to normal heart and circulatory development. In fact, regular vigorous physical activity strengthens the heart and makes the body's circulatory-respiratory system more efficient.

Improving CR Fitness in Children

There is an optimal intensity, duration, and frequency of exercise which is enough to condition the cardiovascular and respiratory system and lead to increased CR fitness but which is not overly strenuous (see Figure 6.2).

Intensity. As mentioned above, there is a *target zone* in which there is enough activity

TABLE 6.3 Nine-minute run percentile norms for ages 5 to 13*

PERCENTILE					Age				
	5	6	7	8	9	10	11	12	13
BOYS									
95	1760	1750	2020	2200	2175	2250	2250	2400	2402
75	1320	1469	1683	1810	1835	1910	1925	1975	2096
50	1170	1280	1440	1595	1660	1690	1725	1760	1885
25	990	1090	1243	1380	1440	1487	1540	1500	1674
5	600	816	990	1053	1104	1110	1170	1000	1368
GIRLS									
95	1540	1700	1900	1860	2050	2067	2000	2175	2085
75	1300	1440	1540	1540	1650	1650	1723	1760	1785
50	1140	1208	1344	1358	1425	1460	1480	1590	1577
25	950	1017	1150	1225	1243	1250	1345	1356	1369
5	700	750	860	970	960	940	904	1000	1069

*Data are presented in yards.
From American Alliance for Health, Physical Education, Recreation and Dance. *AAHPERD Health Related Physical Fitness Test Manual.* Reston, Va.: AAHPERD, 1980, pp. 25–26.

TRAINING PRINCIPLES FOR CR FITNESS

Circulatory-respiratory fitness is enhanced only when large muscle activities are performed in accordance with the following three training criteria:

1. Intensity of the Activity

   The intensity of the activity must be sufficient to increase the child's heart rate to between 70 percent and 85 percent maximum (approximately 160 heartbeats per minute for children 4 to 13 years of age).

2. Duration of the Activity

   A child must remain active between 20 and 30 minutes.

3. Frequency of the Activity

   A child must participate in the activity at least 3 nonconsecutive days each week.

FIGURE 6.2. Training principles for CR fitness.

to achieve CR fitness, but not too much to exceed needed levels. Before a CR fitness training program can be undertaken by a child, the target zone for the child must be determined.

Each child's target zone is between 60 and 80 percent of his or her own maximal aerobic power. Below 60 percent of their capacity children achieve little CR fitness benefit. Above 80 percent there is little added benefit from a great deal of extra exercise. *Maximal aerobic power* (sometimes called maximal aerobic capacity or maximal oxygen intake) is merely the technical term to describe the following situation: There is a point for each child where, despite the child's best efforts, the heart and circulation cannot absorb and deliver any more oxygen to the tissues, and the child cannot exercise much longer or harder without approaching exhaustion.

In normal children the points where maximal aerobic power and maximum attainable heart rate are reached are very close. In fact, the target zone of 60 to 80 percent of maximal aerobic power is approximately the same as 70 to 85 percent of maximum attainable heart rate. Because people are able to count their own heart rate but cannot easily determine their own aerobic power (a procedure that would require laboratory facilities), the heart target zone provides a means of regulating children's exercise performance. The target zone is between 142 and 179 beats per minute for children 4 through 18 years of age.

Duration of exercise. The crucial part of a workout is the duration one stays in the target zone. Aspects of the exercise training pattern are illustrated in Figure 6.3. Usually 20 to 30 minutes in the target zone will provide a significant conditioning effect on the cardiovascular system. The period of time spent on target is called the *stimulus period*. It should be preceded by a warm-up of 5 to 10 minutes so that the heart and circulation are not suddenly taxed. This warm-up is also beneficial to joints and muscles and helps to prevent injuries and soreness.

After the stimulus period there should be a 5- to 10-minute cool-down in which the intensity or strenuousness of the effort is lessened before exercise is stopped. Abruptly stopping exercise when one has been vigorously working out may trap a good deal of blood in the muscles that have suddenly stopped moving. If not enough blood circulates back to the brain, dizziness or faintness may occur. If not enough blood circulates to the intestines, nausea may result.

To determine if a child is in the target zone, the pulse must be counted. Since the pulse count is almost always the same as the number of heartbeats per minute, placing a hand over the carotid artery on one side of the neck will give a child a means of gauging heart rate.

The pulse should be counted before, during, and after exercise (see Figure 6.3). At each of these monitored times the child must stop exercising. Since the heart rate changes very quickly once exercise is slowed or stopped, it is important to count the pulse immediately. The beat must be found within a second and should be counted for 10 seconds. The number of pulse beats counted should be multiplied by 6 to obtain the count

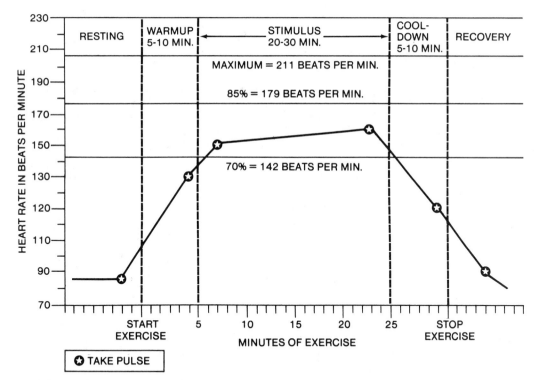

FIGURE 6.3 The exercise training pattern.

for a minute. An appropriate 10-second count for children 4 through 18 years of age is between twenty-three and thirty beats.

By trial and error, the child should develop an exercise pattern that seems easy for 5 to 10 minutes. The pulse should be counted immediately after this warm-up. It should be less than eighteen beats per 10 seconds. The child should then exercise more vigorously to get to the target zone and count again after 3 to 5 minutes to check whether he is doing enough to be on target. If the child's heart rate is below twenty-three beats per 10 seconds, the child must exercise more strenuously. Conversely, if it is above thirty beats per 10 seconds, the child must exercise less vigorously either by exercising more slowly or less forcefully. The counting should be repeated at approximately 5-minute intervals until the child can determine subjectively just how much exercise is necessary to put her in the target zone for 20 to 30 minutes before stopping.

Frequency. CR fitness workouts must be carried out three times weekly, with no more than 2 days elapsing between workouts, or gains will begin to be lost. Exercising Monday, Wednesday, and Friday, or Tuesday, Thursday, and Sunday are popular exercise plans.

Training Effects and How to Deal with Them

After 2 to 3 weeks of regular exercise conducted according to the three training principles previously described, a child's CR fitness level will begin to improve. After 4 to 6 weeks there should be measurable improvement. The child being trained will be able to carry out the exercise more easily, and it will take more exercise for the child to reach the target zone. Resting heart rate will be less, and the body will have become more efficient. The heart will have become a stronger pump. Stroke volume and cardiac output will increase, while resting heart rate will have decreased. The circulatory system will have become more efficient for the diameter of blood vessels; the number of vessels will have increased, while the blood pressure in the arteries will have decreased. The blood will have become a better transporter. The number of red blood cells, mass of red blood cells, and percentage of hemoglobin and blood volume will have increased, while platelet aggregation and the level of blood triglycerides and cholesterols will have decreased. In addition, children being trained may sleep better, may be less tired at the end of the day, and will probably miss the invigorating feeling gotten from a workout if they skip even one scheduled day.

As CR fitness level improves and children become trained, they must increase the vigor of the exercise or they will make no further progress. If a child has been jogging to reach the 70 percent maximal level of target heart rate and is no longer reaching 70 percent, then the child must try running, checking herself out again by counting pulse rate 3 to 5 minutes into the activity and every 5 minutes afterward until heart rate is elevated to a desirable 70 to 85 percent of the maximal heart rate level. The rate with which laps are covered in swimming and the number of skips per minute with a jump rope (metronome may help) can be increased. Children should reevaluate themselves every 4 to 6 weeks and upgrade their programs.

Even for the athlete there is a level of training beyond which no further training is possible. The limits of one's natural endowment are eventually reached when tip-top CR fitness is achieved. This state of CR fitness can be reached in 3 to 6 months.

Once CR fitness is attained, it must be maintained by regular workouts. CR fitness training must become part of a child's lifestyle. If one cuts back to a CR exercising workout once a week, half the previous CR fitness increase will be lost in a mere 10 weeks. If a CR fitness program is discontinued completely, all previous gains will be lost in 5 weeks.

Occasionally certain situations may occur which indicate that a child is doing too much. Even if the child's target zone is correctly based, it is possible that CR exercising in hot weather, at a higher altitude, or under competitive circumstances may cause heart rate to climb faster than is anticipated. Under such circumstances bodily awareness of heart rate level may be inaccurate, and the child may inadvertently overdo it. Nausea or vomiting after exercise is caused when not enough oxygen reaches the intestine. Exercising less vigorously and a gradual and longer cool-down will remedy this condition. Side stitch, or sticking under the ribs while exercising, is a diaphragm spasm and can generally be eliminated by leaning forward while sitting, attempting to push the abdominal organs up against the diaphragm. Abnormal heart action (for example, pulse becoming irregular, fluttering, or jumping or palpitations in the chest or throat) frequently indicates a disorder of the heart. Exercise should be discontinued and a physician consulted before resuming training.

Types of Exercise

Not all types of exercise are equally useful for developing CR fitness. What must be carefully considered is the way in which the CR system is challenged by the exercise selected. Only those exercises which significantly increase the continuous flow of blood through the heart and large skeletal muscles can help develop this fitness component. For example, both weight lifting and isometric exercise (exerting force against an immovable resistance) cause the muscle being strengthened to shorten. This pressure squeezes the blood vessels, letting less blood pass through. By contrast, jogging, requiring continuous movement of the legs and arms, to some extent results in rhythmic tensing and relaxing of muscles. This aids the flow of blood and promotes CR fitness. Of course, exercises which do not improve CR fitness may have other benefits which will be discussed later. For example, they may increase muscle strength or flexibility. Those which improve CR fitness are rhythmic, repetitive, and involve motion.

Certain other exercises enhance blood flow but still do not improve fitness because they cannot be kept up for a sufficiently long period of time. Thus, the second requisite for the right kind of exercise is that it must be capable of being sustained. It must be "aerobic." Aerobic exercise steadily supplies sufficient oxygen to the exercising muscles for as long as the exercise continues. Any rhythmic, repetitive, dynamic activity which can be continued for 2 or more minutes—without huffing and puffing afterwards—is probably aerobic.

Any activity which gets heart rate into the target zone for 20 minutes is suitable, but a child will not become trained for that activity if he switches to others too frequently. Leg muscles become trained after 6 weeks of bicycling, and heart rate response will become slower or evidence CR improvement. However, if the child then works on a rowing machine, for example, that child will again show less of a training response on heart rate since the arm muscles have not had 6 weeks of this kind of exercise. The best type of program is one which uses both arms and legs and achieves the training effect on the CR system by conditioning the muscles of both.

Specific activities which may be used to help improve CR fitness in children include walking, jogging, running, swimming, cycling, aerobic dance and rope jumping.

MUSCULAR STRENGTH AND ENDURANCE FITNESS

Muscular strength is the ability of a muscle or muscle group to produce a maximum force for a brief duration. Muscular endurance is the ability of a muscle or muscle group to produce a submaximal force for a relatively long duration. Muscular strength and muscular endurance can be seen as two extremes on a continuum: pure strength representing maximum load and minimum time, pure endurance representing minimum load and maximum time.

To improve muscular strength it is necessary to train progressively (gradually adding more resistance) on a regular basis. To improve muscular endurance it is necessary to train progressively (gradually adding more repetitions) on a regular basis. There is no definite division between muscular strength and muscular endurance, and obviously the two are closely related in most activities. However, the duration of an activity generally reflects the relative importance of each factor. For example, if John can perform only one push-up, the limiting factor is probably muscular strength. However, if Bob can perform 149 push-ups, the limiting factor is most likely muscular endurance. To train for a task that requires predominantly muscular strength, such as the leg strength tasks required by a football linesman, a 10-mile run would do little good. On the other hand, if one desired to run the marathon, maximal load leg presses would make a negligible contribution to endurance level. The child engaged in a specific sport must have the type and amount of muscular strength and endurance necessary to perform in that sport effectively.

How Is Muscular Strength and Endurance Measured?

Muscular strength is most accurately measured in a laboratory by using dynamometer tests, tensiometer tests, or Cybex apparatus. However, several muscular strength measures and a variety of muscular endurance measures may be employed in school settings with reasonable accuracy.

1. Grip strength—The grip dynamometer is used to secure strength scores of the grip of each hand. The scoring dial is marked in pounds and kilograms. Children should be asked to take two trials with each hand, alternating hands. The child should be allowed to bend the elbow slightly. The measured hand should describe a sweeping arc downward on each measurement. Scores should be recorded in kilograms. The best single performance of the child may be compared to normative data (see Table 6.4).

2. Abdominal strength—The student lies on his back with knees bent, feet on the floor, and heels not more than 12 inches from the buttocks. The angle at the knees should be

TABLE 6.4 Grip strength by age

AGE	N	Grip Strength* MEAN (kg)	SD
BOYS
8	22	14.4	3.1
9	37	15.6	2.9
10	53	17.4	3.0
11	56	19.8	4.6
12	45	21.4	3.8
13	55	26.5	6.3
GIRLS
8	20	12.8	2.3
9	30	14.2	3.2
10	54	15.3	2.8
11	47	18.9	4.3
12	44	19.3	3.9
13	55	21.1	4.0

*The better score with either hand was used.
From R. R. Montpetit and L. Laeding. "Grip Strength of School Children, Saginaw, Michigan, 1899 and 1964. *Research Quarterly* 38(1968) 231–240.

less than 90 degrees. The pupil puts his hands on the back of his neck with fingers clasped and places his elbows squarely on the ground. His feet are held by another person to keep them in touch with the surface. The pupil tightens his abdominal muscles and brings his head and elbows forward as he

TABLE 6.5 Sit-up percentile norms ages 5 to 13

PERCENTILE	Age								
	5	6	7	8	9	10	11	12	13
BOYS
95	30	36	42	48	47	50	51	56	58
75	23	26	33	37	38	40	42	46	48
50	18	20	26	30	32	34	37	39	41
25	11	15	19	25	25	27	30	31	35
5	2	6	10	15	15	15	17	19	25
GIRLS
95	28	35	40	44	44	47	50	52	51
75	24	28	31	35	35	39	40	41	41
50	19	22	25	29	29	32	34	36	35
25	12	14	20	22	23	25	28	30	29
5	2	6	10	12	14	15	19	19	18

From American Alliance for Health, Physical Education, Recreation and Dance. *AAHPERD Health Related Physical Fitness Test Manual.* Reston, Va.: AAHPERD, 1980, pp. 32–33.

curls up, finally touching elbows to knees. This action constitutes one sit-up. The pupil returns to the starting position with his elbows on the surface before he sits up again. The timer gives the signal "ready-go," and the sit-up performance is started on the word "go." Performance is stopped on the word "stop." The number of correctly executed sit-ups performed in 60 seconds is the score. Only one trial is allowed and no resting is permitted between sit-ups. No sit-ups shall be counted in which the pupil does not keep the fingers clasped behind the neck, bring both elbows forward in starting to sit up without pushing off the floor with an elbow, or return to the starting position, with elbows flat on the surface, before sitting up again. The pupil's performance may be compared with normative data (see Table 6.5).

3. Arm and shoulder strength and muscular endurance—for boys the pull-up may be administered. For girls the flexed-arm hang should be administered.

For the pull-up a metal or wooden bar approximately 1½ inches in diameter should be placed high enough so that the boy can hang with his arms and legs fully extended and his feet free of the floor. A horizontal bar, a doorway gym bar, or even the rungs of a ladder may be used. The boy should use the overhand grasp (palms facing forward). After assuming the hanging position, the boy should raise his body by his arms until his chin can be placed over the bar and then lower his body to a full hang as in the starting position. The exercise is repeated as many times as possible. Only one trial is given. The body must not swing during the execution of the movement. The pull must in no way be a snap movement. If the pupil starts swinging, check this by holding your extended arm across the front of the thighs. The knees must not be raised and kicking of the legs is not permitted. The number of completed pull-ups to the nearest whole number should be recorded. A boy's performance can be compared to normative data (Table 6.6).

To administer the flexed-arm hang to girls, one must have a horizontal bar approximately 1½ inches in diameter. A doorway gym bar or piece of pipe can also be used. A stopwatch is needed. The height of the bar should be adjusted so that it is approximately equal to the pupil's standing height. The pupil should use an overhand grasp (palms facing forward). With the assistance of two spotters, one in front and one in back of the pupil, the pupil raises her body off the floor to a position where the chin is above the bar, the elbows are flexed, and the chest is close to the bar. The pupil holds this position as long as possible. The stopwatch is started as soon as the girl takes the hanging position and is stopped when the girl's chin touches the bar, head tilts backward to keep chin above the bar, or girl's chin falls below the level of the bar. Record in seconds to the nearest second the length of time the girl holds the hanging position. A girl's performance can be compared to normative data (Table 6.7).

The Development of Muscular Strength and Endurance

The manner in which muscular endurance develops may best be understood by examining the results of performance on several muscular endurance tests. Performances of boys 10 through 17 years of age on the bent knee sit-up increase with age. For boys increases are small in prepubescent years, with much larger performance increases each year between ages 11 and 15. Performance levels off between ages 15 and 16 and actually decreases after age 15. For girls performance gradually increases between ages 10 and 15. The performances of girls do not increase with age after age 10 as they do for boys. These findings are in keeping with the fact that muscle mass in girls increases only moderately with age, while muscle mass increases greatly in boys during adolescence. The decrease after age 16 for boys might be a result of the lesser activity levels of boys.

Pull-ups (palms away) and the flexed-arm hang are often used as tests of muscular endurance. Pull-up scores between ages 10 and 12 for boys are between 1 and 3. After age 12 pull-up performances increase proportionately with age. Pull-up performance increases dramatically after puberty. Perfor-

TABLE 6.6 Pull-up percentile norms for boys ages 9 to 13

PERCENTILE	Age			
	9–10	11	12	13
95	9	8	9	10
75	3	4	4	5
50	1	2	2	3
25	0	0	0	1
5	0	0	0	0

From *American Alliance for Health, Physical Education, and Recreation Youth Fitness Test Manual.* Washington, D.C.: AAHPER, 1976, 46.

mances of girls on the flexed-arm hang show gradual increases from 10 to 11 years of age and decreases for each year thereafter.

How to Improve Muscular Strength and Endurance

Muscles increase in strength and endurance when subjected to progressive increases in workload. Changes in workload can be in the form of the number of repetitions required and/or the amount of weight to be resisted or lifted. There are several types of exercise which may be employed to improve muscular strength and/or endurance.

Isometrics—Exercises in which a person exerts static force against a resistance. The muscle does not change length. An example would be pushing against the top of a doorway.
Isotonics—Exercises in which a person exerts dynamic force against a resistance through a

TABLE 6.7 Flexed-arm hang percentile norms for girls ages 9 to 13

PERCENTILE	Age			
	9–10	11	12	13
95	42	39	33	34
75	18	20	18	16
50	9	10	9	8
25	3	3	3	3
5	0	0	0	0

From *American Alliance for Health, Physical Education, and Recreation Youth Fitness Test Manual.* Washington, D.C.: AAHPER, 1976, 40.

range of motion. The muscle changes length. An example would be raising a barbell from shoulders to overhead (this involves a concentric contraction because the muscles shorten to overcome the resistance). Another example would be lowering a barbell from overhead to shoulders (this is an eccentric concentration because the muscles lengthen and are overcome by the resistance).

Isokinetics—Exercises in which a person exerts force against a resistance that pushes back with an equal force. The greater the force the muscle exerts, the greater the force the resistance exerts. An example would be walking in waist deep water. If the leg muscles exert a small force against the water, there is slow movement across the pool. If the leg muscles exert a large force against the water, the water exerts a large force against the leg muscles and the movement across the pool is still quite slow.

Both males and females respond to muscular strength and endurance training by increasing muscular strength and endurance. However, due to physiological hormonal differences during and after puberty, females do not usually experience the muscular weight gains, muscle hypertrophy, or extent of strength and endurance gains that males do.

In order to increase the functional capacity of the muscloskeletal system, it is necessary

FIGURE 6.4. Training principles for muscular strength and endurance fitness.

TRAINING PRINCIPLES
FOR STRENGTH AND ENDURANCE

Muscular strength and endurance fitness is enhanced only when large muscle activities are performed in accordance with the following three training criteria:

1. Progressively increase the workload (strength component) and/or the work duration (endurance component) required of a muscle group. This is called the "overload principle."

2. Perform an activity which achieves the progressive resistance conditions at least three times a week for 8 to 10 consecutive weeks.

3. Ensure specificity of training. Strength or endurance development is specific to the muscle(s) being exercised.

to adhere to several principles, which are summarized in Figure 6.4.

Specific activities which may be used to help improve muscular strength and endurance fitness in children include exercises appropriate for the legs, arm-shoulder area, chest, back, and midsection of the body.

FLEXIBILITY FITNESS

Flexibility fitness is a measure of the capacity of a joint or combination of joints to move through its potential range of motion. Lack of flexibility is one of the most frequent causes of improper or poor movement as well as a reason for many injuries in physical activity. With poor flexibility speed in many activities is limited, since the muscles have to work harder to bring about a maximal movement. For example, in running activities, when the ankle, hips, and trunk are relatively inflexible, muscles have to work harder to bring about a maximum stride from the legs. This extra work results in a greater loss of energy and limits performance. By increasing flexibility of the ankles, hips, and trunk, greater speed can be achieved. Also, great energy savings allow the child to play harder and longer. For the short-legged child, great flexibility in the areas mentioned can help the child perform as well as children with longer limbs who are less flexible.

How Is Flexibility Measured in Children?

In a field setting one practical, fairly easy-to-administer test is the sit and reach test. This test measures the flexion of hip and back as well as the elasticity of the hamstring muscles (rear thighs). During testing the child removes his or her shoes and sits on the floor with the legs extended and the heels shoulder width apart. The feet should be flat against the testing apparatus board. The arms are extended forward with the hands placed on top of each other. The child reaches directly forward, palms down, along the measuring scale four times and holds the position of maximum reach on the fourth

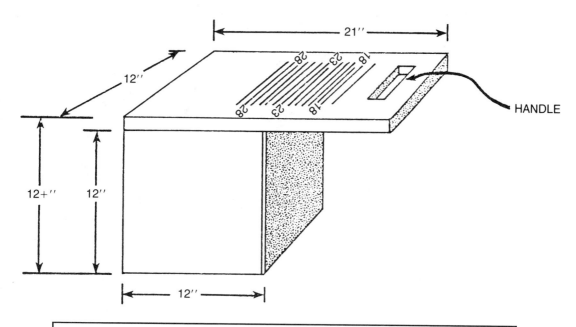

1. Using any sturdy wood or comparable construction material (¾ inch plywood seems to work well) cut the following pieces:

   2 pieces—12 in. × 12 in.
   2 pieces—12 in. × 10½ in.
   1 piece —12 in. × 21 in.

2. Assemble the pieces using nails or screws and wood glue.
3. Inscribe the top panel with one centimeter gradations. It is crucial that the 23 centimeter line be exactly in line with the vertical panel against which the subjects' feet will be placed.
4. Cover the apparatus with two coats of polyurethane sealer or shellac.
5. For convenience, a handle can be made by cutting a 1 in. × 3 in. hole in the top panel.
6. The measuring scale should extend from about 9 cm to about 50 cm.

FIGURE 6.5. Schematic drawing of and directions for constructing sit and reach measurement apparatus. (From American Alliance for Health, Physical Education, Recreation and Dance. *AAHPERD Health Related Physical Fitness Test Manual.* Reston, Va.: AAHPERD, 1980, 70–71.)

trial. The position of maximum reach must be held for 1 second. The test apparatus and directions for construction are shown in Figure 6.5. The test apparatus consists of a specially designed box with a measuring scale where 23 cm is at the level of the feet. The score is the most distant point reached on the fourth trial, measured to the nearest centimeter. The tester should place one hand on the child's knees to ensure that they remain extended. An initial warm-up should precede the test and should consist of slow, sustained static stretches of the lower back and posterior thighs. A child's score may be compared with normative data (see Table 6.8).

The Development of Flexibility

Humans become progressively more flexible from childhood to adolescence and then become progressively less flexible. Girls are more flexible than boys of comparable ages and flexibility is specific to the joint under consideration. A child may be quite flexible in one joint and quite inflexible in many others. Further, the conception that longer limb

TABLE 6.8 Sit and reach percentile norms for boys and girls ages 5 to 13*

PERCENTILE	Age								
	5	6	7	8	9	10	11	12	13
BOYS									
95	32	34	33	34	34	33	34	35	36
75	29	29	28	29	29	28	29	29	30
50	25	26	25	25	25	25	25	26	26
25	22	22	22	22	22	20	21	21	20
5	17	16	16	16	16	12	12	13	12
GIRLS									
95	34	34	34	36	35	35	37	40	43
75	30	30	31	31	31	31	32	34	36
50	27	27	27	28	28	28	29	30	31
25	23	23	24	23	23	24	24	25	24
5	18	18	16	17	17	16	16	15	17

*Data are presented in cm.

From American Alliance for Health, Physical Education, Recreation and Dance. *AAHPERD Health Related Physical Fitness Test Manual.* Reston, Va.: AAHPERD, 1980, pp. 34–35.

length is significantly related to greater flexibility has, for the most part, not received much support in the research literature. In addition, there seems to be wide individual differences in flexibility measures among children of comparable age and sex.

FIGURE 6.6. Training principles for flexibility fitness.

TRAINING PRINCIPLES FOR FLEXIBILITY FITNESS

A number of training principles should be adhered to in order to benefit most from flexibility exercises:

1. Stretch to the point where it is comfortable and not painful. Too much strain keeps the muscles involved in the exercise from relaxing (protective reaction) and defeats the purpose of the stretching exercise.

2. Don't bounce when you stretch. This type of stretching may cause injury and will actually tighten the muscle to prevent it from being injured.

3. If flexibility exercises are to be done in combination with CR endurance and muscle strength and endurance exercises, the flexibility exercises should be done before and after the other exercises.

How to Improve Flexibility Fitness of Children

Numerous investigators have proved that joint flexibility can be improved. The more angles from which a child can stretch a muscle, the more flexible the child will become. Inactivity has the greatest negative effect on flexibility. Any type of physical activity will make a child tighten up to some extent—whether it is running, basketball, tennis, or any other activity—unless the child also does stretching exercises.

All children need a moderate level of overall body flexibility. Such flexibility can be achieved by practicing flexibility exercises. Those who wish to participate successfully in specific sport activities should practice particularly those stretching exercises that involve the joints most importantly involved in those activities in addition to practicing the specific sports skills involved in that sport. (See Figure 6.6 for important training principles.)

BODY-WEIGHT FITNESS

Body-weight fitness is a measure of the ratio of lean body tissue to fat body tissue in the body. Today obesity affects 10 to 15 percent of the school-aged children in the United States. Moreover, one out of four girls and one out of five boys will be at least 10 percent overweight by the time they reach 20 years of age. There is considerable evidence indicating that the incidence of obesity among children is increasing in our country and that childhood obesity persists into adult life.

How is Body-Weight Fitness Evaluated?

Body-weight fitness can be evaluated in a number of ways. However, not all of them are equally accurate, sensitive, or administratively feasible in school settings.

Height-weight charts are commonly used to assess body-weight fitness, but they are not as sensitive as other measures, for they fail to take into account body build and tissue distributions in children. Children who are 10 to 20 percent above their desired weight are considered *overweight*. Persons more than 20 percent above their desired weight are classified as *obese*, and those more than 50 percent over their desirable body weight are considered *superobese*. Unfortunately, it is not unusual for such charts to classify highly muscular and heavily boned children as overweight. In this sense, such charts are limited.

Underwater weighing procedures are probably the most accurate means of assessing body-weight fitness in a laboratory setting. Underwater weighing involves submerging the body completely in water, expelling as much air as possible from the lungs. Based on the amount of water displaced, one can estimate the body's density and specific gravity. These measures are used to estimate the proportion of lean body weight and fat body weight.

At the present time subscapular skinfold measurements provide a good estimate of the percentage of fat in children (see Table 6.9). Normative data are available for both the triceps and subscapular skinfold measures to which the performances of individual children may be compared (see Tables 6.10 and 6.11).

TABLE 6.9 Estimation of percentage of fat in children from subscapular skinfolds*

SUBSCAPULAR SKINFOLD	Boys		Girls	
	9–12	13–16	9–12	13–16
3	13	7	18	11
4	16	11	20	14
5	19	13	22	16
6	21	15	23	18
7	22	17	25	20
8	24	19	26	22
9	25	21	27	23
10	26	22	28	24
11	27	23	29	25
12	28	24	29	26
13	29	25	30	27
14	30	26	31	28
15	30	27	31	29
16	31	28	32	30
17	32	29	32	30
18	32	29	33	31
19	33	30	33	32
20	34	31	34	32
21	34	31	34	33
22	35	32	35	33
23	35	33	35	34
24	36	33	35	34
25	36	34	36	35
26	36	34	36	35
27	37	35	37	36
28	37	35	37	36
29	38	36	37	37
30	38	36	37	37

*Data are presented in mm.
From J. Parizkova, "Total Body Fat and Skinfold Thickness in Children." *Metabolism* 10(1961):794–807.

The subcutaneous adipose (fat) tissue may be lifted with the fingers to form a skinfold. The skinfold fat measure consists of a double layer of subcutaneous fat and skin, the thickness of which may be measured with a skinfold fat caliper. The triceps skinfold is measured over the triceps muscle of the right arm halfway between the elbow and the acromion process of the scapula with the skinfold parallel to the longitudinal axis of the upper arm (see Figure 6.7). The subscapular site (right side of the body) is 1 cm (½ inch) below the inferior angle of the scapula in line with the natural cleavage lines of the skin (see Figure 6.7). The proper method for measuring these skinfolds is shown in Figures 6.8 and 6.9. The recommended testing procedure includes the following:

1. Firmly grasp the skinfold between the thumb and forefinger and lift up.
2. Place the contact surfaces of the caliper 1 cm (½ inch) above or below the finger.
3. Slowly release the grip on the calipers enabling them to exert their full tension on the skinfold.
4. Read the skinfold to the nearest 0.5 millimeter after the needle stops (1 to 2 seconds after releasing grip on the caliper).

Normal Development of Body-Weight Fitness in Children

In Chapter 5 the distribution of subcutaneous tissue for both sexes at all ages was discussed, as was lean body mass for children of different ages and sex. That section should be reviewed if necessary.

Improving Body-Weight Fitness in Children

Although heredity predisposes some children to obesity, and glandular disturbance

TABLE 6.10 Triceps skinfold percentile norms for ages 6 to 13*

PERCENTILE	6	7	8	9	10	11	12	13
BOYS								
95	5	4	4	5	5	5	5	4
90	5	5	5	6	6	6	6	5
75	6	6	6	7	7	7	7	7
50	8	8	8	8	9	10	9	9
25	9	10	11	12	12	14	13	13
10	12	12	14	16	16	19	20	19
5	13	14	17	20	20	22	23	23
GIRLS								
95	6	6	6	6	6	6	6	6
90	6	6	6	7	7	7	7	7
75	7	8	8	9	9	9	9	9
50	9	10	10	11	12	12	12	12
25	11	12	14	14	15	15	16	17
10	14	16	18	19	20	20	22	23
5	16	17	20	22	23	23	25	26

*Data are presented in mm.
Based on data from Johnston, F. E., Hamill, D. V., and Lemeshow, S. (1) "Skinfold Thickness of Children 6–11 Years." Series II, no. 120, 1972; and (2) "Skinfold Thickness of Youth 12–17 Years." Series II, no. 132, 1974. U.S. National Center for Health Statistics, U.S. Department of HEW, Washington, D.C.

TABLE 6.11 Sum of triceps and subscapular skinfolds percentile norms for ages 6 to 13*

PERCENTILE	6	7	8	9	10	11	12	13
BOYS								
99	7	7	7	7	7	8	8	7
95	8	9	9	9	9	9	9	9
90	9	9	9	10	10	10	10	10
85	10	10	10	10	11	11	10	10
80	10	10	10	11	11	12	11	11
75	11	11	11	11	12	12	11	12
70	11	11	11	12	12	12	12	12
65	11	11	12	12	13	13	13	12
60	12	12	12	13	13	14	13	13
55	12	12	13	13	14	15	14	14
50	12	12	13	14	14	16	15	15
45	13	13	14	14	15	16	15	16
40	13	13	14	15	16	17	16	17
35	13	14	15	16	17	19	17	18
30	14	14	16	17	18	20	19	19
25	14	15	17	18	19	22	21	22
20	15	16	18	20	21	24	24	25
15	16	17	19	23	24	28	27	29
10	18	18	21	26	28	33	33	36
5	20	24	28	34	33	38	44	46
GIRLS								
99	8	8	8	9	9	8	9	10
95	9	10	10	10	10	11	11	12
90	10	11	11	12	12	12	12	13
85	11	12	12	12	13	13	13	14
80	12	12	12	13	13	14	14	15
75	12	12	13	14	14	15	15	16
70	12	13	14	15	15	16	16	17
65	13	13	14	15	16	16	17	18
60	13	14	15	16	17	17	17	19
55	14	15	16	16	18	18	19	20
50	14	15	16	17	18	19	19	20
45	15	16	17	18	20	20	21	22
40	15	16	18	19	20	21	22	23
35	16	17	19	20	22	22	24	25
30	16	18	20	22	24	23	25	27
25	17	19	21	24	25	25	27	30
20	18	20	23	26	28	28	31	33
15	19	22	25	29	31	31	35	39
10	22	25	30	34	35	36	40	43
5	26	28	36	40	41	42	48	51

*Data are presented in mm.
Based on data from Johnson, F. E., Hamill, D. V., and Lemeshow, S. (1) "Skinfold Thickness of Children 6–11 Years." Series II, no. 120, 1972; and (2) "Skinfold Thickness of Youths 12–17 Years." Series II, no. 132, 1974. U.S. National Center for Health Statistics, U.S. Department of HEW, Washington, D.C.

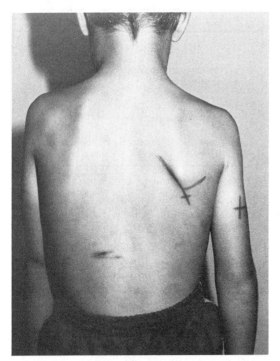

FIGURE 6.7. Triceps and subscapular skinfold measurement sites.

short periods of time. Attempting to prolong such a change can result in adverse physical and mental reactions. Fasting, diets that decrease caloric intake by more than 500 calories per day, diets that restrict foods in any of the major food groups (proteins, carbohydrates, fats, water, vitamins, and minerals), liquid diets (which do not provide the bulk needed for normal intestinal function and elimination), diet pills, and injections are not recommended.

A TOTAL APPROACH TO FITNESS

It is a challenging task to help children develop the attitudes, knowledge, and skills that lead to lifelong fitness. Occasional bouts of calisthenics, lectures about the benefits of physical fitness, physical fitness tests, and sports units, won't—in themselves—accomplish the task. Children must both understand and value fitness if it is to have a signifi-

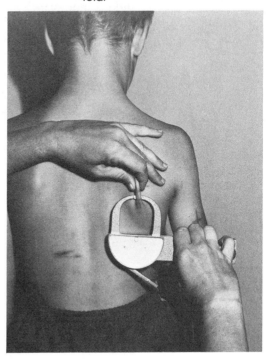

FIGURE 6.8. Measurement of subscapular skinfold.

accounts for less than 10 percent of all cases of childhood obesity, it is the balance between caloric intake and expenditure which is of paramount importance in achieving and maintaining a desirable level of body-weight fitness. To improve body-weight fitness, it is necessary to adhere to certain training principles, which are summarized in Figure 6.10.

To achieve and maintain body-weight fitness, it is generally better to make a small change—rather than a large change—in lifestyle. By decreasing caloric intake just 250 calories (slightly smaller food portions) and increasing activity level by a 250-calorie expenditure each day, one can lose over 1 pound (the equivalent of 3,500 calories) of fat over a 1-week period. The body can readily adjust to this small change in lifestyle. Steady progress can be made toward a target weight without adverse physical or mental reactions on the part of the child. Changes in lifestyle of large magnitude generally fail because such changes can only be tolerated for

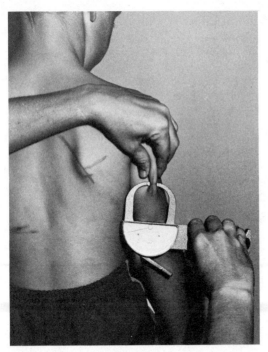

FIGURE 6.9. Measurement of triceps skinfold.

TRAINING PRINCIPLES FOR BODY-WEIGHT FITNESS
To improve body-weight fitness, it is necessary to:
1. Maintain the present physical activity level and decrease caloric intake.
2. Maintain the present caloric intake and increase physical activity level.
3. Decrease caloric intake and increase physical activity level.

FIGURE 6.10. Training principles for body-weight fitness.

cant impact on their lives. They need to be aware of and understand training principles governing the development and maintenance of fitness. They must also be given carefully supervised opportunities to develop skill in obtaining and maintaining personal levels of fitness and must be immersed in experiences and near to people who facilitate positive attitude development. Educators are most likely to help children achieve and maintain physical fitness by systematically sharing fitness knowledge with them, encouraging and offering fitness activities which students find interesting and enjoyable, carefully supervising the planning of individual prescriptive fitness programs of children, and modeling desirable levels of physical fitness themselves.

7

perceptual-motor development

While many assume that children are quite prepared to learn, this is not automatically true. Rather, being ready to learn is a condition that children must acquire or develop. Some children have a great deal of trouble attaining adequate levels of readiness. Why is this so?

In order to attain appropriate levels of readiness, several skills or behaviors must first be acquired. Perceptual-motor development is concerned with the growth of various basic skills or abilities believed to be important in building an adequate foundation for higher, more complex learning. The basic assumption here is that every response that a child makes to his or her environment is in some respects a perceptual-motor response. Some responses may be more complex than others, but all are perceptual-motor in nature; that is, every behavior a child demonstrates involves prior interpretation and processing of sensory information coming into the central nervous system (including visual, kinesthetic, auditory, and tactile information) and the formulation of some kind of behavioral response based on this interpretation of sensory information.

We tend to label the more abstract or complex reactions cognitive, or intellectual, skills or behaviors. The general belief is that although we may not think of the more complex cognitive responses as such, they too are a form of perceptual-motor behavior; they are higher-order, more complex responses to an individual's processing and interpretation of sensory information.

GROSS MOTOR COORDINATION

The child who has difficulty balancing on one foot, walking a line on the floor, walking the length of a low and wide balance beam, skipping, galloping, and hopping; or who displays rigidity, tenseness, and awkwardness when moving the body in general; or who has difficulty learning movements and movement sequences may be demonstrating signs and symptoms of lagging gross motor coordination.

Gross motor coordination relates to the synchronous, rhythmical, and properly sequenced use of the total body in large muscle or gross motor activities. These include the locomotor skills of climbing, walking, running, jumping, hopping, galloping, and skipping as well as balance skills of both a static and dynamic nature.

Locomotor Skills

Humans characteristically develop various techniques in order to move from one place in space to another. Each of these techniques is characterized by its own unique developmental sequence, although all the techniques are influenced by the common developmental denominator of growth. Locomotor techniques evolve sequentially, in a climb, walk, run, jump, hop, gallop, and skip order characterized by considerable temporal overlap. Children become increasingly capable of performing these skills in complex patterns and sequences.

We shall now discuss the unique evolution of each locomotor technique and the sequential development of all the locomotor techniques taken together. The tables in Chapter 4 reflecting the development of increasingly efficient locomotor performance may also be helpful in this area.

Climbing. Climbing tasks involve the integration of arm and leg movements and a reasonable amount of bravery and strength on the part of the maturing child. Stair and ladder climbing develop in similar fashion. In general, the following developmental trends characterize climbing:

1. Increase in the speed with which the apparatus is traversed
2. Increasing tendency to use an alternating leg pattern rather than a marking time pattern
3. Increasing tendency to employ coordinated arm and leg action techniques rather than separating arm movements from leg movements in time
4. Increasing tendency to employ contralateral rather than homolateral leg-arm action techniques
5. Increasing tendency to move backward on climbing apparatus; generally, children climb upward and forward before they climb downward and backward—this explains why we often find children who climb to the top of the apparatus and are then at a loss as to how to come down on their own
6. Decreasing tendency to employ supports such as railings and the hands of adults
7. Increasing tendency to climb to higher levels
8. Increasing tendency to cover more distance in the climb

Various factors influence the manner in which each developmental trend is expressed. With regard to ladders, performance is influenced by the distance between rungs, the diameter of rungs, the width of the ladder, the stability of the ladder, the height of the ladder, and the nature of available avenues of exit after the climb is completed. With regard to stairs, the height and depth of risers and the presence or absence of railings also influence performance.

Walking. A walk is a movement which carries the body through space by a transference of weight from one foot to another. The movement is initiated with a push-off diagonally backward against the ground with the ball and toes of one foot. After the push-off is made, the leg swings forward as flexion is initiated at the hip joint; then the knee and the ankle lift the foot clear off the floor. The weight is transferred from the heel along the outer edge of the foot to the ball and to the toes as the next push-off is made. The feet point straight ahead and the inner borders fall along a straight line. As the arms swing freely and in opposition to the legs, they counterbalance the rotation of the trunk and help carry the upper part of the body forward. There is a brief period of time when both feet are in contact with the floor and a new base of support is established.

The efficiency with which the walk is performed gradually improves with age. The relatively high center of gravity of the infant and young child, which makes balance an issue that limits mechanical efficiency early in life, gradually drops during the elementary-school years due to changes in body proportions. The following developmental trends characterize the walk:

1. An increase in the length of the stride and the consistency of stride length
2. A decrease in flat-footedness. The flat-footed walk is eventually replaced by a walk that is characterized by an initial heel strike
3. A decrease in the width of the step; eventually step width comes within the lateral dimensions of the trunk
4. A decrease in toeing-out
5. A decrease in hip flexion during the leg swing

6. An increase in hip extension at the end of the stance
7. An increase in pelvic tilt and rotation
8. A decrease in arm elevation and elbow flexion and an increase in oppositional arm swing
9. A decrease in time spent in double leg support
10. A decrease in forward trunk inclination

In general, by 2 years of age most children demonstrate all the elements of a mature gait. However, for the next 2 to 3 years there continues to be detectable improvement in rhythm and coordination.

Running. The run is much like the walk. However, there is a period of no support in the run. The foot contacts the ground under the center of gravity, and the weight is first taken on the heel of the foot. The knees are bent more than in the walk and are carried upward and forward. The arms are bent at the elbows and swing in a forward-backward direction alternately with the legs. In order to increase speed quickly, short driving steps are taken, and thereafter the stride is lengthened. Bending the supporting knee more as the weight is taken helps increase speed.

The efficiency of the run gradually improves with age. Strength and coordination increase and body proportions change. The relatively high center of gravity gradually drops, giving the child increasing stability. Toward the end of the elementary-school years girls develop relatively wider hips in relation to shoulder width than boys do. Additionally, for equal stature, boys develop longer limbs than girls. This gives boys a mechanical advantage in running activities that begins toward the end of elementary school.

In general, the running performances of preschool children are erratic, probably due to the fact that the concept of sprint effort is vague to some of them. By age 2 most can run to some extent. There does seem to be a progressive increase in the speed of running during the preschool years, and by age 5 most children have developed reasonably acceptable running efficiency and understand what it means to run fast. The play activities of the preschool years demand an increasing ability to change directions quickly, dodge, and stop abruptly. Gradually children improve in running variable patterns and in running on different surfaces.

Elementary-school children show consistent year-to-year improvement in running speed for both boys and girls from ages 5 to 11, with boys demonstrating a performance advantage at all ages that increases with increasing age. After adolescence males show considerable performance advantage over females.

Additionally, the following developmental trends characterize the run:

1. An increase in the length of the running stride
2. A decrease in the relative amount of upward movement of the body in each stride
3. An increase in the extension of the propulsive leg
4. An increase in the amount of time spent in the nonsupport phase of the stride
5. An increase in the closeness of the heel to the buttock on the forward swing of the recovery leg
6. An increase in the height of the knee at the end of the forward leg swing
7. A decrease in the relative distance the forward foot is ahead of the center of gravity when it makes contact with the ground
8. A decrease in the tendency of the hands to hook toward the midline of the trunk at the end of the forward swing and of the arms to loop outward on the backswing
9. An increase in the extent to which the arms swing through a large arc in the antero-posterior plane
10. An increase in elbow bend
11. A decrease in the extent to which the knee of the recovery leg swings outward and then around and forward in preparation for the support phase
12. A decrease in the tendency to toe-out on recovery

Jumping. A jump is a movement which carries the body through the air from a take-off on one or both feet. The body is suspended in midair momentarily and then drops back to the ground to a landing, where the weight is taken on both feet. The purpose of the jump may be to gain distance forward or to gain height.

The efficiency of the jump gradually improves with age. Strength and coordination increase. Body proportions change, lowering the center of gravity and decreasing balance difficulties. Courage and confidence increase. With puberty girls generally put on a greater proportion of adipose tissue relative to lean body tissue than males. They also develop relatively wider hips in relation to shoulder width. Additionally, for equal stature, they have shorter limbs than boys. This provides males with a mechanical advantage in jumping activities toward the end of elementary school.

The preschool child generally evidences increasing jumping efficiency. The techniques employed increase in difficulty with increasing age. A child demonstrates a jump from an elevation before undertaking the long jump. Hurdling, or jumping over an obstacle, generally occurs after long jumping.

The performances of elementary-school children on the standing long jump and vertical jump increase each year after age 5, with boys generally outperforming girls at all ages; the discrepancy between the sexes increases with increasing age.

Additionally, the following developmental trends characterize the jump:

VERTICAL JUMP

1. A progressive increase in crouch prior to take-off
2. Increasingly more effective arm lift; a sideward elevation of the arms and shoulders, usually both together, eventually drops out and a one arm and shoulder lift replaces it
3. Increased extension of the body in take-off and in flight; initially there is a tendency to lean forward and bring the legs under the body immediately after lift-off—later the jump is characterized by forceful extension of both arms and legs in flight
4. Increasing extension of the trunk at the crest of the reach, with eyes increasingly focused on the target of the jump

STANDING LONG JUMP

1. An increase in the preliminary crouch
2. An increase in preparatory forward trunk lean

3. An increase in preparatory backward arm swing
4. An increase in body extension at take-off
5. An increase in the angle of the body at take-off
6. An increase in the forward and upward swing of the arms during take-off and flight
7. An increase in force absorption upon landing
8. A decrease in the angle of the legs upon landing
9. An increase in the tendency of the arms to be well forward of the body on landing
10. A decrease in the tendency to use a one-footed take-off

Hopping. The body is pushed off the floor from one foot and after a slight suspension in the air is returned to the floor with the weight taken on the same foot. The knee of the inactive leg is bent, and the leg makes no contact with the floor. The arms move upward to help with the body lift. The landing is on the toes, and immediately the weight is shifted to the ball of the foot and then to the heel.

The efficiency of the hop gradually improves with age. Strength and coordination improve. Body proportions change, lowering the center of gravity and decreasing balance difficulties. Courage and confidence increase. Along with these, the speed, distance, precision, and accuracy with which the hop is performed improve.

The earliest attempts at hopping consist of an irregular series of jumps. After the jumps become regular and precise, the child attempts hopping. By age 3½ most children can hop from one to three steps on a preferred foot. By age 4 most children can hop four to six steps on one foot, and by age 5 the number of consecutively performed hops is usually between eight and ten.

Hopping for distance at reasonably rapid speeds is not too difficult for 5-year-olds. Most can hop 50 feet in about 10.5 seconds. Girls sometimes surpass boys at this task, though both sexes perform about equally at ages 6 through 9. Performance of this task increases with increasing age. It has also been found that more than 10 percent of 6-year-old boys and about 2 percent of 6-year-old girls cannot remain on one foot for a distance of 50 feet. For 7-, 8-, and 9-year-olds the percentage of failures among boys and girls is roughly similar. All 10-year-olds are able to do this task.

Rhythmic hopping, requiring that the child alternately hop from one foot to the other, is more difficult. Only 10 percent of 5-year-old boys and a slightly higher percentage of 5-year-old girls can execute a two hop-two hop rhythmic pattern from right to left feet without breaking rhythm. After 6 years of age children are able to perform alternate rhythmic hopping tasks (that is, two hops on one foot with an intermediate transfer to the other foot), with girls outperforming boys at ages 6 through 9. However, it is not until age 8 that more than 50 percent of children of both sexes can be expected to perform this rhythmic hopping task. About 85 percent of 8-year-old girls can perform this task. Findings with other rhythmic hopping patterns are essentially the same. The most difficult hopping patterns are those in which there is an unequal number of hops to be performed on each foot. Most children cannot master these patterns successfully until they are about 8 years old.

In general, boys' performances on the 50-foot hop for speed are similar to those of girls; however, their performances are less proficient than those of girls on rhythmic hopping tasks. This is probably due to the fact that boys have a slight advantage in strength which increases with increasing age and that girls mature earlier, possessing the visual-motor coordination necessary to execute the rhythmic hopping task earlier than most boys of the same age. Additionally, in the American culture girls more frequently engage in tasks similar to rhythmic hopping (for example, *hopscotch*).

Additional developmental trends which characterize the hop include:

1. A decreasing tendency to hold the nonsupport leg high and in front of the body
2. A decreasing tendency to allow a walking step to intrude in the normal rhythm of the hop
3. A decreasing tendency to use the arms for balance

Galloping and skipping. A gallop is a combination of a walk and a run. The same foot is always the lead foot. The skip is a combination of the walk and the hop. One steps forward on one foot, hops on the same foot, and then steps forward on the opposite foot and hops on it. The skip can be executed in any direction, but the pattern is always done on alternate feet with the weight shifting on each walking step. The arms should be swung in opposition to the legs to maintain balance and help gain height, if the latter is desired. The gallop is generally learned before the skip.

These more complex outgrowths of forward hopping patterns are sometimes seen in children as young as 4 years of age; but in general, it is not until about age 6½ that both skipping and galloping skills are achieved. Early attempts at skipping at ages 4 and 5 usually take the form of skipping on one foot and walking on the other foot. In the initial stages of galloping the child tends to change the lead foot and the gait is uneven. Eventually the same lead foot is always used and the gait becomes smooth.

Balancing Skills

Balance may be defined as the ability to maintain equilibrium. It is a basic and complex attribute which underlies a number of performance tasks. If it is deficient, it will probably negatively influence the performance of locomotor as well as projectile activities. Balance is mediated to some degree by the vestibular apparatus, but it is primarily influenced by complex interactions of the visual and muscular systems. Thus, balance tests are good indicators of the integration of the muscular system, visual system, and vestibular apparatus.

Boys and girls age 6 and under are generally unable to balance on one foot with their eyes closed. However, by age 7 they are able to maintain balance with their eyes closed. This ability continues to improve with age.

There are two categories of balance activities. *Static balance* is the ability of the body to maintain a particular body position without moving through space. It is usually measured using stabilometers, balance boards, and stick balances. These instruments record the amount of time balance is maintained or the number of times a child falls off balance. In field settings time in balance and balance errors are measured for heel-toe eyes open, heel-toe eyes closed, right foot eyes open, left foot eyes open, right foot eyes closed, left foot eyes closed, tip toes eyes open, and tip toes eyes closed. *Dynamic balance* is the ability of the body to maintain and control posture while the body is moving through space. Most typically, dynamic balance is measured by walking balance beams of various heights, widths, and lengths, employing various techniques (for example, step-together, cross-over, forward, backward, sideward).

Prior to age 2 children cannot be expected to react positively to much stress when asked to maintain an upright position. Even normal walking and beam walking is difficult. By the age of 3, children can usually walk lines for short distances and can attempt to walk 4-inch-wide beams. By the age of 3 children can usually take one foot off the ground for short periods of time, positioning the other foot in the air for 3 to 4 seconds without losing balance. The balancing skills of 4-year-olds improve rapidly. They can traverse 3- to 4-inch-wide beams and can maintain a position on one foot for increasing periods of time. By the age of 5 a child can be expected to negotiate balance beams of decreasing width and can balance on one foot for increasing lengths of time with and without the aid of arms.

There is a steady increase in dynamic and static balance skill between the ages of 5 and 12. The performances of boys and girls are relatively the same, with younger girls outperforming younger boys. Increases in performance slow down at around age 7 to 8, especially for boys. There is then a period of marked increase in performance for both sexes at ages 8 and 9.

In addition to the trends indicated above, the following developmental trends characterize balance:

1. An increasing ability to perform balances involving a high center of gravity
2. An increasing ability to perform balances involving a small base of support
3. An increasing ability to perform balances involving body parts which are not in alignment over the base of support

GROSS VISUAL-MOTOR CONTROL

Children who have difficulty catching or bouncing a ball, who often hold their hands in the wrong position for a catch, or who react too soon or too late when striking may be demonstrating a lag in the development of gross visual-motor control.

Gross visual-motor control skills are those skills that require movement of the large muscles of the body in close coordination with information derived from visual tracking. These skills always involve the use of a ball and sometimes the use of a bat or racquet. The skills most commonly considered to be gross visual-motor skills are throwing, catching, striking, kicking, and ball bouncing.

Successful performance of these skills requires that the visual system work in close cooperation with the motor system. In throwing, the visual system must gather information about the location and movement of the target. The motor system, in response, attempts movements that will result in a ball being thrown to the target. In catching, kicking, and striking, the eyes must track an oncoming ball and provide the information necessary for the motor response to anticipate its movement and intercept the ball at an opportune time. In ball bouncing, the eyes continuously track the rebounding ball so that movements of the hands may be synchronized with the ball's movement to adjust the speed and direction of the ball.

From birth on children appear fascinated with the movement of objects close to their crib. Gradually the ability to impart velocity (throw, strike, kick) to them precedes the ability to intercept them (catch). In general, all the gross visual-motor control skills develop more slowly than locomotor skills. This is because the visual-motor control skills require that children process more complex visual information prior to their performance.

Each of the gross visual-motor control skills is characterized by its own unique developmental sequence, although the techniques share the common developmental denominators of growth and perceptual development. Such skills also seem to evolve sequentially, with throwing skill preceding the development of kicking and striking skills (that is, when they are performed in a manner that includes ball receipt) and all of these evolving before catching skills—although in a manner characterized by considerable temporal overlap.

Each of these skills is performed as a closed skill (performed when the targets to be struck are stationary and the projectiles to be thrown, kicked, or struck are stationary) before they are able to be performed as open skills (performed when the targets to be struck are moving and the projectiles to be thrown, kicked, or struck are moving). Sensitive teachers acknowledge this characteristic developmental sequence by initially teaching the skills as closed skills and then shaping behavior gradually, so that eventually the children perform the skills as they are characteristically performed in open skill traditional sport and game forms. (You may wish to review Chapter 4 on this material.)

Throwing

Throwing includes any unilateral or bilateral action of the arm or arms in which an attempt is made to propel an object forward. In general, the following developmental trends characterize throwing:

1. Increasing ability to throw successfully at smaller targets
2. Increasing ability to throw successfully at faster-moving targets
3. Increasing ability to throw successfully at targets viewed against increasingly complex visual backgrounds
4. Increasing ability to throw successfully at targets which have low contrast with the backgrounds against which they are viewed
5. The ability to throw at targets moving left to right or right to left before targets moving away from the thrower; targets moving toward the thrower are most difficult

6. Targets which move in a manner that incorporates many and variable speed changes are more difficult to throw at successfully than targets which move in a manner that involves few and consistent speed changes
7. An increasing tendency to throw overhand rather than underhand
8. An increasing tendency to step into the throw
9. An increasing tendency to step forward on the foot opposite to the throwing hand
10. An increasing tendency to rotate along the long axis of the body rather than to move only in the anteroposterior plane
11. An increasing tendency to employ sequential ranges of movement for increasingly larger numbers of body parts over longer periods of time
12. An increasing tendency to follow through at the end of the throw
13. An increasing tendency to use unilateral rather than bilateral hand action
14. With increasing age accuracy, distance, and velocity of ball release improve for both boys and girls; at all ages boys are superior to girls

Catching

Catching involves the use of the hand(s) and/or other parts of the body to stop and control an aerial ball or object. In general, the following developmental trends characterize catching:

1. Children generally learn to throw earlier than they learn to catch
2. Increasing ability to catch smaller balls
3. Increasing ability to catch balls which travel for short distances
4. Increasing ability to catch faster-moving balls
5. Increasing ability to make locomotor spatial adjustments prior to catching
6. Children show yearly improvement in catching skill, with boys generally performing better than girls
7. An increasing ability to catch with a trajectory of lower angle
8. An increasing tendency to track the ball until contact rather than close eyes prior to contact
9. An increasing tendency to move toward the ball earlier
10. An increasing tendency to give with the ball on contact
11. An increasing tendency to not watch the ball through its entire flight; the less skilled the catcher, the more important it is to watch the entire trajectory

12. An increasing tendency to contact the ball with fewer body parts
13. An increasing tendency to hold the arms in a flexed position next to the sides of the body in anticipation of the catch rather than to hold them in an extended position directly in front of the body

Striking

Striking is hitting an object either with the hand(s), fist(s), or some implement under the control of the hand or fist. In general, the following developmental trends characterize striking:

1. Increasing tendency to employ longer striking implements
2. Increasing tendency to employ striking implements with smaller striking surfaces
3. Increasing tendency to strike smaller projectiles
4. Increasing tendency to strike faster-moving projectiles
5. Increasing tendency to strike with heavier implements
6. Increasing tendency to make locomotor spatial adjustments prior to the strike
7. Increasing tendency to strike balls with trajectories of lower angle
8. Increasing tendency to track the ball until contact rather than close the eyes prior to contact
9. Increasing tendency to not watch the entire ball flight; the less skilled the striker, the more important it is to watch the entire flight trajectory
10. Increasing tendency to strike balls with shorter travel distances
11. Increasing tendency to strike balls traveling within complex visual backgrounds
12. Increasing tendency with age to demonstrate yearly improvements in striking performance, with boys generally performing better than girls
13. Increasing tendency to strike forcefully and with greater accuracy
14. Increasing tendency to employ two-arm striking techniques rather than one-arm striking techniques
15. Increasing tendency to swing with increased ranges of motion at the various joints (that is, unfreezing of the unitary rotatory motion)
16. Increasing tendency to employ a forward weight shift and forward step to initiate the strike
17. Increasing tendency to rotate along the long axis of the body
18. Increasing tendency to rotate the hip and trunk prior to initiating arm action in the strike
19. Increasing tendency to demonstrate distinct uncocking of the wrist(s) during the swing
20. Decreasing tendency to separate hands in bilateral striking
21. Increasing tendency to strike balls whose trajectories incorporate more and more variable speed change characteristics
22. Increasing tendency to employ arm-leg opposition in the strike
23. Decreasing tendency to strike downward on a ball

Kicking

Kicking is a movement pattern in which the leg swings in an arc, striking and imparting force to a ball. Children frequently use place kicks and punts and moving balls in play and organized games. In the punt the ball is dropped and then kicked before it touches the ground. In the place kick the ball is stationary when it is kicked. Moving balls are generally kicked while traveling along or near the ground. In general, the following developmental trends characterize kicking:

1. Increasing tendency to kick balls farther and with more accuracy
2. Increasing tendency to kick faster-moving balls
3. Increasing tendency to kick smaller balls
4. Increasing tendency to improve kicking performance with advancing age, with boys outperforming girls at all age levels and the discrepancy between the sexes growing greater with increasing age
5. Increasing tendency to kick balls which have traveled for short distances
6. Increasing ability to make locomotor spatial adjustments prior to the kick
7. Increasing ability to kick balls traveling in trajectories involving more and more variable speed change characteristics
8. Increasing ability to track the ball until contact rather than close eyes prior to contact
9. Increasing tendency to initiate forward movement toward the ball earlier
10. Increasing tendency to not watch the ball through its entire ball flight; the less skilled the kicker, the more important it is to watch the entire trajectory

11. Increasing tendency to increase the range of the preparatory movements at the hip and knee joints of the kicking leg
12. Increasing tendency to increase the total range of motion for the joints of the kicking leg
13. Increasing tendency to demonstrate compensatory trunk lean and arm opposition in the kick
14. Increasing tendency to kick through the ball rather than retract the leg
15. Increasing tendency to use a preferred leg more consistently
16. Increasing tendency to become more adept at adjusting the plant of the support foot
17. Increasing ability to kick heavier balls
18. Increasing tendency to drop the ball forward rather than toss it upward in preparation for a punt
19. Increasing tendency to demonstrate more forceful extension of the kicking leg
20. Increasing tendency to demonstrate straighter angles at the knee and ankle joint at ball contact
21. Increasing tendency of the kicking leg to move toward the midline of the trunk in the follow-through

Ball Bouncing

Many of the games and sports children play involve ball bouncing. Two- and 3-year-old children generally drop and then hit a ball with little accuracy when asked to perform ball-bouncing activities. By age 4 children can perform the two-handed drop and two-handed catch, although the ball is not always under control. By age 5 children are able to use both hands or one hand in an openhanded slapping technique to bounce the ball consecutively for 15 seconds. Between the ages of 7 and 8 children master even rhythmic bounce patterns using alternating hands. By ages 9 and 10 uneven bounce patterns are mastered.

BODY AWARENESS

Children who demonstrate a lack of hand preference; appear confused about the right and left sides of their body; do not seem able to identify various body parts; have difficulty with spatial concepts such as near-far, up-down, above-below, or big-bigger-biggest; or seem lost in a room may very well be demonstrating signs and symptoms of lagging body awareness development.

Body awareness is an individual's awareness, identification, and/or evaluation of the proportions, dimensions, positions, and movements of his or her body, and/or parts. Experts in child development have suggested that the concept of body awareness is an important issue in perceptual-motor development. They hypothesize that young children come to know their bodies and eventually the external space world through changes in sensory-perceptual functioning that are a direct result of the motor experiences in which the children engage during their early years of development. These experts believe that difficulties associated with body awareness development, and thus with spatial awareness generally, are mainly the result of a lack of appropriate sensorimotor experiences.

Body awareness is made up of three basic components: body image, body insight, and body concept.

Body Image

This aspect of body awareness encompasses the feelings and/or opinions which a child develops about the body, particularly with respect to its structure (that is, appearance, height, weight, size) and its performance characteristics. It is how the body appears to oneself, and as such it represents the basic nucleus of personality development. In order for it to form, a child must actively use the body and experience its many capabilities and limitations.

Laterality is one aspect of body image and may be considered a conscious internal awareness of the two sides of the body. Such an awareness may not necessarily be accompanied by verbal labels (that is, right and left) for the two sides. However, when children realize that they have two hands, two feet, two eyes, and two sides to their bodies which are similar in size and shape but different in terms of the positions they occupy in physical space, they may be said to have developed a degree of laterality.

As laterality is established, *sensory dominance* becomes apparent. Sensory dominance refers to the preferential use of one of the eyes, hands, or feet over the other. When an individual develops a preference for the use of the eye, hand, and foot on the same side of the body, that person is said to have pure dominance. If any one of the preferred body parts happens to be on the opposite side of the body, the child is said to have mixed dominance.

Sensory dominance is generally evaluated by asking the child to perform activities such as the following:

1. Eyedness—"Please bring the index card with the hole in it up to your eye until you can see the pencil I am holding."
2. Handedness—"Draw a circle in the air." "Draw an X on the paper in front of you." "Erase the X on the paper in front of you." "Cut a strip of paper with the scissors." "Throw the tennis ball against the wall." "Roll the ball to me."
3. Footedness—"Kick the stationary ball against the wall." "Pick up the ball and punt it to me."

Handedness is relatively stable in 4-year-old children, although ambivalence is more prevalent in 5- through 8-year-olds. There is a return to stable hand preference in the majority of 9- and 10-year-old children. Below 10 years of age as many as 20 to 25 percent of children fail to show clear-cut preferential use of one eye. Older children do show a much greater preference for the use of one eye over the other. Footedness seems to be established by the age of 5, in contrast to eyedness and handedness, and remains quite stable. Preferential use of a given eye with a given hand shows definite age trends. Mixed eye-hand preference is exhibited by 5- and 6-year-olds, while 7- and 8-year-olds are evenly divided (half mixed eye-hand preferences and the other half pure eye-hand preferences). Nine-, 10-, and 11-year-olds show a definite tendency toward pure eye-hand combinations.

The significance of sensory dominance is not clearly understood, although several attempts have been made to link this phenomenon to the development of cerebral dominance. Cerebral dominance refers to the fact that language and interpretive functions of the cerebral cortex are more highly developed on one side than on the other. In nine out of ten human beings the left cerebral hemisphere becomes dominant. Some investigators feel that cerebral dominance is to some extent reflected within an individual by the appearance of sensory dominance. However, to date there is little empirical evidence to support the conception that cerebral dominance is revealed in the hand, eye, and foot preferences of individuals or that there is any direct connection between mixed and/or pure dominance and the perceptual, cognitive, or motor capabilities of the young child.

The values of parents and the way in which they socially reinforce children influence the development of a child's body image. When parents discourage movement opportunities and activities because they fear for the child's safety or do not wish to see their houses in disarray, children may develop body awareness problems.

Success and failure experiences also influence the development of the emotional aspect of body image. Children develop positive or negative feelings about themselves as they experience frustration or success in realizing the movement solutions to problems in their environment. Too much failure or success is undesirable. Generally, the more quickly children master their motor environment, the more successful they will feel, and the more positive their feelings about "self" will be.

Body Insight

Body insight involves the nonverbal knowledge of one's own body and the relationship of its parts to one another. It also includes understanding how the body and its parts move in space. Identification and recognition processes typify body insight activities. The process of accurately naming and/or identifying various parts of the body and their functions is a commonly employed strategy for assessment. The ability to do this progresses at different rates in different children. The rate with which these skills develop is a function of the amount of emphasis and time placed upon the development of such concepts by the adults with whom the child comes into contact. Generally, by 6 years of age children accurately identify major body parts (eyes, ears, hands, knees, head) and fail only slightly in naming more remote body parts (elbows, wrists, heels, nose). After 9 years of age mistakes in identification of body parts are rare.

Body space concepts develop continuously from the child's earliest months. Children can recognize and understand various body space concepts well before they are able to verbalize them. The concept of up-down is understood by the age of 18 months, on-off concepts are known by the age of 21 months, and in-out, turn around, and other side concepts are developed by age 5. Three-year-olds understand over-under, front-back, big, high, long, and tall and often use these words. After 4 years of age such space words get more exact usage and appear in combinations. In later years the space concepts take on expanded meaning as children explore their movement environment.

Body space concepts are evaluated by asking children to do things such as "Lift your hands up," "Move sideways," "Move near me," "Move away from me," "Move behind me," "Put one arm under the other arm," "Put your hand on top of your head," "Put your hand through your legs," "Climb on top of the box," or "Crawl through the tunnel."

Body Concept

Body concept is that aspect of body awareness having to do with the verbalized knowledge one has about one's own body and its relationship to near and far space. Verbalization is important to the process of internalizing body awareness, especially during the early years of development. The child is not only aware of the different spatial features of the body from a sensorimotor viewpoint but is also able to conceptualize about them through the mechanism of verbalization.

The development of body concept includes the accurate and spontaneous verbal identification of body parts and their functions, spontaneous right-left discrimination of body dimensions, and effortless discrimination of the dimensions of external space (directionality).

Right-left discrimination refers to the ability to label or identify the right-left dimension of the body. This may be quickly assessed by asking a child to perform tasks such as "Show me your right foot," "Touch your left ear," or "Pick up the pencil with your right hand." The spontaneity and accuracy of the responses are an indication of the degree of development of the child's right-left discrimination skill. By 6 years of age over 70 percent of children are able to spontaneously distinguish between the right and left sides of the body accurately. However, it is not until about age 9 that this conceptualization process stabilizes in over 90 percent of all children. Below age 5 most children perform at chance level in identifying right and left body parts.

Directionality, the ability to identify various dimensions of external space, is thought to be an outgrowth of conceptualizing the spatial dimensions of the body. For example, in the beginning right and left in external space exist only as they relate to the individual's own body and thus vary according to the position of the body at any given moment in time or space. The concepts of up-down and front-back exist at first in reference to the body and its position in space. The child relies upon the stable spatial referents established for his or her own body in helping to identify and understand the dimensions of the external space world. When children look at the world with their heads between their knees, the world is upside down. Eventually their conception of external space stabilizes and becomes independent of their own orientation in space. In other words, the concept of external space is complete when children can spontaneously identify positions, dimensions, and directions of objects or persons in external space without having to first consciously and deliberately refer to their own bodies.

Directionality is generally evaluated by

asking a child to perform the following activities: "Facing me, touch my left arm with your right hand," "Stand with your front side against my backside," "Tell me if this ball is on my left or right side," and "Am I walking to my left or to my right on this balance beam?"

EVALUATING PERCEPTUAL-MOTOR DEVELOPMENT

Unfortunately, there is at present no single validated and reliable standardized test that can assess lags or deviations in perceptual-motor development. Rather, the use of a combination of tests, particularly those suggested here, along with sensitive observation, seems a more satisfactory solution to evaluation.

Bruininks-Oseretsky Test of Motor Proficiency (BOTMP)

The BOTMP appears to provide a useful evaluation of gross motor coordination, fine motor coordination, and gross and fine visual-motor control. The BOTMP (1978) is an individually administered test appropriate for use with normal, mentally handicapped, and learning disabled children from 4½ to 14½ years of age. There are two forms of the test. The Complete Battery, eight subtests comprised of forty-six separate items—which takes 45 to 60 minutes to administer—provides a comprehensive index of motor proficiency (Battery Composite score) as well as separate measures of both gross (Gross Motor Composite score) and fine (Fine Motor Composite score) motor skills. The Short Form, fourteen items from the Complete Battery, takes 15 to 20 minutes to administer and provides a brief survey of general motor proficiency.

The following subtests are included on the BOTMP:

1. Subtest 1—Running speed and agility (one item). Measures running speed during a shuttle run.
2. Subtest 2—Balance (eight items). Three items assess static balance by requiring that the sub-

ject maintain balance while standing on one leg with eyes open or closed. Five items assess dynamic balance by requiring that the subject maintain balance while executing various walking movements.
3. Subtest 3—Bilateral coordination (eight items). Seven items assess sequential and simultaneous coordination of the upper limbs with the lower limbs. One item assesses coordination of the upper limbs with the lower limbs. One item assesses coordination of the upper limbs only.
4. Subtest 4—Strength (three items). Assesses arm and shoulder strength, abdominal strength, and leg strength.
5. Subtest 5—Upper-limb coordination (nine items). Six items assess coordination of visual tracking with movements of the arms and hands. Three items assess precise movements of arms, hands, or fingers.
6. Subtest 6—Response speed (one item). Measures the ability to respond quickly to a moving visual stimulus.
7. Subtest 7—Visual-motor control (eight items). Measures the ability to coordinate precise hand and visual movements.
8. Subtest 8—Upper-limb speed and dexterity (eight items). Measures hand and finger dexterity, hand speed, and arm speed.

Normative data based on the performances of 765 children ranging in age from 4½ through 14½ years, divided by sex, race, and community size in a manner representative of 1970 United States Census findings, are the basis for the standardization.

Performance on each test item, which is the raw score, is expressed in one of four ways: (a) as the amount of time taken to complete a task, (b) as the number of units completed within a fixed time period, (c) as the number of errors made in performing a task, or (d) as a pass or a fail based on prescribed criteria. Raw scores are converted to point scores for each item. The point scores may be converted to standard scores, percentile ranks, stanines, or age-equivalent scores for comparative purposes.

Frostig Developmental Test of Visual Perception (FDTVP)

The FDTVP (1966) appears to provide a useful evaluation of visual-perceptual skills and fine visual-motor control. The FDTVP is used to screen nursery-school, kindergarten, and first-grade children or older children (generally through third grade) suffering from learning difficulties with regard to fine visual-perceptual skills. The test may be administered individually (in approximately 30 to 45 minutes) or to a group (in under 1 hour). The five tests included are:

1. Eye-motor coordination—Tests the child's ability to draw continuous straight, curved, or angled lines between boundaries of various width, or from point to point without guide lines.
2. Figure-ground—Tests the child's ability to find hidden geometric forms in complex backgrounds.
3. Constancy of shape—Tests the child's ability to recognize certain geometric figures presented in a variety of sizes, shadings, textures, and positions in space and discriminate them from similar geometric figures. Circles, squares, rectangles, ellipses, and parallelograms are used.
4. Position in space—Tests the ability of a child to discriminate reversals and rotations of figures presented in series. Schematic drawings representing common objects are used.
5. Spatial relationships—Tests the ability of a child to analyze simple forms and patterns. These consist of lines of various lengths and angles which the child is required to copy using dots as guide points.

Performance on the FDTVP is recorded on a scoring sheet in the back of each child's test booklet. Raw scores for each of the five subtests are computed. The raw scores can be converted into age equivalents (that is, age of the average performing child on each subtest), and comparisons can be made to determine if the child is performing higher or lower than this figure on each subtest. Scale scores can also be computed from raw scores. Scale scores below 8 on a 5 to 16 scale for any single subtest indicate the need for special training in that area. The scale scores can be converted into a perceptual quotient (total of five scale scores) with a mean of 100 and a range of 68–123. Perceptual quotients may be used to determine whether the child is in the upper, upper-middle, lower-middle, or lower quartile of performance. Generally, children beginning school in the fall who score in the lowest quartile are very likely to experience difficulty in school adjustment.

Southern California Perceptual-Motor Test Battery (SCPMTB)

The SCPMTB appears to be a useful evaluation of various facets of body awareness. The SCPMTB (1969) by Jean Ayres includes a battery of six tests designed to be individually administered to children ranging in age from 4 through 8. Administration time is approximately 20 minutes. The tests included are:

1. Imitation of postures—Requires that the child assume a series of positions or postures demonstrated by the examiner.
2. Crossing the midline of the body—Tests the tendency to avoid crossing the midline of the body with the hand.
3. Bilateral motor coordination—Performing the tasks of this test requires smoothly executed movement of and interaction between both upper extremities.
4. Right-left discrimination—Tests the ability to discriminate right from left on self, another person, and location of an object.
5. Standing balance with eyes open—Tests the ability of the child to balance on one foot with eyes open.
6. Standing balance with eyes closed—Tests the ability of the child to balance on one foot with eyes closed.

The test manual for the SCPMTB contains a description of the tests, a standardization population, directions for test administration, and reliability and normative data. The only materials necessary are a table, chairs, and a stopwatch.

The tests provide raw scores which can be converted into standard scores for children of different age levels so that comparisons may be made regarding the desirability of performance.

8

planning
for
effective learning

No subject matter in the curriculum is ever static. Physical education is no exception. Formal group and individual gymnastics in the European tradition were once considered to form the core of an appropriate physical education program for children. At other times games, utilized primarily for their socialization value, were considered to be the foundation of elementary-school physical education. In recent times many children's programs have been conceptualized as mini-sports programs, introducing young children to the skills and strategies of the major competitive sports. Even more recently there has been great interest shown in reorganizing the elementary-school physical education curriculum around a movement education format. Obviously, there is no one approach that will satisfy all professional physical educators.

The American system of education is well known for its diversity and for the degree to which the teaching professional can have an impact on what is actually taught in the schools. In other countries, particularly in socialist countries such as Russia where education is seen as an instrument of national policy, there is one syllabus for a subject matter and all teachers teach essentially the same

FIGURE 8.1 Effective learning is based on successful participation.

activities at the same time of year to the various age groups. This *standardization* approach has many benefits, and one would be foolish not to recognize them. On the other hand, the *diversified* approach, more typical of American schools, also had much to recommend it.

Many state and local school districts have

tried to achieve some of the benefits of standardization through the development of curriculum syllabi. In these documents overall goals are stated, specific objectives for each activity delineated, methods of organization outlined, and evaluation tools listed. However, these syllabi are seldom strictly enforced. Usually teachers have great latitude in taking the broad suggestions and implementing them in terms of their own professional judgment.

CONCEPTUALIZING THE PROGRAM

Five Approaches to the Curriculum

An examination of current physical education programs indicates that there are at least five fairly distinct approaches to elementary-school curriculum planning. This is not to suggest that each of the five approaches would be equally represented in a survey of elementary schools. In fact, one approach—the eclectic approach—dominates to a marked degree. However, the others are in evidence, and some may even provide a view of the future.

The eclectic approach. By far the most widely used curriculum model for elementary-school physical education is the eclectic model, in which general activity areas such as movement, gymnastics and self-testing, dance and rhythms, games and sports, and aquatics can be found. In this model percentages are often allocated for the various areas by grade level. In the first grade, for example, it is often suggested that movement experiences constitute 35 percent of the program, rhythmic activities 25 percent, stunts and tumbling 20 percent, and simple games 20 percent (Dauer and Pangrizi, 1979). As the curriculum moves from first through sixth grade, those percentages change, and they tend most often to change in the direction of a higher allocation for sports and games and a lower allocation for movement, rhythms, and gymnastics.

The movement education approach. Recently there has been a great deal of interest shown in reconceptualizing the elementary-school curriculum from a human movement perspective. Movement education has become a well-established part of the eclectic approach, but most physical educators consider it to be most relevant and appropriate for kindergarten through third-grade classes. However, movement education proponents have made great strides in providing examples of a total physical education curriculum from a movement perspective (indeed, it would be inappropriate to describe this as a physical education curriculum—instead, one ought to call it a movement curriculum). Here the organizing centers for the curriculum are not the traditional activities but rather movement themes such as striking, gathering, leaping, spatial awareness, and flow. Many of these concepts are directly derived from the work of Rudolph Laban.

Games are not ignored in the movement approach. However, instead of teaching specific games such as soccer and volleyball, the movement enthusiast would more likely develop units on the skills needed to be successful in all games, utilizing concepts such as defensive space to build actual student experiences. Creative games are also favored by movement enthusiasts. Students are asked to utilize their movement skills and games strategies to create games for themselves; they are given some guidance and restrictions by the movement educator. Formal units on competitive games are not likely to appear in an elementary-school curriculum developed from this framework.

Sports program approach. Given the great increase in age-group competition, it is clear that the elementary-school physical education program can be conceptualized as a sports preparation program. This is not to suggest that first grades would be learning full-scale football and baseball skills. Rather, the curriculum would be dominated by activities that are developmentally appropriate and specific to what later will become participation in the major competitive sports in our society. This kind of curriculum would emphasize lead-up games, drills on specific skills, and the learning of strategies and rules for the more popular forms of competitive sports. Dance, rhythms, noncompetitive gymnastics, and other such activity centers would be deemphasized in this model.

This approach to curriculum in the elementary school is not highly regarded in current professional literature, mostly—one assumes—because of the excesses of age-group competition and the all too frequent thrusting of young children into competitive situations long before they are developmentally prepared. Also, there is considerable concern within physical education for an "athletic" approach to teaching in the instructional program. Visions of the elementary-school physical education teacher as a "coach," with teaching strategies dominated by drills, scrimmages, and games and most attention being paid to the better performers, are regarded with horror by most experts in the field.

The recreation approach. Some educators view the major contribution of physical education for children to lie in the area of recreation, providing a time when children can relax and rejuvenate themselves for more academic work. In such cases the program is viewed as a playtime with little instruction and little concern for outcomes beyond those of fun and participation. There is no doubt that this is a minority view that seriously underestimates the potential contribution of a well-planned, competently conducted physical education program.

On the other hand, there are many schools in which classroom teachers conduct the physical education program, and although they openly espouse a sound educational view of physical education, what they actually do is very much like the recreation approach. Classroom teachers often are not prepared to teach physical education, and they do little to reach any educational outcomes, acting instead as playground supervisors.

The fitness approach. Some physical educators still view physical fitness as the major outcome of physical education and plan and conduct their programs to achieve that goal. Such an approach is more popular in the middle and secondary school than it is in the elementary school, but one can nonetheless find cases where the elementary curriculum is conceptualized primarily around fitness activities. The main emphases in such programs are on strength development, flexibility, agility, and endurance. Activities which contribute to these outcomes are favored, as opposed to those that have high skill components but contribute less to the fitness outcomes. In this approach games are used primarily for their fitness contributions and only secondarily for their skill and socialization potentials.

The Scope of the Elementary Physical Education Program

The major portion of the physical education program is accomplished in the regularly scheduled instructional sessions. However, if that is viewed as the extent of the program, the program itself will generally be capable of achieving very limited goals. The factors determining how a total physical education program is designed fit together differently for each school. The best design takes into account the interaction of all these factors in terms of a local situation.

The instructional period. Some elementary-school children receive daily instruction in physical education from a specialist, while others receive only one lesson per week taught by a classroom teacher. Between those two extremes there are wide variations. The scope of an elementary-school physical education program is determined first by the particular pattern of instructional periods available. If only one class per week is possible, then it is often useful to consider using that time to teach the children how to use the school and community facilities so that other "nonattached" time might be used as an adjunct to the instructional physical education period. Thus, if instructional time is utilized to teach children how to use a well-designed playground facility, then time before school, during recess, at the lunch hour, and after school might be utilized to supplement the instructional period. If two or more instruc-

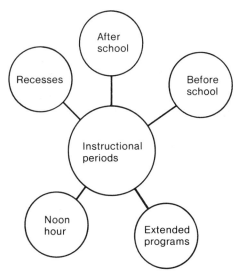

FIGURE 8.2 The elementary-school physical education program.

tional periods per week are available for each child, much more instruction and practice can be provided within the formal instructional program.

Before- and after-school programming. Depending upon the local transportation situation, time before and after school can be utilized for physical education instruction in a voluntary program. This kind of programming can be an extension of the regular instructional programming, with the activity focus changing as the units of instruction change during the regular schedule. Or, this time can be used for programming activities that go beyond the regular curriculum and offer special instruction. A program such as "early bird gymnastics" (Moore, 1980) typifies this latter approach.

Another possibility for these "special" times is an *open gymnasium* where several activities are available at the same time and children are free to choose among them or to rotate from activity to activity. Still a third possibility is to use these times for school intramurals where older students might get extended participation in the activities they have learned during their instructional periods.

Recess programming. Typically, recess in American schools has been a time when children go to the outdoor play space, weather permitting, and play for fifteen minutes in a loosely organized fashion with a teacher acting as playground supervisor—maintaining discipline but providing little in the way of organization and instruction. There is much to be said for this kind of loosely organized approach, simply because it allows children opportunities to organize themselves with all the potential socialization resulting from that arrangement. However, there is also much to be said for an approach where recesses are organized as specific adjuncts to the instructional physical education program. With this latter approach students are first taught how to utilize the outdoor facilities, which are designed to be educationally useful, and are then assigned to certain parts of the playspace, where they engage in certain activities during recess. Assignments are rotated periodically so that students get to take part in all activities, but in a planned and purposeful manner.

In a third approach several activities are made available during the recess, and students are allowed to choose which to take part in. The important point is that a fifteen-minute morning recess and a fifteen-minute afternoon recess provide a potential thirty minutes per day of *practice* time for physical education activities. This assumes that the proper instructional activities are made available and that the entire effort is organized so as to direct children to those activities and maintain their involvement in them during the allotted time.

Noon hour. Depending on the lunch practices at a given school (Do children return home or is there extensive use of a school cafeteria?), there is often time available for activity during the noon hour, although in many schools that serve lunch to students the physical education indoor space is often used for lunch purposes, thus eliminating it as a potential site for noon hour programming. The responsible physical educator will utilize this time as part of the total physical education program. The options for use of this time are essentially the same as those for the before- and after-school hours, except that at the noon hour one is more likely to be able to influence a larger number of students. For this reason the noon hour is an especially good time to program intramural activities, since it ensures maximum participation. Although very strenuous activities probably should be avoided in the noon hour program, there are many activities which meet the needs of the time as an active, happy experience and also work toward the goals of the physical education program.

Extended time. Increasingly physical education at all levels is being reconceptualized so as to include activities which take place away from the school and at times other than regular school hours. While this movement is more prevalent at the senior and middle-school levels, it can also be seen at the elementary-school levels, especially for intermediate-aged children. The resident school camping program fits this description and certainly, if available, should be viewed as a potential time to extend physical education instruction. Weekend trips for activities such as cycling are now common for fifth- and sixth-grade children. Certainly, they require the cooperation of parents and a great deal of planning by the teacher, but they also afford the opportunity to reach goals that are probably not as fully realizable in the "business as usual" instructional program during the school day.

While most authorities recommend that 150 minutes per week of instructional physical education be offered, it is equally true that hardly any schools have the instructional staff and facilities necessary to achieve that standard. This holds true even in those schools that have physical education specialists and good working relationships between that person and the regular classroom teachers. Still, if one takes into account the potential time available in an early morning program, a morning recess, a noon hour program, an afternoon recess, and an after-school program, it is clear that a great deal

can be accomplished through careful programming and administration.

Factors Affecting Planning

Too many teacher education programs equip preservice teachers for an ideal world of work, without imparting any firm sense of the realities of schools. Thus, first-year teachers find out the hard way that what they learned in the preparation program can't be implemented in their local situation and that some compromise must be achieved. This is not to suggest that the world of the school is static and must be accepted as one finds it. There is room for change, but changing things in schools requires careful thought and good "change" skills, which newly certified teachers seldom possess. Thus, an ability to plan realistically is useful—especially when one defines realistic planning as the ability to get the very most out of the actual situation as it exists.

In planning a total physical education program, the following factors must be taken into account.

Community setting. Local control of schools is a closely guarded American value. It allows the teacher much more freedom to develop curricula than would be possible in a system with state-controlled curricula. However, there *are* some liabilities: For example, local values might not be thoroughly consistent with the physical educators' views of what should or should not be done in physical education. Often these values take the form of prohibitions—one might not be able to teach a dance unit in a certain community. Views such as these can be changed, but only over an extended period of time and through careful work.

Communities might have certain views about the role of fitness or the proper emphasis on competition, or they might have certain predispositions toward important activities such as gymnastics or aquatics. Neglecting these community factors when planning a program would be a serious mistake.

Facilities. New, suburban schools in Northern and Western metropolitan centers are likely to have very good elementary-school physical education facilities including a well-appointed gymnasium, adequate outdoor space with hard and soft surface areas, and the equipment to make the spaces educationally useful. Schools in the South and Southwest may not have specialized indoor spaces for physical education, having to teach year round in outdoor spaces. Schools in older areas, whether in cities or in rural areas, probably have spaces designed many, many years ago with little likelihood of replacement or renovation. To ignore facility constraints when planning a program would be foolish; activities requiring specialized spaces or equipment simply cannot be included in programs where the space is unavailable. On the other hand, many physical educators have proven that lack of facilities need not be as constraining as one might believe. There are several ways to adapt space so that activities can be taught. Further, the activities themselves can be modified to fit existing space and facility constraints.

Personal/professional considerations. You are a professional person and, as such, become a factor in planning. You will have your own views on the major priorities in programming. You may have studied in a program that emphasized one thing as opposed to another. These are all legitimate factors to include in your planning. One of the joys of teaching in American schools is the degree of latitude which still exists for curricular innovation. If you have very strong feelings about what constitutes a good elementary-school program, and if you are willing to work hard to convince others of that viewpoint, chances are that your opinion will be a major influence in the designing of your program.

Current professional emphases in physical education. Our professional history is replete with curricular movements that are popular for a time and are then replaced by the next innovation. Some come and go quickly, while others stay longer. Some even become part of what most professionals consider to be a basic physical education curriculum. As a professional, it will be your responsibility to judge the tremendous variety of activities that might be included in your program. Should you do martial arts? Ought there to be a pop dance unit? Should you include roller skating? Skate boarding? Bicycling? Wilderness activities such as backpacking? Certain other factors, such as facilities and community preferences, will help to delimit the potential choices; but in the final analysis, you will have to decide, and you may also have to explain and even defend that decision to parents, other teachers, and administrators.

Educational programming in the school. Is the school one of self-contained classrooms? Is it partially on an open education model? Are the time blocks constant across classes? Is there flexible or modular scheduling? The answer to these questions will seriously affect your planning. You have every right to expect that physical education will be treated as seriously as other academic areas. On the other hand, if the school does operate under a nontraditional format, you have an obligation to show that physical education can work in that format. This may require developing an approach to physical education that reflects the general approach used in the school. For example, you may need a teaching/planning approach that is consistent with the informal classroom model (activity centers, freedom of movement, self-initiated study, and so on) or you may require only a planning change, such as flexible or modular scheduling, while leaving the teaching traditional.

Status of learners. Planning ought to include the status of the learners as a primary concern, taking into account their previous experiences and any developmental data that might be available. For example, in some schools reflecting a higher socioeconomic level children have a great deal of access to private sport instruction in community clubs and private clubs. They may also have valuable summer opportunities.

Therefore, some students in these schools will have had abundant experiences in sport and some will be quite skilled. Also, their expectations will differ from those of children who have not gained access to such experiences outside the school.

Developmental data can be very useful. If the school has none, perhaps that ought to be a matter of concern for the early stages of program planning. Are the students fit? What percentage might not pass a test of minimum muscular fitness? Cardiovascular fitness? What about upper body strength? What do the children know about games? How are their social skills in games playing? Children can vary a great deal within age groups depending on their previous experiences.

All these factors need to be considered when planning the scope of the elementary-school physical education program. Depending on how much instructional and nonattached time you have available and how you intend to integrate the two, these factors will become more or less important. Plan carefully and realistically: Few things are more frustrating for the professional than to design a program that needs to be modified almost immediately because of a constraining factor that was not considered during planning.

DESIGNING THE PROGRAM

Suppose you could arrange an experiment where two groups of children would be equal in all respects such as home opportunities, I.Q., and out-of-school opportunities. The two groups of students would attend schools that were equal in all respects except one. One group would receive regular instruction in physical education throughout their elementary-school years. The other group would receive none. Remember that in all other respects they would have identical experiences, both in school and outside of school. How would the two groups differ at grade six? Can you describe how they might look differently, act differently, know different things, and feel differently? The answers

to these questions are probably the best way to begin thinking about what you believe should be the goals of a school program of physical education.

The physical education group might be considerably fitter, possessing more upper body strength and more endurance. On the other hand, they may be no more fit than the non-PE group, but have identifiably higher levels of sport skills. They might know more about the rules and strategies involved in games and sports. On the other hand, they might not know more about sports, but have a better self-concept about themselves as moving beings. They might display better sportsmanship and be able to play more cooperatively with their peers. One would certainly hope that they would be different in at least some recognizable way that was related to physical education. How you would want them to differ says a great deal about what you believe to be the important goals of physical education. The program you design should help you achieve these goals.

Programs should be designed to ensure that goals are realized to the greatest degree possible. This can be accomplished in two ways. First, only realizable goals should be selected. It does no good to state far-reaching goals that cannot be achieved under current conditions. Second, activities should be selected and programmed that are designed to reach these goals. Not all activities contribute equally to all goals. One ought to be able to infer something about the goals of a program merely by examining the activities taught.

Traditional Physical Education Goals

It has been noted elsewhere (Siedentop, 1980) that physical educators have held a common set of goals for most of this century, a remarkable record of consistency given the shifting tides of educational thought during that time. The goals were originally associated with early twentieth-century progressives in physical education such as Thomas Wood and Clark Hetherington. Hetherington defined the goals as organic development, psychomotor development,

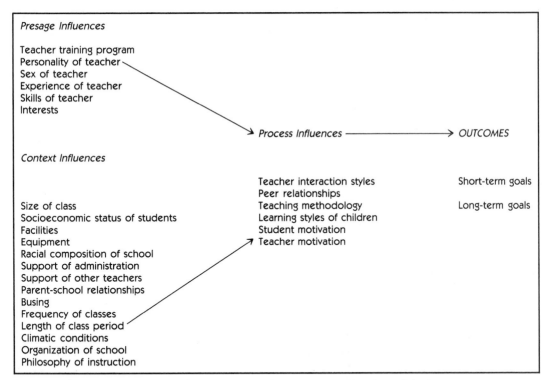

FIGURE 8.3 Influences in designing the physical education program for children.

character development, and intellectual development (Hetherington, 1962). These goals were further popularized by important physical educators such as Jesse Feiring Williams and Jay B. Nash. Bucher (1964) defined these fourfold traditional goals as follows:

Physical development objective: The objective of physical development deals with the program of activities that builds physical power in an individual through the development of the various organic systems of the body.

Motor development objective: The motor development objective is concerned with making physical movement useful and with as little expenditure of energy as possible and being proficient, graceful, and aesthetic in this movement.

Mental development objective: The mental development objective deals with the accumulation of a body of knowledge and the ability to think and to interpret this knowledge.

Social development objective: The social development objective is concerned with helping an individual in making personal adjustments, group adjustments, and adjustments as a member of society. (155,157,160,161)

These goals can be derived directly from the "7 Cardinal Principles" of American education first proposed by the National Education Association in 1918. These time-honored objectives are still accepted by the majority of physical educators. The words used to describe them may be modernized somewhat, but the basic concepts have remained largely untouched as is evidenced by the current AAHPERD (American Alliance for Health, Physical Education, Recreation, and Dance) Physical Education Public Information (PEPI) project goals (Biles, JOHPER, September 1971).

1. A physically educated person is one who has knowledge and skill concerning his body and how it works.
2. Physical education is health insurance.

3. Physical education can contribute to academic achievement.

4. A sound physical education program contributes to development of a positive self-concept.

5. A sound physical education program helps an individual attain social skills.

These broadly conceived objectives allow the physical educator a great deal of latitude in choosing the particular focus of a program design. Certain problems are created, however, if the physical educator assumes that each of the goals must be allocated equal time. Too often this means a watered-down program that achieves little in any specific goal category.

Goals of Physical Education as Play Education

In Chapter 1 we attempted to explain our belief that physical education is best conceived of as a form of play education and that physically active play is the major focus of physical education. If physical education can be viewed legitimately as play education, it follows that the aim of physical education should be to *increase tendencies and abilities to play competitive and expressive motor activities* (Siedentop, 1980). This view suggests that the major effort in teaching physical education must be to increase the degree to which children like to do physically active play; that is, to teach them to love our subject matter.

The major way this is done is by increasing their skills in the subject matter, teaching them what it means to be a player or a dancer, helping them get ready to participate to their fullest extent, teaching them appropriate ways of behaving within the play contexts, and to increasing their knowledge of themselves and their relationships to the play forms. These objectives can be viewed schematically in Figure 8.4.

The major value of the goal hierarchy is to illustrate clearly the relationships among the various levels of the goals. While increased skill is important, it is considered subordinate to helping children learn to love the subject matter. Therefore, teachers must help children acquire skills in an atmosphere and teaching climate which fosters respect and affection for the activities. Knowledge is seen not as a goal in itself but as a means of socializing children into the play settings so that they may play more fully and more meaningfully. The activity counseling function suggests that children need to be guided toward those motor play forms for which they have the most ability and interest. Readiness for participation means that a certain level of fitness and movement capability is necessary for useful participation in play activities. The activities directed toward this goal are not necessarily ends in themselves but rather means through which children can be helped to become ready to learn important skills.

FIGURE 8.4 Hierarchy of program objectives for physical education

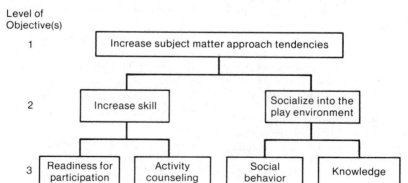

Goals of Physical Education as Human Movement

The proponents of movement education in this country have developed models for planning and instruction that are consistent with their philosophy. Elements of both traditional physical education goals and play education goals can be seen in statements detailing the purposes of movement education. Still, the nature of these statements allows them to stand on their own as a coherent set of educational goals. Typical of such goals are those developed by Schurr (1980).

1. Understand the structure of movement.
2. Move competently and confidently in a wide variety of structured and unstructured movement activities.
3. Develop and maintain fitness.
4. Meet and solve new movement demands.
5. Communicate through, about, and in movement.
6. Interact positively with others through, about, and in movement.
7. Find personal meaning and significance in movement.

It is clear that the content of a program directed toward these goals would differ somewhat from the content of a program directed toward play education goals or traditional physical education goals. A more complete description of movement education can be found in Chapters 14–17. What is important here is to recognize that the selection of goals should form some kind of coherent total concept that reflects as faithfully as possible what a school system, teaching staff, or individual teacher believes about physical education.

Selecting Activities to Meet Goals

There is a point in curriculum planning where a decision becomes necessary about *what* to teach. At this point overall objectives and specific goals provide the framework within which the planner/teacher is confronted with the need to select specific activities/themes. Of course, there are many more activities available than any program can accommodate, so choices have to be made, often among very attractive alternatives. This level of decision making is, without question, the most important; from it emerges what the children will experience. Naturally, there are many constraints upon the teacher/planner and we have tried to highlight these earlier in the chapter. Nonetheless, even with many constraints most teacher/planners will need to make choices. The following guidelines may be helpful.

1. Activities/themes chosen should clearly represent the goal hierarchy of the program. Teachers/planners must be consistent; the activities they select to develop a yearly program should, taken together, clearly reflect the hierarchy of goals they value. Some activities have high fitness payoffs but rather low eye-hand coordination payoffs. For other activities, the opposite may be true.

2. A "good" activity is one that meets program goals. In this sense "good" is a relative term and what is good for your program might not be as good for the program of another professional who has different goals.

3. A good program accomplishes *something*. No program can contribute to all the possible goals that might be developed. Even under the most perfect conditions we would encourage teachers/planners to make sure that their programs accomplished something concrete, be it fitness, sports skills development, positive self-concept, or varied movement skills. We believe that too many programs attempt to reach an unrealistic number of goals and therefore risk accomplishing little of any significance.

4. Know your activities. It is difficult to make sound judgments about the potential of an activity to contribute to program goals unless the activity is understood fairly well. When is it best introduced? How? What amounts of the activity are necessary to contribute to goal achievement? What equipment does it take? Can the equipment be made inexpensively? Can most of the children be active in this activity at the same time? These are all questions that should be answered before an activity is selected for the program.

5. How well does the teacher/planner know and like the activity? You have some rights, too! If you try to teach an activity that you do not like, the feeling will be conveyed to the children. On the other hand, if you really like an activity, not only are you likely to know it better, but you will also teach it better. Further, your enthusiasm for the activity will be conveyed to the children.

BUILDING UNITS OF INSTRUCTION

Once goals and subgoals are developed, the primary planning tasks of the teacher become considerably more specific and more attuned to the day-to-day events of the physical education program in the school. Some of the most important skills that any teacher can acquire are those normally referred to as instructional design skills. Instruction has been defined as "the process of arranging human, material and temporal resources with the intention of facilitating the learning of self and/or others." (Hough and Duncan, 1970) The human resources in planning for instruction certainly include yourself (teacher behavior *is* a factor in instruction), teacher aides, gym helpers, and children within the class. Material resources include facilities, indoor equipment, outdoor equipment, teaching aids, and all other hardware and software that might be used in order to create a better learning environment. Temporal resources, of course, refer to the efficient use of time. The design of instruction, then, involves learning how to use yourself, other people, facilities, equipment, and time in order to optimize the chances of children meeting the goals of the program and enjoying themselves as they do it.

Sequencing Instruction at the Program and Unit Levels

We know that children learn best when instruction is sequenced properly, when they can gradually build new skills on a solid foundation of previously acquired skills, and when the relationships between new learning tasks and previous experiences are clear

and consistent. Planners need to think carefully about sequencing both at the program level and at the unit level. Planning daily lessons will then become much easier.

Programmatic level: Sequencing from year to year. Teachers seldom introduce an activity to second graders without some sense of how the outcome of that activity will relate to other movement/sport experiences the children will have in the program as they advance through it. An activity such as volleyball may not be played in its mature form until the sixth grade, but many earlier activities will be presented which develop skills that are both directly and indirectly related to mature volleyball skills. At the programmatic level it is important for teachers to have a strong sense of how all their plans come together at the end of the program; how all the isolated activities and discrete skills add up to a *coherent physical education.*

A useful aid for helping to sequence instruction at the programmatic level is a progression-analysis divided into stages. The stages we suggest are as follows:

Stage I Basic skill acquisition, practice, and refinement. The student learns and practices gaining control of an object using a particular motor pattern.

Stage II Adding complexity to the setting in which the skill is utilized. The student learns and practices controlling the object under more complex conditions.

Stage III Using the skill in beginning game play. The student utilizes the skill in order to achieve the objective of a simplified game.

Stage IV Using the skill in more complex game play. The student utilizes the skill in order to achieve the objectives of more mature games, often parent games.

The basic goal of Stage I is for the child to learn self-control in relation to an object—to make the object do what the child wants it to do. Stage I involves very early motor skill acquisition, movement exploration, and later skill practice. Even in highly skilled, adult athletic settings, players often spend much time practicing basic skills. Thus, Stage I practice exists *throughout* any instructional program.

In Stage II complexity is usually added by changing the setting in which the skill occurs and by having children practice skills in combination, such as receiving, dribbling, and passing. Here isolated skills are put together in chains that will prove useful in later game play. Stage II practice is also characteristic of all sport and athletic practices, even in their most mature and professional forms.

In Stage III the focus shifts from the skill or combination of skills to the game setting in which the skill is to be used. Here the children learn to use the right chains of skills at the right time in order to accomplish game goals. It is in Stage III that skills begin to take their more mature form in terms of the requirements of specialized games. Limitations imposed by the rules of those games modify the skills slightly and the skills start to become highly differentiated according to the sport for which they are specifically used.

In Stage IV the early games skills are refined and extended as complexity is added in the form of more players, more rules, differentiated position play, more complex defensive play, and more complex offensive play. Learning game cues becomes a large part of the instruction at this stage, as children learn to anticipate game situations so that they will be able to respond properly.

The following chart presents an overall estimate of where the four stages are most likely to appear in an elementary-school program. The chart is intended as an overall guide and might not apply to all local conditions.

	K	1	2	3	4	5	6
Stage I	--						
Stage II		------------------------------------					
Stage III				----------------------			
Stage IV						--------	

Unit level: Sequencing from lesson to lesson. Most teachers in physical education plan and arrange their instruction primarily by units. A unit is a sequence of instructional activities devoted to a specified theme. Activities are sequenced across time to achieve the goals of the unit. Units can be defined in the following ways: (a) by activities—for example, a soccer unit, a jump rope unit, or a track and field unit; (b) by movement themes—for example, a dribbling unit or a striking unit; (c) by experiences—for example, a unit on how to use the facilities of the immediate neighborhood for physical activity or how to do physical education at home; (d) by fitness outcomes—for example, a strength unit, an aerobics unit, or a flexibility unit; or (e) by social outcomes—for example, a cooperation unit, a competition unit, or a sportsmanship unit. Regardless of how the unit theme is defined, it will have an overall set of objectives and a sequence of lessons designed to achieve those objectives. Units, of course, can vary in length, typically getting longer as children's abilities to sustain interest and effort increase.

Task Analysis

Once unit goals are determined, the next step is to perform the necessary task analyses to identify important subskills and sequence instruction properly. A task analysis identifies intermediate goals which the student must learn in order to achieve the final goal; it starts with the final goal and works back toward the entry level skills of the children. A *procedural task analysis* describes a chain of events which together define a meaningful learning unit. Activities such as the long jump, bowling, shooting arrows, and vaulting are typical of those for which a procedural analysis is quite useful. Such an analysis would be diagrammed as follows:

> Instructional Goal
> Complete long jump with proper approach, take-off, and landing
> running approach → last strides → lift-off → float → landing and plant

In the procedural analysis each skill can be learned somewhat independently and then put together in a chain. The learning of a skill does not depend on the learning of the previous skill. However, a major factor in accomplishing the final goal is to put the chain together smoothly. The parts of the chain are easy to learn as discrete skills. It is the coordinated movement of the chain as a whole that is the real skill.

A *hierarchical task analysis* describes all the subskills that must be learned in order to perform the higher order skill. Here there is a necessary relationship between the skills; one skill has to be learned before another can be learned. In a hierarchical analysis one starts with the final goal and asks the question, "What will the student have to be able to do in order to accomplish this task?" This procedure is followed until a level is reached that is commensurate with the entry level skills of the students. A hierarchical analysis would be diagrammed as follows:

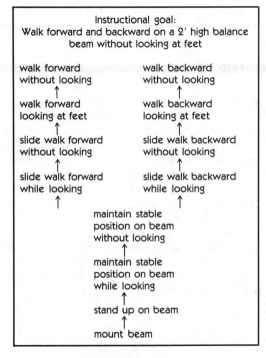

Instructional goal:
Walk forward and backward on a 2′ high balance beam without looking at feet

walk forward without looking
↑
walk forward looking at feet
↑
slide walk forward without looking
↑
slide walk forward while looking
↑

walk backward without looking
↑
walk backward looking at feet
↑
slide walk backward without looking
↑
slide walk backward while looking
↑

maintain stable position on beam without looking
↑
maintain stable position on beam while looking
↑
stand up on beam
↑
mount beam

The value of a task analysis cannot be overestimated. It pinpoints exactly what children need to accomplish goals and, in the hierarchical analysis, the order in which skills must be learned. With experience and experimentation teachers can adjust the size of the steps in a learning sequence so that they are best suited to the learning situation. If the steps between skills are too small, children may get bored because of a lack of challenge. On the other hand, if the steps are too large, the children might become frustrated through having little success. An appropriate instructional step in a sequence is large enough to provide some challenge yet sufficiently attainable so that children can have frequent and consistent success.

Planning Individual Lessons

Daily lesson plans are required by many school systems throughout the country. Even where they are not required, they should be considered as essential. First, they provide the teacher with a quick, thorough reminder of *precisely* what is supposed to be accomplished in each lesson and how it is to be accomplished. Second, they provide a standard against which to judge the results of a lesson, thereby modifying lessons continually so as to improve their quality. Third, rereading all the daily lesson plans for an entire unit provides the best way to review and improve units. Fourth, if a teacher has to be absent for some reason, an adequately prepared lesson plan allows a substitute to teach the lesson without disrupting the flow of a unit.

An adequate lesson plan should describe precisely the content of the day's lesson and the development of the content within the lesson. Well-written objectives are probably the best way to describe the overall content (see section on writing objectives). Beyond this, the format used for lesson planning should help the teacher to see the appropriate interrelationships among the various parts of a lesson.

Rink (1979) has provided a useful framework for developing lessons. The framework can be used for lesson planning, too. The basic concept within the framework is the *task*. A task is an activity that makes sense in and of itself—it is a meaningful unit of instruction. A lesson consists of several tasks. The usefulness of the task model is that it enables the teacher to understand the interrelationships among tasks, especially in terms of the degree to which they contribute to the achievement of lesson and unit goals.

Too often tasks in a lesson are thoroughly unrelated. Students participate in a series of tasks that do not progress toward significant outcomes. On other occasions the tasks are related, but not related carefully enough to form a true *progression* of activities. A complete lesson is one in which the successive tasks lead into one another in such a way that learning progresses smoothly and successfully.

The task planning system involves four categories of tasks: informing tasks, refining tasks, extending tasks, and applying tasks. These four categories are defined as follows:

1. Informing tasks—communicate a "do this" message to the child. Informing tasks provide new information to students and new directions. They are the first steps in a new progression. Instructions such as "Let's start with fifteen jumping jacks," "Everybody find their own space," and "Today we will work on dribbling the basketball with our nonpreferred hand" are announcements of informing tasks.

2. Refining tasks—designed to improve the qualitative aspects of performance by helping the child to find better and/or different ways to perform the skill—they are the building blocks in skill progressions. It is through refining tasks that mature forms of skill are gradually shaped. Messages such as "Roll the ball more slowly this time," "Now let's emphasize pointing our toes as we do the cartwheel," and "This time let's get the pass higher" are illustrative of refining tasks.

3. Extending tasks—designed to expand the skill by adding new parts, changing the focus of the skill, seeking a variety of solutions, or combining skills into new chains. Examples of extending tasks would be moving from hitting a ball off a tee to hitting a thrown ball, moving from using a beach ball to a playground ball in volleyball-type games, putting individual stunts together into new routines, and teaching the ball toss and racquet swing separately and then adding them together to form a serving motion.

4. Applying tasks—designed to move the focus from the skill itself to an application of the skill to accomplish a goal. This allows the child a frame of reference in which to evaluate skill development. Instructions such as "Now let's try to hit it ten times in a row" or

"How many times out of twenty can you hit the target?" are examples of applying tasks. The most common applications task is the game or modified game setting.

Typically, one might expect that a well-planned lesson would begin with an informing task, develop that skill further through refining tasks, extend the skill through one or more extending tasks, and finally test the skill in an applying task. However, all too often insufficient attention is paid to progression and the resulting lesson is a series of informing tasks or movement from an informing task immediately to an application task. Below are two lessons which show the progression from informing to refining to extending to application.

EXAMPLE 1 VOLLEYBALL LESSON

TASK	TASK FUNCTION
Volley against wall	Informing
Volley with partner across net	Extending
Volley with group—keep it up competition	Applying
Overhand serve	Informing
Volleyball game	Applying

EXAMPLE 2 MOVEMENT LESSON

TASK	TASK FUNCTION
Exercises	Informing
Jumping jacks	Informing
Touch toes	Informing
Striking ball with different body parts	Extending
Striking with only one part	Extending
Striking with same part to different levels	Extending
Throwing to different levels	Extending
Throwing and catching very softly	Refining
Throwing and catching to see who can do it the greatest number of times	Applying
Chasing game	Applying

There is no magic formula for planning a lesson. Clearly, students have to be introduced to a task (informing function) before they can do it. Also, many feel that each lesson should end with an application task, which allows the children not only to test themselves but to see how the skill is used. The number of refining and extending tasks necessary to fully develop a skill will depend on factors such as the time available and the previous experience of the children. Application tasks should be modified so that they fit the level of skill developed through informing/refining/extending experiences.

Once a lesson has been analyzed in this way, the teacher can be sure that proper attention has been paid to the development of the tasks for the day. The exact format in which the daily lesson plan is written is not terribly important as long as it contains the information about the lesson clearly and precisely.

Evaluating Instruction

Evaluation is often difficult for the physical educator—physical education produces few permanent academic products such as spelling quizzes, mathematics tables, essays, and so on. Children move and perform in physical education, and a teacher is asked to judge that movement and performance as it occurs in order to sort out how well the children are doing at the planned task. Nonetheless, evaluation should be done routinely; it is necessary in order to modify instruction to make it better the next time it is presented. A teacher must have some idea of how well children learned the task in order to make a judgment about how well the tasks were taught. Generating that kind of information is the purpose of evaluation. Grading students is not the first purpose of evaluation, even though progress reports to parents and administrators and to the students themselves can be useful in many ways. The exact nature of the evaluation process will differ from school system to school system. Therefore, we would like to suggest some important ideas and distinctions that relate to evaluation, no matter what format is utilized.

1. Distinguish clearly between measures that are norm-referenced and those that are criterion-referenced. *Norm-referenced measures* look at the performance of a group and evaluate children on their relative standing within the group. Thus, the AAHPERD youth fitness test might be administered and several children might score 9:30 on the one mile run. This might make them the best in their class. However, on a larger national sample they might only be at the sixtieth percentile. Thus, their standing in a larger group would be less impressive. Finally, despite their relative standing, they might be unfit in terms of endurance fitness if a more absolute standard of fitness were used. *Criterion referencing* provides a standard against which a performance is judged—the performance either did or did not meet the criterion measure. Thus, in an endurance run children would be judged on their performance relative to a standard rather than on how their performance was in relation to other members of the group. It is our judgment that criterion-referenced evaluation is by far the more useful of the two procedures in evaluating instruction, provided that there are reasonable criteria against which to compare performance.

2. Try to achieve the 90/90 rule. Educators should aim at having 90 percent of their students achieve at least 90 percent of whatever constitutes a good performance in a task. In some tasks this is easily calculated. For example, one might aim at having 90 percent of the fourth graders achieve 8:30 in the one mile run. It is less easy to calculate when the task is not neatly quantifiable. Still, it is perfectly conceivable that a teacher in a folk dance unit might expect 90 percent of the students to develop a 90 percent proficiency in the dances.

3. Distinguish between formative and summative evaluation. Formative evaluation provides information about the quality and quantity of task completion as the learning is occurring. Summative evaluation provides information about the degree of attainment of program, unit, or lesson goals after the program, unit, or lesson has been completed. Formative evaluation can be formal or informal. Often something as simple as frequent teacher feedback about progress acts as a very useful formative evaluation. Teachers' comments written on their lesson plans provide good formative unit evaluation for

modifying the unit for next year's program. Summative evaluation is usually more formal, using testing, student evaluations, final performance data, and other procedures.

4. Make sure there is consistency between your goals and your means of evaluation. As Mager (1962) has pointed out so clearly, there needs to be a "match" between your objectives and the criteria you use to evaluate student performance of those objectives. Examples of mismatches would be considering as evidence of attainment of a cardiovascular fitness objective a student's ability to pass a ten-question quiz on fitness, or judging how many children had learned to do the sprint start in a track unit by using their times on the forty-yard dash. Neither of the items used as criteria measures the intent of the objective.

5. Evaluate both the process and the product of your instructional program. When things don't go right, there are always two basic sources for identifying problems in instruction. These sources can best be understood by asking two important evaluation questions. The first—"Did I do what I planned to do?"—is a process question. It asks quite simply whether or not the lesson went as planned. The second question—"Did the students learn what I wanted them to learn?"—is a product question. It asks whether the intended outcomes were achieved. If the answer to the first question is "yes" and things still didn't turn out properly, you can be fairly sure that you have chosen the wrong way to reach your intended goals. If the answer to the first question is "no," you really can't be sure whether your intended plans were the right ones, since you did not really give them a chance. It is important that process evaluation and product evaluation *both* be conducted.

Selecting and Preparing Instructional Goals and Objectives

So much has been written about educational goals and objectives during the past several decades that they will be referred to here only briefly. Much of the discussion in

this chapter concerning the factors that influence planning is directly relevant to the selection of goals and objectives for developing units of instruction. Once goals have been decided in general—taking into account all the factors influencing such decisions—they need to be stated more precisely for the development of instructional plans. Some general guidelines and principles for selecting and preparing goals and objectives are presented in this section.

1. Instructional goals should describe what students will be able to do after they have completed the instructional program. They should describe, as precisely as possible, the kinds of skills, attitudes, areas of knowledge, and values that will accrue to the student as a result of coming into contact with the instructional process.

2. Instructional goals should describe the major culminating or synthesizing behavior which results from the instruction (Dick & Carey, 1978). Instructional units should not have long lists of *objectives;* instead, they should have fairly short lists of instructional *goals.*

3. Instructional goals should be defined in terms of student performance in an applied setting such as a game or the student's daily life. This will keep the instructional designer "on track," working toward meaningful objectives rather than arbitrary performances.

4. Enabling objectives are skills, areas of knowledge, and attitudes that will help achieve the instructional goals. They may be components of the goals or background skills necessary for the achievement of the goals.

5. Enabling objectives should be meaningful units of performance that are worth doing for their own sake, besides leading to the successful achievement of the instructional goals. Higher-order objectives often incorporate more than one meaningful unit of performance, for example, doing a fast break in basketball.

6. Written objectives should describe the task to be accomplished in terms that allow an observer to recognize clearly when it has been achieved. Words such as *dribble, vault, dodge, strike,* and *hurdle* are good behavioral

terms because they refer to things that people can recognize immediately. Terms such as *think, feel, understand,* and *accomplish* are poor terms because they refer to situations that cannot be precisely recognized.

7. Written objectives should describe the situation in which the task is to be accomplished. The description should include the constraints placed on the learner and the basic outline of the setting. The phrase *to bump a volleyball* describes the task well, but it says nothing about the setting in which the task should be performed. Is the setting a return of a serve, a toss across the net, a shorter toss from a partner, or a self-toss by the individual learner?

8. Written objectives should describe a means whereby the child will know when the objective has been accomplished. With regard to the "bump" objective stated above, how well does the child have to bump the ball to meet this objective? How high? How accurately? With what particular form? These things should be answered ahead of time and stated in the objective. Both teacher and learner can then know when an objective has been achieved.

PLANNING SUGGESTIONS FOR THE CLASSROOM TEACHER

In elementary schools where there is no physical education specialist, classroom teachers are responsible for the physical education of their children. This is a difficult assignment for classroom teachers, who often have—at most—the experience of one college methods course in physical education. Also, the classroom teacher's life is busy and hectic, with the additional task of teaching physical education often viewed as a low-priority item. Nevertheless, physical education of children *is* important and classroom teachers who are serious about their responsibilities will try to provide a sound physical educational experience for the children. The following guidelines should help the classroom teacher achieve this goal without spending a large amount of time planning and preparing for the lessons.

1. Choose activities which you know—children will have a better experience if you have some knowledge and interest in an activity.
2. Choose activities whose equipment demands are capable of being handled without large inputs of your time—use playground equipment and spaces already in place, and use activities that require simple, easy-to-acquire equipment (such as rope jumping or volleyball).
3. Choose activities for which children have some previous experience—your teaching time will be utilized most efficiently if it is directed toward refining and extending skills with which children are already familiar rather than introducing children to totally new skills.
4. Choose activities that allow children to be active—always remember that children learn when they are actively involved and not when they are standing in lines or waiting to be in a game.
5. Organize a gym-helper group to assist in the organizational aspects of the lesson—trusted children can get equipment ready and prepare playspaces so that children in the class can move into the lesson immediately upon reaching the site.
6. Outline the lesson before leaving the classroom—management problems will be minimized if children know what they are to do when they reach the site and what will occur during the lesson (rather than waiting until they reach the playspace to inform them).
7. Follow the inform/refine/extend/apply sequence for individual lessons—playing dodgeball every Tuesday for an entire year does not constitute a physical education. Some minimal planning will create simple progressions which lead to real outcomes.
8. Ask for help from specialists—the district should have experts available, whether physical education consultants or curriculum personnel. These persons can often provide materials and equipment which can make the physical education experience easier for you and better for the children.
9. Don't stop trying—don't succumb to the temptation to make the instructional physical education period a supervised play period in which no new learning occurs.

9

current concepts of teaching

For many years researchers have tried to discover the one style or method of teaching that would be maximally effective for all students, all subject matters, and all school contexts. Unfortunately, the search has been in vain. It does not appear that any one specific method is likely to be vastly superior to all other methods. In fact, it appears that different styles of teaching can be equally effective *if they have certain common characteristics.* Teachers are individuals and their individuality becomes part of their teaching style. If all teachers used exactly the same style, schools would be very uninteresting places.

We are not suggesting that any style of teaching is as good as any other style. We do not believe this, nor does research support such a viewpoint. There are some ways of teaching that are better than others. This chapter will discuss the preferable teaching styles.

TEACHER ROLES AND EFFECTIVENESS

The Many Roles of the Teacher

When laypersons think about what a teacher does, invariably they think about those aspects of teaching that involve formal interaction between teacher and student: giving instructions, demonstrating, managing, giving feedback, discussing, and questioning. While it can still be argued that these interactions are the core of teaching, it is important to recognize the many other tasks the teacher performs that contribute to student growth.

The teacher as planner. The well-taught lesson is often the well-planned lesson. A program is something more than the addition of discrete lessons over time. Children need and deserve a sound program of physical education. This requires planning, and planning takes both time and skill. We consider it important enough to devote an entire chapter to it (see Chapter 8).

The teacher as manager. It is not uncommon to find teachers' aides in schools today as well as student teachers from area colleges and universities. These human resources need to be managed in order for them to be most effective. Likewise, there are material resources in the form of equipment and facilities that will not contribute optimally unless they are managed well.

The teacher as professional. Teachers belong to local, state, and national organizations. Also, they may belong to special organizations established to pursue particular subject matter, such as the AAHPERD. Teachers can take advantage of professional journals, new books in the field, and they can attend special meetings. In order for teachers to continue to grow, to learn new techniques, and to contribute their expertise to others, they must have a long-term commitment to professional growth.

The teacher as counselor. Physical educators have served as unappointed school counselors for many years. All teachers do some counseling work with their students. Those teachers who are perceived by their students to be warm and receptive often do a great deal, sometimes to the extent that it overshadows their instructional role.

The teacher as a representative of the school. Fortunately, society has more of a realistic view of teachers than it did years ago, when the teacher was expected to be the one citizen in the community who had no vices whatsoever. Nonetheless, teachers cannot "shed their professional skins" when they leave school in the evening. Even if you live in a community far from that in which you teach, you are still identified as a teacher, and you represent schools and the educational establishment. This is as it should be. Teachers have many opportunities in their "off" hours to enhance the general understanding of what education is all about. By behaving professionally and by being able to speak knowledgeably and articulately about general school issues, teachers have the power to educate the public about the realities of school life.

The teacher as instructor. When all is said and done, the primary role of the teacher today is still that of instructor. The remainder of this chapter explains some facts and ideas about instruction, especially as it relates to children, and even more specifically as it relates to their physical education.

Characteristics of Effective Teaching

As we mentioned earlier, some ways of teaching are better than others. During the past ten years, research on teacher effectiveness has improved to the point where some major findings can be reported. The characteristics that we will discuss are those teacher behaviors that have been correlated with high student achievement across a number of research studies and that are considered by researchers in the field of teacher effectiveness to be highly predictive of effective teaching.

Shows concern for clarity. The effective teacher is likely to state objectives in language children understand, to outline the content of a lesson, to signal transitions between parts of the lesson, to use demonstrations, to emphasize only the important points, to avoid overloading children with too much information, and to summarize the parts of the lesson at its conclusion. Teachers who rate high on clarity don't overwhelm children with information but rather provide relevant information in a concise way. In physical education the effective use of demonstrations and models can greatly contribute to clarity. Specific information feedback also contributes to clarity.

Conveys enthusiasm. The effective teacher is likely to enjoy teaching and convey that enthusiasm to the children. Clearly, in physical education the effective teacher must display an affection for movement, games, and sport. Interactions with children must show enthusiasm for their progress, for the process of learning, and for children as individuals. Positive interaction styles (see Chapters 10 and 11) are characteristic of enthusiastic teachers. It is difficult to be enthusiastic if you are continually involved with reprimanding and/or correcting the errors of your students. Learning to interact in a positive manner is a large part of building an enthusiastic teaching style.

Physical education teachers show their enthusiasm for their subject matter when they participate with their children and when the children see the teachers enjoying the same activities they enjoy. A lesson that moves quickly, has smooth transitions (see page 140), and is lively enhances enthusiasm. Teachers can show enthusiasm in their interactions, but if the lessons drag, the power of the interactions is seriously limited.

Teachers who find ways to convey realistically high expectations for their students are no doubt perceived as more enthusiastic about children than those who do not voice such expectations. The research concerning expectations is quite convincing. Teachers should not "fool" children by expecting more than the children can deliver; however, realistically high expectations not only aid learning but are perceived by children as a sign of caring and enthusiasm. A corollary to this is that teachers must voice high expectations for the learning process. They must find ways to let children know that they value learning and expect the class to achieve well.

Demonstrates flexibility. Effective teachers adjust their instruction to accommodate changes that are either imposed from outside or grow within a lesson. Changes imposed from outside might include a hurriedly called assembly, a fire drill, absenteeism, or a variety of school factors. Changes that grow within a lesson might include a teacher's sense that student interest is waning or that students are too tired to enjoy an activity any further. We are not suggesting that in being flexible (this characteristic is often referred to as *variability* in research on teaching), a teacher merely responds to every ebb and flow in a lesson or to each verbalization from a student. If that were true, as it sometimes is in teaching, the students would be in control of both the pace and content of the lesson. Flexibility refers instead to a sensitivity to the day-to-day and minute-to-minute factors which intrude upon a preestablished lesson plan. Flexibility refers to the skills and control necessary for a teacher to adjust easily and quickly to these changing demands rather than to have a "we are going to finish this no matter what" attitude.

Flexibility also implies the ability to capitalize on unexpected events or incidents that occur during a lesson—what often has been called the "teachable moment." This kind of positive instructional spontaneity shows that a teacher is clearly in control of his or her teaching.

Demonstrates task-oriented behavior. Effective teachers are task-oriented and businesslike about their instruction. This factor is related to the characteristic of clarity. It also involves instructional skills such as pacing (which refers to a sensitivity to the learning rates of children and an ability to adjust instruction accordingly) and the ability to keep children on-task with a positive rather than a coercive style.

Being task-oriented does not mean being a cold, mechanistic teacher. When considered along with enthusiasm and flexibility, such behavior has only positive ramifications. Learning is valued. Learning tasks are stated clearly. The teacher proceeds efficiently and smoothly to help children achieve those learning tasks. Children are mostly on-task and time is not wasted. This is all accomplished with a great deal of enthusiasm and within a positive, supportive climate.

Ensures student opportunities to learn criterion materials. Chapter 2 suggested that opportunity to respond was a major factor affecting the rate at which children acquire skills in school. Providing as many children as possible with as many opportunities to respond as possible (*learning trials* in psychological jargon) is an instructional skill. The traditional method of teaching physical education (in which children spend too much time standing in lines waiting for a turn) violates this characteristic badly.

Opportunity to respond is obviously related to effective management of time. The discussion on movement management and management time in Chapter 11 is relevant here. The less time spent in management, the more time is left for instruction and practice. Paring instruction down to a crisp, effective presentation of the major informational aspects of a game, skill, or activity leaves an optimum amount of time for student-centered practice.

Of course, opportunity to respond assumes that the students' responses fit the general definition of a "quality" response as discussed on page 11. A quality response is one in which the children are motivated to make a legitimate attempt to reach a learning goal and get feedback about their efforts. In other words, we are talking about on-task behavior. Therefore, methods of keeping children motivated and on-task are very important to effective teaching. Berliner (1976), a noted researcher on teaching, said the following:

> A fact of classroom reality is that teacher behavior does not influence student achievement directly. A teacher's indirectness, or questioning, or reinforcement does not simply result in greater mathematics, reading or science achievement. The link that must be considered is the behavior of the student in the instructional setting. We are now convinced that the mediating link so necessary to consider is a student's active time-on-task. If teacher questions, reinforcement, warmth, and clarity are to affect outcomes, they can only do so by engaging and then keeping the student's attention. If the student will attend, the possibility of learning exists. Teacher behaviors that affect student active learning time must be examined carefully. (p. 10)

The implications of this statement for instructional practice in physical education are overwhelming. In the classroom children usually have writing utensils, paper, books of their own, and other learning materials. In the gymnasium it is less likely that children will have their balls, hoops, ropes, tumbling mats, or other equipment that will allow maximum participation.

Also, the gym is a larger place than the classroom and the problems of behavior management are more substantial. Many teachers, fearing a loss of control, attempt to maintain order by restricting the number of children who can be active at any time. Thus, children standing in line or waiting on the side are not uncommon sights in physical education. However, this increased control is achieved at the cost of opportunities to respond. While sometimes necessary, we do not consider it to be, in the long run, a fair trade for children. Thus, we believe that the chapter on managing groups of children cannot be divorced from this chapter on teaching.

Provides academic and behavioral feedback. The effective teacher provides relevant, supportive feedback for both academic performance and social behavior. Criticism, as a general category of teacher behavior, tends to be *inversely* related to student achievement. Teacher behaviors such as praising, showing warmth, complimenting, supporting, and encouraging tend to be positively related to student achievement. A rather detailed analysis of positive, interactive teaching styles is available in chapters 10 and 11.

A Question of Style

The characteristics of effective teaching noted in the previous section are not specific to any style of teaching. They are generic in the sense that they can be present or absent in any given style. The argument we are trying to make is that the presence or absence of these characteristics is probably more important than the choice of style. While that may seem like heresy to many physical educators, we believe it to be true, and we further believe that it is supported by research on teaching effectiveness.

"Wars" between proponents of opposing teaching styles are counterproductive. The war that needs badly to be waged is between those whose teaching reflects the relevant characteristics and those whose teaching does not. The most prominent enemy among those who do not reflect the important teaching characteristics are the few physical educators who simply have stopped trying, who keep children orderly and pretend that this discharges their responsibilities as teachers. Second on our enemies list are those who do not organize instruction so as to optimize the children's opportunity to respond, to take part, to be active. Such a teacher is likely to value neat lines rather than participation. Third on our list are those who do not help children to clarify learning goals, who do not set limits which help children to identify relevant feedback, and who do not organize learning tasks into small, meaningful steps. Fourth are the coercive teachers who deliver nothing but criticism, nags, and corrective feedback.

A Note on Direct Instruction

Recently a number of impressive research efforts focusing on instruction in the elementary school have produced significant results (Rosenshine, 1976). It should be noted that the studies were done primarily in schools with low socioeconomic levels and that the achievement outcomes were mainly in math, reading, and science. However, the results of the various studies were very similar and reflect to a large extent the generic characteristics cited in this chapter.

Rosenshine (1976) has labeled the general pattern of effectiveness revealed by teaching research *direct instruction*. In direct instruction a great deal of time is devoted to achieving learning goals (time on-task, opportunity to respond). Teachers tend to control the flow of the lesson with fairly narrow questions and instructions (clarity). Academic and behavioral feedback is frequent and predominantly positive. Learning is approached in a direct, businesslike manner. Goals are clear and known to the students. The teacher, within this setting, is warm, friendly, and supportive (enthusiasm, positive feedback, and so on). Teachers monitor and supervise student work closely so as to keep students on-task.

This is not a revolutionary new teaching style; no doubt, many successful teachers have for many years used what is now referred to as direct instruction. It is a good style of teaching because it has embedded within it the important generic characteristics of effective teaching.

While other, more exotic, styles of teaching may be defended on theoretical grounds, it is unlikely that anyone will mount a defense on empirical grounds. Thus, one should not look at the organizational setup of an open classroom and immediately consider it good while automatically discounting a traditional classroom with chairs in neat rows. If the traditional classroom teacher is enthusiastic, has clear learning goals, possesses a positive teaching style, and reflects the other characteristics described above, that teacher may influence learning more than will the atmosphere of an open classroom.

MODELS FOR INSTRUCTION IN PHYSICAL EDUCATION

When students learn what their teacher (or they and their teacher together) has intended them to learn, we can say that *instruction* has taken place. This allows for the following situations. (Duke 1978)

Incidental teaching: what the teacher actually teaches that he or she did not intend to teach.
Teaching omissions: what the teacher failed to teach that he or she intended to teach.
Incidental learning: what students learned that the teacher did not teach.
Learning omissions: what students did not learn even though the teacher taught it.

Thus, we cannot say that all learning is attributable to instruction. Nor can instruction be said to have occurred when no learning is achieved. This emphasizes the importance of instruction, and also implies that the ultimate judgment on the utility of an instructional style rests with its effects on student achievement.

Mosston's Spectrum of Styles

No model for instruction in physical education has had the impact of that developed by Musska Mosston (1966). Mosston's model is based on the assumption that decisions about the processes and products of educational experiences should move from being teacher-centered to student-centered, from student dependence upon the teacher to student independence. In order to build this spectrum of styles, Mosston analyzed teaching styles by analyzing who made decisions.

He focused on three sets of decisions: those made *before* the learning experience (preclass decisions), those made *during* the learning experience (execution decisions), and those made *about* learning while it was going on (evaluation decisions). The spectrum of styles is graphically portrayed in Figure 9.1.

Command style. In command teaching the teacher makes all preclass, execution, and evaluation decisions. This is the most prevalent form of teaching in physical education. Basically, the teacher decides what is to be learned and gives instructions to the students; the students respond to the instructions. The teacher offers evaluative comments. The pace of the class is totally teacher-directed.

Command teaching has gotten a bad name because it appears at one end (the minimum developmental end) of Mosston's spectrum of styles. However, there can be good and bad command teaching. Our previous discussion of direct instruction places it clearly within the command style.

Task teaching. In task teaching some of the decision making is shifted to students. Teachers still decide what tasks will be learned and usually in what order and to what degree of skill. Within that framework, however, students begin to make execution decisions. The main feature of task teaching is that students tend to go at their own pace. They also begin to participate in evaluating decisions, since criteria for achievement of tasks are usually part of the task description.

This often allows students to match their performances against the stated criteria. Teaching by "stations" and many forms of contingency management teaching (Rushall and Siedentop, 1972) are clearly within the task style.

Reciprocal teaching. Task teaching differs from command primarily in that *execution* decisions are more in the hands of the students. In reciprocal teaching the students are more involved in evaluation decisions as well as in execution decisions.

A teacher cannot watch every response of each child and provide relevant information feedback. This fact points up a serious drawback to traditional forms of teaching. In the reciprocal teaching style students are paired and one responds while the other evaluates. Naturally, time has to be spent teaching children how to evaluate—what to look for and what to communicate to one's partner. Doers and observers change roles frequently.

Small-group teaching. A variation of the reciprocal style is that of small-group teaching. The basic features are identical except that much more social interaction occurs because of the presence of a larger group. Here there are doers, observers, and recorders. The addition of the recorder formalizes the evaluation process and produces learning data that the teacher can use to chart student progress.

Individual programs. The shift in decision making in this style is not only away from the teacher but also away from any in-

FIGURE 9.1 Mosston's spectrum of teaching styles. (Musska Mosston, *Teaching Physical Education.* Columbus: Merrill, 1966.)

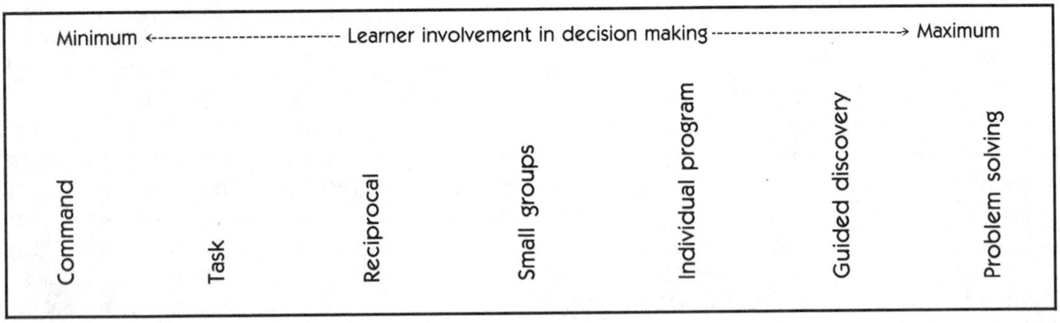

Minimum ◄-------------------------- Learner involvement in decision making -------------------------► Maximum

Command   Task   Reciprocal   Small groups   Individual program   Guided discovery   Problem solving

terdependence among peers. In both execution and evaluation decisions the student performs independently.

Mosston identifies five operational designs within this style. Using tasks, children can self-evaluate their performances and check off each task completed. A second design allows children to make quantitative decisions about themselves by finding their maximum performance relative to the stated task. A third design allows children to decide how well they did by making qualitative decisions about performance relative to task criteria (not how much or how far, but how well they did something). A fourth variation is to combine quantitative and qualitative decisions into multiple levels of performance differentiation. Students may begin to address their own abilities in a fairly complex manner. The final variation is programmed instruction. While the first four variations focus on self-evaluation variables, programmed instruction also includes some instructional design elements that require careful specificity of tasks, small progressions between tasks to ensure success, and reinforcement of each step in the sequence.

Guided discovery.

The final two styles on Mosston's spectrum are different from the others; Mosston believes that they involve the learner in a totally different learning relationship. This new relationship emphasizes higher-level cognitive activity in which learners *discover* answers, *solve* problems, and gain *insight* into skill acquisition.

Guided discovery teaching is very difficult. It has strong similarities to programmed instruction. The teacher must arrange a set of questions, cues, and/or prompts to gradually lead the learner to the learning outcome. Like all programming, guided discovery teaching requires many trials in which teachers learn to anticipate student responses and adjust the learning distance between questions/cues. During execution, several rules pertain. First, the teacher never *tells* an answer, always waits for the student response, and always finds a way to reinforce gradual approximations to success.

Evaluation in guided discovery consists of the child's own personal evaluation and the reinforcement by the teacher of each step in the sequence. As you can see, guided discovery requires careful planning. Beginning teachers prepare what amounts to a script for each lesson. With experience step sizes are adjusted, divergent responses are anticipated, and more relevant questions/clues are utilized.

Problem solving.

The final style on the spectrum requires the highest cognitive engagement between the learner and the subject matter. In guided discovery students respond to a careful sequence of question/cues and their responses are mostly anticipated. If they deviate too far from the goal of the sequence, the teacher can provide a remedial prompt to bring their responses back toward the established sequence. In problem solving, divergent responses are not only condoned, but teaching is arranged so as to maximize the different ways students might choose to solve a movement problem. The child explores alternatives and through that exploration finds an acceptable solution.

Preclass decisions again require carefully arranging problems that are most likely to elicit divergent student responses. Problems can be presented verbally, in which case instruction is primarily group-paced. Or, problems can be presented on task cards or a sequence of problems can be presented as a task list. Students can then move along at their own pace.

Clearly, execution decisions are primarily in the hands of the students. Evaluation in this style is very different and complex. Students must evaluate their own efforts and weigh the various solution strategies they have tried. The teacher's role is primarily to be supportive of diversity, to value different solutions rather than to judge the rightness or wrongness of any given solution. Teacher evaluations that are made are usually to help students "get on the right track."

A comment on the Mosston model.

It is clear that the Mosston model values higher-level cognitive activity in physical education. There is a strong implication that creativity and a sense of self-worth derive from the guided discovery and problem-solving styles. While this may be true, it is largely a matter of belief or of logical argument. If skill development was the primary value, the styles might be placed in a different order on the spectrum.

One should also recognize that there are striking similarities between command teaching and teacher-controlled forms of guided discovery and problem solving. The teacher is at the center of the learning process, controlling the pace of the lesson. The model of direct instruction described earlier could apply to command, guided discovery, or problem-solving styles.

If the spectrum of styles seems too complex, it might be helpful to compress it somewhat so that it involves the following three general styles:

1. Direct instruction styles
2. Task styles
3. Inquiry styles (guided discovery and problem solving)

It might also be helpful at this point to examine these instructional styles in light of the major factors which influence learning (see pages 10–12). Do students get a clear idea of what it is they are supposed to learn (a clear direction from a teacher, a clearly written task, a carefully sequenced progression of problems)? Do they get to respond often (at their own pace, multiple trials, no waiting)? Do they get clear, informative feedback (criteria defined both qualitatively and quantitatively, teacher-augmented feedback, plentiful peer feedback)? It is the presence or absence of these factors that affect learning.

The Environment as Teacher

Teachers are here to stay. Their roles may change, but no trends or evidence indicate that they are becoming outmoded. We have frequently alluded to the fact that one teacher cannot monitor all student learning at the same time or provide relevant, informative feedback to all children when they require it. Task teaching, the open gymnasium, and many other variations on individualized instruction are similar in that they imbed *in the environment* some of the teaching functions. Task cards present clear descriptions of what is to be done. A child doesn't have to wait to get the teacher's attention to find out what is to be done next. Setting specific performance criteria helps children to self-evaluate properly. Arranging tasks that have high levels of intrinsic feedback (see page 11) also helps to place in the environment one of the main learning factors.

Much can be gained by reading the chapter on equipment design and generalizing its main principles to all of teaching. Equipment can be built so that it elicits specific kinds of student behavior. Feedback devices can be built into the equipment. Within this general setting children can have many opportunities to respond with the right kinds of motor responses and get good, informative feedback immediately. Motivation can even be built in by designing some natural reinforcement into the equipment: for example, a light may go on when a target is hit or a bell can be rung when a child climbs to the top of an apparatus. The basic concept here is that of *environmental design*. While it is a reasonably new concept in education, we suspect that within it one can get a clear glimpse of future teaching.

CURRENT INNOVATIONS IN ORGANIZING FOR INSTRUCTION

There are many delightful ways to organize good instruction for physical education in the elementary school. As we have suggested, each of these approaches no doubt reflects some of the essential characteristics of effective teaching. While the approaches may *look* different to the casual observer, the more experienced educator will see that in each approach children have clear direction as to learning goals, frequent opportunity to respond, plentiful feedback and encouragement, and an atmosphere conducive to learning and to personal growth. What follows are brief descriptions of some of the current approaches being utilized by physical education specialists and classroom teachers.

Contracting

A learning contract can be arranged on an individual basis with one student in a class who may need this kind of specificity, or it can be used as a basic teaching strategy with all students. A learning contract is quite simply an agreement made between the teacher and the student. Contracts usually include (a) a specific description of what is to be accomplished, (b) the time frame within which the contract is to be fulfilled, (c) the criteria by which completion will be judged, and (d) a specific description of what will accrue to the learner as a result of completing the contract. An example of a contract is shown on page 149.

Contracts can be used with almost any style of teaching. They need to be very simple with young children but can grow quite complex as children mature and have greater experience with the contracting process. Contracts are especially useful for out-of-class work. For example, certain children may need extra fitness work or specific kinds of skill practice that simply can't be accommodated within regular class time. Contracting for out-of-class practice is one of the best ways to achieve these kinds of goals.

As children gain experience in contracting, they can begin to build their own contracts. The contracts can become more sophisticated, even to the point of building independent study units. The maturity and independence learned through such educational experiences is invaluable. However, like all skills, the ability to contract is acquired slowly through careful progressions. Thus, in the beginning contracting should be simple with short-term outcomes. Also, students should be rewarded immediately when they complete their early contracts. Later, as they grow more experienced in contracting, the rewards for contracting can be deferred for considerable amounts of time. Many teachers have had great success with point systems where children earn points for completing contracts. Points are than accumulated and lead to certain kinds of recognition or reward.

Programmed Learning Units

One of the advantages that typical classroom teachers have over their counterparts in physical education is the availability of many attractive learning programs. However, units of learning can be prepared in physical education that will enable students to learn the activity at their own pace. Given sufficient physical space and self-control on the part of the learners, it is even possible to allow children to choose different learning packages, which they can pursue independently or in small groups.

A programmed learning unit is a set of instructional materials of sufficient specificity that a learner can achieve the goals of the unit with only minimal intervention and supervision from the teacher. While developing programmed or packaged learning units requires much teacher effort, once they are developed, they can be used again and again. A programmed learning package contains (a) clear objectives arranged in a careful sequence, (b) a sufficient amount of information for the learner to know what to do, when to do it, and how to do it, (c) clear criteria for completion of each of the steps in the learning sequence, (d) identification of resources necessary for doing the tasks, and (e) methods of evaluation, both during and at the end of the program.

Learning programs for younger children (or any beginning efforts at using learning programs) should be short and simple. Children need help to acquire the independent study skills necessary to utilize learning programs. However, once these are acquired, students can begin to participate in the formation of their own learning programs.

Use of learning programs requires the development of learning resources in the form of illustrative charts, loop films, instructional pamphlets, instructional books, pictures, and teacher-made materials. Such programs are greatly facilitated by the development of a learning resource center where all the resources are available. This should be a place where children can easily find the resources they need, utilize them, and return quickly to their activity area. Such an area could be developed in one part of a gymnasium or in an adjacent office or storage room. Or, the resource center of the school might be used, especially in an open school plan where children are accustomed to moving about freely and have developed the skills necessary to pursue independent learning.

The Open Gymnasium

The open gymnasium is an instructional strategy that has developed over the past several decades with the advent of *open* or *informal* models for elementary education. This strategy stresses independent learning skills, learning at one's own pace, personal responsibility, choice among learning materials and goals, and individualization of curriculum and process in learning. These goals, and the open settings designed to achieve them, have developed as part of what has been described as the *humanistic* education movement.

The major instructional feature of an open education setting is the *interest area*. Several interest areas are arranged within one setting, and children are free to move around the setting as their needs and interests dictate. The open gymnasium, therefore, has several activity stations available, and children are free to choose which of them they want to pursue. Open education settings are very compatible with task card and programmed learning approaches, discussed elsewhere in this section.

If the open gymnasium concept is used as a major instructional strategy, the teacher must spend a great deal of time helping children to learn how to operate independently in such a setting. This is especially true for the self-control skills (Siedentop, 1977) necessary to ensure that children remain on-task despite frequent interruptions and high activity level. Many physical educators have utilized the open gymnasium concept as an adjunct to their regular instructional program. It has been used in the early morning, at noon, after school, or during regularly designated periods throughout the week. Children might come for extra help or for especially interesting activities, or they might earn the right to extra physical education through combinations of achievement, improvement, or appropriate behavior in the classroom or the regular physical education program. When used as an adjunct, teachers need to determine what activities will be available and then publicize them throughout the school. This requires the cooperation and approval of classroom teachers and the school principal.

When utilizing an open gymnasium approach, the teacher must establish a clear set of "gymnasium rules" (see chapter on managing groups of children) and must already have worked carefully with the children to help them learn how to operate within those constraints. The physical space (gymnasium, multipurpose room, or outdoor space) needs to be clearly marked off into various interest areas. Instructions for the use of interest areas need to be specified clearly and placed in an easily accessible place within each interest area.

An open gymnasium might have several activities available within a particular unit, such as gymnastics. In this case the space would be divided among mats and several pieces of apparatus. Each area would have specific instructions or suggestions. Clearly, the features of task cards and programmed materials lend themselves to this strategy. Another use of the open gymnasium concept would be to have several different kinds of activities available. One corner of the gym might have tumbling mats, while one wall might be reserved for wall ball or a similar striking game. A jump rope interest center might occupy still another corner. Still another space might be available for tasks related to shooting baskets. The only limitations to devising open settings are the physical space constraints, the managerial skills of the teacher, the availability of equipment, and the imagination of the teacher. Usually spaces can be found, management skills can be learned, and inexpensive equipment can be made. What remains, then, is the need for imagination and desire on the part of the teacher.

Stations

Stations have been used in sport coaching and secondary teaching for many years and form the basis for most weight training programs (where it is known as *circuit* training). Stations can also be very effective in the elementary school. A station approach to organizing instruction requires that the teaching space be divided into separate instructional stations. Students practice different skills at the different stations. Certain stations may require individual skill practice. Others may be designed for small-group efforts. Still other stations might involve larger groups of children.

The use of stations also requires some form of task, contract, or programmed learning strategy. At each station there must be information about what to do, how to do it, and how to assess it. Students rotate among stations for their complete lesson.

At the outset students should be assigned to an initial station and then rotate in some preconceived pattern, usually according to the time/sound signal. As students learn to work more independently and to remain on-task without direct teacher intervention, they may have some choice as to both the station at which they begin and the station to which they move. Movement among stations might also depend on students meeting some criterion at one station before moving on to another station. In this latter, more flexible approach students will constantly move among stations, with the signal for movement coming from their own performance rather than from an external source.

If the stations represent progressive steps in a learning sequence, then the order in which they are attempted is fixed. In this case there probably needs to be a limit to the number of children that can work at any given station. This ensures maximum participation, minimizes waiting time, and prevents discipline problems that might result from overcrowding and waiting at any given station.

Station teaching lends itself well to activities such as fitness development, strength development, ropes, stunts, and tumbling.

However, with some imagination and preparation, stations can also be used effectively to teach the skills and strategies of team sports. For example, in a volleyball unit stations might be arranged for several different levels of passing skill, bumping, setting, serving, and spiking. Other stations might combine several of these skills, such as bumping and setting, into small-group tasks. At each station the task can be made into a game to enhance motivation.

Task Cards and Task Teaching

Task cards and task teaching refer to different strategies but will be considered together here simply because they are so often confused with one another. A task card is simply a written, visual description of a skill or strategy to be learned with a clear statement of a criterion children can use to assess the degree to which they have completed the task. Task cards can also include information about how to do the skill. They can be used with learning packages, contracts, open gyms, and station teaching. Their major advantage is that they allow for individual pacing, and they present information to the learner precisely at the time the learner needs it. Task cards can be small, handled individually by students, or they can be large, posted at appropriate places in the learning setting. Task cards should be attractive, very clear and explicit in their language, written or drawn at a level commensurate with the skills of the children, and complete in the sense that the children will seldom require any further explanation from the teacher.

Task teaching is one of the teaching styles identified by Mosston and described earlier in this chapter (see page 116). Such teaching can be of several varieties. In the single task multiple station children work at stations but each work on the same task. In the multiple task multiple station children work on different tasks at different stations. In the former it is clear that the teacher can still be the source of information for the task. In the latter that instructional function must be shifted to task cards, learning programs, or some other form of environmental design.

Teaching Aides

A major innovation in organizing instruction in physical education for children is the increasing use of extra personnel who can help the physical educator or classroom teacher with instructional duties. Aides can be recruited from a number of different sources. First, parents of children often are happy to come to the school occasionally to help out in physical education. Such adult help is especially useful in after-school programs, noon programs, and special gym times when there are likely to be a larger number of children needing attention than in the regular program. Aides can serve as assistants to the teacher, helping with equipment, helping to organize children, and even helping in certain aspects of instruction.

Many elementary physical educators have formed "gym helpers" clubs. Gym helpers are usually those students whose skill, motivation, and good behavior make them ideally suited to provide help to the teacher. Gym helpers usually have assigned duties, often related to equipment storage, preparation of the gym for a particular lesson, changing equipment for different lessons, helping to keep records, helping to keep score, officiating during competitions, and other related duties.

Peer teaching is another option that many physical educators have begun to explore. Peer teaching involves the utilization of children to teach their classmates. Often, but not always, the "peer teacher" is one who presents a particularly good model for a skill or game strategy. Peer teaching taken to its ultimate form is what we have described previously (see page 116) as reciprocal teaching, a strategy in which peers take turns helping one another by giving feedback and direction to learning progressions. For peers to act as teachers, they should be prepared as fully as possible. This means that the teacher will need to work with children so that they understand the skills necessary to be a peer teacher; they must particularly understand appropriate and inappropriate forms of teaching interaction. Also, if peers are expected to provide feedback for their class-mates, they need to be instructed as to what to look for in their classmates' performance. This kind of instruction needs to be quite specific. It doesn't suffice to tell a fourth grader to help a peer by "watching her form." It is much easier to instruct peer helpers to watch to see if their partners keep their legs straight, if they stop without losing balance, or if they twist their trunk in the preparatory movements of a throw. They must then be *shown* the more appropriate and less appropriate versions of what they may see.

Cross-age tutoring refers to a movement within elementary schools in which older children provide some instructional help for younger children. Research has shown that cross-age tutoring can be a very effective instructional resource. Here too the older children who act as instructional aides need to be given some information as to what their role will be, how they should act, and what kinds of things to avoid. When children are used as instructional aides, the teacher's main role is to provide feedback for the peer or cross-age teachers so that they can improve their techniques. Having developed a group of student instructional aides, the teacher's ability to provide instruction is greatly enhanced. Children can then be divided into smaller groups, each with its own "teacher." The resulting experience, if properly planned, can be of benefit both to the students receiving the instruction and to the students providing the instruction.

IMPROVING OUTCOMES

Enhancing Cognitive Outcomes

There are many ways in which the elementary-school physical educator or classroom teacher can help children to learn more about physical education, sport, dance, and exercise. Naturally, children will learn about games and skills as they participate in the physical education class. However, these learnings can be enhanced and extended.

Attractive, educational bulletin boards are useful aids in helping children learn more about physical education topics. Bulletin boards are often placed either in the physical education space or near it in a hallway. Often the physical educator has access to a bulletin board near a central lobby of the school and can, from time to time, use this strategically placed space for furthering cognitive objectives. It should be noted that not only are good bulletin boards educational, but such devices can also serve to raise the general motivational level of the children. Bulletin boards should be (a) topical in the sense that each board has a theme, (b) attractive, (c) done at a level the children can readily understand, and (d) oriented toward learning about an activity, a person, a place, or some other related topic. For example, physical educators have done bulletin boards on the following topics: the Olympics, women sport heroes, cardiovascular fitness, games of different countries, sport costumes from different lands, youth sport safety guidelines, cycling, wilderness activities, and nicknames of local teams.

Most elementary schools have libraries or learning resource centers. Physical educators should see that books, filmstrips, and other kinds of learning media on physical education and related topics are available in this facility. The physical educator should then encourage children to use the available resources. This can be done by developing book lists, planning independent studies around physical education topics, arranging for small groups of children to view audiovisual materials, and providing some recognition in class for those who take advantage of the school's resources. As a physical educator's own professional resources increase, the educator can develop a mini-center for physical education resources either in the physical education space or as a specially designated part of the learning center. Many corporations and agencies provide free educational materials relative to physical education, sport, dance, and exercise. These can be ordered and placed in such a mini-center.

Some physical educators prepare a regular newsletter which is given to children to take home to their parents. It is typically designed to be shared among children and their parents. Such an effort has three major purposes. First, it can be used as an educational tool to help children and their parents learn more about physical education. Second, it can be used as an important public relations vehicle to improve communication between teachers and parents and, subsequently, to gain parental support for the physical education program. Third, it is an important way to provide recognition for achievement in physical education. For example, all the children who completed a particular set of rope climbing tasks might be listed in the newsletter as members of the "Top-of-the-Rope Club." This kind of newsletter can be typed by a school secretary and duplicated on school duplicating machines, either mimeographed or stenciled. Since no mailing costs are involved, the expense is minimal compared to the potential benefits of such an undertaking.

Another useful strategy is to have special "days" or special "weeks" throughout the school year. For example, there is a week each year specified nationally as "sports week." There could also be a special "fitness day," a "dance day," or an "international sport week." The physical educator should secure the support of the school principal for special events during these times. Special announcements could be made over the school public address system. A daily "sports quiz" is both fun and educational for the children. Special activities in the regular class program could also be arranged. The overall effect of such "special" programming is to underscore the importance of the subject matter, to increase motivation for participation, and to improve the children's understanding of the many facets of physical education.

Enhancing Affective Outcomes

Most elementary-school physical educators and classroom teachers are very concerned about outcomes in the affective domain—the attitudes and values children derive from their participation in physical education. There are two primary outcomes in the affective domain that we would like to emphasize. The first is the development of a positive attitude toward participation in physical education in all its forms. The second is the development of a healthy, positive self-concept, particularly as it relates to participation in physical education.

The best way to create positive attitudes toward participation is to ensure that children learn a lot in physical education, that what they learn is appropriate to their developmental needs, that the learning is success-based, and that the atmosphere within which the learning occurs is positive and supportive. These factors have been addressed consistently throughout this text (readers are encouraged particularly to review Chapter 2 Learning Motor Skills and Chapter 10 Developing a Climate for Personal Growth).

Likewise, the development of a sound self-concept, particularly in relation to physical education, is a natural outcome of a program planned and conducted in a manner similar to that described above. However, there are special techniques teachers can use both to improve attitudes and to enhance self-concept development. There is no doubt that self-concept is enhanced each time a child accomplishes something important and that accomplishment is recognized in an appropriate way. The strategy, therefore, has two facets. First, it is important that children learn important skills. This is partially a function of planning and curriculum building, but it is also a function of emphasizing to children the meaning and importance of the activities. Once the importance of an activity has been established in the eyes of children, accomplishment in that activity will be more highly valued. It is important that teachers find ways to emphasize the importance of *all* activities. Children must come to understand that achievement is important in a wide range of activities, not only in those that happen to be most important in the local culture. If children view an activity as important, success in that activity will improve self-concept; the children will see themselves as having accomplished something of value. This sense of accomplishment will be enhanced when *others* also recognize the accomplishment.

This does not mean that trumpets need to be blown and a school assembly called for each objective reached in physical education. It does mean, however, that teachers must find a number of small, yet significant ways to recognize achievement in physical education.

Some techniques that teachers have used successfully include the following: (a) "I can" charts, which are large poster boards on walls of the gym—children can sign their names when they have completed an important task as part of a unit; (b) "Me charts" (Schurr, 1980), which are personal records of what children have accomplished and what they hope to accomplish; (c) physical education newsletters as mentioned in the previous section; (d) school achievement records—children can compare their performances with those of children from previous years; (e) publicly posted records where task completion can be noted with checks or stars; (f) listing of names in special clubs for children who have done important work outside of class, such as a "50-mile club" for children who run regularly outside of class; or (g) home reports—a periodic record of accomplishment (not a grade card) is sent home to be shared with parents.

If a physical educator or classroom teacher thinks it important for children to reflect on their physical education experiences, they can encourage the keeping of a physical education diary, a movement journal (Schurr, 1980), or a personal record of goals and accomplishments. These self-reports can be shared with teachers and parents if the children so desire. The physical educator should encourage the children to include thoughts about how they *feel* about their experiences and how their performances and accomplishments relate to those feelings. The purpose of such reports, of course, is to foster in children understanding of their relationship to the subject matter of physical education and to other persons as they participate in physical education.

10

developing
a climate
for personal growth

Recently American educators have felt the pressures of two movements which reflect different views of what schools should be like. The pressure for achievement (not new in American education) is now being felt more than ever because of publicity concerning lower achievement levels on standardized tests. Also, there is a growing concern for the manner in which schooling affects the social-emotional aspects of student growth.

The achievement-oriented student is highly motivated by grades and by the idea of "getting ahead"; often such a student is not very concerned about what must be done to others in order to achieve personal goals. Jerome Bruner (1960) described the system fostering such students as a meritocracy and wondered what happened to the many students who were weeded out in the competitive system of testing and grading.

As a reaction to the above, different kinds of schools have been explored in the past several decades. In these schools achievement has been downplayed totally in favor of techniques and approaches that promote a well-integrated, well-adjusted student. At its extreme this movement tends to produce what Skidelsky (1969) has so aptly labeled

"well-adjusted mediocrity," a student who is emotionally stable but hasn't learned much.

There are ways in which the goals of achievement and personal growth can be pursued together, and these ways do not necessarily represent some compromise position between the two extremes. Indeed, it can be argued convincingly that *real* achievement cannot be won without high levels of personal integration. It can also be argued that to be well integrated, one has to achieve a level of knowledge and skill that is commensurate with personal goals and ambitions.

PERSONAL GROWTH AND STUDENT-TEACHER INTERACTIONS

Factors in Personal Growth

A well-integrated person has a positive self-concept, views oneself realistically, has useful and positive interaction skills, and is secure enough to be unafraid of venturing into new areas, whether they be in interpersonal relations or in learning. That a person can truly achieve this state of personal growth without "learning" in the school sense is unlikely in our culture. Thus, the view promoted here is that personal growth and school achievement are very much related and that each can contribute to growth in the other area. Indeed, they are probably so intertwined during childhood that it is somewhat artificial to discuss them separately.

Developing a climate for personal growth involves decisions in curriculum, teaching strategies, and student-teacher interactions. Personal growth is not achieved in a six-week unit—it is something that happens over a longer period of time. Many factors must coalesce to create an environment that touches each student in a meaningful way. Certainly, a crucial factor is success. Each child must learn in a way that optimizes success. This has implications for curriculum and teaching. Children must learn valuable skills— skills that count in the real world. Competition should be used where appropriate but always kept in check, and the consequences of competition should be temporary, ordinarily confined to the activity itself. Children must be encouraged to be expressive not only in their movement and about their movement skills but also about their feelings toward activities and persons. Most of these factors are discussed in detail elsewhere in the text. The focus of this chapter is on the personal interaction between student and teacher. We are convinced that who the teacher is, that is, how the teacher behaves, is the most important ingredient in developing a climate for personal growth.

Student-Teacher Interactions

When asked to describe themselves, most teachers will say that they are caring, supportive teachers who are concerned with the personal growth of students. While these intentions are clear at an attitudinal level, we have been unable to verify their existence at the behavioral level. A supportive, caring teacher would, at the behavioral level, show strong tendencies toward positive interactions with students. Recent research describing the interaction styles of elementary-school physical educators (Quarterman, 1978; Stewart, 1977) shows clearly that many

FIGURE 10.1 Effective teachers express high expectations for learning and having fun.

physical educators engage in corrective and punitive interactions to a far greater degree than they engage in positive interactions. In one study (Quarterman, 1978) interactions were distributed as follows:

INTERACTIONS BASED ON STUDENT SKILL ATTEMPTS:

Positive: 6.9 per 30 minutes or 15%
Corrective: 20.1 per 30 minutes or 80%
Negative: 1.8 per 30 minutes or 5%

INTERACTIONS BASED ON STUDENT SOCIAL BEHAVIOR:

Positive: 0.9 per 30 minutes or 6%
Nags*: 17.2 per 30 minutes or 83%
Nasties*: 1.0 per 30 minutes or 6%

During the past ten years much evidence has been gathered to show that undergraduates can learn to be positive interactors (Siedentop, 1982). They do this by learning a series of skills. As with all skills, their first attempts might seem fairly clumsy and simplistic, but progress comes quickly and the level of interaction skill achieved by the student teacher is remarkable.

*The difference between the "nags" category and the "nasties" category is primarily a difference in degree. Comments such as "Be quiet," "Get that line straight," "Quit fooling around," and "Let's pay attention" would each be counted as nags. When a teacher really gets angry at students and speaks loudly and angrily to them, the comments are counted as "nasties."

Building Positive Interaction Skills

Any teacher or teacher-in-training can learn to be a positive interactor. All data that we have suggest that very few physical educators have developed these skills on their own. They may believe that they are primarily positive, but their behavior does not reflect that belief. Data from a number of studies (Quarterman, 1978; Stewart, 1977; Cheffers and Mancini, 1978) show the following results.

1. When physical education teachers react to student behavior other than skill attempts (social and managerial behavior) they do so almost exclusively in a negative or corrective way.
2. Teacher reinforcement of appropriate student social and managerial behavior occurs infrequently.
3. Teacher reactions to skill or game behavior of students is primarily corrective; teachers look for errors and correct them.
4. Teachers seldom reinforce appropriate skill and game behavior.
5. Rate of skill and game behavior feedback by teacher is typically low (not often more than one per minute).
6. Teachers use nonverbal communication infrequently.
7. Teacher interaction related to the affective domain is almost nonexistent.

It is our experience that the young men and women preparing to become physical educators are very caring about children. However, they simply don't have the skills to translate that caring into teaching behavior. Below we will suggest a series of skill development steps that will foster positive teaching styles.

Shift from negative/corrective to positive statements. The best first step is to practice saying positive things. In our experience as teacher educators we have used peer teaching, microteaching, or simply teaching to a video camera. Students need to overcome the discomfort most of them feel initially when beginning to say positive things. When working with children, teachers should look for things the children do right, following the adage "Catch them when they are good." We often set criterion goals for a teaching session (Siedentop, 1982). For example, a typical goal for a student teacher might be 1.5 positive reactions per minute to social/managerial behavior and 2.0 positive reactions per minute to skill behavior. We have found that most students achieve such goals easily.

Expand the variety of positive statements. Invariably, students first learning to be positive interactors have a limited repertoire of things to say: For example, they often react by saying "Good job," "Way to go," or simply "Good." These students need to find new ways to react to children. We have had success having interns add at least two new interaction statements at each successive teaching episode, be it in a microsetting or in a field setting.

Be more specific. The limited repertoire of beginning students normally has a high percentage of general reaction statements rather than specific reaction statements. The difference is important. It is well established that specific feedback is likely to account for more behavior change. Telling a child "Good pass" is fine, but it is not as useful as telling the child why it was a good pass or what about it was good. "Good pass, Jocelyn, you got it to him at just the right moment" not only serves to reinforce the child but tells specifically what was done well. After a teacher or teaching intern has improved the rate and variety of positive interactions, we set some criterion goals for specific and general reactions, usually starting with a 50 percent goal and gradually moving toward the point where 70 percent of the interactions are specific rather than general.

Increase nonverbal interactions. For professionals whose major concern is movement behavior, which is largely nonverbal, physical educators show little inclination to interact nonverbally (Cheffers and Mancini, 1978). Educators and psychologists have for some time promoted the notion that nonverbal communication is important, especially for personal growth in the affective domain (Galloway, 1971). Simply put, physical educators have not shown much inclination to touch children as a way of communicating approval. When we reach this stage of interaction skill development with interns, we encourage them to use nonverbal positive signals (thumbs up, a circle with the thumb and first finger, clapping, and so on) and also to touch children as a way of communicating approval for social/managerial behavior or skill behavior. Again, we usually set some criterion goals in terms of rate per minute and help the interns achieve a variety of ways of communicating nonverbally.

Adding value content to interactions. Children not only need specific information about what they are doing but also information about *why* it should be done that way. An interaction with value content describes why the behavior should or should not be done in a particular way: "Brenda, if you keep your arm straight, the ball will go up instead of out." "Betsy, you jumped so high that time because your knees were bent before you jumped." "Boys and girls, because you paid attention so well and got the equipment away quickly, we have time left for a game." Interactions with value content help children to develop standards for behavior. While interactions with value content need not occur with great frequency, they can be quite important, especially when directed toward a group of children.

Various methods exist for collecting information about interaction skills (Siedentop, 1982). Typically, a simple behavior category system should be developed to include the relevant interaction skills that will be monitored. Supervisors or peer-interns can count the interactions in each category as they occur. We also have tape recorded teaching lessons (Dessecker, 1976) and coded the interactions later. Once their skills have been fairly well developed, teachers can simply write reminders to themselves on their lesson plans to focus on certain kinds of interactions or to focus on interacting with certain children.

A Word about Punishment

The typical way of interacting with children in order to maintain effective discipline is to punish offenders, either by verbal reprimand or by some more formal method. Chapter 11, Managing Groups of Children, details many alternative ways to maintain effective discipline without resorting to punishment. That chapter also makes some suggestions about how punishment should be used when it is necessary. The primary message of that section is that punishment that is part of a system which is known to the children is clearly most effective.

The primary danger of inflicting punishment out of anger or punishment that is not part of a systematic program known to children is what in psychology is called the "spread of effect." Too often teachers try to remediate minor misbehaviors by verbal reprimands—"Be quiet." "Boys, pay attention!" "Sh-h." "Put that ball away." In our category system we call these behaviors "nags" (see page 126). Often nags don't work, and if they do work, the misbehavior stops only momentarily. Frequently there is a buildup of tension to the point where the teacher yells angrily at a child or a group of children (in our category system this is a "nasty"). After such a scene, the children tend to feel that the teacher doesn't like them or that they are not worthy. A punishment should always be specific to the behavior that needs to be stopped. When the punishment gets out of hand, it tends to "spread its effect," so that the worth of the child is called into question. Certainly, there have to be limits, rules, and punishment, but they must be used skillfully and systematically. No child needs to be yelled at angrily by an adult who has lost self-control. The goal should be to turn off the inappropriate behavior, not to turn off the child.

Believability, Sincerity, and Positive Teaching

High rates of positive interactions will do little to promote personal growth unless they are believed, that is, unless children perceive them to be sincere. There are various skills which can help build a believable style.

The most important ingredient in believability is consistency in interactions. You can't reward a child for speaking out of turn on one day (the smile, the chuckle, the "O.K. now, Tommy"), punish him the next day ("Tommy, be quiet"), and still expect that child to "believe" in you. If students' behavior isn't treated consistently, the children become confused.

A second factor in believability is that interactions should be directed toward significant aspects of student behavior. Children don't need to be reinforced for trivial behavior. They *know* when they have accomplished something and they also *know* when they are being praised for something insignificant. Obviously, what is significant behavior for one child may not be for another. The child who has had trouble learning to play with others can be praised highly for small amounts of successful interactive play behavior. The same praise for the same behavior in a more socially skilled child would seem insincere.

A third factor in believability is that the positive interaction should be commensurate with the task or behavior to which it is directed. A reaction such as "Incredibly good" to some behavior that was only marginally significant and maybe deserved a "Nice" soon wears out as you try to outdo your own superlatives. Further, when the child really does accomplish something important, the resulting "superlative" interaction will seem too common.

A fourth factor in believability is the degree to which your positive interactions are distributed across the range of children with whom you work. Teachers tend to interact with very highly skilled children more often than with other children. They also may interact frequently with some of the very low-skilled children because the latter are perceived to need "extra attention." The great majority of the children in the middle get ignored. Paying attention to all your children is more a matter of skill than of good intentions. Again, little reminders noted on lesson plans or clipboards help ensure that teachers pay attention in some systematic way to all the children. We have found that increasing the frequency of positive interac-

tions tends to distribute them more evenly— but that in and of itself is seldom enough. Some direct attention needs to be paid to the problem. All children with whom you work should have a chance to see their good behavior and successful physical education work be the object of your positive attention. After all, you are a very important person to each of them and a word from you, or a pat on the back, or a smile can be a big event in their day.

The Personal Touch

By advocating a skills approach to student-teacher interactions, we do not mean to suggest that all aspects of interpersonal relations can be reduced to discrete skills. There is much about warmth, caring, and loving that goes well beyond the interaction skills suggested here. However, the skills we have outlined can make you a better interactor and help you put your good intentions to better use. There are two more aspects of interpersonal interaction skills that warrant consideration because they are directly related to what might be called a "personal touch" in teaching.

One of the ways children learn that you care about them is through interactions based on nonschool factors. Certainly, it is good strategy for teachers to know more about their children than IQ scores and other school achievement data. It is also valuable to know something about their home background. When children learn that you are concerned about them in ways other than "school" ways, they will probably be more willing to enter into the kind of relationship that results in personal growth. It must be remembered that relationships are two-way streets. It is unlikely that you can help a child grow personally unless that child trusts and likes you well enough to be influenced by you. Interactions based on nonschool factors are one strategy to use toward this end.

A second factor contributing to the personal touch in teaching is creating a climate where students feel free to express their feelings. Since expressing feelings about things is not characteristic of our culture, this will not occur automatically and you might have to prompt it by asking often how children feel about things—about their progress in learning a skill, about their movement capabilities, about a game, or about being in the gymnasium. Expressions of feelings on the part of the student must be *accepted* by the teacher. Acceptance implies a lack of judgment; that is, you can't ask children to express their feelings and follow it with a corrective or negative interaction. Empathy means that you can understand how children feel, and if you can communicate through your interactions your empathy for children, you are much more likely to be able to build a climate of trust.

Growth through Enthusiasm

Research has shown that effective teachers are more enthusiastic than their less effective counterparts (Gage, 1972; Rosenshine, 1970). In Chapter 9 we discussed enthusiasm in some detail. We suggested that teachers need to be enthusiastic about what they are teaching (the content), about improvement and progress, and about their students.

It was suggested that components of enthusiasm might be (a) a positive teaching style, (b) participation in activities, so that you model your enjoyment of the content of what you teach, (c) active, energetic classes in which transitions are smooth and do not drag, (d) high but realistic expectations for your students, and (e) appreciation for learning.

In terms of personal growth the expectations you have for your students and your appreciation shown for improvement are probably key factors; you can find ways to express realistic—but high—expectations for their sense of confidence in themselves or for their feelings of worth about their movement skills. Combined with this should be frequent positive interactions directed specifically at personal growth areas such as self-confidence, positive verbalizations of self-concept, and verbalizations of good feelings about physical education.

Student-Student Interactions

While the authors believe that the teacher is the main factor in creating and maintaining a climate for personal growth, it would be shortsighted to ignore the clear implication that students must also treat each other in a positive, supporting way for a beneficial climate to endure. Children can be painfully cruel to one another. They also can be positive, supportive, and caring. The teacher's job is to see that the latter behaviors prevail. This means that teachers must voice expectations for supportive, caring social behaviors among their children, remind children often about what those behaviors are and why they are important, and interact positively with children who behave that way. Caring, supportive environments don't *just happen.* When they do occur, they are almost always the result of some skillful planning and execution on the part of a professional who knows what to do and how to do it.

COMMUNICATION SKILLS

Effective climates for personal growth in schools are multidimensional. Certainly, effective instructional design and competent, positive styles of teaching contribute to the personal growth of students. Behaviorally oriented, positive interactions are also important facets of this multidimensional picture. In several chapters we have attempted to explain clearly the major aspects of instructional and behavioral interaction skills. Nevertheless, while effective *inter*personal communication skills are quite important, such skills are often characteristic of readers who are in touch with themselves, who have effective *intra*personal skills. Thus, one's ability to communicate clearly with oneself is the foundation for eventually developing a climate for personal growth.

Intrapersonal Communication Skills

The elementary-school classroom teacher and physical education specialist live in a world of children. Their adult contacts are infrequent, and their contacts with children extensive, demanding, and continuous. Nobody who has not had the responsibility of teaching groups of children on a daily basis can understand the continuous pressure of that assignment. In order to develop a nurturant climate for personal growth among children, the teachers must first be reasonably well in touch with their own feelings and behaviors: They must know themselves fairly well, and they must accept themselves if they are to be of optimum service to the children with whom they work.

The first step leading toward more effective intrapersonal communication skills is *self-awareness.* Who are you? What do you feel? What do you believe? How do you behave around children? How do you react when you are tired? How do you approach your teaching when you have many other things on your mind? How do you treat children who are of a different race? How do you react to physical handicaps in children? Do you treat "cute" children differently than "homely" children? Why do you want to teach? The answers to these questions and many others like them will gradually build up a reservoir of self-knowledge that is necessary for effective communication skills.

The second step is *self-disclosure.* There are areas of feelings, attitudes, and behaviors that we all tend to keep from ourselves. We must be honest with ourselves and then find out whether others perceive us as we perceive ourselves. The process of self-disclosure means sharing your self-perceptions with others (empathetic listeners) and securing feedback from those persons about how they perceive you. It is impossible to clarify any misconceptions you have about yourself until you go through this process of self-disclosure. If you do it with people who are genuinely interested in your own development as a person and as a teacher, the experience itself will help not only to improve your own intrapersonal skills but also to develop a useful and satisfying relationship.

The third step is *reducing dissonance.* If you perceive yourself to be quite warm and outgoing but your teaching behavior and the reactions of those around you indicate that you do not come across that way in your teaching, then you have some dissonance (a discrepancy between self-perception and actual behavior). This can be reduced in one of two ways. First, you can adjust your self-perception so that it fits your behavior more precisely. Second, you can adjust your behavior so that it fits your perception more closely. It has been our experience that most teachers want to adjust their behavior so that it better fits their beliefs about themselves. This can be a very satisfying experience. The steps outlined earlier in this chapter can help you to achieve that goal.

The final goal in effective intrapersonal communication is *self-acceptance,* which, we believe, comes with the process of reducing dissonance between how you see yourself and how others see you (between what you believe and how you behave). Each of us has an ideal self, an image of who we would like to be, of what kind of teacher we would like to be. Each of us also has a real self, the person who actually behaves as a teacher and whose behavior is interpreted by children and others. As you reduce the dissonance between your self-perceptions and your actual behavior, you will gradually adjust both your ideal self and your real self until they come closer together. Self-acceptance is usually defined as the amount of agreement or congruence between the ideal self and the real self. There is no quick way to achieve self-acceptance. Like most other things, it needs to become a goal and to be worked at consistently and persistently. Our degree of self-acceptance influences our ability to communicate effectively with those around us. Research has consistently confirmed that people with higher levels of self-acceptance are more effective communicators. They are more assertive, take more initiative, are less likely to be defensive, and are more likely to be helpful. Teachers who have higher levels of self-acceptance are much more likely than others to develop and maintain climates for personal growth for the children they serve.

Interpersonal Communication Skills

When communication takes place, it always has three elements: a *sender,* the person who communicates the message; the *receiver*, the person to whom the message is directed and who will respond to it; and the *message* itself, whether conveyed in words, expressions, or (usually) a combination of the two. Teachers need to be effective communicators. When communications are not effective, they lead to misunderstandings and confusion, which often creates problems for both teachers and students.

If teachers are to develop climates for personal growth, they must effectively communicate certain kinds of messages ("I value you," "You are accepted," "It is all right to take risks," "I recognize your achievement," "I want you to succeed"). Effective communication doesn't often happen by chance, nor is the skill innate. Most effective communicators develop their skills through attention and hard work.

Sending skills. It is not always easy to say what you mean. Often we convey one message through our words and another through our actions. Sometimes those verbal and nonverbal messages are very different. The following sending skills are important for effective communication.

1. Speak for yourself. You know what you want to say better than anyone else and you demonstrate clearly the ownership of the communication when you use pronouns such as *I, me, my,* and *mine*. Identifying an idea, feeling, or need by saying "I think," "I feel," or "I need" makes the source of the message quite clear. Often people use words such as *someone thinks* or *it is felt*, substituting a vagueness about ownership of the message. When you speak for yourself, you convey a sense of trust and openness.

2. Describe rather than judge. When you send a message to a child, it is important that you describe clearly the focus of the message but that you do so without being judgmental. Being judgmental tends to stifle communication—without communication personal growth is much less likely to occur.

3. Take the child's viewpoint into account. We tend to see things from our own perspective, which is also an adult perspective. Teachers can see things better from

their children's perspectives by being sensitive to what the children say, how they react to things, and how they behave nonverbally. These factors can then be taken into account when sending messages to them.

4. Be aware of your feelings about yourself and your listener(s). How you feel about yourself has some consistent components and some components that vary according to the many stresses which affect your daily life. The more comfortable you feel about yourself, the more likely you are to communicate effectively. It is also important to be aware of how you feel about the child to whom you are sending the message, be it an individual child or an entire class of children. We have observed, both in ourselves and in other teachers, that an identical message can be delivered quite differently to two different classes. What changes, other than the time of day, is how we feel about each class. If one class is eager, presents no discipline problems, and is fun to be with, our messages tend to be more relaxed, effective, trusting, and positive. A message with identical word content can be delivered to another class, perhaps one that presents discipline problems, with an entirely different mood and a very different set of nonverbal behaviors. Clearly, even though the word content of the message is identical, it is received quite differently.

5. Be aware of your nonverbal cues. Effective communicators tend to have direct eye contact. Their facial expressions are congruent with the theme of their message. They show happiness and positive nonverbal expressions if the message is positive. Body posture obviously sends messages of its own. Rigidity of body tends to stifle communication. Relaxation, leaning toward the listener, and touching tend to denote warmth and involvement in the communication. Too many of us are unaware of what messages our bodies are sending.

Receiving skills. Communication is always a two-way enterprise. Most of us like to give information, to *send* messages. Too few of us really work at becoming good listeners. Certainly, there are few skills more valuable for working effectively with children than good listening skills. It is important to note that the skilled communicator is always *involved* in listening as much as in sending. Several receiver skills are described below.

1. Use paraphrasing. Paraphrasing means restating in your own words what the sender has just said, including what you perceive the sender feels and means. Paraphrasing helps to avoid unfortunate instances of judging and unnecessary evaluating. Paraphrasing is quite valuable to the sender also because it provides immediate feedback about the clarity with which a message was delivered. Paraphrasing also clearly indicates to the sender that you are indeed listening, that you are involved in the communication. Finally, paraphrasing helps you to gain insight into the perspective of the person who sent the message.

2. Use effective attending skills. Attending skills are all those overt behaviors you emit while you are listening, particularly the nonverbal behaviors. Behaviors such as eye contact, posture, and facial expressions all carry messages to the sender. When a child comes to you, effective communication requires that you momentarily attend to the child. Do not expect to listen to a child while looking elsewhere and still have that child perceive you to be someone who cares.

3. Pay attention to the nonverbal cues of the sender. You can tell a lot about a message by observing carefully the nonverbal behavior of the sender. You can tell how much emotion is involved, how important the message is, what it might mean to the sender, and many other things just by observing carefully things such as eye contact, posture, facial expression, and the gestures used to communicate the message.

4. Be aware of your own feelings. When you are nervous, angry, or defensive, you tend not to hear what is said. Misinterpretation becomes more likely when the receiver is involved in a strong emotional feeling or when the receiver is distracted, thinking about other things. You can avoid interpersonal communication problems before they occur simply by being sensitive to your own feelings as a message is conveyed to you by a child.

Roadblocks to Communication

Certain ways of responding tend to produce negative reactions in those with whom you are trying to communicate, thus blocking further efforts at communication (Gordon, 1974). Varying degrees and intensities of these kinds of responses can slow down communication, inhibit one or more of the parties to a communication, or bring the communication to a complete halt. Major kinds of communication roadblocks are described below.

1. Ordering, commanding, or directing. Example: "You stop complaining and get back in line."
2. Warning or threatening. Example: "You had better begin to pay attention or I'll have to have a talk with your classroom teacher."
3. Moralizing or preaching. Examples: "You should know better than that." "You ought to behave better than that."
4. Advising or offering solutions prematurely. Example: "You'll just have to have your mother help you get your gym clothes ready on time."
5. Lecturing or giving logical arguments. Example: "You should know better; not everybody can have their own ball."
6. Judging, criticizing, or blaming. Examples: "You are just lazy." "You are always causing trouble in here."
7. Stereotyping or labeling. Example: "You're acting just like a second grader."
8. Analyzing or diagnosing. Example: "You're just trying to get out of having to do it."
9. Giving positive evaluations prematurely. Example: "I'm sure you will figure out some way to get it done."
10. Sympathizing or consoling. Example: "You're not the only one who ever finished last."
11. Interrogating or cross-examining. Examples: "Why did you wait so long to ask for help?" "What did you do that for?"
12. Distracting or diverting. Examples: "Why don't we talk about something else." "Now just isn't the time to discuss it."

Each of us has used these kinds of responses to children who seek to communicate with us. You might recognize numbers 2, 3, and 11 as occuring with particular frequency in elementary schools. If the goal is effective communication or, in problem situations, to help students reach effective solutions, these roadblocks can inhibit the process, slow it down, or even shut it off completely. Avoiding responses that block the communication process is an important communication skill.

COPING MECHANISMS USED BY CHILDREN

Some fundamental facts about children need to be recognized in order to develop a climate that fosters personal growth. First, children generally respond to adults—they seek the approval of adults, they vie for the attention of adults, and they tend to be strongly rewarded when an adult praises them. Second, in most teaching situations there are many, many more children than there are adults, thus creating much more demand for adult attention than can ever be delivered by a single teacher. Third, when a teacher and child (or group of children) interact, there is an established structure for that interaction and that structure is based on an *imbalance* of power in favor of the adult. This is true for any adult and child. It is even more true for teachers, because even more power is vested in teachers due to their role in the school and the school's role in society. You are unlikely to change these facts and probably will not want to. They are the givens within which teachers and children must learn to communicate effectively.

Because of the imbalance of power and the strong desire among most children to secure the attention of their teacher, children develop coping mechanisms which help them to deal with the situation. It is extremely important to understand that these behaviors are coping mechanisms and are not necessarily symptomatic of character disorder. Gordon (1974) has identified and described the major kinds of coping mechanisms that teachers encounter as they try to help children to grow.

1. Rebelling, resisting, or defying. Can take the form of momentary open defiance or more likely subtle defiance in terms of stalling, doing less than asked, and so on.
2. Retaliating. Particularly likely among students whose teacher tries to dominate through authority.
3. Lying or sneaking. Students feel that it is either unsafe to tell the truth or that the truth is not sufficiently spectacular to merit attention.
4. Blaming others or tattling. Particularly likely when punishment is frequent. This is simply a way of avoiding punishment or trying to gain favor.
5. Cheating. Particularly in games before children have sufficient skills to exert control; they are likely to cheat in order to gain the necessary control.
6. Organizing or forming alliances. Unable to cope with a situation alone, children often gain power by joining together in a common cause.
7. Submitting or complying. Sometimes children learn quickly that the best way to get some attention and to avoid a lot of punishment is to submit or comply quickly with any teacher request.
8. Apple polishing. Young children are often overt and clumsy in gaining the attention of a teacher by responding to the teacher favorably. As children get older, they become more skilled at this important mechanism.
9. Withdrawing or regressing. Often, when children have found other coping mechanisms to be inadequate, they simply start to withdraw or regress, sometimes only momentarily (pouting), but more continuously in serious cases.

We should say again that these are coping mechanisms that children learn in order to "make it" in school. From another point of view, they are the behaviors that school teaches the children. They do not necessarily reflect the character of the child, and when they are recognized for what they are, they can be dealt with effectively. The teacher should create a climate where such mechanisms are less necessary. This does not suggest that behavior such as lying, defying, or blaming should be excused or tolerated. Quite the contrary, it needs to be dealt with openly, quickly, and forthrightly. However, it also must be understood rather than merely condemned, dealt with constructively rather than punished and forgotten about.

THE HELPING RELATIONSHIP

Teachers are inevitably thrust into the role of helper. Not only are they responsible for student growth within their subject matter, but traditionally they have also been expected to help children grow and mature as persons. *To help* means to facilitate. The goal of helping is to create conditions within which children learn how to behave more appropriately, more maturely, and with greater independence. The elementary-school classroom teacher and physical education specialist are in unique positions to offer help over an extended period of time. The communication skills discussed in this chapter can provide the expertise necessary to help more efficiently and more sensitively. The interaction skills discussed in the earlier parts of this chapter can help to create the climate within which children seek help and profit from interaction with a skilled helper.

There are four major conditions for effective helping. They are *empathy, respect, warmth,* and *genuineness.* These conditions are really a set of skills that can be acquired, perfected, and ultimately incorporated into a teaching style and even into a lifestyle. In counselor education these skills have been recognized for some years. They have been systematically practiced and shown in research to be valuable contributors to the helping relationship. Again, *wanting to help without knowing how to help is a frustrating experience.* If you are properly motivated, the skills introduced below can help you be the kind of teacher you would like to be.

1. Empathy. Empathy refers to the skill of perceiving a problem from the point of view of the person who has the problem. It does not mean sympathy. Most counselor educators believe that empathy is the most important dimension of the helping relationship and a necessary precondition for providing help.

2. Respect. If a teacher respects a child, he believes that the child has it within her to solve a problem. This is consistent with the notion that helping is a facilitative relationship—the helper acts in such a way that the problem is actually solved by the person who has the problem. Respect means supporting the children as they attempt to solve problems. It does not mean that the teacher should always provide the solution for the child.

3. Genuineness. This dimension refers to the helper's attempt to deal honestly with the child. The teacher's verbalizations to the child should be as congruent as possible with the teacher's feelings. Children will eventually spot insincerity. Once they perceive that a teacher is not genuine, they will be less likely to establish a meaningful relationship.

4. Warmth. This dimension creates the climate within which the helping can actually take place. By now you no doubt understand that warmth is a product of skillful interaction styles—emphasizing positive interactions—and that nonverbal behavior is particularly important. Smiling, touching, eye contact, and other such nonverbal behaviors are crucial to establishing a warm relationship.

11

managing groups of children

When asked about problems in teaching or what teaching skills they would most like to improve, elementary-school classroom teachers often rank classroom management and discipline at or near the top of their lists. These problems are magnified during physical education periods. The space for teaching (gym, multipurpose room, playground, and so on) is larger than the classroom. Children are usually excited when they begin the physical education period. The nature of the subject matter produces more student interaction than is found in the typical classroom. The subject matter emphasizes movement. It is no wonder that management skills are crucial for success in teaching physical education.

The authors firmly believe that straight lines and quiet children are seldom signs of a good manager at work. In fact, they are more often signs of ineffectiveness. The "hard-liner" who believes that the only responsible approach to management is through toughness and frequent doses of punishment will find no comfort in these pages. Likewise, the teacher who believes that all management and discipline problems are simply a matter of good teaching and of

finding interesting things to teach will find little solace here either. The former view is self-serving and often cruel. The latter view is naive and romantic.

We believe that management and discipline are legitimate topics in their own right. While they often are related to effective instruction, they are not identical to it. We believe that management and discipline are best defined as those strategies and techniques which help students and teachers to reach their goals most efficiently. We believe that children need structure and that they grow and develop optimally when they are in situations with defined limits (indeed, nothing is clearer than the fact that children, when left on their own, very quickly develop boundaries and limits to behavior in order for their group to function). We believe that self-management and self-discipline can be learned and that education experiences should be arranged so that children gradually assume more and more responsibility for their own management and discipline.

Furthermore, we believe that skills in the area of management and discipline are essential for those who work with children in educational settings. Many experts in the area of teacher effectiveness (Berlinner, 1979) now believe that teachers influence student learning in an indirect rather than a direct manner. A number of different research studies, from different research perspectives, have found that teachers whose students learn more have a common characteristic: They tend to teach in a manner that keeps children on-task a greater percentage of time than do less effective colleagues. For children to learn, they must be motivated to pursue the subject matter vigorously, whether it be reading skills or gymnastic skills. Teachers who keep children motivated are usually effective regardless of the specific instructional strategy they utilize. Thus, it appears that management and discipline skills are the foundations of effective teaching.

MANAGEMENT AND DISCIPLINE

Management Defined

Children enter the multipurpose room excitedly but sit in a circle before the first activity begins because their teacher doesn't have all the equipment ready. This is a management problem.

The first part of the lesson calls for using hoops for solving movement problems. The second part of the lesson calls for using ropes. There is a point where the hoops have to be put aside and the ropes put in place. Who does it? How long does it take? Are discipline problems more frequent during this managerial transition?

You decide to take your children outside for their lesson. You have to get them from the building to the playground space, which is about fifty yards away. How do you get that done? What is out there waiting for children when they arrive at the playground space? Those are management issues.

You are teaching and one of those teachable moments occurs when you need the attention of your children, all of whom are scattered about the playspace. Perhaps you want to show them something, or give them some positive feedback, or point out a particularly troublesome aspect of a skill or game. You need to get their attention. What signal do you use? How long after the signal is given do *all* the children attend to you? Do the well-behaved children have to wait for what you are going to say while you attend to the less well-behaved children?

Management refers to time devoted to organization and transition before, during, and subsequent to a teaching lesson. Theoretically, it is a time when no instruction is given and no practice occurs. Therefore, it follows that a major goal of good teaching is to reduce managerial time. A managerial episode (Siedentop, 1976) is the amount of time devoted to any one such instance; that is, the time it takes to get a class started once they enter the gym, the time needed to get the group's attention, the time needed to move from place to place, or the time needed to put away or get out equipment as the lesson changes.

There is some evidence that elementary-school physical education specialists are not always good managers. Descriptive research studies (Quarterman, 1977; Stewart, 1977) show that on average as much as 37 percent of all class time is devoted to management. Some teachers spend as much as 52 percent of their time in managerial activities. On the other hand, it is clear that teachers can learn to reduce the amount of time they devote to management as well as learn to manage more efficiently and positively (Dodds, 1976; Darst, 1976; Hutslar, 1976). In research studies, physical education student teachers have demonstrated enough skill so that no more than 10 percent of class time is devoted to management; several have become so skilled that less than 5 percent of class time is required for managerial chores. Obviously, this increases the amount of time for instruction and practice and also reduces the chances for behavior disruptions. It seems obvious that behavior disruptions tend to occur more frequently during management time than during instruction or practice time. We have found that by reducing the time devoted to management, we often achieve a corresponding decrease in disruptive behavior.

Discipline Defined

There are two perspectives from which the concept of discipline can be viewed. One perspective is to consider the term *discipline* to be synonymous with the term *punishment*. This view is implied whenever one uses the term *discipline* as a verb, as in "I had to discipline Bobby today." What is really meant is "I had to punish Bobby today." This view is also implied whenever someone asks, "Do you have a discipline problem?" That sentence can usually be translated as "Do you have a group that you have to punish frequently?"

Again, it is important that you understand our perspective on discipline. Punishment is a behavior management technique that is sometimes necessary in working with children. The sole purpose of punishment should be to redirect disruptive or otherwise inappropriate behavior to more appropriate directions. There are many punishment techniques that can be used skillfully without resorting to emotionally laden, angry outbursts at students. We shall outline several of these later in this chapter.

Punishment, however, is an overused and basically unproductive technique that is fraught with potential problems. There is too much punishment in schools, mainly because teachers do not possess the skills necessary to develop and maintain appropriate behavior through positive techniques. The perspective on discipline advocated here is that appropriate behavior should be developed and maintained primarily through positive supports rather than through punishment. We are not so naive as to believe that punishment need never be utilized, but neither are we convinced that problems of management and discipline can be effectively met through focusing on what children do inappropriately or wrongly. Appropriate behavior does not mean merely the absence of inappropriate behavior. The primary discipline task of the teacher is to help children develop appropriate ways of behavior so that educational goals can be achieved. Clearly, the most direct way to accomplish this task is to focus on the development and maintenance of appropriate behavior.

Changing Concepts of Discipline and Management

Issues involving discipline and management in educational settings have always been intimately tied to our conception of how to raise a child. Throughout most of the history of Western civilization our conception of human development has been based on a doctrine of original sin, in which there was thought to be a need to harness the energy of the strong-willed child. The social and religious climates of most Western societies considered qualities such as obedience and submission to authority as appropriate characteristics needed by children and instilled primarily by strong, overt control, most often through physical force or the threat of physical force.

The Greek slave who was entrusted with the education of the young Greek boy carried a long staff. From what we know about Greek education, it is clear that the staff was used to "keep the boys in line." The Greek slave was called a *pedagogue*, the root from which our term *pedagogy* derives.

There is little doubt that schools are more humane places than they were a hundred years ago. Methods of discipline have become more tolerant of the developmental needs of children. Teacher-student interaction patterns which foster appropriate physical, social, and emotional development as well as academic improvement have become quite important in the preparation of teachers. To lose sight of this gradually improving state of affairs in elementary schools is to lose perspective. Increasingly we are finding methods for dealing with management and discipline problems that do not impair the growth of children physically, psychologically, or emotionally. However, that does not mean that old problems do not persist or that new problems do not occur.

One hundred years ago one might have

been able to catalog instances of school violence in which teachers abused children. Increasingly one is able to cite instances in which students abuse teachers. Surely, the incidence of student attacks on teachers is more widespread at the middle- and senior-high-school levels, but certainly it is not unheard of in the elementary school.

Traditionally teachers have been able to rely on the fact that parents trained their children to behave well at school. An extremely common discipline tactic among teachers has always been to warn children that if their misbehavior persists, a note might have to be sent home to parents. For many children in our schools that threat is no longer relevant. They may well have only one parent at home, and that one parent may show little concern for what goes on at school.

The pervasive use of drugs and alcohol has started to reach its ugly hand into the elementary school. No one can be sure how widespread it is or what direction it will take. Also, teachers increasingly have to be able to deal with children who show the effects of drugs that are prescribed rather than illicit. The phenomenon called "hyperactivity" is treated typically with drugs, the most common being Ritalin. Depending on what part of a drug schedule a child might be on, a teacher may have to deal with a child that is either nervous and shaky or subdued and unresponsive. Both these impairments are heightened in physical education because of the degree to which the motor behavior of children is affected.

AN OUNCE OF PREVENTION

The best way to deal with discipline and management problems is to be sensitive to when they might occur and to take steps to avoid their occurrence: An ounce of prevention *is* worth a pound of cure. Preventive management and discipline falls loosely into two categories: that achieved through appropriate planning and that achieved through appropriate teacher behavior.

Initial Activity Control

When children come to physical education classes, they are often excited. We get excited, in this anticipatory sense, when we are about to engage in something we enjoy a great deal. Therefore, the excitement of children as they approach their physical education period is something to be nurtured and prolonged rather than criticized or prevented. Obviously, this excitement must be kept within bounds, but children are usually capable of doing that. What is crucial is that the excitement of the children be translated into activity very quickly or else discipline problems will tend to emerge. When children enter the playspace or gym, there should be some designated activity for them to do. The means by which this management episode is efficiently implemented can vary. Classroom teachers can inform the children as to where to go and what to do before leaving their room. The physical education specialist can post instructions near the entrance to the gymnasium or playspace. The instructions should tell briefly and clearly what the children should do to begin the class. The instructions can be written or they can be graphic. They can be displayed on a blackboard, on a poster, or on an instruction sheet posted on the door.

Children must be taught to use this initial activity indicator. One should not expect all children to respond to it the first time. Those students who do respond should be praised. This is the quickest and best way to teach this kind of behavior. The group as a whole can be praised as they increasingly respond to the initial activity communication quickly and properly. Children not only need to be praised for learning to behave this way, but they need to understand why it is important to get organized quickly upon entering the playspace. Clearly, the best reason is that it leaves more time for playing.

Getting the Attention of a Group of Children

Regardless of the style of teaching used in physical education, there are times when the teacher wants the attention of the entire group. The teacher might want to point out something interesting, provide some group feedback or praise, or give instructions for another activity. Typically, it takes the less-skilled teacher up to a minute or ninety seconds to finally get the children's attention. Often this kind of management episode is one in which the teacher has to interact frequently with individual children due to their lack of attention or their failure to respond quickly enough. Successful teachers take time to *teach* a signal for attention. Whenever children hear that signal, they know that they should respond immediately by ceasing activity, quieting down, and watching the teacher.

Some teachers use a whistle. Some use a hand-clap. Others use a verbal signal—a key word. All take time to teach it. Others use a verbal signal—a key word. All take time to teach it. They do not simply issue the signal and expect children to respond appropriately. Again, the simplest and most direct way to teach a signal is to praise individual students who respond quickly and to alert the group as to their total response. In teaching this signal, some physical educators have had great success making a "game" out of it and holding up one finger for each succeeding second it takes the children to attend. The goal of the game is usually to see if the entire class can be attentive within five seconds. Once this level of response is achieved, the teacher can occasionally praise the group for their quick attention.

Changing from Place to Place or Activity to Activity

If you are teaching gymnastics by stations, there will be times when you want your groups to change stations. If you are teaching games, you will want to move from one game to another. If you are doing a movement lesson, you may want to use hoops at one point and scarves at another point. In each case you have to change activity, space, or equipment. It is in the process of these managerial shifts that many disruptive behaviors tend to occur.

There are several key points to be made here. First, this kind of managerial shift is much easier if you have taught a signal for attention. Once you have the attention of the group, you can then issue your instructions. Instructions should always be statements which require compliance rather than questions which might imply the alternative of noncompliance. For example, you would say "Squad one quickly over to the mats" and not "Would squad one like to come over to the mats now?"

The key element here is time. The less time needed for the shift, the better. Therefore, a time criterion is a useful strategy teachers can employ in teaching management behavior: "Class, on my signal put the hoops away and each get a ball and let's do it in less than twenty seconds—Go!" The class can then be given some feedback about how well they did. Again, a "game" is played and a reason for praising the children who behave well is provided.

Activity, equipment, and space shifts cannot be accomplished without effective prior planning. If you have a large box of balls in an equipment room and ask children to get their own balls, you have created a situation in which children will have to line up and get them one at a time. This takes too much time. You must plan and arrange equipment so that it can be put away and gotten out quickly and efficiently. Likewise, if you have children move quickly from one place to another and then have nothing ready for them to do at the new place, you have defeated your purpose.

Activity, equipment, and space shifts are crucial managerial episodes. Often teachers like to use a variety of activities within one lesson or have different children work on different activities at the same time. This requires shifts. Unfortunately, it is during these shifts that lessons are too often lost. Children interact improperly as regards equipment or they begin to misbehave because they are waiting for something else to happen. The time spent planning for efficient managerial shifts and teaching children how to change spaces, handle equipment, and change activities is, in the long run, well worth it. Given the right treatment, children can learn how to manage themselves quite well in physical education.

Develop and Teach Class Rules

In any group situation there are rules. In the absence of formal rules children quickly establish their own rules in group play. Teachers may never announce or post class rules, but they all have them. Children usually learn the rules gradually by having the teacher respond negatively to them when they break a rule. Unwritten rules sometimes change from day to day, depending on how a teacher feels. Children behaving one way on Monday might go unnoticed, while the same behavior might get a reprimand on Wednesday. It is no wonder that children sometimes get confused or afraid.

Every physical education teacher ought to establish rules for appropriate behavior during physical education. Since there is no such condition as "no rules," it is far better for the rules to be stated openly. Rules should be posted clearly in the physical education area and children should be taught to comply with them. Rules should not be thought of as impositions and/or restrictions on children. Instead, they should provide a common base of appropriate behavior that allows children and teachers to reach their goals in physical education. The following guidelines may be helpful:

1. Make the rules short and directly to the point.
2. Use no more than seven rules so that you do not confuse students.
3. Whenever possible, state rules in a positive manner.
4. Keep a tally as to the number of times you review rules with each class during the period of teaching rules.
5. Remind the class (prompting) about the rules at times other than those cued by the breaking of a rule.
6. Present the rules in a manner appropriate to the age of the students.
7. In the beginning praise students frequently for complying with the rules. (Madsen et al., 1968)

It is important that you understand clearly the need to *teach* class rules for appropriate

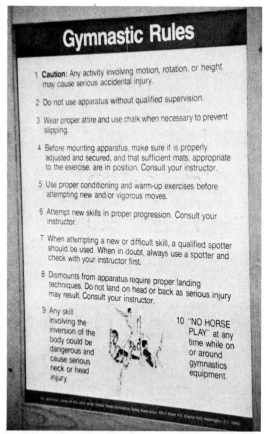

FIGURE 11.1 Rules should be posted clearly in the physical education area and students should be taught to comply with them.

behavior. Young children should not merely be *expected* to behave well in the gym or on the playground. Most of them will never have been in that kind of an environment when they first come to school. Teachers need to approach this kind of learning in the same way they would approach the learning of a motor skill, starting with the basics and gradually helping children until they are able to behave more skillfully.

Managing the Flow of Activities

It appears that effective teachers are first of all effective managers. Certainly, it is clear that little of any value can be taught when teachers devote too much time to managerial chores and waste their energies on negative forms of discipline. One might logically reach the conclusion that effective management means effective disciplining. However, research (Kounin, 1977) has shown that a preventive feature of classroom management—the effective management of the flow of activities—is of even greater importance than effective discipline skills. The rationale is that when a teacher manages the flow of activities within a lesson smoothly and has quick, clean transitions from one phase of a lesson to another, that teacher has prevented situations from occurring in which disruptive behaviors appear.

The two sets of concepts described below illustrate the basic skills needed to manage the flow of activities (Kounin, 1977). One set of concepts describes the teacher's smoothness in handling the flow of activities. (The opposite of this state is "jerkiness" in handling the flow of activities.) The other set of concepts focuses on maintaining the momentum in a lesson and is understood to be the opposite of "slowdowns," which destroy momentum.

The teacher who manages lesson transitions smoothly and keeps the momentum of the lesson going without slowdowns has probably done a great deal to prevent disruptive behavior. Preventing disruptive behavior from occurring is always better than dealing with it after it has occurred.

Getting hung up with an intrusive event. You are busy teaching and some event (person or thing) pops into the picture (a student enters the gym with a message from another teacher). How do you handle that intrusive event? If you become immersed in it, the smoothness of the class is lost. Can you attend to the event and also continue to attend to your class? If you can, then you are a "smoothie."

Thrusting yourself improperly into the children's activity. You decide it's time to stop one activity and start another, or you decide it's time to stop the activity to show or tell the students something. At what point do you interrupt the activity? What is your sense of timing? The jerky teacher bursts in on ongoing activities on the basis of personal intent and purpose and disregards the children's involvement with the activity. The smoothie, on the other hand, times the point of entry on the basis of the flow of the activity. To be smooth on the entry, you might have to wait momentarily; nevertheless, the price of thrusting yourself into an activity that is at a high point may be disruptive behavior.

Dangling activities. You interrupt an activity to attend to another matter and then you return to the activity. The children are left dangling. They were involved with an activity, and the reason for the interruption probably won't seem so important to them. Worse yet, you might interrupt an activity and not even return to it. Or, you could do the old flip-flop—terminating one activity, starting another, and finally returning to the first activity. Your lesson plan might indicate that you are going to do activity B. The children are thoroughly involved in activity A, but a plan is a plan. So, you stop A and do B for a while, returning to A after completing five minutes of B. You then wonder why the children don't get back into activity A so easily. Be smooth—not jerky!

Slowing down by overdwelling. Nothing destroys the momentum of a class more quickly than a teacher who overdwells on student behavior, on equipment, or on a task. A teacher who spends thirty seconds nagging a squad about the fact that a line wasn't straight is overdwelling. A teacher who spends too much time getting hoops placed around an activity space is overdwelling. A teacher who spends four minutes explaining how to do a skill or an activity is overdwelling. You can't maintain the momentum of a lesson if you slow it down while you explain some details at length, get out or put away equipment, or attend to a behavioral disruption. Overdwelling on the behavior of a student, on equipment, or on an explanation produces *waiting* among the majority of students. *Waiting* is the arch-enemy of momentum and the chief ally of disruptive behavior. If you want to ensure that you will have behavior problems, make your students wait.

Fragmenting the group or the activity. Is there ever a time when you have one child doing what the entire group could be doing? If so, you're guilty of group fragmentation. Group fragmentation produces waiting, an enemy of smooth teaching. You can also commit the error of activity fragmentation. This occurs when you fail to make the focus of the activity a meaningful unit in itself. For example, in sports skills teaching we often break down an activity into separate skills for practice. We know that when put together into a game, the skills form a meaningful whole—but do the children know that? Skills practice has to be made meaningful in and of itself, not merely because it will later become meaningful in a game.

Handle transitions smoothly and maintain the momentum of the lesson. Avoid jerkiness and slowdowns. These are the main ingredients of what Jacob Kounin (1977) has called "movement management." Kounin's research indicates clearly that techniques of successful movement management are more important in controlling behavioral disruptions than are the techniques of behavior management. An ounce of prevention *is* worth a pound of cure.

Components of a Positive Interaction Style

Helping children to keep on their toes. Children need to be reminded about class rules and appropriate kinds of behavior within the physical education setting. Teachers often remind children only *after* an instance of misbehavior. In this way the level of misbehavior among children tends to control the degree to which the teacher offers reminders. Children need reminding often, especially as they are learning appropriate ways to behave, and they need to have those reminders offered in a positive manner. In psychology and instructional technology the value of *cues* and *prompts* has long been understood. When teaching a new skill or idea, the teacher offers many prompts and cues to guide the learner. Then, as the learner progresses, the cues and prompts are gradually omitted so that the learner does not become dependent upon them.

Focusing on appropriate behavior. Teachers are very stingy about praising a child for good behavior. That observation is based not only on our own experience in schools but also on research findings. Typically, teachers react negatively or correctively to inappropriate behavior at fairly high rates. There are many "Be quiet," "Pay attention," "Stop fooling around," and "That's enough" kinds of reactions. On the other hand, there are far too few "Thank you," "Jane, you have been very good today," "How nice that everybody paid attention so well" reactions. Some teachers have told us that they simply expect children to behave well and don't feel that children need to be rewarded for things that they *ought* to be doing anyway.

There are many more teachers who see themselves as positive, humane people who believe that children do indeed deserve to be complimented when they behave well, but who can't seem to translate that desire so that it shows up in their teaching.

It is our contention that classroom management goals can be reached just as effectively by focusing on appropriate behavior as by focusing on misbehavior. Much has been said in American education during the past seventy-five years about the climate of the classroom. All agree that it is important for the classroom climate to be warm, accepting, and generally supportive of the students who live within it. The quickest way to achieve this kind of climate is to shift your focus of attention from inappropriate to appropriate behavior, to reward the many things that children do well rather than nagging them when they make mistakes. The literature on positive classroom management is now quite large and convincing. A more detailed explanation of positive teaching styles in physical education can be found in Siedentop's *Devel-*

oping Teaching Skills in Physical Education (1982).

Ignoring inappropriate behavior.

How many times do you cast a knowing glance at a youngster who is engaged in some mild form of misbehavior? How many times have you put your finger to your lips to say "Sh-h" to make a group quiet? How many times have you said, "John, don't do that"? None of these interactions is made in anger and none is sufficient to create a negative climate in your classroom or gymnasium. But, if you emit two or three of these per minute, there would be seventy-five such interactions in a thirty minute class, and that *is* enough to affect the climate of your classroom. In fact, two or three such comments per minute is not unusual, especially for physical education student teachers (Siedentop, 1981).

In the long run nags do not produce good behavior. If they did, they wouldn't occur so frequently. Some teachers nag day in and day out over the course of their teaching career. We don't believe that you want to be that kind of teacher.

When you shift your focus to appropriate behavior, as outlined in the previous section, you must also begin to ignore inappropriate behavior. In psychology this technique is known as extinction; when it is paired with positive reinforcement for appropriate behavior, what results is a very powerful combination. Some nags probably function as rewards for the many children for whom the attention of the teacher is a powerful reinforcer: You may think you are stopping a misbehavior when, in fact, you are rewarding it.

You must decide for yourself what level of minor misbehavior you can tolerate while you shift to a positive style of management and discipline. Once this is decided, you can begin to reward more and nag less. Very quickly you will experience a change among your children and you will have less opportunity to nag, simply because those minor misbehaviors will occur less often. When children find out that attention and approval is contingent upon good behavior, they will begin to behave that way more frequently.

However, if they can still get your attention with minor misbehavior, this might be enough to keep them behaving that way.

Building Positive Interaction Skill

Through a number of research studies designed for physical education teachers and for students preparing to become teachers, we have learned a great deal about the stages people go through when they switch to a positive teaching style. (These stages were explained more fully in chapter 10.)

Stage one: the global good. The first change involves increasing positive behavior statements without much regard to the content or specific focus of those statements.

Stage two: increased variety. From complete dependency on three to five statements, teachers broaden their verbal and nonverbal repertoire so that they have a variety of ways to compliment and reward their students.

Stage three: specific information content. Once rate and variety are increased, the teacher usually begins to include specific information in the praise statement.

Stage four: adding some value content. Once information content is more frequently specific, teachers begin to add information to their praise statements which indicates *why* it is important to behave in a particular way.

Stage five: becoming less dependent on misbehavior cues. As teachers learn to be positive classroom managers, they most often initiate a praise statement because they see an instance of misbehavior. The problem with this is that as misbehavior decreases in frequency, so too does the teacher's rate of praise—since praising is tied so often to the cue of misbehavior. Really skilled positive teachers emit high rates of praise regardless of the level of misbehavior.

A POUND OF CURE

At the risk of belaboring a point, we want to reiterate that effective management and positive discipline techniques help to *prevent* management and discipline problems from occurring. However, there are times when children misbehave and when misbehavior has to be stopped. There are also times when groups of children become unruly. Some classes are extremely difficult to handle. Some children within classes may need special kinds of treatment. The skills and techniques in this section speak to those situations.

Stopping Misbehavior

All teachers occasionally have to reprimand a child or a group of children. Clearly, how this is handled makes a difference. There are several characteristics of effective desists that warrant our attention. We are indebted to Jacob Kounin (1977) for the research effort on which most of these suggestions are based.

The first characteristic of an effective desist is clarity. This factor refers to the information content of the desist and is highly similar to our discussion of information content in positive behavior interactions (page 127). The offending children must know exactly what they were doing that was wrong. A simple "Stop that" isn't sufficient.

A second characteristic of an effective desist is firmness, which can be defined as the degree to which the teacher follows through on the desist. Following through might mean some eye contact with the offending child or moving a bit closer to that child. Desists that lack follow through simply occur one moment and are gone the next.

An effective desist is also well timed. This means that the teacher recognizes the misbehavior and stops it immediately. Bad timing occurs when there is a substantial time lag between the misbehavior and the teacher's reaction to it.

An effective desist must be properly targeted. If a desist is directed to a child who is an onlooker rather than an initiator of misbehavior, a targeting error has occurred. If you stop a less serious misbehavior while ignoring a more serious misbehavior, another targeting error has occurred.

One might think that the roughness or harshness of a desist is correlated with its effectiveness; that is, the more harsh the desist,

the more quickly and effectively it works. However, this is not the case. It is important that you understand clearly that harshness is not merely an extension of firmness. It is an entirely different quality and has a totally different effect on classroom behavior. Firmness is a characteristic of effective desists. Harshness or roughness is not. A harsh or rough desist does seem to have one typical outcome: It makes all the children uncomfortable. According to Kounin (1977), "Rough desists did not make for better behavior in the watching children—they simply upset them." (p. 13)

Changing Behavior

When we talk about curing classroom behavior problems, we are really talking about changing behavior. Changing behavior can mean two things. First, it can mean teaching children new ways to behave. Second, it can mean reducing the frequency of some ways of behaving and increasing the frequency or regularity of other, more appropriate forms of behavior. The techniques involved in both situations are basically the same.

Behavior changes (increases/decreases) when we change the situation in which it occurs and/or change the consequences that it tends to produce. Of the two (situations and consequence), it is clear that changing consequences is the more powerful stimulus. A consequence can be defined loosely as anything that follows a behavior and affects that behavior; a consequence can maintain a behavior, strengthen it, or weaken it. The following are basic principles for changing behavior.

1. Be specific—the behavior you want to change must be defined very specifically. You must avoid the temptation to try to change behavior categorized by ill-defined concepts such as "fooling around."
2. Define the contingency carefully—a contingency is the relationship between a behavior and a consequence. It must be defined very carefully: "if you do 'X,' then 'Y' will happen."
3. Think small—don't try to change the entire personality of the child. Start with a small but significant behavior and accomplish your specific goals with that behavior.

4. Move gradually—be satisfied with small, consistent improvement and then change gradually to other behavior problems.
5. Be consistent—stick to your contingency and apply it in the same manner all the time. Nothing confuses children more than to have contingencies applied differently from time to time.
6. Begin at the child's current level—don't expect children to behave in socially mature ways until they can first demonstrate some very basic social behavior capabilities. The first behavior change should be at their current level of functioning.
7. Know what you are doing—make specific goals, monitor the behavior of the child frequently, check your results, and make changes if you are not achieving the desired results.

Whether you are trying to reduce the degree to which a child is misbehaving or increase the likelihood of appropriate behavior, the basic principles are the same. Small, specific changes in behavior are won by applying contingencies in a very consistent manner and gradually moving to larger, more expanded chunks of behavior. A word of caution is necessary at this juncture. Too often behavior change strategies are thought of simply as ways of reducing or eliminating inappropriate behavior. Faced with a behavior problem, the teacher wants to eliminate it quickly and efficiently. The problem with this one-sided view of behavior change is that it tends to ignore the fact that *the child is misbehaving for some reason.* For example, if a child is misbehaving in order to win the attention of peers, reducing that misbehavior by some teacher-imposed contingency in no way abates the child's need and desire. Sooner or later (sooner in most cases) the child will try again to achieve the desired end—the attention of peers—and the manner in which that is done may again be viewed as inappropriate by the teacher. Often it is helpful for the teacher to think of behavior change as a two-sided problem: reducing the frequency of the inappropriate behavior and substituting a behavior pattern through which the child can gain reinforcement similar to that received by means of the inappropriate behavior pattern.

Behavior change techniques have often been criticized because people feel that children should not receive special privileges, rewards, and the like for what these adults view as "expected" behavior. When people first begin to use behavior change techniques, they often dream up very large rewards to use as consequences. However, a principle generally adhered to in behavior change programs is the "principle of least intervention"—using the least amount of reward or punishment necessary to accomplish the goal. If you can achieve a behavior change simply by using your own behavior as a teacher (praising children frequently), privileges or material rewards are unnecessary. If a small privilege will suffice to effect an important change in student behavior, use it rather than offering a larger privilege.

Above all, it is our judgment that in 99 percent of the cases of behavior change in the elementary school, it is absolutely unnecessary to use reinforcers that are "special" in the sense that they are not part of the day-to-day scene in the school. Candy bars or special books, for example, usually violate the principle of least intervention. The elementary school is an environment rich in rewards for children. There are special places such as the gym or playground; special times such as recess, noon hour or after school; special things to use such as books or balls; and special things to do, such as helping a teacher or going on a nature walk. In all our research with behavior change in elementary schools, we have utilized three primary kinds of rewards. First, we have found that extra gym time is a uniformly powerful reward for children. Second, we have found that helping the teacher is a privilege for which children will work diligently. Third, we have found that access to favored activities is a powerful incentive for good behavior. None of these rewards costs anything. In fact, there is no reason why building a strong reward system should cost the school any additional funds. Finding powerful rewards is much more a problem of managing the many good things you already have than it is of bringing in new things to the school.

Decreasing Inappropriate Behavior

Obviously, the fundamental strategy for behavior change is gradually building a base of appropriate behavior through systematic reinforcement, mostly in the form of attention and approval from the teacher. This is the most neglected strategy. The child who is trying to behave well in school seldom gets recognized for that effort. Thus, as we introduce you to the major behavior change strategies that have been proven useful in elementary-school settings, keep in mind that each of the strategies should be accompanied by a program of building appropriate behavior through reinforcement.

Omission training. In this strategy a child is rewarded for *not* engaging in a particular behavior. Ronnie earns one point for every gym period he participates in without arguing with a classmate. When he accumulates five points, he gets to help the gym teacher with another class. The result is that arguing decreases.

Positive practice. In this strategy a child must engage in an appropriate behavior a specified number of times each time she engages in an inappropriate behavior. A child does not put her equipment away properly. As a result, she must get out and put away equipment properly five times for each infraction. The result is that putting equipment away improperly occurs less often.

Reward cost. In this strategy a child loses "X" amount of reward for each incident or inappropriate behavior. A child often cheats in games. A contingency is developed whereby an instance of cheating results in loss of five minutes of intramural gym time. The result is that cheating decreases.

Time out. In this strategy a child loses "X" amount of time from physical education for each infraction. A child hits another child. Hitting is against the class rules. Child must be in time-out area for two minutes. The result is that hitting decreases. It is important in this strategy that the time-out area be devoid of opportunity for reinforcement. A special part of the gym or play area is set up as a time-out area. Children should not even

have visual contact with classmates if that is reinforcing. An egg timer or some similar device is useful for keeping time.

Reinforcing other behavior. In this strategy the teacher frequently praises the child for virtually anything other than the inappropriate behavior the teacher is trying to reduce. Gradually the inappropriate behavior occurs less often. A small child sometimes does not engage in social play. The teacher praises the child often for any kind of involvement in the physical education period. This strategy is usually combined with an extinction procedure; for example, when the child refuses to engage in social play, the teacher ignores the child.

Extinction. In this strategy the teacher ignores the child when the child is engaged in the inappropriate behavior. A child uses inappropriate ways to get the teacher's attention. When the inappropriate attention-getting behavior is seen, the teacher ignores it and attends to other children. Inappropriate attention getting gradually decreases.

Notice that in none of these strategies did we suggest any method that remotely resembles physical punishment. There are too many educational settings where the "paddle" is still used. Notice too that we have not talked at all about yelling and dressing-down youngsters, except to point out that such a strategy is largely ineffective and makes children upset and uncomfortable. Almost all the strategies we have advocated fit the psychological definition of punishment: They are contingent events that decrease the likelihood of a behavior recurring. Although they fit the psychological requirements for punishment and do indeed have the desired result (the inappropriate behavior decreases), they are not the emotionally laden, punitive kinds of tactics one normally associates with the term *punishment.*

Formalizing the Behavior Change Strategy

The teacher can do much to reduce inappropriate behavior and to help children learn appropriate behavior patterns simply by using teaching behavior in a systematic way. Reminding (prompting/cueing) children of good behavior, posting rules, ignoring attention-getting forms of minor misbehavior, and being very liberal with compliments for children who behave well can, over a period of time, not only produce high rates of good behavior, but also set an appropriate climate for personal growth. Nevertheless, there are times when even systematic use of one's own teaching behavior is insufficient to achieve classroom management goals. At that point the teacher is wise to consider formalizing the behavior change strategy in one of the following ways.

Behavior proclamations. A behavior proclamation is a formal statement of contingencies that might apply to an individual student, a group of students, or even to an entire class. The proclamation states the behavior to be achieved (and perhaps the behavior to be avoided) and the rewards that can be earned for fulfilling the contingency. The teacher decides both the level of behavior necessary and the amount of reward that can be earned. The behavior is monitored frequently and the reward is earned when the specified amount or length of behavior has been achieved. An example of a behavior proclamation is found in Figure 11.2.

Naturally, the behavior proclamation has to specify its terms with sufficient clarity that the child/children can understand what it is they are to do or not do. Also, the reward specified must be sufficiently strong so as to motivate the good behavior.

Behavior contracts. A behavior contract differs from a behavior proclamation in that the child/children have a role in defining the behaviors, deciding on a reward, and establishing the precise contingencies (how much, for how long, and so forth). Teachers should not use behavior contracts unless they are willing to negotiate with children on these matters. From a learning and development point of view, the behavior contract is an important step forward from the behavior proclamation and starts the child/children on the road to self-control. The elements of the contract are the same as for the proclamation. It is important that all parties sign the contract and many teachers who use contracts successfully have a third party attest to the contract, thus underlining the importance and seriousness of having each party fulfill his or her side of the bargain. An example of a behavior contract for an individual child is shown in Figure 11.3. It should be emphasized that contracts can also be written for groups of children.

Good behavior games. One of the quickest ways to "turn around" a group of children who are misbehaving too frequently is to use a behavior game. Behavior games have been used successfully in many different kinds of elementary-school physical education settings (Young, 1973; Huber, 1973; Siedentop, Rife, and Boehm, 1976; McKenzie,

FIGURE 11.2 Example of a behavior proclamation.

GOOD BEHAVIOR

Sally Brown _____ will 1) take part in all activities
                                              2) not argue with classmates for
                                              four (4) weeks in phys. ed.

For this good behavior Sally _____ will get to help Mr. Castle after school 10
minutes a day for two (2) weeks

                                    Mr. Castle
                                    Physical Education Teacher

```
┌─────────────────────────────────────────────────────────────┐
│                    BEHAVIOR CONTRACT                        │
│                                                             │
│  Sarah Caldwell and Mr. Roman agree that the following      │
│  plan will be in effect for the next four weeks.            │
│                                                             │
│  Starting date January 6          Ending date February 3    │
│                                                             │
│  Sarah will:                                                │
│                                                             │
│      1. remember to bring her gym clothes for each p.e.     │
│         day,                                                │
│      2. not disturb the class by talking or fooling around  │
│         with Melanie, and                                   │
│      3. participate in all activities and try hard to       │
│         improve skill                                       │
│                                                             │
│  Mr. Roman will:                                            │
│                                                             │
│      1. give Sarah individual help on the balance beam,     │
│      2. count one point for each day Sarah meets the three  │
│         points stated above, and                            │
│      3. let Sarah help with the 4th grade class each day    │
│         she earns a point during this contract.             │
│                                                             │
│                    Signed _____   │
│                           _____   │
│                           _____   │
└─────────────────────────────────────────────────────────────┘
```

FIGURE 11.3 Example of a behavior contract. (Siedentop, 1982)

1976). Many different kinds of behavior games can be developed. What follows is a description of the most common game format we have used to reduce inappropriate behavior quickly (Siedentop, 1982).

1. The class is divided into four groups. Groups are allowed to choose a name for their team.
2. It is emphasized that each team can win and that teams are competing against a behavior criterion rather than against each other.
3. Four to six behavior rules are explained thoroughly (see section on rules in this chapter).
4. Rewards are discussed and decided on by the group.
5. The game is explained. Points will be awarded each time a signal goes off (the students won't know when the signal will occur). The teacher will check each group when the signal occurs. If all members of the group are behaving according to the rules, the team gets one point. If any member of the group is breaking any of the rules, the team gets no point.
6. A cassette tape is preprogrammed with a loud noise that will sound periodically (a bell or a

buzzer work well). Eight signals are programmed. The intervals between the signals vary. Several tapes are programmed. When class begins, the teacher simply turns on the tape recorder with the volume up (often the teacher doesn't know when the signals will occur).

7. When the signal occurs, the teacher quickly glances at each team and makes a judgment as to their behavior. Teams that win points are praised and told about their point. Teams that do not win a point are told why (after doing this for a few days, the teacher can usually manage this kind of behavior game easily, not taking more than fifteen to thirty seconds at each signal to record and announce points).
8. At the end of the period the teacher totals the points and posts the scores for the day.
9. At the end of a specified period (ranging from one day to as long as eight weeks), the rewards are earned by each team that has met the present criterion.
10. If one player on a team loses more than two points for his or her team two days in a row, the team gets to meet and decide whether this

player should sit out from gym class for a day (this doomsday contingency very seldom needs to be used).

11. With each consecutive game played, it is possible to reduce the number of signals per class and increase the length of the game. As good behavior becomes the norm for the class, the game can gradually be phased out.

With eight checks per day and a three-week game for a class that meets twice weekly, a team might have to accumulate forty-two out of forty-eight points to earn a reward. The extra gymnasium time is combined with access to favored activities and has been, in our experience, sufficiently powerful to motivate good behavior. With very young children or a particularly unruly class, the contingency might have to begin as a daily game where the reward is five minutes of free gym time at the end of the period (if they don't win, they return to their classroom five minutes early). Once good behavior has been achieved, the game contingencies can be stretched out.

The criterion for winning the game can also be made progressively more stringent, thus allowing the teacher to get continually better behavior for the same amount of reward. The number of behavior checks programmed on the cassettes can be reduced gradually so that less time is taken to manage the game.

Behavior games have also been used successfully in situations where poor management has been the problem rather than disruptive behavior (Siedentop, Rife, and Boehm, 1976). The game in this case was played with the entire class. All students had to comply with the rules of the game to earn the points. If any one student in class did not comply, the entire class missed the chance to earn the point. The rules were as follows:

FIGURE 11.4 Management time was reduced for three student teachers who used the management behavior game.

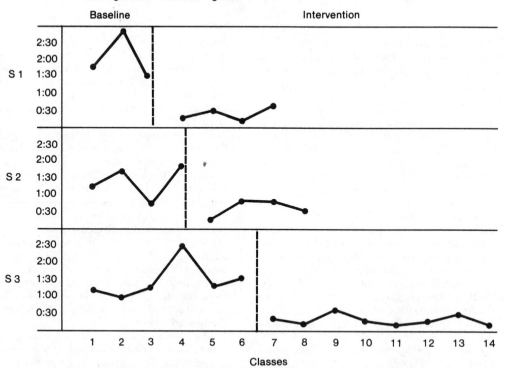

Mean time of managerial episodes in classes taught by three student teachers.

Rule 1: When entering the gym, students should read the instructions posted at the door and be in the proper formation or place when the official starting time occurs (two minutes of free time earned for each successful class beginning).

Rule 2: When the teacher signals for attention, the entire class is attentive within five seconds (one minute of free time earned for each instance).

Rule 3: When changing activities or changing sides in a game, all students will be in appropriate place fifteen seconds after the teacher signals for the change to take place (one minute of free time earned for each successful instance).

The teacher simply keeps records of the number of free-time minutes earned by the class. The free-time minutes can be used daily or they can be accumulated until the class has earned enough for a free period. "Free time" has always meant that several activities are made available and the children can engage in them as they want to (or the entire class can agree to play a favored game). Figure 11.4 shows the reduction in total time in management for three physical education student teachers who used this management behavior game.

Token economies. The most fully developed, formalized system of behavior change is known as a token economy. In this strategy all social and academic behavior can be combined into one system. The token economy has been used in elementary schools with great success. Token economies are usually point systems that incorporate both the social behavior and academic performance of the child into one overall program. Thus, children earn points for being prepared, for behaving properly, and for learning. Token economies are usually accompanied by a "general store," which is a separate place within the gymnasium (or classroom) or, if several or all classrooms in a school are operating in the same token economy system, a special room within the school. The "general store" includes rewards that are small and require only a few points (thus allowing for frequent, more immediate rewards) as well as large rewards that require students to save

their points (thus establishing long-term goals and the ability to work for deferred rewards). The rewards are usually items that are common to the elementary school and can include activity rewards such as extra gym time or working as a teacher's aide as well as material rewards such as pencils, gym socks with school colors, and access to special school field trips.

Toward Self-Management

Children enter the physical education space and immediately go to the area where they had been working during their last instructional period. They get the necessary equipment to begin their practice. They do not interfere with one another's activity. They seek help from the teacher when they need it, but they do not pester her just for attention. They stop to help a classmate who is having some trouble getting started. They compliment each other on progress and occasionally stop to help evaluate the progress of a classmate. They change activities quickly and seldom need prompting as to what to do or how to do it. They participate joyfully and the setting is full of happy noises, yet no one is so rude as to distract a fellow classmate. These children have learned to manage themselves in the physical education setting so as to extract from it the most learning and the most joy.

Few would disagree that the scenario just described represents a desirable goal or end state for management and behavior in activity settings for children. However, many do argue about the best way to achieve that goal. We cannot represent all those views adequately here, but we can tell you what we believe to be the main features that any such approach must have.

Clarity. It is clear from everything we have examined in this chapter that children learn best and most quickly when things are made clear to them. We continually tell children that they have to "share" or "cooperate," without giving them specific, concrete examples of what those concepts mean. One of the best ways to build clarity in these concepts is to use students as models: When good examples of sharing and cooperation are seen, they must be pointed out to the rest of the children.

Good behavior must be valued. There is simply no way to refute the notion that children tend to behave better when it is made clear to them that good behavior is valued in the setting. Our suggestions about positive interactions and reinforcement systems are simply ways we like for showing children that we value their good behavior.

Children must learn about consequences. All behavior produces consequences: A child pushes another child and gets pushed back; a child pushes another child and the teacher yells at him; a child pushes another child and the child runs away crying; a child pushes another child and the child becomes submissive—four examples of "pushing" that result in different consequences. Some consequences are immediate and obvious, while others are deferred and more subtle. The immediate and obvious consequences are strong. The deferred and subtle consequences are generally weak. The consequences that are produced by behavior such as sharing, cooperating, helping, and learning are often sufficiently deferred in time to be relatively weak in the degree to which they affect the child's behavior. Teachers must help children see, understand, and eventually respond to the consequences that good behavior naturally produces. "Do unto others as you would have them do unto you" is a statement of consequences, but it also refers to consequences that are generally deferred in time and weak compared to some of the immediate things that children's behavior produces.

Go one step at a time. Children don't learn to do a cartwheel on the first trial. Nor do they learn to "pay attention" on one trial. Nor do they learn to "help one another" in one class period. In physical education we have made much about the necessity for skill progressions. We should also understand the necessity for behavioral progressions.

It doesn't just happen. We know that highly skilled performance is achieved through careful planning and a long series of graded progressions in which situations are often contrived to represent special aspects of games and skills. A large amount of practice is required with frequent feedback. While teachers plan for these kinds of skills, they often assume that good behavior will automatically emerge from children. However, good behavior is learned just as surely as is a good spike or a good throw. Teachers need to teach good behavior just as specifically and carefully as they teach the substantive aspects of their subject matter.

12

the
exceptional child
in physical education

Adapted physical education, as a special field within the broader context of professional physical education, grew out of World War II. Corrective physical education—the use of activity and exercise as remedial agents—had long been of interest to physical educators but had not developed fully as a field in its own right. The large numbers of disabled veterans in World War II created a need for the study of physical education in relation to those disabilities, both in terms of helping to correct them and in terms of providing a meaningful and pleasurable activity experience for people who could not partake fully in regular activity programs. Thus, adapted physical education grew both as a means for remediating physical conditions (the corrective tradition) and as a means for modifying activities to enable handicapped persons to enjoy play (the adapted tradition). During the 1950s and 1960s adapted physical education became an important field, producing a large number of textbooks and accompanying materials. Professional preparation in physical education often included a course in adapted physical education because regular physical education teachers in schools often were assigned classes made up primarily of students with physical and mental hand-

icaps. During the past several decades it has not been unusual for the elementary-school physical educator, or the classroom teacher, to have to prepare lessons for small classes of physically handicapped or mentally retarded students.

Society's treatment of the handicapped has not produced a record of which we can be proud. Most handicapped people have been discriminated against in many ways. Society tends to ignore them, making no provision for their special needs. Traditionally most handicapped students have been removed from the mainstream of education by being placed in special schools or in special classrooms within schools. Society, and teachers, tend to have low expectations for such students. If they are physically handicapped, we tend too often to attribute low mental ability to them also. If they are of low mental ability, we tend to assume they can learn little and that society will have to "take care of them" for the remainder of their lives.

It has been known for some time, if not widely publicized, that handicapped people with all kinds of disabilities can achieve much more than society has generally considered to be possible. Retarded persons move from

153

sheltered workshops into responsible jobs within the community. Hearing and sight impairments do not restrict persons from living full, useful, and active lives. Physical disabilities do not require that a person's mobility be thoroughly restricted. Learning disabilities do not mean that children can never achieve as well as so-called "normal" children. While new therapies and rehabilitative techniques have been utilized to make considerable advances with special children, it is much more important that society has begun to accommodate these children, to allow for their fuller participation, and to remove some of the obstacles which have prevented such children from achieving in the mainstream of education and society.

PUBLIC LAW 94-142

Purposes and Provisions

On November 29, 1975, House Bill S.6 was signed by President Gerald Ford and became Public Law 94-142. The title of the law was the Education of All Handicapped Children Act, and it changed forever the manner in which special children will be treated in this society. The main feature of PL 94-142 is to ensure that all handicapped children receive a free, appropriate public education which includes services necessary to meet their unique needs. One of the striking features of the PL 94-142 is that physical education is the only curriculum area that is included in the defined elements of special education. This means that physical education in all its forms—including special physical education, adapted physical education, motor development, sports and games, dance, intramurals, and lifetime sports—must be made available to handicapped children (Ersing, 1977).

PL 94-142 provided for a transition period from 1975 to 1980 for states to provide the required services. It stipulated that by September 1, 1980, all children between the ages of three and twenty-one would be prop-

erly served unless there were specific state laws waiving the three to five and eighteen to twenty-one age groups. The law has six main provisions: zero reject, free appropriate education, nondiscriminatory and multifaceted evaluation, least restrictive environment, due process, and confidentiality. These provisions are explained below.

Zero reject. This provision means that all children must be served. In order to receive federal funds, states must determine the number of children currently not being served. Priorities in planning and implementation are then given to those who are not being served currently and to the profoundly handicapped who possibly are not being served appropriately. No child is to be denied the right to a free, appropriate education. The legal basis for this portion of the law is the same as that used to support the civil rights legislation of a decade earlier, primarily the famous case *Brown versus the Board of Education* in Topeka, Kansas. This court ruling disallowed exclusion from educational services on the basis of any irrelevant characteristic, such as skin color or handicap.

Free appropriate education. The mechanism through which a free and appropriate education is to be made available to all handicapped children is the Individual Education Program (IEP). The IEP is a written plan, prepared cooperatively by agency representatives, school representatives, parents, and the child—if appropriate. It is quite likely that physical educators and classroom teachers will be asked to help prepare IEPs. Each IEP must include the following features:

1. Evidence of the child's present level of functioning.
2. The specific goals to be achieved.
3. The degree to which the child can participate in the regular classroom activities.
4. The special services to be provided.
5. The duration and extent of the services.
6. An evaluation plan to determine if the goals outlined in 2 are being achieved.

The law requires that IEPs be reviewed and updated frequently, no less than annually.

Nondiscriminatory and multifaceted evaluation. This provision was made to guard against children being placed in classes on the basis of one single test, such as an IQ test. It requires that instruments used in evaluation be free from cultural bias. The evaluation must also be presented to children in their native language or mode of communication. The evaluation must be conducted by competent and qualified persons. This means that physical educators must be skilled in administering diagnostic tests of motor development, perceptual-motor functioning, and other batteries because they will be viewed as the relevant, competent professional on the IEP team. Tests used in developing IEPs must be valid for the purposes for which they are to be utilized. No single evaluation should be used. This requires that a battery of instruments be available and utilized, which results in a multifaceted evaluation. Relevant instruments are suggested later in this chapter.

Least restrictive environment. The purpose of 94-142 is to ensure that handicapped children receive their education in settings from which they can benefit the most. This is rendered operational in the concept of the least restrictive environment. It is this portion of the law that has received the most publicity and is known widely as the "mainstreaming" provision. The current view is that children should be placed in regular classrooms to the maximum extent possible, with assistance provided by supplementary aids and services. However, mainstreaming is not always the best solution to the least restrictive environment provision of the law. There are numerous alternatives ranging from the regular classroom to full, residential hospital confinement. The best current thinking is that these options should be arranged hierarchically so that a student is placed originally in the setting that is least restrictive for the handicap in question. Then, the student should have the opportunity to move to a different setting as he or she makes progress. The basic premise is that the setting that constitutes the "least re-strictive environment" will change as the student improves.

Due process. Due process is a concept that is fundamental to our constitutional rights as citizens, and 94-142 has extended that right specifically to the procedures used in providing education for handicapped children. Its purpose, of course, is to protect the rights of the child. It requires that parents be notified prior to evaluation and placement. It also requires notification if changes in placement are to be made, for example, in moving a child from a regular classroom to a special classroom. Parents have the right to be present during the preparation of the IEP and must consent to the evaluations and placements. If parents disagree with any of the procedures, they have the right to appeal.

Confidentiality. The specifics of the procedures used to fulfill this law and the results of testing are to be kept confidential. They are not to be used by persons who are not directly involved with an individual case. The data on individual handicapped children are not to be made public.

Implementing PL 94-142

The Education of All Handicapped Children Act presents many opportunities for the American educational system to fulfill one of its fundamental commitments—to extend the concept of equal opportunity to children who have handicaps. Still, the law presents many difficulties for administrators, programmers, classroom teachers, and elementary-school physical education specialists. It is clear that teacher education must include those skills necessary for teachers to operate successfully within the context of 94-142. To do less than this would seriously jeopardize the new teacher's ability to deal with one important requirement of professional teaching. Teachers who are already on the job will need serious in-service training to acquire the specific skills necessary both to understand and implement this important law. Jansma (1977) has outlined the major topics that need to be addressed in order to prepare the physical educator or the classroom teacher to be able to operate successfully within the provisions of the law and to be able to help handicapped children fulfill their educational destinies—especially in reference to physical education. He suggests that attention be paid to the following:

1. Skills in managing student behavior.
2. Knowledge of handicapping conditions or diseases.
3. Thorough knowledge of laws (state and local) which affect teachers directly.
4. Skills in selecting and administering motor, perceptual-motor, and fitness tests for diagnosis and assessment.
5. Skills to formulate individual prescriptions (IEPs).
6. Skills to formulate learning progressions, especially in fundamental motor skills.
7. Understanding how to use special equipment and facilities.
8. Understanding the multidisciplinary nature of dealing with the education of handicapped children.
9. Knowledge of resources—including literature, tests, specialized professionals, and materials.
10. Understanding the movement limitations and capabilities of handicapped children.
11. Development of a helping and positive attitude toward handicapped children and their potential.

Many of these skills are addressed in this chapter. Other skills, such as managing student behavior and formulating progressions, are addressed elsewhere in the book.

The implementation of 94-142 will differ, depending on the type of handicap involved. The law does provide specific guidelines as to what children come under the umbrella of the general term *handicapped children. Specifically,* it means those children who have been evaluated as mentally retarded, hard of hearing, deaf, speech impaired, visually handicapped, seriously emotionally disturbed, orthopedically impaired, other health impaired, deaf-blind, multihandicapped, or as having specific learning disabilities that cause them to need special education and related services. These handicaps

will be defined more clearly later in this chapter.

Identification, Assessment, and Evaluation

The three major components of dealing with exceptional children in physical education are identification, assessment, and evaluation (Ersing, 1980).

Identification refers to procedures through which children are determined to be in need of special physical education or are covered under PL 94-142.

Assessment refers to procedures through which identified students are examined so as to establish current levels of skills and abilities so as to provide adequate programming through IEPs.

Evaluation refers to procedures through which students are examined to ascertain the degree to which program objectives have been met.

Some children will be identified for the physical educator and classroom teacher. These children will have been determined to be learning disabled, mentally retarded, or emotionally disturbed. They will come as referrals from the appropriate educational and medical personnel and agencies.

Some children will have medical problems and will be referred by a physician. The medical doctor is the person legally responsible for suggesting that certain activities are inappropriate for children with medical handicaps. School nurses may refer a child to a physician but may not prescribe activities themselves.

The classroom teacher and the physical education specialist can each contribute to the identification process, particularly in those areas where disabilities involve posture, physical fitness, motor efficiency, and perceptual-motor function. These problems can best be identified through the use of screening devices. A list of suggested screening tests and evaluations are presented in Figure 12.1. This list includes the problems for which the devices are appropriate as well as the developmental levels for which the devices were intended. A bibliographical

INSTRUMENTS	Developmental Levels			Areas of Concern				
	PRESCHOOL	PRIMARY	INTERMEDIATE	GROWTH	POSTURE	PHYSICAL FITNESS	BASIC MOTOR SKILLS	PERCEPTUAL-MOTOR DEVELOPMENT
1. National Center For Health Statistics Growth Charts (see Chapter 5)	*	*	*	*				
2. New York State Posture Rating Test (included in this chapter)	*	*	*		*			
3. Krauss-Weber Test of Minimum Muscular Fitness (Krauss & Hirschland, 1954)	*	*	*			*		
4. AAHPERD Youth Fitness Test (see Chapter 6)		*	*			*		
5. AAHPERD Health Related Physical Fitness Test (see Chapter 6)		*	*			*		
6. OSU Scale of Intra-Gross Motor Assessment (Loovis & Ersing, 1979)	*	*	*				*	
7. OSU Fundamental Motor Skills Inventory (see Chapter 4)	*	*	*				*	
8. Frostig Developmental Test of Visual Perception (see Chapter 7)	*	*						*
9. Bruninks-Oseretsky Test of Motor Proficiency (see Chapter 7)	*	*	*					*
10. Southern California Test Perceptual-Motor Test Battery (see Chapter 7)	*	*						*

FIGURE 12.1 Physical education screening instruments for exceptional children.

source is provided for each device so that interested readers can learn more about the procedures involved in each test.

Children identified by classroom teachers and physical education specialists should be referred to the proper medical person, usually the family doctor of the child involved. The school should then receive a referral form from the physician detailing clearly the degree to which the student can or cannot be involved in regular physical education activities and describing any special activities from which the student might benefit.

Children who have initially been identified and referred can then be assessed further to establish their current level of functioning relative to the handicap. Information developed through the identification and assessment procedures can be used by the IEP team to prepare an appropriate plan for the child. IEPs must include statements of current levels of educational performance; statements of annual goals, including short-term instructional objectives; statements describing the degree to which the child will be able to participate in regular programs; the projected date for initiating the program; the duration of the program; the evaluation procedures, including the criteria by which judgment will be made; and a schedule for determining on an annual basis whether the instructional objectives are being achieved.

Programming

Once an IEP has been completed, the resulting prescriptions represent a program to be implemented by the various teachers and aides who work with the child. Ersing (1980) has suggested a useful category structure for classifying the types of program involvement likely to be encountered by physical educators and by classroom teachers who have responsibilities for physical education. The structure has four main levels:

1. Unrestricted (totally mainstreamed)
2. Modified (partially mainstreamed)
   a. Vigorous
   b. Moderate
   c. Mild
3. Remedial (partially mainstreamed)
4. Developmental

A description of the purposes of the various levels and the kinds of children for whom they are applicable is found in Table 12.1. It should be pointed out that the nature of PL 94-142 is such that many children will move from one programming level to another as they acquire the physical, mental, and social skills to advance. Placement at one level *does not* condemn a child to that particular approach forever. It is true that the nature of certain disabilities is such that they cannot be improved through regular physical education programming. For these children the goal will always be to modify activities so as to provide the proper physical education and recreation outcomes that are achieved by children through regular programming—including skills in sports, games, dance, and aquatics. Other children may actually be helped to improve, relative to their specific disability, through a planned physical education program. The objectives written for these children will reflect that expectation, and programming to meet those objectives will be different than for children

FIGURE 12.2 Programming levels for exceptional children in physical education

LEVEL	GOAL(S)	TYPES OF CHILDREN
Unrestricted	Same as for regular program.	Students with no physical or medical disability. Students with acute and temporary disability (problems that will disappear within days).
Modified	Same as for regular program but achieved through modified activities or modified participation.	Children whose disabilities will not allow participation in the near future. Children whose disabilities cannot be remediated by specific exercise rehabilitation program. Children with chronic conditions which restrict strenuous participation. Children with a physician's recommendation to avoid vigorous activity. Children restricted from any form of gross body exercise.
Remedial	To improve conditions through prescriptive exercise and to stabilize through exercise.	Children with severe postural deviations. Children with cerebral palsy who are not enrolled in a therapy program. Children with low levels of physical fitness. Children with degenerative conditions in which progress can be retarded through exercise. Children returning after serious injuries.
Developmental	To develop basic perceptual and motor skills	Children who deviate markedly from average on perceptual-motor screening assessments. Children whose skill abilities are so low as to preclude satisfactory participation in regular program.

who need adapted activities to meet objectives similar to those for regular children.

As teachers work with handicapped children, they become more highly skilled at providing the kinds of modifications that are of greatest educational value. Remember that a modification of an activity is a means of achieving specific educational goals as outlined in the IEP. Activities should be modified only as necessary in order to ensure successful participation by the handicapped person. Generally, the ways of modifying activities for handicapped children are quite similar to the ways in which games and activities can be modified for regular children in order to meet specific instructional goals. Thus, the chapter on games, especially those sections detailing ways of changing games to meet goals, will be relevant to the discussion here.

Teachers should attempt to maintain the basic nature of the game because in so doing they normalize the child as much as possible. Changes should enhance successful participation and create adequate safety constraints while still maintaining as much of the parent activity as possible. A list of ways in which physical education activities and objectives can be modified to achieve specific goals for handicapped children is presented in Figure 12.3.

It is important that physical educators understand that most children, no matter what the source of their exceptional condition, can improve in physical education—they can meet objectives and show progress. If activities are planned to fit their needs, they will progress just as do children who have no disabilities. The manner in which activities are changed should be determined on the basis of the individual needs of each special child.

FIGURE 12.3 Modification of activities: writing objectives and programming activities.

1. Reduce playing area to restrict movement.
2. Use larger equipment to make game easier or slower.
3. Use extra players to reduce activity of individual players.
4. Shorten distances.
5. Change rules to specifically limit excess activity.
6. Shorten duration of games or time periods of activity.
7. Rotate players frequently to provide rest.
8. Reduce point requirements for winning.
9. Eliminate competition by not keeping score.
10. Use free substitutions.
11. Plan frequent rest periods.
12. Allow balls to bounce or be caught in games such as volleyball.
13. Allow two hands instead of one where accuracy/power is involved.
14. Allow substitute runners.
15. Use lighter equipment.
16. Use guide wires, ground surfaces with different textures, handrails, and similar devices.
17. Lower baskets, nets, and so on.
18. Substitute walking or jogging for running.
19. Disallow specific movements which might harm individuals.
20. Substitute skill practice for games.
21. Decrease repetitions in exercise programs.
22. Reduce tempos in rhythmic activities.
23. Soften landing spots with mats.
24. Increase the size of striking implements and targets.
25. Substitute accuracy for distance in projectile activities.
26. Substitute walking for rhythmic movement such as leaping or skipping.
27. Use stationary ball-handling games.
28. Use quiet table games.
29. Simplify cues that are parts of games.
30. Simplify rules.
31. Stress form instead of performance.

Managing Behavior

For certain disabilities the management of student behavior will not present any problems that differ from those presented by all children. The basic techniques and strategies needed to manage behavior humanely and effectively are explained at some length in Chapter 11.

Certain kinds of disabilities are likely to produce behavior problems as well as instructional problems. In fact, they are more likely to produce behavior problems. Children who have been labeled emotionally disturbed or hyperactive are particularly difficult for the physical educator or classroom teacher who conducts a physical education lesson. The larger spaces in physical education settings, the exuberance of the other children, the increased noise level, the increased activity level, and the management problems these factors create all lend themselves to the production of a situation in which children with behavioral problems, emotional problems, or hyperactivity problems often lose control, thus creating discipline problems not only for themselves but also for many of the other children in the group.

One hyperactive child who has lost control can destroy the discipline of twenty-five other normally well-behaved children. This is the "other side of the coin" of the mainstreaming issue. Children who have emotional, behavioral, or hyperactivity problems are among the most likely to be mainstreamed and also among the most likely to create discipline problems for the teacher.

Hyperactive children often take drugs prescribed by a physician. The drugs frequently produce a very low level of physical activity such that the child will appear to be quite lethargic and unwilling to participate in an activity. However, children who are taking these kinds of drugs have to be periodically withdrawn from them. When they are in a withdrawal phase, they can be hyperactive to the point of being unable to concentrate and unable to behave in a manner conducive to good order within the class. Thus, the same child may be quite passive one day in the physical education lesson and wildly active the next.

There is no easy way for a teacher to deal with these kinds of behavior problems. The most teachers can do is to apply their behavioral skills more clearly and with greater frequency. This means that all cues and prompts should be clear, simple to understand, and repeated frequently. Praise for good behavior should be more frequent. Reprimands, when delivered, should be firm, thoroughly consistent, and associated with class rules whenever possible.

A totally disruptive child should be removed from the class situation. Time out (see page 147), a usually quite effective, noncoercive punishment technique for regular children, may not be as effective with the mainstreamed child. The teacher may need to decide at some point whether it is appropriate to include a special child in the physical education class. While certain children may be able to participate in a regular physical education class (even though they cannot profit from a normal classroom situation), the opposite is probably true too. There may be children who can participate in a regular classroom but who need a special physical education class. The physical educator and/ or classroom teacher should be instrumental in reaching this kind of decision. This problem is not an easy one. There might be a tendency to remove any child with behavior problems from the mainstream physical education class and place that child in a "special" physical education class. While this might be easier for the teacher involved, it is not always best for the student, and PL 94-142 is written to guard the interests of the student. On the other hand, a regular physical education class might be *too restrictive* for certain children simply because they have not yet acquired the behavioral skills necessary for participation in the group. For this kind of child, the least restrictive environment might be a special physical education class, at least on a temporary basis, until the child learns the basic behavioral and/or motor skills necessary for beginning participation in a regular class.

HANDICAPPING CONDITIONS

Certain kinds of handicapping conditions are medical in nature, need to be diagnosed by a trained medical person, and often result in specific suggestions from a physician about the kinds of activities most appropriate for the child with the condition. Other kinds of handicapping conditions are more educationally disabling than physically disabling. These are often diagnosed by educational psychologists as well as physicians, but the physical educator or classroom teacher is less likely to receive specific advice about programming activities for such children.

Public Law 94-142 presents a legal definition of "handicapped children." Within the context of that law children evaluated as being mentally retarded, hard of hearing, deaf, speech impaired, visually handicapped, seriously emotionally disturbed, orthopedically impaired, other health impaired, deaf-blind, multihandicapped, or as having specific learning disabilities are considered handicapped if those impairments need special education and related services.

Brief descriptions of common handicapping conditions are presented below with some suggestions for the physical educator and/or classroom teacher who has to deal with children who manifest these conditions.

Anemia

Anemia is a blood condition in which there is a deficiency of hemoglobin, either within the red corpuscles themselves or due to an insufficient number of red corpuscles. The result is a reduced ability to provide oxygen to cells in order to maintain adequate metabolic functioning. Signs include easy fatigue, paleness, increased respiration rate, and headaches during exercise. Anemic children must be placed in activities that are within their ability to withstand fatigue, usually some moderated or mild form of the activities normally pursued within the program. For activities that do not require vigorous exercise, the anemic child can often take part without modification.

Arthritis

Arthritis refers to a number of conditions which involve joint inflammation. Arthritis is not uncommon among children and is often due to rheumatic fever. Joints involved are typically restricted in their range of motion, and the muscles which move these joints often tend toward atrophy due to lack of use.

Remedial programs are usually called for in arthritis cases among children to prevent permanent deformity and atrophy of muscle groups near the impaired joints and to build up a normal range of motion in the impaired joints. The aid of a physical therapist is often required for severe cases, but the child might also have a specific, remedial exercise pro-

gram within the physical education program. Such a program would emphasize strength development in affected muscle groups and range of motion exercises. Aquatic activities are especially useful for children with arthritis. Exercises can be done in the water. The water reduces the problem of working against gravity, thus reducing the potential for pain during exercise. As the child improves, he can begin to take part in more regular activities, albeit in a mild or moderated form.

Cardiac Disorders

Medical examination may reveal that a child has one of the diseases of the heart and blood vessels that is included under the larger heading of cardiac disorders. The problem might be congenital, having occurred during the fetal period of pregnancy; it might be a rheumatic heart disease, due to rheumatic fever; it might be the result of hypertension; or it might be a hardening and narrowing of the arteries, known as arteriosclerosis. Cardiovascular disease is quite common among adults and more frequent among children than is commonly recognized.

The American Heart Association has provided guidelines for prescribing activity for children with cardiac disorders. The system categorizes cases into four classes. Class I is for children who have a heart disease but for whom there is no need to limit physical activity. Class II is for children with cardiac disorders who can take part in limited activities, who are comfortable at rest, but for whom ordinary physical activity results in undue fatigue, palpitations, or anginal pain. Class III is for children whose cardiac impairment requires serious limitations on activity levels and who, although comfortable at rest, experience discomfort with even moderate levels of activity. Class IV is for children whose cardiac disorder prevents them from taking part in even mild forms of activity and who may experience cardiac discomfort even at rest.

Children with cardiac disorders should have referrals from their physicians specifying the degree of involvement in the modified program, either at a vigorous, moderate, or mild level. For most of these children a remedial program of carefully programmed progressive exercise is beneficial. Physical educators and classroom teachers have to be very attentive to signs of cardiac discomfort, such as shortness of breath, palpitations, or anginal pain. Activities need to be adapted in terms of distance traveled, duration, and intensity of involvement. Highly competitive activities should be avoided.

Cerebral Palsy

Cerebral Palsy (CP) is a condition resulting from lesions in the central nervous system during its developmental period. The lesions result in motor dysfunction and are nonprogressive, although the symptoms of CP vary markedly with age as well as from child to child. Cerebral Palsy is classified into six types, each of which has a specific set of symptoms. *Spastic CP* is the most common and is often accompanied by mental retardation. Spastic CP children have muscular stiffness, exaggerated stretch reflexes, inward rotation of the legs, knee flexion, and a scissors gait.

Athetosis is the second most common CP condition. Its main symptom is unpredictability of movement, resulting in postural problems. Emotional problems often accompany this condition, probably due to the high frustration level resulting from the unpredictability of movement. A third type of CP is *rigidity,* a condition characterized by uncoordinated reciprocal muscle groups and impaired stretch reflexes. The other three types, *ataxia, tremor,* and *atonia* are not sufficiently common to warrant consideration here.

Children with cerebral palsy will be under treatment by a physician. That treatment may involve braces, drugs, surgery, and a rehabilitation effort. It is in the rehabilitation effort that the physical educator or classroom teacher may become involved. The remedial prescriptive exercise program for CP children may be partially carried out within the context of a physical education program.

Such programs may be designed to increase range of motion, facilitate relaxation skills, or develop strength—particularly of reciprocal muscle groups. They may include postural exercises and gait training and may result in the normal strength, endurance, skill, and social outcomes that derive from an increased ability to be a part of play activities.

The physical educator can contribute much to the improved functioning of the CP child. The muscular rehabilitation effort is very important. Children with CP also benefit from activity involvement that increases their perceptual skills, particularly as regards balance, spatial relations, visual discrimination, ocular tracking, and figure-ground orientation (see Chapter 7, Perceptual-Motor Development). The CP child is also usually in need of activities through which social development might take place. Physical therapy sessions are useful in many ways but do not ordinarily contribute to social development, especially in terms of peer group relations. Thus, the CP child should become involved in game and play activities as much as possible.

Epilepsy

Epilepsy is a broad term referring to different types of seizures which are caused by electrochemical imbalances in the brain. Seizures are usually classified as one of six types. *Jacksonian seizures* have alternating contractions of muscles in a single, localized part of the body, progressing from the center outward. *Minor motor seizures* have localized nonprogressive contractions of muscles in one part or one side of the body. *Petit mal seizures* involve loss of consciousness for very brief periods of time, usually lasting only a matter of seconds. *Grand mal seizures* are much more complicated, having three distinct phases. The first phase is characterized by sudden rigidity, usually with the child falling down. The next phase involves contractions in the major muscle groups, causing writhing and jerking movements. The final phase is a relaxed period where the child may be confused or may even fall into a deep sleep. *Psychomotor seizures* involve haphazard and poorly coordinated movement, incoherent speech, mental confusion, and often aggressive or destructive behavior. The final form of seizure is called *autonomic* and is characterized by sweating, rapid heart rate, high blood pressure, and expressions of fear and anxiety by the child. Screening for epilepsy is a medical matter, but children are often first identified by seizure complications which occur at school. Treatment is by a physician and usually involves therapeutic drugs to control the seizures.

There is no reason why most epileptic children cannot take part in regular programs of physical education with the same goals as those set for nonepileptic children. Occasionally, in extreme cases activities may have to be modified to allow for less vigorous participation. These recommendations usually come from the physician. Seizures may occur sometimes and the physical educator or classroom teacher must handle them calmly so that other children do not become upset. Epileptics have had a long history of social discrimination. We have only lately come to understand the nature of the handicap and to make efforts to ensure that epileptic children do not become social outcasts among their peers.

Diabetes

Diabetes mellitus occurs when the hormone insulin is not produced in sufficient supply by the pancreas. Insulin serves an important function in the bloodstream, transporting glucose into cells for energy production. Lack of insulin shows up in behavior characterized by apathy, appetite increase, increased thirst, excessive urination, vomiting, and dizziness. Unless treated, the problem can progress into shock and finally into coma. Treatment by a physician usually involves some diet control and regular injections of insulin. The condition is usually diagnosed by a physician, but like epilepsy, it might first be spotted by a teacher through observation of symptoms mentioned above. Other symptoms include slowly healing infections, boils, gangrenous sores, and sudden changes in visual skills.

Exercise and physical activity seem to help this condition. Often diabetic children are overweight and a systematic program to reduce weight can also be beneficial. A regular or modified program may be indicated depending on the severity of the problem. Children will need extra doses of sugar following exercise and should be cautioned to have them on hand. As much as possible, the goals for a diabetic child in physical education should be similar to those for nondiabetic children. Social skills need to be emphasized because of stigmas attached to this kind of handicapping condition.

Severe Emotional Disturbance

Emotional disturbance is specifically mentioned in PL 94-142, yet remains one of the least well-defined of the handicapping conditions. Unfortunately, it is also quite prevalent among children—most elementary-school classroom teachers and physical education specialists will have to deal with mainstreamed children who have been identified as emotionally disturbed. A number of behavior patterns can lead to such an identification. Among them are depression, behavior that is thoroughly inappropriate for normal situations, inability to develop or maintain relationships, learning problems which defy normal explanation, inability to delay gratification, and extreme fear. The term does not refer to children who are maladjusted socially and who have not yet learned what are considered to be normal, age-appropriate social skills. It does apply to serious psychiatric impairments such as autism and childhood schizophrenia.

Emotional disturbance seldom involves physical education programming that is atypical in terms of physical activity. For the teacher the problem is not "what activity" but rather how to get the child into the activity and keep her there in a productive relationship with the activity and peers. In other words, the problem is a behavior management problem rather than an activity programming problem. The skills outlined in the chapter on behavior management are very useful with these children, especially if they are applied carefully, consistently, and frequently. Clearly, the social goals of the physical education experience are most important for a child who is emotionally disturbed. Learning how to play with other children can be a valuable step forward for children with emotional problems.

Hearing Impairments

Auditory impairments are usually of two kinds. One kind exists when a child simply does not receive a sufficient auditory input to respond, the volume of auditory input being too low. A second kind of impairment exists when auditory input is distorted in some way so that messages do not get through clearly. Obviously, since teachers communicate with children mostly through verbal behavior, an auditory problem can create many difficulties for a child. Auditory impairments are sometimes discovered in routine medial examinations. However, it is not uncommon for such problems to exist for some time without being diagnosed correctly.

Children who do not respond to directions, have indistinct speech patterns, shown excessive amounts of vocal play, have many misunderstandings with their peers, tend to have tantrums, show high levels of frustration, and react strongly to affection might be suffering from an undiagnosed auditory impairment. In the past many children with hearing handicaps have been thought to be retarded or emotionally disturbed.

Deafness is an extreme degree of hearing impairment. The legal definition of *deafness* refers to hearing impairments which are sufficiently severe that a child's ability to process verbal information, with or without amplification, interferes with the child's educational performance. Many children who are "deaf" can hear some things and can hear many things through amplification, that is, through hearing aids.

There is little reason why a child who has been diagnosed adequately and treated with the proper aids, should not take part in a regular program of physical education. Auditory input is not as essential in physical activity as in other educational settings. Hearing impaired children will need slightly different instruction, with greater emphasis on demonstrations, visual details of skills, written handouts, and other instructional forms that substitute for verbal instruction.

Learning Disabilities

If a child's academic achievement lags far behind his academic aptitude, he is referred to as learning disabled. A learning disability may be related to several different problems, including perceptual, motor, speaking, writing, or socializing problems. Children with learning disabilities have the aptitude to learn and achieve, but for some reason they are not doing so. This discrepancy between aptitude and achievement often results in social problems with peers and emotional problems for the child. PL 94-142 defines the term *specific learning disability* as a handicapping condition in which one or more of the basic psychological processes involved in understanding or in using language—spoken or written—manifests itself in an imperfect ability to listen, think, speak, read, write, spell, or do mathematical calculations.

Many terms are currently used to describe children with learning disabilities, including *minimal brain dysfunction, perceptual handicaps, dyslexia, brain injury,* and *developmental aphasia.* Unfortunately, sometimes these terms (and others like them) are applied without sufficient attention to the specific criteria which define them. The term *learning disability* specifically excludes learning problems that are traceable to actual visual, auditory, or motor handicaps. It also excludes all forms of retardation. Most importantly, it excludes learning problems that are related primarily to environmental, economic, or cultural conditions.

The area of learning disabilities is so large and so diverse that no single form of physical education programming can be said to be appropriate for children with such problems. At times children with learning disabilities might profit from specific perceptual-motor development programs (see Chapter 7). Quite often learning disabled children can be helped considerably by emphasizing the social outcomes of physical education, particularly peer-group approval. The teacher must also be constantly aware of limited social skills and reinforce those that do occur in the physical education period. Chapter 10 (Developing a Climate for Personal Growth) is particularly relevant to this task.

Mental Retardation

PL 94-142 defines the mentally retarded child as one who has significant subaverage general intellectual functioning and poorly developed adaptive behavior patterns. These problems manifest themselves during early development and affect the child's educational performance adversely. The American Association on Mental Deficiency (AAMD) provides an even more specific set of criteria for classification. They too refer to deficits in intellectual functioning and adaptive behavior, but they go further and list four categories of mental retardation based on IQ testing. *Mildly retarded* children are those whose tests fall in the 55–69 IQ range. These children have often been referred to as the "educable mentally retarded." While slower academically, these children are more nearly normal in motor functioning. The *moderately retarded* (IQ from 40–54) are handicapped in the academic, motor, and self-help areas. These children have historically been referred to as the "trainable mentally retarded." The *severely retarded* have IQ scores from 25–39. The *profoundly retarded* have IQ scores from 0–24. Each of the last two groups requires custodial care.

Screening for mental retardation is currently more advanced and complete than ever before. The major change has been to include measures of adaptive behavior along with tests for intellectual functioning. Physical education for the mildly retarded need not differ in purpose from that for normal children. However, the teaching strategies need to be very specific to the children's abilities with clear, unambiguous directions, careful progressions, expert feedback, and strong reinforcement. Physical education for the moderately retarded requires changes both in goals and in teaching strategies. Basic motor skills and self-help skills form much of the curriculum, with emphasis on social and motor skills that lead toward greater independence for the child. The clear and sequential nature of learning needs to be emphasized and progressions must be very small, with reinforcement following even minor progress.

Visual Impairments

Visual impairments range from total blindness to a large number of lesser handicapping conditions. PL 94-142 does not require that a child be blind or near blind in order to qualify as a visually handicapped child. Instead, the law describes visual handicaps as those which, even with correction, affect a child's educational performance adversely. This means that children with glasses are considered visually handicapped if their condition is severe enough to affect their educational performance.

Visual handicaps may stem from a number of different problems, including myopia, hyperopia, cataracts, glaucoma, infectious diseases, muscular problems, neurological problems, and congenital blindness. Many visual handicaps can be improved through use of glasses or contact lenses. Sometimes surgery improves a condition.

The visually handicapped child can often be helped by physical education simply because of the opportunity it provides to develop other modes of sensory input—tactile, auditory, and kinesthetic. Often children with visual handicaps have had a restricted movement experience and may, thus, have fallen behind the normal development of their peers. This kind of developmental deficit can only be remediated through an increased quantity of movement experience.

More seriously, visually handicapped children may need to have the play environment modified somewhat for them so that they may take part successfully. Usually this means the substitution of a different sensory channel for information ordinarily acquired through sight. For example, ropes or buoys

POSTURE RATING CHART

Grade 4 5 6 7 8 9 10 11 12
Rater's Initials
Date of Test

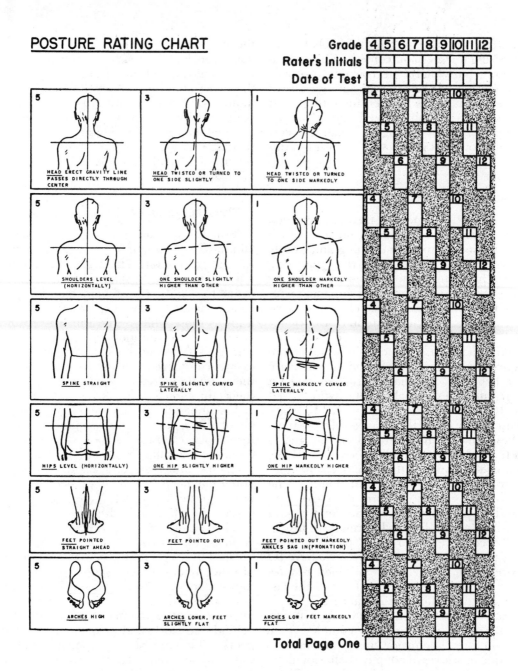

5	3	1
HEAD ERECT GRAVITY LINE PASSES DIRECTLY THROUGH CENTER	HEAD TWISTED OR TURNED TO ONE SIDE SLIGHTLY	HEAD TWISTED OR TURNED TO ONE SIDE MARKEDLY
SHOULDERS LEVEL (HORIZONTALLY)	ONE SHOULDER SLIGHTLY HIGHER THAN OTHER	ONE SHOULDER MARKEDLY HIGHER THAN OTHER
SPINE STRAIGHT	SPINE SLIGHTLY CURVED LATERALLY	SPINE MARKEDLY CURVED LATERALLY
HIPS LEVEL (HORIZONTALLY)	ONE HIP SLIGHTLY HIGHER	ONE HIP MARKEDLY HIGHER
FEET POINTED STRAIGHT AHEAD	FEET POINTED OUT	FEET POINTED OUT MARKEDLY ANKLES SAG IN (PRONATION)
ARCHES HIGH	ARCHES LOWER, FEET SLIGHTLY FLAT	ARCHES LOW FEET MARKEDLY FLAT

Total Page One

FIGURE 12.4   Posture rating chart. (From New York State Education Department, Bureau of Physical Education and Safety Education.)

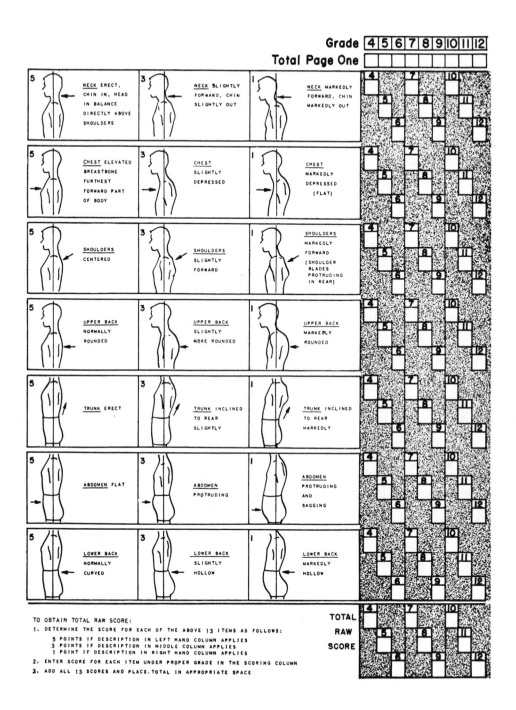

Grade 4 5 6 7 8 9 10 11 12

Total Page One

5 NECK ERECT, CHIN IN, HEAD IN BALANCE DIRECTLY ABOVE SHOULDERS
3 NECK SLIGHTLY FORWARD, CHIN SLIGHTLY OUT
1 NECK MARKEDLY FORWARD, CHIN MARKEDLY OUT

5 CHEST ELEVATED BREASTBONE FURTHEST FORWARD PART OF BODY
3 CHEST SLIGHTLY DEPRESSED
1 CHEST MARKEDLY DEPRESSED (FLAT)

5 SHOULDERS CENTERED
3 SHOULDERS SLIGHTLY FORWARD
1 SHOULDERS MARKEDLY FORWARD (SHOULDER BLADES PROTRUDING IN REAR)

5 UPPER BACK NORMALLY ROUNDED
3 UPPER BACK SLIGHTLY MORE ROUNDED
1 UPPER BACK MARKEDLY ROUNDED

5 TRUNK ERECT
3 TRUNK INCLINED TO REAR SLIGHTLY
1 TRUNK INCLINED TO REAR MARKEDLY

5 ABDOMEN FLAT
3 ABDOMEN PROTRUDING
1 ABDOMEN PROTRUDING AND SAGGING

5 LOWER BACK NORMALLY CURVED
3 LOWER BACK SLIGHTLY HOLLOW
1 LOWER BACK MARKEDLY HOLLOW

TO OBTAIN TOTAL RAW SCORE:

1. DETERMINE THE SCORE FOR EACH OF THE ABOVE 13 ITEMS AS FOLLOWS:

    5 POINTS IF DESCRIPTION IN LEFT HAND COLUMN APPLIES
    3 POINTS IF DESCRIPTION IN MIDDLE COLUMN APPLIES
    1 POINT IF DESCRIPTION IN RIGHT HAND COLUMN APPLIES

2. ENTER SCORE FOR EACH ITEM UNDER PROPER GRADE IN THE SCORING COLUMN

3. ADD ALL 13 SCORES AND PLACE TOTAL IN APPROPRIATE SPACE

TOTAL RAW SCORE

in a swimming pool allow a partially sighted or blind child to know where to go and how to proceed. Often the partially sighted child may need the help of a peer to move in a game setting. This help entails directional guidance only. Special sound stimuli can also be added to movement and game settings to provide special cues for the visually handicapped child.

Postural Deviations

Postural deviations are of two types. *Functional deviations* refer to those caused by inappropriate development of the antigravity muscle groups. *Structural deviations* refer to those involving skeletal abnormalities. While physical educators may be able to help in the treatment of structural deviations—on the advice of an orthopedic physician—it is functional deviation that can most often be improved through a well-planned physical education program.

Many children are diagnosed as having functional postural deviations. One means of evaluating posture which may be useful is that included in the New York State Physical Fitness Test. This assessment involves thirteen areas of the body. The rating chart (Figure 12.4) shows three profiles for each area: the correct position (five points), a slight deviation (three points), and a pronounced deviation (one point) from the correct position. The examiner rates each area on the five-three-one basis, and the total point value is the student's score.

The testing area consists of a plumb line suspended over a line on which the subject stands. This line is three feet in front of a screen. Another line is drawn at a right angle to the first line and extends ten feet farther back from the screen (a total of thirteen feet). This is where the examiner is positioned in order to view the student against the screen.

The student is rated from two viewpoints. In one position the child stands facing the screen, so that the plumb line bisects the back of the head, runs down the spine, and passes down between the legs and feet. Lateral deviations are assessed from this position:

Tilted Head. When a child habitually tilts the head toward right or left, the tilt is often symptomatic of vision or hearing impairment. Usually such individuals are unaware of the tilt; when given opportunities to become more aware of head position by aligning the head over the shoulders when facing a mirror, the tilt frequently corrects itself. Over time the head tilt may cause a shortening of the neck muscles on the side of the tilt. Slow static stretch and hold exercises for the muscles on the side of the neck opposite the tilt often corrects this problem.

Wry neck results from a shortening of one of the strong neck muscles. This causes a rotation of the head to the opposite side and a tilt to the same side. The condition may be acquired or congenital. When acquired, stretching exercises are recommended in combination with remediation of the visual or auditory loss which generally precipitated the problem. When congenital, the condition may be corrected at an early age by surgery and/or bracing. When observed in schoolchildren, referral to a physician is appropriate.

Uneven shoulders. Wry neck is often accompanied by a raised shoulder. The lateral spinal curvature in the neck and upper back region may eventually provoke a compensatory lateral curvature in the middle back. When the two shoulders are of unequal height, scoliosis should be suspected.

Lateral curves of the spine. Scoliosis is a lateral curvature of the spine. Although the condition begins with a single curve, it usually consists of a primary curve and a compensatory curve in the opposite direction. Usually appearing in early childhood, scoliosis may arrest itself without treatment. Often, however, it becomes progressively debilitating. It is more serious than any of the other common posture deviations and should be referred to a physician.

Scoliosis is more prevalent in girls and among thin and frail children, but it is not confined to either. About 75 percent of the known cases are due to disease, about 12.5 percent are congenital, while the other 12.5 percent result from paralysis or partial paralysis of muscles on one side of the spinal column. Many individuals seem to have mild lateral curvatures and other asymmetries of disease origin which do not affect their health, happiness, or productivity. When scoliosis is not identified as such until the early adult years, the condition has probably arrested itself and should not be a matter for undue concern. However, the younger the child, the more serious the condition, since there are more years of growth ahead.

Uneven hips. Differences in hip height may be caused by scoliosis, uneven leg length, or the habit of standing on one leg for long periods of time. If simply due to habit, an awareness of body position—which can come from aligning body segments in front of a mirror—will generally solve the problem. If associated with scoliosis or uneven leg length, the child should be referred to a physician.

Pronation. Of all the postural foot defects, pronation is the most common. It involves taking the weight of the body on the inner borders of the feet and rolling inward on the ankles. Flat-footedness is a closely related disorder. Students with pronated feet often tend to toe outward and to complain of foot discomfort and ache in the calf muscles. The tendons in the back-ankle portion of the foot bow outward. Markedly pronated feet should be examined by a physician.

Pronation may occur in early childhood as well as during other growth periods. In affluent areas well over 10 to 20 percent of the children may wear corrective shoes prescribed by a physician, which are designed to ameliorate the condition. In these shoes the medial border is built up in such a way as to force the weight of the body to be taken on the outer border of the foot. Children who wear corrective shoes should not change to gymnasium shoes for physical education. Also they should not go barefooted without the permission of their orthopedist.

Flatfoot. Flatfoot may be congenital or postural. The black race is predisposed to congenital flatfoot. If the muscles of the legs and feet are strong and flexible and the body is in good alignment, the congenital flatfoot is not considered a postural deviation. Infants are born with varying degrees of flat feet. Strong arches develop as the natural consequence of vigorous kicking and strenuous locomotor activities. Faulty body mechanics and improper alignment of the foot and leg may create an imbalance in muscle strength, which in turn prevents maintenance of the longitudinal arch in the correct position. Almost always the same poor posture practices which cause flatfoot result also in pronation and toeing outward. Knock-knees frequently accompany flatfoot also. If flatfoot occurs with pronation, toeing outward, and/ or knock-knees, referral to a physician is appropriate.

The child then turns to the left and stands sideward, so that the plumb line passes in a line through the ear, shoulder, hip, knee, and ankle. The left lateral malleolus (ankle bone) must be in line with the plumb bob. Anteroposterior posture is rated from this position.

Forward head and neck. When the ear lobe is not in alignment with the tip of the shoulder, forward head and neck is diagnosed. In its mildest form the head tends to droop forward with the condition generally increasing so slowly that most persons are unaware of it.

In the mild stage the best ameliorative exercise is practice in discriminating between good and poor alignment. Balancing and carrying relatively heavy weights on the head while performing locomotor movements increase head and neck position awareness, as does movement in front of a mirror. Exercises which help correct and prevent this condition are (a) alternately rotating the head slowly to one side until the chin touches the shoulder and then turning to the other side and (b) touching the ear to the shoulder, alternating sides.

Forward head and neck may eventually become normal carriage in our sedentary society, where emphasis is placed on early book learning and a large proportion of the population holds desk jobs. It is estimated that 70 percent of all American schoolchildren have some degree of forward head and neck.

The more severe cases are usually accompanied by kyphosis, round shoulders, a prominence of the seventh neck vertebrae, and excess adipose tissue over the seventh vertebrae. This condition requires the attention of a physician.

Hollow chest. The most common of the chest deviations, hollow chest, denotes the relaxation and depression of the chest which normally accompanies round shoulders and/or kyphosis. It requires the attention of a physician.

Round shoulders. Round shoulders is a forward deviation of the the shoulder girdle in which the scapulae are pulled sideward and tilted, bringing the shoulder tips in front of the normal gravitational line. Round shoulders should not be confused with kyphosis. They are distinctly different problems.

The incidence of round shoulders is high among persons who work at desk jobs, among persons in poor health, or among those who demonstrate general body weakness. Athletes often exhibit round shoulders because of overdevelopment of the arm, shoulder, and chest muscles resulting from sport and aquatic activities which stress forward movements of the arms. This tendency may be counteracted by engaging in an exercise program designed specifically to keep the back muscles equal in strength. Perhaps the easiest way to do this is to swim a few laps of the back crawl each day. Certainly, the well-rounded athlete who enjoys many different activities is less likely to develop round shoulders than one who specializes almost exclusively in tennis, basketball, or volleyball.

Exercises for round shoulders should simultaneously stretch the tightened front muscles and strengthen back muscles. The following exercises are effective. (a) Assume a front lying position on a bench. The hands grasp dumbbells on the floor to each side of the body. The weights are lifted toward the ceiling as far as possible, keeping the arms straight. This position should be held and the chin should remain on the bench. (b) Sit cross-legged with the head and back flat against the wall. The arms are bent at shoulder height with the palms facing the chest, fingertips touching, and the elbows against

the wall. Keeping the head and spine against the wall, press the elbows back with as much force as possible. (c) Lie on back, arms out to side, palms down, knees flexed, and feet spread. Raise hips and arch back so that shoulders are off mat, supporting weight on feet, hands, and back of head in a modified wrestler's bridge.

Protruding shoulder blades. Sometimes the scapulae are pulled to the sides away from the rib cage. This condition is considered normal when it occurs in preschool and elementary-school children but abnormal when it occurs in pubescent or older individuals. Hanging and climbing activities help ameliorate the condition.

Many girls in our society do not outgrow winged scapulae as do boys. The condition is often accompanied by round shoulders. If this condition is pronounced or accompanied by other postural deviations during or after puberty, a physician should be consulted.

Kyphosis. An exaggerated spinal curve in the shoulder and upper back region is the condition commonly known as kyphosis, humpback, hunchback, or round upper back. Although severely retarded individuals whose mobility is limited often exhibit kyphosis at a young age, this condition is rarely found among normal children in the public-school setting. Kyphosis is usually, but not always, accompanied by round shoulders, hollow chest, and forward head and neck. When observed in a child, referral to a physician is appropriate. Exercises which prevent or ameliorate the condition strengthen the back muscles and stretch front chest muscles. The following exercises may be helpful. (a) Prone, lying on a table with head and trunk hanging downward, head supported on a chair. In this position, with hands clasped behind the neck, raise the trunk slowly to a horizontal position. (b) Prone, lying with hands on hips. Raise head and shoulders approximately two inches off floor. (c) Prone, lying on a table with arms in overhead position. Do breaststroke. (d) Hanging, facing outward, from stall bars or a horizontal bar. e) Sitting in chair, top of chair at about midthoracic level, hands behind head. Lean trunk backward as you adduct scapula and pull arms backward.

Protruding abdomen. Abdominal protrusion is normal in the young child and is usually accompanied by lordosis. Participation in the vigorous activities of the elementary-school years should result in a flat, taut abdomen in adolescence and early adulthood. Abdominal exercises in a physical education class are a poor substitute for natural play activities. They are not recommended as long as the child derives pleasure from running, jumping, climbing, hanging, and skipping. However, if exercises are necessary, several are particularly appropriate. (a) Cross-lateral creeping, in which the right arm moves forward at the same time as the left knee moves forward. (b) The angry cat exercise, in which one alternates humping the back and letting the head hang down with extending the spine with the head held high. (c) Drumming by striking alternating feet against the floor while lying on the back. (d) Alternate knee and elbow touch in opposition with hands behind the neck. (e) Sit-up with trunk twist for maximal activity of abdominals. Feet should not be held down.

Lordosis. Lordosis, also called sway or hollow back, is an exaggeration of the normal curve in the lower back. This condition causes the pelvis to be out of correct alignment. Correction of this condition, at least in the early stages, is largely a matter of increasing body position awareness so that the student can feel the difference between an anterior and a posterior tilt. Alternating anterior and posterior pelvic tilts should be practiced while lying, kneeling, sitting, standing, and performing various locomotor activities. Activities such as the backbend, which emphasizes backward bending of the lower back, are contraindicated.

Weak abdominals almost universally accompany lordosis. For this reason strength exercises for the abdominals should be undertaken along with stretching exercises for the tight lower back muscles. The following exercises prevent and help improve lordosis. (a) Bicycling motion of legs while lying supine with back flattened to maintain contact with the floor. (b) Paint the rainbow. From a supine lying position, flex hips until feet are vertically overhead and twelve to eighteen inches from it. (c) Angry cat exercise. (d) Cross-sitting forward bend. From a cross-sitting position with hands clasped behind neck, bend forward so that head approaches floor without lifting the seat. Maintain a slow stretch for several seconds.

It is important that an instrument such as this be used with children so that problems can be identified and remediated as soon as possible. The longer a problem goes unidentified, the harder it becomes to remediate.

13

developmentally engineered equipment and playgrounds

The physical environment has an enormous impact on the development and learning of motor skills and on the development and maintenance of physical fitness and normal posture. Abundant evidence indicates that youngsters are highly responsive to the challenge of an appropriate environment and equally susceptible to the deprivations of an impoverished one. Children who are provided with environmental opportunities to learn motor skills and develop fitness generally do so. On the other hand, when environmental opportunities are limited or unavailable, motor skills are often poorly learned and fitness levels generally remain low.

Most of a child's motor education derives from informal play experiences in home and school environments. Such play experiences are predominantly interactions between the child and whatever equipment and apparatus the environment contains. Yet, commercially available motor education equipment and playgrounds rarely acknowledge and facilitate motor skill acquisition and physical fitness in a sensitive manner.

Educators and parents directly responsible for the design of these environments need to select commercially available equipment and apparatus effectively. Addi-

tionally, they may need to supplement such equipment with homemade items. This chapter suggests design strategies that may help in the selection and construction of developmentally appropriate equipment and playgrounds.

DEVELOPMENTALLY ENGINEERED EQUIPMENT

Accommodating Physical Growth of Young Children

Young children differ widely in growth status and growth rate with regard to body weight, body height, proportional growth of various body segments, skeletal ossification, distribution of fat and muscle tissue, postural characteristics, and somatotype. Each child's potential for learning to perform motor skills well is limited and shaped to a significant extent by the child's unique configuration of growth characteristics. No two children are alike.

Research has suggested that the learning of sport skills by children may be facilitated by the use of lighter-weight equipment. The *Proposed Safety Standard for Public Playground Equipment*, prepared by the National Recrea-

FIGURE 13.1 Vertical ladders.

FIGURE 13.2. Staircases.

tion and Parks Association (1976) for the Consumer Product Safety Commission, suggests that playground apparatus be designed by manufacturers for specific age groups and be labeled as such before being marketed. Designs should be based on appropriate anthropometric data (for example, maximum heights, gripping contact surface, clearance, step height, and so on). Additionally, three equipment design strategies seem to be particularly successful in acknowledging the characteristically wide ranges of growth rate and status normally encountered among preschool and elementary-school children.

The first equipment design strategy is to provide children with several pieces of equipment which are the same shape but which differ in size. For climbing, such apparatus might include the following: three vertical ladders, each with rungs a different distance apart (Figure 13.1); five staircases, each with different stair heights (Figure 13.2); three horizontal bars, each at a different distance from the ground (Figure 13.3). Examples appropriate to throwing include: three yarn balls of similar weight but differing in size; three suspended hoop targets differing in diameter (Figure 13.4); four balls, 8½" in diameter, differing in weight. Examples appropriate to catching include: several beach balls differing in diameter; bleach containers differing in size, with the bottom removed or funnels differing in size (Figure 13.5); four different-size sponge balls suspended from inverted hangman's nooses (Figure 4.19). Examples appropriate to striking include: several plastic bats differing in length but similar in weight and width of striking surface area; several racquets of similar length and weight but dif-

FIGURE 13.3. Horizontal bars.

FIGURE 13.4 Hoop targets.

fering in size of striking surface area. Examples appropriate to running include: three inclines differing in steepness and three running distances of different lengths. Examples appropriate to jumping include: six rubber balls, each suspended at different heights from pieces of sash cord, in graduated order (Figure 13.6); five wands supported by blocks of different height (Figure 13.7).

A second equipment design strategy is to provide equipment which children may change in order to accommodate their own

FIGURE 13.6 Six rubber balls suspended at different heights from pieces of sash cord.

FIGURE 13.5 Bleach containers and funnels.

FIGURE 13.7 Wands and blocks.

unique growth status. For climbing, such apparatus might include: an inclined sliding board which children can raise or lower on trestle bars; a balance beam which children may change so that either a two-, four-, or six-inch wide balance surface may be used for balancing activities (Figure 13.8); a ladder which has removable rungs (Figure 13.9). Examples appropriate to throwing include: a metal hoop target of adjustable height; a small piece of black rubber floor matting with two yellow footprints painted on it which children may move toward or away from a target; a moving target sus-

FIGURE 13.9 Ladder with removable rungs.

FIGURE 13.8 Balance beam of adjustable width.

FIGURE 13.10 Pendulum target.

FIGURE 13.11 Pin targets and coiled rope ball support.

pended on the end of a flexible plastic rod which children may choose to move pendularly at rapid or slow speeds (Figure 13.10). Examples appropriate to kicking include: a goal of adjustable width made of traffic cones which children may choose to place close together or farther apart; plastic pins or Indian clubs that serve as targets which children may space at varied distances from one another (Figure 13.11). An example appropriate to catching is a large muslin sheet whose incline may be adjusted. Children can catch balls rolling off of it (Figure 4.18). An example appropriate to jumping and leaping activities is a pair of standards and a crossbar which children may raise or lower (Figure 13.12). Examples appropriate to striking include a ball which may be adjusted in elevation by means of an inverted hangman's noose from which it is suspended, and a batting tee of adjustable height with a funnel top (Figure 4.13). An example appropriate to climbing is a graduated Swedish Box. Children may use one, two, or three sections, depending on the level they select.

A third equipment design strategy is to provide children with pieces of equipment that incorporate gradual gradations in size. For climbing, examples might include: a walking board which is wide at one end and increasingly narrower toward the opposite end (Figure 13.13) and a horizontal ladder which has rungs spaced close together at one end and increasingly farther apart toward the opposite end. An example appropriate to leaping and jumping is a long elastic cord fastened to the ground at one end and to a standard five feet from the ground at the other end (Figure 13.14). An example appropriate to kicking is a *Three-Tiered Kicking Target* made of muslin (Figure 4.12).

FIGURE 13.13 Narrowing walking board.

FIGURE 13.12 Hurdle standards and wands.

Equipment that Provides Knowledge of Results (KR)

It is well known that information about the acceptability and correctness of facets— or of the whole—of a motor skill performance very much facilitates the learning and performance of that skill. KR may be defined as a score presented verbally or mechanically to a performer as a representation of the outcome of a movement. KR serves informational, motivational, and reinforcement functions.

A number of equipment design strategies which are sensitive to the major functions of KR seem particularly capable of facilitating the learning and performance of motor tasks by preschool and elementary-school children. Color may be manipulated to serve KR functions. Examples include: rope and vertical ladders with rungs of different colors; lines of different color placed at gradated distances from throwing targets; sections of a long elastic cord inclined from the floor to a four-foot elevation to which are attached whiffle balls of various colors (Figure 13.14); and a rubber floor mat, to be used for long jumping, which is divided into equal sections, each section colored differently (Figure 4.5). Numbers, letters, and words, depending on the reading skills of the child, may also be used to serve KR functions. Examples include: a jump and reach task in which the child must touch a piece of chalk to a progressively numbered piece of vinyl af-

FIGURE 13.15 Jump and reach vinyl strip.

fixed to a wall (Figure 13.15); and a rubber floor mat, to be used for long jumping, which is divided into equal sections, each section labeled with ordered single letters of the alphabet.

Timing devices may be used to provide KR. For running, examples include a graduated hourglass device made from large plastic containers that have been filled with birdseed (Figure 4.4) and a large clock with a single arm which is started and stopped by pressure-sensitive mats. Sound may also be managed to serve KR functions. Examples include: a sheet metal target; a bicycle horn at the top of a vertical ladder; a series of aluminum pipes suspended from a wooden dowel rod by string, which serve as a kicking target (Figure 4.9); a stabilometer which

FIGURE 13.14 Inclined elastic cord.

FIGURE 13.16 Snoopy Kicking Target.

"buzzes" when the balance platform is parallel to the ground; and a *Snoopy Kicking Target* that rings when kicked because of bells attached to the target face (Figure 13.16). Light may also be manipulated to serve KR functions. An example would be a throwing target incorporating four circular targets of different size which, when struck by a thrown ball of yarn, depresses microswitches which cause light bulbs of similar color to the

targets to light up and stay on for adjustable amounts of time (Figure 13.17).

The movement of different pieces of apparatus may be manipulated to serve KR functions. Examples include: a *Cookie Monster Windowshade Target,* mounted on a wooden board and hung from a wall, which will "pop-up" when struck by a ball (Figure 4.1); a *Sylvester and Tweety Bird Target,* made of two thicknesses of cardboard, which has Tweety Bird fall on the floor out of Sylvester's arms when struck by a ball sent with sufficient force (Figure 13.18); a *Dr. Seuss Space Ship Target* which, when struck by a ball, spins around a central axis that is parallel to the ground (Figure 4.11); a *Bugs Bunny Target,* whose teeth will fall forward on a hinge if they are struck with sufficient force (Figure 13.19). Encapsulation is another means of providing for KR functions. Children are often effectively motivated to persevere in kicking, striking, and throwing activities when the balls that they are sending toward targets disappear into the target. Yarn balls thrown into the opening of a large box-like *Flower Target* disappear and later reemerge via an internal ramp that sends them back in the direction of the thrower (Figure 4.2). *Mouth Targets,* muslin sheets with large holes in them, which are suspended from lengths of sash cord sewn into a top hem and decorated to resemble a mouth or cave, can be

FIGURE 13.18 Sylvester and Tweety Bird Target.

FIGURE 13.17 Pink Dragon Target.

FIGURE 13.19 Bugs Bunny Target.

presented singly or in series to encapsulate balls sent toward them in striking, kicking, and throwing activities (Figures 4.10 and 4.15). Balls that are struck, kicked, and

FIGURE 13.20 Tornado Target and coiled rope ball support.

thrown can be caught and held in the long tail of a net cage-like target called a *Tornado Target* (Figure 13.20).

Facilitating the Acquisition of Ballistic Skills

Throwing, striking, and kicking stationary balls at stationary targets, long jumping for distance, and vertical jumping for height to a stationary target are all motor skills which are primarily ballistic in nature. A key to the successful design of appropriate apparatus for such activities is acknowledging the unique mechanical demands that learning these skills makes on children. The feature which is central to efficient performance of all ballistic skills is effective force production. Consequently, ways of encouraging force production need to be incorporated into successful apparatus design.

Effective force production is influenced by the distance and size characteristics of targets. Targets need to be established at challenging distances in order to encourage children to produce forceful movements. They also need to be large enough so that children will not attend to the need to be accurate at the expense of producing forceful executions. Targets which are too small and too close to the performer seriously interfere with the ballistic character of throwing, striking, and kicking performances. Examples of targets that illustrate these distance and size characteristics include the *Mouth Targets* (Figures 4.10, 4.14 and 4.15), *Cookie Monster Target* (Figure 4.1), *Sylvester and Tweety Bird Target* (Figure 13.18), *Dr. Seuss Space Ship Target* (Figure 4.11), *Flower Target* (Figure 4.2), *Snoopy Kicking Target* (Figure 13.16), *Three-Tiered Kicking Target* (Figure 4.12), and *Tornado Target* (Figure 13.20). Low rope and traffic cone barriers (Figures 4.1 and 4.2), *Neat Feet* (Figures 4.1, 4.13, 4.15 and 4.16), and coiled rope ball supports (Figure 13.20) are effective devices for defining desirable distance requirements.

Additionally, employing targets which provide only positive feedback when desirable amounts of force and accuracy are produced by a performer facilitates the learning of ballistic skills. Windowshades (Figure 4.1) which "pop-up" only when struck with sufficient force and which can be adjusted by loosening or tightening the central core are an example of such targets. Another example is a *Bugs Bunny Target* (Figure 13.19), whose teeth fall forward on a hinged support only when it is struck with sufficient force and accuracy. Still another is the *Dr. Seuss Space Ship Target*, which rotates at increasing speeds around a central axis when struck with increasingly forceful kicks (Figure 4.11). The *Sound Curtain Target*, made from lengths of aluminum pipe suspended from a long dowel rod, which makes noise when struck by a kicked ball, is another example of such a target (Figure 4.9).

Devices that encourage weight shift in striking, kicking, and throwing activities significantly contribute to performance efficiency. *Neat Feet*, yellow footprints painted on black floor-runner material, serve to remind children of the need for weight shift (Figures 4.1, 4.13, and 4.15). Similarly, when a pressure mat connected to a light bulb is used in conjunction with *Neat Feet*, it also serves to encourage a desirable weight shift (Figure 4.2).

Two additional devices encourage pelvic-spinal rotation, opposition, and sequential movement of body parts, which are part of efficient striking, kicking, and throwing performance. An inclined plastic rope fixed to a basketball hoop and floor plate (Figure 4.3) provides a useful example for throwing. When children attempt to sling a foot-long plastic pipe, two inches in diameter, up the rope toward a cymbal and colored tape markers, efficient force production is facilitated. A plastic ball inside a mesh bag which hangs from a piece of sash cord that is parallel to the ground and slightly above the head level of a child will encourage efficient force production when the task is to strike the ball over the supporting sash cord as many times as possible (see Figure 4.16).

Adjustable supports and other devices which do not interfere with the natural trajectory characteristics of struck or kicked balls also encourage desirable force production and accuracy. Examples include: an ad-justable batting tee (Figure 4.13); a detachable ball supported by an inverted hangman's noose with a velcro fastener (Figure 4.14); the *Striking Machine*, which employs an air jet to support foam balls (Figure 4.15); a coiled rope support for balls which are to be kicked (Figures 4.9, 4.11, and 4.12).

The length, surface area, weight, and grip characteristics of striking implements also influence the efficiency of force production. Racquets and bats are most effectively grouped by similar weight but gradated length, and by similar length but gradated size of striking surface. In striking activities implements that are shorter, lighter, and have larger surface areas are easier to use than implements that are longer, heavier, and have smaller surface areas. Examples of striking apparatus that demonstrate these concepts include oversized plastic *Monster Bats* (Figure 4.14), ping-pong paddles, junior-size tennis racquets, badminton racquets, and racquetball racquets. Care must also be taken to see that children can grip racquets and bats comfortably.

The size, weight, and rebound characteristics of balls used in ballistic activities should also be carefully considered. Children should be encouraged to progress from larger to smaller balls and from fairly lightweight to heavier balls in striking and kicking activities. Children should progress from lightweight, easily held balls to larger and heavier balls in throwing activities. Balls which do not rebound or which have limited rebound characteristics are far more desirable than balls that do rebound.

Jumping activities are also ballistic in nature. Consequently, force production is essential to efficient performance of all jumping skills. Practitioners must identify different types of apparatus that will encourage the production of force in jumping activities. For example, the child can jump toward a tin can target of adjustable height that is suspended from sash cord which is located at a 45-degree angle from the floor in front of the child. The can makes noise when the child jumps and touches it during flight (Figure 4.8).

Facilitating the Acquisition of Receipt Skills

Motor skills involving the receipt of projectiles include all catching, kicking, and striking skills in which a performer is required to respond to a moving object. A key to the successful design of developmentally appropriate apparatus for activities involving these skills is acknowledging the unique visual-perceptual information-processing demands that learning these skills makes on children. Young and unskilled children appear less capable of (a) processing as much visual information, (b) processing visual information as rapidly, or (c) discriminating task-relevant visual information in receipt task performance situations, as compared with older and more skilled children.

The equipment design strategy should control the amount of visual information which must be processed in receipt activities. For example: children should be asked to respond to stationary balls, balloons (balls) dropped through the air, balls rolled along the ground, balls rolled down ramps, balls traveling in pendular trajectories, balls bounced along the ground, and aerial balls, in that order. The amount of visual information which must be processed increases as the complexity of the movement change characteristics increases. Responding to the stationary ball is easiest, since it does not move. A balloon dropped through the air travels very slowly and at a consistent speed due to air resistance. A ball rolled along the ground travels at progressively slower speeds due to friction. A ball rolled down a ramp travels at increasingly faster speeds due to gravity. Balls with pendular trajectories increase speed as they travel toward the bottom of their arc and decrease speed as they travel toward the top of their arc. A ball bounced along the ground increases speed as it leaves a bounce, slows at the top of a bounce, and speeds once again as it drops from the top of a bounce. Aerial balls, due to spin, wind resistance, and speed present the most difficult information-processing situations.

The equipment design strategy should consider the speed with which visual information must be processed in receipt activities. For example: large wooden, cloth, and net ramps (Figure 4.18) which may be adjusted in terms of their length, incline, and elevation from the ground allow for a good deal of additional control over the amount of time and speed balls of various size and weight travel down the ramp prior to a required gross motor receipt response. As children become more skilled, visual information-processing demands may be intensified by increasing the incline of the ramp, decreasing the length of the ramp, decreasing the size of the ball, or increasing the weight of the ball. Adding increasing amounts of masking tape to a balloon dropped through the air for striking or catching activities provides another application of the same equipment design principle, since it progressively increases weight. Still another application involves increasing the traveling distance of a ramped ball, a ball traveling along the ground, or a ball bouncing along the ground. When you increase the traveling distance of balls, you give a child more decision time in which to make needed spatial adjustments.

The equipment design strategy should acknowledge children's limited visual-perceptual discrimination capabilities. Initially high contrast should be provided between the color of the projectile being responded to and the color of the background against which it moves. A yellow ball traveling against a grey background is more desirable than a white ball traveling against a white background. Additionally, the complexity of the background against which the projectile moves must be minimized. A solid-colored ball traveling through the air against a solid-colored wall is more desirable than a yellow ball traveling through the air against a wall on which are painted many primary-colored geometric shapes. As children become more skilled, the contrast and background complexity requirements of the tasks may be made more challenging. Target movement characteristics should also be considered. Initially targets should move from left to right and right to left in front of the performer. More skilled children should be given opportunities to respond to targets that move toward them and away from them.

Encouraging Normal Posture and Physical Fitness

The posture of preschool and primary-school children is characterized by protruding abdomen, exaggerated lumbar curve, and prominent scapulae. However, by the end of the intermediate grades these postural characteristics may no longer be considered normal. Such posture, along with rounded shoulders, pronated feet, and forward head testify to our inability to provide formal instructional opportunities and/or playgrounds throughout the preschool and elementary-school years that nurture the development of sufficient muscular strength. The development of normal posture does not occur unless the abdominal, shoulder girdle, arm, and leg muscles increase in strength with growth. They increase in strength only when repeatedly stressed in climbing, hanging, and swinging opportunities provided over long periods of time on playgrounds and in other physically demanding formal instructional settings. For this reason the provision of challenging and demanding hanging, climbing, and swinging opportunities on playgrounds is a necessity.

The physical environment of the school can do a good deal to establish and maintain each of the several components of physical fitness: cardiovascular-respiratory fitness, muscular strength and endurance fitness, flexibility fitness, and body-weight fitness. The provision of vita parcours, or fitness trails, which have activity stations at the beginning and end designed to increase flexibility fitness; stations in the middle designed to increase muscular strength and endurance; and which demand that users jog or run the length of the trail serve not only the needs of schoolchildren but also those of the adult community. Challenge courses, or obstacle courses, serve a similar function, though their contribution to the development of cardiovascular-respiratory fitness is generally negligible (Figure 13.21). Quar-

ter-mile tracks and cycling/jogging trails strongly encourage cardiovascular-respiratory fitness, while swimming pools encourage strength and cardiovascular-respiratory fitness.

Providing for Children's Safety

Three major types of hazards are related to equipment and playground apparatus: hazards associated with defects in construction and design, hazards associated with improper equipment installation and maintenance, and hazards resulting from human error. At the present time there is no mandatory safety standard regulating the construction, design, installation, or maintenance of private or public playground apparatus, sports equipment, or hand-constructed apparatus normally found on playgrounds. In general, however, the following recommendations reflect the safety factors most often considered by playground and small-equipment manufacturers.

1. Equipment should be designed for a specific developmental range and should be used by the group for which it is developed. Three- to five-year-old children may be exposed to unnecessary hazards (maximum height, gripping surface of ladders, step heights) on equipment designed for nine- to twelve-year-olds. This standard may be accommodated by employing the recommendations made earlier in this chapter with regard to physical growth and by constructing separate play areas for different age groups. Elementary schools may provide one play area for kindergarten through second-grade children and another for third- through sixth-grade children. This arrangement not only provides for the involvement of larger numbers of children in a given time period, but the duplication of certain types of equipment at different scales cuts down on equipment wear.

2. Equipment used on playgrounds must be durable. Materials should have a demonstrated record of durability or they should be tested. Manufacturers increasingly subject their apparatus to load tests after they are fully assembled. This is necessary for deter-

FIGURE 13.21 Obstacle courses encourage the development of desirable levels of muscular strength and endurance as well as flexibility. (Courtesy of Miracle & Jamison, Grinnell, Iowa.)

mining whether linked parts will collectively and individually withstand the loads to which they will be subjected under normal use. Equipment needs to be installed in a manner that will prevent tipping and sliding while in use. For heavy equipment this usually implies fixing the equipment in concrete or attaching equipment to anchor bolts set in concrete footings. Locking devices should be provided for all bolts so that they do not work loose or so that they may not be removed by hand. Hooks and rings should be manufactured from high carbon steel to ensure their durability. All exposed bolts must be covered by a permanent cover that cannot be removed by hand or they must be countersunk or recessed.

Definite policies should be established for repairing, marking, and maintaining large and small equipment. When a piece of equipment falls out of repair, a teacher must make a decision as to whether the item needs to be withdrawn for repair, used in its pre-sent state, or discarded. Often items requiring repair need attention outside of class hours. Occasionally equipment is best used in a state of disrepair until it can no longer be salvaged. Sometimes equipment in disrepair is unsafe and should be withdrawn from use immediately. Rubber balls can, in some cases, be repaired by means of a vulcanizing patch. For others, a hard-setting rubber preparation is useful. Broken wooden bats need to be discarded. Taping around the breaks will not make them safe. Balls need to be inflated to the recommended pressure marked on the ball using an accurate gauge. Ball pressure should be periodically checked. The needle used to inflate the ball should be moistened before it is inserted into a valve. Children need to learn not to sit on balls or kick balls not specifically made for kicking. When not in use, balls should be slightly deflated. Leather balls should be cleaned with an approved ball conditioner. Mats should be stacked or hung. Plastic or plastic-covered mats should be periodically cleaned with soap and water, as should other plastic equipment. Equipment that is likely to warp should be laid in a flat position. Bats should be taped to prevent slippage. Wire baskets are often good containers for small equipment and can be placed on shelves for easy viewing and accessibility. Wooden equipment should be periodically inspected for rough edges. Sanding, repainting, or varnishing should be done when necessary. All equipment should be marked. Marking can be done with indelible pencils, paint, stencil ink, or a marking set available at sporting goods establishments. Unfortunately, few marking systems are permanent, and re-marking at regular intervals may be necessary. Electric burning pencils and stamps are also useful on some equipment. If equipment is issued to classrooms, a color system could be established to keep track of each classroom's equipment.

3. The potential impact of swinging elements must be within certain safety tolerances. Swing seats may be purchased that are made from rubber, wood, plastic, or metal. Only the belt-type rubber seats are acceptable—the others frequently cause injuries. There should be sufficient clearance between moving elements and between moving elements and fixed structures to prevent collisions under normal use. Swings that travel in a straight line require less space on each side than do horizontal tire swings which move in a 360-degree range.

4. The velocity of rotating equipment should be limited. This refers to the speed of the outer edge of the equipment. The outer edge should be of a smooth, circular design, and the base should have no openings accessible to any part of the body. This standard is directed at equipment such as merry-go-rounds. Speed controllers and improvements in design have led to a new look for this particular piece of equipment.

5. Slides should be designed in such a manner that speed of descent and landing are within a safe range. Landing speed from a slide is influenced by the type and condition of the sliding surface, the incline and length of the slide, and the speed of the child

upon entry. In addition, the distance from the exit end of the slide to the ground and the type of landing surface are relevant safety considerations. A sand pit provides a cushion. Guide rails help ensure that the child will not fall off the side of the slide. The tall, narrow slide connected directly to a ladder is now being replaced with lower, broader structures.

6. Height of walkways, landings, and decks should be limited according to users. In general, play structures should be no higher than what is required for child users to walk under them without danger of colliding with the understructure. Play surfaces on climbing equipment should be enclosed by railings, except for entrance and exit areas. In general, ladders leading to platforms should be installed approximately 90 degrees from the horizontal, and stairways should have a gradual incline of 25 to 35 degrees. A protective surface should be installed and maintained under and around all climbing and moving equipment. Sand, eight- to ten-inches thick, is sufficient for most purposes. It should extend across zones where children may fall and should be contained by a border. Sand needs to be regularly maintained to ensure absence of foreign materials such as broken glass. It should also be replenished or rearranged as needed in heavy-use zones.

DEVELOPMENTALLY ENGINEERED PLAYGROUNDS

Encouraging Motor Activity

A good deal of research indicates that the use of a playspace over time is related to the complexity and novelty of that playspace. Novelty apparently has the power to elicit responsiveness, and complexity has the power to sustain interest.

In order to attract the attention of long-term users, playgrounds in school settings need to change periodically. New pieces of small and large equipment need to be added, and old, unused small and large equipment needs to be removed at regular intervals.

Playgrounds must also be complex. When children are exposed to relatively uncomplex play environments that do not change over time, the amount of motor activity evidenced in the play environment decreases, while the amount of social activity increases. Decreases in motor activity are undesirable, since they reflect reduced opportunity for learning motor skills and developing desirable levels of fitness.

In order to provide for such needed complexity, a number of strategies can be employed. Playgrounds take on high levels of complexity when children are provided with the opportunity to readily obtain and use small, loose equipment such as balls, ropes, tricycles, bicycles, wagons, ladders, sliding boards, rope ladders, sand equipment, bats, racquets, nets, climbing ropes, targets, horizontal bars, cargo nets, and trestles. The larger the amount of mobile small equipment that is provided in accessible storage units located on the playground site, the more complex the playground becomes and the more it becomes capable of sustaining child interest over long periods of time. Many interesting multifunction storage units can be built. Some serve as playhouses and climbing towers as well as storage units.

The incorporation of large, permanently embedded, unchanging pieces of apparatus should be avoided; particularly when they are single-function structures. The functional complexity of a slide, a teeter-totter, a swing, a spring-base animal, a merry-go-round, or a set of monkey bars is limited. If large, permanently embedded, unchanging pieces of apparatus are to be incorporated on playgrounds, they should be complex multifunction structures (Figure 13.22). However, such apparatus is often extremely expensive and takes up a great deal of physical space.

Perhaps the most desirable response to the need for complexity would be to install basic skeletal support structures on playgrounds to which many pieces of loose apparatus (taken from a nearby storage unit) could be attached. One example is to set four timbers (six inches by six inches) six feet high into the ground; one in each of the four corners of a twelve-foot-square configuration. To this basic skeletal structure (the only elements on the playground when the playground is not in use) can be attached: horizontal bars that have spring-load fit into the posts; staircases, ladders, and sliding boards that rest on the horizontal bars at different inclines; a cargo net that is attached to the ground at various distances from the posts; climbing rope, rope ladders, and a trapeze that are suspended from horizontal bars;

FIGURE 13.22 Complex multifunction structures are appropriate for intermediate-school playgrounds. (Courtesy of Big Toys, a Division of Northwest Design Products, Inc., Tacoma, Washington.)

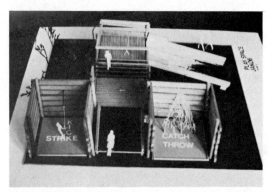

FIGURE 13.23 Stalls provide safe striking, kicking, and throwing areas.

and a nylon tent that fits over a horizontal bar and attaches to permanently installed ground rings, which may serve as a playhouse. All the attachable elements could be stored on brackets in a storage house, at levels that make the equipment accessible to child users.

Another solution to the need for complexity would be to build stalls around a central wall on a playground (Figure 13.23). Targets for kicking, throwing, and striking activities (obtained from storage) could be attached to the wall of a stall, thus eliminating potential safety problems that generally result in the severe restriction of these activities on most playgrounds. Racquet games, as well as a number of throwing and kicking games, could also be safely engaged in by children in such stall areas.

Provide for All Forms of Motor Play

If many motor skills are to be experienced and learned, normal posture and physical fitness developed and maintained, and game and sport rules and strategies practiced and understood, the playground must speak effectively to many forms of motor play.

Playgrounds for preschool through second-grade children.

Preschool and early primary-school children need to develop and learn to perform efficient fundamental motor patterns that are prerequisites to the specialized skills demanded of intermediate and older children in our culture. These fundamental motor patterns include the overarm throw, underarm throw, running, overarm strike, sidearm strike, underarm strike, place kick, punt, catch, vertical jump, broad jump, hurdle jump, jump from a height, stair climb, vertical rope climb, inclined ladder climb, rope ladder climb, vertical pole climb, hop, skip, gallop, slide, and leap. Preschool and primary-school children also need to develop normal posture and desirable levels of fitness.

Stalls, as previously discussed, are excellent places for throwing, striking, kicking, catching, and vertical jumping activities. Climbing activities are best provided with utilitarian and complex adjustable climbing apparatus set up on deep sand. The apparatus should acknowledge the physical dimensions and variability of children in this target age group. Hopping and jumping diagrams painted on hard surfaces encourage the development of hopping and long jumping skills. A jump-the-creek diagram and a graduated long jump diagram painted on a hard ground surface are appropriate in playspaces designed for preschool and primary-school use (Figures 4.5 and 4.6). Standards and a bamboo pole accompanied by a large sand pit landing surface develop hurdle jumping and high jumping skills.

The use of running, throwing, and catching skills in relatively uncomplicated game settings appropriate for this age group requires the delineation of rectangular and circular areas. Playspaces designed for preschool and early primary-school children should have such boundaries painted on hard surfaces and chalked on turf surfaces.

The development of strength that comes with pulling wagons loaded with other children and pumping pedals on small vehicles may be accommodated with a vehicle path or area that incorporates gradual slopes, straightaways, curves, and a variety of surfaces (for example, rough pebbles set in concrete, smooth concrete).

The greater the variety of surface types included on playgrounds, the greater the potential range of movement opportunities afforded the children. Hard surfaces generate different movement possibilities than do soft surfaces. Level surfaces stimulate different movement opportunities than do inclines. Gravel and sand encourage still other movement possibilities.

Playgrounds for third- through sixth-grade children. Intermediate-school children need to apply previously learned fundamental motor patterns in specialized sport-form settings that are popular in our culture. They also need to develop and maintain normal posture and physical fitness.

Further development of climbing skills and of some components of fitness may be effectively acknowledged through the provision of large, permanently embedded, multiuse apparatus configurations that cover large amounts of physical space on a playground. These areas should be covered with eight to ten inches of sand. Such climbing configurations must be enormously complex and acknowledge the physical dimensions of the children who are to use them.

If children are to learn the rules, strategies, and skills of popular sports, court diagrams for four square, tetherball, hopscotch variations, basketball, volleyball, tennis, and badminton need to be painted on concrete or asphalt surfaces. Standards and other necessary permanently embedded equipment should be installed. Turf field spaces need to be chalked for soccer, softball, football, and speedball. Goal areas and backstops need to be installed where necessary. Stalled areas need to be provided on hard level surfaces for racquetball.

The addition of vita parcours/fitness trails, cycling/jogging trails, and quarter-mile tracks encourage the improvement and maintenance of fitness and the learning of lifetime sports skills.

Large vandal-proof storage units, housing nets, racquets, bats, bases, balls, ropes, and other small equipment need to be effectively located so that materials can be easily checked out and returned during play sessions. Often such a storage area is located within a school, near an exit which is close to the playspace. Such an equipment storage area can be supervised by students.

14

movement education

The term *movement education* describes an approach to elementary-school physical education that has evolved in the past few decades, primarily as a reaction against traditional sport-oriented programs for children. Although there are many variations, the term is used most often to describe a total program with the following characteristics.

Purpose The primary purpose of a movement education program is to develop each child's potential for versatile and skillful movement in a variety of movement settings.

Content Content is divided into the areas of games, educational gymnastics, and educational dance. Content is primarily developed using the movement analysis framework of Rudolph Laban and is organized by movement concepts rather than by the activity itself or the equipment being used.

Process Goals, emphasizing the cognitive and affective aims of education, are achieved through attention to the learning process itself. The methodologies used are primarily child-centered and humanistic in nature.

Movement education began to gain acceptance in this country in the latter part of the 1950s, probably as a result of the programs established in England. Although to most movement educators change has been all too slow, movement education has had a profound influence on physical education programs in this country. Traditional programs as they existed twenty-five years ago are probably difficult to find.

DISTINGUISHING CHARACTERISTICS

The goals of physical education have already been discussed thoroughly in Chapter 8. Generally, the goals of movement education do not differ considerably from those of other models of physical education. Movement educators are concerned with skill acquisition, affective gains, attitude development, social skill, and physical well-being. However, the means they have developed to reach these general goals and the conception of skills to be developed do differ considerably from those of traditional physical education. In some cases the distinguishing characteristic is a matter of emphasis. In other cases there are substantive differences.

1. *The subject matter of physical education is defined in movement.* Movement skills and concepts, rather than the activity itself, are the focus of the curriculum. The organizing elements of traditional programs are usually

formed by the activities and the equipment used, such as in basketball, parachute play, floor hockey, or relays. The organizing element of movement education programs is typically a movement concept such as weight bearing, striking, or awareness of space. The movement education program is generally divided among games, gymnastics, and dance; in more traditional approaches games and sports receive more attention.

2. *Movement education stands directly opposed to motor elitism.* Movement education is for every child, the unskilled as well as the superstar, the disabled as well as the able. Its very nature, and the instructional strategies associated with it, tend to preclude the development of "stars." Movement concepts are developed by presenting movement tasks that allow students to participate successfully at their own levels and to progress at their own rates, without compromising the emphasis on quality movement and skill development.

3. *Movement education stands for the maximum amount of activity for children.* One of the most important contributions of methodology associated with movement education has been the elimination of lines and the elimination of waiting to play in a game. Movement methodology has always assumed that all children should be involved at all times, thus increasing the amount of activity time children receive in a typical lesson. Research has shown that children usually have the opportunity for activity only a small percentage of the time available for physical education. Typical circle games and low-organization games for children limit the time each child has to practice skills. Movement education has been a strong, positive influence in correcting this problem.

4. *Movement education is child-centered rather than activity-centered.* This characteristic is borne out by the willingness of movement educators to modify and adapt activities to the needs of children rather than expecting children to adapt to the activity. In creating games and in modifying games that extend manipulative skill work (see chapter on games), the central imperative is always how the game will fit the needs of the children and, if it doesn't, how it can be altered so that

it will fit those needs. Emphasis on success-structured learning and progressions designed to fit the developing abilities of children also represent the child-centered thrust.

5. *Affective education is sought directly rather than as a byproduct.* Physical educators have always promoted value development, attitude formation, and socioemotional well-being as outcomes in their programs. However, these values were seldom taught directly and were seldom visible in curriculum and lesson planning. Movement educators tend to seek these goals directly. Responsible decision making, inventiveness, self-direction, and productive social relationships are built into movement experiences.

6. *The learner is involved cognitively in a more direct way.* Physical educators have always included cognitive goals in their program explanations. Nevertheless, movement education is probably the first program of physical education to involve the child cognitively as part of the learning process in a way that is different from learning rules and strategies. In movement education children are asked to become consciously aware of their movement responses, to become involved in problem solving cognitively as well as motorically, and to do so at a cognitive level beyond that of memorization and rote learning.

7. *The educational design is success-structured.* Because children in movement education programs work at their own level of ability, movement education programs are success-oriented. This means quite simply that the good movement education lesson is sufficiently challenging to spark the children's interest, yet within reach of their developing abilities. Thus, chances for continued success are optimized. The importance of success-structured learning cannot be over-emphasized. It can and should be a characteristic of all school learning and all forms of physical education. Movement education has done much to focus the attention of physical educators on this important factor.

8. *Competition is defined more humanistically.* Movement educators have often gained the reputation of being anticompetition, and we suspect that some of them may have over-

reacted to the unfortunate misuse of competition in children's sport. Nevertheless, movement education is not anticompetition. Rather, it has reassigned competition to a role that tends to reflect its child-centered and humanistic values (Krueger and Krueger, 1977). Competition is a very healthy experience for children and one that has enormous potential for motivating children in physical education. However, adult-style competition forced on young children without concern for the skill, social, cognitive, or emotional demands of a competitive situation can be counterproductive. The key here is *appropriate* competition rather than the elimination of competition.

9. *Movement education focuses on the motor development of the child.* Such programs are opposed to the introduction of specialized sport skills as program content until the child has developed both versatility and skillfulness in the more general motor patterns that form the foundation for these specialized skills. For example, a movement education program spends a great deal of time working with developing striking patterns with and without implements. Movement educators believe that specialized sport skills such as the volleyball serve, tennis stroke, and hockey slap shot will be more easily learned if basic patterns are fully developed before the specialized skill is introduced.

10. *Skills are developed primarily as open skills.* The elementary physical program deals primarily with motor skills that are open (where the conditions under which the skill is used are always changing). Movement educators teach skills in the three content areas (gymnastics, dance, and games) as though they were open skills. Progressions involve increasing difficulty and varying conditions. Versatility is developed by providing students with experiences that help them to react skillfully to changing conditions.

11. *More emphasis is placed on expressive movement and the quality of a movement response.* In most sport skills training (except for sports such as gymnastics and diving), the exact form of the movement is subordinated to the outcome of the movement. If you can hit the longest ball or sink the most baskets, nobody will say much about the form with which you accomplished those feats. Likewise, except in an occasional dance unit, almost no attention is paid to the expressive or qualitative aspects of the performance itself. In movement education children work with expressive movement in the dance area and are asked to examine their movements in terms of the quality of the movement response. Cues, instructions, and feedback from teachers often relate to the qualitative aspects of the performance.

12. *The learner is treated as decision maker.* Because of movement education's emphasis on cognitive involvement above the memory level of learning, it is natural that children are involved in making decisions. At the simplest level the child might decide what to do to answer a teacher probe such as "Can you find another way to balance on three body parts?" At a more advanced level decisions can be made in creating simple games. At a still more advanced level decision making becomes very much a full-time activity as the learner has more and more responsibility for making movement decisions, whether in educational dance, gymnastics, or game settings. Children are encouraged to take more and more responsibility for managerial behaviors in lessons and to become self-directed in the way in which they handle routine matters. While this emphasis on the learner as decision maker is not uncommon in other forms of physical education, it is more visible in the curriculum and lesson planning of movement education.

The characteristics described above tend to differentiate movement education from more traditional programs of elementary-school physical education, although none of these characteristics apply solely to movement education. Indeed, there is no reason why they should not be characteristic of most physical education programs for children. The influence of movement education has been such that traditional elementary-school physical education programs reflect many more of these characteristics than they did two decades ago. This is a positive trend in elementary physical education. As we have stated continually, the real battle is not between movement educators and physical educators who support a more traditional approach. Rather, the real battle is between all physical educators who respect children, who want to contribute to their development, who utilize appropriate methods, and those who see the elementary program simply as a mini-sports program, who see children as young athletes to be coached, or who are so unprofessional as to see the elementary physical education program as supervised recreation with few educational outcomes.

CONTENT

The content areas of movement education are educational games, educational gymnastics, and educational dance. Each requires the development of different but interdependent movement skills and abilities.

Games develop the gross motor manipulative skills and abilities involved in sending and receiving objects. The manipulative patterns are used in this text to organize the content and are defined as throwing, receiving, striking, and dodging patterns. Development begins as the individual masters control of an object in the simplest conditions. Conditions grow more difficult and complex and eventually become gamelike and more closely related to the popular sport activities of our culture.

Educational gymnastics skills are related to control and management of the body itself. Control begins with mastery of basic body management skills and progresses as the difficulty and complexity of the conditions under which these skills are performed are increased. Movement themes in educational gymnastics are developed from the content areas of locomotion on the feet and other parts of the body; transferring body weight; and stillness, weight bearing, and balance. The end product of educational gymnastics is not precisely defined Olympic gymnastics skills but rather body management related to a movement concept.

Educational dance develops and expands the abilities of the child to use movement in an expressive way. Educational dance is process-oriented rather than performance-oriented and is closely related to programs of creative dance. Content is structured in the dance area using the progressive themes developed by Rudolph Laban, which are discussed below.

THE MOVEMENT FRAMEWORK OF RUDOLPH LABAN

Movement educators have drawn heavily upon the work of Rudolph Laban and the system he designed to describe movement. If we were to ask each of you to do a gesture in space with your hand and arm and then ask you to describe what you did to another person, you would begin to get some appreciation of the difficulty involved in communicating body action to another. In the simplest sense Rudolph Laban gave us a language to talk about movement. This language is useful to the movement educator as a framework for designing experiences as well as for extending and developing the quality of movement responses of children.

Chart 14.1 presents the four major constructs of Laban's system. They include:

Body: What the body or its parts are doing
Space: Where and how the action is using space
Effort: The quality of the movement
Relationship: How the movement relates to other parts of the body, other people, or objects

People in many fields have adapted Laban's constructs for their own use. Chart 14.1 is similar to the work of Russell, Stanley, Logsdon, et al., and others. It is useful to note that Laban applied his work directly to the dance area. It is for this reason that the language under each of the major constructs is most suitable to dance. When the system is used for games and gymnastics, the language changes slightly and expands to meet the specific needs of these movement settings.

What the Body Is Doing

This first construct is body-oriented and attempts to label the action itself and the shape of the body or its parts.

CHART 14.1 An adaptation of Laban's movement framework

WHAT *BODY* IS DOING	USE OF *SPACE*	THE *EFFECT* ASPECT	*RELATIONSHIP* ASPECT
Body Actions	*Areas*	*Time*	*Body Parts*
Curl	Personal space	Sudden/sustained	Meeting/parting
Stretch	General space	Quick/slow	Symmetrical/asymmetrical
Twist	*Directions*	*Weight*	Above/below
Body Part Actions	Forward	Firm/fine touch	Behind/in front of
Support body	Backward	Strong/light	On/beside
Lead movement	Sideways	Heavy/light	*Other People*
Apply force	Diagonally	*Space*	Contrasting
Receive force/weight	Up	Direct/indirect	Alternating
Body Activities	Down	Straight/flexible	Successive
Locomotion (move from	*Levels*	*Flow*	Mirroring
one space to another)	High	Bound/free	Matching
Nonlocomotor (remain in	Medium	Stoppable/ongoing	Following
same space)	Low		Copying
Manipulative (sending and	*Pathways*		Above/below/behind/over/
receiving objects)	(Air or floor patterns)		under/in front of
Body Shapes	Straight		Supporting
Wide	Curvy		Lifting
Round	Zig-Zag		*Apparatus*
Twisted	*Planes*		Near/far
Straight	Pivotal direction		In/out
Angular	Around axes of body		Over/under
	Extension		Onto/off of
	Small/large		*Other Stimulus*
	Near/far		Visual/auditory/tactile

Body actions. The body is capable of producing movement through the actions of *curling* (bringing body or part in toward center), *stretching* (extending body or part from center or joint; and *twisting* (rotating on its axis). It is not by accident that these are the actions by which all movement is produced and which are synonymous with the language of flexion, extension, and rotation. The terms *curl, stretch,* and *twist* are used directly in the dance and gymnastics areas.

Body part actions. Body parts can *support* the body by becoming a base upon which all or part of the body weight is taken. They can *lead* movement by initiating a movement and having the whole body or other body parts follow the movement of a single part. They can *apply force* to create a body action or activity or *receive the force* of body action or activity. They can be *emphasized* in an action or play a major role in *gesture*.

Body activities. The body activities of locomotion, nonlocomotion, and manipulative skills form the basis of content organization for the gymnastics and games areas. *Locomotion activities* involve all those actions that take the body from one place to another. Most of us are familiar with those locomotor actions which involve the feet only, such as walking, running, skipping, hopping, and so on. In the gymnastics area we will extend locomotor actions to those that involve other parts as well.

LOCOMOTOR ACTIONS
FEET ONLY

Walking	Skipping
Running	Jumping
Hopping	Galloping

OTHER BODY PARTS

Steplike actions	Sliding
Rolling	Flight

Nonlocomotor actions take place with the body occupying the same space. Twisting, turning, spinning, rising from the floor and sinking to the floor, opening the body from its center and closing the body toward its center, pushing and pulling, gesturing, and bal-

FIGURE 14.1 Educational gymnastics skills are related to control and management of the body itself.

Body shape. The construct of *body shape* describes the pattern of the whole body. The terms *wide, round, twisted, straight,* and *angular* are self-explanatory in their meaning. The idea of body shape is most useful to the areas of gymnastics and dance.

The Use of Space

A second major part of Laban's system concerns the use of space. Use of space is a theme in the dance area and is used in the games and gymnastics area to extend and refine body activities.

Areas. The term *areas* describes the broad use of space. *Personal space* is the space surrounding our body as we move or stay in one spot. *General space* is the space structured by the limitations of a room or defined boundaries. We often ask children to "find their own space," which means an area within the defined boundaries of a room or outdoor space that gives them the largest possible work area. This is sometimes confused with the phrase *personal space,* which we actually take with us at all times.

Directions. The body can produce movement in a *forward, backward, sideways, diagonal,* or *up and down* direction either by changing the part of the body that is facing the line of direction or by orienting the body in a different degree relationship with a point of origin (N, S, E, W). We usually want children to actually move in a forward, sideways, or backward direction when we ask them to change direction. The ordinary use of the word *direction* (changing direction—of a car, for instance) does not mean to change the facing: so the teacher will have to clearly define direction for students. The concept of direction is used in all program areas to ex-

ance are all actions that essentially do not take the body anywhere. Experience with nonlocomotor actions are important in all three content areas but play a major role in the dance and gymnastics areas.

Manipulative actions are in reality nonlocomotor actions but are more specifically defined here so that the reader can associate them with the content of the games area and a body activity. Basically, our bodies allow us to send objects away from us, receive objects, and maintain possession of objects. These broad categories are the content of the games area and can be further defined as follows:

SENDING OBJECTS	RECEIVING OBJECTS	MAINTAINING POSSESSION OF OBJECTS

Throwing
  without implements
  with implements
Striking
  without implements
  with implements
	Catching
	  without implements
	  with implements
	Collecting (controlling object
	  without actually stopping it)
		Carrying
		Propelling (includes dribbling
		  actions)

pand the experience of a body activity—doing that activity in different directions.

Levels. *High, medium,* and *low* levels are defined relative to the task being performed. Children can toss a ball at a much higher level in space than they can jump or balance. The concept of levels is used frequently in all program areas to increase students' range of experience with many body activities such as tossing balls to different levels, balancing at different levels, and rising and sinking to different levels.

Pathway. The term *pathway* is often confused with the term *direction*. The pathway of a movement is the *floor pattern* or *air pattern* the movement makes through space. Children can be helped to understand this concept if they are told to think about having chalk on their feet and then told to look at the pattern the chalk makes on the floor after they have moved. Air patterns can be explained by using the example of sky-writing airplanes. The concept of pathways is used most often in dance and gymnastics to expand children's use of space as they move. It is a useful term in the manipulative area, since it helps children understand the patterns of offensive and defensive plays and helps describe the single action of a body part through space in the performance of a skill.

Planes. Planes of movement describe the use of space over the axis of the body. These actions (the sagittal, frontal, and horizontal planes) are part of Laban's system but are not used in the elementary-school program.

Extension. The concept of *near* and *far* extensions involves the distance of the movement from the body. The notion is useful in helping children make movements bigger or smaller and in helping them to understand the near/far relationships of actions involving objects with the body.

The Effort Aspect

All movement has a *time* dimension, a *weight* dimension, a *space* dimension, and a *flow* dimension. These qualities of movement are used extensively in all three content areas. It is the blend of these qualities (strong, quick, direct, and free, for instance) that makes movement expressive and dynamic. It is the proper blend of these qualities which makes a movement skill effective and efficient.

Time. The *time* quality of a movement is commonly associated with speed (fast/slow), and it is indeed in this manner that children first get a feeling for this quality. Laban intended that time be a contrast between sudden, quick movements and the more sustained, ongoing quality of movement. In this respect movement can be very fast and still not be sudden.

Weight. The *weight* quality of movement refers to the inner tension of a muscular action. It can include either firm (strong, tight, heavy) or light touch (weak, loose, delicate). The concepts of firm and light touch are used extensively in all areas. In the games and gymnastics areas combinations of quick, strong movements produce the explosive power necessary for many gymnastic and manipulative actions. A lighter and more sustained action is needed to receive force effectively. In dance children work with these qualities directly to create expressive movement experiences.

Space. The *space* dimension is not to be confused with the use-of-space dimension. This spatial factor relates directly to the qualitative aspect of the use of space. An action either uses space in a very direct way (straight line—gets there right away) or indirectly (flexible, wavy—takes its time to get where it wants to go—playing with space). Most of our functional movements use space very directly. It is in the dance area that children learn to play with space and experience the expressive quality of this dimension.

Flow. Movement can either be *bound* or *free.* The distinguishing characteristic here is that bound movement is stoppable and free movement is not. Bound movement is restrained and characterized by continuous control. There is a point in free movement that is an abandonment that cannot be regained after the action is initiated. Ballistic movements in the games area (striking, for instance) have a free quality to them. Spring actions and flight in gymnastics have a free quality to them. Bound and free movement create different expressive qualities. Children are usually not asked to focus on the flow quality of movement until late in their elementary-school experiences.

The Relationship Aspect

The last major construct of Laban's system concerns the relationship aspect of movement. The relationship construct gives meaning to the interaction between individuals and their environment. People interact with others, with their physical environment, and with external stimuli. The relationship aspect defines these interactions.

Body parts. Individual body parts can have a relationship with each other. These relationships are used primarily in the dance area and consist of *meeting and parting* with each other (coming together and moving apart); *symmetrical and asymmetrical* relationships (two similar parts doing the same thing or different things); *above and below* each other; *behind or in front of* each other; *on and beside* each other.

Other people. Children relate to others in all program areas. In the games area both cooperative and competitive relationships with others are established. The specific relationship of one person's movement to that of another is focused on most frequently in the dance and gymnastics areas, but it is important to the games area as well. The descriptions used for this dimension are self-explanatory: Children *contrast* their movement to the movement of another, *alternate*, make their movement *successive* to, *mirror, match, follow,* or *copy* the movement of another person or persons. They can relate to another by moving *above, below, behind, over, under,* or *in front of* the other person, or they can *lift* and *support* each other.

Apparatus. Children can make their movement relate to apparatus through conscious attempts to be *near or far from* it, *over and under* it, *in and out of* it or *onto or off of* it. Near and far relationships are useful for all program areas. The concepts of in and out, over and under, and onto and off of are most useful in gymnastics and sometimes in dance.

Other stimuli. The dance area is closely tied to the establishment of relationships between movement and *sound*. Other stimuli for dance include *poems* and *tactile* (touch) and *visual* stimuli. Children can be helped to establish expressive relationships between all these stimuli in the dance area. The student in the games area is most often asked to relate to externally imposed rules, boundaries, and so on.

USING MOVEMENT ANALYSIS TO DEFINE AND DEVELOP CONTENT

Physical education programs with a movement orientation draw content from the movement analysis of Laban or a similar movement analysis, but they may do so in different ways. You will recall that there are four major factors or movement components to Laban's analysis: what the body is doing, the use of space, the effort factor, and the relationship factor. Although it is not the orientation of this text, it is possible to study the use of space by employing gymnastics, games, and dance experiences. It is also possible to develop a program based entirely on the major movement constructs as the organizing element of curriculum—across various movement settings. There are successful programs which have used variations of this approach. We will develop the areas of games, gymnastics, and dance as separate content areas (recognizing the overlap that occurs, particularly with younger students). We will develop these areas primarily through the use of movement themes.

Part of Laban's work was the development of sixteen movement themes for the dance

CHART 14.2 Themes

LABAN'S FIRST EIGHT DANCE THEMES	BARRETT'S GAMES THEMES	LOGSDON'S GYMNASTICS THEMES
Themes concerned with the awareness of the body	Awareness of the body, with emphasis on general locomotion and the use of body parts	Awareness of the body and the parts, with emphasis on how the body can move
Themes concerned with the awareness of resistance to weight and time	Awareness of space, with emphasis on general, personal, directions and extensions	Awareness of space, with emphasis on areas, levels, directions, extensions, and pathways
Themes concerned with the awareness of space	Awareness of weight and time, with emphasis on using different amounts of force and speed	Awareness of time, with emphasis on body actions and activities
Themes concerned with the awareness of the flow of the weight of the body in space and time	Awareness of the flow of movement, with emphasis on the integration of first three themes	Awareness of relationships, with emphasis on body shapes and actions of the body
Themes concerned with the adaptation to a partner	Awareness of simple relationships (cooperative in nature)	Awareness of weight, with emphasis on activities of the body
Themes concerned with the instrumental use of the limbs of the body	Awareness of the body, with emphasis on specific locomotor and nonlocomotor patterns	Awareness of flow and continuity, with emphasis on selection and refinement of movement in sequences
Themes concerned with the awareness of isolated actions	Awareness of space, with emphasis on pathways and levels	Awareness of relationship to others, with emphasis on partner and small-group work
Themes concerned with occupational rhythms	Awareness of time, weight, and space combinations, with emphasis on effective and efficient movement	Awareness of rhythm, with emphasis on creating, repeating, and refining rhythm patterns in movement sequences
	Awareness of complex relationships (cooperative and competitive relationships)	

area. A theme is a major content focus that is (a) part of a progressive total view of the development of subject matter, (b) important to the movement setting being studied, and (c) discrete in its contribution to the whole. Laban's sixteen basic themes are reproduced in Chart 14.2 in condensed form. Following Laban's lead, Barrett and Logsdon (1977) developed parallel themes for the games and gymnastics areas, respectively. Barrett also reduced the content of the elementary-school program to the first seven of Laban's themes. These themes are presented in Chart 14.2.

Content in this text is defined and developed in the dance area primarily through the use of Laban's movement themes. In the games area content is organized primarily in terms of the manipulative and games strategy skills unique to that area. A suggested progression for the development of games skills is proposed in terms of four progressive and overlapping stages. Gymnastics content is developed in terms of themes representing gymnastics actions that are also progressive and overlapping.

As the reader studies the development of the games and gymnastics material through the charts that are presented for the development of each theme, the influence of Logsdon and Barrett's themes will be recognized. As the teacher develops more experience in working with movement content, the relationships which blend all three content areas will become clearer and more useful in developing material independent of the charts provided.

Versatility and skillfulness in performance are developed by extending the complexity and difficulty of the use of an activity, expanding the ways it can be performed, and refining the quality with which a movement is performed. The following examples from the three content areas should illustrate the use of movement analysis in the development of a movement activity. The movement descriptors, taken directly or indirectly from the work of Laban, are underlined.

MOVEMENT ACTIVITY	EXTENSION	REFINEMENT
Tossing and catching a beanbag	To high, medium, and low *levels* with different *body parts* To different parts of *personal space* In *general* space With *another person*	Receiving *softly*

GYMNASTICS AREA

MOVEMENT ACTIVITY	EXTENSION	REFINEMENT

Moving onto and off of small boxes	*Feet* only
	  Together
	  Apart
	Moving off with different *body shapes*
	Using different *body parts* on and off
	Showing a change in *direction*
	Following another
		Achieving flight in the jump
		Making *body shape* clear
		Landing *softly*

DANCE AREA

MOVEMENT ACTIVITY	EXTENSION	REFINEMENT
Rising from the floor and sinking to the floor with different body parts leading	Show a clear change in *time quality* (sudden and sustained) Change your *base of support* Show a clear change in *weight quality* (flow, pathway)	Use at least three different *body parts* Get to all parts of your *personal space*

In the preceding illustration a movement activity from each of the three content areas is given. The information in the Extension column describes how that activity can be developed using Laban's movement analysis. The information under the Refinement column describes the qualitative concern in the performance of the movement activity. The material in the games, gymnastics, and dance sections of Part Three of this text includes information on how to extend and refine the movement activities discussed.

The movement analysis is useful to help structure the development of movement activities. This does not mean that all parts of the analysis can be used for every movement activity or movement theme. The question the designer must ask is, "What does it mean to be skilled at the movement activity?" The movement themes of Laban, Barrett, and Logsdon can guide in the use of analysis to develop content but they cannot replace a clear notion of the relationship of even the single movement task to the whole.

DESIGNING MOVEMENT EXPERIENCES

Movement educators develop content with students through the presentation of movement tasks. Movement tasks direct students to do something related to the content the teacher has planned, usually a theme or small part of a theme. Four criteria are suggested for evaluating a movement task.

1. The task must deal with content designed to help children move skillfully and in a versatile manner.
2. The task must be appropriate for the different experiential levels of students.

3. The task must involve an organization that provides maximum active participation.
4. The task should seek to involve the students affectively and cognitively as well as motorically.

Helping Children Move with Skill and Versatility

Children enjoy activity, and there are many enjoyable things a teacher can do with children. Because movement educators feel so strongly about the unique role of physical education in developing versatility and skillfulness in movement, they are reluctant to support activities for their "fun" value alone with limited program time. Movement tasks must therefore seek primarily to develop the movement abilities of the child.

Different Experiential Levels of Students

Movement educators seek to present tasks that allow students to work at their own level

FIGURE 14.2 Versatility and skillfulness in performance are developed by extending the complexity and difficulty of the use of an activity.

and progress at their own rate. This is done with careful attention to progression and student learning. It is also done through the presentation of movement concepts. Movement concepts can best be understood by contrasting the following tasks.

Task 1: Everybody do a headstand and end in a forward roll.
Task 2: Take a balance that is comfortable for you and see how you can make a free body part lead you out of that balance into a roll.

In the first task the students have little freedom for individual response. Students who cannot do a headstand or who can perform balances beyond the headstand are not permitted to work at their own level. In the second task the teacher asks the students to balance and therefore is permitting a range of correct responses that should be within the ability levels of the class. There are times when the teacher might want to present a more limited task, but a movement educator would be reluctant to do so unless the task was definitely within the experiential level of all the students. Movement tasks that are concepts rather than specialized movement skills permit diversity of response.

Providing Maximum Active Participation

The most important factor in learning a motor skill is the amount of time one has to practice that skill. Movement tasks must maximize opportunity to learn. Teachers can make this easier by asking themselves how many people are necessary to perform the skill involved. If there is enough equipment and space, then there are few reasons why students should not be organized in small practice groups. If teachers cannot control an environment where every child is moving, they need to give serious thought to developing a learning environment where this can occur.

Involving Students Affectively, Cognitively, and Motorically

There are many ways in which a teacher can involve students affectively and cog-

FIGURE 14.3 There are many ways in which a teacher can involve students affectively and cognitively in motor experiences.

nitively in motor experiences. Consider the following examples:

Task 1: Move onto the apparatus with one part or combination of body parts and move off with a different part or combination.

Task 2: In groups of four continuously pass the ball on the move, making each member of your group important.

In both of these tasks a cognitive or affective component is present. The important thing to note however is that the motoric emphasis is not lessened in these experiences. The cognitive and affective concerns are added to the experiences primarily through shifting the responsibility for student behavior to the student. In all psychomotor tasks there are always cognitive and affective components. Teachers can create richer learning experiences by giving thought to student involvement in these areas of learning.

15

developing games skills

The American culture is a sport and games culture. Sport participation and observation consume a large part of our leisure activity. Children are socialized early into the sport culture. Sport heroes, adult game forms, and children's interpretations of adult game forms play a major role in childhood. Educators have a major responsibility to use the child's interest in constructive ways.

Sport is not inherently "good" for children. For every example of positive influence we could probably cite an example where sport and game participation has had a destructive effect upon the self-concept, development, and approach tendencies of a child toward sport and game participation. Too often our programs have been used as a screening program to eliminate the less-skilled and to ensure that they will remain unskilled and nonparticipants. Too often our programs have been defended by people claiming that sport teaches people how to win and lose—although the same students continue to win and the same students continue to lose. In response to these problems some programs have opted to ensure the success of every student by eliminating competition in any form and by making little demand on the development of skill. This position is equally unfair to children.

The approach to games and sports outlined in this chapter is designed to provide a progressive and developmental program that will help children become versatile and skillful games players—and to do so in a way that increases rather than decreases a student's desire to become a lifelong participant.

PROGRESSION OF GAMES SKILLS

The development of the games program can be conceptualized as having several spiraling and overlapping stages:

Stage I: Obtaining control of an object using a particular motor pattern
Stage II: Controlling the object under more complex conditions
Stage III: Using skills in beginning game play—focus remaining on control of object
Stage IV: Using skills in more complex game play

In Stage I we are concerned with helping the individual make the object do what he or she wants it to do. For sending patterns (striking and throwing) control consists of the ability to direct the object where one wants it to go with the intended force qualities. For receiving objects (catching and collecting) control consists basically of obtaining possession of objects when they are coming right to you from straight-on directions with little force. As difficulty is increased, one must move to receive the objects as they come from different directions and with varying amounts of force.

In Stage II we begin to add more complex conditions to the use of a skill. Students begin to combine several skills together, such as receiving, propelling, and sending skills. They are asked to relate to another person using a skill in both cooperative and competitive ways, with the emphasis still on mastering control of the object.

In Stage III we begin to take the focus off the skill itself and use the skill in competitive settings that demand both offensive and defensive beginning strategies. At this point we assume that the ability to direct an object to a desired place, receive objects, and propel objects is developed. We now work on helping students decide where and how to manipulate an object and move their bodies in relation to a game under very basic game conditions. At this stage we can also begin to limit the ways in which skills are performed (not solely for safety) to make them consistent with how the skills will be used in specialized forms of sport (example: illegal hits in volleyball, charging and traveling rules in basketball).

When students reach Stage IV, we assume that fairly high levels of individual skills have been established and also that students have acquired the basic strategies used in simplified game conditions. For example, we assume that they can defend against an offensive player in basketball or that they can place the ball away from an opponent in a net activity. We then begin to increase the complexity of the conditions under which skills and strategies are used. This is done by

1. Adding players—both offense and defense
2. Increasing the complexity of the conduct of a game (how started, procedures for rule infractions, scoring, out-of-bounds play, and so on)
3. Differentiating positions on the same team where appropriate

Students do not leave one stage when they are ready for another. Increasing levels of mastery and control at each stage are developed as a new stage is added. Even professional athletes spend time during every practice session mastering basic control of an object (Stage I). Readiness to move to a more advanced stage can only be determined by the acquisition of minimum levels of mastery over a previous stage. Moving to a more advanced stage before a minimum level of skill is acquired can only prove frustrating. The assumption that students will pick up earlier stages during practice of a more advanced stage is not valid. Consider the number of college students in a basketball situation who have not learned how to move out from in back of a defensive player to receive a pass, or the number of tennis players who cannot use spatial concepts for offensive or defensive play. These basic Stage III abilities should be learned much earlier. They can be learned much more easily in less complex situations.

The following chart presents a gross estimate of where in a continuous program these stages are likely to begin.

	K	1	2	3	4	5	6
Stage I	→————————————————————————→
Stage II			→————————————————→
Stage III					→————————→
Stage IV					→————————→

Stages I and II are developed in this chapter separately from Stages III and IV. Stages I and II are organized by the manipulative patterns essential for well-rounded games participation. The development of these patterns is presented in chart form. Stages III and IV are developed in terms of basic games strategies essential for games activities appropriate for the elementary-school program. Basic games strategies for keep-away games and net-oriented games are presented in a progressive order.

THE MANIPULATIVE PATTERNS

Stages I and II in the development of games skills involve helping the child gain control of the manipulative skill patterns common to the sport activities of our culture. Children must be able to send, receive, and move with objects alone and with others. If we look closely at the specialized skills involved in sports participation, we find that many have a common skill pattern, as described below.

The primary organizing elements we will use for the games content are shaded in the chart below. The main responsibility of the elementary-school program is to establish a high level of skillfulness in these patterns so that a student has a strong base of experiences and abilities from which to draw in learning the more specialized forms of these patterns. As the child moves into the fifth and sixth grade, some of this work will be channeled into the more specialized skills of the sports listed; however, the primary emphasis of the program remains with establishing strong patterns.

SKILL IN MANIPULATIVE PATTERNS

If we were to ask a college varsity player to dribble a basketball across a gym and we then analyzed the performance, we would probably find that the player was using a mature and mechanically efficient movement pattern. We might also take some eight-year-olds, ask them to do the same thing, and find that they too have a mature and mechanically efficient movement pattern. However, no one would say that the eight-year-old was s good a dribbler as the college basketball player. What then is the difference between the ability level of these performers?

The difference is obviously that varsity basketball players can adapt the way they use the skill to game conditions. They will dribble the ball way out in front of them to move fast—hug it close when defended—change the level of the dribble, use their bodies be-

ANALYSIS OF SKILL PATTERNS USED IN GAMES

Sending	Striking	With implements	Racquets—tennis, badminton, racketball, squash
			Bats—softball, baseball
			Sticks—floor hockey, ice hockey, field hockey
		Hands only	Volleyball, handball
		Feet only	Football, soccer
		Other body parts	Soccer
	Throwing/Tossing	With implements	Lacrosse, jai alai
		Hands only	Basketball, softball, baseball, soccer
Receiving	Catching	With implements	Softball, baseball, lacrosse, jai alai
		Other body parts	Soccer
		Hands only	Basketball, softball, baseball, soccer
	Collecting	With implements	Floor hockey, ice hockey, field hockey, lacrosse
		Other body parts	Soccer
Propelling	————————	With implements	Floor hockey, ice hockey, field hockey
		Bouncing	Basketball
		Tapping with feet	Soccer
Dodging	People		All sport forms to some extent
	Objects		

tween the ball and defender, move smoothly from the dribble to a pass or a shot at the basket, change direction of the dribble, quickly change hands, and so on. The basketball dribble is an open skill, like the skills of most sport forms appropriate to the elementary-level program. The conditions surrounding the use of an open skill are always changing, and skillfulness is in reality adaptability to these conditions.

How do we teach people to be adaptable players like the varsity player? Logically, we begin teaching a skill in the simplest of conditions and then continuously increase the difficulty and complexity of those conditions until a student is prepared to use a skill in the most complex conditions surrounding the sport itself. We also have to accept the fact that elementary-school students may not be ready for all the complex conditions by the end of the elementary-school grades.

Some of the conditions affecting early stages of control in manipulative skills include:

The size, weight, and shape of the equipment
Number and relationship of other players (cooperative or competitive)
Stationary or moving objects (angle, speed, and trajectory)
On-the-move or stationary players
Number of skills combined in one action (example: receiving and throwing or striking)
Intended direction and speed of object

Using this framework, a student does not learn to throw and catch and then become ready for softball or baseball. Throwing and catching skills are developed first in very simple conditions. Students progress in throwing and catching as they become more able to adapt throwing and catching abilities to ever-increasing demands and conditions. Teachers must recognize that all students in the same class will not be ready for the same level of experiences at any one time. They must therefore structure game experiences to meet these individualized needs by structuring tasks that permit a range of responses, providing separate tasks to different learners, or modifying tasks during activity for different students.

Teachers should also note that students will very likely be at different stages in different skills. Striking skills, for instance, require much more work at the lower stages. Although general guidelines for age levels can be described, many factors help determine the appropriate stage of students in developing games skills.

Using the Chart Material

The content material presented in this section is divided as follows:

Sending skills	Tossing/throwing
	Striking
	Different body parts
	Hands only
	Feet only
	Implements
Receiving skills	Catching
	Collecting
Dodging skills	People
	Objects

To assist the teacher in planning learning experiences with these skill patterns, the material is presented in terms of four constructs:

The major task: A major learning experience with a skill pattern
Extension: How the learning experience can be extended
Refinement: Important aspects of the quality of response
Application: How the learning experience can be used in an applied (self-testing or competitive) experience

Major task. This column represents a major breakdown of the type of experience included under the specified skill pattern. For instance, in the tossing/throwing section major tasks include (a) tossing to self-space, (b) tossing to a different space, (c) tossing to target areas, and (d) tossing in relation to another person. The major tasks presented are progressive in the sense that a similar idea is continuously presented (example: tossing to self-space followed by tossing to a different space). There are times in any progression when the teacher can choose between more than one type of experience at the same level—in this case adding targets or adding people. The order of these experiences was arbitrarily selected.

Extension. The extension column represents a progressive list of experiences students should have with the major task. Consider the following example:

MAJOR TASK	EXTENSION
Catching objects from a personal toss→self-space	Slight release out of hand→high toss Catch at medium levels→off the ground catches and near the floor catches Directly in front→side→slightly back

The extension column lists the simplest condition under which the major task is performed and how to increase that condition to make it more difficult as students gain control.

Refinement. The refinement column addresses the qualitative aspects of performance—not what the student is doing, but how the student is doing it. In some instances the concern is with the mechanical aspects of the performance; in some, with the extent of control expected in an experience; and in some, with the level of student responsibility in the performance of a task.

In the examples below the teacher is guided in what to look for in the quality of the student's response to receiving objects from a personal toss in self-space. If student performance is not consistent with these guidelines, the teacher will want to focus on making students' performance better. The teacher can also use this information to redesign an experience that will help focus on the quality needing work. The suggestions for refinement indicated for early experiences are assumed to apply to later experiences as well.

Application. The application column is devoted to experiences in which the student can use the major task in a self-testing or competitive setting. When teachers design an experience in an applied setting, they are taking the students' focus off the performance itself and asking students to concentrate on using the skill to accomplish something outside of the movement itself.

Teachers must not use experiences with an applied competitive setting until they are sure that students can perform the skill itself. In competitive experiences the skill level will initially drop. However, competitive experiences motivate students and are therefore useful educational experiences. They also add a gamelike condition to the use of a skill and therefore are important to the development of skillful games players. Competitive experiences must be used with care, however.

Self-testing activities are useful to provide the students with feedback in terms of their

MAJOR TASK	EXTENSION	REFINEMENT
Catching objects from a personal toss in self-space	Slight release out of hand→high toss Catch at medium levels→off the ground catches→near the floor catches Catch directly in front→side→slightly back	Extending to meet object with the hands—flexion to receive force of object (arms and whole body if necessary) Tossing object only to a height within the ability to control object and still be challenging Tracking the object with the eyes (see the beanbag in the hands) When catching at different levels, students should be helped to make the catch near the floor as well as high off the floor and to vary their levels

own needs. Competitive activities against others are useful only when students have enough confidence and competence in their own skills. Students themselves should be part of the decision-making process in deciding when to use their skills in competition against or with others, and application conditions should not add a complexity that has not been added in a noncompetitive experience.

PLANNING LESSONS

Long-Term Planning

It is unlikely that a teacher will want to take a major idea from a manipulative pattern and develop it completely in one lesson in the early primary grades. Students will need a lot of practice mastering aspects of control, and the teacher will want to repeat a movement idea many times. For example, beginning kindergarten students may not advance beyond practice with sending objects out of their hands at very low and medium levels. To move further in the progression would not be wise until this minimum level of control is mastered. On the other hand, these same students do not have an attention span that allows them to practice any one task for any length of time. The teacher must give them a lot of beginning-level tasks with many movement ideas. A plan must provide for several lessons with a skill pattern and often for more than one skill pattern in a lesson. These lessons are returned to frequently, since the early primary student spends a great deal of time in Stage I establishing rudimentary control of an object.

As students get older and more experienced, they can be asked to stay with a task in Stage I and Stage II until they have achieved a level of control of that task. Teachers can more fully develop ideas using the extension, refinement, and application columns of the charts. Lessons take on a more specific focus, and several lessons that focus on the same pattern may be used and returned to often.

At the third- and fourth-grade levels most students still receive a lot of work in Stages I

and II but begin to take these experiences into Stage III. Material begins to be developed in full-blown progressive units that continuously interrelate experiences with all three stages of games playing.

Long-term planning for students in the fifth and sixth grades takes the children into Stage IV experiences if they are ready, but does not neglect the first three stages. At this point games playing becomes a mixture of modified sports activities and teacher- and student-designed activities. The key to Stage IV is determining if play can be continuous when made more complex. If it is not continuous, students should probably remain in Stage III or should perform less complex experiences in Stage IV.

GRADE LEVEL	TYPE OF EXPERIENCES
K	Numerous skill patterns with a lot of different equipment at beginning levels repeated continuously throughout the year.
1	Primary emphasis is on rudimentary control and variety—almost exclusively Stage I.
2	Development of beginning major tasks in one or two skill patterns at a time. Continued emphasis on variety, but beginning emphasis on mastery and development of a movement idea using refinement, extension, and application columns. Continuity from one lesson to another. Units are repeated often but go further each time. Time equally divided between Stages I and II. Stage I and II experiences taken to competitive development using primarily self-testing and single-skill activities.
3–4	Material developed in full-blown progressive units that combine Stages I, II, and III. Units tend to focus on one major pattern or one major task within a pattern (except in the case of catching, which is always present in throwing). Time divided 20 percent for Stage I, 60 percent for Stage II, and 20 percent for Stage III.
5–6	If students have had sufficient experience with earlier stages in a pattern or major focus of a pattern, experiences can be developed through Stage IV. Units become longer in length and are not usually repeated throughout the year. Time divided 15 percent for Stage I, 25 percent for Stage II, 40 percent for Stage III, 20 percent for Stage IV.

As with any "canned" progression, the above material should be used only as a gross guide to planning. Student needs differ depending on children's experiences both outside the school setting and within the physical education program. With some skill areas, such as striking with implements, many students probably do not have a great deal of prior experience and will need to stay with the lower stages for longer periods of time.

Using the Charts and Games Strategy Material

After a teacher has chosen a long-term major focus of work, which in some cases might be a large, fully developed unit or a focus for a few lessons, the teacher must decide exactly what children are going to be asked to do (the major tasks) and how the material will be developed. Many decisions are contingent on the responses of students to a task. There are, however, decisions that a teacher can make in planning.

Let us consider the plan of a teacher who has decided to work with a group of second graders in the areas of tossing/throwing. The teacher is working with students who are in Stages I and II of games skills development and has tentatively decided to spend at least four days in this area of work and to return to it several times during the year.

The teacher defines the objectives. Students should be able to:

1. Maintain control of a ball in self-space, tossing to different levels and directions around that space
2. Move in different directions to receive a ball with control
3. Toss a ball to a partner from different levels using an appropriate amount of force for the abilities of the partner
4. Work at an appropriate level of ability

TASK	WHAT TEACHER IS LOOKING FOR	RESPONSE	DECISION
Toss the ball to yourself with control in your own space.	Are they tossing ball?	Yes No———→	Stop work—reemphasize or reinforce on-task behavior.
	Are students staying in their own space with the ball in control?	Yes No———→	Emphasize that there shouldn't be any more balls hitting the floor.
	Are balls "bouncing" out of students' hands?	Yes———→	Design a task to help students "give" with the ball—such as catch the ball "softly" or keep the ball at a lower level, if that is the problem.
See if you can change the level of your toss so that sometimes it is high, sometimes it is just out of your hand, and sometimes it goes to all levels in between.	Are students using all levels?	Yes No———→	As an example, indicate a student who is using all levels or otherwise communicate what "different levels" means.
	Are students using high levels that are challenging but still within limits of own ability?	Yes No———→	Individually make a judgment whether to ask for more control or for more challenge.

(continued)

TASK	WHAT TEACHER IS LOOKING FOR	RESPONSE	DECISION
Toss the ball to different places around your own space—front, back, to the side—and still keep control.	Are tosses to different directions controlled?	Yes No———→	Remind students to stay in own space Ask them to reduce the height of the toss so that they can better control it. Ask students not challenging themselves to send it a little further.
Look for a new space, toss your ball into that space, and be there to catch it.	Are students aware of others moving so that they are moving safely?	Yes No———→	Slow group down—focus on looking for other students and empty spaces.
Toss your ball to a space so that you have to move forward, backward, or sideways to get it.	Are balls going to all directions?	Yes No———→	Reemphasize possibilities for different directions. Ask students not to go in the same direction twice.
As you get better, toss the ball further away to different directions.	This increases speed. Awareness of others as well as distance of toss becomes a factor.		Go back to earlier emphasis if necessary.
We're going to work on tossing the ball to a partner now. Get a partner and practice sending it back and forth.	If students need help organizing for this, the teacher should break down the directions. Eventually students should be able to get a partner, put one ball away, find a good space to work in, and begin working immediately without further teacher cues.	Yes No———→	Break down directions as necessary—encourage independence by combining parts of directions.
Toss the ball to your partner so that you're tossing from above your head.	Are children using appropriate hand patterns to throw? Two hand (overhead) Chest pass (middle levels) Two-hand underhand pattern (low levels)	Yes No———→	If widespread, stop whole group to demonstrate. If not widespread, help children individually or give cues while students are active.
Now combine all levels so that you don't toss twice from the same level.	Are students using all the levels interchangeably?	Yes No———→	Tell students that they cannot pass twice from the same level. Reinforce idea of three different levels.

The above lesson was designed using the content charts. The tasks that comprise the lesson were obtained by using the major task and extension columns of the chart. Teachers must know what qualitative aspects of performance they are looking for when students respond to a task. The charts are designed so that the refinement column provides much of the information needed to help students improve the quality of their

CHART 15.1 Tossing/catching in relation to others. Developed in relation to: individual quick passing; passing and dribbling; cooperative with three; competitive two on one; and competitive two on two.

Students should be able to:
1. Maintain control of a ball, dribbling it with an offensive player trying to tag the ball
2. Receive and send a ball from a wall quickly to different levels
3. Pass and receive a ball on the move in relation to three other students effectively using space
4. Maintain control of a ball with a partner sending and receiving with one/five defensive player(s).

TASK	WHAT TEACHER IS LOOKING FOR	RESPONSE	DECISION
When you come into the gym, start dribbling the ball. (Basketball dribble at different speeds, changing direction and pathways.)	Do they get a ball and start to work immediately?	Yes No ⟶	Remind, reinforce those on-task, or stop group to reinforce compliance
	Are children complying with all elements of the task?	Yes No ⟶	Have group put their balls away and try it again if necessary. Reward those who do if not widespread. Redirect those off-task.
Dick, Jane, and Tamie will now try and touch your ball as you keep moving.	Can students maintain control with an offensive player?		
Choose a distance at least 4 feet from the wall and see how many times you can get the ball to the wall in 30 seconds. Try it again and see if you can beat your own score. Try it again and this time send the ball from above your head, below your waist, and chest height, alternately.	Distance should be appropriate to skill level.	Yes No ⟶	Repeat task with same emphasis.
	Are patterns being alternated?	Yes No ⟶	Repeat task with same emphasis.
Now let's see if we can keep the ball on the move in groups of three. Get with two others you want to work with, find some space, and begin.	Are students moving into a space to receive a pass and timing this move so that they are in a good position to receive it when they get there?	Yes No ⟶	Work individually or with whole group, demonstrating if necessary.
	Are passes timed so that they are ahead of the moving receiver?	Yes No ⟶	Reemphasize or go back to partner work, passing ahead.
When you can keep the ball going without any misses ten times in a row, make one of you a defensive player in the middle trying to get the ball or add dribbling and passing	Students should be able to decide when to move on and when to stay with the cooperative task or to add dribbling.		Help those students who are not making a move decision.
	Does the defensive player stay with one receiver? Does the offensive player move out behind the defensive player to receive a pass? Are the passes quick and accurate?	Yes No ⟶	Ask students what the best strategy is. Find a group doing it and a group not doing it. See if students can tell the difference. Summarize good strategy and ask students to focus on that.

(continued)

CHART 15.1 (*Continued*)

TASK	WHAT TEACHER IS LOOKING FOR	RESPONSE	DECISION
Ask group how many think they are ready to add another defensive player. Give them as a guideline the idea that they must be able to make at least ten passes without defense being able to touch ball. Reorganize groups where necessary.	In order to deal effectively with two on two, the above skills must be established. The need for quicker passes, better-timed cuts, and "faking" your intended direction offensively is put at a premium.	Yes No ⟶	Return to previous experience as necessary.

responses. However, the teacher must redesign tasks based on how students respond to the original task. *Teachers should not continue to extend a task using more difficult conditions if the qualitative aspects of performance are not being met by students or if the learning environment is not productive.*

When students move into Stages III and IV, skills are used in gamelike conditions and students are introduced to games strategies. A lesson involving games strategies is developed in Chart 15.1.

In the sample lesson presented, the teacher has selected aspects of Stages I, II, and III in designing the lesson. The work in Stages I and II is taken from the charts—giving students practice with propelling skills and tossing and catching skills in situations demanding high levels of control under not-so-complex conditions and adding both self-testing and competitive elements to the practice of the skill. The offensive and defensive work is taken from the games strategy section presented later in this chapter.

It is important to note that the teacher was very sensitive to the stages of readiness in adding more complexity to the progression and made allowances for students who were not ready to go on when the task was presented. It is not uncommon to have many groups at many levels in one class all functioning with the same movement idea but at very different levels of complexity.

DEVELOPING THE MANIPULATIVE PATTERNS

Tossing/Throwing

Good games players must be able to toss/throw objects:

1. Of different shapes, sizes, and weights—primarily without implements but occasionally with implements
2. Using sidearm, underhand, and overhand patterns
3. To different directions and levels, using varying amounts of force
4. From a stationary as well as on-the-move position and in combination with other skills, players, and externally imposed game conditions

The first major theme and manipulative pattern is tossing/throwing. Tossing and throwing have been separated from each other because they require different kinds of experiences for development. The amount of force needed in sending an object is primarily what distinguishes throwing from tossing. Throwing patterns require using the whole body to produce force. Throwing usually involves increasing force production because of (a) greater distance, (b) a need for increased speed, or (c) the use of heavy objects that need to be sent. Tossing patterns usually do not involve the total body in force production.

In order to develop throwing patterns, students must be put in a situation where maximum force production is encouraged. Students at beginning stages cannot receive objects that are coming with great force. Therefore, the teacher must involve the students initially in learning experiences requiring near maximum force production and those in which the force of an object is considerably reduced.

It is difficult to separate tossing experiences from catching experiences. Often the teacher will want to combine these skills for emphasis at beginning stages of development. The teacher will also want to include tossing experiences that use a variety of different kinds of balls.

The major throwing tasks are designed to develop mature skill patterns in the overhand and underhand throw (See Chart 15.2). These skill patterns form the basis for basic striking patterns and for many specialized sport skills (volleyball serve, tennis serve, bowling, and so on.).

The reader is encouraged to consult Chapter 4, which discusses efficient performance of these skills.

CHART 15.2 Tossing and throwing

MAJOR TASK	EXTENSION	REFINEMENT	APPLICATION
Tossing in self-space *SAMPLE TASK* Toss the ball to different levels in your own space without letting it hit the floor.	Initially no implement Implements Initially soft, light objects—larger, heavier, harder objects Control of level of toss Control direction of toss Imparting force with no concern for receiving object	Application of force under object Remaining within own ability to receive object Using total body to impart force Follow through in line of direction	Self-testing Self-designed Teacher-designed
Tossing to a different space *SAMPLE TASK* Toss your ball to a new space and be there to catch it.	Toss in front Toss moving forward, backward and sideward Continuous change in direction Tossing from high level (overhand) Tossing from low level (underhand)	Awareness of others while moving Continuous tracking of object Judging distance accurately Working at limits of own ability Stopping with each reception—on the move continuously	Self-testing Self-designed Teacher-designed Call ball
Tossing to target areas *SAMPLE TASK* Toss your beanbag from a high level above your head to the high target. When you can hit the target three times in a row, move back a step away from the target.	Changing target: size (large—small); level (med—high or low) Distance from target (knock down targets→ increasing force) Specifying level of release		Self-testing Self-designed Teacher-designed
Tossing in relation to another person *SAMPLE TASK* Find out how far up or out to the side your partner can stretch away from his or her space to receive the ball (beanbag).	*Stationary* Changing distance apart Change level of toss Toss to make partner move to receive object (sideways, backward, forward)	Responsibility of catching is on the tosser, not receiver Understanding limits of partner ability to receive and getting object to these limits	

(continued)

CHART 15.2 (*Continued*)

MAJOR TASK	EXTENSION	REFINEMENT	APPLICATION
Tossing in relation to another person *SAMPLE TASK* Standing in your own area, pass the ball to your partner while they are moving and see if you can get it to them so that they don't have to break stride to receive it.	*To a moving partner* Changing distance Changing level of toss so that partner does not have to break stride Partner cueing direction Slow speed→increasing speed	Tossing object ahead of individual Choosing appropriate level, force, and direction Getting rid of objects immediately	
Both partners moving Both moving in same direction→different directions Limited space→increasing space *SAMPLE TASK* Staying in your own area, continuously pass the ball to each other using all the space available to you.	Getting rid of object quickly Use of entire space available to group Moving into a space to receive object *Note:* With the increased size of space, pattern moves from a toss to a throw. Timing pass to individual coming to meet it		
Tossing in relation to others continuously on the move *SAMPLE TASK* In groups of three, continuously pass the ball to each other on the move without holding the ball and trying to utilize all the space in your area.	*Groups of three, four, five* Increasing size of group Increasing size of space	Moving into a space to receive Awareness of all others moving at the same time	Hot potato (variation)

Tossing in relation to offensive and defensive roles
 	
(Move to basic games strategy for keep-away activities.)
 	
SAMPLE TASK
In groups of three, two of you pass the ball back and forth and one of you try to get the ball away.
	One defense/two offense
	Designated area
		Offense
		  Cutting into open space to receive object
		  Timing—pass ahead of receiver
		  Choosing appropriate level in relation to defense
		Defense
		  Closing up space
		  Staying with receiver	

(*continued*)

CHART 15.2 (*Continued*)

MAJOR TASK	EXTENSION	REFINEMENT	APPLICATION
Throwing: establishing an overhand throw pattern (no concern for receiving) *SAMPLE TASK* Stand somewhere behind this line and try to get a hard throw to the wall—hitting the wall at a high level.	Objects that are easily gripped (bean-bags)→objects more difficult to grip because of hardness, size or weight Hard throw with no concern for accuracy Throw to a high, broad target area or over a restraining object (net, rope, stick) Throw to different directions Throwing for distance Throwing for accuracy using increasingly smaller targets Throwing to a continuously changing target area Throwing to a moving target—(people, balls, other objects)	Mechanical principles of overhand pattern Opposition Sequential rotation Transfer of weight Attending to angle of release Making movement bigger to produce force Direction of release (see throwing, chapter 4) Throwing to space in front of moving object *Note:* Catching behavior develops behind the ability to throw and will restrict the development of the throwing pattern if required too early in the child's throwing experiences.	Ball pass Norwegian ball Newcomb Bombardment Wall dodgeball Busy ball Pig in the middle Crackabout
Throwing: establishing an underhand throw pattern *SAMPLE TASK* Stand somewhere behind this line and use an underhand pattern to hit the wall near the floor. Try to make it a hard throw and keep the object close to the floor.	Using objects easily gripped with some weight—larger, heavier objects Using target areas on floor or close to floor—using target areas at higher and changing levels Changing distance from target areas Increasing concern for accuracy	Choosing appropriate point of release Using body to produce force Follow through in desired direction Stepping into throw, transferring weight to the forward foot (opposite to hand being used)	Bowling Self-testing activities

Catching/Collecting

Good games players must be able to catch/collect objects:

1. Of different weights, sizes, and shapes with the hands only, different body parts, and with and without the use of implements
2. From different directions, levels, distances and coming with varying amounts of force
3. From stationary as well as on-the-move positions and in combination with other skills, players, and externally imposed game conditions

This theme involves the manipulative skills of receiving objects. A distinction is made between catching, collecting, and trapping skills. We usually associate catching skills with the use of the hands, but implements such as scoops and lacrosse sticks can also be used for catching. When we catch an object, we absorb the force of the oncoming object and completely control it, maintaining possession.

Collecting objects usually involves body parts other than the hands. We do not maintain possession of the object with our body parts. We absorb the oncoming force and redirect it to maintain control of the object. Collecting skills are most common in soccer, where the chest and feet are often used to absorb the force of an oncoming ball and redirect it to the ground in front of the player, where it can be played.

Trapping skills stop the force of an object completely and keep the object in a still position. Trapping skills are used primarily in soccer. Players place their foot on a soccer ball coming on the ground to stop it completely. They also use the lower part of the leg to trap the ball between the shin and the ground.

CHART 15.3 Catching and collecting

MAJOR TASK	EXTENSION	REFINEMENT	APPLICATION
Catching objects from a personal toss in self-space SAMPLE TASK Catch the beanbag so that it is sometimes very close to the ground before you get it, sometimes far above your head, and sometimes in between.	Note: Large objects are likely to be easier for a child to track. Smaller objects will elicit a more mature pattern. Balls of all sizes should be used, but weight quality should move from light to heavy and objects that can be gripped easily should precede those not easily gripped. Slight release out of hand→high toss Catch at medium levels→off the ground catches→and near the floor catches Directly in front→ side→slightly back	(See catching, Chapter 4) Extending to meet object with the hands—flexion to receive force of object (arms and whole body if necessary) Note: Phrases "catch softly" or "give with it" are often effective. Tossing object only to height within the ability to control object and still be challenging Tracking the object with the eyes (see the beanbag in the hands) When catching at different levels, students should be helped to make the catch near the floor as well as high off the floor and to vary their levels	Self-testing Teacher-designed Student-designed Call ball Boundary ball Newcomb Bombardment Busy ball Running score Keep away Pig in the middle Wall ball Bases on balls Low levels High levels Keep away
Move to meet a self-tossed object SAMPLE TASK Toss the ball to different directions around your personal space and be there to catch it.	Walk with small toss Toss to a new space and be there to catch it Toss sideways/backward and move to receive	Toss should be within limits of student's ability Maintain an awareness of other students while moving	
Catching an object tossed by another SAMPLE TASK Toss the beanbag to your partner and see how far your partner can stretch from his or her own personal space to receive it. Try to get your partner in a full stretch up or to the side.	Both partners stationary Changing distance between partners Changing level ball is received (high/on ground/medium levels) Changing direction (left-right-back) Testing the limits of your partner's self-space	Responsibility of sender to place ball within limits of partner's ability Varying levels→use of all levels Partner should be at complete extension when ball is received (the point at which partner almost misses) up, down, and to the side	

(continued)

CHART 15.3 *(Continued)*

MAJOR TASK	EXTENSION	REFINEMENT	APPLICATION
SAMPLE TASK Send the ball to your partner at different levels while partner is moving.	Making partner move to receive object Changing distance through controlling space available Receiving low balls on the move/high balls/medium balls/balls that bounce	Encourage students to select a distance that will give them enough time to move into position to meet ball without having to deal with force levels that are too difficult Emphasis should be on receiving object without breaking forward momentum	
SAMPLE TASK Both you and your partner send the ball back and forth continuously on the move in your own work area.	Both partners on the move continuously Changing direction Moving in the same direction	Keeping eye on ball while moving away or toward ball from different directions or same direction	
SAMPLE TASK Send the ball back and forth to your partner, but this time you must send the ball to your partner from whatever level you receive it.	Receiving and sending in a smooth action Sending object from same level from which it was received To same level To different level Changing distance	Emphasis is on being able to receive ball just long enough to control it before sending it again	
Catching an object off a wall *SAMPLE TASK* Choose a comfortable distance and send the ball to the wall so that it comes back to you at different levels.	Sending object to a wall to receive it With bounce—without bounce Increase distance Change levels of rebound, include bouncing balls Change direction of throw	Toss *up* is the easiest to receive and students should be encouraged to cause a high arc before dealing with more difficult low bouncing and line drive balls Students will need help trying to send the ball to the wall so they have to move to receive it—change in angle of throw only needs to be slight to cause a need to move to the right or left	
Catching a thrown object from a partner	Similar progression as a tossed ball from a partner, only distance between partners should elicit a definite throw pattern (must be able to catch from a toss a short distance with a great deal of accuracy before throw is introduced)	Partner that throws the ball has responsibility for sending the object at a force level that is challenging but not above the abilities of the receiving partner	

(continued)

CHART 15.3 *(Continued)*

MAJOR TASK	EXTENSION	REFINEMENT	APPLICATION
Receiving (collecting) objects without use of the hands *SAMPLE TASK* Send the ball up in the air and break the momentum of the ball with different parts of your body so that the ball drops in front of you.	Different body parts from a self-toss *Note:* Work with receiving beanbags similar to the progression preceding striking patterns should precede this work as well as catching ability with hands only Light, medium-sized nerf or plastic balls—heavier soccer balls Tossing ball up and "giving" with ball to place it in front of you Using different body parts (chest, knees, feet) Increasing size of toss Increasing need to move forward, backward, or sideways to receive	Toss from partner must be high enough to allow receiver to move under ball The level and arc the ball is coming from will determine the appropriate body part Students should understand that they are trying to reach out with the receiving part and then move back (give) with that part—the longer the time and space they use to give with the object, the more force they can absorb	
SAMPLE TASK Choose one part of your body that you feel comfortable with (not hands) and work at receiving the force of the ball from a toss from your partner until you get really good using that part.	Different body parts—from a partner toss Increasing distance between partners Using different body parts→getting good at at least one	Continue to encourage tossing partner to keep the ball high Increasing need to move forward, backward, sideways to receive Feet only from a partner	
SAMPLE TASK Have your partner roll the ball to you and see if you can use your foot to stop the ball completely.	Trapping a ball (stopping it still) using the feet, shins/1 foot and 2 feet Increasing need to move to meet ball (up, to right and left)	Students should be encouraged to place their foot behind the ball to stop it, not on top Weight should not be transferred to the foot stopping the ball	
SAMPLE TASK Have your partner roll the ball to you so that you have to move either to the right or left to receive the ball. See if you can control the ball without stopping it and send it right back.	Controlling ball with feet without bringing it to a dead stop Increasing speed of ball Increasing need to move to meet ball (up, to right and left)	Ball should remain within self-space after it is controlled Encourage students to move out to meet the ball and not wait for it to come	
Receiving objects without hands and placing them in a position to play them	Combining receiving an aerial ball with different body parts with passing the ball with the feet		

(continued)

CHART 15.3 *(Continued)*

MAJOR TASK	EXTENSION	REFINEMENT	APPLICATION
	Toss to self, receive with different body parts, pass to a wall	Encourage students to start slowly and then to increase speed	
	Toss from partner—receive with different body parts send back with feet	Ball should be placed where it can be easily played	
	Changing distance between partners	Encourage students to choose the appropriate body part for the level and arc of the ball	
SAMPLE TASK	Sending and receiving continuously with partner stationary and occasionally attempting to lift the ball into the air so that partner can play it high	Ball should be placed where it can be easily played	
Continuously pass the ball back and forth to a partner in your area slowly, with both of you on the move.	Sending and receiving continuously with partner (small group) on the move	Sending ball to a space in front of moving partner Moving into a space to receive object	
(Move to basic games strategy for keep-away activities.)	Slow→increase in speed Short distance→long distance	Choosing an appropriate force level for partner	

Students in elementary school are all at different stages in their ability to receive objects. The size and weight of the object is a critical factor in catching. Students put in situations using objects that are too hard, too heavy, or coming too fast for their ability are likely to resort to immature patterns of catching as well as develop a fear reaction to catching (example: closing the eyes and turning the head when a softball or kickball is hit/kicked to them). Teachers must be sensitive to the child's stage of development in catching and ensure that the conditions under which the child is asked to catch are congruent with the child's ability.

The material developed in this theme begins with catching/collecting/trapping under the simplest of conditions and provides direction for expanding the conditions under which students receive the force of objects. Before working in this theme, the teacher should review the developmental stages and analysis of the catching pattern described in Chapter 4.

Striking

Good games players must be able to strike objects:

1. Of different weights, sizes, and shapes with different body parts, the hands only, feet only, and with sticks, bats, paddles, and racquets
2. Using sidearm, underhand, and overhand patterns
3. To different directions and levels, using varying amounts of force
4. From stationary as well as on-the-move positions and in combination with other skills, players, and externally imposed game conditions

Children can develop mature striking patterns at an early age. Often striking skills are not introduced in our programs until late in a physical education program. There are many reasons for this. For example, practice in striking balls and other objects can be a managerial nightmare for the unprepared teacher and in situations where students have not yet learned on-task behaviors.

Striking skills are critical to many of our

FIGURE 15.1 Striking skills are critical to many of our sport activities.

sport activities, particularly those that are used in adult life. They can be introduced to elementary-school children in Stages I and II beginning with the first grade. Students will develop mature patterns of striking early but cannot be expected to gain high levels of accuracy with most striking patterns. Striking skills are more difficult than throwing skills and require a great deal of guided experience before students can move on to using these skills in Stages III and IV. Many elementary-school children will not be ready for striking experiences that move beyond early cooperative/competitive experiences in Stage III.

Major tasks have been organized progressively and according to the type of striking skill used. Experiences using hands only, feet only, and a variety of body parts as well as sticks, bats, and racquets are all necessary striking experiences. They can be developed generally at first and then later treated in detail as the child advances through the elementary-school program.

Striking work, as it is developed in this chapter, begins with beanbags and balloons. Body parts in general, and then specifically, are then introduced with balls before work is started with implements. Actually, these areas can be developed simultaneously if need be. Although the word ball is used in most instances, the reader should be alert to the idea that badminton shuttlecocks and patecas can be used as well with the advantage that speed in flight is reduced with these objects, and they are usually easier to track. See Chart 15.4, page 218.

Dodging

Good games players must be able to dodge:

1. Different numbers of people moving in different amounts of space at different speeds and in different ways
2. Objects of different sizes and shapes, aerial and not aerial, coming at different speeds from different directions and with different amounts of force
3. From stationary as well as on the move positions and in combination with other skills, players, and externally imposed game conditions

It is difficult to distinguish where actual dodging skills begin and abilities relative to an awareness of others and objects and moving in relation to stationary objects leave off. The bulk of this initial work and moving in relation to others belongs to body management skills developed in Chapter 16, but it must be recognized that these areas are interrelated. See Chart 15.5, page 226.

DEVELOPING BASIC GAMES STRATEGIES

Many of our more popular games and sports in the United States share the same basic strategy orientation. Soccer, field hockey, basketball, ice hockey, lacrosse, and some less common sports have a similar orientation. Tennis, badminton, volleyball, and many other racquet sports have much in common. As a result, the basic games strategy skills

CHART 15.4 Striking

MAJOR TASK	EXTENSION	REFINEMENT	APPLICATION
Sending beanbags with different body parts *SAMPLE TASK* Send your beanbag as straight up in the air as possible from a part of your body below your waist.	*Note:* Basic skills necessary for striking can be established first with sending and receiving beanbags to enable students to position themselves and body parts in relation to object. Resting beanbag on a part of the body and sending it as straight up as possible (catch with hands) Change the level the beanbag goes into the air Send with parts of hands and arms Send with parts of the legs Send with parts of the trunk	Controlling direction of follow-through Producing force with whole body Responsibility to keep object within personal space	
Receiving beanbags on different parts of the body from a self-toss *SAMPLE TASK* Toss your beanbag into the air and see if you can catch it on a part of your body above your waist but not your hands.	Choosing a part easy to control Choosing a part above the waist Choosing a part below the waist Choosing a part hard to control	Controlling the force and choosing a direction of the toss so that it can be received by a particular part Positioning the body part so that it is as flat as possible to receive object Absorbing the force of the object with the body part being used and the whole body (receiving softly)	
Tossing and receiving beanbag with different parts *SAMPLE TASK* Toss your beanbag up in the air with one part of your body and receive it with the same part.	Tossing with one part and receiving with a different part Tossing and receiving with the same part Changing level of toss Changing direction of toss	Controlling level of toss so that it is appropriate for the receiving part Moving out to meet beanbag and "giving" with it	
Establishing basic striking patterns using balloons (lightweight balls) *SAMPLE TASK* Keep the balloon up in the air using different	Hands only Keeping the ball up in the air Keeping the balloon above the head Sending the balloon from below the waist	Containing the balloon within perimeters of personal space Tracking the balloon with the eyes Striking the balloon under object	Self-testing

(continued)

CHART 15.4 (*Continued*)

MAJOR TASK	EXTENSION	REFINEMENT	APPLICATION
parts of the hand to strike the balloon.	Different parts of the hand	Choosing appropriate striking pattern for level of balloon when it is struck	
	Continuously changing the level from which the balloon is sent	Contacting balloon at an appropriate stage of the striking pattern	
	Changing the level of the balloon in the air	Positioning part of the body to strike balloon	
	Minimum and maximum use of force		
	Different body parts	Tapping object for minimum levels	
	Specifying part	Encourage experiences that require the use of the total body to produce force (e.g., head)	
SAMPLE TASK	Child choice		
Keep the balloon up in the air using different parts of your body, sometimes hitting it as hard as you can and sometimes just tapping it very lightly.	Changing direction of the balloon		
	Keep balloon up in air with different parts		
	Using minimum and maximum levels of force		
	Using above ideas with a partner		
Striking medium-sized plastic or nerf balls	Using a wall		
	Tossing ball to the wall and striking it back with different parts of the body		
	Tossing ball to the wall and striking it back to wall continuously using a bounce	Toss should initially be up so that student has time to move under it or behind it	
	Changing to a heavier ball (soccer or volleyball)	Encourage students to stay with a part until they can control it	
	Specifying body part		
SAMPLE TASK	One partner specifies the level of toss desired and strikes ball back— one partner tosses ball to other partner and catches the ball after it has been struck	Tossing ball to partner so that it can be easily struck	Self-testing
Toss the ball to your partner at a high or medium level and see if your partner can strike it back to you so that you don't have to move. Partner should use different parts of the body. Change off after a few tries.		Controlling force of striking so that it can easily be caught	Keeping object going
	Striking the ball to different levels		
	Striking the ball to different directions to make partner move	The ball should go to the receiving partner—do not permit "wild" striking at the ball	
	Increasing distance between partners		
	Using a net, rope, or other boundary to strike over, under, or between		

(*continued*)

CHART 15.4 (*Continued*)

MAJOR TASK	EXTENSION	REFINEMENT	APPLICATION

SAMPLE TASK
One partner should stand in different places in the court on one side of the net. The other partner should stand as far back on the other side of the net as possible and still hit the ball to the receiving partner so that the partner can catch it.
	Striking the ball to a wall
	  Overhand, sidearm, and
	    underhand patterns
	  Changing distances
	  Large target areas and
	    small target areas
	  Changing use of the
	    hands
	Striking ball over a net,
	  rope, or other object
	Overhand, sidearm, and
	    underhand patterns
	  Keeping ball within
	    boundaries
	  Placing object in differ-
	    ent areas of the
	    court
	  Choosing a pattern and
	    working for
	    consistency
		(See volleyball serving
		  patterns)
		Encourage
		  Step into the hit
		  Extension of arm
		  Accurate toss up or
		    drop to strike	

Striking (controlled tap) the ball with hands only, with a partner *SAMPLE TASK* Keep the ball at high level, sending it back and forth to each other using your fingertips to tap the ball.	Keeping the ball up in the air with a bounce if necessary No bounce High level only Low level only Alternating high and low Increasing distance Across a net or other boundary	Do not permit students working at a high level to send it back at a low level—ask them to catch balls not high enough, so that they learn to move under the ball When the underhand ac-tions (bump or hand striking pattern) is in-troduced, both high and low can be prac-ticed together	
Striking (controlled tap) the ball in small groups (of three, four, or five) *SAMPLE TASK* In small groups keep the ball up in the air using your hands and arms only.	Keeping the ball up in the air with a bounce if necessary No bounce High level only (Move to basic games strategy for net activities)	Stress keeping ball at a high level to give play-ers a chance to move under it	
Striking the ball with the feet only (kicking); equipment recommen-dation: rubber balls or large nerf balls, de-flated soccer balls	Sending the ball to a wall using your feet (catch in between; stationary ball; stationary kicker) Stationary ball, moving kicker (few steps)	Encourage students to have the ball come back to them—if they want to kick harder, they can move back, but the ball must be controlled	

(continued)

CHART 15.4 *(Continued)*

MAJOR TASK	EXTENSION	REFINEMENT	APPLICATION
SAMPLE TASK Stand a few steps away from your ball and move toward it, kicking it to the wall directly in front of you so that it comes back to you.			
Continuously striking the ball with different body parts in groups of five *SAMPLE TASK* In groups of five keep the ball going using different parts of your body to strike the ball and a bounce in between if you need it. Remember to keep the ball high so that other players have time to move under it.	Bounce in between—all parts No bounce in between—all parts	Choosing appropriate part for level of ball Sending ball at a high level so that it can better be controlled by other players Moving to meet ball Establishing spatial boundaries with team members to avoid collision (signaling)	Group self-testing

Striking the ball with hands only
 	
SAMPLE TASK
Keep the ball moving to the wall with a kick, controlling it before you kick it back.
	Using different parts of the hands to strike ball
	Keeping ball above the head (tapping)
	Keeping ball below the waist
	Note: Initial attempts at underhand striking pattern will produce what will eventually become illegal volleyball hits. These should be tolerated initially and ultimately phased out as a definite hit pattern can be obtained such as the bump and dig (see page).
	Using different parts of the foot
	  Changing distance
	  Raising the ball in the air to different levels
	  Continuously kicking, stopping, or controlling object in between
		Contacting ball at highest level possible
		Use of fingertips
		Light action (see volleyball set)
		(see volleyball bump)
		
		Ask students which part of foot gives them more control (inside)
		Ball can be raised by applying force under it	

SAMPLE TASK Punt the ball to the wall, first trying to get a low	Starting with object in the hand (punt) Changing level of ball on the wall	See kicking, Chapter 4 Encourage students on the punt to toss it out	

(continued)

CHART 15.4 (*Continued*)

MAJOR TASK	EXTENSION	REFINEMENT	APPLICATION
level and then a high level at the wall.	Changing distance, kicking for accuracy against wall at different levels	from them to get a punt and step into the kick with the opposite foot	
SAMPLE TASK Dribble your ball in general space. When you come to wall, kick the ball to the wall, receive it again, and keep going with your ball.	Traveling with the ball/ propelling with a dribble, and kicking into a large target area—increasing speed—increasing distance from target	Speed should be only as fast as student can go and still maintain control of the ball	
Striking the ball to a partner with the feet *SAMPLE TASK* Kick the ball back and forth with your partner, stopping the ball before you send it back to your partner.	Ball stationary and partners stationary Each partner stopping the ball before sending the ball back Keeping ball on ground and getting ball into the air	Do not allow students to return ball without stopping it first Encourage students to move up to meet the ball and then move back into position	
SAMPLE TASK Keep the ball going back and forth in your own area with both you and your partner continuously moving and using all the space in your area.	Changing distance Ball stationary to a slowly moving partner (partner stops ball and passes back) Controlling the ball but not stopping it Sending ball to a stationary partner while on the move Increasing speed of traveling Increasing distance Passing to a moving partner while on the move Increasing speed Increasing distance Same direction Different directions	Pass should be ahead of receiving partner at an appropriate speed When ball is not stopped, it still should be controlled—do not allow students to lose control Students should keep the ball controlled within a designated area The ball should be controlled and then immediately passed Passes should be ahead of moving partner	
Striking the ball in relation to two others (See keep-away development later in this chapter.)	Passing the ball continuously on the move With a stop and without a stop Increasing speed Increasing size of space Encouraging getting ball up in the air and use of body parts other than hands	Encourage players to move into a space to receive it and to use all the space If ball isn't stopped, it still must be controlled	
Establishing striking patterns with imple-	Keeping the balloon up in the air with the racquet		

(*continued*)

CHART 15.4 (*Continued*)

MAJOR TASK	EXTENSION	REFINEMENT	APPLICATION
ments—balloons and nylon racquets	Changing level of balloon Changing direction in personal space		
SAMPLE TASK Sometimes just tap your balloon and let it go off your racquet a little bit. Sometimes hit it hard so that it goes to a very high level off your racquet.	Striking the balloon at different levels in relation to the body Keeping balloon above the head Waiting for balloon to almost hit the floor All levels in between Changing level continuously	Students will have a hard time waiting for the ball to come low. Encourage them to experience all levels	
SAMPLE TASK Get as far away from the balloon as you can and still strike it. Make your body really stretch to get it.	Striking the balloon when it is away from the body Using the extremities of personal space (side, up, out, and low)		
SAMPLE TASK Send the balloon back and forth to a partner.	Striking the balloon with a partner Taking turns hitting balloon up Sending balloon to a partner	Distance will have to be fairly close	
Striking using paddles and balls (nerf balls, tennis balls) (*Note:* This sequence can be used without paddles as well.)	Keeping the ball on top of the paddle, continuously tapping With a bounce if needed Changing level Varying direction of tap		
SAMPLE TASK Keep the ball going on top of your paddle, sending it to different directions (right, left, forward, backward) around your personal space.	Striking object down Continuously Changing level Striking alternately up and down Striking against a wall Tapping object using a bounce	Control direction so that you don't have to move out of personal space Changing paddle position smoothly Maintaining a force factor within the individual's ability to control object	
SAMPLE TASK Send the ball to the wall with your paddle so that it comes back on your right side, then left, then right, alternating sides.	Increasing distance Keeping ball to right side/left side Alternating sides Striking ball close to and far from body Striking ball close to the floor/far from floor	Changing body position so that opposite sides are to net and feet get all the way around Follow through with a transfer of weight to front foot Striking object at a point where body and arm are extended in a full stroke	

(*continued*)

CHART 15.4 (*Continued*)

MAJOR TASK	EXTENSION	REFINEMENT	APPLICATION
Striking using paddles and balls, with a partner *SAMPLE TASK* Alternate hits against the wall with your partner, being sure to give your partner enough space to hit the ball.	Alternating hits against a wall—cooperatively Short distance/tap Increase distance/stroke Trying to place the ball in a difficult position for partner to hit	Choosing a level below/ up to strike object Placing ball so that partner can easily move into position Getting out of the way as soon as your hit is made	Self-testing to keep ball going with a partner
Striking with a partner over a line/rope/folded mat/bench	Keeping ball going Placing ball in a position hard for partner to hit	Boundaries will ultimately have to be designed for this activity—at first they should be kept informal, increasing in size as students can control force element	
Establishing underhand striking patterns with sticks (golf clubs, hockey sticks, whiffle balls, plastic nerf balls, pucks, small balls) *SAMPLE TASK* Travel with your stick and ball. When you come to a wall, send the ball to the wall, pick it up again, and keep going until you come to a new wall. Try to do it so that you don't have to stop and wait for the ball to come back.	Sending an object to a wall, using an underhand striking pattern Stationary ball Changing distance Stopping ball in between—controlling ball Lifting object into the air From propelling ball Receiving ball on the move without stopping and then striking	Refinement of this pattern can include rule instructions as to the height of the stick—no restrictions if a full underhand pattern is desired (in close group work the rule restriction is a necessity) Positioning ball in front and to the right before striking Rotation on backswing and follow-through Lifting object by getting stick under the object	
Striking in relation to another person *SAMPLE TASK* Travel with your partner, sending the ball back and forth. Hang on to the ball just long enough to control it.	Sending object to a partner Both partners stationary Object stationary Changing distance Controlling object but not stopping it first Receiving partner on the move (forward, backward, sideward) Increasing speed Getting rid of object quickly	Responsibility of sender to make object manageable to abilities of receiver Sending object ahead of partner on the move Moving into an appropriate space to receive object from partner	
Striking in relation to others continuously on the move (propelling becomes a necessary skill)	Groups of three, four, five Increasing size of group Increasing size of space	Awareness of all other players Moving into a space to meet a pass	

(*continued*)

CHART 15.4 (*Continued*)

MAJOR TASK	EXTENSION	REFINEMENT	APPLICATION
SAMPLE TASK In your small group keep the ball going back and forth on the move, using all the space available to your group.			
Striking in relation to offensive and defensive roles *SAMPLE TASK* One person in your group of four tries to get the ball away from the others, keeping the ball in your own area.	One defense/three offense Designated area Goal area for offense (Move to basic games strategy for keep-away activities.)	Defensively cutting off space or possible angles at goal/placing self between object and goal Offensively using each other to open space/quick passes	
Establishing sidearm striking patterns with bats	Hitting a stationary ball *Note:* Ball can be kept stationary through the use of batting tees, hung from string, reversed vacuum cleaners, etc.) Large, light ball→small, heavier ball Light, large bat→heavier bats Hitting a tossed ball Slow speed→increasing speed Controlling the direction of the hit/left-right/up-down	Placement of left hand on bottom, right hand close and on top of left hand, bat up and off shoulder Elbow out Open stance rotation on backswing and follow-through Increasing concern for level swing, transference of weight forward Placing bat down after swing (if turn is over or other skills are being used in conjunction with batting)	

that are used in playing these games are similar.

The two basic games strategies for which elementary-school students should be prepared are keep-away activities and net activities. Keep-away activities involve two teams, shared space, and a defended goal. Soccer, field hockey, ice hockey, basketball, lacrosse, touch football, and speedaway are all keep-away activities. The manipulated object changes and the way in which a person can travel with, send, and receive the object changes. The idea of the game does not change.

Net activities involve either one player, two players, or teams of players who are sep-arated from each other by a net. The purpose of the activity is to send the object so that the other team cannot return it. Volleyball, tennis, badminton, and other racquet sports share this orientation. The size of the ball changes, the skill used to strike the object changes, but the basic intent of the activity does not change.

Many teaching programs have assumed that an individual who has the ability to control an object will know what to do with the object offensively and defensively. This is a false assumption. Games strategies develop progressively, like any other skill, and this development must be guided progressively. Such progression assumes that the manip-

CHART 15.5 Dodging

MAJOR TASK	EXTENSION	REFINEMENT	APPLICATION
Dodging people: moving in relation to others in a specified general space	Large space→small space Slow→fast movement Small group→large group Uncluttered environment→cluttered environment Move to application in tag activities	Group should use all the space available Individuals should move so that they are avoiding each other and moving into empty spaces In tag situations students should move in relation to the tagger, maintaining an awareness of others	Freeze tag Safe tag Partner seat tag Steal the bacon Steal the treasure Pussy wants a corner

Moving in relation to one other	Partners facing
	  Shadowing directions of partner (forward, backward, sideways)
	  Seat tag attempting to tag each other's seat
		Making shift with partner
		Playing both offensive and defensive role	

Dodging moving objects	Dodging rolled objects→low objects Balls: fleece balls, nerf balls, beanbags, yarn balls *Note:* Having partners use a wall is a way to avoid retrieval problems Beanbag tied to end of rope (See Application) Groups of three with dodger in the middle Small groups, varying number of dodgers and throwers	Timing jump or shift to right or left in relation to oncoming ball (slow down object if this becomes a problem) Keeping object at a low level Partner turning, keeping object at a low level Shifting in relation to anticipated direction of throw	Ball pass Poison pin Crackabout Wall dodgeball Jump the brook Dodge ball

ulative skills are already present. It then works on increasing the number of offensive and defensive players, rules related to manipulative infractions, scoring skills, and special environments.

Suggestions for Implementation

Rules. Students can be helped to understand the need for rules if they have a role in deciding what rules will be included and have the option to design and add rules as necessary. Teachers should guide the development of rules by adding only those necessary (a) for safety, (b) to prevent the long-term practice of skills done in a way that will eventually be considered illegal, and (c) to maintain the flow of the game. If a rule destroys the flow of the game, change or modify the rule or the game.

Individual skills. Practice of individual skills should not be stopped once game play begins. The need for more practice of a specific ability outside of a game situation will probably be made even clearer by game play. Teachers should not be afraid to go back and to work simultaneously with different stages.

Progression. Teachers should not be afraid to move continuously back and forth to different levels of the progression as necessary.

Individualization. It is conceivable and in fact probable that different students will be at different levels of the progression at any one time. Students should have the option of working at an appropriate level for themselves, even if this results in four or more different groups at four different levels of ability in one class.

The process of decision making. Students can be helped to make rule decisions and decisions regarding their own progression if they are encouraged both to go through a process of decision and to play with and evaluate their decisions during and after play.

Maximum activity. Progressions are designed so that all students can participate in an organizational format that allows them maximum opportunity to practice. The smallest number of players necessary to develop a strategy or skill should be used.

Adaptation of progression. No progression, game, or activity is sacred. Learning experiences should be modified to meet the needs of students.

Strategies for Keep-Away Activities

One offense—one defense. Assume that students have enough control of an object in a noncompetitive environment to (a) change the speed, direction, and distance of the object from their own bodies and (b) be able to concentrate on the presence of another person trying to get the object away.

Activity: Propelling or carrying an object while (a) another person is trying to make a player lose control, (b) another person is trying to obtain possession, (c) the teacher adds simple rule limitations on how object may be protected and how defender may attempt possession.

Abilities developed: (a) Quickly change direction and speed of object in relation to defender; (b) Protect object with body where rules permit; (c) Stop and start quickly.

Two offense—one defense. Assume that students can control an object with deliberate and intentional moves in the face of a defender.

FIGURE 15.2 Students can control an object with deliberate and intentional moves in the face of a defender.

Activity: Continuously passing and receiving object with a partner with one defensive player trying to obtain possession with (a) on-the-move receiver and stationary partner and (b) propelling as well as passing alternative.

Abilities developed: (a) Quick passes to the receiver; (b) Opening up space by moving into a spatial position clear of defense; (c) Passing ahead of receiver on the move; (d) Defensively closing up space by placing oneself with the receiver at an angle that closes off anticipated pass, and continuously repositioning oneself.

Two defense—two offense (not goal-oriented). Assume that offensive players can keep the object from one defensive player with little effort.

Activity: Partners moving in a defined space attempting to keep object from two defensive players. Continue to phase in rule limitations on maintaining and obtaining possession of the ball and temporary penalties for infractions if necessary. Add boundaries as necessary.

Abilities developed: (a) Increased ability to time pass to a receiver and make a quick pass; (b) Increased ability to time cut into space to receive object, receiving pass on the move and clear of defense; (c) Increased emphasis on defensively making an accurate pass difficult for passer by placing oneself between passer and intended receiver.

Two offense—one defense (goal-oriented). Assume that (a) students can use a partner to maintain possession of an object with two defenders when the activity is not goal-oriented or direction-oriented; (b) students can combine skills of receiving, propelling, passing (and shooting if appropriate) in smooth actions.

Activity: Most scoring in keep-away activities is done primarily with a target skill—shooting. Initially this should be simplified by (a) moving across a line to score after a certain number of passes and (b) increasing the size of the target or simplifying the skill used to score. This is particularly essential in basketball, where the skill is more advanced. Some possibilities for scoring include

a. Tossing or throwing ball to the backboard from inside a restraining line
b. Hitting a target on the wall with the ball from inside a restraining line or after a designated number of passes
c. Passing the ball across an end line to a teammate after a certain number of passes
d. Sending the ball between two markers (soccer)

Abilities developed: (a) Keeping the ball going in a forward direction in the face of a defender; (b) Combining propelling, passing, and receiving skills with a target skill; (c) Defending a space rather than a person.

Two offense—two defense (goal-oriented). Assume that students can score easily using a cooperative effort when one defensive player is included.

Activity: Initially experience should include only one goal so that defensive players do not attempt to go in the other direction upon obtaining possession. When the role of defending a goal is clear, two different goals can be added.

Abilities developed: (a) Defensively playing to defend space and not the player (beginning zone defense skills); (b) Defensively playing to guard a single person (player to player); (c) Defensively playing to combine ideas of defenses.

Three offense—two defense (goal-oriented). Assume that students (a) can relate to other players using offensive strategy of well-timed passes and timed moves into space to maintain possession of the object;

(b) can use both player to player and spatial patterns of defense.

Activity: Offensive players move object down the space. Defensive players combine player-to-player with zone strategies of defense.

Abilities developed: (a) Using three offensive players to maintain possession of the object. (b) Using player-to-player defense to force a pass and zone defense as play approaches goal area.

Three offense—three defense. Assume that offensive players can use all three players effectively; defensive players can use both a player-to-player and zone defensive strategy appropriately.

Activity: Initially work should be one-goal-oriented and then two-goal-oriented, with players shifting into both offensive and defensive roles.

Abilities developed: Relating offensively and defensively to a third player.

Note: It is at this point that the conditions of the eventual game will most affect the appropriate offensive and defensive roles. The size of the space and the ability of students to deal with more forceful manipulative skills determine whether the positions are differentiated as in soccer and most field sports or whether it is good strategy for players to play both offensive and defensive roles, using the full space as in basketball. Initially students should have experience in a more limited space, with no role differentiation on one team. As the size of the space increases and there are more than three players, offensive and defensive positions become separated and space is divided strategically for games in which this is necessary. For example:

a. *Basketball:* The progression for basketball continues as above by adding additional players and more sophisticated rules that have not already been added: for example, free throws for rule infractions, jump balls, and three-second lane violations.
b. *Field Sports:* The progression for field sports continues as above by increasing the number of players, size of space, and rule limitations that have not been added (such as corner kicks, specialized goalie privileges, and limitations on

the throw-in). As four players are added, offensive and defensive positions can be separated to include (a) goal defender, one back and two forward positions and, (b) one goal defender, two backs, and three forward positions. Students will need help in understanding the implications of offensive players moving back into defensive territory and defensive players moving too far up into offensive territory. They will also need help and practice in understanding how to play a space and not the ball. These skills should be established well before great numbers of players are added.

Strategies for Net Activities

One on one—cooperative/competive. Assume that students have enough control of an object working alone in self-space or against a wall to be able to change the direction of the struck object, control the force of the object, and keep the object going continuously for a reasonable period of time.

Activity: The challenge of beginning play in net activities is a cooperative/competitive challenge. Students attempt to work cooperatively with each other to keep the object going to beat their own score, the score of other partner groups, or a standard set by the teacher. This may progress from (a) against a wall to open space, (b) limited space to a larger space, (c) no object to hit over to a line, rope, net, folded mat, or other obstruction to move over and, (d) unclear boundaries to defined boundaries.

Abilities developed: Initially skill developed in sending the object to a partner so that it can be easily controlled. In the case of wall work the additional skill of moving out of the way after a hit so that the partner can play the ball will also need to be developed.

One on one—competitive. Assume that students can keep the object going in a cooperative way under conditions that are going to be used for the competitive environment.

Activity: Students attempt to make it difficult for partner to return the object by (a) placing the object in a different part of the space, (b) using the force of the object (great

and limited) offensively, (c) changing the level of flight and trajectory of the struck object. The initial focus should be on testing the limits of the partner—to make it difficult, but not impossible, to return, using the above strategies singly and then in combination. Later experiences should be completely competitive, playing within assigned boundaries and rule limitations regarding net, illegal hits, and so on. Few elementary-school students are ready for this level of play. Before this time game play should be started with a throw, courtesy serve, or set, depending on what the students choose.

Abilities developed: Skill development cuses on (a) placing object in a space difficult for partner to cover, (b) changing the force used to strike the object from maximum to minimum as an unanticipated change, (c) changing the flight trajectory of the object to make it difficult for the partner to return the object or to give the offensive players time to reposition themselves. Defensive skills involve primarily (a) positioning oneself to best cover the defined space, (b) returning to that space quickly when pulled out of position, and (c) anticipating the direction of a partner's play.

Note: Some students at this point may be ready to go on to doubles work in racquet sports. Space and facilities may require that the teacher take students to doubles work. Concepts of doubles play should emerge from student recognition of the need to come to some agreement as to the best way to cover space. Initially side-by-side patterns will seem most logical and in many instances there may be no need to go beyond this. As offensive skills develop, more sophisticated combinations with up-and-back strategies can be introduced.

Volleyball is a team sport and therefore the progression must continue to build skills up to a six-on-six activity. The rest of this progression is for volleyball.

Two on two—competitive. Assume that students can work competitively against one another in a limited space, using offensive and defensive skills and that they can receive an object from one direction and send it to another with accuracy.

Activity: The space needs to be made larger and students need to have an opportunity to play with each other with no focus other than to share the space with another team member. The shape of the space can be changed to produce side-by-side or up-and-back patterns. Rules should permit as many hits on a side as necessary to get the ball over the net (rope, mat, or other object) without letting it hit the ground. Students should be encouraged not to move across another's space and to call balls that are not clearly in their space or in their partner's space. Activity should include a cooperative activity with four players before moving on to a competitive activity.

When students can share space with each other, they will need to be helped to use each other offensively. This can be encouraged by scoring a point every time there are two hits by different players on each side before the ball goes over the net.

Abilities developed: The skills at this stage are primarily practice in a competitive situation of the manipulative skills that enable students to receive an object coming from a specific direction and send it to a partner with accuracy and with a flight pattern easy for the partner to play. Offensive-defensive strategy remains the same as one-on-one strategy, but a larger space and two players change the vulnerability of opponents, which should be pointed out to students. The most difficult concept to apply at this level is relating to a partner and developing an awareness of what space each is responsible for defending.

Four on four. Assume that students can share space with one another on a court in both side-by-side and up-and-back positions.

Activity: The space needs to be made larger and students need to play in a two-up-and-two-back position with each other. The focus should first be on encouraging passes from one player to another and points might be given for three hits on a side. At this point several other game elements should be added: (a) Starting the game from a throw outside the back boundary by designated server; (b) enforcing rule regarding illegal hits/lifting or pushing ball instead of clear hit; (c) giving students the option of a regulation volleyball or lighter nerf volleyball or plastic ball (regulation ball should only be used after skills have been developed with this ball as well); (d) regulation scoring; and (e) rotation of players. Student work should then be focused on passing the ball from one front-line player to another. Point incentives might be used to encourage passes.

Abilities developed: (a) Setting ball up to a front-line player. (b) Setting ball from front line to front player. (c) Continued emphasis on offensive strategy. (d) Continued emphasis on defending space as a stable assignment and introducing the idea of covering a larger space for a player pulled out of position.

Note: The next stage of the progression is six on six, which is a regulation number of players. Elementary-school students should be spending most of their time in games of a modified nature and in the early stages of this progression. The serve, because of the force it produces, should be added to game play with a regulation ball very late in the progression, if at all. Elementary-school children can perform the skill necessary to receive the serve in decreased force level conditions, but in most instances they cannot produce the force necessary to receive with any degree of accuracy the serve coming with great amounts of force. If the serve is to be introduced into game play, lighter balls are almost a must in all but very exceptional situations. Play that includes a serve tends to become a game of serves, wild attempts at returning it, and little team play.

16

educational gymnastics

Educational gymnastics differs from Olympic gymnastics programs both in purpose and in process. The purpose of Olympic gymnastics is to perfect precisely defined and specialized skills. The process involved in teaching such skills usually involves a progression—teaching skills in order of difficulty and then combining them into routines.

The purpose of educational gymnastics is body management; the ability of an individual to manage his or her own body in objective movement under increasingly difficult conditions. The contrast between the programmatic goals of body management and the perfection of a specialized skill can best be illustrated with the example of rolling. In Olympic gymnastics the elementary-school student is expected to perform a forward and backward roll with a standard starting and ending position. The end product is the performance. The learning process usually involves perfecting the skill until it is done exactly the same way each time. In contrast to this, elementary-school students in educational gymnastics explore different ways of making their bodies round to pro-

vide a surface for rolling. They explore and refine rolling in different directions, attempting to understand the use of the hands in rolling and the dissemination of force when using the roll. They work with the ability to roll from different heights, from both balanced and off-balance positions and from different speeds. Also, they roll in combination with other skills. The end product is skill in rolling under increasingly difficult conditions. Experiences may include the specific skills of the forward and backward roll, but they also include all other possible ways of rolling. The end product is body management appropriate to the conditions of the situation.

The process of teaching educational gymnastics involves the presentation of movement tasks which permit a wide range of students with different skill abilities to choose a correct response consistent with their own abilities and inventiveness. Concepts of movement are presented which permit a range of responses and increase the children's cognitive and kinesthetic awareness of their bodies in movement. The skilled mover can and does adjust to the movement demands of a task, one's own unique abilities, and the physical environment which is both anticipated and unanticipated.

THE CONTENT OF EDUCATIONAL GYMNASTICS

Educational gymnastics deals with objective movement and not with expressive movement. The goal is to master control of the body—not to manipulate an object or accomplish a purpose outside the movement itself (such as a game) or to express or communicate feeling (as in dance). Many content organizations have been proposed for teaching educational gymnastics. The interrelatedness of the content and the process involved in developing body management skills makes a completely satisfactory analysis difficult. The analysis of content and process presented in Figure 16.1 will hopefully get beginning teachers started in this area.

Gymnastics actions are developed by presenting tasks to students which focus the students' work on the process variables involved in the gymnastics actions. The development of the themes in this chapter increase the variety of ways in which a student can perform a gymnastics action, the level of control of the action, and the difficulty of the conditions under which the action is performed.

Gymnastic Actions

Locomotor movement. Locomotor movements take the body someplace. The body is transported in different ways from one space to another; thus the term traveling is used. The body is capable of traveling using different bases of support in steplike actions on a wide variety of parts. Ultimately the hands and feet will receive the most attention as useful appendages to transport the body either in steplike actions (walking on hands or feet or combinations of hands and feet) or in wheeling actions (such as the cartwheel).

The body can also move from one place to another through rolling and sliding actions and on equipment by gripping and releasing actions.

Stillness, weight bearing, and balance. Stillness, weight-bearing, and balance actions are related concepts. Stillness is one of the first concepts to be developed and con-

FIGURE 16.1. The content and process of educational gymnastics

GYMNASTICS ACTIONS	PROCESS VARIABLES FOR GYMNASTICS ACTIONS

Locomotor movement—the traveling actions
  Stepping and wheeling actions: feet, hands and feet,
    hands only, other body parts
  Rolling
  Sliding
  Gripping and releasing
Stillness—weight bearing—balance
Weight transference
  Rocking and rolling
  Sliding
  Step-like actions
  Flight
	Body aspects
	  Part(s) receiving, bearing weight, or producing force
	  Body shape
	  Twisting, turning, and spinning actions
	  Stretching and curling
	
	Space aspects of movement
	  General space and personal space
	  Levels: high, medium, low
	  Directions: forward, backward, sideways, up-down
	  Pathways: floor
	  Extension: near, far
	Dynamic aspects of movement
	  Speed: fast and slow
	  Weight: heavy (strong) and light
	  Flow: bound and free, stoppable and ongoing
	Relationship aspects of movement
	  People
	  Equipment

cerns itself with the ability to maintain an alert stillness with body tension; to arrest action—not merely to stop moving. Weight bearing relates to developing the ability to support the weight of the body on different parts and combinations of body parts. A more specialized form of weight bearing is the concept of balance, which usually implies narrow and more difficult to maintain bases of support.

Weight transference. The body transfers weight when it travels or when it moves into or out of supported or balanced positions. Weight transference is a separate area of concern because it focuses on the transferring action itself; how the action moves from one base of support to another. It also deals with ways to get from one base of support to another (Example: How to get from head and hands to the seat as a base of support). All the locomotor actions are ways to transfer weight. The body can also twist, spin, or turn to accomplish these actions.

The Process Variables

The process variables listed in Figure 16.1 form a useful framework to design experiences that expand the variety of ways and the skill with which children travel, support their weight, and transfer their weight. The reader will recognize these constructs as part of the analysis of movement presented in Chapter 14. As in the games area we are concerned with expanding the variety of ways in which a student can produce these actions, and we are also interested in helping the child master control of these actions in increasingly difficult ways.

Themes in educational gymnastics. The movement theme has provided a useful organizing element for gymnastics content. Teachers can design their own themes and with experience will want to do so. The themes identified in this chapter are meant to be progressive and spiraling in their development. This means that an idea is never really left as you go on. It is returned to in the same way or in a different way.

The themes include:

    I. Locomotion and stillness—feet only
   II. Locomotion—traveling with different body parts
  III. Locomotion—rocking and rolling
  IV. Weight bearing
   V. Locomotion—hanging and swinging
  VI. Locomotion—the jumping actions
 VII. Balance
    A. Achieving balance on different body parts
    B. Moving into and out of balanced positions
VIII. Transferring weight—twisting, turning, and spinning

The themes are developed in detail on pages 239–253 through the use of a chart having three columns: (a) the major task, (b) ways in which the major task can be extended, and (c) how the task can be refined to produce quality-controlled responses. It is unlikely that a teacher will completely develop one theme before moving on to another. A child returns to a theme or major task with new abilities, new confidence, and ideas not possible the first time a theme is experienced. It is for this reason that educational gymnastics themes are said to spiral.

The role of equipment. Equipment plays a major role in gymnastics work. Managing the body in relation to different kinds and arrangements of equipment is a large part of the content itself. Equipment motivates and brings out movement possibilities not possible in floor work alone.

The major tasks in the themes outlined on the following pages are developed in three environments: floor work, small apparatus work, and large apparatus work. These three environments are considered progressive for planning in educational gymnastics.

1. Floor work—with mats or without mats
2. Small apparatus
   a. In and out (ropes laid flat to form shapes, hula hoops flat or raised, and so on)
   b. Over and under (blocks and canes or milk cartons with paper canes, and so on)
   c. Onto and off of (very low boxes, benches, folded mats, and so on)

3. Large apparatus
   a. Benches, boxes, stools
   b. Balance beams
   c. Ladders, Whittle equipment, inclined planks, bars
   d. Ropes, rings, and swinging equipment

Equipment companies produce equipment for educational gymnastics. Many of the essential pieces can be made inexpensively, such as vaulting boxes, beams, and benches. In addition, Olympic gymnastics equipment can be used in novel ways to achieve the ends of educational gymnastics by grouping and arranging pieces together.

Because the type and availability of equipment vary so much from one situation to another, very specific recommendations for its arrangement are not made in this chapter, except where necessary to illustrate a point. When planning the purchase of larger apparatus, teachers should give consideration to supplying a great enough variety of equipment to support the activities of moving onto and off of, swinging, hanging, sliding, gripping, and releasing.

Mats play a different role in educational gymnastics. Mats are used at all times as a piece of equipment to move over or across, and not merely for landing. Equipment is arranged and rearranged to elicit different locomotor actions. Figure 16.2 illustrates arrangements of a hoop, block and cane, and a mat, which are considered small apparatus.

Each of the different arrangements and the varying distances between the equipment would promote or discourage different actions as the students attempt to use all these in continuous movement. There is no single line of direction for most equipment organization. Students are encouraged to approach the equipment from different directions.

The arrangement of large equipment provides a similar challenge as one considers how to arrange the equipment to promote changes in level, direction or pathway, speed, and so on. Teachers must continuously ask themselves how to arrange and rearrange the equipment to promote both variety of response and quality of response to a major task.

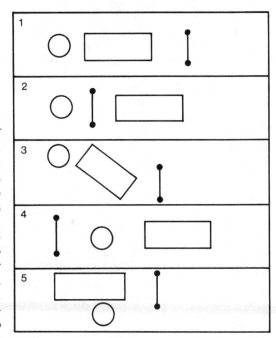

FIGURE 16.2 Arrangement of small apparatus.

GYMNASTICS LESSONS

Long-Term Planning

Gymnastics work with elementary-school children is not restricted to a long unit once a year. Teachers should move into and out of gymnastics work throughout the year to promote continuous development. Long-term planning consists of introducing basic ideas in all three content areas (locomotion; stillness, weight bearing, and balance; and weight transference) and extending these ideas as students gain control of their bodies, develop a movement vocabulary, and develop a willingness to explore in productive ways their own potential movement abilities.

Young children will initially want to explore both practical and impractical ideas, such as using the nose as a partial base of support or traveling by sliding along on the seat. These responses, although initially encouraged as inventiveness, are ultimately discouraged as inefficient and not gymnasticlike. Although educational gymnastics both supports and encourages creativity,

creativity is not encouraged as an end in itself. It is encouraged as a means to expand the movement potential of the student.

Older students are more interested in perfecting and repeating movements that are challenging for them. Older students can be encouraged to work on something until they do it as well as they can. This does not mean that variety should not be sought. Rather, it adds a concern for practice, which makes movement better.

As with other areas of the program, the size of units in gymnastics changes with both the choice of the content itself and the age of the student. The older student can be expected to participate in longer units, perhaps combining several themes. Movement ideas for the very young child cannot be as fully developed, although the ability of the young child to repeat experiences and particularly to explore movement ideas with equipment should not be underestimated. A unit for the younger child might consist of only a single beginning major task from the beginning themes with an emphasis on small and large apparatus work.

The Gymnastics Lesson

Lessons in educational gymnastics usually have several phases—the warm-up, floor work, small apparatus work, and large apparatus work.

The warm-up. In this part of the lesson teachers attempt to get the students "with them"—focused and moving. Sometimes specific locomotor action tasks are used, such as (a) travel and stop, (b) travel on different parts of the body, or (c) practice ways to get your body into the air. Self-directed students can use this time to come into the gym and practice a movement of their choice.

Floor work. Movement concepts are best presented on the floor with or without mats. Ideas are developed first in very simple and concrete ways to introduce concepts. They are then expanded to increase variety and extended to increase the difficulty of the condition under which the action is performed.

Small apparatus. Many movement ideas can be more fully developed if small apparatus is used before large apparatus. Small apparatus, like floor work, tends to make it easier for children to remain focused on the task and to develop a clearer understanding of the potential of a task.

Large apparatus. The large apparatus section of the lesson should be designed to promote the task. Apparatus is very stimulating to students, but the need to work with conscious attention on the task during work on the apparatus must be continuously reinforced.

The following sample lesson plan illustrates the development of a concept related to the theme of rocking and rolling (pages 243–244). This particular lesson might take more than one class period, with floor work being divided between the two periods and one lesson applying the concepts to small apparatus and the other to large apparatus. Lessons giving children opportunities to practice rolling in different directions can also be the focus of a single lesson.

In the lesson presented, opportunities are provided for children to be successful at their own level of ability in rolling. The concepts of soft placement of the body, the use of the hands, and a rounded body surface for rolling receive emphasis regardless of the ability of children to make their bodies roll in all possible ways.

EDUCATIONAL GYMNASTICS (SAMPLE LESSON PLAN)

Major Focus of Work: Locomotion—rocking and rolling
Objectives: Students should be able to:
1. Lower themselves onto different body parts and roll with control
2. Move into and out of a roll in different directions from a variety of other movements
3. Incorporate a roll in continuous movement in relation to small apparatus and large apparatus

---

(continued)

TASK	WHAT TEACHER IS LOOKING FOR	RESPONSE	DECISION
WARM-UP			
Come into the gym and practice a move you want to get better—one that you were trying last time.	Are the students directed in their efforts and working independently?	No——→ Yes	Reinforce or if necessary provide a task with more structure, such as "Travel about the room, stopping quickly and with stillness when I clap my hands."
FLOOR WORK			
What can you think of that rocks back and forth?	The obvious answer here is a rocking chair, but be prepared for others.		
Can you make your body rock? What other parts can you use? What parts are good to rock on? Why? What other parts can you make round to rock?	Are the students rounding the part or combinations of parts used?	No——→ Yes	Encourage students to feel every part of the body surface used. Select students for a demonstration who are really making parts round. Select a variety of responses to encourage further exploration.
	Are students using both front parts of the trunk and back parts of the trunk? Are they going in different directions?	No——→ Yes	Focus a task on directions—forward and backward, side to side, and in between.
Let your rocking movement take you to a new space. Rock so hard that it goes to a new place.	Are students producing enough force and keeping round enough to move into a new position?	No——→ Yes	Reinforce the idea of a round surface. Encourage students to take a few rocks before they move into a new position.
Select one of your rocking movements—first let it go to a new place. Then rock and see if you can stop the movement before it goes someplace else.	Are students opening up the round surface and making it flat, or are they adding a part that would stop the motion?	No——→ Yes	Choose students responding correctly to the task to demonstrate, or specifically ask students to make the surface flat when they want to stop.
As you move into a rolling action from the rocking motion, pay attention to the way you are using your hands. What are they doing? What can they do?	Are students using the hands to direct the roll? Holding onto the knees to keep tight?	No——→ Yes	Encourage students to use the hands to direct the rolling action or to support weight so that parts such as the head can be lifted.
Start on your feet. Lower a hand or your two hands to a spot around your feet and see if you can continue on into a roll.	Are students keeping the body tight and lowering themselves softly to the mat?	No——→ Ues	Encourage no sound and soft movements.
Slowly Increase speed	Are a variety of directions being used?	No——→ Yes	Give specific tasks related to direction. Hands in front Hands in back One hand only To the side
Can you bring your roll back up into a stand again?	Is enough force being generated by a tight curl and directed action of the hands to bring the movement back up to a stand?	No——→ Yes	Encourage students to increase the speed of the movement and to keep the body tucked.

(continued)

TASK	WHAT TEACHER IS LOOKING FOR	RESPONSE	DECISION
Walk slowly and lower yourself into a rolling action Changing directions Increasing speed	Actions should continue to be controlled with the soft placement and lowering of body parts.	No⟶ Yes	Decrease speed. Have all students try the same action with teacher before going on to variety of moves again.
SMALL APPARATUS			
Travel through your equipment, using a roll at some point in your work. Equipment: hoop, block and cane, folded mat, and landing mat.	Are the students moving continuously from one piece of equipment to another? Are they using all the equipment?	No⟶ Yes	Reemphasize or use a demonstration.

○ ▭ ❘ ▭

H   FM   BC   LM

	Are their movements controlled?	No⟶ Yes	Slow the movement down and reemphasize careful placement of parts.
	Are they using different body parts or the same parts? Are they changing direction?	No⟶ Yes No⟶ Yes	Use a task asking for a change in level as the focus. Use a task with a change in direction as the focus.
Rearrange equipment or have student select arrangement.			
LARGE APPARATUS			
Move onto and off of your equipment, using a roll at some point. Equipment: single pieces initially—low boxes, benches, bars, stools, etc. Later, combinations of pieces of equipment that promote a roll from one piece to another. Change in direction	Initially the roll will be used primarily after the landing. Students will need time to work with this task. A landing and roll in different directions can become a specific task. With time students should be encouraged to roll to their equipment, to use a roll at some point on their equipment, and to roll off equipment as appropriate.		
	Are the students using a roll at some point? Are the rolls coming at the same point in the movement each time?	No⟶ Yes No⟶ Yes	Reinforce task, use demonstration of on-task responses. Select students with different responses for demonstration or reinforcement.

Establishing a Safe and Productive Learning Environment

In educational gymnastics spotters are not used. Spotters tend to give students a false sense of security, which encourages them to lose control and to try movements they are not ready to control independently. Spotting is also an advanced skill that very few elementary-school children are able to perform adequately. Students in educational gymnastics learn how to control and use their body weight. The emphasis is on safe placement and control as the body moves in and out of a position.

Gymnastics activities can be dangerous.

Educational gymnastics is not "free-play" on mats or equipment, and control of movement and safety must be a primary and ever-present concern of the teacher and students. The characteristics essential to a safe learning environment in educational gymnastics are as follows:

Independent work. Students work by themselves unless otherwise directed by the teacher. Students do not assist or interfere with the work of other students in any way. Physical contact with another student during their work (except when part of the task) is not permitted.

Awareness of others. Students will be working in an environment in which mats, equipment, and floor space will be shared in ultimately unstructured ways (no lines or specific paths of action). In order to do this safely, students must be taught how to share space and equipment safely with others. Initially this may mean developing a conscious awareness of each other and shared space as a lesson focus. Later this awareness becomes part of the student's way of working that is continuously reinforced. Collisions are not acceptable. They are not an unavoidable stage in the learning process.

Emphasis on control. Students must begin to develop a conscious awareness of and concern for controlled movement. This control is developed through a concern for *soft* controlled landings and the *placement* of parts onto mats and equipment. Speed is a major factor in lack of control and slow, controlled work should be a beginning emphasis.

Resting off the equipment. When students begin work and when they are stopped or resting, they should not sit on the equipment or mats. This helps the teacher establish the use of the equipment for serious work and avoids countless managerial problems. At stopping time students should be asked to bring their work to a close rather than being directed to interrupt their work at once.

Appropriate dress. Students must be dressed in clothes that allow them to move freely and safely. Shorts (slacks if shorts are not possible) and bare feet are appropriate. Heavy shoes, dresses, and floppy blouses are not appropriate.

Teachers must insist upon a safe and productive learning environment at the start of the child's experiences and continuously reinforce it until it becomes part of the children's natural response to the gymnastics environment.

Using Charts to Develop Lessons

Theme I: Locomotion and stillness—feet only. Theme I is designed to develop versatility in the use of the feet for traveling actions, to introduce major concepts important to later themes, and to build a movement vocabulary. The younger elementary-school-aged child is still at a stage where basic locomotor patterns using the feet are being refined and in some instances developed. This child will need to return to these ideas often. The older child can move through much of this material quickly and with much more concern for the efficient production and reduction of force in the movements. Older students will easily be challenged by large equipment arrangements for this theme. This theme is essential for establishing a safe and productive learning environment. See Chart 16.1, page 239.

Theme II: Traveling with different body parts. Theme II is designed to help children develop the ability to use various body parts as bases of support for traveling actions and to help them begin to manage the transitions as the body changes from one base of support to another. Because many gymnastics actions require the ability to receive weight and support body weight on the hands either alone or in combination with other body parts, very specific attention is paid to experiences that take weight on the hands, even though the latter is actually a weight-bearing task.

As other themes are developed more fully, they can be combined with this theme. New combinations of equipment will elicit

CHART 16.1. Theme I: Locomotion and stillness—feet only

MAJOR TASK	EXTENSION	REFINEMENT
Traveling in general space, using the feet in a variety of ways. Stopping with alert stillness (freezing) when the teacher signals *Sample Task:* Travel using your feet in different ways, changing your direction continuously. *Comments:* The teacher is looking first for a variety of patterns and awareness of space and of others. Use of space implies (a) that when students stop, there are no large empty spaces not being used and (b) students are seeking space not being used and are moving away from others.	Different locomotor patterns Feet together, apart, together, and apart Change in direction Change in speed Combining several ways of moving, using the feet in a pattern that is repeated the same way over and over Changing pathways Variety implies that each student is experiencing a large range of movements, not just the class. This is encouraged through the development of tasks from the extension column.	Awareness of others moving through space Use of all the space Arresting action of movement to produce a quick stop
Using the feet in light ways *Sample Task:* Travel throughout the space as high as you can, getting your feet off the floor in different ways. *Comments:* This ability is absolutely essential for further work and should be greatly exaggerated through this stage of the learning process. Teachers should encourage "quiet feet."	Projecting the body up from the floor and landing lightly on the spot Both feet increasing height One foot Combinations Traveling in a variety of ways with a concern for lightness in the feet (bring back ideas from first major task if necessary)	Absorbing force by "giving" in the ankles, knees, and legs if necessary (quiet feet) Smooth transitions from one locomotor pattern to another
Moving over, in and out of, and onto and off of small apparatus Using the feet in different ways—equipment Something to move in and out of (hoops, ropes, or circles) Something to move over and under (two milk cartons with a paper cane stretched across) Something to move onto and off—folded mats, small boxes—should not be more than 18″ off the ground *Note:* Each child can have the same equipment or different equipment. If possible, there should be enough equipment for each child to have his or her own. *Sample Task:* Move over, in and out of, or onto and off of your piece of equipment, sometimes keeping your feet together and sometimes keeping them very far apart.	Changing direction Actions involving one foot Actions involving two feet together; one and two feet Actions bringing the feet off the floor a "little bit" and off the floor "a lot" *Note:* The equipment will act as a stimulus for movement and children should be permitted time to work on the task "using your feet in different ways" before being asked to focus on a more specific task. Teachers should insist on correct responses—that is, use of the feet and not other body parts as well as "quiet feet." Moving to a piece of equipment (in and out, onto and off of, or over) and then moving to another piece Using feet in different ways to get there as well as at the equipment	"Quiet feet"—absolutely no hard landings Working independently and slowly Variety of uses of the feet Equipment left in its original position Students should be helped to understand how to use the whole body to project it off the ground Slow, controlled work increasing speed as increase in control of movement is developed Reinforce awareness of space and of others If this is the first experience sharing equipment in general space, students will need help in Getting to all the equipment Not interfering with others Moving to a piece of equipment not being used—no lines Keeping this movement continuous

(continued)

CHART 16.1. (*Continued*)

MAJOR TASK	EXTENSION	REFINEMENT
Using the feet in different ways to combine locomotor movements Without equipment With equipment (same as preceding task, arranged in a variety of patterns using different combinations of equipment) *Sample Task:* Move continuously from one piece of equipment to another, using your feet in different ways and showing a very clear change in direction.	Move from one piece of your own equipment to another, using your feet lightly without a break in the movement Showing a change in direction Showing a clear change in speed—some part must be fast, some part must be slow Combining feet together and feet apart Showing a clear change in distance of the feet from the floor Rearrange your own equipment to help you show a different pattern of movement Move from one set of equipment to another (development above can be used if necessary)	Patterns should be smooth with no breaks—ask students to practice them until they are smooth, if necessary Students out of control should be slowed down Space between equipment is part of the task and not a resting area
Using the feet to develop patterns we can do with a partner *Sample Task:* One partner travels from one piece of equipment to the other and sees if the other partner can do it in the same way.	All the above ideas in the floor work as well as small apparatus or large apparatus can be used as the focus for tasks with a partner (experienced primary-school students) Following the movement of a partner Matching the movement of a partner (simultaneous) Patterns utilizing movement toward and away from partner Contrasting the movement of a partner	Students should be required to remain with the focus of the task, even though an additional focus (the relationship with a partner) has been added Movement should be matched in quality (speed, spatial aspects, force) as well as kind of action Patterns should have a clear beginning and ending

different traveling actions and combinations of traveling actions.

Young children need to spend a long time working with the ideas included in this theme. As students gain more experience, they can be expected to focus on more specific ways of traveling, on the transitions, or on combinations with arriving and balance actions. See Chart 16.2 on page 241.

Theme III: Locomotion—rocking and rolling. Theme III is designed to develop rolling skills as a specific locomotor action. The theme is introduced with rocking actions, which are then extended into rolling actions. Children should eventually be able to roll in all directions, from different levels and speeds, and from balanced and off-balance positions. Low equipment will help children develop rolling skills as they attempt to lower themselves from equipment, taking their weight on their hands.

Qualitatively, most rolling involves being able to take weight on the hands as the first body part that absorbs the weight of the body. The head should not be used to take body weight in rolling and children should be encouraged from the start to do "no head-touching rolls."

With very young children undue emphasis should not be placed on mastering every type of roll. Experience with equipment and combining other actions will do much to develop the confidence and abilities needed to perform these actions. With older students more direct teaching of specific actions is appropriate if the students have not developed these skills. See Chart 16.3 on page 243.

CHART 16.2. Theme II: Locomotion—traveling with different body parts

MAJOR TASK	EXTENSION	REFINEMENT

Travel (move from one spot to another, taking your weight on different parts of your body)
Sample Task: Travel using different parts of your body continuously, changing your level as you move.
Comments: It is unlikely that the teacher will want to develop this material fully in one lesson. This task should be returned to often with the same and different emphases as a warm-up to equipment work and using the focus given to such work.
	Bringing out variety
	  Using three parts, four parts, two parts
	  Facing up, facing down
	  Parts high—knee, foot, hands, chest, seat, head
	  Ways to use hands and feet alone
	  Feet leading, hands leading
	  Feet together, apart, combination
	Changing the pathway of the movement
	Using the same movement to go in different directions
	Combining movements to go in different directions
	Contrasting speed
	Changing the level of the movement
	Advanced Work: After other themes. Combining traveling work with balance actions, including other themes as a must in a sequence—partner work, copying, simultaneous actions, and so on.
		Combined emphasis on placement of parts on the floor and "quiet feet"
		Use of space and awareness of others
		Correct responses to the task
		Children should be encouraged to experience the full range of the concepts of pathway, levels, and directions before moving on to another
		Eventual emphasis on smooth transitions and actions; which flow from one to another

Taking weight on hands
  Put your hands on the floor and bring your feet up off the floor and down as quietly as you can.
  Take your feet off the floor only as far as you can bring them down with no noise
Sample Task: As you bring your feet off the floor, sometimes bring them down close together and sometimes, far apart.
Comments: Weight on hands is an essential gymnastics skill. It is introduced here quite specifically and should probably be a part of warm-up work in all lessons.
	Bringing feet down close to hands
	Bringing feet to different spots around the hands
	Bringing feet far apart
		This is a rather specific task and can be demonstrated to show the absolute control the teacher is demanding
		Head should be up to prevent roll over
		Elbows should be straight
		Lift should be from the hips
		At least one foot should come down under hips and close to the hands
		Students who can get extension of legs up should not be prevented from doing so if their movement is controlled

Moving into and out of, onto and off of, and over and under small equipment, using different body parts Hoops or ropes, small boxes, folded mats, canes and blocks (or milk cartons) *Sample Task:* Move into and out of, onto and off of, and over and under your equipment, using your hands and feet together in some way.	Possibilities for development include appropriate ideas suggested in first major task Moving on equipment with one part off, with another on	Slow work and reemphasis on placement of body parts and landings of parts on the floor

(continued)

CHART 16.2. (*Continued*)

MAJOR TASK	EXTENSION	REFINEMENT
Combining ways of moving on different body parts to get continuous movement Equipment possibilities same as preceding task with different combinations *Sample Task:* Travel continuously, using all your equipment and showing a clear change in pathway somewhere in your sequence.	Try to keep going as you travel (placing your weight on different parts of the body) Show a clear change in level as you travel Show a clear change in direction as you travel Show a clear change in pathway as you travel Developing a pattern with a partner (following, matching, toward and away from, contrasting, and using a focus on changes in level of direction or speed)	Continuous emphasis on (a) slow, controlled work and (b) light landings Real changes in level Real change in direction Real change in pathway
Traveling on different body parts using large apparatus; equipment possibilities are limited only by what is available and should include equipment that encourages continuous movement with a variety of locomotor actions including Climbing Gripping and releasing Steplike actions Limited flight Rolling Receiving weight on hands from a variety of positions Equipment can be rearranged to elicit different combinations of movement *Note:* Mats should be considered and arranged as a piece of equipment to travel over. *Sample Task:* Using your set of equipment, put together a sequence of traveling actions that takes weight on hands at some point in your sequence.	Initially traveling from one piece of equipment to another, using different body parts The direction the teacher chooses for further development should be guided by the responses of the student and the equipment possibilities; children need a lot of opportunity at an initial stage to explore their own ideas without being asked to focus more specifically on an extension of the task—the equipment will provide the stimulus and focus for these experiences The apparatus can make other ideas possible such as (a) traveling with hands only or hands and feet and (b) including a swing to get from one place to another Later developments Contrast of speed (Space aspects) clear change in direction, level, pathway Advanced development (after additional work in these areas) Contrasting stretching and curling actions Combining with balance Contrasting symmetrical and asymmetrical movements As later themes are developed, they should be incorporated into this theme—to improve both the locomotor and balance movements	If these are the first experiences of children on large apparatus, they will need constant monitoring of (a) speed of work, (b) awareness of others, (c) ground rules regarding use of equipment, and (d) light landings The initial "attack" of children in their approach to apparatus, which is an exercise of enthusiasm, will have to be controlled and "slowed." As children have increased opportunity to work on the apparatus, a more conscious awareness of what they are doing can be developed and should be insisted upon. Teachers should encourage refinement of individual actions Students select, individually, helping students make their actions more controlled, extended, and smooth

(*continued*)

CHART 16.2. (*Continued*)

MAJOR TASK	EXTENSION	REFINEMENT
Traveling on equipment in relation to a partner or small group *Sample Task:* One partner takes a position that is a shape with good balance. The other partner moves under, over, or around that shape, using different body parts to support the weight. *Comments:* Group and partner work on large apparatus should only be attempted after students have considerable experience working independently of each other.	Following a partner Developing a sequence with a partner or small group Matching actions Following actions Contrasting actions Moving toward or away from partner Using partner as a piece of equipment Partner takes a position on a stable (or later, unstable, base) other partner moves over, under, or around this shape without contact	Partner work should be focused on helping students to develop sequences or actions that clearly relate to each other in the way the task focus specifies Give students time to practice patterns to make them better

CHART 16.3. Theme III: Locomotion—rocking and rolling

MAJOR TASK	EXTENSION	REFINEMENT
What parts of your body can you rock on? What parts can you put together to make a round surface for rocking? (Floor or mat) *Sample Task:* What parts of your body can you use to rock in a sideward direction?	Cues for variety if necessary Rocking forward and backward Rocking sideways Rocking directions between sideways and backward	Smooth rocking motion by rounding surface of the body Feeling each part of the body surface touch the mat or floor
Let your rocking movement take you somewhere to a new position; as you move into your rolling action from the rocking motion, think about how you might use the hands to help di- *Sample Task:* Try different ways to rock and see if you can go from that rocking action into a roll.	Continuous movement should begin to produce a roll, but it is initiated through a rocking movement Start your rocking motion and then stop it by making the body flat Ensure variety by using comments related to direction or parts of body used in the movement	Production of force by rocking should lead to a new position Concepts of roundness to produce movement and flatness to stop movement should emerge Use of hands to direct the action and to take the weight for the head to be tucked under without touching the mat
Start your rolling action on your feet by lowering your hands or hand to a place around your space and rolling in that direction *Sample Task:* Place your hands in a different spot around your space and lower yourself into a roll, using your hands to guide the direction of your roll.	Placing two hands down and moving over them slowly and smoothly into a roll Placing one hand down and moving over Lowering yourself to other body parts and moving into a roll slowly Coming up to stand to complete action Increased speed in lowering	Slow and deliberate placement and smooth transfer of weight rounding body surface to receive the weight should be emphasized

(*continued*)

CHART 16.3. *(Continued)*

MAJOR TASK	EXTENSION	REFINEMENT
Moving into a roll from a moving position *Sample Task:* Move only as quickly as you can and still maintain control in lowering.	Walking slowly and lowering yourself into a roll Change in direction to produce backward and sideways rolls Increasing speed	Slow speed is essential Placement of part to mat and rounding surfaces for rolling
Run, jump, land, and roll *Sample Task:* Take a few steps and get your body into the air—sometimes with a turn to land—and roll in different directions	Slow speed→increase in speed Forward direction→other directions	Emphasis on controlling force of jump in the landing before going into the roll
Rolling after landing from equipment (equipment should be low initially and then increased in height)—any equipment that provides an opportunity to jump off and land is suitable *Sample Task:* Come off the equipment with a jump into the air, land softly, and roll.	Jumping down to a landing—jumping up off of equipment Jumping in a forward direction (much later), adding a turn and roll in a different direction Combination with body shape in the air before landing	Jumping skill and landing softly from equipment should be developed before this task Absolute emphasis on controlled landing before moving into the roll Jumping up instead of down
Rolling onto, on, or off of equipment (vaulting equipment, beams, benches, boxes) *Sample Task:* Use a roll to get onto your equipment. Move off of your equipment or travel along your equipment.	Including a roll at some point in your use of the equipment Different directions Initiated with different body parts	Controlled work and particularly slow speeds are essential here to begin with

Theme IV: Weight bearing. Theme IV is designed to develop skills and awarenesses related to supporting the body on different parts and combinations of parts. The body can be supported on parts it cannot use to travel, although this theme will help expand possibilities for traveling actions as well as for balance actions.

Equipment plays a major role in this theme as we can hang, balance, rest, and in other ways use equipment to completely or partially support our weight. Weight bearing does not demand either complete stillness or complete extension of the body in a supported position. The emphasis in this theme is primarily on experiencing a wide variety of ways to support the body.

Young children will need lots of time to explore the potential of the beginning major tasks in this theme. Older children can move through the beginning tasks more rapidly and spend more time in the later aspects of this theme, which naturally may move into balance actions. See Chart 16.4.

CHART 16.4. Theme IV: Weight bearing

MAJOR TASK	EXTENSION	REFINEMENT
Taking weight on different parts of the body (floor work)	Bringing out variety Different ways to support yourself on three parts of the body, four parts, two parts	Balance on extension is not the concern here, but a clear pause at a position should be demonstrated

(continued)

CHART 16.4. *(Continued)*

MAJOR TASK	EXTENSION	REFINEMENT
Sample Task: Take your weight on three parts of your body, then carefully and with control move to support your weight on three different parts.	Different levels (close to ground, medium levels, and high off the ground) Moving continuously from weight supported on one group of body parts (or a part) to another group (change at teacher's signal if necessary) Selecting a position and moving to at least three positions different from the original position Finding ways to make different body shapes with weight supported on different parts—round, wide, long, combined	With older students begin to insist upon smooth transitions from one position of support to another Smooth transitions from one base of support to another
Taking weight on different parts of the body (equipment work) Equipment should include that which will allow hanging work at a fairly high level (bars, ladders, ropes, rings, etc.) as well as apparatus which will support a larger surface of the body at a lower level (low boxes and bars, vaulting horses, etc.) *Sample Task:* On your piece of equipment see how many different ways you can find to have the equipment support different parts of your body. Move into and out of the support with absolute control. *Comment:* Many more opportunities for weight bearing are made possible with the use of equipment, including the actions of hanging and using the equipment to support the hips and other parts of the body. If these do not emerge from the students' work, they need to be encouraged.	Finding a way to support your weight on different parts of your body All parts on equipment Some parts on equipment, some parts off the equipment Return to ways to bring out variety in previous task if necessary Move from one means of support to another on the equipment—see how long you can go from one support to another, continuously changing how you are supporting your weight	The action is one of support and not of traveling—students should be encouraged to hold a momentary point of stillness in the support and then show a clear intent to continuously change the support
Using partner as a means of support *Sample Task:* Find all the different ways one partner can support part of your weight while other parts are supported by the floor. *Comment:* Only mature children who can work with others productively and with care for safety should move to this task. Work should be developed so that student focus is on moving safely into and out of the supported position.	One partner finds a stable position and holds it still; other partner finds a way to support different parts of the body, using the base of the still partner Partial support (some parts still supported on the floor) Total support	Teachers should watch carefully for mismatches in size and strength If variety is not being produced, teachers can encourage use of specific parts or combinations of parts

FIGURE 16.3 Theme VI revisits the idea of locomotion using the feet with a specific emphasis on the jumping actions.

Theme V: Locomotion—hanging and swinging. Theme V is a natural extension of Theme IV (Weight Bearing). It is designed to develop the student's ability to use the body as a lever to produce momentum and to carry it to a new position. It is a rather specific theme, but a critical and often neglected aspect of our gymnastics work. Hanging, gripping, and releasing actions are natural parts of this theme.

The theme begins with hanging actions encouraging support on a variety of parts. Moving to a new position from a hanging position should begin to encourage swinging actions as more emphasis is put on continuous movement from one hanging position or base of support to another. Low bars as well as higher bars, ladders, ropes, and rings or raised beams (whittle) are useful for this theme. Young children should be expected primarily to explore the hanging positions as well as ways of getting into and out of them carefully, and to swing without really going to a new position. Older, more able, students

should be guided to eventually produce enough force with a swinging action to feel the point of weightlessness and to use that to change position. See Chart 16.5.

Theme VI: Locomotion on the feet—the jumping actions. Theme VI revisits the idea of locomotion using the feet, with a specific emphasis on actions which project the body into the air: the jumping actions. Although jumping is usually conceived of as a two-to-two foot action, the term is used here to include all the possible combinations of take-offs and landings which produce a moment of unsupportedness. The main intent in this theme is to focus on producing power with the legs and the total body action to get the body off the ground. Power is both a function of speed and the strength of muscle contraction and extension. A companion emphasis to this is the ability to land from flight in a way that absorbs the force of the body weight.

Both young children and older children

CHART 16.5. Theme V: Locomotion—hanging and swinging. This theme needs equipment that is suitable for hanging and swinging actions. Horizontal ladders, lind climbers, bars of all heights, ropes, rings, and so on are suitable.

MAJOR TASK	EXTENSION	REFINEMENT
Supporting the body in ways that allow other parts to hang freely *Sample Task:* Using your equipment, find as many ways as you can to hang from different parts of your body.	Use of variety of different body parts to support a hanging position Hands and arms Trunk Legs Moving from one support to another	Safety must be assured for these skills—students should be encouraged to move out of the hanging position the same way they moved into it, unless they can safely place a body part to transfer the weight
Produce swinging from a stable hanging position Find a stable position from which you can hang and see if you can get your body swinging Swinging with a release to a landing on feet (where appropriate) *Sample Task:* From a stable hanging position get your body swinging and see if you can swing into a new position of support.	Producing force with swing (minimum→maximum) Swinging changing body shape in the air Swinging into a new position of weight support	Extension is necessary to produce a longer lever and thus more production of force for "swing" Students most likely will need to be encouraged to progress with this task individually rather than in group work as the equipment and different levels of ability are likely to have a great influence on success and safety Feeling the point at which the body becomes weightless before gravity takes it in the other direction should be emphasized

should initially explore the possible take-off and landing combinations. Ultimately the one-to-two foot combination will be found to be the most efficient in transferring the speed of preliminary steps to flight. Older students should be challenged with unassisted arrivals onto equipment and ultimately assisted flight with take-off boards, mini-tramps, and so on. This theme can then be combined with quick movements onto and off of equipment and other traveling and balancing themes. See Chart 16.6.

Theme VII: Balance actions. Theme VII builds on work done in weight bearing. Balance is different from the weight bearing work in that it puts an emphasis not only on the body parts used as a base of support but

CHART 16.6. Theme VI: Locomotion on feet—the jumping actions

MAJOR TASK	EXTENSION	REFINEMENT
Floor work		
Experiment with different ways to use your feet and get up in the air	Provide structure if necessary to help students experience all combinations—variety of patterns	Emphasis remains on light use of feet
One to same foot	Adding a short run before take-off	Students should be encouraged to feel and focus on the parts of
One to other foot	The following patterns should receive increased emphasis	the body producing elevation;
One to two feet	One to same foot (hop), producing force emphasizing complete extension	the power is produced through flexion and powerful extension of
Two to one foot		the ankles, knees, and hips—the
Two to other foot		role of the arms in producing
Two to two feet	One to other (leap), emphasizing extension and flight in the air of both legs	total body action should also be emphasized
Sample Task: Take a few steps and get your body into the air with a powerful and quick push with your legs. How can you get the most power?	One to two feet (hurdle), emphasizing power of take-off and positioning feet to stop action	
	Determining which pattern gives better height or distance	
Equipment		
Moving over and off of and onto equipment using different patterns for elevation	Using different patterns	Emphasis should be on production of force using whole body for
Some equipment possibilities are:	Emphasizing each one separately	height and distance and controlled landings
Cone hurdles placed individually or in combination	*Advanced work:* Can include moving onto equipment of greater	Landings from height: Students should experience arresting
Mats folded or flat	height without the use of the hands and assisted flight using	movement completely to a stop as a focus—they should also have
Benches	mini-tramps and take-off boards	ample opportunity giving with the
Low boxes	(heavier mats should be included initially as height of landing	movement and going with the movement to disseminate the
Sample Task: Move onto the equipment, landing on your feet with as strong a take-off as you can. Make your action an explosive, strong action.	increases)	force when landing is an off-balance position
		Do not neglect the need for controlled landings—students may use a roll if necessary
Combining jumping actions with quick on-and-off actions on equipment	Landing on equipment with different body shapes	
Sample Task: Move onto and off of your equipment as quickly as you can, using feet only or hands and feet.	Quick on-and-off actions	
	Feet only	
	Hands and feet	
	Landing on equipment in balanced positions	

asks the student to achieve stillness and body extension in positions having narrow bases of support. To support your weight on a body part or combination of parts is qualitatively quite different from stretching out that balance and holding it still.

The second part of this theme focuses on ways to move into and out of balanced positions. This is actually a weight transference theme since the focus is on the transition from one position to another. It is included here because it is a logical extension of balance actions. The emphasis in this section is on careful preparation before the balance and thoughtful, controlled actions out of balanced positions.

Both young and older students will enjoy the challenge of finding balanced positions. Younger children will be encouraged to find controlled ways to move into and out of balanced positions. Older students will be expected to explore more difficult and inventive ways to move into and out of balanced positions, with an emphasis on the continuity and flow of the movement.

Advanced work in this theme encourages students to feel or develop a conscious awareness of the loss of balance both in still positions and from positions involving dynamic balance, and to apply their balancing skills in combination with locomotor skills and in relation to a partner. See Chart 16.7.

CHART 16.7. Theme VII: Balance actions

MAJOR TASK	EXTENSION	REFINEMENT
Floor		
Balancing on different body parts	Balancing with different numbers of parts supporting the weight	Balance should be experienced as a controlled and refined tension with sensitive movement to adjust to the balanced condition
Sample Task: Choose a three-part balance you can hold stable. See if you can change the shape of your body in this balance.	Balancing with different parts high	
	Understanding factors related to stability	Balances should be encouraged to be absolute stillness (6 seconds as a guide)
	Ask students to find very stable positions—ask what stable positions have in common (low center of gravity, weight over base of support)	The body should be extended out or up as appropriate for extended position or brought in close to the body for curled positions—the body shape should be clear and purposeful
	Ask students to experiment with moving from stable positions to unstable bases of support	
	Producing inverted and noninverted balances	Initial work should encourage slow, well-thought-through movements in and out of balanced positions; later work should encourage more fluuid movements as students are encouraged to
	Producing balances with	
	Wide shapes	
	Long and narrow shapes	
	Round shapes	
	Producing asymmetrical and symmetrical balances (balances where both sides of body are the same and balances where similar parts are doing different things)	Feel the loss of balance—the point at which balance is lost
		Prepare for the balanced position in the move that precedes it
Moving into and out of balanced positions	Take any balance you would like; find three different ways to get into that balance smoothly	Reemphasize need for stillness and extension in the balance
Sample Task: Start in a still position. Move slowly into your balance, find an interesting way to move out of it, and end in another still position.	From your balanced position, find three different ways to move out of your balance	If the term *twist* is unclear, go back to defining it as one part remaining stationary as other parts of the body move
	Twist out of balance	
	Turn out of balance	

(continued)

CHART 16.7. (*Continued*)

MAJOR TASK	EXTENSION	REFINEMENT
	Combine a sequence that includes a way to move into the balance, a balance, and a way to move out of your balance Choosing balances at different levels to move into and out of Low level Medium levels High levels Choosing inverted balances and noninverted balances	Encourage slow loss of balance so that the point at which balance is lost can be felt
Balancing supporting weight on small apparatus and single pieces of large apparatus Small apparatus: hoops, canes, small boxes, benches *Sample Task:* Find as many different ways as you can to balance, placing some parts of your body inside the hoop and some parts outside of the hoop.	Different body parts high Inverted and noninverted balances Specifying body parts or numbers of body parts Finding ways to balance using the space in and out of hoops; over and under canes, and on and off of boxes and benches	After initial exploration encourage extension and stillness Push students to explore all possibilities
Feeling the loss of balance *Sample Task:* Start moving slowly. Stop and let your weight keep going, passing through the balance point on your feet. Catch your balance and try it again.	Take a balance you can hold well; tip the balance slowly and try and bring yourself back into balance; tip it again and find the point at which you can't bring it back to a balanced position anymore; move out of your off-balance position safely Experiment with different bases Move into a balance from an action that has momentum (a traveling action); move through the balance point and feel the loss of balance Traveling and stopping on the feet, letting the momentum of your traveling carry you through the point of balance to a roll Traveling and stopping in inverted balances and passing through the balance point Arriving on equipment and feeling the loss of balance Feet only Inverted balances	Feeling the loss of balance requires a sensitivity that is more easily developed if actions are slow Loss of balance does not mean loss of control; speed of action should be that which the student can control safely
Using equipment to feel the loss of balance (any type or combination of equipment may be used)	Using the equipment to completely support different parts of the body (parts can be specified if more structure is needed)	Allow students to explore possibilities before requesting extended form and absolute control of actions

(*continued*)

CHART 16.7. (*Continued*)

MAJOR TASK	EXTENSION	REFINEMENT
Sample Task: Develop a short sequence on your equipment that includes a balance and shows a clear change in level.	Using the equipment to partially support the weight of the body while other parts remain on the floor Finding ways to move into and out of balanced positions on large apparatus—slowly Developing and perfecting short sequences on single piece of equipment—move into a balance and out of a balance Show a clear change of level	Give students time to work on moving into and out of balanced positions
Combining locomotion and balance *Sample Task:* Travel along your group of equipment, using all the equipment and at some point showing a balance	Incorporating a balance into longer sequences of traveling along equipment Show a clear change in level Show a clear change in direction Using stretching and curling actions	The ongoingness of locomotor actions sometimes causes students to forget to hold the action of the balance Achieve clear body shapes They need reminding
Balancing in relation to a partner *Sample Task:* Develop a smooth sequence with your partner that at some point allows each of you to at least partially support each other.	Matching balance of a partner Using a partner as support for a balance Partial support Total support Finding different ways to move into or out of the support with a partner Combining support actions with a partner with traveling actions into a sequence that at some time allows both students to support and to be supported Finding a different way to move into or out of a balance you can do with a partner Floor work Equipment	Teachers should insist that both partners be able to do the balance that is used Working with a partner in this way requires good self-management skills and students who are task-oriented and "deliberate" movers Teachers can encourage variety of balances through ideas related to Level Direction Number of parts used Specifying inverted or not inverted balances Specifying the part or combination of parts being used

Theme VIII: Transferring weight—twisting, turning, and spinning. Up until now students have been experiencing this theme in simpler ways in relation to hanging and swinging, weight-bearing, balance, and traveling actions. This theme introduces more advanced ways in which weight can be transferred through twisting, turning, and spinning actions.

Turning actions change the direction the body is facing, and although they occur most often on the feet, other body parts should be encouraged to participate in the shift in body weight. Twisting actions put the body in an off-balance position as one body part stays and the body shifts around that part. Spinning actions use a body part which is a narrow base of support to rotate around. Floor work in this theme should be fully developed before moving onto equipment.

Theme VIII is more appropriate for experienced groups of students. See Chart 16.8.

CHART 16.8. Theme VIII: Transferring weight—twisting, turning, and spinning

MAJOR TASK	EXTENSION	REFINEMENT
Taking weight on different body parts, use a twist to transfer that weight to a new body part *Sample Task:* Move from one base of support to another, attempting to twist to the new base of support.	Keeping your feet stationary, twist to transfer the weight to the hands and a new position Select a different part to which to transfer the weight, still keeping your feet stationary Select a different part to keep stationary, and see if you can twist and receive the weight on a different part Knees Shoulders Hips Hands Move through different bases of support, quickly twisting as you transfer the weight	Students should be encouraged to "move through the base of support receiving the weight"; it is not meant to be a balance If idea of "twist" is not clear, guide students to experience twist with different bases of support
Taking weight on different parts of the body, use a turn to change your direction and smoothly move through another base of support *Sample Task:* Develop a sequence of four actions that uses a turn to transfer weight from one action into another.	Turning with weight supported on different parts of the body to a new base of support Feet only Travel on different parts of your body, linking your movements with a turn Half turn Quarter turn Full turn Combining turning actions with traveling actions, emphasizing stretching and curling Turn in the stretched position	Help children experience turning from a variety of bases of support Turning action should incorporate a smooth controlled transfer of weight Encourage students to experience turning actions in both stretched and curled positions
Creating momentum by spinning on different parts of the body into a new base of support *Sample Task:* Use the momentum of your spinning action to help you face a new direction, and transfer your weight to a new part of your body.	Choose a part of your body that can create a base for spinning action; see how fast you can get your body going (stomach, seat, knee should be suggested if they do not emerge) Let the spinning action take you into a new base of support	Encourage students to use only enough momentum to get to where they want to go
Using twisting, turning, and spinning actions on the apparatus, maintaining a base of support and transferring the weight to a new base of support (bars, ropes, rings, and other hanging types of apparatus should be included as well as stools, boxes, benches, beams, etc.) Equipment should be placed at angles to each other to encourage turns and twists when possible	Support yourself on different parts of your body on the equipment; turn or twist to a new base of support; find ways to spin using different bases of support Travel along your equipment showing at some point A turn to a new direction A twist to a new base of support A spin on a body part	Allow students enough time to explore separate actions before combining sequences Variety can be encouraged with a focus on body parts supported or receiving weight, level, direction, or invertedness

(continued)

CHART 16.8. (*Continued*)

MAJOR TASK	EXTENSION	REFINEMENT
Sample Task: Transfer your weight on the same piece of equipment, showing first a twist, then a spin, and then a turn. *Comment:* Each of these actions can be explored separately or in combination. Some are more appropriate for particular pieces of apparatus than others.		

17

educational dance

Educational dance is that part of the physical education program that helps the child use movement expressively. The young child whirls and jumps and spins because whirling and jumping and spinning feel good. The child receives different sensations from different movements and uses movement to express inner feelings of joy, happiness, frustration, and aggression. The child gives movement feeling, and movement can give feeling to the child.

Dance has not received a large share of program time in physical education programs. This is due partially to the preservation of the notion that physical education is synonymous with sports and athletics. It is also due to teachers who themselves are insecure with expressive movement. It is sometimes due to incorporating dance in music education rather than in physical education. The material in this chapter can help a teacher feel more secure with the content of dance.

WHAT IS DANCE?

Dance is abstract. It is not an expression of an act but an expression of the feeling of an act.

It is in this way that dance differs from creative dramatics and mime. An educational dance program is designed not only to give students experiences in expressive movement, but to develop the ability of the students to express themselves in movement. This is done through progressive experiences which develop kinesthetic and cognitive awareness of movement.

Teachers can give students an expressive experience in movement. We can ask first graders to be an elephant, a cloud, or a leaf and ask them to move freely to music. We will probably be successful in giving the children an expressive experience in movement. These experiences, however, will do little to help the children continue to develop their expressive movement potential. If the experience is left at imagery the student is aware of the movement of the elephant, the cloud, or the leaf but not his own movement. It is not the movement of the cloud that is expressive—it is the light, floating sustained, and flexible movement of the child. It is not the falling leaf that is expressive. It is whirling and suddenness that give sensation to the child.

The child who is aware of the characteristics of movement can use these characteristics in other progressive movement experiences. It is our view that the teacher should use any means available to define and elicit movement from the child, and this includes imagery and other types of support to be discussed later. Developing an awareness of movement means that children must be helped to understand the characteristics of their movements and be able to produce them in other experiences, with and without the aid of supports.

THE CONTENT OF EDUCATIONAL DANCE

The content of educational dance is drawn directly from the movement analysis presented in Chart 14.1 on page 192. The first seven of Rudolph Laban's themes are used in the elementary-school program. They are described in detail later in the chapter. You will recall that Laban's analysis consists of four major constructs: what the body is doing, the use of space, the effort aspect, and the relationship aspect. The first seven themes highlight one of these four constructs. They are designed to expand the children's ability to use each movement theme in their dancing through varied experiences which focus on developing an awareness of that aspect. Awareness is both kinesthetic and cognitive. The student must be able to feel and produce the movement and be able to label it. Consider the weight quality of movement that is part of Theme II. Firm/strong movement and fine touch/light movement produce very different sensations. In Theme II light and firm movement will be experienced in different actions of the body and its parts; by using space in different ways; in contrast with each other; and through different relationships to other people, music, poetry, and so on. The reader will note that the theme was taken from the effort column of the movement analysis. The material that is used for development will come from the other three columns of the analysis (body, space, relationship). The student will be asked to produce light movement and strong movement. Experiences

will be provided to ensure that students feel the sensation of these opposing qualities and know the name of the quality they are experiencing.

The seven themes as designed by Laban are meant to be progressive. The first three themes in particular establish a very firm base of experiences in the elementary-school program. When a teacher leaves one theme and moves on to another, work from previous themes is not forgotten but is returned to with a new perspective of increased awareness. Students beginning educational dance in the later grades of elementary school will still need to begin with experiences in Theme I. However, they will move through these themes more rapidly and will experience the theme with more sophistication.

Each of the seven major themes is developed in this chapter. Major tasks under each theme are listed. Material to develop major tasks is provided as well as information helpful to improving the responses of children. This information is not meant to be complete in any way. It is designed to give the beginning teacher a place to start with children and to illuminate the nature of the theme presented.

THE DANCE LESSON

Begin a lesson with a structured vigorous activity. Many groups of children come into a gym eagerly anticipating vigorous activity. Children will be more likely to function as a group and be ready to listen if the teacher begins with a vigorous warm-up that is primarily teacher-directed. Action words familiar to the children or past work are useful for this part of the lesson.

> Example: When I say *go*, travel quickly to a new spot. When you hear the drum, freeze. Good. This time when you hear the drum, freeze, turn quickly and move on to a new spot.

Defining the Movement Concept

The movement concepts of educational dance are abstract. In order to communicate a concept to children, the teacher must find a way for the children to come to know the concept—to be aware of the concept in their own movement and to be able to identify it.

Teachers can define a movement concept by guiding children from the known to the unknown. If, for example, I wish to have children experience quick, direct, and firm movement with different parts of the body, I can go from a punching action with the hands, to talking about the characteristics of the punch, and then to asking students to reproduce it with other parts of their bodies.

Teachers can define a movement by creating an environment that would produce the movement characteristics desired. If I want very firm traveling movement, I could suggest to students that they have been dropped in a jar of very heavy and thick molasses and ask them how their movement would change. Once we have felt the movement desired, we would then drop the idea of molasses and develop the concept of firm, sustained movement.

Teachers can guide students to a movement concept through a series of tasks that increasingly approach the concept to be developed. If a concept has a time, weight, and space characteristic, a teacher can ask students to do something having one of those qualities and then gradually add the other characteristics. If, for instance, I want children to engage in a wringing action, I might ask them to do something that twists the body or its parts. I can then add the quality of firmness and sustained action to get wringing actions.

Teachers can define a movement concept through demonstration. A teacher can do the demonstrating with or without another student, being careful to make clear that this is an example of *one* way to do the action. If I want to get across the idea of rhythmical conversation with another, I can ask a student to be my partner. I can do a short rhythmical phrase—be still—and have the partner do something to answer me. I can comment on what we did and then ask the students to carry on their own conversations.

Teachers can define a movement concept in terms of characters or actions familiar to the students (clouds, Incredible Hulk, wind, waves, chopping, and so on). As we pointed out earlier, care must be taken using this method. If I use the Incredible Hulk to help define strong movement, I must be careful to translate only the strength characteristics of the character and not the restricting additional characteristics as we move beyond the imagery.

Developing the Movement Concept

Once children have a feeling for a movement concept, the teacher should develop it more fully. Development has two major parts: expansion, having children experience the concept in different ways; and refinement, having the children improve the quality with which they experience a concept.

Ideas for expanding a child's experience with a movement concept are limitless. Theoretically, one movement concept can be experienced with attention to any other. Practically speaking, some concepts go more naturally with others. Understanding the purpose of a movement theme and experience with movement will help the teacher choose wisely. The material in the development columns of the charts provided in this text can help a teacher get started.

Teachers should expect children to attend to the concept being developed and to experience it to the limits of their own ability. If a task involves different body parts, the child should be using different parts. If the task involves quick movement, the action of the child should be quick. If partners are to meet and part, then they should meet and part. Students should remain on-task and should be expected to produce a high quality of response.

Structuring Movement Experiences

Teachers can design movement tasks for students with different degrees of structure. Structure is related to the number of decisions in an experience left to the student. If I ask children to stand on a line and jump into the air when I say *go*, I have left to the students the decisions related to the characteristics of the jump, but little else. If I ask students to move quickly in their own space, I have left more decisions to the student. Teachers will want to design experiences in dance with different degrees of structure.

Students who do not have a great amount of experience with a movement idea will need more structure. Many beginning teachers are reluctant to give more structure to an experience because they fear they will destroy the creativity of the children. However, children who do not have experience with an idea are limited in their potential responses. Narrowing the number of decisions a student has in an experience is helpful in making responses more creative. If, for example, I want children to move to music that should help develop free turning and spinning actions, I may want to structure the experience first by having the students move just their hands and arms to the music on the spot. I can then add traveling actions and actions of the whole body. I will probably be more successful in developing creativity because I have expanded the students' idea of the concept.

The amount of structure a teacher gives to a movement experience is related not only to the child's experience with a task but also to the ability of students to remain productively on task. Teachers whose children are self-directed and good listeners can give experiences less structure. Students who have not developed these skills will need more structure, although the amount will decrease as their ability to handle more decisions increases.

Teachers can add structure to experiences by:

1. Having a clear starting and stopping time for an experience
2. Giving a limited choice of ways to exhibit a movement concept (specify the action, body part to be used, on the spot or traveling)
3. Using percussion instruments to support the quality
4. Making sure the children understand and are focused on the task before they begin to move—this can be done through questioning or by asking one or two students to show you what you asked them to do
5. Having initial experience performed in a limited space

Producing Expressive Movement

The objective of educational dance is expression. In order for a child's movement to be expressive, the student must be totally involved in the movement idea. Expression is feeling, and in dance feeling involves cognitive, affective, and psychomotor involvement. The following guidelines will help in creating an environment for total involvement.

1. Respect the uniqueness of a student's response. Each child moves differently and enjoys some movement sensations more than others. It is the goal of educational dance to provide experience with a full range of movement, but this does not mean that some students will not prefer one kind of movement to another.

2. Use your voice to communicate characteristics desired. One of the most useful tools a teacher has is the voice. Quickness, sustained movement, lightness, strength, and rhythm can all be communicated using the dynamics of the voice. Consider the task, "Quickly travel to a new spot and sink slowly to the ground." Say it now with the dynamics of movement in mind.

3. Participate with the students with care. Teacher participation can help more fully involve students. It gives them a sense of security. However, teachers must be careful when they participate that they do not narrow a child's perception of a task. They should carefully monitor their own responses for variety.

4. Use repetition of movement phrases often. Expression in movement is largely a function of rhythm. Rhythm is repetition. Students should repeat sequences several times in order to feel the rhythm of the action.

5. Respect those students who are not easily involved. Some students, particularly in early experiences and particularly older students, will need time to become involved. Try not to draw attention to the child's lack of involvement. This does not mean that the child should be allowed to be off-task. It means that you allow children to participate at their own level of involvement.

6. Use demonstration with care. Student demonstration is useful to communicate a concept. It also tends to motivate students to higher levels of performance. Teachers must take care that students who are asked to demonstrate are ready to have others view their work. Teachers can avoid some of the problems connected with demonstration if groups of children demonstrate at the same time and if children who are insecure in their expression are not selected.

Demonstration should be used for a purpose. Teachers need to focus students' observation on an aspect of the task they want to clarify or a concept they want to communicate. Students should view with a purpose and teachers need to question students to assess the degree to which they saw what they were supposed to see.

7. Carefully observe student responses. Teachers should carefully observe the responses of students to a task. In order to further develop a movement concept in relation to the needs of students, a teacher must be able to analyze the responses of students in terms of the four major constructs of the analysis: What body action are the students performing? How are they using space? What time, energy, and space factors are involved? Are the children relating to another (others)? When the teacher can look at the child's response to a task relative to the full meaning of the theme and instructional objectives of a lesson, the teacher will be able to select further development congruent with the child's movement ability.

8. Choose support material that has a great deal of movement potential. Support material should expand and not restrict a child's experience with a movement concept. Stimuli of many sorts can be used to involve the students: students can use or design their own stories involving events of nature, living processes, or people having movement characteristics. They need to move beyond the single dimension of an event or character, such as the sun rising or an old man walking slowly.

Music for children's dance should be dynamic and not stay for too long with one movement idea. Short sequences of recorded music from a wide variety of sources can be used. Teachers can design their own tapes combining folk, classical, and percussive music as needed to support a movement idea.

When students dance with scarves, sticks, percussive instruments, bells, or other implements, teachers should help the children explore the full potential of these supports.

9. Don't call it dance. With older children teachers will find that preconceived notions about dance interfere. Teachers can avoid initial problems by not calling what they are doing dance but rather movement.

10. Use percussion instruments. They are a valuable tool for teaching dance. Teachers should practice using them to produce quickness, sustained movement, heavy and light and even and uneven rhythmic patterns.

11. Bare feet are essential. Clothing that does not restrict movement and bare feet will help to bring out the children's movement potential. Teachers who have not asked students to remove their shoes and socks before may find some resistance. Accept the resistance and proceed. With time children will not attend to the idea that they are in bare feet.

A sample lesson plan is included on the next few pages. The plan is taken from work in Theme II and assumes experience in Theme I.

MAJOR FOCUS OF WORK: CONTRASTING QUICK AND SUSTAINED MOVEMENT

Each student should be able to:
1. Contrast quick and sustained movement both on the spot and traveling in a variety of ways
2. Demonstrate a clear beginning and ending to their sequence

---

(continued)

TASK	WHAT TEACHER IS LOOKING FOR	RESPONSE	DECISION
Find a space and show me something you can do that is very quick—something that is over in a flash.	Are the movements quick?	Yes No⟶	Choose a child who is doing something very quickly. Reemphasize that the movement must be over almost as quickly as it begins.
	Have the children chosen total body actions or actions of single parts?	Total⟶	Use a percussive drum beat to help give a task that requires them to explore quick actions of single parts.
		Single⟶ Parts	Give a task that requires them to explore quick actions of the total body.
		Mixed⟶	"I observed some of you using your whole body and some using only a part. Can you mix both, making all your actions very different?"
Put three very quick actions together and stop very still. What we will have is quick, quick, quick, and still. When you find a combination you think is interesting, do it several times.	Stillness to start: A change in body part or action being used Really quick actions Stillness at the end of sequence Rhythmical pattern	Yes No⟶	If doing three actions is too difficult, go back to contrasting one quick movement with stillness. Reemphasize aspects of the task. Use demonstration if need be.
This half of the room sit. The other half of the room will show us their sequences. As you watch, look to see who is really quick and who really has stillness at the beginning and end of what they do. Reverse demonstrating group.	As children are demonstrating, the observers should be focused on their task. A short discussion of good sequences and what made them good should follow.		
Move your feet as quickly as you can in your own space— I will help you with the drum: quick and stop quick and stop.	The feet should be moving quickly on the toes so that time is not wasted with the full placement of the foot.	Yes No⟶	Demonstrate—teacher or student.
Now let your quick feet take you some place, quick, quick, quick, and stop. I'll help you with the drum to start.	The temptation will be for children to move *fast* but not quick.	Yes No⟶	Reemphasize that the feet must be moving quickly.
Let's see if you can do it by yourself. Really quick feet and stop.	This will be difficult for them. The traveling action should be short.	Yes No⟶	Demonstrate one possibility. Reemphasize quick traveling that gets there quickly.
Now put several together with a moment of stillness before you start again.	The moment of stillness will decrease as students work independently	Yes No⟶	Have them count to 6 or take three deep breaths before being quick again.
Add a quick turn or spin to your sequence either at the beginning, while you are traveling, or at the end. See where you like it.	Give students time to try putting this together in different ways. Comment on the different possibilities you see them trying.		

(continued)

TASK	WHAT TEACHER IS LOOKING FOR	RESPONSE	DECISION
	Are they losing the rest of the sequence in their attempt to explore turns and spins?	Yes———→ No	Give them time to explore and then reemphasize that it is part of their sequence.
Everyone start very still and do your sequence twice for me. Be very quick and very still when you should be. Do quick traveling and very still beginnings—putting a spin or a turn in there where you would like.	Are sequences quick with stillness?	Yes No———→	Challenge them to make quick quicker and still very still.
	Have they included a spin or a turn?	Yes No———→	Ask them to go back and try it again, being sure to include the turn or spin.
Everyone find a good space. What would happen if we made that turn very slowly. Try a slow turn. It's hard, but be very slow.	Initial reactions might be just turning the feet slowly with the rest of the body inactive. Accept this for now and concentrate on the slowness of the action.		
Try to make the way you turn interesting. Can you think of a way to use the space differently as you turn?	Look for: Changes in level Twisting actions of upper body Variations in body shape Gesturing actions with the upper body—taking up a lot of space	Yes No———→	At this point the teacher can seek to develop any of these aspects of the turn if they are not present. If some of the children included some of the aspects in their work, use several of them to demonstrate and ask observers to see if they can identify what it is that makes the turn interesting.
Can we add this slow turn to our sequence? A quick travel, slow turn, and quick travel. Be sure to start and stop very still.	Have children maintain quickness and then slowness.	Yes No———→	Reemphasize quality. Use drum or tambourine if necessary. Encourage them to let the slow keep going as long as it can.

DEVELOPING THE THEMES

Theme I: Body Awareness

Theme I is probably the most critical theme in the elementary-school program. It is this theme that helps the child to become aware of the potential of the body for expressive movement. It explores actions of the total body and its parts—as well as stillness—for their expressive nature. Expressive movement is not new to the young child, who twirls and hops for the sheer sensation of it. If this expressiveness is to be extended and produced with awareness, it must be nurtured and guided in its development.

A sound base of experience should be provided with the exploration of total body actions beginning with the actions most familiar to the child. These actions should be contrasted with stillness as the young child has difficulty arresting movement. The teacher will then want to blend lesson material from different sections of this theme.

Older students can be expected to relate their movement to others, to poetry, and to other factors in more sophisticated ways. Younger students will need to limit their relationships to those involving the teacher. The teacher must help them develop their work on sequences, guiding them to explore each part of the sequence and then combine actions. Younger students will initially depend on percussive help and lesson material that changes often. Older students can practice, explore, and refine their responses.

CHART 17.1. Theme I—body awareness

MAJOR TASK	EXTENSION	REFINEMENT
*Total Body Actions** Exploration and combination of the following actions: Locomotor actions (run, skip, creep, rush, slither, hop, gallop, dart, flee) Vibratory actions (shiver, shake, wobble, quiver, tremble, patter, shudder) Turning actions (spin, whirl, twist, whip, swivel, pivot) Stopping actions (freeze, hold, perch, grip, anchor, pause, settle) Percussive actions (stamp, punch, explode, pound, erupt) Closing actions (shrink, shrivel, contract, surround, clasp) Opening actions (grow, expand, release, open, spread, release) Sinking actions (collapse, sink, lower, drip, drop, fall) Rising actions (lift, rise, suspend) Advancing actions (reach, approach) Retreating actions (recoil, withdraw) Jumping actions (leap, toss, prance, soar, bound, bounce, fly)	Exploring individual actions to define and expand the action Body parts or the part of a body part important to the action Example: As you skip, make your knees really important Size of the movement Example: Make your shivering bigger. The time, weight, space, or flow quality that is the essence of the action or a variable in the action Example: Make your slithering as smooth as you can. Doing the action in a different direction or using different areas of personal space Example: As you rise from the floor, get to the back area of your space as well. Changing base upon which action is performed (where appropriate) Example: What other body parts can you spin on? Contrasting actions with opposites	Actions should be *defined* using material children can relate to and then brought back to the idea of the movement itself. Children can swirl with the quality of a leaf in the wind, but they cannot be a leaf in the wind. To leave the definition at imagery prohibits further exploration of that quality.
	Examples Locomotion and different kinds of stillness (freeze and settle): travel and freeze—travel and settle Locomotion and movement on the spot Rising and sinking actions Contracting and expanding actions Advancing and retreating actions	Actions should be explored in terms of the role body parts play in the action. Example: The head and chest in lifting and rising actions, the knees in skipping actions. What each part is doing in the action becomes important as well as awakening an awareness of making the total body participate in the action.

(continued)

CHART 17.1. (*Continued*)

MAJOR TASK	EXTENSION	REFINEMENT
	Combining actions into sequences or movement sentences (usually at least one locomotor movement, one nonlocomotor movement, and a quality of stillness is effective in getting total involvement)	
	Examples Slither, spring, settle Rise, travel, freeze, and sink Rush, pivot, sink, open, and freeze Advance, pounce, collapse Advance, pounce, withdraw Twirl, travel, pause, travel Relating Movement	Students should be encouraged to precede and follow actions with a moment of stillness to give a beginning and ending point to their movement. Stillness involves an alert tension, not a total release.
	Examples To own sounds	Children need to be helped to keep their sequences short. For young children the task run may never end unless first structured by the teacher.
	Example: What does a slither sound like? A spring? A settling action. Make these sounds. Add these to your move.	
	To percussion sounds of teacher	Teachers need to be alert to the ability of the child to involve the total body in the action. Observe for parts that are left out of the action and if necessary focus on them.
	Example: Teacher selecting movement of skip or gallop with an uneven rhythmic beat of drum or tambourine.	
	To props that help children involve themselves in movement	Help students to make their actions bigger, lighter, quicker, or more sustained as appropriate.
	Example: Scarves or ribbon wands (large streamers attached to a small stick that can float, snap, twirl, fly, etc.)	Observe for ways to help children produce more variety as well as quality in their actions.
	To the teacher—following or contrasting the actions of the teacher—	
	Example: Rising and sinking, advancing and retreating.	
	To percussive sounds self-made	
	Example: Combine some sounds that suggest an action(s) to you and see if you can duplicate these actions in movement.	
	To an action piece of poetry (self-written or other)	Teachers need to be careful that pantomime does not take over

(continued)

CHART 17.1. (*Continued*)

MAJOR TASK	EXTENSION	REFINEMENT
	Example: Night has come—the birds are still The petals on the flowers are closed But the sun pops up to open the day And the petals on the flower now want to play.	here. It is the quality of the movement and not the object moving that is to be expressed.
	To music Example: Music can be used to bring out particular locomotor patterns as uneven rhythm for gallops and skip. It can also be used for bouncing, swirling, or other actions with definite weight qualities as well as more interpretive experiences that merely suggest a variety of experiences. To a small group or partner Example: One group: advancing, pouncing, and retreating Another group: rising, exploding, and advancing	Encourage children to listen to the music and if necessary clap a rhythm or use just a body part before using a total body action
Actions of Body Parts Using body parts in isolated actions	Exploring the ways in which different body parts can move using total body actions applied only to individual parts and other development material Example: (a) Take your weight on a part of your body other than your feet and show me how the knees can move. Where can they go? How fast can they move? How slowly? How high from the floor can they go? Take your weight on another part(s) of your body. Can your knees do more or less in this position? (b) Tap your hands lightly on the floor. Keep them going very quickly. Use the other side of the hands. Let them come off the floor and tap the space around you.	If necessary for emphasis, ribbons, bells, or some other way to draw attention to a part may be used when exploring parts of the body.

(*continued*)

CHART 17.1. (*Continued*)

MAJOR TASK	EXTENSION	REFINEMENT
	Meeting and parting of different body parts Meeting in one part of space and parting to a new space as far away from each other as possible Meeting and parting, contrasting the time quality—quick and sustained Continuous changes of parts being used Change of base of support to free other parts	
	Using a total body action emphasizing a part that is to be made clear or important in the action—locomotor, turning, stopping, percussive, contracting, expanding, resting, advancing, and retreating actions are all useful for emphasizing parts of the body	There are certain body parts that are important for certain actions: For instance, the knees in skipping; the head and chest in rising; and the pelvis area in sinking actions. Young children will explore unimportant parts as well.
	Example: Travel throughout the space using your feet in different ways. As you travel, emphasize or make important one part of your body. I'm going to be looking to see which part you are making important, so make it very clear.	Older children should be helped to understand the role of these parts in an action.
Leading actions using different body parts	Leading nonlocomotor actions with different body parts Rising and sinking actions Turning actions—twisting actions Traveling with rising and sinking actions	It is possible to perform locomotor movements, leading with different parts of the body. It is difficult for young children to do this without merely extending a part out and carrying it as the body moves rather than leading the movement. A *carry* is different from body lead. A body lead unfolds with the movement rather than prior to it.
	Example: Collapse to the floor. Let's pretend you're a puppet with strings on different parts of your body. If I pick up the puppet slowly by only one of those strings, what would you look like. Let's try it. You're really collapsed and I'm going to lift the puppet from the head *very slowly* and now let it go very quickly. Now I'm going to lift the puppet by its elbow very slowly. When I lift using one of the strings, I am making you lead your rising action with one part of your body and you are coming up very straight. Can you lead your rising action with some different parts of your body not coming up so straight.	

*Adapted from Boorman, 1969.

Theme II: The Awareness of Weight and Time

Theme II is designed to give the student experiences in using the qualities of weight and time. These are the first qualities of the effort factor to be introduced to the student. It is the quality of the movement which adds dynamics and texture to movement, making it expressive.

The time quality is not to be confused with mere fast and slow movement. The contrast is between actions which are quick and over soon and those which have an ongoing, or sustained, quality about them. The terms *slow* and *fast* are useful in helping children begin to experience this quality, but the ideas of quickness and ongoingness should be added as soon as the teacher structures the experiences.

The weight quality of contrasting firmness and fine touch is meant to focus on the inner tension of the movement. The words we most associate with this quality are *strong* and *light*. They should be developed with the idea of the inner attitude that produces them.

With many groups the quality can best be explored first with actions of single body parts or nonlocomotor actions. Teachers should not dwell on one extreme of a quality for too long (e.g., fine touch) before introducing and contrasting it with the other extreme of that quality (fine touch and firmness). These qualities can best be understood in terms of their opposites. It is also difficult to move continuously with one quality.

Students should be encouraged to use extremes in their work with this theme. Firmness should be as firm as possible, quickness should be as quick as possible, and so on. Movement phrases and sequences should not be too long, otherwise the quality of the movement will be lost.

Some students will find great involvement in movements requiring strength. Lightness will be more difficult for them. For some children the opposite will be true. Both experiences should be provided.

As soon as both time and weight qualities have been fully explored separately, they should be combined and the students, particularly the older students, should be able to participate in group and partner work structured so that children design short sequences demonstrating their ability to use and contrast these qualities.

Theme III: The Awareness of Space

Theme III focuses on developing the child's awareness of the spatial factors in movement. The children have been using space in their movements when working with Themes I and II. It is Theme III however

CHART 17.2. Theme II—The awareness of weight and time

MAJOR TASK	EXTENSION	REFINEMENT
Sudden and Sustained: Feeling sudden movement	Producing quick actions in isolated parts of the body Single action of body parts Combined actions of two parts Meeting and parting of body parts Example: When you hear the drum, do something with your finger that is very quick—hands—feet—head Producing quick actions with the total body	Students will need help being quick at first. Percussive music or the sound of your voice may help. Quickness is over fast and should not be confused with ongoing fast movement. Teachers can help by giving a stopping point at first. Music with quick, explosive percussive sounds is helpful but should be withdrawn as the feeling of quickness is developed.

(continued)

CHART 17.2. *(Continued)*

MAJOR TASK	EXTENSION	REFINEMENT
	Example: Hold a position. When I say *go,* make your whole body change its position very quickly. Move to the floor very quickly—away from the floor—turn, get some place quickly and then stop. Turn and go to a new place. Meet somebody, turn quickly, and meet someone else.	
	Designing short sequences of quick actions—teacher-designed	
	Example: rush-whip-freeze-dart-pound-collapse	
	Student-designed.	
	Example: Put together a movement sentence that takes you quickly to a new spot. Do something quick at that spot and travel to a new spot. Finish your sentence with a quick stopping action.	
Feeling sustained movement	Producing sustained actions in isolated parts of the body Single actions of body parts Combined actions of parts Meeting and parting of body parts	Children have trouble moving in a sustained way. The sound of your voice may help, or sustained tapping on a drum or tambourine may also help. Sustained actions should be combined with quick actions as soon as children have a feeling for the quality. Variety in meeting and parting experiences can be obtained with encouragement to use different parts of the body, different bases of support, and to use all parts of personal space.
	Example: Put your hand somewhere in your personal space. Have your hand move through your personal space slowly and with a feeling that it's never going to stop. It's just going to keep going. Choose another part and see if you can make it do the same thing. Can it meet another body part and then have that part take over?	
	Producing sustained actions in non-locomotor movements Rising and sinking Opening and closing Stopping actions Turning actions	The concept of slow motion photography that children are familiar with may be useful to communicate the sustained quality of movement.
	Example: Take your weight on a part of your body other than your feet and slowly bring all parts of your body into the center—very slowly. Now very slowly let them move from the center, maybe at one time, maybe one at	

(continued)

CHART 17.2. (*Continued*)

MAJOR TASK	EXTENSION	REFINEMENT
	a time. This time can you open up slowly to a new base of support and start again, closing?	
	Traveling with sustained actions Action words—creeping, slither, flow, weightless, bouncy Changing level Example: Pick a spot that's close to where you are. See if you can get to that new spot very slowly. When you get there, pick a new spot and get to that spot very slowly. Can you get there moving at a different level but still keeping your action slow? Designing short sequences of sustained actions Example: Creep and settle Rise slowly—pause—melt	Slow traveling actions are difficult for young children and should not be dwelled on too long as the quality will be lost. The teacher should attempt to introduce some variety in traveling actions through the concept of varying levels, direction, or pathway while maintaining the sustained quality.
Combining suddenness and sustained movement in contrasting actions	Meeting and parting of body parts Example: Put your hands together. When you hear the drum, bring these parts apart from each other as far as you can to a space around you. Now bring them together in a new place as slowly as you can. Contrasting single action of body parts Example: Do something quickly with your shoulders. Now try to do that action as slowly as you can.	When contrasting qualities are combined, students should attempt to use the extremes of the quality. The teacher should not be satisfied with less.
	Contrasting nonlocomotor movements Rising and sinking Opening and closing Stopping actions Turning actions Example: Show me how you can turn very quickly. Now try turning very slowly and settling to a still position.	Variety in nonlocomotor actions can be achieved through emphasizing or leading actions with different body parts, using the space differently, or varying the base of support.
	Contrasting locomotor actions Stepping slowly and with quickness Varying size of movement Varying direction of movement	

(*continued*)

CHART 17.2. *(Continued)*

MAJOR TASK	EXTENSION	REFINEMENT
	Advancing quickly—retreating slowly in relation to a spot, to another, or to a group Combining sequences of action words having qualities of suddenness and sustainment Pause, collapse Explode, freeze, settle Pound, float, grip Example: (a) I have put actions on one side of the blackboard that are very quick. I have put actions on the other side of the blackboard that are very slow. Put together a movement sentence from these words that shows us you can be very quick and very slow. (b) Find a quick way to travel, , a slow way to turn, and a slow way to end your action	Students will need time to choose and develop their sequences. Once they have chosen a sequence, they should be held to producing the quality of that action. Students should be helped to observe these qualities in the actions of other students. "Let's watch Freddy's sequence. What is he doing?"
Firmness and Fine Touch: Feeling tension and firmness	Producing muscular tension in isolated parts of the body Example: When you hear the drum, make a part of your body very light. Thrusting and shooting actions of isolated body parts Example: Shoot an arm out into the air very strong and very quickly. Percussive and explosive actions of the total body Example: Take any position you would like. When you hear the drum, explode from that position. What other ways can you think of to explode? Combining traveling and gripping actions Example: Travel a short distance and then grip the floor with your feet very slowly. Contrasting tension with the release of tension Example: Do something that is very strong. Freeze and hold that strength. Then see if you can completely release that strength.	Children need to be helped to feel the inner tension that is firmness. "Let me see you feeling strong." Firmness in traveling actions should be felt in the pelvic area and legs as well as the feet.

(continued)

CHART 17.2. (*Continued*)

MAJOR TASK	EXTENSION	REFINEMENT
Feeling fine touch and lightness	Feeling a light quality in different parts of body (initially primarily the hands and feet) Example: (a) tap the floor with your hands—all different places around you very, very lightly. Now tap the air around you. Can you tap with your feet? Other parts of your body? (b) Move your hands in a very light, dreamy way around your space—just kind of floating. Feeling lack of tension in non-locomotor actions of rising and sinking and expanding and contracting Examples: Take a position very close to the floor. If we could move from the floor like steam off a road, how could we come off the floor?	Lightness is difficult for children to feel in the whole body. Work with lightness in individual parts only as necessary to communicate this quality. Talk about things that move lightly. Children may need help in timing these actions. The rising and opening actions should make clear the role of the chest, shoulders, neck, and head in producing lightness. Variety can be achieved by emphasizing and leading with different body parts, changing the use of space or base of support
	Feeling lack of tension in locomotor actions and stopping actions (flee—float—perch—settle) Example: Move lightly across the floor to a perch on a line. Keep finding new ways to move lightly and a new line or spot to perch on.	A perch is a light stopping at a point and the lightness of this quality should be emphasized.
Combining firmness and fine touch in contrasting actions	Meeting and parting of body parts Example: Put any two parts together. Bring them apart with a very strong action. Now bring them together with a very light action. Keep changing the parts and the space you are using.	Percussive help may be needed here initially. The contrast should be clear.
	Contrasting single actions of isolated parts of the body Example: Do something with your leg. Now make that action very strong—now very light. What other actions can you try that you can do both very strong and very light with different parts of your body?	Teacher can give students an action at first and then ask the children to explore other parts and actions
	Contrasting nonlocomotor movements Rising and sinking Opening and closing	

(*continued*)

CHART 17.2. (Continued)

MAJOR TASK	EXTENSION	REFINEMENT
	Stopping actions Turning actions	
	Example: Start in a low position. Come off the floor in a firm, strong way and move to the floor very lightly.	
	Contrasting locomotor actions Stepping lightly with strength Advance and retreating Skipping, hopping, and running with contrasting qualities	Teacher indicates change first and then students do action in their own time.
	Example: Let's pretend the floor isn't very strong and if we hit it too hard we will fall right through. How would you step? Now if we wanted to break through that floor how would we step? Can you start in a very still position, put these two actions together, and show us when you are finished by again having a very still position?	
	Combining sequences of action words having qualities of firmness and fine touch Stamp—explode—settle Flee—perch—erupt Travel—twirl—freeze	The actions can first be defined and worked with separately before being combined. Students can choose their own combinations or they can be defined by the teacher.
Combining the weight quality and time quality: Firm—sudden/strong-quick Firm—sustained Fine touch—sudden Fine touch—sustained	Contrasting time/weight qualities with actions of individual body parts Head nodding, hands grasping, actions of the arms and legs moving into personal space Meeting and parting of body parts	Younger students may not be able to work with all four combinations at one time and will need to work only with one example: Firm—quick Fine touch—slow
	Example: Let your hand and arm explore the space around you. Make your action very slow and very strong. Can you change the action to very slow and light; quick and light; quick and strong? Pick two of the qualities you'd like to contrast with a different action using another part and let's see if we can really tell when you are changing	

(continued)

CHART 17.2. (Continued)

MAJOR TASK	EXTENSION	REFINEMENT
	Total body actions on the spot contrasting time/weight qualities. Opening and closing Rising and sinking Stopping and turning actions Combining above with body parts leading	Produce variety in these actions by suggesting a different use of space, base of support, or change in lead or emphasis on body parts
	Example: Close your body up very tightly. Let one part come out at a time and let it come out a different way. I'll help you the first time, using a drum when the action should be strong and a triangle when the action should be light. You decide on the speed.	
	Total body actions traveling and on the spot Action sequences	Teacher and students can combine action words or qualities in many ways. Simple poetry the children write or interpret and interpretive music are very useful here.
	Example: (a) Rise slowly and lightly from the floor, gallop in a strong way, and melt slowly to the floor. (b) Press up from the floor, pause, and explode. (c) Whirl quickly and lightly through the air. Freeze and pounce.	
	Contrasting actions with a partner/ teacher/group Doing the opposite of a partner movement, answering in the opposite Leading and following—same action Advancing and retreating with opposite actions Rising and sinking, contrasting actions Opening and closing, contrasting actions Contrasting actions of a single body part with a partner In relation to sounds—one partner or group moves on strong, quick, and another on strong, slow sounds Designing group sequences that contrast the time/weight quality	Younger students should probably keep their movements related to the teacher only. Group work can be structured in terms of coming toward each other with one quality, mingling with another, and parting with another.

that seeks to develop a more varied use and awareness of that space.

Children have been introduced to the basic ideas of general space, personal space, direction, and level before they get to this theme. A rudimentary idea of "own space" and "general space" is necessary for the scattered organization pattern used in the games and gymnastics area of the movement education program. The idea of levels and direction has been used to expand the variety with which children perform actions in all content areas as well. In Theme III a more comprehensive study of these spatial concepts is made. Pathways and extensions are fully explored and for the intermediate-aged student the idea of focus is explored and incorporated into the child's dancing.

Students need to be helped to feel the difference between movements that make different air and floor patterns. These differences should be emphasized as the body leans into the curvy pathways and prepares for changes in direction in zig-zag pathways with an inner tension, or flows with the rhythmical action of spiraling movement.

The concept of extension is very useful in helping children to use large expressive, dancelike movements. Once this is incorpo- rated into the child's movement vocabulary, a simple "Let's make your movement much bigger" will help the teacher bring out much expression in the child's movement.

Variety in direction and level makes children's movement more interesting. These concepts become critical to interesting group and partner work and essential for extending children's ability to gesture (movement of a part that is free). We normally associate direction with locomotor actions, but forward, backward, up and down, and sideways are critical for on-the-spot actions as well.

Much of this theme can be built upon work done in the first two themes. However, the spatial concepts of the work are the central focus, and lessons should be designed to reflect this.

CHART 17.3. Theme III: The awareness of space

MAJOR TASK	EXTENSION	REFINEMENT
Awareness of personal space and general space	Defining and exploring general space Identifying a spot and moving quickly to that spot; choosing a spot in front of you, behind you, to your side Getting to all parts of general space before you stop, never coming to the same spot twice Finding a spot not in the defined general space Defining personal space Space of the whole body— reaching up and out as far as you can go—to the back of your space Reaching out as far as you can go and losing your balance, carrying you into general space Penetrating personal space with different body parts Shooting parts into space Exploring the area that each body part can use within personal space Example: What part of your space can your feet get to; your head; your elbows? Really get to all those parts.	The assumption here is that children can remain within a boundary identified by the teacher and that they can find a single space within that boundary that is as far from others as possible. If not, then staying within a defined general space and finding a personal work area within that space should receive priority. The image of a bubble surrounding the body is a useful one to help children understand the concept of personal space. Think about touching the bubble, breaking it, getting to all its space, filling it with body surfaces and cutting through it with sharp actions.

(continued)

CHART 17.3. (*Continued*)

MAJOR TASK	EXTENSION	REFINEMENT
	Exploring personal space with total body actions Fill your space with the biggest shape you can think of Take up only a little room in your space, making your body as small as you can Continuous changes filling the space and using only a part of it	Children should be encouraged to use space in the back and lower regions of their personal space.
	Example: Make a shape that takes only a little space. Let that action grow until it gets as big as it can and then make it small again.	The first response to being big and little will be a round ball shape that grows to be a tall stretched shape. Encourage students to seek other ways of being small.
	Combining actions using personal space and general space	
	Example: Travel to a spot inside this space that you haven't been for a while. When you get there, do something that first takes up a little space and then let it grow and get as big as it can. Pause and then start over, going to a new space.	Encourage students to look for the space they want to move into before they start to move. This will eliminate long traveling actions.
	Awareness of space created by others/objects Moving in and out of; over and under; near to and far from the space created by others/objects (stationary objects/people are useful to start with before moving people)	
	Example: Everyone get a partner. One of you make a shape in the space that you are in. The other see if you can find a shape that fills the space (uses the low space; covers some of your partner; uses the space in back of your partner. You must not touch your partner. Just use the space your partner created.	Encourage students to make shapes that use space in interesting ways.
	Moving with a small group in a limited general space, trying to keep as much of the space filled as possible	Teacher will need to draw children's attention to space close to ground as well as high space.

(continued)

CHART 17.3. (*Continued*)

MAJOR TASK	EXTENSION	REFINEMENT
Awareness of concept of extension (big and little movement)	Contrasting extension in locomotor actions	
	Example: Hopping, skipping, running, galloping, and using the feet in different ways to travel first with very small movements and then with as big a movement as you can make.	Actions will be made bigger by involving the total body in the action and exaggerating the main action of the movement.
	Contrasting nonlocomotor movements with movements that remain close to the center of the body and far away from the center	
	Stopping actions that are big actions vs. small actions	
	Turning, using a lot of space vs. only a little space	
	Rising movements that keep body parts close vs. rising movements that take body parts far from the center, contrasting with sinking actions	
	Opening and closing movements—opening up all the way—opening a little vs. closing really tightly	Children should explore limited vs. full extension of body parts in these actions.
	Example: Take a deep breath and fill your lungs with air, raising your body from the floor. Try it again and take up as little space as you can as you move up through your personal space. Take another deep breath and have the air fill your whole body and make it reach to fill as much space as you can as you move up through the space.	The idea of breathing in lightness is a useful concept here for rising actions.
	Extending action of body parts to the whole body	
	Example: Do something with your finger that is a very small action. Now add your hand to that action, your elbow, shoulder, trunk, head, whole body. Try another action with another body part. Start it small and let it grow. Let it grow out of your personal space if you can.	These experiences should help children understand the idea of making actions bigger as well as extending action from the center of the body.
Awareness of direction (up/down, sideways, forward, and backward)	Exploring directions with locomotor actions—running, skipping, hopping, rushing, slithering, galloping	

(*continued*)

CHART 17.3. *(Continued)*

MAJOR TASK	EXTENSION	REFINEMENT
	Example: (a) travel through general space using the feet. Try what you are doing going sideways, forward, or backward. Keep changing the way you are using the feet and the direction you are using. (b) As you travel, sometimes take your action up into the air or down close to the ground.	Students should make the transition from one direction to another smoothly; they should also be encouraged to try all movements in different directions.
	Adding the concept of direction to action sequences	
	Example: Rush backward, spin, and flee forward.	
	Exploring concept of direction in nonlocomotor actions Use with exploring personal space with different body parts (up, down, sideways) Rising and sinking actions, moving forward or backward Opening or closing actions, moving to the side Combining opening and closing actions with rising and sinking actions	
	Example: Using your hands, explore your personal space with movement that goes sideways/up and down/forward and back.	
Awareness of levels—high/medium/low	Taking a position or body shape at a high/medium or low level Changing base of support Wide, narrow, and round shapes Moving into levels of personal space	Each level may have to be explored separately by young students to assure full understanding of getting the body high and low in different ways and also to develop an awareness of middle levels.
	Example: Travel lightly and when you hear the drum, move into a shape that is at a high/medium/low level.	
	Contrasting the level of body shape of a partner or small group (still and moving)	Partner and group work should be reserved for students who can work with each other productively; the quality of the work will initially be lower in group work. This should be expected. However, the teacher should work for the quality.
	Example: One partner make a shape. The other partner must make a shape that is at a different level.	
	Example: (moving) Continuously move from one body shape to	

(continued)

CHART 17.3. (*Continued*)

MAJOR TASK	EXTENSION	REFINEMENT
	another with your partner, making sure that you are not at the same level as your partner.	
	Combining actions at different levels in movement sentences Example: Do something that has a beginning part, a middle part, and an ending part. It may take you to a new spot, or you may stay where you are. Have one of your actions be at a high level, one at a medium level, and one at a low level. Make your levels really clear.	Sentence can first be structured with specific actions by the teacher and then given to children to structure in a more open way. Once introduced, the idea of levels is one that can be reinforced continuously in other dance experiences.
Pathways—floor patterns and air patterns	Producing floor patterns with locomotor actions—spiraling—curvy—zig-zag—straight combinations Identifying the pattern, moving to the pattern—identifying the body sensation—repeating the action, emphasizing the body sensation Exploring different patterns in movement, identifying the pattern and sensation Starting floor patterns at different points Making the patterns bigger or smaller Changing direction with a change in type of action Combining floor patterns and action sentences Teacher-designed or student-designed Swirl—dart—pounce Run—spin—shrivel—settle	The concept of chalk or paint on the shoes that paint on the floor can be used initially to get the concept of floor pattern across to the children. Children should be encouraged to feel the difference in the body adjustment to moving through space using these patterns.
	Example: Write your floor pattern on the floor with your finger. Do it again until you know it by heart. Choose a different action for each of these parts.	You may want to limit younger children to locomotor actions for their sentences.
	Exploring air patterns with different body parts Moving the hands through personal space making zig-zag, straight, curvy, spiraling pathway. Choosing pathways that have round actions or pointy actions in space. Exploring air patterns that other parts can make	Two different sensations are evident—that of using space flexibly (curvy and zig-zag) vs. directly (straight) as well as the sharpness of the changes in the direction of the pattern.

(*continued*)

CHART 17.3. (*Continued*)

MAJOR TASK	EXTENSION	REFINEMENT
	Using body parts to lead the whole body in an air pattern	
	Example: (a) Exploding from a low position, using the hands to lead the action in a straight air pathway. (b) Wiggling your way up out of a tight hole, using your hands to help you. (c) Spinning actions, having the elbows lead in slashing pathways.	
The concept of focus	When children are able to use many of the spatial concepts, and when they begin to become involved in their movement without being self-conscious, the teacher can begin to introduce the concept of focus. Focus is directing the eyes and attention of the mover to a space, object, or person in the environment. A useful way to begin to introduce this concept is with the idea of pathways that lead someplace. Asking the students to focus on the destination in a pathway and to explore the idea of no focus in pathways can help. When focus is introduced, it can begin to be reinforced in all actions, particularly those of reaching, rising, closing, meeting, parting, fleeing, etc. Children should contrast differences in "looking far away" and "looking close." It will take on more significance to children as they begin to relate their movements to each other and other aspects of the environment. The challenge "Keep your eyes on your partner" will become significant. It is also useful, however, as it is introduced in exploring the effects of different focuses on individual body actions.	

Theme IV: The Awareness of the Flow and Space Quality of Movement

Theme IV is designed to develop an awareness of the flow of the weight of the body in space and time. The flow quality (bound and free) and space quality (direct and flexible) take their place behind Theme II in introducing the child to the effort qualities of movement. They are more difficult than time and weight for the child, since they do not play as direct a role in the child's everyday actions.

Each of the separate qualities introduced in the following pages should first be experienced and then brought together as a combined focus. Previously children have been encouraged to move spontaneously and freely and to experience the bound or tight quality of movement. These sensations will therefore not be entirely new to them. It is in this theme that children are made aware of this quality and its potential for inner expression. The spatial direct/flexible quality likewise has surfaced in earlier work as children used space in different ways. The direct quality, however, has probably characterized their movement more often than the indirect quality. Opportunities to use both extremes and to become aware of their different expressions are given priority in this theme.

Themes I, II, and III are basic themes for the primary grades and should be fully experienced before Theme IV or V are introduced. The spontaneity of the young child's movement should not be sacrificed in order to intellectualize content. If handled correctly, Theme IV can add expression to movement experienced in the earlier themes. In any case, combining two effort qualities requires an ability to maintain an awareness of two very separate experiences. This is well within the reach of intermediate-aged children and experienced late primary students.

Flow should be experienced as an inner

tension and abandonment. Images are useful here (as suggested in the next pages) to help the child experience this quality. Children whose actions tend to be overcontrolled will have a hard time with free flow. The teacher will have to totally immerse these children in the sensation of free flow in creative ways, perhaps initially combined with music to bring out the inner feeling. Tightness and inner tension can be more easily experienced at first with actions that are on-the-spot. It is easier for a child who prefers a freer quality to experience inner tension than it is for a child who prefers more controlled movements to experience free flow.

Direct and flexible contrasts should awaken in the child a willingness to play with space. An inner feeling of unhurriedness should emerge from the child's work with the flexible quality of movement.

CHART 17.4. Theme IV—The awareness of the flow and space quality of movement

MAJOR TASK	EXTENSION	REFINEMENT
Awareness of the flow quality of movement Bound/free	Exploring the free and bound quality of actions with single body parts Example: (a) Send your arm and hand into the air like it is not going to come back—other body parts. Send your other hand into the same space, but this time send it so that if I say *stop* at any point, you can stop it. What is happening that makes your arm feel different inside?	The free action you are looking for here is abandonment—a launching and letting go of the movement. The bound action is tight and careful.
	Different body parts Different weight qualities Different time qualities Different pathways Exploring bound and free actions with the total body Example: Fling yourself into the space—turn-run-jump and just let your whole body go with the movement (drum accompaniment if necessary). Now let's try moving through space more carefully, stopping so that you can stop at any point, sinking to the ground very carefully and then exploding from the floor. Contrasting the flow quality of rising and sinking actions and opening and closing action (varying the weight quality if children are ready, or the body part leading the action)	Don't push for combined emphases too soon. Use this material to bring out variety at this point. Abandonment can be associated with uncontrolled jazz. Bound stepping can be associated with the way you might walk through a mine field—unsure whether to let your weight go. Other useful images might be the weightless environment on the moon or resistance created with heavy air.
	Action sequences, teacher-designed and student-designed, that contrast bound and free flow	Free movement has an excitement about it that should be encouraged. Bound movement tends to be more serious.

(continued)

CHART 17.4. (*Continued*)

MAJOR TASK	EXTENSION	REFINEMENT
	Partners reacting to the flow quality of each others' movement Contrasting Meeting and parting sequence Reacting to each others' movement, traveling and on-the-spot; sometimes joining in on the free movement, sometimes reacting to that movement with very bound actions Example: Start away from each other. Travel to each other very freely with complete abandonment. Collapse freely, rise very tightly gradually moving away from each other—pause and freely part.	Experienced students should have little difficulty choosing the actions or order of their contrasts.
Awareness of the spatial quality of movement Direct/flexible	Exploring direct and flexible actions with different body parts Example: Look at a spot in space you would like to take your finger. Go to that space as directly as you can—get there right away. Bring your finger back to where it started. This time let your finger play around with the space along the way. Don't get there right away—move off your pathway. Different body parts Different time qualities Different weight qualities Different pathways Exploring direct and flexible actions with total body actions Locomotor actions with pathway Example: Move to a spot as directly as you can. How would we describe your pathway? Still keep your straight pathway now, but use the space to either side of your pathway as you get there—sometimes with just your traveling action and sometimes maybe exploring the space with actions that use your whole body or different parts of your body. Variety in locomotor action Different time quality Different weight quality	A blackboard might be useful to help children understand flexible actions as "off-your-pathway" kinds of movements. Draw a pathway and show children what happens when the space is used flexibly. It is important to communicate that a flexible use of space does not only involve actions of the feet or a change in pathway. The body should be more totally involved in using the space. Actions of free body parts will take the work into gesturing.

(*continued*)

CHART 17.4. (*Continued*)

MAJOR TASK	EXTENSION	REFINEMENT
	Combining direct and flexible with directional words (up/down, forward, back, sideways)	Up/down movement becomes a rising and sinking action. Encourage variety in these actions, particularly with flexible actions. Use of body parts leading can be reintroduced.
	Example: Move up in a flexible way and forward in a direct way. Can you do it the other way around, going up in a direct way and traveling forward in a flexible way?	
	Contrasting the use of space with a partner/small group	
	Example: (a) Your partner stands in one spot very still. You don't know whether she is friendly or not, so you don't want to go right to her. You just move around the space around her trying to decide how close to go. Finally you stop still right in front, and then your partner has to decide what to do with you. When both of you have made up your mind that you are "okay" people, move directly toward each other and stop. (b) All of us are shopping. We're moving around the store, having lots of time to look at everything, try things on, stop and get a coke, and do lots of things that show we don't really have to go to any place directly. What do you think could happen to make us move someplace very directly? What kind of action should the first part be? The second part? Let's try it.	
Combining flow and space qualities with the weight and time qualities: Flow/space Flow/time Flow/weight Space/weight Space/time	These combinations can be experienced using the previous material in this section or in Theme II, where the emphasis was on contrasting time/weight qualities. Experiences in the following areas should be included: Total body actions—locomotor and nonlocomotor Actions of different body parts Partner work and small-group work Flow/space qualities: Flexible and free (unrestricted twisting, turning, winding)	Stimuli and images can help these combinations by suggesting situations that would elicit the com-

(*continued*)

CHART 17.4. (*Continued*)

MAJOR TASK	EXTENSION	REFINEMENT
	Flexible and bound (restricted wringing, twisting, turning, screwing)	bination, like being let loose and not knowing where to go for flexible and free movement, or trying to wring the water out of a wet towel.
	Direct and free (unrestricted ongoing, linear, aimed movements)	
	Direct-bound (overcontrolled, restricted, tight movements that are linear)	
	Flow/time qualities:	Children can be helped to understand these actions by selecting feelings and actions that help them to move in that way. The actions should not be pantomimed and should be fully explored as very separate qualities.
	Sudden and bound (quick, tight movements—jerky)	
	Sudden and free (bouncy, rebounding movements)	
	Sustained—bound (stalking, slow-motion movements)	
	Sustained—free (lazy, ongoing, endless, slow actions)	
	Flow/weight qualities:	
	Firm and bound (tight, strong, restricted movements)	
	Fine touch and bound (delicate but tight movement)	
	Firm and free (strong swinging movement)	
	Fine touch and free (flying, buoyant movement)	
	Weight and space qualities	
	Firm and flexible (strong twisting actions)	
	Firm and direct (strong actions)	
	Fine touch and flexible (gently spiraling, roundabout actions)	
	Fine touch and direct (gently aimed actions)	
	Space/time qualities:	
	Direct and sudden (sharp, pouncing, tapping actions)	
	Direct or sustained (smooth, long-aimed actions)	
	Flexible and sudden (twisting, fluttering, whipping actions of short duration.	
	Flexible and sustained (yawning actions, twists of long duration)	

Theme V: Relating Movement to Another

Although we have been using simple relationships in our work with the first three themes, it is Theme V which directly focuses on the idea of relationships and helps students begin to establish a cognitive awareness of how to relate to others.

Simple relationships with a partner and with encounters have already been experienced. The teacher has probably already observed how partner and group work initially tend to reduce the creativity and spontaneity of the children's movement—this is natural. Teachers will recognize success in this theme as they take children through that initial stage and bring them to spontaneous and expressive movement once more. This time, however, it will be with an ability to relate their movement to others. If relating isn't imposed on children too early, Theme V will be a natural extension of the child's dancing.

Theme V develops gradually, even as children begin Theme I. It can be incorporated into work on other themes or it can be taught as a very separate theme. The needs of the students and preferences of the teacher will determine how it is presented.

Theme VI: The Use of the Body

Theme VI is the second theme to deal with the use of the body. It can, in fact, be incorporated as extended work with Theme I.

CHART 17.5. Theme V—Relating movement to another

MAJOR TASK	EXTENSION	REFINEMENT
Relating to another person	Encounters with others Traveling through space—establishing eye contact with another and responding Example: Wander through the space. When your eyes establish contact with another, move quickly to that person—freeze—and turn slowly away to find another. Finding an action another is doing that you would like to do too Example: Use your feet in different ways. As you are moving around the space, if you find someone doing an action you would like to try, move behind, alongside of, or in front of that person and move in the same way until you find something else you would like to try. Relating your ending shape to another Example: (a) When you hear the drum to end your action, slowly reach toward another in the room, keeping your attention on that person. (b) Extend a body part to someone who is close to you. (c) End your action at a level that is different from those around you.	Encounters are brief moments of relationship. They have the advantage of not needing a long-term cooperative relationship with others and can be highly teacher-directed for students who need more initial structure in their work with others. Movement may deteriorate initially as children work with each other. The important part of the lesson is the adjustments children are making to each other; this should receive the teacher's attention.
	Meeting and parting relationships Contrasting movement characteristics Pathways Traveling actions	Sequences should be short and preceded and followed by stillness. Contrasting actions should be very clear contrasts

(continued)

CHART 17.5. (*Continued*)

MAJOR TASK	EXTENSION	REFINEMENT
	Time quality Weight quality Spatial relationships Levels The body part emphasized	Sequences may be teacher-directed at first with the teacher cueing students when to start and when to part.
	Example: Start in a position away from your partner. Travel toward your partner with lively, quick actions. Meet and move away with actions that are careful, slower actions.	

	Adding meaning to the meeting
	  Mingling
	  Passing by
	  Meeting and leaving together
	  Clashing
	  Dancing together before
	    parting
	  Chatting before leaving
	  Combination of above
	With attention to:
	  Body shape
	  Level
	  Time quality
	  Weight quality
	  Flow quality
	  Rhythms
		When mingling or other actions of meeting are introduced, the characteristics of these actions should first be explored before sequencing.

	Example: (a) Start away from your partner (or group). Travel toward your partner. When you get there, one person holds stillness while the other talks in movement—maybe a short question, such as "Would you like to go?" (Bum ba bum ba bum) The other person answers in movement and then you travel off together to finish your sequences with stillness. (b) Start away from each other (group) and come together with very sustained movements that use a lot of space. When you come together, make your actions very quick and very strong. Leave each other with fleeing movements or retreating movements, whichever you like.	

	Copying and contrasting
	  relationships
	  Shape
	  Level
	  Time quality Successive or
	             Simultaneous
	  Weight quality
		Students should be helped to vary the quality being contrasted and be helped to challenge the partner with difficult actions.

(*continued*)

CHART 17.5. (*Continued*)

MAJOR TASK	EXTENSION	REFINEMENT
	Flow quality Rhythm	
	Example: (a) One partner take any shape you want and hold it very still. The other partner try to make the exact same shape. The fingers should be the same; the head and every part should be the same. (b) Start to move around the space that is yours and your partner's. If your partner is moving with actions at a high level, you move with actions that are at a medium or low level. Your actions can keep changing—sometimes on-the-spot, sometimes traveling, sometimes maybe just pausing, but always at a different level from each other. I'm going to give a signal for both of you to pause so that I can see everybody at different levels. (c) One partner do something very quick. The other partner try to do the same action in a more sustained, slow way.	Simultaneous relationships require much more concentration and skill in continuous movement and should be reserved for the more experienced groups.

	Interacting conversational relationships (the choice of the reaction to another[s] is the child's in these relationships, without an attempt to define the reaction in terms of copying or contrasting)
	    Rhythmic conversations; With or without specific attention to body shape, level, time quality, weight quality, or flow quality
	    On-the-spot conversations
	    Traveling conversations
	    Combinations
		Conversational relationships are real *relating* relationships. The expressive communication created by one student should elicit a response from the other. The teacher can take part in a demonstration with other students to help children feel secure in the experience.

	Example: Each child has a rhythmic instrument (which could be just two lumme sticks) to accompany their movement. One student says something to another (maybe several quick hard beats with a traveling action that encircles the other). The other partner reacts to this sequence, either choosing to answer, or maybe choosing to turn slowly and ignore the other person, or maybe moving in front of, behind, or in back of the other.	

(*continued*)

CHART 17.5. (*Continued*)

MAJOR TASK	EXTENSION	REFINEMENT
	Relating group movement to music, poetry, or another source Using movement that has simultaneous strong and light sounds—or different instruments with very clear parts; each member of the group would choose one part of instrument Using poetry that suggests different movement characteristics; different groups can assume different parts or members of the same group can assume different parts	The clarity of the music determines the degree of difficulty in this experience.
	Example: *THE CATERPILLAR* Brown and furry Caterpillars in a hurry, Take your walk To the shady leaf, or stalk, Or what not, Which may be the chosen spot. No toad spys you, Hovering bird of prey pass by you, Spin and die, To live again a butterfly. (Christina Rossetti)	Again, the teacher must be careful that students do not mimic the character but instead copy the movement quality of that character. When poetry is used, it will take time to develop and should not be hurried. The action and possibilities should be fully explored.
	The key parts in this are (a) the hurried, spinning, and then still action of the caterpillar; (b) the searching, jumping toad who never makes eye contact with the caterpillar; (c) the hovering, swooping bird of prey who never makes contact with the toad; and (d) the final butterfly action with the quck, light, and indirect pathways. Each part needs to be discussed in terms of the quality of movement that is appropriate. All children can try all parts at first before breaking into groups. Groups of at least three are necessary. When the poem is read, all are still until their part comes in. They may continue to move after they are introduced or may hold stillness when the reading passes their part.	

The emphasis in Theme I is on experiencing the total stir of the body with little attention to the specifics of the action. Theme VI is designed to help the student use the body and its parts with more intent and with more attention to differences in actions and how the action is being produced. It culminates with experiences combining different body activities.

Theme VI is to be used in intermediate classes where a good background has been established with earlier themes. In the first major task, actions of everyday living are transferred from mime to the more abstract communication, which is dance. If children do not have sufficient experiences in using their total body and its parts, they will not easily grasp this idea. This is equally true of the second major task, designed to focus the student's work on gesture, which is the movement of free parts of the body in an action. Gesture was introduced to some extent in experiences emphasizing different parts of the body while moving and in experiences such as meeting and parting of body parts. Theme VI extends the idea of parts, using space freely with a meaning that may not be an essential part of the action but which adds meaning to the action.

Jumping activities are more familiar to the students. These actions can be approached from an almost athletic orientation or as effort orientation. Both orientations are presented with the idea that practice, with both focuses, is essential. To some extent the body activities defined in this theme have been experienced to some degree during other themes. In Theme VI they are fully explored, developed, and then combined into sequences.

CHART 17.6. Theme VI—The use of the body

MAJOR TASK	EXTENSION	REFINEMENT
Actions of everyday living transferred to the whole body	Selecting an action from everyday living—miming this action and enlarging the action to include total body involvement Activities involving tools (hammers, forks, spoons) Personal care activities (dressing, combing hair, washing, etc.) Nonverbal communications to others (stop, go, no, yes, come here) Job-related activities (factory workers, waitresses, dishwashers, typists, doctors, dentists, construction workers, etc.) Example: Show me how you brush or comb your hair in the morning. Take that action and make it bigger. Make it so big that it uses your whole body. Make it so big that it takes you into general space.	These activities may resemble mime in the beginning stages and should be expected to. Gradually the movement should express the meaning the action has for the performer and not just the action itself.
Focus on gesture	Returning to total body actions of Theme I with attention to how individual body parts can freely use the space in the action (locomotor, vibratory, turning, stop-	

(continued)

CHART 17.6. (Continued)

MAJOR TASK	EXTENSION	REFINEMENT
	ping, percussive, closing, opening, sinking, rising, advancing, retreating, jumping)	
	Example: Show me a way to turn. Now show me a way to turn that is made more interesting because your hands, elbows, head, or leg uses the space around you in a little more interesting way as you turn.	This is the first time students have been encouraged to use the free parts of the body without a highly structured intent. The teacher should be patient with their early attempts.
	Defining the gesturing actions of gathering, scattering, and penetrating (gathering—parts coming together at a point in space; scattering—parts moving away from each other that begin with a spatial focal point; penetrating—piercing, stabbing, cutting into space)	
	Work with individual body parts (hands in particular) in self-space	The idea is to focus on an object rather than on a point in space. It may be useful to first communicate gathering or scattering gestures.
	In conjunction with work on actions from everyday living	
	In conjunction with stepping actions	
	Example: As you step back from your space, scatter the space; using your hands, make your whole body participate.	
Expanding the concept of the jumping actions	Exploring ways in which jumping can be done	Students can explore the possible jumping actions, seek to get
From one foot to the same foot	Number of feet for take-off and landing	more control over them, and then experiment with effort
From one foot to the other foot	Distance (linear)	qualities and combinations with
From one foot to both feet	Height	other body activities.
From both feet to both feet	Weight quality (forceful, hard, light, bouncy)	
From both feet to one foot	Time quality	
	In combination with locomotion and on-the-spot actions, particularly those of turning and stepping	
	To even and uneven rhythmical beats (self-designed and teacher-designed)	
	Combining different patterns of jumping	
	Example: Most of us think of jumping as this (demonstrate two feet to two feet jump). There are lots of ways of getting into the air.	

(continued)

CHART 17.6. (Continued)

MAJOR TASK	EXTENSION	REFINEMENT
	See how many different ways you can find to get your body into the air—a little or a lot.	

Sequence of body activities of
  Gesturing while stepping
  Stepping or weight transference
    during locomotion
  Traveling while turning
  Turning jumps
  Gestures during jumps
  Gestures and locomotion
  Traveling jumps
  Step-jump rhythms
  Stepping during turns
  Turns with gestures
	Exploring each body action with
	  appropriate material from Themes
	  I, II, III, and IV
	  Time quality
	  Weight quality
	  Direction, level, pathway
	  Body shape
	  Flow quality
	  Direct/indirect actions
	
	Example: As you travel and turn, be
	  concerned about what shape
	  you are making in your turn and
	  vary it.
	
	Developing rhythmical sequences
	  for the individual action
	
	Example: Think of a rhythmical pat-
	  tern you would like to try and
	  clap it with your hand—for exam-
	  ple, short, short, long. Add that
	  pattern to your gestures and
	  jumping actions.
	
	Combining body activities into
	  sequences
	
	Example: Gathering gestures with
	  stepping actions combined with
	  jumping and turning. (The young-
	  er the student, the more help the
	  student will need with rhythmical
	  or voice accompaniment, or
	  more guidance will be needed in
	  the use of space or effort.)
		If students still need help with ges-
		  turing actions, provide structure
		  with ideas related to
		  Emphasizing different parts
		  Relating parts to each other
		  Defining the specific gesturing ac-
		    tion to be used.

Theme VII: The Awareness of Basic Effort Actions

Theme VII is the last of Laban's themes considered appropriate for the elementary-school physical education dance program. Theme VII is actually the combination of Theme II (weight and time) and Theme IV (space and flow). These are the themes that focus on the four components of the effort quality of movement (time, weight, space, and flow). When combined, very specific actions are expressed. For the elementary-school student, these actions are best studied as contrasts.

Each of the effort actions has certain activities associated with it. This means that although technically any action can be performed in a thrusting way, for example, stamping and jumping activities are more common and the effort quality is more easily experienced in these actions. The associated activities are listed under each major task to help guide the teacher. The words that will help elicit the effort quality desired are listed in the teaching hints column along with the percussion instruments that will help with that quality.

The contrasting effort actions are developed in a consistent way throughout the development section of the theme. Ideas for helping the students get the feel of the effort quality are listed first. These experiences should be short, as it is not possible to stay with one effort without giving the body a rest from that quality (which is why the effort actions are presented as contrasts). The teacher should use any support necessary to help the student experience the effort quality (percussion, imagery, descriptive words, music, poetry) and then help the student make the transition from these supports to being able to produce the effort quality without the support. Whether the teacher develops the vocabulary of the effort actions (thrusting, slashing, floating, and so on) depends on the group and the teacher. The important consideration is that the student understand and be able to produce the actions.

This is an advanced theme in terms of the students' ability to be cognitively aware of the time, weight, and space quality of their movement simultaneously. Younger children can become involved with these effort actions without this cognitive awareness. The intermediate-aged child should be able to maintain this awareness. Experiences can be less teacher-structured in terms of the amount of guidance the student receives describing the body activity used.

Example: Do something with a pressing action on the spot and travel with a flicking action.

Rhythm should play a major role in contrasting these qualities. Short sequences should be repeated several times until the rhythmic pattern is clear.

Example: quick, quick-slow; quick, quick-slow; quick, quick-slow.

Group and partner work can be exciting and should be used frequently with these major tasks in simple ways (contrasting and matching) and in more complex ways where students actually formulate dances with others.

CHART 17.7. Theme VII—The awareness of basic effort actions

MAJOR TASK	EXTENSION	REFINEMENT

Thrusting and floating
Properties of the action
  Thrust = firm, direct, sudden
  Float = fine touch, flexible, sustained
Activities associated with action
  Thrust = stamping, jumping, chopping, heartbeat
  Float = gesturing, gathering, on the toes
	Defining the thrusting action—firmness, suddenness, directness
	  Hard pushing off the floor with step actions leading to elevation; exploding actions that are direct and lift the body into the air
	  Punching actions of the hands into different parts of personal space
	  Rhythmical patterns of thrusting actions with a pause or rest
	
	Example: Push off the floor hard as you step. Put a few hard steps together and then rest. What does your pattern sound like? Clap it (push-push rest, or whatever). Repeat your pattern several times until it sounds the same each time.
		Useful words to elicit the quality:
		  Thrust (vigorous, pierce, pound, lunge, jolt, hammer hit, powerful)
		  Float (gentle, buoyant, soft, stir, dreamy, drifting)
		Useful percussion to elicit the quality:
		  Thrust—drum or tambourine
		  Float—cymbal, singing

(continued)

CHART 17.7. (*Continued*)

MAJOR TASK	EXTENSION	REFINEMENT
	Defining the floating action—fine touch, flexible, sustained	The actions are defined using the body parts most closely attached
	On-the-spot movement of the hands, wrists, and elbows floating on the air supporting them	to that action. Others can be explored, but in some cases it is difficult to "feel" the quality.
	Stepping buoyantly with an emphasis on the rising, floating sensation in the upper part of body (filling the lungs to rise buoyantly)	
	"Dreamy" turns and stepping through space contrasted with pauses in rhythmical patterns (assisted with a light tap on a cymbal or other "spacy" music)	
	Contrasting thrusting and floating actions	Floating can be assisted with the idea of a scarf as it moves down
	Combining hard, straight thrusting actions with a soft action on-the-spot (body part gesturing and total body actions)	supported by air. The scarf is also useful for younger students to move with, with music.
	Example: In your own space put together a sequence of actions that are hard, soft, hard.	Thrusting actions are easy for children to associate with (for instance, the punch), and rocket explosions are most familiar to them.
	Contrasting thrusting and floating actions, traveling and on-the-spot.	
	Example: Let's try putting dreamy traveling and turning actions with sudden, hard turning actions. I'll help you first using the cymbal and drum. Then see if you can find another way to put this all together.	
	Contrasting floating and thrusting actions with a partner or small group	
	Matching Meeting and parting Contrasting Mingling Following	
	Example: Meet with hard thrusting actions. Mingle with dreamy floating actions that change levels, and part with hard thrusting actions.	
Slashing and gliding *Properties of the action:* Slashing = firm, flexible, sudden Gliding = fine touch, direct, sustained *Activities associated with the action:*	Defining the slashing action—sudden, flexible, firm Splashing the space with quick turning actions Flinging things madly into the air—making the action bigger to include the whole body	*Useful words to elicit the quality* Slash = hitting, whipping, beating, swiping, flinging, splashing, ripping Glide = smooth, calm, stroking, gentle, straight Slashing actions should be easy. It is more difficult for children to get

(continued)

CHART 17.7. (*Continued*)

MAJOR TASK	EXTENSION	REFINEMENT
Slash Jumping turns, scattering gestures, twisting shoulders *Glide* Pathways, sole of the foot, palms	Combining hard "flings" into space with a hard twist to the floor Defining the gliding action—sustained, direct, fine touch Stepping actions which allow the step to go on forever as almost a gesturing action of the feet and legs Gliding gestures in different directions with the arms and legs Combining actions on the spot and with limited traveling Example: Show me you know what gliding looks like with your hands and arms. Make it look like it could go on forever—very gentle, very straight. Put a few of these together with one or two gliding steps and come to a gentle stop. Contrasting gliding and slashing actions Hard slashing actions of the total body contrasted with gentle gliding gestures of the arms in on-the-spot or traveling actions. Example: Jump and turn, jump and turn—land low on your second jump. Glide up using your hands and arms (with and without percussive assistance).	a feel for the ongoingness of the straight gliding action. The idea of gliding on ice and a sliding action will help children relate to this action.
Wringing and dabbing *Properties of the action:* Wringing = firm, flexible, sustained Dabbing = fine touch, direct, sudden *Activities associated with action:* Wringing = on-the-spot, twisting, wrestling action of the total body Dabbing = hopping, patting, skipping, toes, fingertips	Defining the wringing action—hard, twisting, slow Wringing actions of the arms, singly and in combination Total body hard, twisting, sinking to the floor Example: Twist your body hard and slowly into the floor. Rest, rise gently, and do it again. Defining the dabbing action—sudden, fine touch, direct Light dabbing of the space—as an artist would dab paint on a canvas Light—toe dominated skipping and hopping Example: I'm going to use the triangle to help you be really light	*Useful words to elicit the action:* Wringing, twisted, knotted, screwing Dabbing, darting, shooting, pointed, tap *Useful percussion to elicit the quality:* Wring: sustained hard drum Dab: wood blocks, lumme sticks

(*continued*)

CHART 17.7. (*Continued*)

MAJOR TASK	EXTENSION	REFINEMENT
	with your hopping and skipping. Let's try a pattern like this ♩♫ ♩♫♩♫♩ and rest.	
	Contrasting wringing and dabbing. Light, quick dabbing steps with jumps or hops contrasted with sustained hard wringing actions to the floor *or* Hard, wringing sustained actions from the floor contrasted with light, quick dabbing steps into general space Rhythmic patterns on-the-spot contrasting dabbing and wringing gestures of the arms and hands Partner or group work—matching, contrasting, meeting and parting, mingling	
Pressing and flicking *Properties of the action:* Pressing = firm, direct, sustained Flicking = fine touch, flexible, sudden	Defining the pressing action Stepping actions which press into the floor (limited traveling) with the flat part of the foot leading Actions of the hands (palms in particular) pressing space up, down, and away from the center of the body Advancing and retreating actions—pulling and pushing Example: Let's pretend the air is very heavy and hard to move around us. We just can't send our parts out into the air to move us. We must push the heavy air out of our way. Let's start small and see if we can press up on the air so that we can at least get off the floor. Press out to give us some room. Step out into the air, pressing the air away so that our foot can find a place on the floor.	*Useful words to elicit the quality:* Pressing, pulling, squeezing Flecking, flickering, fluttering, twitching, rippling *Useful percussion to elicit the quality:* Press: hard, sustained drum Flick: triangle, bells, tambourine
Activities associated with the action: Pressing = palms into floor or space Flicking = jumping, turning, leaps, little fingers, leg gestures	Defining the flicking action Quick turns, jumps, and leaps which use the space flexibly with particular emphasis on the flinging actions of arms and legs in the action Quick gestures of fingers and wrists in particular	The idea of a nervous action is useful in communicating the flick. The flick is a quick abandonment and flexible use of space. The fluttering of a butterfly is another useful idea to help communicate this action.

(*continued*)

CHART 17.7. (*Continued*)

MAJOR TASK	EXTENSION	REFINEMENT
	Twitching of total body	
	Example: Send the body into the air with a very quick and light turn, flinging the body around so that you maintain the looseness of the action.	

	Contrasting pressing and flicking
	  Light, quick dabbing jumps, turns, and leaps contrasted with pressing actions to the floor—quick, quick-slow rhythm pattern
	  Pressing stepping actions forward or backward contrasted with quick turns and changes of direction
	  Contrasting gestures of the fingers, hands, and arms, creating rhythm patterns of variations of slow and quick and changes in part of body or surface receiving the emphasis
		Pressing is easier to communicate. Surfaces of the body are more dominant in this action.

	Example: I'm going to give you a pattern to do with your palms pressing into space and your fingers flicking. My pattern is slow-quick-quick. Let's do it several times to get a feel for it. Now you think of a combination of 3 or 4 different actions that can contrast these actions with a different rhythm.	

	Partner and group work
	  Meeting and parting
	  Matching
	  Contrasting
	  Answering
	  Creating rhythms together
		The teacher should not be reluctant to demonstrate or participate in learning experiences to help children clarify the intent of the experience.

	Example: I'm going to be Bob's partner. Bob is going to put together a short sequence that tells me something—like pressing toward me and then quickly turning away (demonstration). I'm still while Bob is talking. When he is still, I get to answer him. I might circle about him with quick leaps and turns and again press toward him to get his attention. Bob must then decide how he's going to answer me. Make your actions really pressing and really quick flicking actions. Don't make your sentences too long.	

18

games

Games have been an important part of the physical education program for many years. Physical educators use games to teach important skills and to increase motivation. Physical educators also teach games that are important culturally. Typically, texts on physical education methods have included sections on such games and the activities that best "lead up" to them. More recently our concepts about the role of games has expanded in some very exciting ways. Many physical educators now help children develop their own games. Other physical educators focus on games that require cooperation among players rather than competition. Still others are growing more sensitive to how "traditional" games can be changed so as to be more developmentally appropriate. All in all, the "games" movement in physical education is one of the healthiest directions that the profession has recently taken.

GAMES AND HOW TO PLAY THEM

What Constitutes a Game?

Each of us grew up learning games. Each of us now takes part in a number of games during our leisure hours. Tennis, volleyball,

golf, and softball differ greatly, yet each is a game. A game is a form of playful competition in which outcomes are determined by physical skill, strategy, or chance. In physical education we are concerned mostly with games that combine physical skill and strategy. Brian Sutton-Smith (1968) suggests that games are recreative and have rules, sides, winners, and competition.

Games are competitive. Recently it has been suggested that there should be non-competitive games, but that is a contradiction in terms. It would be more precise to suggest that one kind of competition should be replaced by another. In that sense games can include competition of:

One individual against another
One team against another
One individual or team against an object
One individual or team against a standard

It is also possible to propose certain additional rules in competitive games so as to discourage or diffuse the identification of one player with one team. For example, not only can volleyball players rotate on one side of the net, but at a certain point (after they serve perhaps) they can rotate to the other side. Thus, when the game ends (fifteen points are scored by a team), any individual player is likely to have been on both teams for part of the game.

What Characteristics of Play Manifest Themselves in Games?

It is obvious from our own experiences that games can be less than playful and may not be recreative at all. Yet each of us also has experienced game situations that are very playful and recreative. It is extremely important that we keep in mind which characteristics of play are present in games and how those characteristics can be compromised so that the game loses its playful quality.

Games are more playful if they are freely entered into. When one "has to play," the playfulness is diminished. Games typically have boundaries, and this adds to their playfulness. Play is said to be "separate" in the sense that it is set apart from real life either in a purely physical sense—as with a golf course, tennis court, Jungle Gym—or in a mental sense—as with fantasy and make-believe. Play is uncertain, meaning that its outcome is not known in advance. Games are more playful when the outcome is constantly in doubt, even up to the last moment of the game. This has implications for choosing sides and creating rules which allow for as much evenness between the competitors as possible. The same is true when the competition is against a standard. If the standard is too difficult, the challenge too great, children lose interest. Likewise, if it is too easy, they quickly give it up. When left to themselves, children tend to make their own games consistently more difficult so as to maintain a sense of challenge and uncertainty. Play most often has rules and so too do games. As children grow and develop, these rules become more fixed and more complex.

Play also produces no serious consequences. It is here that we have failed most often in protecting the playful nature of games for children. Winning and losing matter a great deal during the game, for that is in the nature of play: For it to be otherwise reduces the playfulness of the experience. Yet when the game is over, winning and losing should not matter at all. It is when winning and losing matter outside of the game and away from the playspace that the playfulness of the experience is jeopardized.

Developing Game Skills

One might be inclined to say that game skills are developed by playing games. However, while this is true as a general proposition, definite suggestions can be made about how children might learn more game skills in a happier, more efficient manner. Being sensitive to the development of games skills requires attention to their learning characteristics, the developmental stages of children, and the demands of specific games. The following suggestions should be noted.

1. Participating in a game requires a large number of response patterns, which are cued by a constantly changing game situation. Learning how to perform one skill in one way in one situation is counterproductive to games playing. Barrett (1977) has argued convincingly for a skills learning approach which emphasizes variation in terms of the setting and the response of the child to the setting.

2. Young children may be hesitant to participate in games. Typically, the child moves from being an onlooker to being an associate and finally to being a cooperative player. A very gradual process may be necessary in order to slowly bring certain children along toward the status of player. As in teaching a child to be in water without fear, the process requires careful steps in which a supportive setting reduces anxieties.

3. Children enjoy playing when they have the necessary skills to be successful. Play occurs when children are sufficiently skilled so that they are in control, and the game does not exert control over them. This is what Sutton-Smith (1968) had described as the "transformation of power" concept. This has several implications. First, one must sort out the many skills required for successful participation in any game. If they are too difficult for the current skill level of the children, the game must be altered, or the prerequisite

skills must first be learned. Robertson (1977) has made this point quite convincingly.

> In short, the teacher must analyze the game into its separate motor, perceptual, cognitive, and affective demands. If the children will not be successful at each of these tasks, then the game should not be played or it should be *changed*. The key is to simplify the tasks and, then, gradually rebuild the complexity until it approximates the original game situation. This procedure is called "teaching for game readiness." (p. 25)

You should understand that if children want to participate in a game and can't control their participation through skill, they may resort to cheating. In this sense cheating can be understood as a stage in games playing development. Denzin (1976) has presented evidence for this hypothesis, and it should be noted that cheating gradually diminishes as skills increase, until children simply don't cheat any longer.

4. Games can increase in complexity and become more fixed as children move up the developmental ladder. Typically, games during early childhood are considerably different than those played during the later stages of childhood. Entry to and exit from the game are much looser among younger children. Rules tend to change constantly because the game changes in complexity in order to stay interesting. Physical and spatial arrangements are more flexible. Membership is less important. Teachers need to be sensitive to the simplicity and flexibility of children's games and also to the constant feedback they will receive from children when the games need to be altered. Forcing children into adult patterns of play in terms of fixed rules, permanent boundaries, and fixed role behaviors is inappropriate and counterproductive to children's development as players.

5. Games are fun for children. A teacher may have some keen sense that a simplified game involving a ball, a net, throwing, and catching might help develop physical and strategy skills that will someday "lead up" to volleyball skills, but one should never make the mistake of assuming that it is a lead-up game for the children playing. For them it is important now, for its own sake, and is enjoyed for that reason. Sometimes lead-up games, or games of "low organization"—as they are sometimes called in our field—are not given as serious consideration as the games we call volleyball, floor hockey, and soccer. That is unfortunate. It is the result of seeing the world of games through the eyes of an adult rather than being sensitive to how children see the games.

6. Skill training is a capability that is very gradually acquired. An adult will take an hour on a weekend and hit a tennis ball against a board in order to improve his or her backhand. Another adult will spend an hour on a putting green. Competitive athletes spend many hours each week in routine skill practice. They constantly take part in drills that are designed to help develop specific skills through many repetitions. In order to take part in drills and skill practice of this type, one must have some idea of goals for a game, possess the ability to delay gratification derived from game participation, and demonstrate numerous other behaviors. Young children have none of these attributes. They will learn them gradually to be sure, but it is thoroughly inappropriate to treat a group of young children as if they were an athletic team, running them through a series of drills and skill practice situations. If children's skills need to be practiced, one should create a game in which appropriate participation will contribute to the necessary skill development.

Games Can be Changed

A number of professionals have recently turned their attention to the question of how games can be analyzed and modified to meet specific developmental and educational goals (Morris, 1976; Mauldon and Redfern, 1969). Games *can* be changed in a number of ways to facilitate the goals of the teacher and the needs of the children:

1. Change the number and/or organization of players.
2. Change the equipment used.
3. Change the rules.
4. Change the scoring contingencies.

Naturally, the number of players in a game influences the degree of participation of the individual players and the relative roles they assume. Fixing players in assigned spaces produces a different set of roles for individual players than letting them move about at will.

Changing equipment will also change the nature of the game, especially as it affects the level of skill needed for successful participation. The size ball used, the size of a target, the length of an implement used to strike a ball, the height of a net, or the amount of air in a ball—affecting the degree to which it bounces—can each change the nature of a game substantially.

Perhaps the simplest and most direct way to change games is to change the rules which govern play within the game. Rules can be introduced to increase participation, to emphasize certain skills, to decrease individual identity with a particular team, or to prevent a team game from being dominated by more highly skilled players. In basketball-type games, for example, adding a rule that all players have to be over the half-court line before the ball is moved over the half-court line eliminates the "fast-break" type of helter-skelter play that so characterizes early attempts to learn that game. Likewise, stationing yourself as teacher at the center court area and insisting that the ball be thrown to you each time it comes across the half-court line allows you to make sure that many players get a chance to handle the ball rather than just the few who are more highly skilled.

Games have outcomes. "Keeping score" is a means not only of determining the winner but also of knowing as the game progresses who is further along toward the final goal; that is, who is "ahead." Since our society tends to emphasize winning and competition, most children get socialized very early to a competitive attitude and become very interested in "who is ahead" in any game they play. One of the quickest ways to change games is to modify the scoring contingencies; that is, to change the manner in which points are scored. Using basketball again for our example, in the typical basketball game points are scored for shooting the ball through the hoop. If done from the floor during regular play, two points are awarded for each such act. If done from the free-throw line as the result of a foul, one point is scored: But why not award points for other parts of the game?

We have experimented with changing game contingencies and have found it a very successful strategy to influence the kinds of skills used in the game (Jones, 1978). If we want more passing, we award points for good passes as well as for shots made. If we want good rebounding, we add some points for that. Since players try to accumulate points in order to win the game, it follows that they will try to do whatever it is that earns them points. Thus, a teacher can greatly influence the kinds of skills used in a game by adjusting the scoring contingencies.

Stressing Cooperation in Games

Many physical educators believe that competition has been emphasized too much in our culture in general and in motor play activities specifically. It is clear that we live in an achievement-oriented, competitive culture and we *know* that the games children grow up with in a culture tend to prepare them for adult roles in that culture. Thus, it is not surprising that most of the games children play in childhood are highly competitive. It should also be noted that many adults think that this kind of highly competitive childhood play is appropriate. Nevertheless, many physical educators believe that we have emphasized competition too much, especially at the expense of cooperation.

Recently cooperative games have started to become more popular among physical educators. These games not only emphasize cooperation but require it for successful play. Orlick (1977; 1977a), a leader in this movement, has suggested that successful cooperative games have four components: cooperation, involvement, acceptance, and fun. Players have to work together to "win" the game. All players are involved at all times, players feel that they have a contribution to make, and everybody has fun.

Cooperative games are created by changing the rules and scoring contingencies of more traditionally competitive games (see page 296 for ways of changing games). Orlick cites three categories of cooperative games: games with no losers, collective score games, and reversal games.

In cooperative games with "no losers" the goal is always to compete against a standard. The standard is achieved through cooperation among players. For example, musical chairs—in which the goal is to have all children sitting in whatever chairs remain—requires children to cooperate to achieve the standard of having all children still in the game work together to sit on the one remaining chair that marks the end of the game (Orlick, 1977).

Collective score games involve scoring contingencies where points are awarded when two teams cooperate to achieve a common goal. Typically, for example, volleyball lead-up games are played with points awarded for balls that are thrown or hit over a net without being caught or hit back by the other team. A cooperative approach would be to score one collective point each time a ball is thrown over the net and caught successfully by the other team.

Reversal games tend to deemphasize team membership and consequently reduce the degree to which children associate with the score outcome of the game. If children are rotated from one team to the other *during* a game, they will be less concerned with the score outcome because they will have contributed to each team.

Orlick (1977) suggests that semicooperative rule changes be introduced as lead-ups to cooperative games. In a volleyball-type game, for example, all children on one side of the net might have to handle the ball before it goes over to the other side. Or, all members of a team in a soccer or basketball-type game might have to touch the ball before a shot can be taken.

Help Students Create Their Own Games

Most games taught in the physical education curriculum are predesigned. They may be culturally institutionalized games, such as soccer or volleyball, for which there are rules, strategies, and histories. They may be games designed to prepare young children to eventually participate in those "adult" games. However, there are also "made-up" games. Increasingly, these "creative games" are being viewed as opportunities for students to employ their imagination and creative abilities in ways that lead not only to skill outcomes but also to enjoyment.

Creative games are usually thought to emphasize process goals such as creativity, decision making, and problem solving. Reilly (1977), however, has pointed out that skill outcomes need not be neglected either. Indeed, there is no reason why the process goals of creativity and problem solving cannot exist along with some more specific skill outcomes.

The physical educator can help to direct the nature of the games created and the skills required by manipulating the kinds of spaces and equipment and movement responses that serve as the essentials from which a game might develop. For example, if five children are given a hoop and two balls and asked to create a game that emphasizes throwing and catching, the stage has been set for producing certain kinds of skill outcomes.

Graham (1977) has suggested six guidelines for teachers who help students design their own games:

1. Begin gradually. Students will need more structure at the outset as they learn gradually to handle the decision-making skills. Students will produce quite simple games to begin with.
2. Don't interfere too much. Students will learn the consequences of their decisions as they play their newly created games.
3. Safety remains your responsibility. If an unsafe situation has been created, notify the students and require them to develop an alternative.
4. Students must enforce their own rules. Teachers as referees and umpires imply too much adult control. Students must be responsible for monitoring their own game participation.
5. Be flexible. Creative games will change. Children will want to make them more complex as they master the skills involved.

6. Be patient. Sometimes young children don't make decisions very quickly. Children must be given the opportunity to *learn* the skills of decision making and problem solving.

The creative games movement is another sign of the healthy state of the elementary-school physical education scene. An imaginative teacher can use creative games not only for specific skill development but also to achieve important process learning in the areas of decision making and problem solving. Too many educators have been mistaken in the notion that skill outcome goals and creative process goals cannot be achieved together. The creative games movement proves them to be wrong.

GUIDELINES FOR TEACHING GAMES

Whether a teacher decides to use a creative game, a cooperative game, a regulation game, or a modified game, there is still a need to select and teach the game properly. When appropriately selected and well taught, games can enhance the learning experience for children tremendously and help to achieve the goals of a unit more quickly and more enjoyably.

Games should be selected for a particular instructional purpose: They should contribute to achieving the goals of the instructional unit. For this reason experienced physical education teachers most often "create" their own games to achieve a particular instructional goal. These games are usually slightly modified versions of typical elementary-school games and sports, but it is in the "slight modification" that the game becomes a better instructional activity. Ways of changing games have already been addressed earlier in this chapter, so that it is easy to see how any game can be changed by modifying the number of players, the organization of the players, the equipment used, the rules, or the scoring contingencies.

Games should also be selected so that the rules and strategies are at a level of complexity that is appropriate for the skills and backgrounds of the children playing them. Generally speaking, the fewer and simpler the rules, the better the game and the more direct its contribution to instructional goals. Games of elimination should be avoided, simply because children should be as actively involved as much of the time as possible. If elimination is absolutely necessary, players should return to the game as quickly as possible. Another possibility is to have a practice area for children who are eliminated so that they may practice skills while they wait to return to the contest.

The following are practical guidelines for teaching games to children.

1. Have students learn skills and skill combinations before using them in the game. A game is not a good setting in which to first acquire a skill. Instead, a game is a setting to refine and further develop a skill already learned in a safer, more controlled setting. The practice of skills can be made "game-like," so that the generalization from practice to game settings is optimized.

2. Have all equipment ready and accessible before starting a game. Once a game is introduced, the children should be able to begin it as quickly as possible. A transition period for getting equipment ready not only diffuses the children's high expectations about the game but also creates a situation where disruptive behavior is more likely to occur.

3. Mark boundary lines or goals clearly. Pointing to a red line already on a gym floor is probably not enough, because it is simply one line among many and not sufficiently highlighted. Teachers use shoe polish, tape, chalk, and other materials to temporarily highlight the major boundaries until they are learned sufficiently.

4. Arrange games for maximum participation. More on this important topic will be discussed later in this chapter.

5. Know the game well before teaching it. Teachers should know the rules, safety considerations, major teaching cues, scoring, and major difficulties to be encountered prior to the time they teach the game to children. This will improve the teacher's clarity of presentation and help the teacher to anticipate learning difficulties.

6. If groups or teams are to be used for

the game, get students into those groups quickly. A transition time to count off for team membership is most often a waste of precious instructional/learning time. A teacher can list teams on posters or on a chalkboard, hand out colored wristbands as children enter the gym, or have prearranged teams that stay fixed no matter what the activity.

7. Don't hesitate to modify a game to meet equipment or space constraints or specific instructional goals. A slightly smaller ball, one with less air pressure, a larger goal, a different scoring system, or a different rotational system can each modify a game slightly so that it better fits the needs of the situation.

8. It is a good idea to have a "trial run" without keeping score until all rules and basic strategies are learned, at least to a minimum level. Children may then participate successfully in the beginning attempts at the game.

9. If teams will intermingle in the game space, use some kind of identification so that children know who is on their team and who is an opponent. Whatever is used should be easy to get on and off yet be sufficiently sturdy so that it is not loosened easily as the children move. Colored wristbands are very good, as are pinnies.

10. Teach the rules of the game along with skills with which they occur while children practice the skills. Rules should be incorporated as much as possible in skill practice and not wait until the game begins. For example, a high stick rule in floor hockey should be introduced during passing rather than wait until the first game is organized.

11. Rules should be enforced consistently and fairly. It does a child no good to have a rule "bent." In case of arguments, a standard procedure should be adopted so that time is not wasted and constant bickering among children is avoided. A typical procedure would be (a) go to the teacher, (b) review the incident, (c) discuss the rule, and (d) consult a rules list or chart. A list of basic rules should be posted at the playspace. Students can learn to call infractions for their own group and act as referees. Students can also learn to call their own fouls as they play. These social skills, however, are learned; unless a teacher takes the time to teach children how to do them, it should not be expected that they will be done automatically or done well without practice.

12. Try to maintain "fair" sides. This can be achieved partly through selection to team membership. It can also be accomplished through rotation and changing sides at opportune times. Also, players should rotate positions and/or jobs in the game so that each gets experience at the various requirements of different positions, such as goalie, forward, defense, and so on.

13. As the game goes on, the teacher should be actively teaching, providing cues for skills and strategies, giving feedback and encouragement, and gradually introducing the subtler nuances of the rules and social skills inherent in the game. The teacher should not stop the game too often for purposes of feedback and clarification. Instead, most of these comments should be made as the children play.

14. If a major problem or misunderstanding or teachable moment occurs, stop the game, clarify the situation, and begin the game again as quickly as possible. A very good strategy for such situations is to stop the game quickly, emphasize the right way to do something, show how children were doing it improperly, show the right way again, and begin the game again. This positive modeling–negative modeling–positive modeling is thought to be a very useful teaching strategy to help youngsters learn the difference between proper and improper skills and strategies. It can be done quickly, often in twenty seconds or less.

15. Try to use the same formation for many games, changing the skills and rules to fit the specific instructional goals. In this way children will spend more time learning skills and less time learning formations.

Techniques for Maximizing Participation

Children learn best when they get to make many, many learning responses. Techniques for maximizing the opportunity to respond are among the most important of all teaching techniques. In games it is very important that children get as much playing time as possible. What follows are some techniques for achieving a maximum participation goal in game settings.

1. Get as much equipment as possible. The old excuse "I just don't have the equipment" is seldom valid, given what we now know about inexpensive homemade equipment. The chapter on building play equipment should be of great help in this area. Teachers can also trade equipment with other schools. As long as other schools are not in the same unit at the same time, equipment can be shared. In fact, in a school system where there is more than one elementary school, it makes sense to stagger the presentation of units so that equipment can be shared.

2. Use more than one game space. If the game calls for one large circle, change it so that you can use two or three smaller circles. Three or four small games are not only just as good as one big game, but they are no doubt much better in providing places to learn the skills and strategies of the games.

3. Maximize the use of space. Go outside whenever possible, where there is likely to be more space available. Tape, lime, shoe polish, or chalk can be used to mark game spaces outdoors.

4. Have children who are temporarily not involved in the game practice the skills in an adjoining space. You can use a stage or a hallway, if feasible, or anywhere where children can get some extra practice while they wait their turn to play in the game. Naturally, we recognize that fulfilling this strategy is directly related to your ability and confidence to maintain discipline.

5. Choose games that allow for maximum participation. Instead of playing one softball game, modify the game so that you can have three games, even though you may have only two bases in the modified game. If a game requires a lot of inactivity, then perhaps it is not a good game to select for your program.

6. Be on the watch for children who are "in" the game but not doing anything. Careful assignment of children to positions, rotating, and other techniques can be used to make sure that all the children "in" the game are actually participating. Also, this presents another key situation in which a slight modification can help to create more widespread participation. For example, in court games that require moving across a middle line, the teacher can stand in the middle and a rule can be inserted that requires passing to the teacher every time the team crosses the midcourt area. In this way the teacher can then pass the ball/puck to a child who is less involved and prevent the "hogging" of the ball/puck by the more assertive and skilled children.

The goal of maximum participation is a worthy one, intimately related to the teacher's ability and confidence. Usually when teachers create lines, it is to maintain order rather than because they believe in this procedure as an instructional strategy. A beginning teacher might be afraid to implement some of our suggestions here because of insecurity about maintaining order. The chapter on managing groups of children can be a big help in providing techniques that will allow you to create and maintain enough order so that you can begin to think about maximizing participation.

19

introductory games

The games in this chapter use basic skills in both cooperative and competitive ways. They are called introductory games because they are less complex than the sport activities described later in the text. They have been selected according to the guidelines described in the previous chapter, which emphasize

1. Maximum participation
2. Nonelimination
3. Worthwhile skill goals
4. Flexible structure that can easily be modified to change the skill being used or to increase or decrease the complexity of the game (number and organization of players, equipment, rules, and scoring contingencies)

The games in this chapter have been designed as original activities or modified from traditional games for children. They are designed to be used as part of an instructional program with clear skill goals. Even the most basic of these games requires that children use skills within rules of competition or to relate their movements to those of another. Skill practice does not begin at this point. These games and activities do not introduce a skill to students; rather, they provide practice for these skills under more complex conditions after children have gained a reasonable level of competence and confidence in the skill itself.

The games are presented with the following information:

1. The *organization* of the game, in terms of the number of players and their relationship to each other and the playspace
2. The *skills* used in the game, in terms of the dominant major skill patterns used in the game
3. A *description* of the game, in terms of the object of the game and any necessary rules basic to the activity
4. *Suggestions* on how to achieve better game play or modify the game for student needs.

The teacher is encouraged to use, modify, and adapt all facets of these games to meet the needs of a whole class or of small groups of students within a class. As stated in the previous chapter, students should also be involved in the process of game design. Phrases such as "How can we make this game better?" or "How can we make a rule to solve this problem?" or "What rules would your group like to add (take away) to (from) this game?" are all used by teachers who are concerned with process and helping children to understand games. No game is sacred—a game is a tool to be used in the educational process.

ADAPTING GAMES TO THE NEEDS OF STUDENTS

Organization

The games described in the following pages have been reduced to the lowest number of students who can participate without changing the nature of the activity. Teachers can add complexity to these games by increasing the number of players where the increase would add complexity to the use of the skill and *not* decrease the opportunity to use the skill in the same way.

Example: If I add players to a net game, I am asking students to relate to teammates and therefore I am adding complexity to the use of the skill. If I add a player to a game where children basically take turns practicing the same skill, I merely decrease the opportunity to learn by adding more players.

Example: When the game of keep away is played with a soccer ball using foot dribbling and passing skills, the teacher may want to give the advantage to the offensive team, even up to three against one. The rationale for this is that offensive skills in soccer take a long time to develop, and the outcome will be more equitable with this advantage.

Teachers may justifiably add players if equipment or space is limited and the game is considered a critical part of games skills development. In this case stations should be set up for students not actively playing to practice skills on the sidelines.

Equipment

A variety of equipment alternatives are listed under the description of games in this chapter. As discussed in Chapter 15, the equipment a child uses in the practice of a skill is a condition which can make a skill easier or more difficult. The size, weight, and material of which the equipment is made can change the child's degree of success with a skill. Where equipment is having a detrimental effect on performance (too small, too large, too heavy, too hard) the equipment should be changed, even if this means that some children are using one type of equip-ment and other children are using another type.

The type of equipment used also affects the organization of a game or activity. In striking games, in particular, some objects bounce more or can be struck farther than other objects. The farther an object travels, the more playspace is needed; in some instances more players are needed to cover that space. With objects that travel farther or pose a safety problem, more space is needed. The teacher can reduce the space needed by choosing equipment that will not create these needs.

Skills

The basic skills used in each game are described in the following pages. These skills can be changed or modified to meet student needs. Many of these possibilities are discussed in the suggestions section of the game presentation.

Teachers may want to specify the type of pattern to be used.

Examples: (a) Games involving throwing—specify overhand or underhand patterns; (b) games involving jumping—specify jump with two feet, jump from a stand, jump from one foot to another foot, and so on; (c) games involving striking with different body parts—specify body parts.

In addition, many games can be used for a variety of purposes using entirely different skills patterns.

Examples: Games involving striking can substitute throwing, or vice versa.

Description

The description of the game gives the object of the game and rules regarding play. Any of the rules can be adapted as needed. Generally, as skill level in a game increases, children find the "loopholes" in a game. Restrictions on play can then be added. A good rule to follow in determining when to add rules and when to remove them is to add or take away rules or procedures in order to keep the flow of the game going. If the game is no longer a challenge, add a restriction that makes the game more difficult. If the flow of the game cannot be maintained, decrease the restrictions or rules on play.

Example: (a) If a softball-type game uses pitching and the game does not flow, have the teacher pitch, add a batting tee, or change the game to a throw; (b) if in a tag-type game the tagger can't tag anyone, add a tagger or decrease the space.

As discussed earlier, scoring rules should be changed to accomplish specific goals.

Example: If passing to teammates is an objective in game play, a rule can be established that a score cannot be made before a certain number of passes are made.

Suggestions

A minimum number of variations and ideas for encouraging better play are listed in this section. The teacher should be alert for teachable moments, needed adaptations, and concepts that need to be communicated to students.

Ability Levels of Games

The games in this chapter are divided into three ability-level classifications: Levels I, II, and III. These levels are used to distinguish both the difficulty of the skills used and the complexity of the game iteself. They correspond approximately to the following breakdown:

Level I — Grades K, 1, 2
Level II — Grades 2, 3, 4

Level III — Grades 4, 5, 6

The breakdown does not at first appear to be very discriminating, but it is consistent with the levels of game skill development presented in Chapter 15. Early primary-level students are operating at early stages of development in manipulative skills and spend most of their time trying to learn how to control objects and deal with competitive activities that are self-testing in nature. Most of the games described in this section for this level are competitive activities using locomotor skills (dodging, jumping, tagging), not manipulative patterns.

Most of the Level II activities are appropriate for the third and fourth grades and advanced second grades. These students are beginning to use skills in combination and under more complex conditions. There is great variability in the competitive conditions used in these games and the teacher should choose wisely. Games that are simpler in nature should be used for the second and third graders and the more complex should be used for the fourth grades. Teachers at these levels should ensure that children have had ample time to develop these skills in less complex and noncompetitive environments before using these skills in games.

The fifth and sixth grader needs opportunities to practice skills with games that involve a lower organization. Even adults enjoy playing games that are not highly organized and assure high levels of success. Students this age will also begin orienting their play in the direction of more specific sports.

TABLE 19.1 Index to games included in this chapter

NAME	PAGE	SKILLS	LEVEL
Call ball	305	Throwing and catching	I
Freeze tag	305	Dodging and tagging	I, II
Safe tag	306	Dodging and tagging	I
Norwegian ball	306	Throwing and catching	I, II
Boundary ball	306	Throwing and catching	I, II
Wall dodgeball	307	Throwing and dodging	II
Partner seat tag	307	Dodging and tagging	II
Partner steal the bacon	307	Dodging—reaction time	II
Newcomb (variation)	307	Throwing and catching	II

(continued)

TABLE 19.1. (*Continued*)

NAME	PAGE	SKILLS	LEVEL
Bombardment	307	Throwing and catching	II
Tag ball	308	Dribbling, defending, offensive guarding	II, III
Jump the shot	308	Jumping	I
Steal the treasure	308	Running, dodging, tagging	II
Busy ball	308	Throwing and catching	I
Running score	309	Throwing and catching or striking skills	II
Pig in the middle	309	Base running, throwing, and catching	III
Wall ball	309	Batting and catching	III
Throw baseball	309	Base running, throwing, and fielding skills	III
Hot potato (variation)	310	Catching and throwing	I (upper)
Jump the brook	310	Jumping	I
Poison pin	310	Dodging, striking with different body parts, throwing and catching, trapping	II
Pussy wants a corner	310	Dodging and tagging	I
Ball pass	311	Dodging and throwing	I
Bases on balls (variation)	311	Kicking, running bases, throwing and catching	II
Bat ball (variation)	311	Striking, throwing and catching, running bases	II
Crackabout	312	Dodging and throwing	II
Circle pole ball (variation)	312	Throwing and catching, defending	III
Low levels	312	Throwing and catching	II
High levels	313	Throwing and catching	II
Handball (modified)	313	Striking	III
Partner defense	313	Basketball dribbling and defensive skills	II
Keep away	313	Throwing and catching (basketball orientation)	II
Keep away	313	Dribbling, passing, and receiving (soccer and hockey orientation)	II
Keep away	313	Passing and defending (football orientation)	III

GAMES

CALL BALL (LEVEL I)

Organization. Groups of three or four players

Equipment. One ball per group—size of ball varies with skill ability

Skills. Throwing and catching

Description. Group decides what shall be considered in bounds. One child throws the ball into the air and calls out the name of another player, who must catch the ball before it bounces. If the ball is caught, the catcher becomes the new thrower. If not, the thrower must throw the ball again.

Suggestions. Help children set appropriate boundaries. If they continuously miss, decrease the size of the boundaries. One variation is to have each player throw it for every other player—trying to find a level of throw that will challenge the person to whom they are throwing.

FREEZE TAG (LEVEL I, II)

Organization. Scattered formation within a designated boundary; size of space decreased according to ability of students

Equipment. None

Skills. Running with quick changes in direction, awareness of space and others; tagging

Description. One player is "it" and tries to tag other players lightly on the seat. Players tagged must freeze and then become frozen taggers. Frozen taggers must keep one foot stationary but may tag anyone they can reach. Players who are tagged by the person(s) designated "it" or by frozen taggers, or those who step out of bounds or collide with another, become frozen as well. The last person left untagged becomes the new "it."

Suggestions. It is easier to avoid being tagged in a larger space. As children become more skillful, decrease the size of the space. This game can also be played going in one direction from line to line with the frozen tagger.

SAFE TAG (LEVEL I)

Organization. Scattered within a designated boundary

Equipment. Colorbands to designate who is "it"

Skills. Running with quick changes in direction, awareness of space and others; tagging

Description. One or more players may be "it." Each "it" has a pinney, scarf, or something else to let others know that he or she is "it." Player tagged becomes the new "it." Player can avoid being hit by squatting, putting one hand on the floor, lifting one foot, and so on.

Suggestions. Vary the size of space according to ability. Use different locomotor patterns. Vary the safe position according to the time it takes to get into that position.

NORWEGIAN BALL (LEVEL I, II)

Organization. Two teams of students behind opposite lines of the playspace

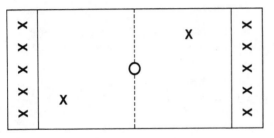

Equipment. Approximately one ball for each player and one heavier larger ball for the center

Skills. Throwing and catching

Description. A heavier ball, such as a basketball, is placed in the center of the playspace. On the signal "Go" each team armed with balls (playground, volleyball, plastic balls) attempts to send the center ball over the line of the opposite team. Players may not touch the center ball with any part of their bodies nor step over the line to retrieve balls. A retriever for each team may be designated, whose job it is to send loose balls back to their own team. They may not stop a shot or shoot themselves. The game is started again in the center when a team scores.

Suggestions. Choose a size space that is within the overhand throw capabilities of students. The game will go quicker with a lighter ball in the center. Vary the throw pattern required (overhand, underhand, sidearm).

BOUNDARY BALL (LEVEL I, II)

Organization. Two teams, each scattered on half the playspace, with a goal line in back

Equipment. One ball for each player

Skills. Throwing and catching

Description. Size of space is designed to ensure that students cannot easily throw over the goal line of the opposite team. Object of the game is for one team to score by getting a ball across the goal line of other players. Game ends after a designated number of points.

Suggestions. Size of space determines difficulty. Students should soon learn the importance of catching as well as throwing. Older students may want to designate defensive players. The teacher may want to have a rule regarding traveling with a ball in one's hands if students move up to the center line to throw.

WALL DODGEBALL (LEVEL II)

Organization. Three or four players and wall space

Equipment. One volleyball, nerf ball, or playground ball per group

Skills. Throwing and dodging

Description. One player is the thrower and stands at least 8 feet from the wall, depending on skill level. The thrower tries to hit the players—who are standing with their backs to the wall—below the waist with the ball. Player becomes the thrower when hit.

Suggestions. As throwing skill increases, distance and size of ball can be changed.

PARTNER SEAT TAG (LEVEL II)

Organization. Partners facing each other

Equipment. None

Skills. Dodging and tagging skills

Description. Partner attempts to tag the seat of the other players without touching any other part of the body. Points needn't be kept.

Suggestions. Students should be restricted to a space. Turning and running is not good strategy.

PARTNER STEAL THE BACON (LEVEL II)

Organization. Partner standing around an Indian club, beanbag, or softball, a designated distance apart on a goal line

Equipment. One club, pin, or ball

Skills. Dodging, quick reaction time

Description. On the signal "Go" each partner moves from his own goal line and tries to get the club (pin or ball) back to his own goal line without being tagged by his opponent.

NEWCOMB (VARIATION) (LEVEL II)

Organization. Two teams of three or four each on opposite sides of a net, rope, or other obstacle

Equipment. One ball (playground, plastic, or volleyball), one divider (net, stretched high rope, folded mat, and so on)

Skills. Throwing and catching

Description. Groups are spaced out with boundaries of their choice (increase size for more skilled). One player in the back part of the space tosses the ball over the net to the other team. If the ball is missed and lands within the designated boundaries, thrower's team scores a point. If the ball is caught, whoever caught the ball can throw it either over the net or to a teammate.

Suggestions. The game was originally designed to be played like volleyball but using throwing and catching skills. The teacher can add players and increase the size of the space as players get more skilled. Rotation of players in a circle from the back line to the front line can then be introduced. The height of the net will also determine offensive play. As players start to direct the ball down, increase the height of the net. Scoring can be designated by the teacher (either time or points) or students can make this decision.

BOMBARDMENT (LEVEL II)

Organization. Two teams each on half of the playspace; a center line divides the team and an end line is to the back of each team; at least six Indian clubs, bowling pins, or plastic milk cartons are placed behind the end line of each team

Equipment. Enough balls so that there is one for every two students; twelve Indian clubs or pins

Skills. Throwing and catching

Description. Balls are equally divided between the two teams. One team tries to knock down the pins of the other team. Player may not cross the center line or the end line. The team that knocks down all the pins of the opposing team wins.

Suggestions. The size of the playspace should vary with student ability. A variety of ball sizes may be used in the same game or in different games. The type of throw pattern to be used may be specified.

TAG BALL (LEVEL II, III)

Organization. Each child has a ball scattered throughout the playspace; boundaries are designated

Equipment. One playground, plastic, volleyball, or basketball per child

Skills. Dribbling; defending; offensive guarding

Description. One or two players are designated "it" and do not have a ball. They must try to tag the ball of the other players without touching any part of their bodies. Players whose balls are tagged or who lost control of their balls must hold their balls until the end of the game.

Suggestions. Start this activity with partners first—one offensive and one defensive player before moving to the whole group. Encourage students to defend their balls by placing their bodies between the ball and the player trying to get the ball away.

JUMP THE SHOT (VARIATION) (LEVEL I)

Organization. Partners or groups of four children

Equipment. One jump rope with a beanbag tied to the end for weight

Skills. Jumping and turning a rope

Description. One player turns the rope from one end, not allowing the beanbag to come off the floor more than a few inches. The other player attempts to jump the shot without getting caught in the rope. As players get better, they can keep track of how many times in a row they can jump.

Suggestion. Help children learn how to turn the rope, keeping it low to the floor.

STEAL THE TREASURE AND CAPTURE THE FLAG (LEVEL II)

Organization. Two teams, each on opposite sides of a center line in the playing area; a section on each team's side holds the treasure or flag

Equipment. Six pins or clubs for treasure and pinnies, belts, or armbands to designate one team

Skills. Running, dodging, and tagging

Description. Each team tries to steal the treasure of the other team without being tagged behind enemy lines. Players tagged must return the treasure if they have it in their hands and become prisoners of the opposite team. Players venturing into opponents' territory may steal one piece of treasure or free one prisoner if they can do so without being tagged. Prisoners who are freed must hold hands with the person releasing them until they get back to their own side and may be retagged on the way. At the end of the game the team who has the most treasure wins.

Suggestions. Capture the flag is a similar game. Instead of treasure each team has a flag they are trying to defend. When one team gets to the flag without being tagged, the game is over. One variation is to have released prisoners be safe in opposing territory as long as they are holding the hand of the player who freed them.

BUSY BALL (LEVEL I)

Organization. Teams of three to six players across a net from each other

Equipment. One ball for every two players

Skills. Throwing and catching

Description. Balls are equally divided between two teams. On the signal "Go" each team must try to get rid of the balls on their side of the net. *No net* The game ends at the end of 2 minutes or at a prearranged time. The team that has the fewest number of balls on their side wins a point and the game begins again.

Suggestions. Designate boundaries according to skill ability. Keep episodes short. Encourage students to receive and send the ball in one action. Have students catch and then strike the ball back over the net as a variation.

RUNNING SCORE (LEVEL II)

Organization. One to six children on a team across a net from each other (low or high for different skills)

Equipment. Balls of any size; paddles and balls; a rope barricade of some sort or a net

Skills. Throwing and catching or striking skills

Description. Each player or team of players cooperates with the player or team on the other side of the net. The object of the game is to see how many times the object (ball, bird, or pateca) can be sent back and forth across the net without hitting the floor or bouncing once, if that is the rule. If the object hits the floor (or bounces more than once) the player must start counting all over again. The group that keeps it going the longest is the winner.

Suggestion. Use low nets, folded mat, or low rope for striking skills involving paddles and balls, or use the hands with a small ball. Use high nets for throwing and catching or striking with different body parts with large balls.

PIG IN THE MIDDLE (LEVEL III)

Organization. Groups of three and two bases 15 to 25 feet apart

Equipment. One ball (small or large) and two bases per group

Skills. Base running, throwing, and catching

Description. Base runner starts on one base and attempts to score a point by running to the other base before being tagged by the baseman with the ball. If a base runner is tagged with the ball, the runner changes places with the tagger. The base runner who is not tagged getting to the new base scores a point and continues until put out.

Suggestion. Use soft balls until children are well skilled.

WALL BALL (LEVEL III)

Organization. One batter about 20 feet from the wall; one pitcher and two fielders; one catcher

Equipment. Softball-size whiffle or fleece ball and plastic bat; home base

Skills. Batting and catching

Description. Pitcher pitches ball underhand to batter, who tries to hit the ball, run and touch the wall, and run back home to base. Batter can score by calling the level of the hit against the wall (high, medium, or low) or by beating the ball back home. Fielders try to catch the ball off the wall and send it to the catcher. Each player stays up at bat until hitting the ball. Positions change after each play according to a preestablished rotation.

Suggestions. Students should have a choice of using a batting tee or a pitched ball.

THROW BASEBALL (LEVEL III)

Organization. One batter, three basemen, one pitcher, and one catcher; three bases and home plate (short dimensions between)

Equipment. Three bases; a small ball (whiffle ball preferably); one home plate

Skills. Base running, throwing, and fielding skills

Description. Batter throws ball into the field and then attempts to make it to all three bases and home before the ball. Fielders must send the ball to first, second, and third base before sending it to the catcher. The catcher must try to tag home plate with the ball before the runner gets there. If the ball gets home before the runner, the runner is out. If the runner gets home first, the runner scores a point. Players rotate positions after each batter has had a turn. Players keep their own individual scores.

Suggestions. Vary the size of the playing field with throwing and catching abilities. Teach beginning skills regarding base running, covering space in the field, and placing the ball offensively. Teach beginning rules regarding fly balls.

HOT POTATO (VARIATION) (LEVEL I UPPER)

Organization. Four players (one defense, three offense); scattered playspace

Equipment. One ball or beanbag of any size or shape

Skills. Quick throwing

Description. The three offensive players must pass the object among themselves without holding it more than 5 seconds or getting tagged with the ball in their hands. The defensive player must try to force a bad pass or tag a player who is holding the object. A player tagged or making a bad pass exchanges places with a defensive player. Player may not move.

Suggestions. Vary the size of the space between players, depending on skill level. Put contingencies on the level of the pass (high, medium, low).

JUMP THE BROOK (LEVEL I)

Organization. Groups of no more than six or eight children

Equipment. Two ropes or lines that form a brook to jump over

Skills. Jumping

Description. The brook is designed so that the lines converge, creating a brook wider at one end than at the other. Students attempt to jump the brook at the widest point they can without stepping on the lines or between the lines.

Suggestions. Encourage students to try different jumping patterns (two feet to two feet) (one foot to two feet) (one foot to one foot) (two feet to one foot) and to use a running start. Rule must be made that children land on their feet.

POISON PIN (LEVEL II)

Organization. Groups of five or six

Equipment. One bowling pin, Indian club, or narrow tall can; playground ball or plastic ball

Skills. Dodging, striking with different body parts, throwing and catching, trapping

Description. One player stands in the center of a circle of other players. Each player attempts to knock the pin down in the center of the circle by throwing a ball at the pin. Center player attempts to protect the pin by diverting the ball.

Suggestions. Players trying to knock down the pin should be encouraged to pass the ball to each other quickly to prevent the center player from getting into position. Center player will initially just meet the ball to prevent it from striking the club. Later the distance can be increased and players in the center can be asked to attempt to trap balls as they are sent low.

PUSSY WANTS A CORNER (LEVEL I)

Organization. Groups of five to twenty-five players

Equipment. One base for every student except one (bases can be made from hoops, chalked circles, cardboard, tape, rope, and so on)

Skills. Dodging, tagging

Description. Every child has a base except one. The player who does not have a base calls "Pussy wants a corner" or "Change." On that signal every player must find a new base, including the caller. The player without a base becomes the new caller.

Suggestion. Use bases that will not slide or trip the children.

BALL PASS (LEVEL I)

Organization. Groups of five to ten players

Equipment. One base for every student except one (bases can be made from hoops, chalked circles, cardboard, tape, rope, and so on); one playground ball 5 to 8½ inches, plastic ball, or volleyball nerf ball.

Skills. Dodging, throwing

Description. Every player has a base except the rover, who has the ball. Players on base may exchange bases with another at any time. Player with the ball attempts to steal a base that is left free or hit a player off base below the waist with the ball. If a player is hit with the ball, that player becomes the free player. Players may not travel with the ball.

Suggestions. Vary the number of players and the distance between bases according to the throwing ability of the students.

BASES ON BALLS (VARIATION) (LEVEL II)

Organization. Five fielders and a catcher take their place on a softball diamond (distance between bases adjusted for skill level); one player is the kicker

Equipment. One playground ball or preferably a soccer nerf ball; three bases and a home plate

Skills. Kicking, throwing and catching, running bases

Description. The kicker places the ball on home plate and kicks it between first and third base. A kicker can have as many chances as needed for an in-bounds ball. The kicker then attempts to get to as many bases as possible before the fielders can get the ball home to the catcher. The catcher must tag home plate and say "Stop." The runner then adds up the number of bases touched. Players then rotate one position to the right with the third baseman becoming the new kicker. Players keep track of their own scores.

Suggestions. As catching, throwing, and kicking ability increases, the following rules may be added:

1. If a fielder catches a ball on the fly, the kicker is automatically out and cannot advance.
2. A pitcher is added to roll the ball to the kicker.

BAT BALL (VARIATION) (LEVEL II)

Organization. Groups of six players (one batter and five fielders)

Equipment. One pylon or other type of marker to run around; one batting tee, plastic bat and whiffle ball; one home base.

Skills. Striking a stationary object with a bat, throwing and catching, running bases

Description. The batter places the ball on the tee and attempts to strike it, run around the pylon, and make it back home before the ball gets to a player who must touch the pylon with the ball and then send it home to the catcher, who must, in turn, touch home with the ball. Player who beats the ball home scores one point. After a player has batted, all players rotate positions in a prearranged order. Players keep their own individual scores.

Suggestions. Vary the distance between the pylon and home plate according to the throwing skill of players. Encourage students not to throw the bat. Add rules for fly balls and out-of-bounds balls as necessary.

Striking a small ball with the hand or with a paddle may be used as well as throwing to substitute for striking with a bat.

CRACKABOUT (LEVEL III)

Organization. Groups of at least four and no more than ten, scattered in their own area of the playspace

Equipment. One plastic ball, volleyball, nerf ball, or playground ball per group

Skills. Dodging and throwing skills

Description. Players must remain within the designated playing area. One player attempts to hit other players below the waist with the ball. The thrower may go anywhere in the playspace and is "it" until successful. As soon as a player is hit, the thrower calls "Crackabout," and the ball may be picked up by any player to start again. Players who throw balls without hitting anyone are responsible for retrieving them out of bounds.

Suggestions. To avoid a rush for the ball, make a rule that the first player who touches the ball becomes the new "it." Have a contest to see who can be hit the fewest number of times.

CIRCLE POLE BALL (VARIATION) (LEVEL III)

Organization. Two teams of four or five, each designated by pinnies or other means; one center circle with a pole in the center

Equipment. One playground ball; pinnies (or other means to designate teams); some kind of center pole (volleyball standard or similar item)

Skills. Throwing and catching in relation to offensive and defensive player

Description. Each team has a player within the center circle. Other players may not enter the center circle. One team starts the ball outside the play area and must pass the ball until they can get it to their teammate within the center circle. The center player can score by tapping the center pole with the ball. The nonscoring team then gets to start the ball out of bounds. Players may not run with the ball or defensively touch any other player. The center circle player may not interfere with a pass from the opposing team but may otherwise go anywhere within the center circle.

Suggestions. Game should be played initially without dribbling. Later dribbling may be added as well as other more specific basketball rules. A circle and poles may be added at either end of a playspace or center player may be required to hit the backboard to score using the key area as the center circle. In this case players would be shooting for goals at opposite ends of the playspace.

LOW LEVELS (LEVEL II)

Organization. Two players facing a wall with one line about 8 feet from the wall; side boundaries can be established if necessary

Equipment. One ball (a variety of ball sizes can and should be used, resulting in practice of different skills)

Skills. Throwing and catching

Description. Players stand between the lines. One player starts by throwing the ball against the wall so that it bounces before the 8-foot line between the side boundaries and comes through the play area at a low level. The other player must catch the ball, without letting it pass. The receiver then becomes the thrower. Players keep track of the number of catches in a row they can make without a miss.

Suggestions. Players should be encouraged to use an overhand pattern, causing the ball to bounce before the line. This should be practiced first. The line can be adjusted to accommodate different skill levels. Game can be combined with "High Levels" so that student doesn't know the level of the ball.

HIGH LEVELS (LEVEL II)

Organization. Two players facing a wall with a line 20 feet from the wall; side boundaries can be established if necessary

Equipment. One ball (a variety of ball sizes and weights can and should be used resulting in practice of different skills)

Skills. Throwing and catching

Description. Players stand anywhere inside the restraining lines. One player starts by throwing the ball against the wall so that the ball comes at a high level and bounces before the 20-foot line. The second player must catch the ball before it bounces. The receiver then becomes the thrower. Players keep track of the number of catches in a row they can make without a miss.

Suggestions. Players may be encouraged to use either an overhand or an underhand throw pattern. They should practice throwing the ball so that it bounces before the line before play is started. The line can be adjusted to accommodate different skill levels. Game can be combined with "Low Levels" for a different game.

HANDBALL (MODIFIED) (LEVEL III)

Organization. Two players and a wall with designated back lines and sidelines

Equipment. Small nerf ball, soft whiffle ball, tennis ball, handball, or other small ball

Skills. Striking with the hands

Description. One player bounces the ball and hits it against the wall. The other player must return the ball to the wall, using a striking pattern with the hand after ball bounces. Fair balls bounce within a designated area. If a player misses the ball or fails to return it to the wall, the other team member gets the point. Players can play for time or points.

Suggestions. This game can be modified to be a cooperative/competitive activity

by asking students to see how long they can keep the ball going. It can be made more difficult by

1. Putting a line away from the wall beyond which the ball must cross to be a legal hit (increases the force level)
2. Adding rules of handball, such as serving behind a line and scoring only when you have served or requiring the serve to go beyond a 13-foot service line

A piece of plywood a little larger than the hand with two elastic bands can be used as a transition between hand activities and more racquet-oriented activities.

PARTNER DEFENSE (LEVEL II)

Organization. Partners

Equipment. One medium-sized playground ball, basketball, or plastic ball

Skills. Basketball dribbling and defensive skills

Description. One partner must keep the ball bouncing. The other partner must attempt to make the partner with the ball lose control or tag the ball without touching any body parts.

Suggestions.

1. Encourage players with the ball to defend it by placing their bodies between the defense and the ball.
2. Have students select boundaries if necessary.

KEEP AWAY (THROWING AND CATCHING) (LEVEL II)

Organization. Groups of three (two offensive and one defensive player)

Equipment. One medium-sized playground ball, plastic ball, or basketball

Skills. Throwing and catching in relation to a defensive player; defending against players with the ball

Description. Two players try to keep the ball away from the player without the ball. Players may not move with the ball but may move when they do not have the ball. If the defensive player touches the ball, the player who threw the ball exchanges places with the defensive player.

Suggestions. Use this game to encourage

1. Offensive players without the ball to cut to a space to receive the ball
2. Offensive player to pass quickly
3. Defensive players to stay with one player and close up their passing options

Add rules allowing dribbling as students can handle the passing game and make the right decision about when to use the dribble and when to pass right away. Add equal number of offensive and defensive players as play skills increase. Points can be awarded for five passes in a row (or any number) without defense touching the ball, when offense and defense have equal numbers and completely change sides with a turnover.

KEEP AWAY (SOCCER-ORIENTED) (HOCKEY-ORIENTED) (LEVEL II UPPER)

Organization. Groups of four (three offensive and one defensive player)

Equipment. One soccer ball; deflated playground ball or soccer nerf ball (plastic hockey sticks and pucks/balls)

Skills. Passing, receiving, and kicking skills (striking)

Description. Three players try to keep the ball away from a defensive player by moving with the ball and passing it with their feet. If the defensive player gets control of the ball, the last offensive player to touch the ball must then become the defensive player.

Suggestions. Encourage offensive players to:

1. Control the ball before they pass it
2. Use the soccer dribble to move clear of a defensive player before they pass

3. Cut into space to receive a pass

Encourage defensive players to attempt to gain control by blocking a pass or tackling the player with the ball (using their foot [stick] to clear the ball away from offensive player). Add equal numbers of defensive players as game skills increase. Award points for consecutive passes when offense and defense is equal.

KEEP AWAY (FOOTBALL-ORIENTED) (LEVEL III)

Organization. Groups of five (three offensive and two defensive players)

Equipment. Whiffle footballs, nerf footballs, junior-sized footballs

Skills. Football passing and defensive skills

Description. Three players try to keep the ball away from two defensive players by passing the ball back and forth. If a defensive player touches the ball or if an offensive player fails to catch the ball, the offensive player who threw the ball changes places with the defensive player. Players may not run with the ball.

Suggestions. Encourage offensive players to

1. Pass ahead of a receiver
2. Pass quickly
3. Move into an empty space away from a receiver

Encourage defensive players to

1. Try to force a bad pass by keeping the hands high in front of a passer
2. Place themselves behind the passer and possible receiver

Add equal numbers of defensive and offensive players as skill increases. Count the number of completed passes in a row for scoring when teams are equal. Exchange offensive and defensive teams completely when teams have equal numbers.

20

classroom
and
playground games

PLAYGROUND GAMES

The games played most often on elementary-school playgrounds before and after school and during the noon hour and recess are self-regulating, needing little, if any, supervision. They reflect children's constructive use of leisure time and represent meaningful opportunities for children to further realize the fitness and physical skills objectives of the school physical education curriculum. They require (a) limited initial instruction, which can easily be provided for in the school physical education program, (b) the painting of game diagrams on hard surfaces on the school playground, and (c) the provision of a limited amount of accessible loose equipment.

TETHERBALL

Tetherball requires a pole 10 feet high and 2 to 4 inches in diameter, set permanently in a concrete base (or placed sturdily into a mobile heavy base). The pole is located in the center of a circle 20 feet in diameter. A stripe is painted around the pole 5 feet from the top. A tetherball is attached to the top of the pole with a 7-foot length of sash cord. The circle is divided into two neutral zones (each 90 degrees) and two play zones (each 90 degrees) by two painted lines. The neutral zones separate the two play zones.

Generally, two players are needed for tetherball. One player stands in each of the two play zones. The server, chosen by lot, puts the ball in play by striking the ball around the pole in either direction. The opponent must not strike the ball on its first swing around the pole. On the ball's second time around, the opponent's task is to strike the ball back in the opposite direction. The object is for either player to strike the ball repetitively so that the rope winds around the pole and the ball eventually touches the pole. The first player who succeeds wins the game and becomes the server for the next game. If a player hits the ball with any part of the body other than the hands or forearms, catches or holds the ball during play, steps outside the play zones, hits the rope with the forearm or hands, throws the ball, or winds the ball around the pole below the 5-foot mark, the game is awarded to the opponent. The player who first wins four games wins the match.

Variations of this game may be played using a tennis ball and paddles, and with four, rather than two, players (doubles).

FOUR SQUARE AND TWO SQUARE

A 16-foot square, divided into four 8-foot squares, serves as the bounded area for the game of four square. Each of the four squares is consecutively numbered, 1-2-3-4, in a counterclockwise fashion. A 3-foot long diagonal line, designated the service line, is located across the outside corner of the first square. A utility ball, 8½ inches in diameter, or a volleyball is used in this game.

One player stands in or just outside of each square. The player in the first square must stand behind the service line and put the ball in play by dropping the ball and striking it underhand on the bounce into any of the other three squares. If the serve hits a line, the server is out. Any player receiving the ball must keep it in play by striking the ball underhand after it has bounced once in that player's square. The ball may be redirected to any of the other squares. Play continues until one player fails to return the ball, causes the ball to land on a line between squares (ball landing on an outside boundary is considered good), steps into another square, strikes the ball overhand, catches or carries a ball, or allows the ball to touch any part of the body but the hands. When a player misses or fouls, he or she goes either to the end of a line of children waiting, or, if no children are waiting, to the fourth square. All other players move up one square and/or the first person in the waiting line moves into the fourth square. The ball is always served by the player in the first square.

A variation of this game, called two square, may be played on the same court. The basic rules are the same as for four square, except two players and two squares are used. If extra players are waiting for a turn, the active player who misses or commits a foul can be eliminated. If there are only two players, a score can be kept. In this game the ball is served from behind the base line of the first square (boundary line that is farthest from the opponent's square).

HOPSCOTCH

Hopscotch is a game played by two to five people on a painted, hard-surfaced, bounded area, using laggers (for example, stones, buttons, pennies, checkers). In the most common form of this game (Figure 20.1, Diagram A) the first player starts the game by tossing a lagger into the first box. He or she then hops over the first box and into the second. On the same foot, the player hops into the third box. When the fourth and fifth boxes are reached, the player jumps into them (one foot in each box). The goal in this game is to hop on one foot in single boxes and to jump, with one foot in each box, into the double boxes. When the seventh and eighth boxes have been reached, the player must jump, turn around, and place the feet in opposite boxes. Afterward, the player hops back into the sixth box, jumps into the fourth and fifth box, hops into the third box, and then into the second box. When the second box is reached, the player bends down, picks up the lagger, hops into the first box, and then hops out. The player then tosses the lagger into the second box and repeats the routine. The player continues hopping and jumping into the other boxes with the lagger until all eight boxes are covered.

Certain rules should be followed. The player may not hop into the box where the lagger has been tossed. The player must pick up the lagger on the way back by stopping in the adjacent box. Only after the lagger has been picked up can the player hop into the box. A player who tosses the lagger into an incorrect box or on a line loses a turn. Falling, stepping on a line, touching a hand to the ground for balance, missing a box, or stepping into a box where a lagger is positioned result in the player losing a turn. Players who have gone through the boxes may write their names in any box. In future play no player may step in that box except the person whose name is in the box. The player

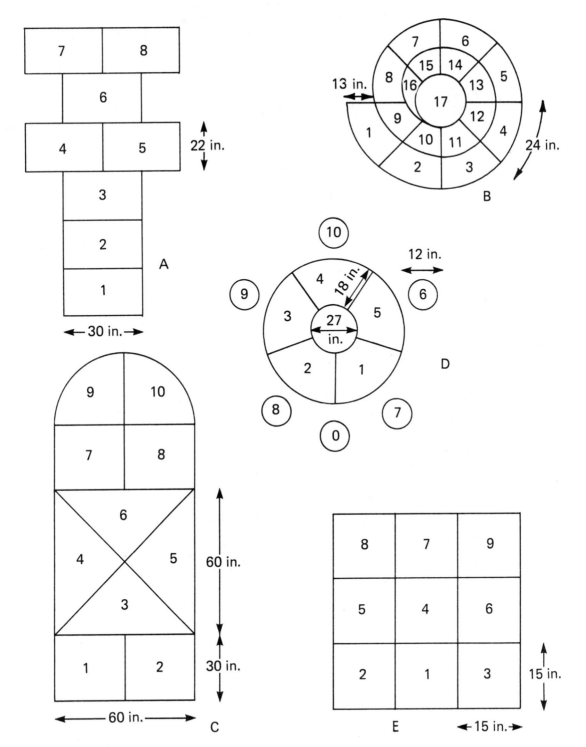

FIGURE 20.1 Hopscotch diagrams.

whose name is on the largest number of boxes wins.

There are many other forms of hopscotch. In snail hopscotch (Figure 20.1, Diagram B) a player attempts to hop from one section to the next until the circle is reached. This procedure is then reversed and the player hops out. Players who complete the snail are allowed to claim a section of their choice by writing their names inside. No one may touch this section except the owner. The owner may stand in this section to rest. The player with the largest number of sections wins.

Tournament hopscotch (Figure 20.1, Diagram C) requires that the player first toss a lagger into the first box, hop into the first box, pick up his or her lagger, and then hop out of the box. Next the player tosses the lagger into the second box, hops into the first box, then the second box, picks up the lagger, hops to the first box, and then hops out. This process is continued through all the numbers.

Numbers hopscotch (Figure 20.1, Diagram D) is another interesting variation. Starting with the number 1 and progressing through the number 5, each number is added to and subtracted from each of the numbers on the boxes of the diagram. The middle circle represents the number being added or subtracted. From the 0 starting position the player hops to the first box and then to the middle circle (adding 1), then to the second box, which represents the answer. From the second box the player hops to the middle circle (adding 1) and then hops to the third box, which represents the answer. From the third box the player hops to the middle circle (adding 1) and then hops to the fourth box, which represents the answer. The player continues in this manner until the tenth box is reached. The reverse procedure is then employed, subtracting, starting from 10. After adding and subtracting 1, add and subtract 2, 3, 4, and 5 when the middle circle is hopped into. Proceed in the following manner. Begin from the 0 starting box, hop into the first box, then to the middle circle (adding 2), and then hop to the third box, representing the answer. From

the third box, hop back to the second box, then to the middle circle (adding 2), and hop to the fourth box, representing the answer. Continue this process until the tenth box is reached. Reverse the procedure to subtract. When moving from the middle circle to an outside circle, a jump is used.

Chinese hopscotch (Figure 20.1, Diagram E) requires that the player jump into the middle square of the near row of three squares. The player jumps again with spread legs and lands with the left foot in the left square and the right foot in the right square of the near row. The player jumps again, returning both feet to the middle square. The player then jumps backward, landing outside the diagram at the starting position. Next the player jumps over the near row and repeats the previous procedure, using the middle row of three squares. He or she jumps backward to the near row, repeating the procedure, and finishes by jumping backward to land outside the bounded area at the starting position. The entire sequence is repeated, starting with a standing long jump to the far row, repeating the sequence, and working backward through the middle row to the near row. The sequence is then repeated from each of the four sides, working diagonally from each of the corners.

ROPE JUMPING

Three basic rhythm patterns are employed in short jump rope activities:

1. Slow-Time. The performer jumps over the rope, jumps in place as the rope passes over the head, and then executes the second step or repeats the original step a second time.
2. Fast-Time. The performer jumps only when the rope passes under the feet. There is no rebound jump in fast-time.
3. Double-Time. The rope is turned at the same speed as for slow-time, but, rather than taking the rebound, the performer executes another step while the rope is passing over the head. Double-time is difficult because there is a tendency to also speed up the rope.

Most steps can be done in slow-time, fast-time, and double-time. Once children have become skilled in the two-foot basic step, the alternate-foot basic step, the swing-step forward, the swing-step backward, the rocker-step and spread legs forward and backward, in slow time, the same steps may be introduced for fast-time and double-time. The alternate-foot basic step and spread legs forward and backward are steps that lend themselves well to an introduction to double-time jumping.

1. *Two-foot basic step.* With feet together, jump over the rope as it passes under the feet and take a preparatory rebound while the rope is overhead.
2. *Alternate-foot basic step.* As the rope passes under the feet, the weight is shifted alternately from one foot to the other, raising the unweighted foot in a running position.
3. *Swing-step forward.* Same as alternate-foot basic step, except the free leg swings forward. Keep knee loose, and let foot swing naturally.
4. *Swing-step sideward.* Same as swing-step forward, except the free leg is swung to the side. Knee should be kept stiff.
5. *Rocker step.* One leg is always forward in a walking stride position in executing the rocker step. As the rope passes below the feet, weight is shifted from the rear foot to the front foot. The rebound is taken on the front foot while the rope is over the head. On the next turn of the rope, the weight is shifted from the front foot to the rear foot, repeating the rebound on the rear foot.
6. *Spread legs forward and backward.* Start in a stride position, with the weight distributed equally on both feet. As the rope passes under the feet, jump into the air and reverse the position of the feet.
7. *Cross legs sideward.* As the rope passes below the feet, spread legs into a straddle position sideward. Take the rebound in the sideward straddle position. As the rope passes under the feet on the next turn, jump into the air and cross the feet with the right foot forward. Repeat with the left foot forward. Alternate forward foot.
8. *Toe touch forward.* As the rope passes below the feet, swing the right foot forward. Alternate, landing on the right foot and touching left toe forward.
9. *Toe touch backward.* Similar to the swing-steps sideward, except the toe of the free foot touches to the back at the end of the swing.
10. *Shuffle step.* When the rope passes under the feet, push off with the right foot, side stepping to the left. Land with the weight on the left foot, and touch right toe beside left heel. Repeat in opposite direction.
11. *Heel-toe.* As the rope passes under the feet, jump with weight landing on the right foot, touching left heel forward. On the following rope turn, jump, landing on the same foot, and touch left toe beside right heel. Repeat, using opposite foot.
12. *Heel-click.* Do two or three swing-steps sideward in preparation for this. When the right foot swings sideward, instead of a hop or rebound when the rope is above the head, raise the left foot to click the heel of the right foot. Repeat on the left.
13. *Step-tap.* When the rope passes below the feet, push off with the right foot and land on the left. While the rope is turning above the head, brush the sole of the right foot forward and then backward. As the rope passes under the feet for the second turn, push off with the left foot, landing on the right, and repeat.
14. *Crossing arms.* Crossing arms during forward turning is easier than crossing behind the back during backward turning. Children should be told that during crossing the hands exchange places. This means that during forward crossing the inside of the elbows are close to each other.
15. *Double rope turning.* After doing a few basic steps in preparation for the double turn, as the rope approaches the feet give an extremely hard flip of the rope from the wrists. Jump from 6 to 8 inches into the air and allow the rope to pass under the feet twice before landing.
16. *Going from forward to backward jumping without stopping the rope.* As the rope starts downward in forward jumping, rather than allowing it to pass below the feet, the performer swings both arms to the left (or right) and makes a half-turn of the body in that direction (turn facing the rope). On the next turn, spread the arms and start turning in the opposite direction.
17. *Schottische step.* The schottische can be done to double-time rhythm or it may be done with a varied rhythm. The pattern is step-step-step-hop, step-step-step-hop, step-hop, step-hop, step-hop, step-hop. In varied rhythm, three quick turns in fast-time are made to conform to the three steps and then double-time prevails.

Long jump rope activities are generally participated in by groups of three to five children. Appropriate introductory skills require the child to (a) turn the rope effectively; (b) jump over a stationary rope; (c) jump over a pendularly swung rope; (d) jump once while the rope is turning; (e) run through a turning rope, entering the front door; and (f) jumping once and exiting through the front door.

1. Turning the rope
   a. Tie one end to a metal pole about 3 feet from the ground. Encourage the child to turn the rope with a fully extended elbow, with the arm moving in a large arc. The rope should strike the ground each time. The speed of the movements should be regular.
   b. When two children turn together, they should be encouraged to watch one another and synchronize their movements so that the rope strikes the ground each time and the speed of the rope movements are regular.
   c. Children should learn to take a turn at rope turning after they have taken a turn at jumping.
   d. While turning with one other person, attempt to turn the rope over and under a ball that has been tossed upward and into the rope turning configuration so that it bounces in place. Turners must learn to adjust the speed of their turning as the ball bounces become smaller and more rapid.
2. Entering
   a. Jumpers should enter the rope at approximately a 45-degree angle, establishing a path of entry that is comfortable.
   b. The children should enter from the *front door* (side where the rope is coming down).
   c. Later, as children become more skilled, they may enter from the *back door* (side where the rope is coming up).
3. Exiting
   a. Jumpers should exit the rope from the front door.
   b. Later, as jumpers become more skilled, they should attempt to exit the back door.
4. Jumping over a stationary rope
   a. Building a house—Child jumps forward, backward, and sideward over a stationary rope held first on the ground and then at increasing heights from the ground.
   b. Inclined rope—Turners hold the rope taut; one end of the rope should be held 5 feet from the ground, the other end should be held on the ground. Jumpers select where to enter and leap over the rope.
   c. Ocean wave—Turners make waves in the rope by moving their arms up and down. Jumpers try to time their entry and leap to get over the waves without touching the rope.
   d. Snake—Turners make snakelike movements with the rope by moving their arms from side to side. Children try to time their entry and leap to get over the snake without touching the rope.
5. Jumping over a pendularly swung rope—Child stands with side to the rope. The teacher swings the rope in a pendular fashion, allowing the child to jump repetitively with the rope passing under the feet each time. The rope never goes above the child's head level.
6. Single jump and exit while teacher turns—Child stands in the center between the turners. The rope is carefully turned in a complete arc over the jumper's head. As the rope nears the child's feet, the child jumps over the rope and then exits the front door.
7. Jumping outside the turning rope—While the rope is turning, children can stand to one side outside of the rope and practice timing their jump. Word cues such as "Jump" can be used by the teacher to help them with the skill. Loud (jump) and soft (rebound jump) claps can also help children with timing.
8. Running through a turning rope without jumping—The child should enter the front door and exit the rear door. Generally, kindergarteners can master this skill.
9. Running into a turning rope, jumping once, and running out—First graders should be able to master this skill. As the children become more skilled, more jumps should be attempted inside before exiting. An additional jump for each grade level is not an unrealistic expectation.

Intermediate skills require that the jumper be able to (a) enter the front door, jump repetitively, and exit the front door; (b) enter the front door, jump repetitively, and exit the rear door; and (c) enter the rear door, jump repetitively, and exit the rear door. Once these skills are mastered, students can participate in interesting and intricate routines.

1. Run in the front door, jump a specified number of times, and exit the front door without chanting.

2. Same as 1, with chants that specify the number of jumps.

I like coffee, I like tea,
How many boys (girls) are wild about me?
One, two, three, et cetera.

Lady, lady at the gate,
Eating cherries from a plate
How many cherries did she eat?
One, two, three, et cetera.

3. Enter through the backdoor—Introduce this skill with the game of Kangaroo. When a jumper enters the back door, the jumper resembles a kangaroo. In the game the student calls out "Kangaroo," enters the back door, and exits. The second time, the jumper calls out "Kangaroo One!" and adds a single jump. Additional jumps are added and called out.

4. Vary the techniques used to jump—Two-footed jumps, right hops, left hops, heel-and-toe steps, straddle jumps, feet together jumps, forward stride jumps, and backward stride jumps may be employed.

5. Vary the techniques by adding quarter and half turns.

6. Add stunts as directed by selected chants.

Teddy Bear, Teddy Bear, turn around.
Teddy Bear, Teddy Bear, touch the ground.
Teddy Bear, Teddy Bear, show your shoe.
Teddy Bear, Teddy Bear, you'd better skidoo.
Teddy Bear, Teddy Bear, say your prayers.
Teddy Bear, Teddy Bear, go upstairs.
Teddy Bear, Teddy Bear, turn out the light.
Teddy Bear, Teddy Bear, say good night.

7. Hot pepper—The turners turn the rope increasingly faster for the jumper, who attempts to keep up. Some chants are appropriate for this activity.

Ice cream, ginger ale, soda water, pop.
You get ready 'cause we're gonna turn hot!

Pease porridge hot, pease porridge cold.
Pease porridge in the pot, nine days old.
Some like it hot, hot, hot!

8. Calling in—A first jumper calls in a second jumper by name. Both jump three times holding hands, and then the first jumper runs out. The second jumper calls in a third jumper and both jump three times holding hands, after which the second jumper exits. Children can be called in while chants are employed. The initial jumper chants while others wait to be called in.

Calling in and calling out,
I call . . . in and I'm getting out.

9. High water—The turners turn the rope so that it gradually becomes higher. Chants may be employed.

At the beach, at the sea,
The waves come almost to the knee.
Higher, higher, et cetera.

10. Stop the rope—During a chant, a jumper can stop the rope by (a) letting the rope hit her, (b) straddling it, (c) crossing the feet and trapping the rope between them, and (d) stamping on the rope.

Junior, Junior, climb the tree.
Junior, Junior, slap your knee.
Junior, Junior, time to miss.
(for girls, use "baby doll")

11. Multiple person jumping—Two, three, or four children jump at the same time. They can run in, jump a certain number of jumps, and run out, keeping hands joined. Starting as a small circle with hands joined, two, three, or four can run in, jump in a circle, and run out maintaining joined hands.

12. Jumping with a ball—A jumper can bounce a ball while jumping or play catch with a person on the outside of the rope while jumping.

13. Follow the leader—Several jumpers must duplicate the jumping actions of the first jumper, in turn. If someone misses, they must go to the end of the line.

14. Jumping with an individual rope inside a large rope—At first both ropes should be turned in the same direction. Later the jumper can try the opposite direction. Partners can try this, also.

15. Jumping with two long ropes—Simultaneously turning two long ropes requires skill and arm strength. A number of techniques may be employed:
   a. Double Dutch—The two ropes are turned alternately. The rope near the jumper is turned front door while the rope away from the jumper is turned back door.
   b. Double Irish—The two ropes are turned alternately. The rope near the jumper is turned back door while the rope away from the jumper is turned front door.
   c. Egg beater—The two long ropes are simultaneously turned at right angles by four turners.
   d. Two long ropes are turned while a jumper uses an individual rope.

DECK TENNIS

Deck Tennis is played by four children with a single deck tennis ring on a rectangular bounded area (Figure 20.2). The court is divided in half by a volleyball net hung at regulation volleyball height. The rules of this game are similar to those of volleyball. The server continues to serve as long as points are scored. The server must stand behind the right side of the base line and throw the rung underhand into the opposite half of the court, diagonally across from the server. The rung must be caught with only one hand and returned immediately to the opposite side of the court. A point is scored by the serving team if the receivers fail to return the ring or return the ring so that it falls outside the boundaries of the opposite side of the court or in the dead ground. A ring that falls into the court within the bounded area is considered good for the thrower. When the server makes an error, the receiver becomes the server and no points are scored.

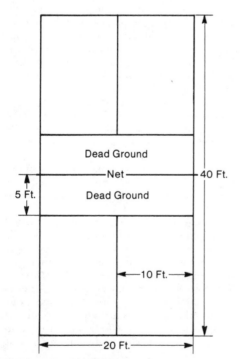

FIGURE 20.2 Deck tennis and volley tennis court diagrams.

This game can be played by two people using a singles court (half the width of the doubles court). If singles are played, diagonal serving is not employed.

O'LEARY

O'Leary is a ball game played by one person, or it may be played by a number of children who take turns when a player makes an error. Generally, the ball used is a solid rubber or playground ball 2 to 4 inches in diameter. To the tune of "Ten Little Indians," the child chants, "One-Two-Three O'Leary, Four-Five-Six O'Leary, Seven-Eight-Nine O'Leary, Ten O'Leary, Postman." While chanting, the child dribbles the ball in place with one hand, keeping time. Whenever the word "O'Leary" is said (four times), the child gives the ball a higher bounce and performs a stipulated task. When the word "Postman" is said, the child catches the ball. The following tasks are done in order:

1. Right leg swings outward over the ball.
2. Left leg swings outward over the ball.
3. Right leg swings inward over the ball.
4. Left leg swings inward over the ball.
5. With hands grasped and arms forming a circle, ball passes through the arms from below.
6. Same as 5, but ball passes through arms from above.
7. Ball passes through a circle formed by the forefingers and thumbs, from below.
8. Same as 7, but ball passes through hands from above.
9. Alternate 1 and 2.
10. Alternate 3 and 4.
11. Alternate 5 and 6.
12. Alternate 7 and 8.
13. Do 1, 2, 3, and 4 in order.
14. Do 5, 6, 7, and 8 in order.
15. End with a complete turn around.

SIDEWALK TENNIS

Sidewalk Tennis is played on a rectangular bounded area (Figure 20.3) that is divided by a 3-foot-high net. It is played with a tennis ball or other small rubber ball by two (singles) or four (doubles) players. When two

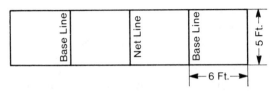

FIGURE 20.3 Sidewalk tennis court diagram.

play, the game starts when the server bounces the ball behind the baseline and hits the ball underhand into the opponent's court. After the ball has bounced, the opponent must return the ball over the net with an open palm. On the return the ball may be hit while in the air or on the first bounce. If the server fails to make a good serve or return, that side loses the serve. If the server steps over the base line when serving, the serve is lost. Causing a ball to land outside the bounded area is considered a fault. A ball landing on a boundary line is considered good. Hitting a ball with any part of the hand or body other than the palm is considered a fault. In doubles partners alternate on returns and service. All games are for fifteen points. If the score is tied at fourteen-all, one person (or one team) must make two consecutive points to win.

VOLLEY TENNIS

Volley Tennis is played with a volleyball on a 20-by-40-foot court resembling that used for Deck Tennis (see Figure 20.2). The only difference is that there is no dead space area in Volley Tennis as there is in Deck Tennis. The court is divided by a net 3 feet high.

Two teams, comprised of two to six players each, participate. The game combines features of both volleyball and tennis. The players on each team are usually positioned in two lines, front and back. Play starts with a serve from the right side of the back court line of the serving team. The same server continues to serve until that side has committed a fault, at which time the other team gets to serve. Only the serving team may score. A team rotates positions when it receives the serve.

To serve, the server must strike the ball after it has bounced once so that it goes over the net and into the opposite court, where it must bounce before it may be played. A serve which touches the net is considered a fault. At all other times a ball which touches the net and drops over is considered good. The ball may be played after the serve and on any other play by batting it with the hand after it bounces or by volleying it, as in volleyball. The receiving team may only touch the ball three times before sending it into the opposite side of the court. Players on the same team may volley or bounce the ball to each other three times before sending it over the net. Any ball that touches a line is counted as being inside the court which the line bounds.

In order to be considered good, a ball must go directly across the net (not bounce) and land in the opponent's court. If the ball touches any player before it touches the court's surface, it is considered good. Any ball that bounces twice before it is hit or twice between hits is a fault. A game is usually for fifteen points and a team must win by at least two points. Play is continued until this occurs.

CLASSROOM GAMES

There are certain unavoidable situations where physical education might need to be conducted within the confines of the classroom or general academic space rather than in the physical education space or playground. It is understandable that there will be certain events which will take the gymnasium or indoor playspace away from phys-

ical education, although teachers should see that such events are kept to an absolute minimum. Some schools are used for voting, and on voting days the gymnasium or indoor playspace is used all day for this purpose. On other occasions a school play or other such assembly activity might take precedence over the regular use of an indoor space for physical education. Normally, when such events occur, the physical educator or classroom teacher should plan to take the children outdoors for their physical education period. However, rain, wet grounds, or cold weather may preclude such plans. On days such as these, physical education should not simply be set aside but rather should be conducted as well as possible in the confines of the classroom.

If physical education is conducted by a specialist, that person will have to be very thoughtful in using the classroom so as not to disrupt the ongoing activities of the classroom teacher. If physical education is conducted by the classroom teacher, then he or she can plan for physical education in the confined space.

Much of what is possible in the classroom is determined by its physical arrangements. In schools where there are fairly permanent desk arrangements, the physical education activities chosen will be greatly constrained. In open classrooms the space is much more flexible, thereby allowing for a wider variety of classroom activities. The teacher should certainly take the nature of the physical space into account when choosing the activities for a classroom session of physical education.

The teacher must also be aware of the noise that is generated by a physical education period in a classroom. In a self-contained classroom with permanent walls, the noise level can be higher without unduly disturbing neighboring classes. However, in an open classroom facility high noise levels from one class may severely disrupt other classes in the same general area.

As in all physical education classes, the basic goal of the classroom period should be to maximize participation in some meaningful activity that is also fun for the children. The space and noise constraints will determine the degree to which the activity can be of a semiactive nature, using aisles or open spaces for movement. Teachers should not be afraid to use these infrequent periods for enjoyable, cognitive-oriented activities directly relating to physical education outcomes. A sport quiz, a competitive group ac-

tivity oriented toward rule recognition and definition, or other such "mental" activities are perfectly legitimate for these infrequent classroom periods.

The teacher might also want to utilize some semiactive or inactive games for the classroom period. The following are descriptions of some commonly utilized classroom games.

DO THIS, DO THAT

Equipment.   None

Formations.   In aisles next to desks with leader in front of room or in circle facing in with leader in center

Description.   When the leader says "Do this," each member of the group must imitate the leader's actions. When the leader says "Do that," any child imitating the action has a point scored against her. The leader may choose any movement that does not require changes in space. Leaders change often.

DUCK FLY

Equipment.   None

Formations.   In aisles next to desks with leader in front or in circle facing in with leader in center

Description.   The leader calls out the names of animals with the word *fly* after each ("Ducks fly!" "Birds fly!"). When the name indicates an animal that does fly, the children go through the motions of flying, using their arms. When the animal named does not fly, the children should remain still. Anyone who "flies" at the wrong time or does not "fly" when supposed to is "it" and becomes the leader.

I SAW

Equipment: None

Formations. Children seated at desks or seated in a circle; leader in front of room or center of circle

Description. The leader starts the game by saying, "On my way to school this morning I saw. . . ." The leader then shows what was said through nonverbal movements. The children try to guess what was said. The child who guesses correctly becomes the leader. If no one guesses, the leader gets to do another "I saw."

WHAT TO PLAY?

Equipment. None

Formations. In aisles next to desks with leader in front or in circle with leader in center

Description. Using the tune from "Mary Had a Little Lamb," the game is started with children singing "Mary, show us what to play, what to play, what to play, Mary show us what to play, show us what to play." The leader then says "Play this" and leads the group in a pantomime action, either an exercise the children know or a nonverbal behavior familiar to the children. This continues until a signal is given to stop and then another leader begins the game anew.

HUCKLEBERRY BEANSTALK

Equipment. Small objects such as pencils, erasers, and so on

Formations. Children in seats

Description. A leader is chosen. An object is chosen and shown to all the children. The children then put their heads down and close their eyes while the leader hides the object. Once the object is hidden, the leader signals for the children to begin to hunt for the object. Any child that sees the object returns to his or her seat and calls "Huckleberry beanstalk." The object should not be hidden higher than eye level or inside cabinets. The child who first sees the object can lead for the next try.

RABBIT AND THE FOX

Equipment. Two sponge balls (or beanbags), one red

Formations. Small circles, six to eight children to a circle, seated

Description. The "rabbit" is the red sponge ball and can only be handed to the right. The "fox" is the other sponge ball and can be passed either to the right or to the left. The game begins with a child passing the rabbit to the right. Another child starts the fox by passing it to the left or right. The object of the game is to have one child holding both the rabbit and the fox. The balls can be passed only to a child next to the child with the ball. When the fox catches the rabbit, a new game begins. The red sponge ball is used for the rabbit so that the children can remember that "red is passed to the right."

SPIN THE PLATTER

Equipment. Tin pie plates

Formations. Small circles, six to eight children in a circle, standing or sitting

Description. Each child has a number. A leader spins a tin pie plate on the floor in the center of the circle. While spinning the plate, the leader also calls a number. The child whose number is called tries to reach the plate and catch it before it stops spinning. If the child whose number has been called is successful, that child starts the game again. The size of the circle can be changed to accommodate the agility of the children.

NUMBERS

Equipment. None

Formations. Children in seats, seats arranged symmetrically

Description. Each seat has a number which is written on a piece of paper and placed on top of the desk/seat. The game begins by having a leader call a number. The player who occupies the seat corresponding to that number responds immediately with another number. Failure to respond immediately (the teacher must judge the appropriate time lapse) results in a miss. When a miss occurs, the player who missed moves to the last numbered seat with every other player between the number of the miss and the last seat moving up one place. The object of the game is to get to the number-one seat.

CHANGE SEATS

Equipment. Chairs

Formations. Chairs arranged in rows

Description. A leader is chosen (or the teacher can give the commands). The leader has four commands: change right, change left, change front, and change back. Only one command is called at a time. When a command is called, the children must shift in the proper direction. Children in the front rows stand in front one full step when the command "Change front" is given. Children in the back row stand one full step in back when the command "Change back" is given. Likewise, children in the side rows will stand when commands for changing right or left are given. Scoring can be done by rewarding children who stand or sit at attention most quickly, or it can be done by giving a point to the child or children who do it most slowly. Highest or lowest point total wins. Quickness and quietness of change is the object.

RINGMASTER

Equipment. None

Formations. Preferably in a circle facing center with leader in center

Description. The leader is the "ringmaster," who calls out the name of an animal and walks about the circle cracking a pretend whip. The children imitate the animals. The ringmaster changes periodically. If there is sufficient room, the ringmaster may call out "All join the parade," in which case children move around the circle imitating any animal they wish.

ANIMAL TRAP

Equipment. None

Formations. Half the class in a circle

Descriptions. Half the class is in a circle. The other half stands outside the circle. They decide what kind of animal they want to be. When the teacher gives a start signal, the animals run in and out of the circle. When the teacher gives the trap signal (clapping hands), the children in the circle join their hands and form the trap. All children caught inside the circle (inside the trap) are "caught" and have to join the circle. After all the animals have been caught, the children change positions, choose a new animal, and start the game again.

DUCK, DUCK, GOOSE

Equipment. None

Formations. Single circle with children facing in and one child standing outside

Description. The child outside the circle is "it." That child moves around the circle (different movements can be required). The "it" child touches one child and says "duck," touches a second child and says "duck," and touches a third child while saying "goose." The goose chases the "it" child around the circle. The "it" child tries to get back to the goose's place before being touched. If the goose tags the "it" child, the goose becomes "it" and starts the game again.

CIRCLE SPOT

Equipment. Beanbags or similar equipment

Formations. Small circles with eight to ten children per circle and at least 3 to 4 feet between each child

Description. One child is in the center of each circle and is "it." The other children each have a beanbag in front of them. On a signal the children move around the circle (use different movements each time). On a second signal all the children (including the "it" child) try to place one foot on a beanbag. The child who does not have a foot on a beanbag becomes "it" and the game starts again.

BEANBAG STACK

Equipment. One beanbag for each child

Formations. Seated in rows with five to seven children per row

Description. The child in the front of each row has the beanbags for all children in the row behind him. On a beginning signal the front child takes a beanbag and passes it to the child behind, who passes it to the last child, who lays it on the floor. Each succeeding beanbag that is passed back must be stacked in the pile so that only the first beanbag is touching the floor. The first row to have their beanbags stacked correctly is the winner.

HENS AND CHICKENS

Equipment. None

Formations. Children seated at desks or tables

Description. One child is designated as "hen" and momentarily leaves the room. The teacher then designates several other children as "chickens." All children then place their heads on desks, hiding their faces in their hands. The hen comes in and moves about saying "Cluck, cluck." With heads still down, the chickens answer with "Peep, peep." The hen tries to identify the chickens, tapping children she believes to be a chicken on the shoulder. If the designation is correct, the children must sit up straight. If incorrect, the children continue to hide their heads.

CRAMBO

Equipment. None

Formations. Children seated at desks or tables

Description. A child is designated as leader. The leader starts the game by saying, "I'm thinking of something that rhymes with . . . ." The child then names something familiar in school, either inside or outside the room. The other children respond by asking questions: "Is it . . . ?", suggesting an object that rhymes with the word used by the leader. The child who guesses correctly becomes the leader and the game starts again.

BALLOON VOLLEYBALL

Equipment. Balloon or lightweight ball; rope or string

Formation. Children can stand or sit on either side of the rope that is strung across the room, making two teams

Description. Modified volleyball rules can be used with serving, hits on each side, and similar scoring. Children can sit on floor, sit on chairs, or stand, if space permits. The height of the string depends on whether children sit or stand.

21

major sports

BASKETBALL

Source

Basketball is an American sport, invented in 1892 by Dr. James Naismith in Springfield, Massachusetts. Basketball was intended to be a skillful and vigorous indoor sport for those whose activity was restricted during winter months. It has become a popular worldwide sport and is played by both men and women at all levels.

Main Features

Basketball requires a wide range of skills, including dribbling, passing, catching, dodging, guarding, jumping, blocking, and different styles of shooting. It also requires a blend of individual and team performance for success. Played with skill it can be a vigorous game requiring both strength and endurance. It is a low-cost activity requiring little equipment other than a backboard and hoop. It can be practiced alone or with any number up to the official, five-player teams of the parent game. It has endless variations suitable for recreation through the highest levels of amateur and professional competi-

tion. Backyard baskets dot the American landscape and in recent years basketball has become particularly popular in large cities and suburbs.

Scoring

Points are scored by putting the ball through the hoop with any one of a variety of shots. Scores from the field count for two points. Scores made on free throws count for one point. Free throws are awarded as a consequence of certain kinds of fouls committed during play. The game is usually divided into four quarters of equal length, although college basketball is played in two halves. The team that is ahead at the end of play is the winner. A tied contest is resolved in a short overtime period.

Basketball is learned in many places other than school physical education programs. Therefore, children will start with widely differing abilities. Those differences may tend to grow as children who show interest and aptitude for the game take advantage of learning and practice opportunities outside of school.

Teaching Considerations

Basketball for elementary-school children should be taught and played with modified equipment. Baskets should be low in height to begin with and made progressively higher as student abilities increase. Playground balls can be used in early stages, and junior-sized balls should be used with older, more skilled children. Regulation baskets and balls tend to be counterproductive because they encourage inappropriate skill habits due to lack of strength. A regulation game requires five players on a side, although game variations are so flexible that most children can be kept active at all times. The skills of basketball are complex and require a great deal of practice. Therefore, drill-games are very useful and should form a large part of the basketball unit.

Some means of identifying team members is necessary. This can be best accomplished through pinnies, reversible gym shirts, colored bands, or some other identifying characteristic. Providing a large number of balls is useful, since this allows for an optimal level of participation. Playground balls, volleyballs, and rubber balls can often be substituted for junior-sized basketballs and used to extend the degree of participation.

Safety

Basketball is not normally a hazardous game except for minor injuries such as sprained ankles. Elementary-school gyms often have basketball court lines painted on the floor. These lines are often close to walls. Precautions must be taken to see that children are not placed in situations which bring them close to walls in speed situations. Boundary lines should not be used as finish lines for drills unless there is substantial distance between boundary line and wall. Children should have the necessary skills to take part in competitive games. Therefore, games should always be fitted to current skill levels of children.

Important Skills

Passing. Often the ball is advanced downcourt by passing. Offensive play involves passing among teammates to produce a high percentage shot. Passers should be taught to step toward the person to whom they are passing. The ball should be gripped firmly, with main pressure exerted by the fingers. Passers have to be taught how to lead a teammate so that the ball and the teammate arrive at a position at the right moment. Most passing is accomplished with a vigorous extension of the arms and wrist pronation.

Chest pass. Ball is held in fingers at chest level with arms flexed and elbows in close to body, usually with one foot ahead of the other in a stride position. As the pass is initiated, the legs are bent and, in extending, provide much of the power for the pass. The weight should move forward to the front foot as the pass is made.

Bounce pass. The bounce pass is usually done with a technique similar to the chest pass, but it can also be used with a one-hand pass or a two-hand overhand pass. The technique for release is similar to the chest pass and the ball should be aimed so that it bounces up to waist level of the receiver. The point at which the ball should bounce on the floor changes, depending on the total distance of the pass. Children will quickly learn the proper bouncing spot through experimentation. The bounce pass is best used for short passing situations.

Two-hand overhead pass. The ball is held in two hands with the hands to the side

FIGURE 21.1 Chest pass

of the ball rather than in back of the ball. A stride position of the feet allows for forward motion to aid in imparting force. Extension of the elbows and pronation of the wrists provide the primary action. This pass is useful for long passes and is often used to throw the ball over the head of a defender to a teammate closer to the basket.

Baseball pass. The ball is thrown in a manner similar to a baseball, with shoulder and hip rotation playing a larger role than in other passes. A stride position is used and the weight shift to the forward foot aids in imparting force. This pass should not be attempted unless the player's hand is sufficiently large to control the ball being used.

Two-hand side pass. This pass is very similar to the two-hand overhand pass, but it is done anywhere between shoulder and waist height. It is a good pass for passing the ball around a defender to a teammate in situations where the chest pass is not feasible.

Dribbling. Dribbling refers to a repeated, one-hand bouncing of the ball. It is a fundamental skill used to advance the ball downcourt, to maneuver for better offensive position, or to get out of a difficult situation. Dribbling should be done with the head up and eyes focused on the floor ahead of the player rather than on the ball. The ball should be dribbled low when defensive pressure is evident and higher (seldom higher than waist level) when advancing the ball unguarded. The dribble is done with the fingers rather than the hand and with a flexible, supple wrist movement. The elbow flexes and extends to provide force. Dribblers should hold their bodies low, but this should be accomplished by bending at the knees rather than at the waist.

Off-hand dribble. Dribbling with the nonpreferred hand is essential and difficult for children to master. The same technique is used as with the preferred had.

Cross-over dribble. It is important that children learn how to change from a preferred hand dribble to a nonpreferred hand dribble, and vice versa. This is accomplished with a cross-over dribble, where the ball is pushed from one side of the body to the other. This is done in front of the body and as low as possible so that the ball is out of contact with one of the hands only momentarily.

Change-of-direction dribble. This is used when the player wants to change the direction of the advance and maintain the dribble at the same time, as in cutting to the basket from the side of the court. The ball is pushed out ahead of the dribbler and in the direction of the body movement.

Shooting. Shooting basketballs may be one of the most popular recreational pursuits in America. Although other skills are fundamentally important to success in basketball, points are scored by good shooting. Shooters should be encouraged to maintain good balance, to concentrate on a target, to watch the target constantly, to gather for the shot with the entire body from the knees through to the fingers, and to develop a comfortable, relaxed style. The ball should be held in the fingers rather than in the palm of the hand. The elbow on the shooting hand(s) should be kept close to the body. Follow-through is important.

Two-hand push shot. This shot is done with a technique similar to the chest pass except that the ball is aimed higher. Force for the shot is from the knees on up through the release from the fingertips. The hands are not placed directly behind the ball but rather

FIGURE 21.2 Dribbling

FIGURE 21.3 One hand set shot

ket. A two-handed underhand lay-up shot is sometimes taught. The lay-up is taken at the culmination of a driving movement, either with the dribble or after receiving a pass while breaking toward the basket. Players should try to convert their momentum from forward to upward, jumping off the foot opposite to the hand with which the shot will be taken. The lay-up can be shot like the one-hand push shot, with the shooting hand behind the ball, or it can be shot with the shooting hand underneath the ball.

halfway to the side. The contribution of each hand should be equal.

One-hand push shot. This is done from a stride position with the weight shifted forward as the shot is taken. The shooting hand is behind the ball, with the support hand on the side of the ball. The support hand remains in contact with the ball until just prior to the release, which should be accomplished by the ball rolling off the fingertips.

Lay-up shot. A lay-up shot is any shot taken very close to the basket at the end of a drive toward the basket. It is the highest percentage shot in the game. The lay-up is usually a one-handed shot, taken with the right hand if on the right side of the basket and the left hand if taken on the left side of the bas-

Jump shot. The jump shot is a combination of a jump taken from a two foot take-off and a one-hand shot delivered while at the height of the jump. The jump should be straight up rather than forward, sideward, or backward. The ball is held higher than for the one-hand push shot, but the mechanics of delivery are similar. This is the most difficult shot for children to learn.

Hook shot. The hook shot is taken from a pivot position close to the basket, with the player's back to the basket. The arms are outstretched, with the shooting hand underneath and behind the ball and the nonshooting hand providing guidance and support until just prior to release. The shot is taken from a one foot take-off, with the foot opposite to the shooting hand providing the take-off. The shooting arm is straight and the power from the shot comes more from total body movement and wrist action.

FIGURE 21.4 Lay up

FIGURE 21.5 Hook shot

FIGURE 21.6 Defensive stance

Free-throw shot. The free throw is taken from the free-throw line as a result of a foul and can be any shot, although children should be encouraged to use the one-hand push shot. Balance, rhythm, and concentration are quite important in good free-throw shooting. A proper follow-through should be emphasized.

Rebounding. Rebounding refers to retrieving balls after opponent's shoot unsuccessfully. Rebounding is first a matter of position—in between your opponent and the basket. Second, the rebounder should take a spread-out position so as to prevent the opponent from moving closer to the basket. Third, the rebounder should jump to retrieve the ball and secure it in both hands so that opponents cannot steal it.

Screening. Screening is a fundamental offensive skill in basketball and refers to the placement of a player's body in such a manner as to prevent a defensive opponent from moving in a certain direction. The screener should take a spread position and be sure not to initiate contact with the defender (this would result in blocking and be an offensive foul). The best screens are those set on the side of the defensive player, exactly in the direction the defensive player wants to move.

Pivoting. Pivoting refers to changing the direction of your movement by rotating around a fixed point, which is the stationary placement of one foot. It is used often by players who do not have the ball and is a crucial skill for maneuvering with the ball. Players should learn to pivot on each foot. The pivot foot must always be in contact with the floor and must not move (sliding the pivot foot is one of the most common offensive errors—a form of traveling).

Stopping. Basketball is a game played often at near or full speed and also a game in which possession of the ball often changes rapidly, requiring players to move quickly in the opposite direction. Thus, stopping and changing directions is an important skill. Stopping quickly requires that the center of gravity be lowered as much as possible, with

FIGURE 21.7 Pivoting

the feet providing the main stopping force. The stride stop, in which one foot is in front of the other with the weight over the back foot and the center of gravity low, is probably the best stopping movement.

Basketball Drill-Games:
Give it a name, make it a game

Children need to practice skills often to improve. This is usually best accomplished by isolating a skill and practicing it in a controlled, repetitive fashion—what is known in sports training as a drill. However, children like to play games, and drills can easily be made into games by giving the drill a name and providing the main features of a game (see pages 294–97).

PASSING

Against a wall to hit a target
Off a target on the floor and then to a partner
Against a wall for speed (number of passes per unit of time)
In a star formation with players numbered so that as balls go from player 1 to 2 to 3 to 4 to 5, it completes a star
While moving with a partner up and down the court
To other moving players
Working in threes, passing over and around an opponent

DRIBBLING

As an entire group, or signal, left, right, back, etc.
Up and down the court in a controlled dribble (no timing)
Up and down court for speed, stopping at designated lines
Around the perimeter of the court, changing direction at each corner
All of the above with the nonpreferred hand
With a partner, as a keep-away game in a small space
In and out of an obstacle course

SHOOTING

Lay up shooting
Follow the leader, with small groups
Semicircle at each basket, acting as a team
Free-throw shooting
Shooting from designated spots

COMBINATIONS

Dribbling and passing for accuracy and no violations
Passing and shooting, one player cutting for the basket
Dribbling and shooting, changing pathways and shots taken at end of dribble
Dribbling around an obstacle and cutting for the basket for a shot
Three player weave with lay-up shot at end
Passing to a pivot player with cuts by that player, hand-offs and shots

Common Performance Errors

ERRORS	TEACHING CUES/STRATEGIES
PASSING	
Keeping weight on heels	Step toward your target
Lack of arm extension	Keep your elbows in
Improper holding of ball	Demonstrate proper technique
Lack of force	Use your body/snap your wrist/follow through
Lack of control	Use smaller ball
Lack of accuracy	Keep your eye on your target/step toward target/follow through
DRIBBLING	
Slapping at ball	Low, slow dribble/control with your fingers
Watching ball	Keep your head up/use a target on wall for students to look at
Bouncing rather than dribbling	Emphasize low dribble

(continued)

ERRORS	TEACHING CUES/STRATEGIES
DRIBBLING	
Bending at waist to control dribble	Demonstrate bending at knees
Too much arm, not enough wrist	Emphasize low, controlled dribble
Going too fast	Provide a control game
Ball hitting feet	Dribble off to one side of body
SHOOTING	
Elbow held out	Keep elbow close to body
Lack of force	Bend at knees/use entire body/emphasize arm follow-through and wrist snap
Lack of accuracy	Paint/tape target on backboard
Lack of force	Lower basket/use smaller ball
Lack of accuracy	Use wider baskets/smaller balls
Improper holding	Demonstrate for and check all students
Turning head away as shot is made	Usually a force problem/use smaller ball
Uneven contribution of hands on two-hand shot	Lower basket so that less force is required until skill is acquired
SCREENING	
Screen too close	Keep 12″ distance from person being screened
Screen in wrong direction	Walk through proper technique
Screener moves	Hold screen until contact is made
Screener does not use entire body	Screen at right angles to opponent (show)
REBOUNDING	
Failure to get good position	Make a game of positioning/demonstrate
Going after ball too soon	Hold position until ball hits ground

BASKETBALL GAMES/ACTIVITIES

BASKETBALL (PARENT GAME)

Equipment. Balls, baskets, court markings, team identification

Formations. Basketball court and markings with five players on a side, usually designated as two guards, two forwards, and one center

Description. Game is started with a jump ball between centers at center court. Ball may be advanced with dribble or by passing. Offensive players try to move ball into advantageous scoring position where a goal may be attempted and, if made, this counts for two points. Defensive players try to prevent offense from reaching advantageous position and also try to intercept passes or steal ball from dribbler. Fouls made against a shooter result in a free throw, which, if made, counts for one point. All other fouls result in a pass-in from out of bounds for the offended team at a spot near to where the foul was committed. Simultaneous possession by opposing players results in a "held" ball and forces a jump ball by the two players at the nearest free-throw line or center circle. Games are played in equal quarters of halves. Substitutions can be made at any time out.

Variations. (a) Require that the teacher, standing in the center circle, handle the ball each time a team advances the ball downcourt (prevents "hogging" of the ball by better players); (b) require that all members of a team be across half-court before the ball goes across half-court (prevents fast breaks and requires deliberate offensive play); (c) play half-court with ball taken back across a restraining line after a defensive rebound or taken out of bounds from half-court after a basket (allows more children to be active).

Skills. All basketball skills

Strategies. Offensive and defensive formations, zone and person-person defenses, and so on

Major rules. Traveling violations, double dribble, blocking, overguarding, kicking the ball, stepping out of bounds while in possession of the ball, 10-second rule for getting ball across half-court, stepping on free-throw line while shooting free throws, stepping into lane while rebounding on free throws

Safety considerations. Normal precautions

TALLY BALL

Equipment. Balls, court markings, team identification

Formations. Half-court or full court, players spread out, attempting to maintain floor balance while moving toward ball for passes. Teams of five to seven players works best. Using half-court markings with teams of seven, twenty-eight children can be active.

Description. Play is started with one team passing from out of bounds to a teammate in bounds. The goal is to complete six consecutive passes while the opponents try to intercept. One point is earned for each successful pass. After six successful passes, a player from that team attempts a shot from the free-throw line, which, if successful, counts for two points. The ball is then turned over to the other team, which begins play

again with a pass from out of bounds. Winner judged by a set number of points or by highest total within a specified time period.

Variations. (a) Reduce number of passes before shot is taken; (b) require different number of players to touch ball; (c) let each team member attempt a shot after successful pass criterion is met.

Skills. Passing, catching, eluding opponents, pivoting, shooting.

Strategies. Passing and cutting, maintaining floor balance, quick back and forth passing when not guarded.

Major rules. Traveling violations, holding ball more than 5 seconds, defensive fouls, batting ball from opponent's hand, stepping out of bounds; all violations result in free pass in from out of bounds for other team.

Safety considerations. Normal precautions

AROUND THE WORLD OR BASKETBALL GOLF

Equipment. Balls, basketball goals, court markings.

Formations. Determined by floor markings.

FIGURE 21.8   Around the world

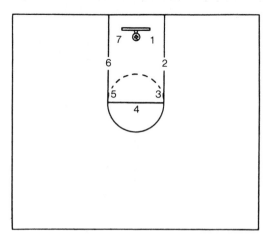

Description. Marks are made at various distances and angles from the baskets in the playspace. Each mark has a number. The numbers can be used in two ways. In "Around the World" the number can be consecutive, giving children direction as to which shot to attempt next. The marks can be progressively more difficult or can be of varied difficulty. Students shoot at each mark until a basket is made. They then proceed to the next mark. The winner is the student who goes "around the world" in the fewest number of shots or most quickly. Marks can also be laid out as a "nine-hole golf course" with "par" for each mark related to the difficulty of the shot. Students keep their own scores for each nine holes they play. Winner is student with lowest score for nine holes.

TWENTY-ONE

Equipment. Balls, baskets, court markings

Formations. Depends on number of baskets available, best done with groups of four to eight per basket

Description. Students can score points in two ways. A "long" shot scores two points. A "short" shot scores one point. A line or semicircle is drawn to designate the point beyond which long shots must be taken. The line should be made shorter or longer depending on skills of students. Students start by shooting long shots. When they have a successful shot, it scores two points and earns students the right to take a short shot, which scores one point. After the short shot the student again moves behind the long-shot line. First student to reach twenty-one points wins. Each student should have a ball.

Variations. (a) Allow a short shot following each long shot attempt; (b) require that the short shot be taken from where the ball is rebounded, thus encouraging students to rebound as close to the basket as possible; (c) have groups at each basket work as teams, keeping a team score and competing with groups at other baskets.

Skills. Shooting, following shots, rebounding

Strategies. Learning easiest angles to shoot, following shots quickly, trying to get shortest "short" shots

Major rules. Not interfering with other shooters

Safety considerations. Normal precautions; special care with congested area underneath baskets

FIGURE 21.9 Twenty-one

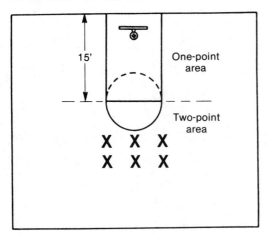

END BALL

Equipment. Balls, baskets, court markings

Formations. Floor is divided into four zones. Forwards play in end zones near baskets. Guards play in center zones, divided by center line. Each team has an equal number of guards and forwards.

Description. Play begins with ball given to guard on one team. Guards try to pass over the heads of opponent guards to teammate forwards in end zone. If pass is successful and ball is caught by a teammate forward, two points are earned by that team. Ball is then given to a guard on the opposing team. Forwards and guards rotate periodically.

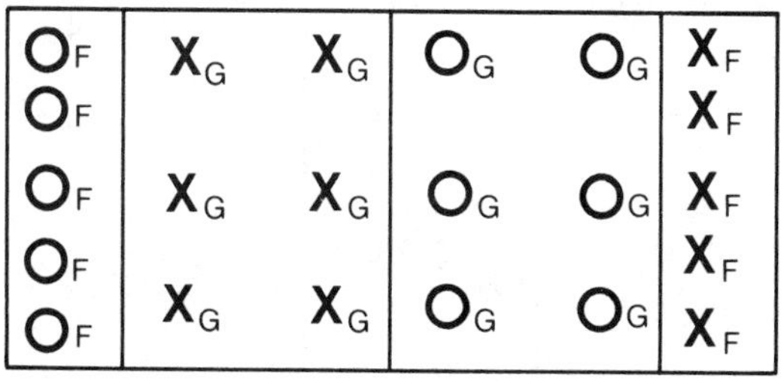

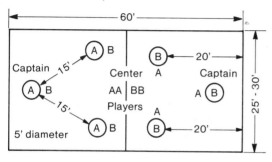

FIGURE 21.10 End ball

Winner determined by number of points reached or highest total after a time period.

Variations. Forwards, after a successful catch, can attempt a shot from where they catch the ball in the end zone. If shot is successful, two more points are earned.

Skills. Passing, catching, shooting, intercepting.

Strategies. Passing among guards to avoid shifting defense of opposing guards; passing as close to basket as possible if shot is to be attempted.

Major rules. Traveling violations, out of bounds, holding ball more than 5 seconds. All penalties result in ball being turned over to opponent guard.

Safety considerations. Normal precautions

CAPTAIN BALL

Equipment. Balls, court markings, team identification.

FIGURE 21.11 Captain ball

Formations. Circle areas where forwards may play. Forwards must have one foot in circle at all times. Forward closest to end line is the "captain." Center players may move anywhere. For each forward there is an opposing guard who stands outside the circle of the student being guarded.

Description. Play begins with a jump ball between two center players. Center players may pass or dribble ball. Their goal is to get the ball to a forward. The goal of the forwards is to pass the ball to their captain. If done successfully, a point is scored. Players should rotate positions periodically.

Skills. Passing, dribbling, catching, pivoting, dodging, guarding

Strategies. Using short passes to advance ball.

Major rules. Traveling violations, moving foot outside circle. Ball is given to an opponent guard.

Safety considerations. Normal precautions

SIX-COURT BASKETBALL— NINE-COURT BASKETBALL

Equipment. Balls, baskets, court markings, team identification

Formations. The basketball court is divided into six or nine rectangular spaces as shown. Players are assigned to spaces, either as guards, forwards, or centers, depending on number of spaces used.

Description. Forwards do all shooting. Guards play defense and then advance ball upcourt to either centers or forwards. Two points for each goal made by forwards. Forwards shoot free throws after fouls are committed. One point for each successful free throw. Players must stay within assigned spaces. They can dribble within those spaces or pass to a teammate in that space or another space. Players rotate periodically.

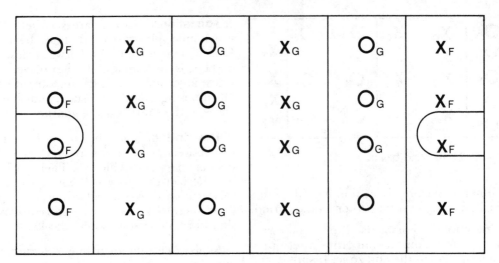

FIGURE 21.12 Six-court basketball

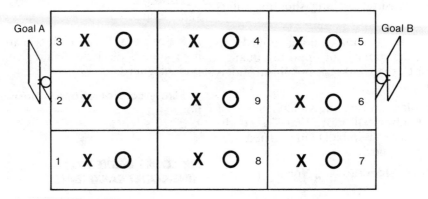

FIGURE 21.13 Nine-court basketball

Skills. All basketball skills

Strategies. Teaches spacing, defensive position, team passing, and ball movement

Major rules. Regular rules plus holding ball within a rectangle for more than 5 seconds

Safety considerations. Normal precautions

FOOTBALL

Source

Football is one of a family of games that are popular worldwide. Its first cousins are rugby and Australian-rules football. Football-type games have origins in early cultures and have been widely practiced in primitive cultures. The first American collegiate game was played in 1869 between Princeton and Rutgers. Football grew rapidly and became a popular collegiate and professional sport early in this century. It is now a very popular sport in interscholastic athletics and has been developed even more recently in age-group programs. There is a great deal of controversy about "pee-wee" football programs, as well there should be. The activity outlined here presents the basic skills of football as a noncontact sport. There is no reason why contact should be part of a football skills unit for elementary-school children.

Main Features

Football is primarily a game of strength, agility, throwing, catching, and courage. In American football the contact aspects of the game have predominated for many years, yet there is still great appreciation for the fine skills and agility shown by players in the skilled positions such as quarterback, receiver, and running back. Touch football, and its many variations, is characterized more by agility, speed, throwing, and catching. Strength and great physical courage are much less important. Interestingly, kicking skills are of relatively minor importance in touch football. Touch football allows a number of children to be active and also to be involved in running, dodging, throwing, and catching. The odd shape of the football makes the throwing and catching skills much more difficult to acquire than would be the case with a round ball.

Football can become a game of elegant strategy. This is one of its most attractive features. Older children love to make up plays and to try to make them work. If they have acquired the basic skills of the game, they can spend hours playing it both in school (perhaps at recess) and in their recreational time.

Scoring

The basic way to score points in touch football is by making a touchdown, which counts for six points. A safety counts for two points. A safety is awarded if the offensive team member with the ball is touched behind his or her own goal line. An extra point counts for one point. An extra point is attempted after each touchdown. The ball is placed 3 yards from the goal line and the team scoring the touchdown has one play to try to make it across the goal line for the extra point. The team with the most points at the end of the allotted time (the game time is flexible—8-minute quarters are suggested for "official" elementary-school touch football games) is the winner.

Teaching Considerations

Teaching the throwing and catching aspects of football requires more time than that needed for sports which involve throwing and catching round balls. Junior-sized footballs should always be used. A regulation-sized football is much too large for elementary-school children to throw properly. Use of regulation-sized balls will tend to promote bad throwing habits. Skills such as centering ball exchanges and punting should also be taught. Blocking and tackling skills should specifically be disallowed as part of elementary-school physical education football programs. Since most children will have seen football played, their expectations will be that it involves blocking and tackling. Thus, it is not enough simply to not mention it. These techniques have to be prohibited in an explicit manner by the teacher.

Team identification will be needed; once a play begins, players are scattered throughout the playing area. Flag football is preferable to touch football. One reason is that flag-type games tend to incur less contact. "Touching" in touch football often results in children getting knocked down. A second reason in support of flag-type games is that there is no argument as to when a player is stopped. If the defender gets the flag from the body of the child with the ball, play is stopped. With one-hand- and two-hand-touch games, many arguments tend to occur. A third factor is that flag-type games involve flags suspended from the waist. This lessens the chances of contact in the head region. Touch-type games, no matter how well the teacher instructs about touching below the waist, too often involve contact above the waist.

Positions should be rotated and all children should have a chance to play the main skill positions. Skilled children should not be allowed to dominate. Lesser-skilled children should have an equal chance to throw the ball, run with the ball, or be a target for a pass. Much time should be spent on team play, patterns of offensive play, and defensive coverage. Once children learn the essence of team play, the game becomes much more intriguing over a longer period of time.

Safety

Flag football, as mentioned above, is a safer game than touch football. It also tends to promote agility over strength and tends to be more appropriate for elementary-school programs. Flags should be suspended at the waist level so as to avoid any contact around the head region. Blocking and tackling should be disallowed and penalties should be invoked for violations of those rules. The ball should be slightly underinflated until children have developed skills in catching. The teacher must always be alert for rough play and prohibit it when it occurs.

Important Skills

The primary individual skills in football are throwing, catching, and dodging. Centering, exchanging, and kicking are also in-cluded. Offensive play-making represents the largest set of group skills, while defensive coverage and field position are also important.

Passing. Throwing a football is similar to throwing overhand in softball in that the body mechanics are alike. However, in football there is the added dimension of throwing the ball so that it spirals (in addition to ensuring accuracy, distance, and velocity). The fingers should be spread and placed on the laces between the middle of the ball and one end. The thumb is underneath. The ball is held toward the end of the fingers rather than back in the palm. The passer should step toward the target and transfer weight as in all overhand throws. The passer should first learn how to throw a spiral, then throw for accuracy, and only after those skills are mastered, throw for distance and velocity.

Receiving. Catching a football is sufficiently similar to catching in other sports that emphasis on giving with the ball as it is caught and watching the ball until it is caught should transfer from previous learning. One difference is that in most other sports where catching is used, the player is facing the ball and often moves toward it. In football the receiver is often moving in the same direction as the pass. In this case balls above the waist should be caught with the little fingers

FIGURE 21.14 Passing

FIGURE 21.15 Receiving a pass

together. However, when the receiver is facing the passer, balls above the waist can be caught with thumbs together.

Lateral passing. A lateral pass is any throw sideward or backward among offensive players (rules allow for only one forward pass per play). A lateral pass can be made overhand, but most often it is done with a sidearm pitch motion. It can be done with one hand, but is more consistent and accurate when done with two hands.

Centering. A centering pass is used to initiate each play. It is made in a backward direction with two hands between the legs of the person playing the center position. The feet are spread outside shoulder width and the knees slightly flexed with the player bent at the waist. Both hands are on the ball. The dominant hand is placed as in passing. The nondominant hand is placed on the opposite side of the ball. The ball is passed back between the legs with a vigorous arm movement and wrist snap.

Exchanging. An exchange between two offensive players must be done so that the ball moves in a sideward or backward direction. This can be done with a lateral pass, as described above, or with a hand-off. In handing off, the ball should be held at one end in both hands. The hand-off should be made into the midsection of the player receiving it. The player receiving the hand-off should wrap both arms and hands around it so that it is received securely.

Carrying the ball. Runners should tuck the ball away when carrying it so that it fits

FIGURE 21.17 Carrying the ball

snugly into the inside part of the elbow and the outside part of the chest. The ball should never be carried in the hands alone.

Stance. Players on the line of scrimmage should start in a three-point stance. The feet are spread outside shoulder width. The body rests on the tripod made with the feet and one hand which is placed on the ground in front of the body. The body is bent at the waist and the knees are flexed so that the head is up and the field of play in sight.

Punting. Kicking in football is similar to the kick used by the goalie in soccer. The ball should be held so that the dominant hand is under the center part of the ball and the nondominant hand is supporting it on the opposite side of the ball. A three-step approach is used, starting with the nonkicking foot (left, right, left for right-handers). The nonkicking foot is planted firmly on the last step and the ball is dropped so that it contacts the kicking foot in front of the body approximately 1 foot off the ground. The kicking leg should be extended at contact with the toe pointed. Eventually children should try to learn to kick a spiral. This is accomplished by the proper dropping of the ball rather than through a different kicking motion. The spiral results when the ball is struck slightly to the inside of the long axis. The ball contacts the foot on the outside part of the instep.

FIGURE 21.16 Three point stance

FIGURE 21.18 Punting

Group skills. Offensive group skills mostly involve learning and executing plays so that players move in predetermined routes and carry out predetermined assignments. Plays are either running plays, passing plays, or plays in which either can be done. In more advanced play a primary goal is to move in such a way that the defense does not know what kind of play is being used. Defensive play is usually a matter of learning specialized roles and maintaining good field coverage. Players can defend either a certain zone or a certain offensive player. Defensive players on the line of scrimmage can rush across to try to bother the passer.

Common Performance Errors

ERRORS	TEACHING CUES/STRATEGIES
PASSING	
Holding ball in center	Grip it between the middle and the end
Failure to spiral ball	Throw it more easily/less distance
Throwing sidearm	Drop opposite shoulder
Not enough force	Rotate upper body/step into throw
Throwing too high	Release ball a little later
Lack of accuracy	Eye on target/step toward target
RECEIVING	
Turning head away	Use softer ball/shorter throws
Bouncing off hands	Give with the ball
Arms too stiff	Bend at elbows/catch it with your whole upper body
Catching out to the side	Get in position to use your body
LATERAL PASSING	
Using only one hand	Toss it with both hands
Lack of accuracy	Shorter passes/eye on target
CENTERING	
Using only one hand	Make sure both hands are used
Passes too high	Move your hands back, not up

Fumbles/bouncing off body	Watch your target/wrap arms around ball
Catching in hands	Receive the ball in your body

PUNTING

Improper drop	Shorten and slow steps/try just for right contact
Kicking too high	Drop ball sooner/point toe
Kicking too low	Drop ball a little later/follow through
No spiral	Angle ball across instep

Football Drill-Games:
Give it a name, make it a game

Passing, catching, and dodging skills can be practiced in drill-games with small groups of children. It is important to have a sufficient number of balls so that drill-game groups can be fairly small. Remember, the purpose of a drill-game is to isolate certain fundamental skills and allow for a large quantity of specific practice. Football skills could be nicely arranged in a "football olympics" format (competitions in passing, kicking, catching, obstacle course running, and so on) and also lend themselves well to station teaching approaches where a different drill-game is going on at each station.

PASSING

For accuracy at a target (suspended tire or hoop)
With a partner—collective scoring

For distance
Over a course with golf-type scoring

RECEIVING

With a partner—collective scoring
Kicks and passes

CENTERING

For accuracy to a target

RUNNING

In and out of a cone course

COMBINATIONS

Catching a pass and running
Kicking, returning a punt, dodging a course
Passing to a receiver with defenders present
Running up and down with a partner lateraling the ball

FOOTBALL GAMES/ACTIVITIES

FLAG FOOTBALL (Parent game)

Equipment. Balls, team identification, flags, field markings

Formations. The field is 30 × 60 yards with lines marked each 20 yards and an end zone line 10 yards behind the goal line. Teams may have six to ten players with two smaller games preferable to one large game. A certain number of offensive players are linemen and must line up on the scrimmage line. Defenders can play anywhere.

Description. The game begins with one team kicking off (with a punt) from their own goal line. Offensive teams have four downs to advance the ball into a new offensive zone (where they get a new four downs). Teams may pass or run. No blocking is permitted (players may "get in the way of defenders," but no contact is permitted). One is downed if one's flag is removed by a defender (each player should have two flags hung from the waist). A team may punt but must announce when they intend to do so. No rushing is allowed on a punt. A touchdown scores six points. Teams have one play to try for one extra point from the 3-yard line. Halves or quarters can be played.

Variations. (a) The number of downs to

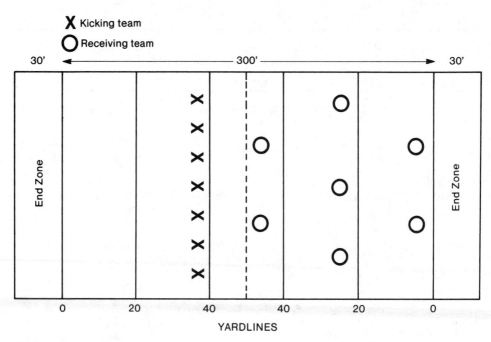

X Kicking team

O Receiving team

30' ←———————— 300' ————————→ 30'

End Zone | End Zone

0   20   40 | 40   20   0

YARDLINES

FIGURE 21.19 Flag football

move from zone to zone can vary; (b) the zones can vary (there may only be a midfield line making two such zones); (c) only passing can be allowed; (d) the size of the field can be made smaller.

Skills and strategies. All football skills and strategies

Major rules. Each team has 25 seconds to put the ball in play after a play has ended. A safety is scored (two points) if offensive players lose a flag in their own end zone. A touchback is when players intercept a ball or down a punt in their own end zone. The ball is then started from the 20-yard line. Five-yard penalties are given for illegal forward passes, delaying the game, off-sides. Fifteen-yard penalties are given for contact on offense or defense, rough play, or any unbecoming conduct.

Safety considerations. Normal considerations

ZONE FLAG CHASE

Equipment. Balls, flags, field marking

Formations. A field is marked into three or four zones of equal distance (approximately 15 yards). The width of the field is about 20 yards. One defensive player is in each zone. Offensive players are at one end line. Three of these games should be played rather than one large game.

Description. The offensive player starts at the goal line and tries to run to the opposite goal line without losing the flag. The offensive player carries a ball. Coming into each defensive zone, the defender attempts to pull off the flag. Offensive and defensive players should rotate often.

Skills. Dodging, defending, ball carrying

Major rules. Defenders must stay in their own zones. Out of bounds for offensive player results in loss of flag. Out of zone for defender counts as touchdown for offense. Offensive player who makes it from end line to end line scores six points. Two points can be scored for every zone the player successfully passes.

Safety considerations. Normal precautions

FOOTBALL END BALL

Football end ball is played just like end ball (see page 336) except that a football is used.

FOOTBALL PASS BALL

Equipment. Balls, team identification, field markings

Formations. Rectangular field; five to ten players on a team. Two smaller games is preferable to one large game.

Description. Players may play anywhere on the field. One team starts with the ball. Members may pass it anywhere to a teammate. The ball may not be held by one player longer than 5 seconds. No player may move more than three steps while in possession of the ball. The object is to complete a specific number of consecutive passes without being intercepted or dropping the ball (the number can increase as the skills of the children increase). Defenders try to intercept but cannot contact an offensive player. One point is scored for the passing team each time members reach the criterion number of successive passes. If a ball hits the ground, the sequence begins again if ball is recovered by the passing team. When the defenders get the ball, they begin their own sequence.

Skills. Passing, receiving, dodging, defending

Strategies. Offensive space, patterns, team defense

Major rules. Contact is forbidden. Violations result in a point for the passing team.

More than three steps by the passer is a violation and results in turning the ball over to the other team with an out-of-bounds pass. Dual possession results in a jump ball at that point.

Safety considerations. Normal precautions

ONE-DOWN FOOTBALL
(Fourth Down)

Equipment. Balls, team identification, flags, field markings

Formations. A rectangular field with a midfield line; five to nine players on a team. Smaller teams preferable to larger teams.

Description. Play begins from the midfield line. The team has one play to try to score a touchdown. The ball is put in play by centering. The offensive team may pass or run. Once the ball is in play, the offensive team may make any number of passes in any direction. The defenders try to get the flag of the player with the ball. If they do, play begins again with the ball changing sides at the midfield line. Team with highest point total wins.

Variations. (a) Two downs may be used rather than one with the ball marked for the second down at the point where the first play was stopped; (b) offensive players who have the ball and are not moving may be immune from tagging.

Skills. Passing, receiving, dodging, defending

Strategies. Offensive plays, defensive field coverage

Major rules. No offensive player may hold the ball more than 5 seconds without passing or running. Illegal contact by either team results in a touchdown (for offensive team) or a turnover (for defensive team).

Safety considerations. Normal precautions

FLOOR HOCKEY

Source

Hockey-type games are played throughout the world. They have roots in several ancient and primitive games. Floor hockey, as an elementary-school game, is a first cousin to field hockey and ice hockey and a second cousin to the Gaelic games of hurling and shinty. In cold climates hockey is played on ice. In warmer climates it is played on a large field. Both field hockey and ice hockey are contested in the Olympic games. Field hockey has long been a popular sport for girls and women in America. It is also played by men in many regions of the world.

Main Features

Floor hockey is a fast sport that requires skill with a stick, dodging ability, speed, and teamwork. It has become a very popular sport for elementary-school physical education and is also widely played in middle- and junior-high-school programs. It is best played in a fairly large indoor space so that players can spread out and move the puck up and down the space via passes and dribbling maneuvers. Floor hockey should be played with plastic sticks (or other safe materials) and the rules should be such that protective equipment is not needed.

The purpose of hockey is to score goals. The goal is a small area tended by a goalkeeper, whose job it is to prevent scoring. Players advance the puck up and down the floor via passes and dribbling. Teamwork is essential for offensive success.

Floor hockey can be played outside using a ball instead of a puck. At the elementary-school level this is often advisable since elementary-school indoor spaces are typically too small for more than one hockey game at a time.

Scoring

Points are scored in hockey via goals, which count for one point each. The goal shot must come from a shot off a stick or a deflection from another player. Pucks (balls) cannot be kicked through the goal. A full-scale game usually consists of three 8-minute periods. The team with the highest point total at the end of regulation play is the winner.

Teaching Considerations

Hockey should not be attempted in a space that is too confining. The skills of dribbling and passing need space, since they involve utilizing a stick to propel the puck. Therefore, consideration should be given to teaching hockey as an outdoor activity with a ball instead of as an indoor activity with a puck (if space indoors is small). A ball can also be used for indoor hockey. Hockey requires a certain amount of equipment (sticks), which must be safe to use. Plastic sticks are advisable and enough equipment should be available so that each child has a stick.

Children will have had limited previous experience utilizing implements to propel and control a puck or ball. Therefore, patience and careful progressions are necessary to ensure that children acquire the basic skills properly. Without adequate skill development, hockey becomes an "all chase the ball" activity where several skilled children dominate the play and the majority of the children experience little more than some helter-skelter running.

The fact that children concentrate on using their sticks means that they concentrate less on people in their path. Therefore, consideration should be given to avoiding collisions due to lack of attention. Also, children might have seen ice hockey on television and think that all hockey is played with much contact. As stressed with football teaching, the absence of contact must be pointed out and enforced during early game play.

Safety

Much care must be exercised during hockey units, especially if the game is taught inside as floor hockey. Carrying the stick above the waist or swinging it above the waist (highsticking) should be specifically disallowed and penalized when it occurs. Excessive roughness and contact (body checking) should also be specifically shown to the children as rule violations. While children are learning the fundamentals, they must at the same time learn to be careful with their sticks and to make sure that when they try to hit the puck, they do not swing the stick high. Also, when taught inside, the confines of a small space with many active and exuberant children often produces unintentional collisions. Children should be cautioned to be considerate of teammates and opponents as they move around during practice and game play. Proper equipment must be utilized.

Important Skills

Hockey is similar to soccer in the types of skills used, most specifically dribbling, passing, receiving, and shooting. The difference, of course, is that in hockey the player carries the implement with which to accomplish these skills. The basic skills are few but take a bit longer to acquire due to the children's lack of previous experience utilizing implements in skilled situations.

Dribbling. Dribbling is moving the ball with the stick while moving yourself. The stick is gripped in two hands. Right-handers usually have the left hand at the top of the stick and the right hand almost halfway down the throat. The stick is gripped firmly

FIGURE 21.20 Stance with stick

in the hands with the fingers wrapped around the stick. The stick should be kept low at all times. Dribbling involves pushing the puck (ball) ahead of the stick. In early attempts children will want to push the ball fairly far out and run after it. As they gain skill, they can control the puck closer to the stick with soft taps as they move. When moving downfield, the stick should be carried to the right side of the body (right-handers). When maneuvering in and about other players, the puck should be kept close to the stick and guarded so that defenders cannot steal it.

Receiving. Receiving a puck is much like receiving a pass in soccer. The puck (ball) must first be stopped, then controlled, and then something else must be done with it. This stopping-controlling-playing triad represents the basic progression of skill levels taught in receiving. The puck should be stopped with the flat side of the blade of the hockey stick. To do this, the player must get in position to be able to utilize the stick to receive a pass or intercept an opponent's pass. The player must continually concentrate on the puck and use the stick to absorb force, so that the puck does not bounce away so far that it cannot be controlled. Once the puck is stopped, it should be controlled with the stick as quickly as possible so that further play (either a dribble or pass) can be initiated.

Shooting. A shot on goal in hockey is usually referred to as a drive. A long pass can also be called a drive. The stick is taken back to waist level on the side of the body and swung in an arc directly through the puck at the intended target with a follow-through coming up to waist level on the other side. In this manner the puck is actually struck rather than lifted and slung. Shorter drive shots require less backswing and therefore can be made more quickly and deceptively. The shooter must bend at the waist and keep an eye on the puck as the shot is taken.

Passing. A pass is a short, quick hit of the puck in order to send it to a teammate. As short a backswing as possible is taken in

FIGURE 21.21 Shooting

order to generate the appropriate force. To further accuracy, the feet should be spread and the body in good balance as the pass is made. The lower hand on the stick is the guiding hand and is used to aim and direct the puck. The movement of the stick through the puck should be in line with the intended target.

Tackling. Tackling refers to taking the puck away from an opponent with your stick.

FIGURE 21.22 Tackling

The stick should be held low to the ground, as this is the most likely point at which to steal the puck. The blade is quickly moved to intercept the ball or take it from the opponent's blade. Once taken, the puck should be dribbled in such a way that the opponent cannot take it right back. Since rough play and body checking is not allowed, skill and speed should be emphasized as the most necessary ingredients for successful tackling.

Bullying. A bully or face-off is used to start the game after a goal has been scored or in a held-ball situation. The players line up so that each faces an opposite sideline with their backs to their own goal. The players hit the floor on their side of the puck and then hit each other's stick over the ball lightly. They repeat this three times. After the third hit of the sticks, they each try to gain control of the puck, either with a dribble or by passing it quickly to a teammate. The bully or face-off is also done by having the two players set themselves as indicated above, with a referee dropping the ball/puck between them.

Common Performance Errors

ERRORS	TEACHING CUES/STRATEGIES
DRIBBLING	
Missing the puck	Keep your stick on the floor/watch
Running too fast	Keep control/slow down
Dragging stick behind	Keep the puck out in front of you
Hitting at puck	Keep your stick down and let the body do the work
Puck stolen too often	Keep the puck closer to you/use the stick to protect it

Blade too stiff/puck bounces off	Give with the puck as it comes to you
Missing puck	Keep your eye on it until you have control

SHOOTING

Lack of accuracy	Shots too long/start closer/watch puck/follow through
Lack of force	Take blade back/swing through
Poor puck contact	Head down/watch the puck

PASSING

Lack of force	Use the wrists/snap it
Lack of accuracy	Lead your teammate/watch the puck
Poor puck contact	Head down/watch the puck
Too hard	Just flip it with the wrists

TACKLING

Turning head away	Start with less threatening situation
Stick too far away	Get closer to your opponent
Jabbing with stick	Get the stick in and out quickly
Bumping opponent	Steal it with the stick, not the body

Floor Hockey Drill-Games: Give it a name, make it a game

Children will need a great deal of practice in controlling the puck with their stick and then passing it to teammates. Without these skills games become wild and are not conducive to further skill acquisition. Drill-games should be used to provide the necessary repetitive, controlled practice of basic skills. As skills increase, the drill-games can become increasingly more complex as combinations of skills are added, so that game play is more and more approximated. Guidelines for creating games can be found in Chapter 18.

DRIBBLING

Up and down the floor for control (each child with a stick and puck)
In and around obstacles
For speed and control together
With a partner, as a keep away game in a small space

PASSING AND RECEIVING

To wall targets for accuracy (or floor targets)
To partners for accuracy—partners stationary
Between partners moving down the floor
Between partners with an opponent in between
With two partners, moving down the floor
In small circles, passing back and forth

SHOOTING

For accuracy to wall targets/gradually increase distance
In a semicircle, shooting into a goal
To a goal, with a goalkeeper
With partners to a goal, with a goalkeeper

TACKLING

One-against-one play in a confined area
Two-against-two play in a confined area

COMBINATIONS

With partner, passing and then shooting on goal
With partner and one opponent, passing and shooting
Three-against-three play in smaller area (like half-court basketball)

FLOOR HOCKEY (PARENT GAME)

Equipment. Sticks, pucks (balls), goals, floor markings, team identification, identification for centers.

Formations. Six players per team. One is a goalkeeper who may use hands, feet, or stick to stop shots. Two players are forwards, who play only on the offensive half of the floor. Two players are guards, who play only on the defensive half of the floor. One player is a center who can move anywhere (must be identified with special color). A center line divides the court in half.

Description. Play begins at center with a bully. Games consist of three 8-minute periods. The purpose is to score goals. Pucks out of bounds can be put in play by other team or with a bully. Type of shot allowed for score depends on type of goal used. Goals should be short to disallow high shots. With no self-contained goal, only shots on the ground are allowed as goals. Puck must be shot or deflected into a goal.

Skills. All hockey skills and strategies.

Major rules. Loss of playing time for highsticking, rough play, blocking, striking with the stick, tripping, and pushing. Loss of puck for off-sides (guard in offensive area or forward in defensive area), touching puck with hands, kicking puck, stepping on the puck, or holding the puck down with the body.

Safety considerations. Normal precautions as for other hockey activities.

SQUARE HOCKEY

Equipment. Hockey sticks, pucks (balls), floor markings, team identification.

Formations. A square playing area with a diagonal line dividing the square in half. The size of the square depends on the number of players. Two smaller games are preferable to one large game. Each game has two teams. Players on each team numbered consecutively, starting from one corner of the diagonal.

Description. The teacher calls several numbers indicating the players from each team who can enter the field of play. The puck is placed in the center of the square. The players try to gain control of the puck and move it so that they can shoot it through the end line of the opposing team. Players whose numbers are not called are goaltenders. After each score, a new set of numbers is called. The number of players called depends on the space and the total number of players in the game. A minimum of two players should be called so as to develop teamwork and passing skills. The team with the most goals wins.

Skills. Dribbling, passing, shooting, tackling, goalkeeping

Strategies. Floor balance, defensive space, passing lanes

Major rules. Highsticking, roughness, contact fouls result in loss of playing time. Minor violations such as kicking the puck result in loss of puck to the opposition.

Safety considerations. Previous instruction about contact, highsticking, and other infractions; appropriate equipment

BEGINNING HOCKEY

Equipment. Sticks, pucks (balls), floor markings, team identification

Formations. A rectangular space with goals at each end of the field or court. The space should be large enough to allow for movement and passing with players spread out. Depending on space available, five to eleven players per team. Two games with fewer players are preferable. The size of the goal (marked with cones or similar markings if no net goal is available) should be adjusted (made smaller) as skills increase.

Description. Play begins with a face-off (bully) at the center of the space. Children may move anywhere at any time. They attempt to dribble and pass the puck downcourt until they can attempt a shot. Defenders try to tackle and intercept. No goalie is used. A bully starts play after every goal scored. Team with most goals wins.

Skills. Dribbling, passing, receiving, tackling, and bullying

Strategies. Beginning team play, offensive space (depth and width), defensive coverage, passing lanes

Major rules. Highsticking, roughness, contact fouls result in loss of playing time (have a time-out penalty area). Minor violations such as kicking the puck result in loss of puck to opponents. Out of bounds results in loss of puck to opponents.

Safety considerations. Previous instruction about contact, highsticking, and other infractions; appropriate equipment

SIDELINE HOCKEY

Equipment. Hockey sticks, puck (ball), floor markings, goals, team identification

Formations. Equal number of players per team (six to twelve). Two smaller games preferable to one large game until skills de-velop. Two to four players from each team play within the boundaries. Other players line their respective sidelines. No goalie is used.

Description. Play begins with a bully at the center of the space. Teams try to move the puck downcourt and score. They can use players on their own sidelines to help to advance the ball. The sideline players must stay outside the boundaries, but the puck can be passed from in bounds to out of bounds and back. The puck cannot remain out of bounds for more than 3 seconds without being turned over to the other team. Thus, the out-of-bounds players try to return the puck to play as soon as possible. Team with most goals wins. No goalie is used.

Variations. (a) A goalie may be used; (b) number of players in bounds may increase or decrease depending on skills and space; (c) a rule requiring the use of out-of-bounds players may be installed.

Skills. All hockey skills and strategies

Major rules. Highsticking, roughness, and contact penalties result in loss of playing time. Minor infractions result in loss of puck. Puck out of bounds across end line is turned over to the other team. Bully starts play after every goal. Players rotate after each goal.

Safety considerations. Normal precautions as for other hockey activities

PADDLE, RACQUET, AND STRIKING GAMES

Source

Striking games using the hands, paddles, and racquets have been played in most civilized cultures. Some games are rebound-type games where the ball is hit off a wall, such as handball, paddle ball, and squash in our culture. Other games, such as tennis and badminton, are played with a net separating opponents. Tennis is thought to have evolved from an ancient Greek game and was played in France in the twelfth century. Lawn tennis was first played in England in 1873 and in America a year later. Badminton was devel-oped in the British Empire and is considered to be the national sport in Malaysia, Indonesia, and Thailand. It is also played actively in Western Europe. Other striking games played in courts are rugby five and jai alai (also known as pelota).

Main Features

Paddle and racquet sports can be enjoyed for a lifetime, and often are, by an increasing number of people. Some racquet and paddle sports are played indoors (such as squash, paddle ball, and badminton) while others are played primarily outdoors (such as tennis). However, in recent years indoor tennis and outdoor badminton have become popular, too. These sports can be played quite enjoyably at different levels of skill by men and women alike. They tend to be fast games with ample room for strategy and skill. The games are typically short and often a match consists of two out of three games.

The basic skills necessary to begin playing enjoyably are fairly easy to master. Thus, modified paddle and racquet games can be enjoyed by young children during the years in which their skills are increasing. On the other hand, high levels of skill require years of patient practice. For many people devotion to a racquet, paddle, or striking sport forms the foundation of their leisure life.

While these sports tend to be played in small spaces (as compared to hockey or football), they are also played by only two to four people. Thus, the space per person needed is quite high. Many schools do not have the amount or kinds of good spaces necessary to institute racquet and paddle sports units for children without modification. However, since these skills are fun and can be played for a lifetime, every effort should be made to create adaptations of games that require the use of skills that will later transfer to tennis, badminton, or paddleball-type games.

Scoring

Scoring in most paddle and racquet sports is accomplished when a player hits a shot in bounds that is not returned by the opponent. In some sports, such as table tennis, the serve alternates every five points. In other sports, such as lawn tennis, one player serves for an entire game, and then the other player serves for the next game. Matches are usually two out of three games. Many of these sports have provisions for playing off a tied game.

Teaching Considerations

To develop a paddle or racquet unit, a teacher should have enough equipment so that each child has an implement. There should be balls, birds, and the like so that children receive a sufficient quantity of practice without having to share implements or spend all their time chasing balls. Short implements should be used for early units. Often these can be made, or else they can be purchased. Balls should be sufficiently large to begin with that they can be hit easily, and they should not rebound so quickly or gain velocity so quickly that children cannot participate at a high level of success. The beginning of skill development in these activities goes back to the time when children strike balloons with their hands.

Often wall space is extraordinarily useful for practicing these skills and playing rebound-type games. Nets can be improvised for early attempts at tennis and badminton type-skills and games. In most elementary schools, these sports are often easier to teach outdoors than indoors, primarily due to space constraints. It may be that the parent games (badminton, tennis, and the like) are never played in the regular elementary-school program. However, if children have experience with aerial darts, wall ball, and modified forms of the parent sports, they will be ready to utilize longer implements, faster balls, and larger court spaces when they become available.

Early emphasis on appropriate form is quite essential, even though a specific, stereotyped form should never be imposed on a child. Skills such as the backhand stroke, when learned properly in their gross form at an early age, can last the child a lifetime. However, if early skill attempts produce bad stroking habits, they become more and more difficult to change and correct as the child grows older—and those bad habits will seriously limit the degree of enjoyment the player may eventually be able to get from participation in one of the parent games.

Safety

When children swing implements attempting to hit an object, there is always a risk of injury, especially when a child chasing a ball enters the swing space of another child.

Proper spacing for skill practice is therefore essential as is proper instruction about being aware of other children nearby. Homemade equipment should be fairly light and have blunt edges. Rules should be established for how and when children chase objects (birds, balls, and so on) they are hitting.

Important Skills

Although the skills necessary for success in the parent games of tennis, badminton, paddleball, squash, handball, and so forth are specific to those sports, the general skills underlying them will be presented here. If variations are important from the beginning, as between the forehand stroke in tennis and badminton, they will be noted here. The general skills necessary for success in this family of games are the forehand stroke, the overhand stroke, the backhand stroke, the nondominant hand stroke, the volley, and the underhand stroke.

Forehand stroke. The implement (racquet or paddle) is gripped as if the player were shaking hands. The thumb and fingers form a "V" along the handle and the implement is gripped securely in the fingers and hand. The forehand stroke is basic to success in paddle/racquet sports. The first aspect of the skill is to prepare sufficiently; that is, to have the implement drawn back in anticipation of the upcoming shot. The shoulders and waist should rotate away from the line of flight. The body should be turned so that the left side (for right-handers) faces the

FIGURE 21.23 Forehand shot with short paddle

intended direction of the shot. The forehand stroke should be level. To move up or down for a higher or lower shot, the player should bend or extend the knees rather than the waist. The tennis forehand is hit with a fairly stiff wrist and elbow, the major movement coming from the shoulder. The ball (bird, and so on) should be contacted just in front of the body. Follow-through should be emphasized along with stepping toward the intended target.

Backhand stroke. The backhand stroke is one of the more difficult motor skills for most people to learn. The backhand grip is slightly different than that used for the forehand. The easiest way to teach it is to simply have children learn to twist the racquet one-quarter revolution to the left (for right-handed children) so that the thumb is now on the back side of the handle. The grip adjustment should be made during the preparatory stages of the backhand. Therefore, teaching children to distinguish between situations that require the use of the forehand

FIGURE 21.24 Backhand shot with short paddle

or backhand becomes an important learning goal. The right side (for right-handers) is turned toward the net (or wall). The body rotates away at the shoulders and waist as the racquet is brought back in the direction of the body rotation. The stroke itself should be level and in the intended direction of the shot, with the body weight shifting forward as the stroke is made. A rhythmical, flowing stroke is preferable to a choppy, striking kind of stroke. Backswing, stroke, and follow-through should form one continuous, flowing motion.

Overhand stroke. The overhand stroke is used for the serve and smash in tennis and the clear and smash in badminton. Although each movement differs somewhat, the basic stroke pattern is similar. The forehand grip is used. The body is turned to face the net (wall) so that the implement-hand is to the rear. The overhand shot should be contacted slightly in front of the body and above head level. The backswing phase is taken with a flexed elbow and much shoulder rotation, keeping the racquet above shoulder level. The stroke phase uses the shoulder rotation, elbow extension, and a wrist snap, while the follow-through is down and across the front of the body.

Underhand stroke. The underhand stroke is used for serving in badminton, the underhand clear, and also forms the basis for lob shots in tennis. The body is turned to face the net, as with other shots. The backswing phase involves shoulder and waist rotation with the racquet taken back and up,

the elbow flexing only slightly. The stroke phase is a smooth pendular motion, with the object contacted about 1 foot off the ground midway between the two legs in a strike position (about at the midline of the body). The follow-through is up and across the body, with a weight shift accompanying the strokes and follow-through phases as with other shots.

Nondominant hand stroke. In non-implement striking games (such as handball), players must learn to execute shots with their nondominant side. The mechanics for the nondominant forehand stroke are identical to those for the dominant hand, but much more time and patience are necessary to acquire skills with the nondominant hand. Progressions need to be in much smaller steps and a greater quantity of practice is usually necessary because most children have little skill background with the non-dominant hand that will transfer to this learning situation. Children will tend to be very stiff and use the entire body for non-dominant side shots. They will have to learn to be more flexible, using the wrist and arm as they can usually do so easily with the dominant hand.

Volley shot strokes. Volley shots are used to intercept the object in flight and change its direction quickly and drastically without imparting much force to the shot. The volley shot at the net in tennis and in badminton are important skills in those parent games. The volley shot can be done on

FIGURE 21.25 Underhand shot with badminton racket

the forehand or the backhand side. The shot should be contacted above the level of the net if possible. The racquet is held firmly with the face square to the intended direction of the volley shot. The shot seldom needs any force other than that which the object brings to it in a rebound from the face of the racquet or paddle. There is no follow-through with this shot, nor is there a backswing.

Strategy skills. The major strategy in this family of games is that of attacking weak spots and getting the opponent to move by hitting a variety of shots, both long and short. Many skilled players in these games rely as much on finesse as they do on strength. Therefore, from the outset children should be taught to try to control their shots as much as possible.

Common Performance Errors

ERRORS	TEACHING CUES/STRATEGIES
FOREHAND	
Hitting with weight back	Step forward as you hit/shift weight
Not prepared to stroke	Take your backswing early/get the racquet back
Hitting too high	Swing level
Jabbing at the ball	Stroke smoothly/follow through
Not turning side to net	Side to net/turn your side
Too much wrist (tennis)	Hit with a stiff side/stiffen up that wrist
Too little wrist (badminton)	Cock your wrist in the backswing
Poor accuracy	Swing at your target/follow through toward your target
BACKHAND	
Not switching grip	Turn one-quarter revolution to the left
Hitting with weight back	Shift your weight to your front foot
Hitting with bent elbow	Keep the elbow straight/swing from the shoulder
Hitting ball too close to body	Line it up so that you have to reach for the ball
Jabbing at ball	Swing smoothly/stroke the ball
Halting at contact	Follow through
OVERHAND	
Ball contacted at wrong place	Contact just in front of you
Elbow bent	Straighten your arm/swing from shoulder
Lack of force	Emphasize backswing and then stroke
Not turning side to net	Side to net/turn your side
VOLLEY	
Too much swing	Let the ball (bird) hit the racquet
Racquet turns in hand	Grip racquet more tightly
Wrong angle on face of racquet	Racquet face square

Racquet and Paddle Drill-Games: Give it a name, make it a game

Skills in racquet, paddle, and striking sports can be practiced in several different ways. If adequate wall space is available, there is great advantage to stroking/striking against a wall. The quick rebound characteristic of this type of practice allows for a great quantity of practice per unit of time.

Children can practice certain skills with partners or in small groups. Also, mass practice (as with serving across a net or stretched line) is occasionally feasible. As with all drills, these exercises work much better if they are given a name and made into a game with simple rules and scoring contingencies (see page 296). Partner and small-group practice is often useful for cooperative game formats.

Toward a wall target for accuracy
Toward a wall for consecutive successful strokes

Between partners (keep it up—collective scoring)
Mass stroking across a net
Alternating strokes on each hit
Serving for accuracy to targets

PADDLE, RACQUET, AND STRIKING GAMES/ACTIVITIES

WALL BALL

Equipment. Rubber balls, wall space

Formations. A rectangular court laid out against a wall. The size court depends on number of players. Best played with four to five players on a court 10 feet wide and 12 feet deep. Players line up behind the end line.

Description. The ball is served by the first player, who drops the ball and hits it. The ball has to hit in a ground-wall-ground sequence within the boundaries. After the first player serves, the second player hits the ball, then the third, and so on. A fault occurs if the ball bounces twice, goes out of bounds, or if the player impedes the hit of another player. Player responsible for the fault leaves the game. The ball is then put back in play by the first player again (or the second player if the first has been put out). Order of being put out is kept and last player wins game and wins right to serve first in the next game.

Skills. Striking, rebounds, spins

Major rules. Ball can't be hit on fly; ball can't bound twice; players can't impede other players.

Safety considerations. Normal precautions

WALL PADDLE BALL

Equipment. Paddles, balls, wall space, and markings

Formations. Two, three, or four players per court. Court dimensions as shown (these are flexible depending on skill levels and space available).

Description. The game begins with a serve from behind the base line. The serve must hit the wall above the net line and land behind the service line. The next player returns the serve so that it hits above the net line and lands within the boundaries. Then, alternating hits, play continues until a shot cannot be returned legally within the boundaries. With three players the server always plays against the other two players. Players keep their own scores. With doubles the serve alternates within each team. Scoring can be done in two ways. First, the server may be the only one that can score and the opponent must win back the serve (as with a side-out in volleyball). Second, each player (or team) may have a fixed number of serves,

FIGURE 21.26 Wall paddle ball

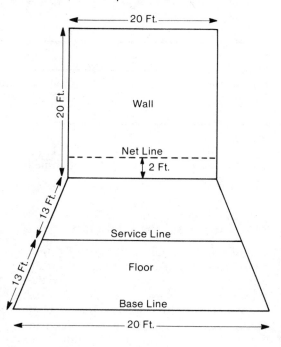

and points can be scored by either player. Number of points needed to win a game is flexible.

Skills. Stroking skills

Strategies. Court coverage, hitting to vulnerable area, moving opponent around, working for angle shots

Major rules. Hit within boundaries; serve must hit above net line and rebound beyond the service line on the fly; legal hits with paddle only.

Safety considerations. Normal precautions

ONE WALL HANDBALL

Equipment. Balls (tennis, sponge rubber, small playground)

Formations. Two, three, or four players. Court same as for wall paddle ball except that net line is not used.

Description. Play is started with a serve from behind the end line. The serve may hit anywhere on the front wall but must rebound behind the service line. Players may hit the ball on the fly or after one bounce. Players alternate hitting until a ball is hit legally within the boundaries and cannot be returned. Three- and four-player games are played and scored as with wall paddle ball.

Skills. Stroking skills with each hand, serving

Strategies. Court coverage, shot making, angle shots

Major rules. Must hit the ball rather than catch it; must hit with one hand only.

Safety precautions. Make sure to use ball that is sufficiently soft to avoid hand soreness.

PADDLE TENNIS

Equipment. Paddles, balls, court markings, net

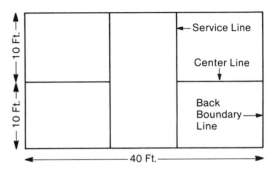

FIGURE 21.27 Paddle tennis

Formations. Two or four players. Court dimensions should be judged by skill of players with court larger as skills improve. Net height should also be adjusted according to skill with lower net for beginners. Sidelines, baseline, and service court lines as in tennis.

Description. Play begins with a serve from behind the base line of the right service court. The server must hit the ball into the diagonally opposite court so that it goes over the net and lands before the service line. The returner must hit it back after it bounces. After that, play continues until a shot is legally hit that cannot be returned. After the serve the ball may be hit on the fly (a volley shot) or after it bounces once. One player serves for an entire game. A game is for four points. Even-numbered points (0, 2, and 4) are served from the right court. Odd-numbered points (1, 3) are served from the left court. If a game is tied 3–3, then a deuce game results and the winner must win by two points.

Variations. The server can bounce the ball and hit it from a bounce.

Strategies and skills. All stroking skills and all game strategies

Major rules. Cannot step over line while serving (foot fault); ball cannot hit surface twice before being hit; players cannot reach over the net to contact a shot.

Safety considerations. Normal precautions

MODIFIED BADMINTON

Equipment. Paddles or short racquets, shuttlecocks, aerial darts, net

Formations. Two or four players per court. Court dimensions should be judged by skill of players with court larger as skills improve. Net height should also be adjusted according to skill, reaching five feet as skills progress. Sidelines, baseline, and service court lines as in badminton.

Description. Play begins with a serve from anywhere in the right service court. Server serves diagonally into opposite service court (serve must go above net and land beyond the short service line.) The shuttlecock must be hit before it touches the surface. Play continues until a legal shot cannot be returned. Only the server can score points. A winning shot by a defender is a "side-out" and the defender becomes server.

In doubles play both halves of a team serve before a total side-out can be won by the defenders. When the serving team score is even (0, 2, 4, 6, and so on) the serve is from the right service court. When the serving team score is odd, the serve is from the left service court. Eleven points wins in singles; fifteen in doubles.

Skills and strategies. Serving, all stroking skills, volleying, court coverage, attacking weaknesses

Major rules. Serve must be hit underhand and contacted below the waist of the server; server must stay in service court until serve is hit; shuttle must be hit rather than carried; shuttles that hit the net and fall into play are fair hits; players must not hit the net with their paddles or their bodies.

Safety considerations. Normal precautions

SOCCER

Source

The term *soccer* derives from *association football,* a form of football that is without question the most popular sport in the world. Soccer is played on all continents and is probably less well known in America than in any major sporting nation. Soccer is the most international of all sports, with major competitions throughout the world—the most famous being the World Cup, which is contested every four years.

Main Features

Soccer is basically a *feet* game, requiring running and dodging skills and the ability to manipulate, move, pass, and kick the ball with the feet. It is among the least expensive of all major games, requiring only a ball and a fairly large playing space. It is a fine activity for physical fitness, especially for speed and endurance in running as well as leg strength for kicking. Soccer-type games can be played with as few as two children and the variations

are virtually endless. It is also a game that can be practiced alone, often with great enjoyment by children. The parent game uses eleven players on a side and is played on a large field, 50 to 100 yards wide and 100 to 130 yards long. At either end is a goal area with a goal consisting of a crossbar and two goal posts (see Figure 21.28).

Scoring

Points are scored for each ball that is legally propelled under the crossbar, between the goal posts, and wholly across the goal line. One point is scored for each such goal. The team scoring the greater number of goals is winner. Tied games can be played off in several ways, either through an overtime period, a complete replay of the game, a series of penalty kicks, or a toss of a coin. The parent game is played in two halves of 45 minutes each, with teams changing ends at half time. Time is continuous with only minor exceptions.

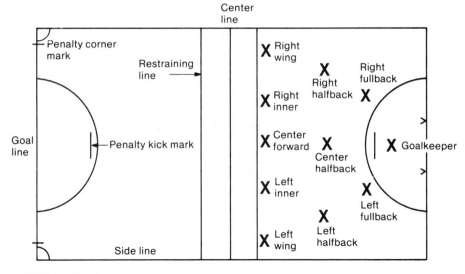

FIGURE 21.28 Soccer

Teaching Considerations

In the United States the major teaching consideration for soccer is the fact that American children have little experience using their feet to manipulate, move, and kick a ball. Therefore, soccer often is a difficult skill for children to learn, simply because they have had little early childhood experience with games that require skillful use of the feet. As with the early attempts at most games, equipment and the dimensions of space have to be changed to accommodate early skill efforts. A ball that is slightly smaller than a regulation soccer ball should be used, and it should be slightly underinflated (producing greater control and less chance of injury from kicking or heading). Field spaces should be considerably smaller than for regulation soccer. Fewer children (than the regulation eleven per side) should play in the space. Team identification will be necessary and especially important since players are so spread out in soccer. Soccer is a vigorous game requiring sustained running when played in its parent form. Therefore, children should be watched carefully for signs of fatigue, and early games should have frequent rest stops—perhaps used to pro-

vide more instruction. The individual skills needed in soccer will require much practice but are not terribly complex. What needs to be emphasized very clearly are the group skills necessary for successful game play. Field position, offensive attacking, and defensive delaying will have to be taught carefully and emphasized consistently, or the games will deteriorate to the point where all children simply follow the ball.

Safety

Soccer is a vigorous game in which children run about often under less than full control. Therefore, they tend to run into one another, push, shove, hold, and other violations. Body blocking should be discouraged in favor of more skillful techniques for stealing the ball. Children should constantly be cautioned to be careful when kicking that they do not kick an opponent. Balls should be underinflated when practicing kicking skills and often slightly underinflated in early game play. Regulation soccer balls are too heavy and, when fully inflated, too hard for elementary-school soccer games. When teaching heading, great caution should be taken and soft, underinflated balls used until skills are fairly advanced and children have overcome the early fears associated with using their head to strike the ball.

Important Skills

Soccer skills will be discussed under four general headings: *striking* the ball; *receiving* the ball; *dribbling* or otherwise individually advancing the ball; and *tackling,* which is a label under which defensive skills are subsumed.

Dribbling. In soccer it is important for an individual to be able to move the ball downfield and also control the ball while moving, even though defenders are trying to gain possession. The series of taps and pushes with which one moves the ball while moving onself is called dribbling. Dribbling is best done with the inside front part of the foot, but it can also be done with the outside part of the foot or the toe. The different kinds of dribbling skill needed in soccer are defined basically by the relative positions of the offensive and defensive players. The major forms are as follows:

Frontal dribble—The two players are facing each other.
Side dribble—The dribbler is sideways to the defender.
Rear dribble—The dribbler's body is between the ball and the defender (dribbler's back is to opponent's goal).
Running dribble—A player moves with the ball and is relatively unchallenged.

Players have to be able to dribble with both the preferred and nonpreferred foot. They also have to learn to change directions while dribbling and, eventually, to feint and fake with the dribble so as to maneuver past defenders.

Striking. The most obvious skill in soccer is striking with the feet, but players also strike the ball with their heads and the goalkeeper can punch the ball with a fist. Scoring is accomplished by kicking or heading the ball through the goal. The major striking skills are as follows:

Instep kick—The toe is pointed downward and the ball is struck on the instep; used for scoring and passing.
Inside kick—The ball is struck with the inside part of the foot; used mostly for passing and sometimes for scoring.
Outside kick—The ball is struck with the outside part of the foot; used mostly for short passes.
Heel kick—Used sometimes for a short pass to a teammate trailing the play.
Punt—Used by the goalkeeper to advance the ball far downfield. The ball is held in the hands and contacted on the instep.
Heading—A method of passing and scoring where a ball in flight is contacted at the top of the forehead so as to change its direction. Most momentum comes from the flight of the ball, but the momentum of the body can help to impart more force.
Punching—The goalkeeper can knock a shot away by hitting it with the hands.

Kicking skills have more in common for beginners than differences. Basically, the nonkicking foot is placed just to the side and slightly behind the ball. With the inside kick the leg is swung across the body. Balls contacted below or above the ball's center of gravity will result in underspin or topspin,

FIGURE 21.29 Instep kick

FIGURE 21.30   Inside kick

changing the velocity and even the flight of the ball. Balls contacted to the right or left of the center of gravity will likewise produce spin that changes the flight of the ball. Generally, as children learn soccer, they should be encouraged to kick the ball in the center. They will learn that kicking below the center of gravity produces a higher kick. The arms should be used for balance, and the eyes should be kept on the ball until it is kicked. As with all striking skills, follow-through should be emphasized.

Receiving.   Soccer is a game of passing and of intercepting passes. Therefore, a major set of skills is involved in receiving the ball, including trapping, intercepting, and catching in the case of the goalkeeper. Receiving in soccer basically involves stopping the ball in such a way as to be able to control it as quickly as possible. The major forms of receiving are as follows:

Bottom of the foot trap—The foot is angled up with the heel down, and the sole is used to stop and control the ball.

FIGURE 21.31   Trapping

Foot trap—The lower inside part of one leg and the inside part of that foot are used to stop and control the ball.

Double leg trap—The player faces the ball directly, bends at the knees, and uses the lower, front part of the legs to stop and control the ball.

Body trap—The thighs and occasionally the chest is used to deflect the ball downward so that the feet can stop and control it.

Catching—The goalkeeper can use hands and arms to catch the ball and should always try to get into position to gather the ball into the chest just as it is caught.

Receiving skills require that children learn quickly about the absorption of force and how to "give" with a ball so as to dissipate the force most efficiently. At the beginning level the child should learn how to receive so that the ball rebounds within reach of another play. The next level would teach how to receive the ball and then execute another skill, such as a pass to a teammate or a kick for accuracy. A third level would stress receiving a ball and then immediately executing another technique against opposition.

Tackling. This group of skills is defensive in nature and has as its main goals the delaying of offensive penetration, gaining possession of the ball, or denying possession of the ball to an opponent. Tackling, as an overall concept, refers to a defender's attempts to use body and feet to achieve one of these purposes and to do so without illegal contact.

Delaying tackles—This is the most conservative form of tackling. No real attempt is made to steal the ball. Rather there is an attempt to maintain position so that the offensive player is seriously delayed from further offensive penetration.

Denying possession tackles—This tackle tries to involve the dribbler in such a manner that he or she loses possession of the ball. The tackler still tries to maintain balance and position.

Winning the ball tackles—This form of tackling aims to take the ball from the dribbler in such a way that the tackler gains possession of the ball.

General skills in tackling involve watching the ball throughout the tackling movements, maintaining good balance, and using a level of assertiveness that is consistent with the three different goals outlined above; for example, a player should not go "all out" when the goal is simply to delay.

Out-of-bounds throw-in. When a ball goes out of bounds across a sideline, the ball is put in play by a player from the other team with a throw-in. The throw-in must be executed with a direct overhand motion, using both hands to support the ball. It may be done from a stand or from a run. A stride position of the feet is best as it allows for a forward weight shift to lend impetus to the throw. The wrists and forearms are snapped vigorously as the ball is thrown, and they should follow through in the direction of the throw.

Group offensive skills. Soccer must be taught as a group game in which all players have a role. Short passes should be emphasized, especially in early games. Children must be taught to maintain sufficient width as they try to advance the ball downfield and they must learn that they should not all follow the ball. They must also be taught to maintain proper depth in relation to one another (it is easier to pass ahead or behind than across a soccer field). Depth allows for diagonal passing, which causes problems for defenders. The main goal for group skills, as for individual dribbling, is to maintain control and not to hurry to get a goal kick.

Group defensive skills. A main skill for the group is to learn how to delay the offensive penetration until the defenders can regroup and get in proper defensive position. Field balance (the defensive equivalent to offensive width) is of major importance. Defensive players must learn to shift so that they maintain position between the ball and the goal (the defensive equivalent to offensive depth). The three kinds of tackling should be understood so that all tackles are not to win the ball, thus jeopardizing defensive balance.

Common Performance Errors

ERRORS	TEACHING CUES/STRATEGIES
PASSING	
Not watching the ball	See your leg follow through
Not leading your teammate	Practice kicking ahead of partner
RECEIVING	
Not giving with ball	Give with the ball
Not getting in line	Move so that the ball comes right at you
Missing (losing eye contact)	Watch till it touches your body
Losing balance	Keep a wide base until you trap it
KICKING	
Kicking with toe	Use your instep
Failure to turn foot out (inside kick)	Turn your leg out as you swing it back
Weight too far back	Kick through the ball
Too little force	Step into the ball and follow through
Poor contact on punt	Hold on to the ball until the last moment
Punting too high	Drop the ball sooner/try to drop it so that you kick it about a foot off the ground
DRIBBLING	
Kicking with toe	Use the inside or outside of foot
Losing control because ball goes too far	Use softer taps
Running faster than kicks go	Kick the ball further in front of you
Missing ball too often	Go slower/watch the ball
HEADING	
Closing eyes	Keep your eyes open and on the ball
Contacting too high or too low	Shorter throw to header
Too little force imparted	Bend at your knees and straighten up
TACKLING	
Missing the ball	Watch the ball until your foot contacts it
Losing balance	Keep a wide base until you reach for the ball
Kicking opponent	Eyes on ball/try just to flick the ball away
Poor timing	Try to reach for it when it is just going away from the opponent's foot

Soccer Drill-Games: Give it a name, make it a game

Children will need a great deal of practice in the main kicking, passing, and receiving skills that form the basis for enjoyable participation in soccer type games. The best way to allow for this kind of controlled, repetitive practice is through a skill drill that has been made into a game. As children's skills increase, the drill-games can be made progressively more complex and more like the competitive, group situations encountered in the parent game.

DRIBBLING

In a circle, each child with a ball
Up and down a field
In and out around obstacles

With a partner, as a keep away game in a small
space
All of the above with the nonpreferred foot
For speed, from line to line on a field

PASSING

In a circle with a player in the middle
Between partners who are stationary
Between partners moving down a field
Between partners with an opponent in between
For accuracy, against a wall
With two partners, moving down the field

RECEIVING

All drill-games using passing also require receiving skills and receiving can be emphasized when
needed

KICKING

Punting for distance

Punting for accuracy
Kicking for accuracy against a wall or target
Kicking for a goalkeeper
Corner kicking for accuracy and height

TACKLING

With partners as a game of keep away, combined
with dribbling
Two against two in small space, combined with
passing and dribbling

Soccer skills can also be practiced individually as children learn to bounce the ball
from foot to foot, from foot to knee, and
many other combinations (juggling the soccer ball with different body parts). If a wall is
available, many different skills can be practiced individually.

SOCCER GAMES/ACTIVITIES

SOCCER (PARENT GAME)

Equipment. Balls, field marking, goals,
team identification

Formations. A rectangular field is used.
Eleven players form a team. A center circle is
marked for kick-offs and a semicircle for the
penalty area around each goal. Five forwards
(left wing, left inner, center forward, right
inner, right wing) are primarily responsible
for advancing the ball and scoring. Three
halfbacks (right half, center half, left half)
assist with both offense and defense. Two
fullbacks (right full, left full) are primarily
defensive players. A goalkeeper guards the
goal.

Description. The game begins with a
kick-off from the center circle by the center
forward of one team. The ball must travel 1
yard and must be touched by another player
before the center forward can touch it again.
The offensive team cannot cross the center
line until the ball does. The purpose is to
score goals which count one point each.
Time is flexible (children should have short
5 to 8 minute quarters with rest periods).

Skills. All soccer skills

Strategies. Major emphasis on player
positioning, team movement, depth and
width of attack, defensive delaying

Major rules. Players are off-side if, when
the ball is played, they are on the offensive
half of the field and nearer the opposing
goal than two opponents and the ball. Ball
cannot be touched with hands, forearms, or
arms. Penalty is an indirect free kick where
ball is placed near to where violation was
committed. Opponents must remain a specified distance from ball when kick is taken
and a goal cannot be scored from this kick.
Players may not trip, hold, kick, or charge. A
direct free kick is awarded for such fouls.
Points can be scored on direct free kicks.
Players cannot intentionally obstruct opponents or charge the goalkeeper (violation results in indirect free kick). Violations that
normally incur a direct free kick and are
committed within the penalty area by a defending player result in a penalty kick taken
from the point of foul. Only the goalkeeper
and the penalty kicker can be within the
penalty area for this kick. The goalkeeper

must stand on the goal line, unmoving, until the kick is taken. A ball out of bounds along the side results in a throw-in for the other team. When offensive team causes ball to go out of bounds across goal line, defensive team puts it in play with a goal kick from the penalty area. When defensive team causes ball to go out of bounds across goal line, offensive team puts it in play with a corner kick taken from the semicircle at the corner of the field (opponents must be a specified distance from kicker).

Safety considerations. Normal precautions

SOCCER KICKBALL

Equipment. Balls, base markers, goal markers, field/court lines

Formations. Fielding team is in a spread formation behind the restraining line. Kicking team has one person kicking, another

FIGURE 21.32 Soccer kickball

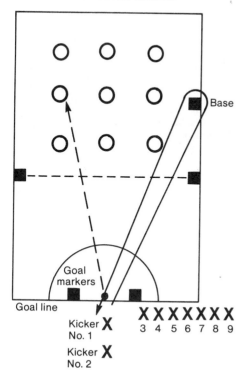

"on deck" retrieving, and remainder waiting a turn (for this reason it is best to keep the sides small and have two games). Teams should have from four to ten players.

Description. The fielders play anywhere behind the restraining line. The kicker kicks the ball anywhere in the playing field and then runs to the base and around it, heading back to the goal line where, if crossed, a point is scored for the kicking team. Fielders must receive the ball and move it only with legal soccer dribbling and passing. The fielders attempt to kick the ball through the goal markers before the kicker passes the goal line. If the ball goes through the goal ahead of the runner, an "out" is scored. After a specified number of "outs," the teams change positions.

Variations. (a) Move the restraining line closer or further depending on skills of fielders; (b) make goal area larger or smaller depending on kicking skills; (c) require several passes among members of fielding team before a goal kick is attempted; (d) line up fielding team in rows and rotate after each out; (e) make teams smaller and have more games going at one time.

Skills. Kicking, trapping, dribbling, passing, running

Strategies. Kicking to a specific spot, kicking on goal, passing among teammates

Major rules. Can't touch ball with hands or arms; can't step into penalty area except to retrieve ball that stops in that area; must run around base before heading back to goal line. Violations result in runs scored if penalty is on fielding team and outs if penalty is on kicking team.

Safety considerations. Prior instruction in how to handle balls received above the waist; prior instruction in blocking and trapping

END ZONE SOCCER

Equipment. Balls, field markings, team identification

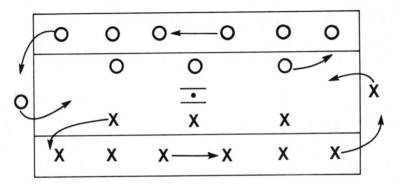

FIGURE 21.33 End zone soccer

Formations. Rectangular playing area with restraining lines 15 feet inside and parallel to each goal line. Kick-off lines marked near center of court field. Number of players is flexible (several smaller games is preferable to one larger game). Forwards are players in the center area. Goalkeepers play within the goal area, marked by the restraining line and the end line.

Description. The purpose is for a forward to kick the ball through the opponent's end zone below waist height. Goalkeepers defend against this. Points are scored for successful kicks. Play is initiated by a forward kicking from player's own kick-off line with all teammates behind the imaginary extension of that line. Opposing forwards act as defensive players attempting to block and intercept the ball. Forwards may play anywhere in the middle area but may not step into the end zone. Goalkeepers may move anywhere in the end zone but may not step into the center area. Players should rotate after designated time or score.

Variations. (a) Use fewer players with smaller playing space and have several games going at once; (b) limit the kinds of kicks allowable; (c) require a minimum number of passes among teammates before a kick on goal can be taken.

Skills. Dribbling, passing, kicking, receiving, blocking, goalkeeping

Strategies. Passing and cutting, field balance

Major rules. Can't use hands. Ball kicked out across sideline is put in play by other team. Kicks higher than waist level result in ball being put in play by other team from spot of violation. Stepping out of your designated playing zone results in ball going over to other team. Pushing, tripping, and other contact fouls result in free kick from where foul occurred.

Safety considerations. Normal precautions

CIRCLE SOCCER, SQUARE SOCCER

Equipment. Balls, court/field markings

Formations. A double circle large enough for the number of players in the game (several smaller double circles is preferable to one large double circle). A line bisects the circles, dividing the playing area in half. The outside circle is the goal line. The inside circle marks the inner boundary line. Children are to remain in the area marked by the double circles except to retrieve balls. Game can also be played with a square as shown (children stay within one step of the goal line in the square soccer version). In each version players rotate after a point is scored or after a specified time period.

Description. The purpose is to kick the ball from your own goal line across the oppo-

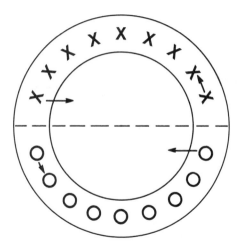

FIGURE 21.34 Circle soccer

nent's goal line below waist level. Opponent's kicks can be trapped before returning the kick. If the ball stops in the center area, it may be retrieved by a player from the team on whose half of the field/court it stops. When a goal is scored, the player on whose right the ball went across the line retrieves it and returns it to a teammate, who then kicks it, initiating play again. Games end after a specified number of points is achieved by one team or after a specified time period, in which case the team with the highest point total wins.

Skills. Kicking, receiving, blocking, passing

Strategies. Passing to achieve best goal kick, kicking for open spot

Major rules. Can't use hands; Can't kick above waist level. Penalties result in ball going to other team.

Safety considerations. Previous instruction in trapping and blocking. Watch inflation of ball in beginning so that it is not too hard. Enforce the below-the-waist kicking rule stringently.

LINE SOCCER

Equipment. Balls, field markings, team identification

Formations. Rectangular playing field, dimensions determined by number of players. Restraining line marked 5 feet in from each goal line; penalty kick line 15 feet from each goal line; and small circle in center of field. Two teams of equal size (two smaller games preferable to one large game).

Description. Players line up across the goal line. One player from each team roams the sideline and is responsible for putting back into play balls that cross sidelines. Play begins with ball in center circle and players from far right of each goal line attempt to win possession and advance ball to where it can be kicked across the opponent's goal line. Goal line players attempt to block the kick. Point is scored for each goal. Players rotate to the right after specified time period or after each goal. Winner is team with highest total at end of specified game length.

Variations. (a) Have two or more players become forwards; (b) require minimum number of passes among teammates before goal kick is attempted.

Skills. All soccer skills, especially dribbling and kicking for forwards and blocking for goal line players

Strategies. One-against-one practice

Major rules. Can't use hands; can't kick above waist level; can't step across restraining line; can't contact opponent forward. Penalty is unguarded kick from penalty line.

MODIFIED SOCCER

Equipment. Balls, field markings, team identification, goal markers

FIGURE 21.35 Line soccer

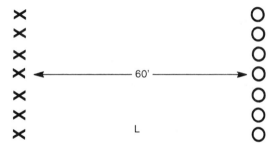

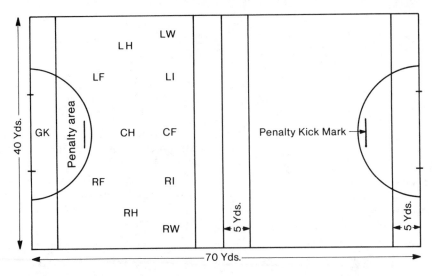

FIGURE 21.36 Modified soccer

Formations. Size of field adjusted to number of players on a side (anywhere from five to eleven). Smaller games of five to seven players per side are preferable. Players are forward line (primarily offense), halfbacks (offense and defense), fullbacks (primarily defense) and goalkeeper.

Description. Regular soccer rules are used. Ball is put in play by a forward from the center circle. No player may cross the center line before the ball. Out-of-bounds balls can be put in play by a kick-in or by a soccer throw-in. A goal is scored as two points. Penalty kicks are scored as one point. If no goal is available, ball must cross the goal line and be beneath the shoulder level of the goalkeeper.

Skills. All soccer skills

Strategies. Special emphasis on field coverage, position play, offensive maneuvers, defensive delaying depth, and width of positioning

Major rules. Pushing, tripping, and holding are violations as is touching the ball with hands or arms. Penalty is free kick from point of foul. If foul is committed in the penalty area, a penalty kick is awarded. Only the goalkeeper can be in the penalty area during a penalty kick (see rules for parent game).

Safety considerations. Normal precautions. If played outside, the condition of the field becomes a consideration.

VOLLEYBALL

Source

Volleyball is an American sport, invented in 1895 in Massachusetts at a YMCA. First used as an indoor sport, it has also become popular as a recreational outdoor sport. Its popularity spread quickly and it has become a highly competitive international sport. It is now played more widely and generally more skillfully in Japan and Eastern Europe than in the United States.

Main Features

Volleyball requires only a small space, compared to other team games. It is inexpensive, utilizing only balls, nets, and standards (which can be easily improvised). It is a skilled, fast-moving game that is sufficiently flexible to be enjoyable for persons of varying background and skill. The parent game has six players on a side. The major skills are striking and receiving. The strategies range from the most elementary patterns to highly complex pattern play on both offense and defense. Boys and girls can play and learn the game together because the culture has provided little direct experience in the game prior to the time it is learned in school. Volleyball is a fine recreational game for the backyard, beach, or picnic area. It can also be enjoyed for a lifetime.

Scoring

Points are scored when the serving team legally propels the ball across the net and within the boundaries and it cannot be returned by the receiving team. One point is scored for each such occurrence. Points can be scored only by the serving team. When the receiving team returns the ball so that it cannot be returned by the serving team, a side-out is scored and the serve changes sides. Penalties committed by the serving team result in a side-out. Penalties committed by the receiving team result in points for the serving team. The game is for fifteen points and the serving team must win by two points.

Teaching Considerations

The major striking and receiving skills in volleyball are few, and their rudiments can be mastered fairly quickly by most children. As in most team games, the major teaching effort should be directed toward concepts of offensive and defensive group play, particularly proper positioning and proper use of the entire team, rather than domination by one or two skilled players. The size of the ball and the height of the net should be adjusted gradually (increase size of ball and raise height of net) as children's skills increase. Very lightweight balls (or heavy balloons) are useful for early skill learning. Ropes with colored string or ribbons attached can easily be substituted for nets. Several small games are

preferable to one large game. Until children are fairly well skilled, it is advisable to have games where the sides are no larger than four children. Using sides of six to ten in early games leaves too many children inactive. Teams should learn quickly how to keep their own score, calling the score out before each serve (the score of the serving team called first—"8 serving 10," and so on). Children can also learn to call their own violations and should be encouraged to do so. When returning the ball to a server, children should roll it under the net rather than throw it across the top. Most striking and receiving skills can be practiced very usefully against a wall (the number of learning opportunities is usually greatly increased with such practice).

Safety

Lightweight balls that rebound properly should always be used and emphasized in early learning, where heavier balls might bruise the forearms. Spiking and blocking should not be introduced until skills in passing, serving, and game play have been mastered fairly well. Balls should be rolled under the net to the server. Early attempts at bump passing should emphasize absorption of force and control rather than striking. When several games or drill-games are being used, instructions should be clear about intruding upon the space of other games.

Important Skills

Volleyball uses receiving/striking skills. The striking aspect is emphasized with the serve, used to put the ball in play; passes, used to receive the ball and send it to a teammate; and scoring strikes, used to attempt to put the defense at a maximum disadvantage. The receiving aspect is emphasized with the bump pass (forearm pass) and the chest pass (set pass).

Underhand serve. For a right-handed player the ball is held in the left hand with the palm underneath the ball. The left foot is forward. A partial fist is used to strike the

FIGURE 21.37 Underhand serve

ball out of the left hand. The arm is swung directly back, then down, and then up and through the ball. The hand follows through in the intended direction of the serve and the eyes watch the ball until it is hit. Weight is shifted forward with the movement of the arm. The knees are first slightly flexed and then extended to help impart force.

Tennis or overhand serve. A stride position with the left foot forward is taken. The body rotates as the arm is in its backswing. The ball is tossed slightly forward of the body and several feet above the head. The striking arm comes through in an overhand motion. The rotation of the upper body and the knee flexion/extension provides force. The ball can be contacted with an open, stiff hand or with a fist.

Hook serve. For a right-hander, the right side is turned toward the court. The ball is tossed as in the tennis serve. The arm is taken straight back and is kept stiff (no elbow flexion as in the tennis serve). The body flexes backward at the hip in the backswing. The ball can be contacted with a stiff, open hand or with the fist.

Bump pass. Used to receive a serve (or any ball below waist level). Hands can be kept open or clasped together. Forearms are kept parallel and straight (no elbow flexion). Ball rebounds from the inside part of the two forearms. Body position is crucial for this skill. Children must learn to bend at the knees rather than at the waist. The angle made with the two forearms determines the direction of the bump. The pass is basically a rebound pass rather than one in which much force is imparted.

Chest pass (set up). Used when the ball approaches at chest height or higher, this pass is especially useful for setting up a potential scoring strike (it can be controlled most easily of all volleyball passes). The player should use a wide, stride base of support and bend primarily at the knees in preparation. Arms are extended above the head and

FIGURE 21.38 Overhand serve

FIGURE 21.39 Hook serve

FIGURE 21.40 Forearm passing

in front of the body with some flexion at the elbows. The thumbs are together and the hands form a wide cup. The ball is contacted with the fingertips at or just above the forehead. The elbows and knees extend to impart force. Emphasis in early practice should be on touch and control.

Dig pass. The dig is a one-handed pass made with an extended arm and with the fist contacting the ball. It is used only in those situations where the player cannot get in position to use one of the other passes, such as when the ball is out to one side and the player has to bend quickly or dive for the ball. The main goal is to strike the ball with the fist so as to keep it up in the air so that a teammate can pass it.

Spike. The spike is a striking shot taken at the net in an attempt to score. Players normally get in position early so as to approach

FIGURE 21.41 Set up passing

the net, jump, and spike. The spike is a one-hand shot, executed in a manner similar to the overhand serve or overhand throw. The player attempts to hit the ball above its center of gravity so as to propel it downward as much as possible. In early attempts spiking can be learned from a standing position with a two-foot take-off for the jump.

Blocking. Defensive players at the net try to block the spiking shots of opponents. Blocking players try to time their jump to coincide with that of the spiker. A two-foot take-off is used for the block. The arms are extended above the head. In two-player blocks, the teammates try to produce a "wall" of arms and hands so as to deflect the spike back into the spiker's court.

Group skills. The major goal for the offense is to return the serve so that it can be set up along the front line, where a front-line player can attempt to spike the ball. This return/set/spike triad forms the basis for volleyball offense. High first passes should be encouraged, as they allow other players to get into position. Defensive play should em-

FIGURE 21.42 Blocking at the net

phasize court coverage and readiness. Balls that reach front line players at shoulder level or above should be let go so that back-line players can play them. Children must be taught position play so that more skilled and aggressive children do not "hog" the ball.

Common Performance Errors

ERRORS	TEACHING CUES/STRATEGIES
SERVING	
Not swinging through straight	Make your arm go toward your target
Ball goes too high (underhand)	Hold ball lower and further away from body
Lack of force	Bend at knees/then extend
Improper contact	Keep eyes on ball
Swinging wildly	Shorten serve to emphasize control
PASSING	
Lack of force	Bend at knees/extend with contact
Improper contact	Eyes on ball until ball is hit
Ball goes to one side	Emphasize dual role of hands and arms and reduce difficulty of task
Hitting too high and hard (bump)	Emphasize absorption and control
Arms extended too quickly (set-up)	Start with catch and throw, then work up to hit
Ball goes too low (bump)	Bend at knees/emphasize proper angle of arms
Turning away from pass	Use lighter, less-inflated balls
Forearms not kept together (bump)	Bring elbows in together

Moving forward into net	Jump straight up
Jumping too soon/late (timing)	Teach hit and jump separately, then combine gradually
Improper contact (taking eye off ball)	Emphasize eye contact
Showing fear of contact	Use lighter, less-inflated balls

BLOCKING

Poor timing	Lower net and gradually raise it
Reaching over net	Just let balls hit your hands
Hands too far apart	Touch your thumbs together

Volleyball Drill-Games: Give it a name, make it a game

Volleyball drills can be made into enjoyable games on an individual basis, in pairs, in trios, or with larger groups. The drill-game isolates a particular skill and allows for a larger quantity of practice per unit of time. The drill-game format can be cooperative or competitive (see pages 297–98). Lines and waiting should be avoided in favor of more active participation.

SERVING

Toward a wall target for accuracy
Across a net and toward a target
Serve to partners (cooperative scoring)
Mass serving across net (cooperative group scoring)

PASSING

To oneself

To oneself off a wall
To oneself against a target off a wall
Partner keep-up
Small group keep-up
From a toss or serve to hit a target
From a toss or serve to hit a target and a height

SPIKING

From a self-toss to hit a target area
From a partner toss to hit a target area
From a set-up pass to hit a target area

COMBINATIONS

Serve and bump pass game with cooperative scoring (one point for successful serve and bump to target)
Serve, bump, and set-up game with cooperative scoring
Bump and set-up partner game with collective scoring

VOLLEYBALL GAMES/ACTIVITIES

VOLLEYBALL (PARENT GAME)

Equipment. Balls, nets, standards, court markings

Formations. Six players on a side (left, right, and center forward—left, right, and center back). Net height should be adjusted according to size and skill of children (6 feet high is close to upper limit for elementary-school children). Size of court is adjustable.

Description. Play begins with serve from behind end line by right-back player. Legal serve must clear net. Opponents try to return ball, using no more than three hits on each side. If opponents cannot return fairly, then serving team scores one point. If opponents return fairly and the serving team cannot, in turn, get the ball back across the net fairly, then a side-out occurs and the serve goes to the opponents. Teams can score only when serving. Serving team continues to serve until a side-out is won by opponents. When serve changes sides, the serving team rotates, with each player moving one place in a clockwise direction. The first team to reach

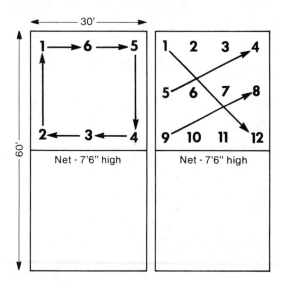

FIGURE 21.43 Volleyball rotation

fifteen points wins, if they are ahead by two points. If fifteen is achieved, but not with two points ahead, play continues until one team achieves a two-point advantage, at which time the game is over. If the serving team commits a penalty, a side-out results. If the receiving team commits a penalty, a point is scored for the serving team.

Skills. Serving, bumping, passing, setting, spiking, blocking, and digging

Strategies. Return of serve to setter, setting for spiker, blocking at the net

Major rules. The following are all penalties and result in side-out or point, depending on whether penalty was committed by serving or receiving team: catching rather than hitting the ball; hitting twice in succession; stepping over line while serving; serve that hits net; stepping on or over center line underneath net; touching the net; reaching over the net to block an opponent's shot; hitting the ball with body part other than forearms or hands.

Safety considerations. Normal precautions. Use slightly deflated ball until children become accustomed to ball striking forearms and hands.

SHOWER SERVICE BALL

Equipment. Nets, standards, balls, court markings

Formations. Children designated as servers are assigned to service area with other children in net area. Adjust service area size to skill level, encouraging children to move to back of service area as skill level increases. Number of players is flexible.

Description. Purpose is to serve ball over the net so that it cannot be caught by a player on the other side. Serves can be made anywhere within the service area at any time by any designated server. Balls caught or retrieved by a child in the net area should be passed back to a child in the service area. A point is scored each time a serve goes over the net and hits the floor. Two scorekeepers are needed, one for each team. Players should regularly rotate between the service and net areas. Number of balls used depends on the number of players on each team. With six on a team, four balls can be used. With twelve on a team, six balls can be used.

Variations. (a) Change size of service area; (b) allow one bounce for the receiving team; (c) require only certain kinds of serves (overhand, and so on); (d) change height of net as skills increase; (e) require children to serve from behind base line; (f) change scoring to emphasize cooperation between server and receiver.

Skills. Serving, catching

Strategies. Serving to specific areas, rotation

Major rules. Points are scored only when ball touches ground after serve (falls cleanly or is dropped by receiver). Winner is team that reaches a certain number of points or highest point total after specified time period.

Safety considerations. Caution children to keep constantly alert for serves, since several may come across net at the same time.

HIGH BALL

Equipment. Balls

Formations. Circles with members facing in toward center. At least five players to a circle, but more circles with five to seven players is preferable to larger circles with more players.

Description. The purpose is to keep the ball in the air by passing or bumping the ball. Competition can be among circles or with a specific time criterion (in which case each circle has a chance to win). Success requires cooperation among players within circles.

Variations. (a) Require only certain kinds of passes; (b) require that each pass reach a certain criterion height; (c) gradually change criterion for length of time ball should remain in play.

Skills. Passing, receiving, controlling ball

Strategies. Cooperative passing, advantage of height in passing

Major rules. Count only the kinds of passes that are designated for each game. Ball hitting ground or passed illegally ceases play for that circle. Ball handled twice in succession by same player ceases play for that circle.

Safety considerations. Normal precautions. Keep safe distance between circles.

ONE BOUNCE

Equipment. Balls (playground, beach), nets, standards, markings

Formations. Volleyball formations with four, six, or nine players on each team. Net is 3 feet 6 inches high but can be adjusted according to skills. Players rotate with each change of service.

Description. The game is started with the ball thrown over the net from behind the end line (which can be adjusted according to skill level). The receiving team must catch the ball on the fly or after one bounce. The player who catches the ball must not move but must throw it back across the net, where the other team must catch it on the fly or after one bounce. A dropped ball or one bouncing twice results in a point for the throwing team. After a point is scored, the team scoring the point starts the game again with a throw-serve. Games are for fifteen points. Players rotate after each point.

Variations. (a) Start game with a volleyball serve; (b) allow for receiving team to pass the ball twice up to the net before throwing it across; (c) introduce scoring system used in regulation volleyball (side-out, and so on); (d) adjust height of net and court dimensions according to skill level.

Skills. Throwing, catching, court balance, passing

Strategies. Passing, court balance, rotation, scoring

Major rules. A dropped ball results in a point for the throwing team. A ball bouncing twice results in a point. The team earning the point begins play again with a serve.

Safety considerations. Normal precautions.

EIGHT-PLAYER VOLLEYBALL

Equipment. Balls, nets, standards, court markings

Formations. Four players on a team. Rectangular court with service line adjusted according to skill level. Line bisecting each side of court indicates area where two net players may play. Back-line players cannot cross line.

Description. The ball is put into play with a serve which must clear the net. The teams then volley until one team cannot return the ball. Any number of hits on one side of net is allowable except that one player cannot hit the ball twice in succession. Players rotate in clockwise direction each time serve changes. Scoring is similar to volleyball in that only serving team can score. Volleyball rules can gradually be introduced with this game. Most gym and outdoor spaces can accommodate four games, keeping thirty-two children active.

Variations. (a) Adjust court size for games involving two or three players; (b) adjust height of net according to skill level; (c) allow only three hits per side; (d) require three hits per side.

Skills. All volleyball skills

Strategies. Team play, set-up passing, blocking at net

Major rules. Same as for parent game (see page 374). Can be introduced gradually as children's skills improve.

Safety considerations. Normal precautions

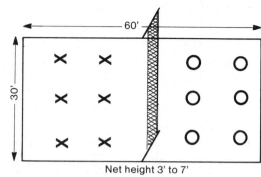

FIGURE 21.44 Modified volleyball

MODIFIED VOLLEYBALL

Equipment. Volleyballs, playground balls, nets, standards, floor markings

Formations. Four, six, nine, or twelve players on a side in volleyball formations. Rotation patterns based on two- or three-row configurations. Net height from 3 to 7 feet depending on skill level. Court size should be adjusted to number of players per team. Two games with six on a side are preferable to one game with twelve on a side.

Description. Serves as the primary lead-up game to regulation volleyball. Thus, rules, strategies, and skills of volleyball should be integrated within this game as children's skills improve. Major changes include allowing for the serve to be made from a point within the court rather than from the base line and then adjusting back to the base line as skill increases. Two service trials can be allowed. An assisted serve may be allowed. More than three hits can be taken on one side. The goal should be to work toward the regulation volleyball pattern of a service which is returned within three hits by opponents. Regular volleyball scoring can be used with a point scored by serving teams and side-out scored by receiving team. Fifteen points per game.

Skills. All volleyball skills

Strategies. All volleyball strategies, with special emphasis on offensive team play (bump, set, and spike), court position, and defensive coverage

Major rules. Same as for volleyball except for modifications based on skill progressions

Safety considerations. Normal precautions

SOFTBALL

Source

Softball was invented in 1859 in Chicago. It is a first cousin to baseball and a more distant cousin to the English games of rounders and cricket. The first rules of baseball were published in 1834 and the first intercollegiate game was played in 1859 between Williams and Amherst. The Civil War helped to spread baseball throughout the

Midwest and South so that by 1870 it was truly a national game. Softball followed closely in its path. Softball is now a national sport in its own right.

Main Features

Softball is a more useful game than baseball (from a participant point of view) for several reasons. First, it requires a smaller space to play. Second, it requires less equipment. Third, it can be played enjoyably at lower skill levels. Fourth, the risk of injury is considerably less. Fifth, it can be learned earlier than can baseball, due to the more complex and risky skills involved in baseball. Sixth, it can be played much later in life.

Softball has developed as a major recreational sport in America. Summer recreational softball leagues occupy the attention of millions of adults. The game is played as a pick-up game, at picnics, in recreational play, in highly competitive amateur leagues, and as a professional sport for both men and women. The games of baseball and softball are deeply embedded in the American sport culture. Thus, most children will know something about the game and will have had some previous experience with the basic skills, such as throwing and catching. Often, by the time children are ready to leave the elementary school, their skills in baseball/softball will be highly developed and they will be competing in age-group summer programs.

Softball requires little more than adequate space and some relatively inexpensive equipment, such as bats and balls. The rules of the game are fairly simple and the game can be played enjoyably with minimal skills, especially if the game is modified to take lower skill levels into account.

Scoring

Scoring in softball occurs whenever a batter becomes a base runner and eventually advances around to cross home plate. A run is scored each time a runner completes the circuit of bases, touching each in turn. The team with the highest run total after a specified number of innings is the winner. An inning consists of three outs. An out occurs whenever a batter fails to reach first base successfully or whenever a base runner is forced out or tagged out at second, third, or home base.

Teaching Considerations

The major teaching consideration for softball is matching the activity or game to the skill level of the children. If an overly mature form of the game is used with children whose skill level is still immature, the consequences are lack of success, boredom, and domination of the activity by several skilled players. This is particularly true for the competitive pitching/hitting dyad. Pitching accurately is a high-level skill. Hitting a pitched ball is a high-level skill. There are many ways to practice softball skills and play softball-type games without having them dominated by the pitching/hitting dyad. Tee ball games eliminate the need for a pitcher, although there is good reason to question the degree to which hitting the ball of a tee transfers to hitting a pitched ball. Having a member of the batting team pitch is a good way to avoid the competition between batter and pitcher. Using larger, softer balls that are easier to see and hit helps to eliminate the slowdowns and lack of success that too often accompany early attempts at regulation hitting and pitching.

Softball can become a game in which children are involved in the field but still inactive for most of the class period. A major teaching consideration is to reduce this inactivity by creating games that require fewer than nine players per side and tend to keep more children active more of the time and by modifying regular softball games to reduce the slowdown aspects—such as the pitching/hitting competition, the time needed to change sides, and the relative inactivity of certain positions as compared to others. It is helpful to have all children on one team bat before changing sides. It is also helpful to rotate children among the various positions.

Early softball units should utilize equipment that is conducive to skill acquisition. Larger, softer balls are helpful. Fleece balls can be used in the beginning. Short, light bats help children to control swings. A larger, flatter surface, such as found with a paddle-type instrument, would be helpful. The distance between bases should be shortened. Pitching should be eliminated. As skills gradually increase, the more regulation aspects of the equipment and game can be introduced at appropriate times.

Safety

Major safety considerations in softball involve instruction and safe practice in proper batting technique, so that the bat is not "thrown" after a swing. Children waiting for a batting turn should be a safe distance from the batting area. Children should be taught to hold onto the bat through the duration of the swing and then to drop it. Rules in early games should provide a penalty for throwing the bat. Soft balls should be used until children have developed adequate catching skills.

If the catching position is taught and utilized in games/activities, catchers should be provided with masks to protect their faces. A body protector might also be used, especially if the catcher is taught to play close behind the batter. In higher grades gloves might be utilized for fielders when a regulation softball is used for a game.

Children should be taught to run bases and bases should be used that minimize the risk of tripping. Bases should be soft or made from rubber. It is not wise to improvise bases from pieces of wood or other materials that are hard and have edges. Sliding is an advanced skill that probably should not be taught or allowed in game play.

Important Skills

Throwing and catching skills are often difficult for children to acquire. Care must be taken to use gradual approximations when teaching these skills. Catching fly balls and fielding ground balls are more specific kinds of receiving skills that also need to be attended to with appropriate progressions. Batting and bunting skills are the other important softball skills. As in most team games, offensive and defensive strategies play a large role in helping children learn how to enjoy softball.

Overhand throw. The ball is gripped with the thumb on one side of the ball and either two or three fingers on top of the ball. When learning throwing, children should use balls small enough so that they can be gripped securely. A stride position is utilized with the foot opposite to the throwing hand forward. In preparation for the throw, the arm is taken back at or above shoulder height and the trunk rotates away from the intended direction of flight. As the throw is made, the weight shifts from the rear to front foot, the trunk rotates, and the arm is

FIGURE 21.45 Overhand throw

FIGURE 21.46 Underhand pitch

brought through in an overhand motion. Stepping toward the target and following through are important.

Underhand pitch. Pitching in softball is underhand. The pitcher stands with two feet together and the ball held in front of the body with both hands. The pitcher then steps forward with the foot opposite to the throwing hand. As the foot goes forward, the throwing arm goes back in a pendular motion. The weight shifts to the front foot as the pendular motion reverses and the ball is thrown. The stride is taken directly at the target (home plate in pitching) and the arm also follows through toward that target. The first goal in pitching is accuracy—to be able to deliver the ball consistently across home plate at about waist level to the batter. Only after accuracy is mastered should pitchers attempt to deliver the ball with greater velocity.

Catching fly balls. The major consideration in teaching catching skills is to help children get in proper position, which in the case of fly balls is directly in line with the flight of the ball—the ball should arrive at the fielder at about forehead level. Children should be taught that it is better to catch fly balls at forehead level with thumbs together and fingers spread. The fielder should "give" with the ball both in the arms and hands as well as with the upper body. Fly balls that are too low to be caught at forehead level should be

fielded as close as possible to waist level with the little fingers together and fingers spread. Again, the hands, arms, and body "give" with the catch to absorb the force. The harder the ball is coming, the more the fielder needs to give with the catch. Children learning to catch often move their heads as the ball approaches, thus losing eye contact. Very soft balls should be used so as to eliminate this fundamental error. In all catching, the arms should be slightly flexed and not stiff—

FIGURE 21.47 Catching a fly ball

this avoids having the ball bounce away from rigid hands and arms. When a fielder cannot move to be in line with the flight of the ball when it is caught, the ball will have to be fielded off to one side of the body. In this case, the arms should be outstretched a bit more, but not so much that rigid arms are produced.

Fielding ground balls. As with fly balls, the fundamental aspect of fielding ground balls successfully is to get in the proper position, which is in line with the flight of the ball; thus, the ball should come directly at the fielder. If the ball is bouncing, the fielder should move so as to intercept the ball at the height of its bounce. The fielder should have feet spread in a parallel or slightly stride position with the knees slightly flexed. If the ball is rolling or bounding close to the ground, the fielder should get down to it by bending at the knees rather than at the waist. The upper body should be kept as upright as possible with the eyes on the ball. As with fly balls, children will shy away from fielding ground balls when first learning. Very soft balls that are rolling slowly can help to abate these fears and establish proper fielding habits. The ball is actually picked up with two hands (even when a glove is used). One hand is placed low with the palm of the hand (or glove) open to the ball. The other hand is placed on the side and is used to trap and secure the ball when it hits the palm of the open hand. Hands and arms should be loose

FIGURE 21.48 Fielding ground ball

and flexible in order to give with the ball and absorb the force. Children should be allowed to go down to one knee if necessary to ensure stopping the ball. This is particularly useful for outfield play, where it is important that the ball does not roll through the outfielder's legs.

Catching. The catcher plays directly behind the batter. The catcher should use a crouch position, with the left leg slightly ahead of the right and the knees flexed. The catcher should be upright at the waist. The arms and hands provide a target for the pitcher. Two-hand catching is used in a manner similar to that of catching fly balls. Ample protection should be provided in terms of masks and body protectors.

Forcing out at base. The person at first base in particular will have to receive throws from other infielders attempting to touch the base with the ball caught prior to the time the runner touches the base. The other infielders may also have to force out runners at their respective bases. The infielder sets up quickly with both feet touching the infield side of the base in a parallel position. As the throw comes, the person at base steps off the base with one foot while continuing to touch the base with the other foot (the infielder should never step on top of the base but rather maintain contact with the edge side of the base). The ball is caught in a manner similar to catching fly balls.

Batting. The bat is held in two hands, with the hands together and the left hand on the bottom for right-handed hitters. Control of the bat should be emphasized early. Control is most easily achieved when the bat is gripped at a point where the leverage is optimized. Thus, smaller, weaker children will have to "choke up" so that their bottom hand is as much as 6 to 8 inches up from the bottom of the bat. The batter stands facing home plate with front shoulder toward the pitcher. The feet should be spread comfortably at about shoulder width and the knees should be flexed slightly. The bat should be held away from the body and toward the rear shoulder. The weight is mostly on the back

FIGURE 21.49 Batting

foot and the hips and shoulders are held level.

As the pitch arrives, the bat is taken further back and the shoulders rotate away from the line of flight of the ball. As this "backswing" movement takes place, the batter strides forward with the front foot (the stride should be relatively short, seldom more than 6 to 10 inches). The bat is swung through as the shoulders rotate back toward the ball and the weight is shifted to the foot. Children should be taught to have a level swing with their arms fully extended at the point of impact, which is slightly in front of their bodies.

Bunting. From a normal batting position the batter steps forward with the rear foot so that the body faces the pitcher with the feet parallel. The knees are flexed, with the upper body upright. The bat is gripped with the left hand (for right-handers) near the bottom of the bat and the right hand just over halfway up the bat. The bottom hand is placed securely around the bat, but the top hand holds the bat loosely in the fingertips. The body moves up and down by knee flexion and extension rather than by movement at the waist. Bunting is nothing more than allowing the ball to hit the bat so as to propel it in an advantageous direction. The batter does not impart force; rather, a good bunt is one in which some of the force is absorbed in the loose fingertip grip of the upper hand and the ball rolls softly in the intended direction.

Base running. There are several kinds of running that are important in softball. First, batters must learn to become runners as quickly as possible, running to first base as quickly as they can. They should be taught not to stand and watch the ball at home base, but rather to become a base runner as soon as they hit the ball. Children must learn to run *through* first base and not to slow down to stop at the base. However, when running from first to second base, they must learn how to reach the base under control so that they do not go past it. Softball runners must remain on their bases until the ball is pitched. Therefore, children can be taught to get a quick start off the base by assuming a stride position with the rear foot in contact with the base and used for a push-off, once the ball is released by the pitcher.

Common Performance Errors

CATCHING

ERRORS	TEACHING CUES/STRATEGIES
Failure to get behind ball	Move so that ball is coming toward you
Rigid hands	Collapse with ball as you catch it
Fly balls above waist	Thumbs together
Fly balls below waist	Little fingers together
Moving head away	Watch the ball/use lighter balls
Catching one-handed with glove	Use both hands/take away glove
Bending only at waist to field ground ball	Bend at knees/get down to the ballfield on knees to block
Catching ground ball off to side	Get behind ball/use lighter ball

BATTING

ERRORS	TEACHING CUES/STRATEGIES
Inadequate control	Bat too long/choke up/tape bat for hand position
Batting cross-handed	Right hand on top (right-handers)
Stance alignment incorrect	Face home plate with side to pitcher
Not ready to hit	Hold bat back and still with weight on back foot
Swinging too hard	Stroke the ball/swing easily—hit for placement
Moving head out	Watch the ball/use softer ball
Holding onto bat after hitting	Drop the bat/practice without pitcher
Swinging just with arms	Weight back to start and moved forward
Swing not level	Keep bat parallel to ground

THROWING

ERRORS	TEACHING CUES/STRATEGIES
No opposition	Left foot forward (right-handers)
No rotation of body	Turn your left side to your target (right-handers)
Using just the arm	Turn your side to target/twist your body/move weight forward as you throw
No follow-through	Go down and touch the ground

PITCHING

ERRORS	TEACHING CUES/STRATEGIES
Incorrect stance	Feet together on the mound
Insufficient accuracy	Move closer/step toward hitter
Inappropriate release	Let ball roll off your fingers
No body follow-through	Bring your right foot up even to your left
Insuffiencient velocity—all arm	Twist your body as you pitch/start with weight back and move it forward

Softball Drill-Games: Give it a name, make it a game

Softball can be among the least active of all team games taught in the physical education program. Far too often children stand around in the field or wait for a turn to bat and are actually involved in action a very small percentage of the available time. Therefore, it is important to develop drill-games that keep children active and allow for many learning opportunities. Softball can be taught in a station format (see page 121) where batting, throwing, fielding, and bunting skills are practiced at different parts of the playing field/space. Or, all the children can be involved in the same drill-game. However, if all are involved, it is better to develop four to five drill-game groups to maximize paticipation.

THROWING

At wall targets for accuracy
Underhand throws to targets
At wall targets for velocity

THROWING AND CATCHING

With partners/cooperative scoring
Throwing and catching flies

Throwing and catching grounders
Throwing to a base

HITTING

Off a tee
From a pitcher (batting practice)
For accuracy to certain parts of the field
With a small group in a semicircle (pepper)
Throwing ball up and hitting it to fielders

FIELDING

Catching fly balls hit by a batter
Fielding ground balls (infield-type practice)

SOFTBALL GAMES/ACTIVITIES

SOFTBALL (PARENT GAME)

Equipment. Balls, bats, bases, field markings

Formations. Nine players on a side. A regulation field is 60 feet between bases and 46 feet from pitcher to home base. For elementary-school children the base distance is better set at 35 feet and the pitching distance at 25 feet. Players are pitcher, catcher, first baseman, second baseman, shortstop, third baseman, left fielder, center fielder, and right fielder.

FIGURE 21.50 Softball

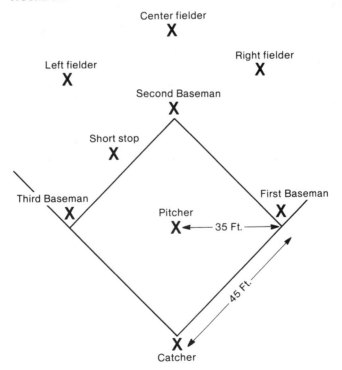

Description. The batting team tries to score runs. One run is scored each time a member of the batting team circles the bases without being put out. Caught fly balls are out. A runner must reach first base before the first baseman touches the base with the ball in hand in order to be safe. Runners can be forced out or tagged out at other bases. A ball and strike zone is established. Four balls leads to a "walk," in which the batter becomes a runner at first base. Three strikes make an out. Balls hit outside the field of play are "fouls." The pitcher must pitch with an underhand motion, having both feet in contact with the pitching rubber when beginning the pitch.

Skills. All softball skills

Strategies. Defensive force outs and double plays; offensive bunting

Major rules. Regular softball rules

Safety considerations. Normal precautions

THROW SOFTBALL

Equipment. Balls, bases, field markings

Formations. As in regular softball, except smaller dimension. The number of children on a team can vary from six to eleven. Two games with fewer on a side are preferable to one large game.

Description. The pitcher throws the ball to the batter, who catches it and then throws it anywhere in the field of play. Once the ball is thrown by the batter, the game is played similarly to softball. The number of outs per inning is flexible. Since changing sides takes time, it is useful to allow all members of a team to hit before the sides change.

Variations. (a) The ball can be kicked instead of thrown (this version of kickball requires that the pitcher roll the ball to the batter); (b) only certain kinds of throws can be allowed in order to limit the difficulty of making an out for a child who can throw the ball far; (c) the batter can be required to run all the way around the bases and an out is called if the ball reaches home base before the runner (often called "Beat Ball").

Skills. Throwing, catching, fielding flies and grounders, base running

Strategies. Throwing to a base, forcing

FIGURE 21.51 Throw softball

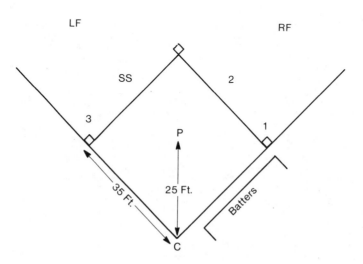

runners, offensive attack to weak parts of defense

Major rules. It is necessary to make a rule specifying where the runner has to be in order to be "safe." Runs are scored as in softball. No lead-offs or stealing is allowed. Balls thrown outside the boundary lines are considered outs. Number of outs per inning is flexible.

Safety considerations. Normal precautions

BOUNCE AND FLY

Equipment. Balls, bats, field markings, batting tees

Formations. Players are either batters or fielders. Fielders may play anywhere within the designated area. The area can be shaped for convenience. Several small games are preferable to one large game. Players not batting help to retrieve balls outside the field of play.

Description. Ball is placed on a batting tee and hit into the field of play. A ball caught on the fly counts for five points for the receiver. A ball caught on first bounce counts for three points. A cleanly fielded ground ball counts for one point. Fielders become batters after a specified time period or when fielding team reaches a criterion number of points. Collective team scoring is used.

Variations. (a) The ball can be thrown up and hit by the batter if skills are sufficiently advanced; (b) ball can be thrown by the batter rather than hit; (c) scoring variations can be arranged so that batting team acquires points as well as fielding team.

Skills. Fielding, batting

Major rules. Scoring rules. Balls outside field of play should count against batting team. A fielded ball is rolled to the sideline where a member of the batting team collects it and carries it to the batting tee area.

Safety considerations. Clear instructions about staying out of the batting area while a player is hitting

TEE BALL

Equipment. Balls, bats, bases, field marking, batting tees

Formations. Players assume regular softball positions. The size of the field should be determined by the skills of the players.

Description. The game is played like softball except that the ball is hit off a tee and there is no pitcher. Winning team is team that scores most runs in a specified number of innings. An inning can encompass three outs or an entire rotation of the members of the hitting team.

Variations. (a) The ball can be thrown rather than hit off a tee; (b) the rule on what constitutes an out can be changed to fit the skills of the children.

Skills. Catching, fielding, batting, base running

Strategies. Forcing runners, throwing to the right base, hitting to weak part of defense

Major rules. Same as for softball

Safety considerations. Thrown bats should count as an out. Children on hitting team should be within a "dug-out" area that is sufficiently far from the home-base area.

LONG BASE

Equipment. Balls, bats, field markings, base

Formations. Number of players is flexible. A common arrangement is six on a side. More games with fewer players is preferable to one large game. One base is used and its distance from home plate depends on the skill of the players.

Description. The pitcher throws the ball to the batter, who catches it and throws it

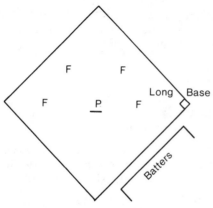

FIGURE 21.52 Long base

than ground balls, cooperative effort to put runner out

Major rules. Ball thrown or batted outside boundaries is an out.

Safety considerations. Normal precautions. Hitting team should be in an assigned area sufficiently far from home base.

SLOW PITCH SOFTBALL

Equipment. Balls, bats, bases, field markings

Formations. Regular softball formations as shown. One extra fielder is used in the outfield (known as the short-fielder or the rover).

Description. Identical to softball with a few exceptions. All pitches must be slow and have sufficient arc. There is no bunting, no base stealing, and no lead-offs.

Variations. (a) Distance of bases and distance from pitcher to hitter can vary according to skill level; (b) balls and strikes can be ignored; (c) an out can be recorded by having the pitcher get the ball back before the runner reaches first base.

Skills. All softball skills

Strategies. All softball strategies

Major rules. Ball and strike zone must be established. No lead-offs. Runner is out if he or she leaves the base before the pitcher releases the ball. No bunting or stealing allowed.

Safety considerations. Normal precautions

anywhere in the playing field. The batter then runs to the long base and back to home base before the fielding team can field the ball and return it to the catcher. The runner is out if the ball is caught on the fly or if the catcher touches home base with the ball in hand before the batter returns home.

Variations. (a) The batter can be allowed to stay at the long base and return home on the throw of the next batter; (b) fielders can also put the runner out by throwing to the long base, where a fielder can touch the base with the ball in hand before the runner reaches it; (c) the batter can hit the ball with a bat rather than throw it; (d) the batter can kick a ball rolled by a pitcher.

Skills. Fielding, throwing, running, batting

Strategies. Throwing to weak part of defense, consequences of fly balls rather

TRACK AND FIELD

Source

Running, throwing, and jumping events are among the first types of contests that cultures develop. Therefore, the specific events of track and field have their origins deep in early cultures. Our specific knowledge of

track and field as a formal set of events comes to us from the early Greek civilizations (circa 400–700 B.C.). When Roman domination of the world was at its height, track and field was contested all across the civilized world and professional athletes made their livings competing at various important meets. The Olympic games were among the largest and most important early Greek festivals. In 1892 they were revived and are now held every four years. Other important games, such as the Pan American games and Commonwealth games, are also dominated by track and field events, even though all such international competitions now embrace a wide variety of sports.

Main Features

The main features of all track and field competitions are strength, speed, and endurance, important qualities that have long contributed greatly to the survival of individuals and their cultures. Children too are interested in "how fast" and "how far" they and their peers can perform in various events. Track and field is a good activity for many reasons. The strength, speed, and endurance gained through participation is valuable. The events can often be practiced outside the formal program. The equipment needs are fairly minimal and equipment is often easy to make or acquire.

Track and field provides one of several opportunities for a festival day or week (see Chapter 25). An annual track and field meet often motivates the children highly and can provide a real boost to school spirit and morale for the several weeks prior to the meet. Track and field is also a good activity because of its inherent variety; there are many events and they can often accommodate the varying interests and talents of many children.

Scoring

Scoring in track and field is by place with five points for first place, four for second place, three for third place, two for fourth place, and one for fifth place. Teams can be formed to ensure equal group competition and a team score for all events can be kept. Records are also used in track and field, since events are standardized. Children can then match their performances with their own previous best performance and with that of their peers. There are many ways to build in healthy competition among children in track and field while still ensuring that all children succeed.

Teaching Considerations

Most youngsters will bring to track and field a quantity of previous experience that is substantially greater than that brought to other sport/game units. Virtually all children learn to run and jump, and many have become fairly proficient by the time they start school. Early Stage I and Stage II experiences (see page 104) will have brought them even further along. Track and field units involve some specific skill learning such as baton passing, sprint starting, high jumping, and hurdling, among others. Children should be ready to achieve quickly in these events.

On the other hand, a major problem in teaching track and field is that it requires fairly extensive organization. As with all skills, ensuring sufficient practice is a major goal. Track and field is most often conducted outside, and children may practice different events at different places in the outdoor space. Station teaching, task cards, small-group teaching, and various kinds of rotational instruction all lend themselves well to track and field. Management issues should be considered carefully and planned for extensively.

Equipment should not be a problem in track and field. Regulation hurdles should not be used. Spiked running shoes should not be allowed. Crossbars for high jumping and hurdles for hurdling can be improvised. A sand pit is useful for the running long jump, but it is not necessary. Two small pieces of wood can be used for a starting signal. Field markings will be necessary and an oval track is highly recommended (see Figure 21.53). Having the children help out and mark the track can be a good project and educationally beneficial. A pit is needed for high jumping but can often be improvised with gymnastic mats and some soft, yielding kinds of undermaterial (underinflated inner tube tires tied together, for example).

FIGURE 21.53 School parking lot can be used for a running track

Safety

There are several instances in which safety is a consideration in teaching track and field. The field used for running events should be clear of debris and hazardous materials such as glass chips and stones. Children should be taught to warm up properly before exerting themselves strenuously. The use of a warm-up period or activity is recommended. Passive stretching is especially important. Great care must be taken if a shot put is used. That area must be marked clearly and children instructed carefully about how to use the area. High jump landing pits should be soft and high. The crossbar used should be such that if it breaks, it does not splinter leaving very sharp edges. Hurdles should fall over easily when touched by a runner. Children should not be allowed to run in bare feet. Progressions are important in events such as the high jump, hurdling, and distance running. Children should not be placed in situations where they are expected to perform tasks well beyond their current capabilities; i.e., hurdles too high, high jump bar too high, a distance event that is too long.

Important Skills

Track and field skills include all the many variations of human movement and allow for skilled performance by a variety of differing ability types. Distance events require a particular combination of abilities and interests. So too do sprint events. Hurdling and high jumping add another dimension. Heavier, stronger students often are better at weight events such as the shot put. All children should be able to learn most of the skills at a beginning level and also find those events for which their talents and inclinations increase the likelihood of success. There are few units in the elementary-school program where success should be more readily obtainable for all children than in track and field.

Sprinting. Sprinting is running as fast as you can: This almost always involves good form. All out helter-skelter running hardly ever yields the fastest time. Sprint form is quite simple. All body parts should contribute to the run. In this sense arm movements in particular become important as they help to drive the body forward. Second, all movements should be directed in a straight line. Swaying and wobbling from side to side are detrimental to good sprint form. The body is fairly upright when at full speed (even though it leans forward at the start). The sprinter should be taught to run in a straight line (drawing that line and running along it often helps) with the arms moving vigorously from hip to shoulder level with the elbows flexed.

Running. Running, for distance events, is a relaxed, upright movement with a comfortable stride and comfortable arm movement. No part of the body should be too tense. Relaxation and efficiency are the keys to good distance running form. There is less arm movement than in sprinting and the arm movement is also less noticeable. Still, the development of a comfortable stride and running in a straight line are important ingredients.

Sprint starting. The crouch start is the most widely used form of sprint starting. The feet are placed in a stride position with the sprinter relaxed and the weight evenly distributed among the feet, one knee, and two hands which are placed just behind the starting line at shoulder width. The fingers are spread to provide a wide base for the hands. This is the "Ready" position. The "Get set" position is achieved primarily by raising the seat to just above shoulder level. This raising of the rear end puts more of the weight on the hands. The head is kept in a comfortable position looking down at the track. When the start signal is given, the hands are thrown back and the feet push off, with most push given to the back foot. The front foot begins the first step (the push is emphasized more if starting blocks are used). The body is kept low in the first few steps and the forward lean is exaggerated. The arms drive forward forcefully. Children should be taught to react to the start signal rather than try to anticipate it.

Baton passing. In relay races around a track a baton is carried by the runner and passed to each successive member of the team. A simple baton pass should be taught to elementary-school students. As the runner approaches the exchange zone, the baton should be carried in the left hand. The

FIGURE 21.55 Passing the baton

next runner should have the right hand extended backward when beginning to run in the exchange zone. The runner with the baton should place it securely into the outstretched hand of the next runner. The lead runner should look back to make sure the exchange is made properly (blind exchanges should be left to more advanced training). The palm of the lead runner should face back with the thumb and fingers pointing down to the ground.

Hurdling. Hurdling is rhythmical running which adds an elongated stride every so often to clear an obstacle. Hurdling should be taught with very low obstacles to begin with (ropes on the ground represent the first progression). Stride length is important in this event; children should be taught to take the same number of strides between each obstacle and to jump each obstacle with the same foot. The lead leg in hurdling is extended fully as it clears the obstacle. The rear leg is flexed at the knee and brought up close to the buttocks. As the lead leg clears the obstacle, the body bends at the waist and the arm opposite to the lead leg reaches forward and down. As children achieve the proper rhythm and step pattern, the height of the obstacle is raised gradually until a comfortable height is reached. Making children hurdle obstacles that are too high for their skill and developmental levels simply produces bad form, fear of the event, and the risk of injury.

FIGURE 21.54 Sprint start

FIGURE 21.56 Hurdling

Standing long jump. The standing long jump is executed from a two-foot take-off with the jumper in a crouched position. Momentum is acquired by rocking from heel to toe and by thrusting the arms backward and then bringing them vigorously forward. The jump is made with an equal push-off from each foot with the arms thrust forward. While in the air, the jumper brings the feet up under the body and then reaches out with them into the pit. The body flexes at the waist as the hands reach forward to ensure that sufficient momentum exists at landing to thrust the body forward in the landing area. The jump is measured from the jump line (or pit edge of the jump board if a board and pit are available) to the point of touch by the body part that is closest to the jump line.

Running long jump. The running long jump is similar to hurdles in that it combines running with an elongated stride. A runway of sufficient length is needed for the jumper to develop speed. A take-off line or board is needed for the jumper to develop speed and in order that fouls can be marked (the jump must be made from behind the line or behind the front edge of the board). Long jumpers should try to run rhythmically in their approach, so that the same number of strides is taken for each jump. Hitting the take-off point in proper stride is among the most difficult aspects of this event. The long jump involves a one-foot take-off. The jumper strides firmly into the jump and uses the arms to gain last-second momentum. The jump is as much up as it is out, height of

FIGURE 21.57 Long jump

jump being important in achieving distance. During flight a running stride can be taken if comfortable. Otherwise, the jumper reaches out with the feet and thrusts the arms forward, bending at the waist so as to throw the body forward at the landing. The jump is measured from the take-off line or pit edge of the board to the back-most point of landing made by any body part.

Triple jump. The triple jump consists of a hop, a step, and a jump taken consecutively. The approach characteristics of this event are identical to that of the long jump. Stride is important, since hitting the take-off board in full stride is necessary to execute the series of skills and obtain a good distance. To help children learn to hit the take-off point properly, have each child mark a checkpoint halfway down the approach. If the runner reaches the checkpoint with the correct foot (right or left), then the proper striding is occurring and chances of reaching the jump point correctly are increased. The first aspect of the triple jump is a hop on the take-off foot. Height as well as distance is emphasized in the take-off. At the end of the hop, the jumper should land with good balance and push off the landing foot for the step phase of the event. Again, the landing from the step needs to be controlled and in good balance, as that landing foot becomes the push-off foot for the jump phase, the final part of the event. At this point the technique becomes quite similar to that used

in the long jump. Children should experiment to see if a right-right-left combination or a left-left-right combination is more comfortable for pushing off for the three phases of the event. As with all long-jumping events, the distance is measured from the take-off line or board to that point in the landing area where any body part first touches down. Further, as with all other jumping events, the take-off foot must be completely behind the take-off line to avoid a foul.

High jump. In this jumping event the goal is height rather than distance. A shorter approach is used, often no more than six to eight strides. As with all jumping events, stride length is crucial, since the jumper must reach the take-off point in proper stride to ensure a fair attempt. Check marks can be used to help jumpers learn proper striding toward the bar (see triple jump description). Speed in the approach is not nearly as important in the high jump as it is in the long-jumping events. The key to high jumping is converting the linear motion to angular motion, changing the straight ahead movement to one which will carry the jumper up and over the bar.

The scissors style is often taught first, although it is not currently used in track and field competition. The jumper approaches the bar from a short angle. The take-off is made from the foot farthest from the bar. The near leg is thrust upwards and the arms are used to aid in this upward thrust. The

FIGURE 21.58 Straddle high jump

take-off leg trails and crosses the bar in a similar motion with a fairly straight knee, thus giving the jump the appearance of a scissors motion.

The straddle role is made from a sharper angle, around 45 degrees from the bar. When approaching from the right side, the right foot becomes the take-off foot. In the last several strides the jumper increases the momentum and gathers to initiate the jump. The left leg is kicked upward and outward with both arms lifting to aid in the jumping motion. The jumper attempts to "lay out" across the bar so that the actual clearance of the bar is accomplished by rolling over it with a body twist. As the left arm, shoulder, and hips roll over the bar, the trail leg is provided with the momentum to carry it over the bar, completing the rolling motion with the jumper often landing on her back in the pit. Very low bar heights should be used to teach this laying-out and rolling technique, so that children can master it and feel comfortable doing it. The major error in starting too high is that jumpers try to "lift" their chest over the bar, thus depressing the lower part of the body, which most often knocks the bar down.

The western roll is quite similar to the straddle roll in approach and take-off. The angle of the approach is similar and the same gathering, lifting, and thrusting motions initiate the jump. The difference is in how the body clears the bar. In the western roll, the jumper clears the bar on the side of the body. The trail leg is brought up more quickly than in the straddle roll and the body of the jumper is laid out across the bar as if in a sliding position. As the body crosses the bar, the right arm (for a right side approach) is thrust downward to provide the momentum for the feet to clear the bar.

The Fosbury flop is the newest technique used in high jump competition. The approach for this technique is similar to others, although more speed is usually utilized and the angle for the approach and take-off is usually less than for the straddle and western rolls. If jumping from the right side, the take-off foot is the left foot. The gathering, push-off, and arm actions are similar to the other jumps. The difference is in how the body clears the bar. As the push-off is being

FIGURE 21.59 Fosbury flop high jump

made, the body begins to rotate to the right (approach from the right side) so that the backside of the jumper is toward the bar. As the jumper reaches the apex of the jump, the upper body (with the back facing the bar) is thrust down, thus providing the momentum to carry the lower body over the bar. The jumper lands in the pit on his back.

Shot put. The shot put is an event in which a heavy ball is pushed (rather than thrown) for distance. A six-pound shot put is adequate for elementary-school units. At the outset softballs may be used while teaching good form. As with too high a bar in the high jump, too heavy a ball in the shot put tends to be counterproductive to the development of good form. The put is made from a circle and the putter must stay within the circle to avoid fouling. The putter begins at the back of the circle with the ball held in the hand at the base of the three large fingers. The thumb and little finger are on the sides for balance. In the gathering position the ball is tucked into the side of the neck and chin with the elbow flexed. The putter begins at the back of the circle with left side toward the front of the circle (for a right-hander). The first movement is backward and downward as the rear leg flexes at the knee and the putter actually bends backward so that the upper body is outside the circle. When in this lowered, gathered position, the putter then initiates the quick movement across the circle by thrusting the left leg up and out. The putter then crosses the circle with a quick hop on the right leg. The lead leg is planted securely at the front of the circle and the weight is thrust forward toward that planted lead leg. The putter develops thrust by rotating the body toward the front of the circle and with the quick, hopping movement across the circle. As the lead foot is secured and the hopping movement completed, the ball is pushed out with a vigorous extension of the right arm directly toward the landing area.

Throw for distance. In some elementary school track and field units, teachers prefer to use a softball throw for distance as a sub-

FIGURE 21.60 Shot put

stitute activity for the javelin event. A running approach is used and the thrower must remain behind the throw line if the throw is to be measured as a fair attempt. The overhand throw is best for this event and is described on page 378.

Common Performance Errors

ERRORS	TEACHING CUES/STRATEGIES
SPRINTING	
Swaying/wobbling	Run a straight line (draw the line)
Short, choppy stride	Lift the knees/stretch out the stride
Arms held tightly	Use those arms/arms like pistons
Landing on balls of feet	Run on your toes
Letting up at finish	Run through the finish line
RUNNING	
Landing on toes	Heel, toe, heel, toe/roll from the heel
Lack of pace over distance	Start slowly/pace yourself
Body leaning forward	Run upright and relaxed
Arms carried too high	Arms comfortably below chest level
SPRINT STARTING	
Weight too far back	Most of your weight on your hands
Feet too close to hands	Spread out a bit more
Rear raised too high	Just above shoulder height
Head held high	Bend slightly at the neck/relax
Standing up at "Go"	Push forward from your feet/throw yourself forward/maintain body lean
Lack of balance on "Ready"	Spread hands slightly (larger base)
BATON PASSING	
Receiving hand too high	Hand below waist level
Pass is too "light"	Slap the baton into the receiver's hand
Lack of accuracy	Have receiver watch the pass/see the pass
Lack of timing	Add verbal signal for receiver to start
HURDLING	
Can't get steps right	Lower barrier/emphasize rhythmical run
Jumping instead of hurdling	Lower barrier/emphasize elongated stride
Lead leg bent	Straighten that lead leg
Trail leg hits obstacle	Point that knee to the side
Trail foot hits obstacle	Snap that trail leg through
Upper body too upright	Thrust that opposite arm toward the lead leg
STANDING LONG JUMP	
Lack of momentum	Practice swinging arms back and through
Unequal push-off	Practice two-foot jumping
Upper body too upright	Throw the arms forward toward the feet
Falling back in pit	Throw yourself over your landing feet
LONG JUMP	
Hitting take-off out of stride	Practice striding/use checkmark

Jump is too low	Practice jumping over a string
Arms not used	Throw the arms forward as you jump
Falling back in pit	Thrust your body over your feet
Lack of control at take-off	Gather in the last three strides

TRIPLE JUMP

| Lack of control in sequence | Practice sequence without going for distance |
| Lack of balance in land | Land with body right over the landing foot |

HIGH JUMP

Hitting take-off out of stride	Practice striding/use checkmark
Jumping too close to bar	Move take-off mark back
Jumping too far from bar	Move take-off mark closer to bar
Jumping out too much	Practice jumping up without bar
Getting trail leg over	Emphasize upper body movements
Bending lead leg	Practice running and kicking leg

SHOT PUT

Throwing rather than pushing	Practice pushing without leg movement
Lack of balance across circle	Practice moving across circle without putting
Lack of rotation in put	Practice rotating and putting while standing at front of circle
Not putting straight out	Thrust the arm straight out to the landing area

Track and Field Drill-Games
Give it a name, make it a game

Track and field events are games in and of themselves in that each attempt produces a performance from which improvement can be marked. The problem with track and field is ensuring full participation. The teacher should avoid having too many children stand around waiting a turn in events such as shot putting, high jumping, and long jumping. Station teaching is one solution, using squads that rotate among the various stations. Early efforts at track and field skills can be accomplished in mass drill-games where all children are kept active. Examples would be having starting and finishing lines 25 feet apart and having the entire class see how many standing long jumps it takes to get across. Another example would be rhythmical running by the entire class in a circle with ropes placed on the ground periodically to simulate the beginning of the elongated stride that eventually will become the hurdle. Baton passing could be practiced in four groups of seven to eight children each, with each runner approximately 15 feet apart. The timing and passing phases of baton passing could be practiced in this formation. In addition, track and field units can take advantage of the following methods of organizing for competition.

Pursuit relays—Run around a track or oval course with four runners to a team.

Shuttle relays—Run back and forth along a straight course with one team in each lane.

Collective scoring—Team with lowest time total of all runners, highest height total of all jumpers, and longest distance total of jumpers and putters wins.

Category scoring—Teams are divided by weight or some other factor to equalize competition. Scoring then done within categories.

Cooperative scoring—Entire class tries to meet a total time, distance, or height criterion as a class achievement.

The Track and Field Meet

Often the culmination of a track and field unit is the schoolwide track and field meet. This event has all the makings of a school festival (see Chapter 25) and can become an important annual event in the lives of the children and school personnel. The meet can be conducted as a special event with regular school schedules rearranged so that all class-

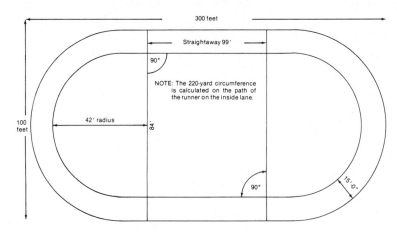

FIGURE 21.61   Plan for a 220-yard running track

es can participate together (grades 4, 5, and 6), or the meet can be held within each regularly scheduled class over a period of a week or two. School records can be kept and records by class can provide a fine incentive for more skilled children. The competitions should be arranged so that not only do all children participate but they also win an award. Competition can be totally individual, or classes can be divided into teams and team points and awards can also be given. If awards can be made at a school assembly, the festive nature of the event is heightened.

A track with lanes is very useful for a track and field meet. A 220-yard track can be constructed temporarily on school grounds. In fact, children can help to measure and line it as part of a school project. The dimensions are shown in the accompanying diagram. The inside lane should be laid out first. Lanes should be 30 to 36 inches wide.

However, a track is not necessary for conducting a track meet. If one or two distance events are considered useful, they can be run around the perimeter of a playspace which can be measured for distance. If adequate practice and instruction has been provided, runs up to 1 mile in length can be included. Sprint events up to 60 yards can easily be run in most outdoor playspaces where lanes are marked in a straight runway fashion. Hurdles can also be run in this manner.

22

gymnastics and aquatics

GYMNASTICS

Gymnastics is a Greek term meaning "naked art" (Baley, 1974). Control of the body in executing graceful yet difficult movements has long been considered an artistic expression as well as a competitive sport event. Although gymnastic-type events have been common to most cultures, it was in eighteenth- and nineteenth-century Europe that gymnastics developed and spread, providing the basis for what is now most commonly referred to as "Olympic gymnastics." Among those who developed gymnastics systems as primary forms of education and competition were Frederick Jahn in Germany, Adolph Spiess in Switzerland, Franz Nachtegall in Denmark, Francisco Amoras in France and Spain, and Johann Guts Muts in Germany.

Most of the early programs in physical education in the United States were composed almost totally of gymnastics systems developed from these European educators. Gymnastics organizations such as the German Turnvereins and Czechoslovakian Sokols were well established in the United States during the later part of the nineteenth century. Gymnastics as practiced today draws primarily from those events included in the Olympic games.

Main Features

Gymnastics in the elementary-school curriculum can be viewed as a series of interrelated levels (Sweeney, 1973). Level one is basic movement with gymnastics-type skills, with or without apparatus. This level is typically accomplished with young children either in an educational gymnastics program (see Chapter 16) or in units dealing with stunts. Wands, ropes, hoops, and benches are the kinds of apparatus normally used with this beginning level.

The second level is a more formal entry into gymnastics as an organized activity in which there are specific skills to be learned and perfected. Tumbling and apparatus work are both included at this level, with utilization of parallel bars, vaulting horses, horizontal bars, rings, balance beams, and trampolines. Most of the material in this chapter is directed toward this second level.

The third level is gymnastics as a sport, a

competitive event, or for use in demonstrations. This level differs from the second level in that skills are put together in combinations to produce routines, and these routines are utilized for competition or demonstration. In competition the routines are scored by judges.

Gymnastics are beautiful activities. The control exerted over the body while performing difficult skills is both pleasant to watch and provides important sources of satisfaction to the performer. Gymnastics is a good fitness activity, particularly for strength and flexibility development. Needless to say, children who practice many hours perfecting their skills also can obtain many other physical, psychological, and emotional benefits, especially if activities are conducted in a strong educational setting.

Teaching Considerations

Gymnastics skills are primarily individual skills. Any group of children will differ markedly in their entry-level skills and the quickness with which they learn new gymnastics skills. Thus, gymnastic units tend to lend themselves to teaching approaches that emphasize some type of self-pacing. If apparatus are used, they clearly limit the number of children that can be engaged in learning (at that particular apparatus) at any given time. Thus, managing time so that learners have as many opportunities to respond as possible is an important part of planning gymnastics units.

Most teachers feel that some combination of task and station teaching is appropriate for gymnastics, especially when learners have moved beyond the very beginning levels or when apparatus are involved. Task cards can be developed for each set of skills; for example, for tumbling, vaulting, the horizontal bar, and so on. Different skills or different pieces of equipment can define the various stations. Task cards should be clearly identified at each station, along with any special safety features specific to that station.

A routine should be developed for moving from station to station. Groups of children will be at each station. They then will move, typically as a group, to the next station to begin practice on a different set of skills. This transition routine should be specifically taught so that children understand the signal for attending to the teacher, for moving to the next station, and for moving so that minimum disruption is created. If a clockwise (or counterclockwise) progression of stations can be developed, the routine is made much easier.

Mats should be used creatively to maximize student opportunity to respond. Children can learn to tumble across the width of a mat rather than standing in line waiting to tumble down the length of a mat. Children should always walk around mats and never across them.

Visual information regarding the skills is important in gymnastics. Demonstrations are useful, but children should have access to sequenced drawings when they are trying to learn skills. Typically, these are best included in the task cards at each station so that the information is close and available when it is needed. Task cards can also include reminders of key points of emphasis in the execution of the skills.

Gymnastics are activities in which children can help each other learn by providing useful feedback pertaining to the key elements in the skill performance. However, if children are to help each other, they must first be educated as to how to be a good watcher and how to give feedback. The key elements in the skills must be identified for the children and they must be given practice in picking out these key elements as their peers move through the skills. They must then be able to deliver specific feedback about what they saw. This kind of visual analysis skill takes practice and cannot be assumed to exist merely because the skill has been explained verbally.

Safety Considerations

Gymnastics skills involve falling, inversion of the body, hanging, and a number of other positions and movements which require safety precautions. In addition, common apparatus utilized in gymnastics require both safe use and appropriate supervision by the teacher and/or aides. Physical and psychological security is necessary if children are to master gymnastics skills. The two kinds of security are intimately related. Most children *feel* safe if (a) they perceive that the task they are asked to do is safe and (b) they have had sufficient previous skill training for the task to be successful. The following are some suggestions for ensuring safety in the gymnastics unit.

1. Ordinary gymnasium rules should be modified for the gymnastics units so that they relate to all pieces of equipment that might be used. A special poster should be developed and displayed. The rules should be emphasized often at the beginning of the unit. Children who obey the rules should be praised. When rules are broken, the child should be stopped immediately, with the emphasis on restating the rule (it is often useful to have the offending child verbalize the rule).
2. Each piece of apparatus utilized should have its own list of specific rules posted on a nearby chart. These rules should include number of children permitted on the apparatus at one time, placement of waiting children near the apparatus, and any special technical concerns. These specific rules should be introduced at the time the apparatus is being introduced.
3. Spotting should be done only by a teacher, a qualified aide, or a student who has been trained to be a spotter. Spotting refers to providing physical guidance with the hands in order to help learners through stunts, particularly those that are rotational. One hand is typically used to support the child as the skill is performed, while the other hand provides additional force in the direction of the rotational movement.
4. General rules should indicate that new skills can be spotted by the teacher only. Other spotting rules should also be made clear. Spotting, if done by aides, must be taught carefully.
5. When using apparatus, it is always better to overpad than to underpad. Always utilize all available padding. When a piece of equipment is approximately the height of the child, a 4-inch mat should be under and/or beside the equipment for safe landings. If the piece of equipment allows the children to climb higher than their height (ropes, cargo net, and so on), an 8-inch mat should be underneath.
6. When asked to move or when moving on their own, children should never move across a mat but, instead, around a mat.
7. Equipment should be checked daily for damage and should be secured so that children cannot use it in an unsupervised situation.
8. Careful progressions should be planned so that children are never asked to advance to a skill for which they have had inadequate preparation.
9. A positive mood of expectation should be developed where safety and previous skills are combined to create both anticipation of new skills and the confidence that the new skills can be mastered.

Introductory Activities

The type and quantity of introductory activities used either as part of or as lead-ups to a gymnastics curriculum in elementary-school physical education depend very much on the experiences children have in the primary grades. For example, if children have had ample movement experiences of the kinds described in Part Three of this text, particularly the educational gymnastics chapter, they will be very much ready for the gymnastics curriculum. If, however, their early experiences have been mostly in a "games" curriculum, they will be less ready and, therefore, need a more carefully planned introductory unit before they begin to perform the gymnastics skills.

The introductory activities suggested here assume that children have had movement experiences of sufficient quality and quantity to allow them to move rather directly into a formal gymnastics curriculum. Thus, the typical "stunts" and "individual and dual stunts" or "self-testing activities" are not included here. If children have had appropriate movement experiences of the type described in Part Three, they will not need the "stunts" experiences.

The introductory activities shown in this section focus on strength, flexibility, jumping, and balancing. These components are essential for skill in gymnastics. Some children may require some remedial work in one or more of these component areas as an adjunct to the gymnastics unit.

Extension press-up. Lying prone with arms extended above heads, toes curled under, and elbows off the floor, children press down and forward to lift body off the floor. Avoid arching the back, lifting the head, or retracting the shoulders.

FIGURE 22.1   Extension press-up

Arching. Prone position with hands clasped behind necks, children pull head, shoulders, chest, legs, and feet off the floor so that stomach provides base of support.

FIGURE 22.2   Arching

Bridge. Lying on back with knees bent, feet flat on floor near the buttocks, hands flat on floor under shoulders, and fingers pointing toward feet, children extend knees and arms to an arch position.

FIGURE 22.3   Bridge

V-sit. Starting in supine position with arms extended beyond heads, children lift legs and trunk off floor simultaneously as they move arms toward legs to form V-sit.

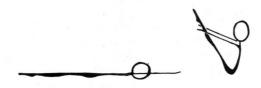

FIGURE 22.4   V-sit

Rocker. From a prone position children grasp ankles so that body can rock forward and backward with stomach as base of support.

FIGURE 22.5   Rocker

Forward bend. Standing with feet apart, children bend forward at the waist to touch the floor. Spread of feet should be such that floor touch is achievable. As flexibility increases, feet come closer together and palms can touch floor, then head to knees, and so on.

Russian dance. Starting in squat position with one leg extended in front, children push off the supporting leg with sufficient force to move the extended leg back to squat and extend the support leg.

FIGURE 22.6   Russian dance

Mule kick. Starting with hands and feet on floor, arms straight at shoulder width, and fingers spread, children see how high they can thrust feet into air.

Jump and tuck. From standing position children jump straight up, lifting and flexing the knees to their chests and grasping arms around lower legs. The grasp is then released and children return to a balanced stand.

FIGURE 22.7   Jump and tuck

Jump and pike. From standing position children jump straight up, lifting legs while keeping them extended and together and reaching with the arms to touch their toes. The head should be held erect and the back kept vertical.

FIGURE 22.8   Jump and pike

Jump and straddle the toe touch.   From standing position children jump straight up, lifting legs with feet apart, legs kept extended, and reaching with arms to touch their toes—head held erect and back kept vertical.

FIGURE 22.9   Jump and straddle the toe touch

Jump and half turn.   From a standing position children jump straight up and execute a half turn before landing in a balanced position. To turn right, the right arm is thrown behind the hips, the left arm is thrown in front of the hips, and the head is turned so that children look over their right shoulder.

FIGURE 22.10   Jump and half turn

Jump and swan.   From a standing position children jump straight up, throw their arms over their heads and behind their shoulders, and pull themselves into an arched position with the arms thrust forward.

Tripod.   From a position with knees on floor and hands placed directly beside knees

FIGURE 22.11   Jump and swan

with fingers spread, the head is placed on a mat in front of the hands and knees so that the child can see both. The right knee is placed on the bridge formed by the upper arm at the elbow, the left knee is placed on the left arm, and the child balances on the hands and head.

FIGURE 22.12   Tripod

Front scale.   From a standing position children bend forward at the waist, lifting one leg backward with no flexion at the knee, while the arms extend forward so that the extended leg and trunk are parallel to the floor and slightly arched with the head up.

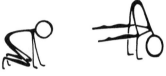

FIGURE 22.13   Front scale

Side scale.   From a standing position one leg is extended with no flexion at the knee, the arm on the same side is extended, the upper body is flexed at the waist in a direction opposite to the extended leg, while the nonextended arm rests on the lower leg so that the extended arm and leg form a continuous line parallel to the floor.

FIGURE 22.14 Side scale

Needle scale. Starting from a front-scale position, children lower the trunk as one leg is elevated. This movement continues until the trunk reaches the support leg and the extended leg forms a continuous line with the trunk—the hands may grasp the ankle for support.

FIGURE 22.15 Needle scale

Squat balance. Starting from a squat position with arms between legs and hands on the floor at shoulder width, the inside of the knees are placed on the upper arms just above the elbows and one foot at a time is lifted from the floor so that children balance on their hands.

FIGURE 22.16 Squat balance

Head balance. Starting from a kneeling position with hands on the floor slightly in front of the knees, children place their heads on the mat in front of the hands so that the head and hands form an equilateral triangle. The hips are then lifted so that they come over the triangle support and the legs are tucked and slowly extended to an arched position.

FIGURE 22.17 Head balance

Forearm balance. Starting from a kneeling position, children place forearms on the mat with the palms down and the hands joined in such a way that the forehead can be placed in the cup made by the hands and fingers. One leg is extended upward, and then the other leg is brought quickly upward so that the children are in a balanced position with both legs extended.

FIGURE 22.18 Forearm balance

One-leg balance. Starting in a standing position, one leg is raised sideward so that the instep of the raised foot can be grasped by the hand of the extended arm on the same side of the body, with the other arm extended in the opposite direction for balance.

FIGURE 22.19 One-leg balance

Tumbling Skills

Tumbling skills typically form the basis of elementary-school gymnastics programs. They can be taught and perfected with no equipment other than adequate mats. They form the basis of floor exercise skills. Many of the skills can be transferred to apparatus in a variety of ways.

Skill in tumbling requires many repetitions with gradual progressions from simple to complex. If tumbling skills are mastered so that children have skill and the confidence to use it, generalization of the tumbling skill to apparatus will proceed quite quickly.

Front tuck role. Starting from a stand or squat, children place hands shoulder width apart on the mat about 15 to 18 inches in front of the feet, with the fingers pointing straight ahead. The legs straighten and the body is pushed forward in a rolling motion over the head, with the head tucked against the chest and the weight borne on the hands and shoulder. As the roll is made and the hands are free of the mat, the hands are brought forward to grasp the shins in a tuck position—the momentum of the roll brings the child to a standing position without the child having to place hands on the mat. Variations include the front tuck roll with the arms between the legs, the roll with the arms outside the legs, front roll from a walk, front roll with a half twist (which is accomplished by crossing the feet as the legs go over the head so that the body twists half a turn as the roll is completed and the child moves to a standing position) and the dive forward roll (in which the children do a short run, take off from both feet, and execute a flat dive that moves into a forward roll).

Back tuck roll. Starting from a standing or squatting position, the child squats and places the hands on the mat slightly behind the feet. The weight is then shifted backward with a push from the feet, and the body rolls on the buttocks and then the back, with the knees brought to the chest in a tuck. The hands are thrown backward and placed on the mat behind the shoulders and next to the ears. The hands then push vigorously against the mat to bring the body completely over to a standing position. Variations include backward roll from a stand, where the beginning motion from stand to squat to roll is continuous; the backward roll with a jackknife position, where the legs are kept extended throughout the roll; and the backward roll with an extension, where the legs are kept extended and the arms extend as the hips come over the base of support during the roll.

FIGURE 22.21 Back tuck role

Front straddle role. From a standing position with the feet spread well beyond shoulder width, children lean forward placing hands on the mat, tuck the head against the chest, bend the arms and roll forward, with the legs kept extended and spread. As the roll is completed and the legs approach the mat, the hands are placed on the mat between the legs, and the body is pushed upward so that the final position is a straddle similar to the beginning position.

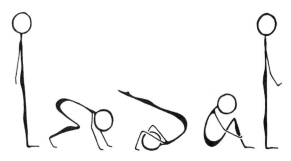

FIGURE 22.20 Front tuck roll

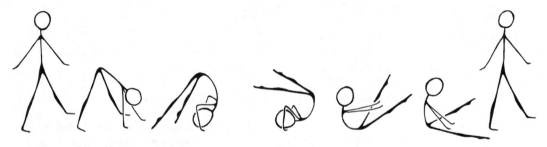

FIGURE 22.22 Front straddle roll

Back straddle role. From a standing straddle position children bend at the waist and reach down so that the hands are placed on the mat behind the feet. The weight is then shifted back onto the hands and into the back roll so that a hands-buttocks-shoulder roll is completed with the legs kept in straddle position. As in the back roll, the hands are then placed behind the shoulders and push vigorously (with the legs still in a straddle position) so that the end position is similar to the beginning position.

FIGURE 22.23 Back straddle role

Handstand. Starting from a standing position, children step forward with one foot, bending forward at the waist and placing the hands 15 to 18 inches in front of the feet, with the fingers spread, pointing straight ahead, the elbows straight, and the shoulder directly over the fingertips. The back leg is then kicked up with the knee extended. As the back leg approaches the vertical, the other leg is brought up to join it with the body as straight as possible. After the handstand is held, the last leg up is the first leg down and then the other follows in a smooth, continuous motion.

FIGURE 22.24 Handstand

Cartwheel. Starting from a standing position with feet spread just outside shoulder width and arms extended, children bend to the side, placing the lead hand on the mat and swinging the other arm across the body at the same time the opposite leg is extended directly upward and over the head and supporting hand. While this is done, the support leg springs off the mat, creating a handstand position as the opposite arm swings across the body and is placed on the mat in a straight line to the intended line of flight. As the hips are brought over the base of support, the arms (first the lead arm and then the following arm) push off the mat to bring the body directly over the hands with the legs extended and finally to a standing position facing the same direction as the beginning position, with the main emphasis on keeping the arms extended and the hips over the head.

FIGURE 22.25 Cartwheel

Front limber. From a standing position children kick up into a handstand. While the handstand is held momentarily, the back is arched and then the body rolls over to the feet, with the head up. The weight is then transferred vigorously from the hands to the feet, maintaining the back arch, and moving to a standing position.

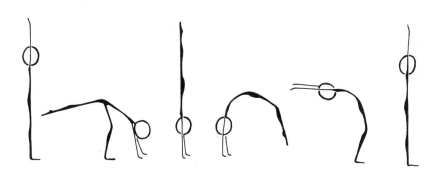

FIGURE 22.26 Front limber

Back limber. From a standing position, children arch backs while they raise their arms in a circular motion over the head and back. The body hyperextends at the waist, leaning backward, and the hands are placed on the mat as close to the heels as possible. The weight is shifted from the feet to the hands, with the arms kept extended. The hips and shoulders are moved over the hands, while the legs are raised off the mat into a handstand position and back to the floor in a continuous motion. The feet push off the floor to bring the body back to a standing position.

FIGURE 22.27 Back limber

Headspring. From a standing position children squat, placing their hands on the mat 15 to 18 inches in front of the feet (as in the front roll). The body leans forward as the legs push, and the head is lowered until it touches the mat, thus forming a three-point base of support (with most of the weight on the hands). The legs are kept extended as the hips are brought over the head to form an inverted L-shape. As the hips pass over the head, the arms push vigorously and the hips extend to an arched position in order to bring the body to a standing position.

Variations. Headspring in a series where the completion of one headspring acts as a lead in to the next; headspring to a straight leg landing with the head and arm push more vigorous so that the landing can be made with legs fully extended; and headspring from a walk, where the skill is initiated from a walk to a two-foot take-off position.

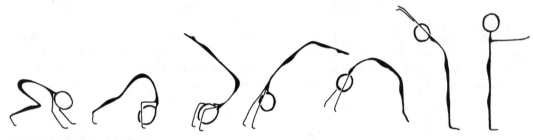

FIGURE 22.28 Headspring

Handspring. Starting from a short run with a final skip, children bend at the waist and place the hands on the mat in front of the feet, with the fingers extended and pointing straight ahead. The legs are kicked up, bringing the hips over the head with the arms fully extended and the head pulled backward as the skill is executed. As the children pass through the handstand position, they should push vigorously upward from

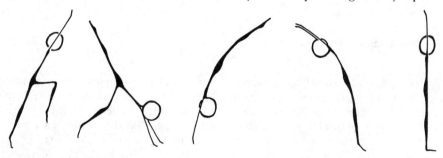

FIGURE 22.29 Handspring

the shoulders and hips so as to bring the body back to a standing position.

Variations. Handspring on a rolled-up mat (sometimes a good lead-up to the regular handspring); walkout handspring, where the final movement is a return to a walk rather than a landing with two feet parallel.

Round-off. Starting from a short run with a final skip, children step forward with the right foot, flex at the waist while placing the right hand on the mat in front of the feet with the fingers pointing sideward. The left foot is thrown up and over the head first with the right foot following. As the legs move over the hips, the body rotates and the left hand is brought down, helping to turn the body 180 degrees from the starting position. Both feet land together, so that the final standing position is in the direction opposite to the starting position.

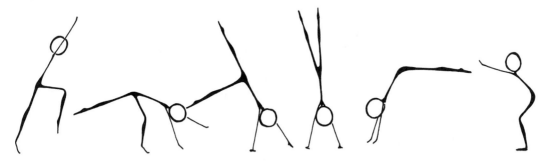

FIGURE 22.30 Round-off

Front walkover. From a standing position children extend one leg forward and flex at the waist, moving the hands to the mat as in a handstand. The other leg extends backward so that the legs split. This position is held toward and past the handstand position, with children landing on one foot and bringing the other leg vigorously through to finish in a standing position.

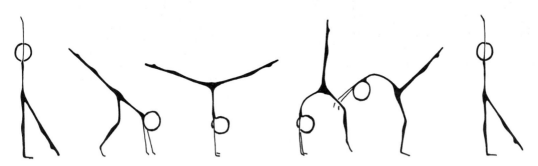

FIGURE 22.31 Front walkover

Back walkover. From a standing position children bend backward, placing the hands on the mat. One leg is then brought vigorously over the head in an extended position; the other follows, thus forming the leg split that is characteristic of the walkover moves.

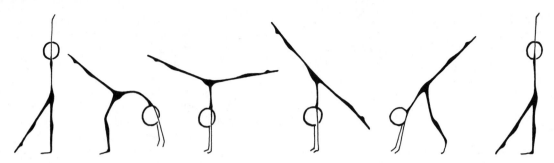

FIGURE 22.32 Back walkover

Back handspring.   From a standing position children swing the arms back and up while displacing the weight toward the rear in a sitting position. As the weight is displaced to the rear, the arms then swing forward vigorously, the head is thrown back, and the back is arched. The push-off is from the heels, with the hips thrown vigorously upward. The extended arms reach down as the body is carried over backward, so that the hands are placed on the mat shortly after the feet leave the mat, carrying the body into a handstand position. The hands push down so that the body is forced to a standing position to complete the move.

FIGURE 22.33 Back handspring

Front somersault.   From a short run a final leap is made, bringing children to a two-foot take-off position with the arms extended above the head. The children then spring vigorously into the air while moving the arms and trunk downward into a tucked position, flexing at the waist, and thus creating the rotational movement for the somersault. Once the turn is completed, the tuck is opened up so that a two-foot landing is made in a standing position. A tight tuck increases the spin of the somersault and the children should strive for vertical height rather than traveling horizontally.

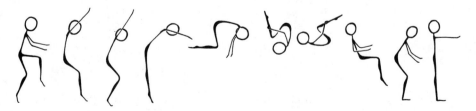

FIGURE 22.34 Front somersault

Parallel Bars

Parallel bar skills can be learned at chest height until sufficient skill is acquired so that the bars can be raised to a higher position. Mats should be placed not only below the bars but also at the ends and on the sides. Parallel bar skills require good arm and upper body strength. Some children may need remedial strength development before trying to learn skills on the parallel bars.

Introductory activities. The following activities are designed to allow children to get the feel of the apparatus and to develop the beginning strength necessary to perform.

Hand walk. With the arms fully extended, children walk the length of the bar, shifting weight from one hand to another.

Bent-arm walk. With the arms flexed so that the upper arm is parallel to the bars, children walk across the bar, shifting weight with each new hand placement and maintaining the bent-arm position.

Inverted walk. Hanging below the bar with the hands placed outside the bars and the arms extended, children flex at the waist so that their feet are between the bars and over their heads. In this position they walk the bar, maintaining both the arm and leg positions.

Bird's nest. Standing between the bars, children grasp the bars with outside grips and lift their legs backward to hook the bars with the heels.

FIGURE 22.35 Bird's nest

Upper-arm swing. With the hands in a regular inside grip and the forearms resting

FIGURE 22.36 Upper-arm swing

on the bar, children swing back and forth, attempting to extend in the backswing and flex in the forward swing.

Cross-arm support swing. Starting with the arms fully extended, children swing back and forth, extending in the backward movement and flexing at the waist in the forward movement.

FIGURE 22.37 Cross-arm support

Still dips. Starting with the arms fully extended, children dip down by flexing at the elbow and then return to the full extended beginning position.

Swinging dips. Using the same dipping movement as above, children swing backward and forward as in the other swings, coordinating the dips and the swings so that the arms are extended at the top of the backward and forward positions.

Introductory skills. The following activities form an introductory set of skills for elementary-school gymnastics units on the parallel bars.

Front rise. Starting in an upper-arm-hang position with the hands grasping the bar and the length of the arm in contact with the bar, children begin a swing. As the legs swing vigorously forward (after a beginning backward swing), the arms push vigorously downward and the hips are extended to bring the body up above the bars.

Back rise. Starting from an upper-arm hang, the swing is initiated as above but in the opposite direction. As the legs swing back and up above the bar, the arms pull forward to bring the body over the hands. The ending position is a straight support position with the arms extended.

Upper-arm kip. Starting from an upper-arm hang, children swing the legs for-

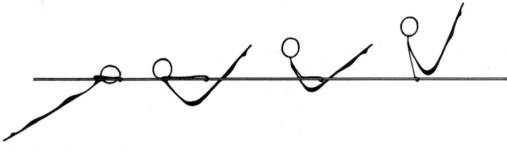

FIGURE 22.38 Front rise

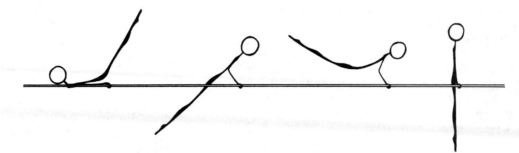

FIGURE 22.39 Back rise

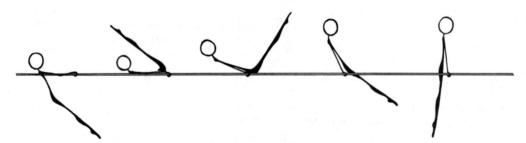

FIGURE 22.40 Upper-arm kip

ward and upward, flexing at the waist so that the feet are above the head with the legs extended. At this point the hips are extended and the arms thrust vigorously downward as the legs extend upward and outward, raising the body to finish in a straight support position.

Kip to a straddle seat. This skill is executed as above, except that during the final extension of the legs, the legs are split to complete the move to a straddle seat position on top of the bars.

Glide kip. Starting from a standing position with arms extended and grasping the bars, children initiate this skill by jumping slightly backward and flexing at the waist. The resulting swing carries the body toward the bars, where the body straightens and then flexes again at the waist as the feet of the extended legs near the bars. As the feet come through the inside of the bars and over the head, the body is pulled vigorously. The body will then begin to swing back again, and as this happens, the children pull hard with the extended arms and the legs are extended vigorously outward and upward (the kip movement). The skill ends in a straight support position.

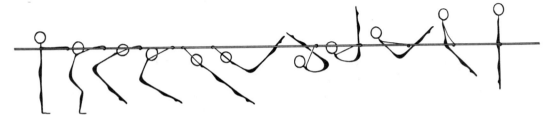

FIGURE 22.41 Glide kip

Pirouette in a straight support position. Starting in a straight support position, children shift weight to the left arm, looking in the same direction, push off with the right hand, and turn to a support position with both hands on the left bar. Children then shift weight to the right arm, look in that direction, and push off with the left hand, completing the turn to finish in a straight support position facing opposite to their beginning direction.

Horizontal Bar

Activities on the horizontal bar can be done at approximately chest height or at a regular elementary-school height of 6 to 8 feet. A double thickness of mats should be utilized. The bar should be grasped firmly. A regular grasp is palms down as the child looks down at the grip. A reverse grasp is palms up as the child looks down at the grip. The "law of thumbs" (Sweeney, 1973) is always followed: The thumbs go around the bar and always lead a circling movement.

Figures 22.42–22.45 show introductory activities designed to allow children to get the feel of the bar and to understand the

strength involved in performing skills on the bar.

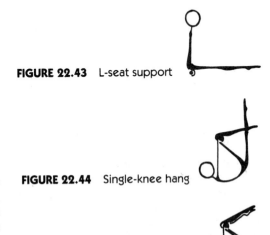

FIGURE 22.43 L-seat support

FIGURE 22.44 Single-knee hang

FIGURE 22.45 Double knee hang

Introductory activities. The following activities form an introductory set of skills for elementary-school gymnastics units on the horizontal bar.

Pull over. Standing facing the bar and using a regular grasp, children swing one leg forward, up, and over the bar, with the other leg trailing slightly in the same pattern. As the legs swing through, the arms pull toward the bar, and the head is pulled back to reach a balanced position of support. The ending position is a straght-arm support.

Single-knee circle mount. Starting from a single-knee hang, children swing the extended leg downward, pull the ar, and rotate to a straddle position on the bar.

Single-knee circle. Starting with a single-knee circle mount, then using a reverse

FIGURE 22.42 Straight-arm support

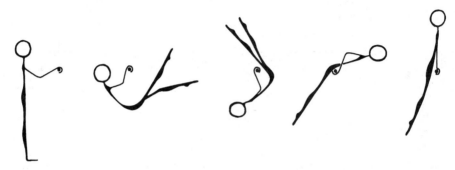

FIGURE 22.46   Pull over

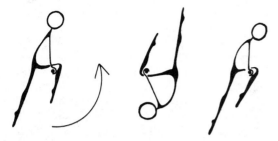

FIGURE 22.47   Single-knee circle

grasp, children swing extended leg forward slghtly so that the flexed knee can hook the bar. The extended leg is then swung vigorously backward as the upper body leans forward over the bar to carry the body in a complete circle.

Single-knee circle backward.   Starting from the same position as above with a regular grasp, children reverse actions to throw the body around the bar in a backward direction.

FIGURE 22.48   Single-knee circle backward

Front straddle circle.   Starting from a single-knee circle mount, children extend both legs to assume a straddle position on the bar with arms extended. The legs are then

thrust backward as the upper body leans forward to make a complete circle around the bar with the legs maintaining the straddle position throughout.

Back double-knee circle.   Starting from an L-seat support, children hook the bar behind their knees and throw their heads backward to develop the momentum to make a complete circle around the bar. When the circle is half completed, children should pull vigorously on the bar to help return the body to finish in a sitting position on top of the bar.

Front hip circle. Starting from a straight-arm support with a regular grasp, the hips are raised so that the upper thighs press against the bar. The head and shoulders are moved over the bar to begin the circle movement. As half the circle is completed, the bar is pulled vigorously and the head is pulled forward to help return the body to the beginning position.

Backward hip circle.   Starting from a straight-arm support with a regular grasp, children swing the legs backward and then vigorously forward, flexing the arms so that the hips can flex as the legs move under the bar in the circle movement. The head is thrust backward and the back is arched. As

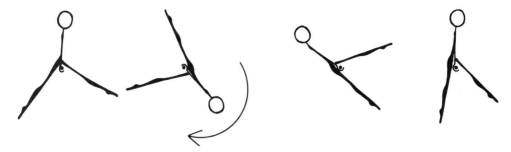

FIGURE 22.49 Front straddle circle

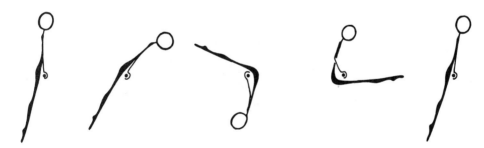

FIGURE 22.50 Back double-knee circle

FIGURE 22.51 Front hip circle

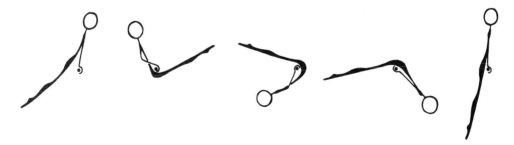

FIGURE 22.52 Backward hip circle

half the circle is completed, the hips are slightly flexed to increase the speed of the rotation.

Underswing dismount. From a straight-arm support with a regular grasp, the shoulders are thrust backward, the arms pull the bar, and the legs swing forward, causing the momentum to carry the legs and hips out and up and the hips away from the bar. At the height of the movement the bar is released and the child lands in a standing position.

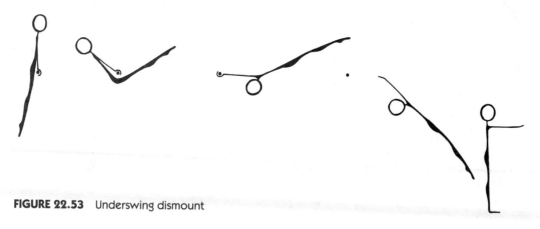

FIGURE 22.53 Underswing dismount

Simple back dismount. From a straight-arm support using a regular grasp, the body is swung under the bar with legs extended and back arched. As the body swings back to the rear, the children pull at the bar and pike at the waist so that the hips move high. At the height of the movement the bar is released, and the landing is completed in a standing position.

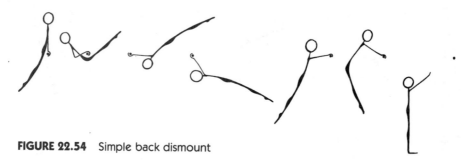

FIGURE 22.54 Simple back dismount

Balance Beam

Balance beam skills can be practiced initially on a line on the floor, then transferred to a low beam, and finally to a regulation beam. Mats should be used both under the beam and at the sides of the beam. Spotters can be used on each side of the beam as skills are performed. Skills can be learned individually and then put into combinations to form small routines.

Introductory activities. The following introductory activities are designed to allow children to get the feel of the beam and to develop the balance skills and confidence to use the beam.

Walk forward. Children walk forward using small steps, with arms extended sideward to aid in balancing.

Walk backward. Children walk backward by placing the toe of one foot behind the heel of the other foot, while arms extend sideward to aid in balancing.

Walk side step. Children move sideways along the beam by sliding one foot to the side and then bringing the other foot alongside with arms extended.

Chaase. Children move forward using the pattern of step, together, step, hold. Arms are extended to aid in balancing.

Side cross step. Starting by standing on the beam facing sideward, children cross one foot in front of the other and then cross the other foot behind to move along the beam.

Run. Children use small running steps to move down the beam, while arms extend to aid in balancing.

Introductory skills. The following activities form an introductory set of skills for elementary-school gymnastics using a balance beam.

One-leg squat balance. Children squat on one leg with arms extended and shoulders forward. The nonsupporting leg is gradually brought forward to a horizontal extended position.

FIGURE 22.55 One-leg squat balance

Turn. Children do a half-circle turn by pivoting on the balls of the feet with arms extended sideward for balance.

Jump turn. Starting from a sideward standing position, children jump into the air and turn a half-circle, landing in a balanced position facing the opposite direction. The head should lead in the direction of the turn, and the arm opposite the turn should be brought across the body to aid in the rotary motion.

Kick turn. Starting facing the length of the beam, children step forward with one foot and lift the other leg forward and up-

ward in an extended position. When the extended leg is at its highest point, the support foot pushes with a half-circle turn in the direction of the support foot (left turn when the support foot is the left foot).

Tuck jump. Starting from a flexed-knee position, children leap upward and bring the knees toward the chest to momentarily assume an open tuck position. The legs are then extended to land on the beam in a standing, balanced position.

Front scale. See page 401 for description of the front scale.

FIGURE 22.56 Front scale

Straddle stand. Starting from a standing position facing sideward, children move legs to a straddle position, flex at the waist to bring the upper body parallel to the floor, and extend the arms sideward.

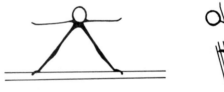

FIGURE 22.57 Straddle stand

Needle scale. Starting from a standing position facing the length of the beam, children execute a front scale, then continue leaning forward until their foreheads touch the lower front of the support leg, with the nonsupport leg raised directly overhead (the beam may be held to aid in the balance).

Straddle hold. Starting from a sideward position, children execute the straddle stand skill and then move their hands down to the beam, gradually shifting the weight from feet to hands, lifting the feet off the beam

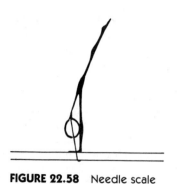

FIGURE 22.58   Needle scale

FIGURE 22.59   Straddle hold

and moving them forward so that the weight is borne by the hands.

Many of the introductory activities described earlier in this chapter can be used as balance beam skills. For example, the V-sit, jump and tuck, jump and pike, side scale, and one-leg balance can all be done on the balance beam. Likewise, some of the beginning tumbling skills can be done on the beam. Descriptions of those skills can be found earlier in this chapter.

Vaulting

The vaulting skills described here can be taught using a variety of equipment. A standard horse (long or pommel) is not necessary or even recommended. Likewise, a beat board is also not recommended because children often do not have the strength to utilize it properly. The pommel horse is expensive and many children lack the arm and upper body strength to utilize it properly.

However, vaulting can be taught over a number of different kinds of equipment that form low obstacles. Balance beams or benches can be utilized, or mats can be stacked to form a vaulting surface. If available, a small, adjustable elementary-school horse is most useful. There are also Swedish vaulting boxes available in small sizes, and these are most often adjustable to different heights. The vaulting skills outlined here are for the kinds of situations in which vaulting is taught across the width of the apparatus rather than down the length, as in the long horse.

Introductory activities. The following introductory activities are designed to allow children to acquire the skills necessary to begin actual vaulting progressions.

Entry. The major entry skill for vaulting is the running approach, which consists of a short run with an elongated final stride, which brings the child to a two-foot take-off position from which momentum is gathered and transferred from the lateral momentum of the run to vertical momentum for the jump. This can be accomplished by having children practice on the floor, jumping into a hoop with no apparatus present.

Jump and turn. Children do the approach and take-off, executing half and full turns during the flight phase, landing in a hoop in a balanced, standing position.

Jump and tuck. Same as above except that a tuck movement is executed during the flight phase.

Jump and straddle. Same as above except that a straddle movement is executed during the flight phase.

Jump and swan. Same as above except that a swan movement with an arched back is executed during the flight phase.

Jump and move. The approach and jump series can be practiced while children perform "fun" movements during the flight phase. Children might clap hands, touch body parts, and create "silly" movements during the flight phase, returning to the floor, landing in the hoop in a balanced position.

Introductory skills. The following activities form an introductory set of skills for vaulting in an elementary-school gymnastics program.

Front vault. Starting from a run and take-off, children place hands on the apparatus and turn their heads and shoulders to the right as their hips and legs rise to pass over the left side of the apparatus. The

FIGURE 22.60 Front vault

weight coming over the hands is borne on the right hand and the left leaves the apparatus to swing the body one-quarter turn as it descends to a balanced, standing position.

Straddle vault. From a run and take-off children place hands on the apparatus and swing the legs through and around in a straddle position to land in a balanced position on the other side of the apparatus.

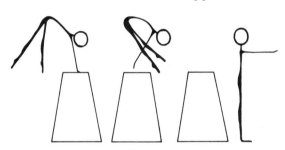

FIGURE 22.61 Straddle vault

Flank vault. From a run and take-off children place both hands on the apparatus. The weight coming up toward the apparatus is borne on the right hand, while the legs are

carried over the left end of the apparatus to land in a balanced position.

FIGURE 22.62 Flank vault

High front vault. The same technique is used as for the front vault except that the hips and legs are thrust higher, so that they are above the shoulders.

FIGURE 22.63 High front vault

Headspring vault (should be spotted). From a running approach and take-off children place both hands on the apparatus and thrust flexed hips over their heads while

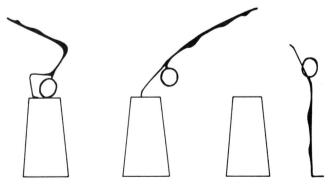

FIGURE 22.64 Headspring vault

placing the head on the apparatus. Head contact is maintained until the weight has gone over the hips. A headspring is then performed as described in the tumbling section.

Handspring vault (should be spotted). From a running approach and take-off chil-

dren execute the first part of the sequence in the same way as for the high front vault. As the handstand position is reached, children execute the handspring as described in the tumbling section.

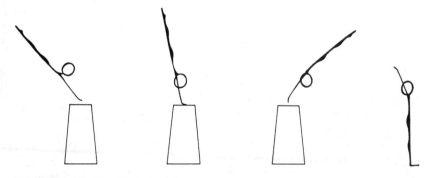

FIGURE 22.65 Handspring vault

AQUATICS

Aquatic activities provide the opportunity for children to develop desirable levels of physical fitness, physical skills, self-concept attributes, interpersonal competencies, and safety skills. Because of this they are appropriate inclusions in the physical education curriculum. The following points should be noted.

1. There is, perhaps, no more perfect activity than swimming for developing physical fitness. Once moderate levels of swimming skillfulness are attained, distance swimming can help children achieve desirable levels of cardiovascular-respiratory fitness. All swimming strokes require isokinetic exercise of all the limbs and motion in many body joints. This results in increasingly desirable levels of muscular strength and endurance and joint flexibility. Additionally, the energy expenditure associated with swimming participation helps children achieve and maintain desirable levels of body-weight fitness.

2. Many floating, locomotion, and diving skills can be learned by preschool and elementary-school youngsters. Ripe periods of neurological maturation and growth provide for economical learning. Since skills range

from the simplest floating activities to the complex techniques of competitive swimming, competitive diving, synchronized swimming, and skin diving, aquatic activities provide an appropriate challenge for every individual.

3. The challenges inherent in aquatic activities make units of instruction which deal with such activities fertile areas for the potential development of feelings of competence and self-worth. The successful negotiation of appropriate risk situations and skill mastery challenges can provide a meaningful dimension to a child's quest for identity.

4. Participating in aquatic activities is invariably "social." In such environments children have the opportunity to observe others' skill levels, compare their performances to those of others, help others to gain skillfulness, and deport themselves in ways which demonstrate competence in both leading and following.

5. With the vast opportunities that people have to come into contact with pools, lakes, and oceans, it is not surprising that over 7000 people drown in the United States each year (American Red Cross, *Swimming and Water*

Safety, 1968). It is imperative that children acquire the knowledge, attitudes, and skills that will eventually make them safe in water environments.

Waiting until a child is in high school before providing aquatic instruction, or leaving it to parents to provide for instruction in public or private recreational settings outside the school, are both indefensible policies. Unfortunately, children younger than high-school age can drown. Not everyone has the means to pay for swimming instruction for their children outside the school domain. Those who are poorest are least able to provide their children with such instructional opportunities. The time to learn to swim is early in life. Extensive research dealing with the swimming behavior of infants and young children has documented that learning to swim early in life is not only feasible but is also economical. Waiting until later may well mean that more time and effort will be necessary in order for learning to occur.

Administration Concerns

Facilities and equipment. Although it would be ideal if all elementary schools had their own swimming pools, having a pool is not necessary for providing aquatic instruction. Arrangements to use pool facilities in junior high schools and high schools in the same school district can sometimes be made. Pools located in public and private recreational centers can sometimes be rented. In warm climates arrangements to use swimming facilities at public beaches may provide a viable option. If arrangements during regular school hours cannot be made, it might be possible to offer such instructional opportunities on weekends, before school, or after school.

Ideally, an instructional pool facility for preschool and elementary-school children should provide an instructional area of chest depth level which is large enough to accommodate the largest class size. It should also offer a second, smaller area of water, well marked and distinguishable, that is over head level in depth. The pool should have abundant and easily negotiated avenues for exit and entry. Wide, nonslippery inclined ramps, vertical and inclined ladders with rung distances of 6 to 8 inches and steps 6 to 9 inches high generally fulfill this requirement. The deck around the pool should be wide, no more than 12 inches above the waterline, and slip resistant. Abrasive stripping and rubber matting help reduce falls on deck surfaces. Grading and good drainage on the deck are essential. The deck should be clear of obstacles that may cause falls or be fallen upon (Figure 22.66).

The water temperature should be maintained at 78 to 85 degrees and the air temperature should be 4 to 6 degrees higher than that of the water. Fixtures should be placed along the walls of the pool at 1-foot intervals so that aluminum poles or taut ropes may be suspended at water surface level or at 3- to 6-inch depths to serve as supports which children may use to learn to float. Storage should be provided to house teaching aids such as ropes, poles, flotation devices, goggles, and fins.

Basic rescue and lifesaving equipment should always be available in the instructional environment, along with a well-equipped first-aid kit. The pool should be locked when not in use to prevent access by unauthorized users and young children.

Staffing. Other staff must be employed, in addition to the instructor, to ensure safety and provide invaluable instructional assistance during teaching experiences. A lifeguard, certified to have completed the American National Red Cross's Life Saving and Water Safety Course, who is trained in lifesaving and water safety techniques, must be present and on duty whenever children are in a water environment. This person must never be expected to assume instructional responsibilities or to go on errands when children are present in the pool setting. No child should be left unattended in a pool area even for the length of time it takes to answer a telephone. At least one responsible staff member should know how to administer artificial respiration and give intelligent first aid.

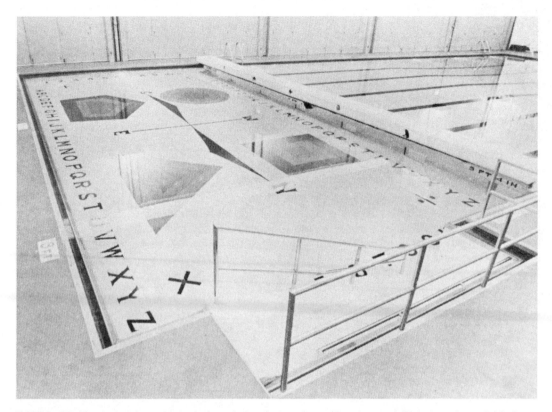

FIGURE 22.66 Swimming pool designed for instruction. (Courtesy of The American Red Cross, *Adapted Aquatics,* ARC, 1977, 121.)

Preschoolers learn best when the ratio of instructional staff to children is minimum (that is, 1 : 1 to 1 : 5). Elementary-school children also learn best when the ratio is quite low, though they tolerate more varied ratios with good instructional results (for example, 1 : 1 to 1 : 15). Parent volunteers and high-school students often can be called upon to assist with management and instruction in the pool environment. These people are particularly desirable when they have received earlier training in swimming instruction (for example, undergraduate physical education, American National Red Cross Water Safety certification). The use of parents and high-school volunteers serves an important secondary purpose—communicating what is going on in physical education to other persons in the school and city community.

Planning and evaluation. Careful program, unit, and daily lesson planning, and effective evaluation, are necessary parts of an instructional experience in swimming. Much that was discussed in Chapter 8, Planning for Effective Learning, should be reviewed, since it is relevant in the aquatic context. The American National Red Cross has developed extensive instructional materials that may be consulted. Local branches of the Red Cross should be contacted for assistance. This organization certifies lifeguards and swimmers at all skill levels.

Lesson length and frequency. There is no one best amount of time for a lesson. In general, 3- through 6-year-olds do well with half-hour sessions. Ideally, sessions should be held once daily for 8 to 10 weeks. But two-day-per-week or three-day-per-week schedules are also acceptable and provide for effective learning. One-day-per-week schedules are to be avoided, since less retention can be expected from one session to the next, seriously interfering with skill acquisition.

Parent releases and medical examinations. It is desirable to have each participant examined by a physician prior to entry into any type of physical activity program. This is especially true for swimming programs. Parents may voluntarily take children in for such a check, or a physician may have to be hired to provide such screening. Parents should be informed about the nature of the aquatic program and sign slips acknowledging that they agree to allow their children to participate. Such written contact with parents may also be used as a means of soliciting volunteer help for the program.

Safety practices and rules. Rules of deportment relative to safety in and around the pool should be made known to all who participate in aquatic activities. Such rules should be consistently enforced by all staff members. It is often desirable not only to communicate these rules repetitively but also to permanently post them in a conspicuous space in the pool area. Stick-figure drawings or pictures can be used to remind even the youngest participants of important rules.

General Instructional Considerations

Sensitivity to different age and developmental levels. After 3 years of age, the child is generally capable of exercising voluntary control over the breathing and limb movements needed in order to swim. At this time, and later in life, swimming instruction is generally most economical.

Children under 7 years of age present unique instructional challenges that are different, in many respects, from those presented by older elementary-school-aged youngsters. Modeling, careful structuring of the pool environment, and manual guidance are effective guidance techniques for all children learning to swim. However, highly verbally oriented styles of teaching and extensive dependence on verbal guidance are most associated with success when employed with older children.

Body support provided by the instructor. The manner in which instructors grasp and support children during instruction are crucial in facilitating learning. The following guidelines are useful.

Tell the learner ahead of time how to expect to be held. Children should be reassured that you do not intend to let go of them. You must never betray a child's trust by doing something other than what you promised. If you do, do not be surprised if the child does not trust you in the future.

Front float position. Let the child hold your hands while facing you with your hands on the surface of the water and extended toward the child. Children should be asked to grasp your hands with theirs, keeping the arms straight. This front facing position is secure for children since they can see you at all times and can use you for leverage should they wish to recover from a prone floating position quickly. Do not grasp the children from the side or from behind before they have experienced floating unassisted in the prone position. Lower your head to the same level as that of the child. This position encourages eye contact and provides reassurance (Figure 22.67).

Back float position. Two support positions work well with this skill. Hold the child

FIGURE 22.67 Holding a child in the front float.

FIGURE 22.68 Holding a child in the back float.

by the head with both hands so that you can easily adjust the tilt of the head backward to facilitate correct floating position and forward to assist the child in recovery. Gradually drop the level of your hands as the child assumes the back float position in the water and raise the level of your hands as the child recovers, as necessary (Figure 22.68). A second method which is effective, particularly if the child is very young, is to hold the child with your arms under the shoulders of the child. Your hands should be placed around the back and sides of the chest; thumbs up along the sides of the chest, and fingers underneath the back. Dip your own body to a lower level in the water as the child assumes the back float position and raise your body and hands to a higher level as the child recovers.

Diving. Position the child's head so that the upper portion of the child's arms are touching the ears. Press gently down on the back of the child's head to keep the child's chin tucked. Place the other hand on the child's legs to remind the child to allow the legs to follow, rather than coincide with, the initial movement of the upper body.

Flotation devices and other instructional aids. In general, flotation devices should not be heavily depended on. When used extensively, they tend to give children a false sense of security and often delay the onset of learning. However, when flotation devices are used sparingly and appropriately, they can facilitate learning.

1. Avoid using plastic inflatable devices such as water wings, arm cuffs, leg cuffs, and vests. They are unreliable.
2. Bathing suits with built-in flotation that can be adjusted by increasing or reducing the air in the suit seem to be promising devices for assisting learners. However, such suits are not readily available through vendors.
3. Kickboards are excellent aids when held while in the front floating position so that the hands grasp the board at the end, thumbs underneath and fingers on top. Holding onto the sides or upper portion of the board does not allow the child to experience the natural buoyancy of the body and delays the learning of the front float (Figure 22.69). To help learners with the back float, two boards should be employed. Each should be grasped in the middle of one long side by each hand, thumbs underneath and fingers on top, with arms fully extended sideward (Figure 22.70).
4. Flotation belts should fit securely around the child's waist. They are particularly useful in helping children learn the dog paddle. Prolonged use of this device is undesirable, as undue dependence on the belt delays the acquisition of the dog paddle and other front swimming skills.
5. Often chemicals in pools irritate the eyes of children and cause delays in learning to open the eyes under water. Goggles often help. Under no circumstances should face masks be employed which cover the nose. These are dangerous, since they seriously interfere with breathing and delay acclimation of the face to the water.
6. Fins are an excellent aid to help children who bend their knees too extensively to effectively propel themselves using a flutter kick. Fins

FIGURE 22.69 Using kickboards in the front float position.

FIGURE 22.70 Using kickboards in the back float position.

generally help the child experience the correct leg movement pattern and provide reinforcement, causing the child to locomote rapidly through the water. Overuse of this device is undesirable, since it creates undue dependence and delays eventual learning.

7. A taut rope or aluminum pole placed 3 to 6 inches under the water and parallel to the bottom of the pool provides a solid support on which to practice the prone float. Two such ropes or poles, set parallel to one another and as wide apart as the child is wide with arms fully extended to the sides, provides an excellent support system on which to practice the back float (Figure 22.71).

8. Weighted rings, hockey pucks, and plastic flowers weighted at the end with metal taped to the end of the stem encourage opening the eyes underwater, underwater swimming, and breath holding.

9. Hoops that are 1 yard in diameter weighted in such a way that they float in a position perpen-

FIGURE 22.71 Using aluminum poles for support in the back float.

dicular to the pool bottom provide excellent obstacles through which to swim underwater, encouraging the development of that skill and surface diving.

10. Sponge balls and beach balls encourage children's adjustment to splashing.

11. Platforms at water level and at graded elevations above the water surface encourage the development of jumping and diving skills.

Establishing a comfortable environment. Anything that reassures, relaxes, and motivates participation by learners is desirable in the pool setting, since it facilitates learning. Anything that threatens, produces anxiety, or results in lack of relaxation is to be avoided, since it seriously interferes with learning.

1. Children do not automatically understand the concept of water depth. The water environment you are introducing them to needs to be safely and systematically explored by the children before they can feel at home in it enough to learn effectively. Walking into the water and trying to touch the bottom with one's feet at different well-marked areas along the side of the pool is one useful activity. Watching you touch the bottom at different depths is another. Placing a long pole into the water and seeing where water wets the pole is a third effective activity. Children need to explore this environment themselves before they truly understand it.

2. Be consistently trustworthy. If you say you will hold the child and then let go, do not be too surprised if the child refuses your offer of support on subsequent occasions.

3. Do not force children to attempt skills they do not feel willing to try on their own. You can encourage and support, but avoid coercion. Reassure children that they do not have to do anything they do not wish to do.

4. Smile and speak softly. Appear as if you are enjoying yourself.

5. Stay close to a learner; proximity communicates security. Keep your head on the same level as the learner's head level so that you can provide reassuring eye contact.

6. Use imagery or fun language. For instance, with the flutter kick on the wall, say "Turn on the rain machine. Show me fast little kicks that

splash the water. I've got my umbrella, let's see if you can get me wet."

Teaching and Sequencing Specific Skills

Selected water acclimation skills (A), floating skills (F), locomotion skills (L), and diving skills (D) comprise a good portion of the content most appropriately taught to preschool and elementary-school-aged children. While there are certain fundamental skills that should be taught in a progressive fashion, there is room for flexibility in the order of their presentation. For example, one instructor may teach a front float, the front glide, the back float, and the back glide, in that order. Another instructor may wish to teach the front float and back float before going on to the front glide and back glide. In general, the skills presented in Chart 22.1 are in an order that generally reflects logical progression. Prerequisite skills, requiring mastery before new skills are introduced, are noted.

CHART 22.1 Aquatic skills inventory

PREREQUISITE SKILLS	SKILLS TO BE TAUGHT AND SUGGESTED INSTRUCTIONAL PROGRESSION
WATER ACCLIMATION (A)	
	Two-Foot Depth Skills
	A1 — Climbing down ladder, side of pool, or steps, into water which is 2' deep.
A1	A2 — Getting body wet in water which is 2' deep.
A2	A3 — Walking on hands and knees in water 2' deep with face out of the water, forward and backward.
A3	A4 — Getting face wet in water that is 2' deep.
A4	A5 — Blowing bubbles in 2'-deep water.
	A6 — Holding breath above water surface in 2'-deep water for 10 seconds.
A6	A7 — Holding breath below water surface in 2'-deep water for 10 seconds.
A7	A8 — Walk on hands and knees in water 2' deep, with face underwater and breath being held 10 seconds.
A6	A9 — Opening eyes under water which is 2' deep.
A6	A10 — Bobbing while holding breath in 2'-deep water.
A6	A11 — Bobbing, expelling air under water, inspiring air above water in 2'-deep water.
A3	A12 — Walking on hands and feet in a supine position in 2'-deep water, forward and backward.
	Chest Depth Skills
A1	A13 — Climbing down ladder, side of pool, or steps, into water which is chest depth.
A2	A14 — Getting body wet in chest depth water.
A3	A15 — Walking in chest depth water, forward and backward, turning around.
A4	A16 — Getting face wet in chest depth water.
A5	A17 — Blowing bubbles in chest depth water.
A6	A18 — Holding breath above water surface in chest depth water.
A7	A19 — Holding breath below water surface in chest depth water.
A10	A20 — Bobbing while holding breath in chest depth water.
A11	A21 — Bobbing, expelling air underwater, inspiring air above water twenty-five times in chest depth water.
A19	A22 — Flutter kick in prone position while holding the wall in chest depth water, recover to feet.
A9	A23 — Open eyes under chest depth water.
A23	A24 — Being splashed and splashing in chest depth water.
A22	A25 — Flutter kick in supine position, holding the wall in chest depth water, recover to feet.

(continued)

CHART 22.1 (*Continued*)

PREREQUISITE SKILLS		SKILLS TO BE TAUGHT AND SUGGESTED INSTRUCTIONAL PROGRESSION

FLOATING (F)

Front Float

A19	_____	F1 — Front float, holding with both hands onto a fixed bar which is 3 to 6" below the surface of the water, holding breath in chest depth water, recover to feet.
F1	_____	F2 — Front float, very lightly holding with both hands a fixed bar which is 3 to 6" below the surface of the water, holding breath in chest depth water, recover to feet.
F2	_____	F3 — Front float, very lightly holding with one hand onto a fixed bar which is 3 to 6" below the surface of the water, holding breath in chest depth water, recover to feet.
F3	_____	F4 — Front float, releasing a fixed bar (held in both hands) which is 3 to 6" below the surface of the water, holding breath in chest depth water, recover to feet.
F4	_____	F5 — Front float in water of chest depth level for 15 seconds, recover to feet.

Back Float

A12, F5	_____	F6 — Back float, holding onto two fixed bars (one in each hand) that are located 3 to 6" below the surface of the water, parallel to the learner and as far apart as the child is wide with arms almost fully extended sideward, chest depth water, recover to feet.
F6	_____	F7 — Back float, very lightly holding onto two fixed bars (one in each hand) that are located 3 to 6" below the surface of the water, parallel to the learner and as far apart as the child is wide with arms almost fully extended sideward, chest depth water, recover to feet.
F7	_____	F8 — Back float, releasing two fixed bars located 3 to 6" below the surface of the water, which are initially held one in each hand, parallel to the learner and as far apart as the child is wide with arms almost fully extended sideward, chest depth water, recover to feet.
F8	_____	F9 — Back float in water of chest depth for 15 seconds, recover to feet.

LOCOMOTION (L)

Front Glide With Flutter Kick

A22	_____	L1 — Front glide with flutter kick using a floating dumbbell or kickboard, face out of water except for chin, chest depth water, recover to feet, start with a push-off from bottom.
A19, L1	_____	L2 — Front glide with flutter kick using a floating dumbbell or kickboard, face in the water, breath holding, chest depth water, recover to feet, start with a push-off from bottom.
F5, L2	_____	L3 — Front glide with a push-off from bottom, recover to feet in chest depth water, holding breath, face submerged.
L3	_____	L4 — Front glide with push-off from the wall, recover to feet in chest depth water, holding breath, face submerged.
L3	_____	L5 — Front glide with flutter kick starting with a push-off from bottom, recover to feet in chest depth water, holding breath, face submerged, 3 yards.
L5	_____	L6 — Front glide with flutter kick starting with a push-off from wall, recover to feet in chest depth water, holding breath, face submerged, 3 yards.

Dog Paddle

| F5 | _____ | L7 — Dog paddle arm stroke with face out of water except for chin, waist belt flotation device worn, push-off from bottom, recover to feet, chest depth water. |

(*continued*)

CHART 22.1 *(Continued)*

PREREQUISITE SKILLS	SKILLS TO BE TAUGHT AND SUGGESTED INSTRUCTIONAL PROGRESSION
A22, L7	_____ L8 — *Dog paddle arm stroke and flutter kick with face out of water except for chin, waist belt flotation device worn, push-off from bottom, recover to feet, chest depth water.*
L8	_____ L9 — *Dog paddle arm stroke and flutter kick with face out of the water except for chin, no flotation device worn around the waist, push-off from bottom, recover to feet, chest depth water, swim 5 yards.*
L9	_____ L10 — *Dog paddle, push-off from wall in water well above head level, swim 5 yards.*

Changing Direction on the Front

L9	_____ L11 — While swimming the dog paddle in chest depth water, turn to the right or left and swim back in the direction from which you came.

Back Glide with Flutter Kick

F9	_____ L12 — Back glide with push-off from bottom, recover to feet in chest depth water.
L12	_____ L13 — Back glide with push-off from wall, recover to feet in chest depth water.
A25, L12	_____ L14 — Back glide with flutter kick starting with a push-off from bottom, recover to feet in chest depth water.
L14	_____ L15 — Back glide with flutter kick starting with a push-off from bottom, recover to feet in chest depth water, 3 yards.
A25	_____ L16 — Back glide with flutter kick starting with a push-off from side, in chest depth water, recover to feet, 3 yards.

Initial Backstroke

F9	_____ L17 — Back glide with finning arm action under the surface of the water, waist flotation belt worn, push-off from bottom in chest depth water, recover to feet.
A25, L17	_____ L18 — Back glide with finning arm action under the surface of the water, waist flotation belt worn, flutter kick, chest depth water, push-off from bottom, recover to feet.
L18	_____ L19 — Back glide with finning arm action under the surface of the water, flutter kick, no waist flotation belt worn, chest depth water, push-off from bottom, recover to feet, swim 5 yards.
L19	_____ L20 — Initial backstroke, push-off from wall in water well above head level, swim 5 yards.

Changing Direction on the Back

L19	_____ L21 — While swimming the initial backstroke in chest depth water, turn to the right or left and continue swimming back in the direction from which you came.

Turning Over

L9, L19	_____ L22 — While swimming the dog paddle, turn over and swim the initial backstroke; keep going in the same direction.

Front Crawl

A2, A22	_____ L23 — Front glide with flutter kick using a floating dumbbell or kickboard, face in water and lifted upward, alternately expelling and inspiring air, chest depth water, recover to feet, start with a push-off from bottom.

(continued)

CHART 22.1 (*Continued*)

PREREQUISITE SKILLS		SKILLS TO BE TAUGHT AND SUGGESTED INSTRUCTIONAL PROGRESSION
L23	_____	L24 — Front glide with flutter kick using a floating dumbbell or kickboard, face in water and turned to side, alternately expelling and inspiring air, chest depth water, recover to feet, start with a push-off from bottom.
L1	_____	L25 — Front glide with arm over arm front crawl arm stroke, holding breath, chest depth water, start with a push-off from bottom, recover to feet, face in water, waist flotation belt optional.
L25	_____	L26 — Front glide with arm over arm front crawl arm stroke, face in water, head turning to side, alternately expelling and inspiring air, chest depth water, push-off from bottom, recover to feet, waist flotation belt optional.
L24, L26	_____	L27 — Front crawl with arm over arm crawl arm stroke, flutter kick, face in water, head turning to side, alternately expelling and inspiring air, chest depth water, push-off from bottom, recover to feet, swim 5 yards.
L27	_____	L28 — Front crawl, push-off from wall in water well above head level, swim 5 yards.

Back Crawl

L12	_____	L29 — Back glide with arm over arm back crawl arm stroke, chest depth water, start with a push-off from bottom, recover to feet, waist flotation belt optional.
L16, L29	_____	L30 — Back crawl with arm over arm back crawl arm stroke, flutter kick, chest depth water, start with a push-off from bottom, recover to feet, swim 5 yards.
L30	_____	L31 — Back crawl stroke, push-off from wall in water well above head level, swim 5 yards.

Jump

A13, A15, A19, A20	_____	D1 — Feet first jump from water level into chest depth water, recover to feet.
D1	_____	D2 — Feet first jump from a 6″ elevation into water of chest depth, recover to feet.
D2	_____	D3 — Feet first jump from a 12″ elevation into water of chest depth, recover to feet.
D3	_____	D4 — Feet first jump from an 18″ elevation into water of chest depth, recover to feet.
L10, D4	_____	D5 — Feet first jump from water level into water well over head level, level off and swim.
D5	_____	D6 — Feet first jump from a 6″ elevation into water well over head level, level off and swim.
D6	_____	D7 — Feet first jump from a 12″ elevation into water well over head level, level off and swim.
D7	_____	D8 — Feet first jump from an 18″ elevation into water well above head level, level off and swim.

Sitting Dive

F5	_____	D9 — Front sitting dive from water level into chest depth water, level off and recover to feet.
D9	_____	D10 — Front sitting dive from a 6″ elevation into chest depth water, level off and recover to feet.
D10	_____	D11 — Front sitting dive from a 12″ elevation into chest depth water, level off and recover to feet.
D11	_____	D12 — Front sitting dive from an 18″ elevation into chest depth water, level off and recover to feet.
D5, D12	_____	D13 — Front sitting dive from water level into water well above head level, level off and swim.
D13	_____	D14 — Front sitting dive from a 6″ elevation into water well above head level, level off and swim.
D14	_____	D15 — Front sitting dive from a 12″ elevation into water well above head level, level off and swim.
D15	_____	D16 — Front sitting dive from an 18″ elevation into water well above head level, level off and swim.

(*continued*)

CHART 22.1 *(Continued)*

PREREQUISITE SKILLS	SKILLS TO BE TAUGHT AND SUGGESTED INSTRUCTIONAL PROGRESSION

Kneeling Dive

D9	_____ D17 — Front kneeling dive from water level into chest depth water, level off and recover to feet.
D17	_____ D18 — Front kneeling dive from a 6" elevation into chest depth water, level off and recover to feet.
D18	_____ D19 — Front kneeling dive from a 12" elevation into chest depth water, level off and recover to feet.
D19	_____ D20 — Front kneeling dive from an 18" elevation into chest depth water, level off and recover to feet.
D13, D20	_____ D21 — Front kneeling dive from water level into water well over head level, level off and swim.
D21	_____ D22 — Front kneeling dive from a 6" elevation into water well over head level, level off and swim.
D22	_____ D23 — Front kneeling dive from a 12" elevation into water well over head level, level off and swim.
D23	_____ D24 — Front kneeling dive from an 18" elevation into water well over head level, level off and swim.

Crouching Standing Dive

D17	_____ D25 — Crouching standing dive from water level into chest depth water, level off and recover to feet.
D25	_____ D26 — Crouching standing dive from a 6" elevation into chest depth water, level-off and recover to feet.
D26	_____ D27 — Crouching standing dive from a 12" elevation into chest depth water, level off and recover to feet.
D27	_____ D28 — Crouching standing dive from an 18" elevation into chest depth water, level off and recover to feet.
D21, D28	_____ D29 — Crouching standing dive from water level into water well over head level, level off and swim.
D29	_____ D30 — Crouching standing dive from a 6" elevation into water well over head level, level off and swim.
D30	_____ D31 — Crouching standing dive from a 12" elevation into water well over head level, level off and swim.
D31	_____ D32 — Crouching standing dive from an 18" elevation into water well over head level, level off and swim.

Standing Front Dive

D25	_____ D33 — Standing jump-away front dive from water level into chest depth water, level off and recover to feet.
D33	_____ D34 — Standing jump-away front dive from a 6" elevation into chest depth water, level off and recover to feet.
D34	_____ D35 — Standing jump-away front dive from a 12" elevation into chest depth water, level off and recover to feet.
D35	_____ D36 — Standing jump-away front dive from an 18" elevation into chest depth water, level off and recover to feet.
D36	_____ D37 — Standing jump-away front dive from water level into water well above head level, level off and swim.
D37	_____ D38 — Standing jump-away front dive from a 6" elevation into water well above head level, level off and swim.
D38	_____ D39 — Standing jump-away front dive from a 12" elevation into water well above head level, level off and swim.
D39	_____ D40 — Standing jump-away front dive from an 18" elevation into water well above head level, level off and swim.

(continued)

CHART 22.1 (*Continued*)

PREREQUISITE SKILLS	SKILLS TO BE TAUGHT AND SUGGESTED INSTRUCTIONAL PROGRESSION

Surface Dive

A13, A15, A19, A20	_____	D41 —Front tuck surface dive in chest depth water, touch bottom, return to surface.
L10, D41	_____	D42 — Front tuck surface dive in water well above head level, dive to a 5′ depth, return to surface.

Other Diving Skills

Other diving skills, such as springboard diving employing an approach and hurdle, may be introduced as children are ready.

23

traditional dance

Traditional dances are the dances of a country or nation that have been handed down from one generation to the next and which reflect the customs, rituals, occupations, and beliefs of the people of that country or nation. They include international folk dances, American play party games and singing games, as well as American contra, round, circle, mixer, and square dances.

These traditional, structured dances represent an important art form which serves to connect us to our past and helps us to appreciate and understand other cultures. They require that children demonstrate basic locomotor movements and dance steps, formations, positions, and figures in specified patterns and sequences. Many of them are sufficiently physically demanding so that they facilitate the development of various components of physical fitness. Since these dances are generally learned in social settings, providing them in the curriculum may also provide an opportunity for developing many desirable interpersonal skills. For these reasons such dances are often included in elementary-school physical education programs.

AN INTERNATIONAL SURVEY

Traditional dances which come from countries other than the United States are often referred to as international folk dances. English folk dances are of three forms: *sword, morris,* and *country* dances. The sword dance is the oldest form and was introduced into England during Roman times. It is for men only and involves simple running steps with complex figures. Morris dances are also performed by men only and were originally a fertility rite and part of religious ceremonies. They are thought to be an offshoot of sword dances because of their many similarities. They involve the execution of precise routines in which sticks are knocked together rhythmically, or large handkerchiefs are waved in various manners. English country dances are participated in by both men and women. They are danced in circles, lines, squares, or by couples. They are characterized by light running steps, and flirtation or coquetry is related to all movements.

German folk dances were not influenced by many cultures because Germany did not suffer the great invasions or waves of settlement endured by peoples of other countries. The *turning couple* dance is characteristic. The dances follow the same form and pattern as country dances, longways sets, quadrilles, or cotillions and tend to be lusty, with a heavy peasant quality punctuated by a stamp or heavy step. Dances from the north tend to be serious and those from the south are more lighthearted.

Modern folk dance in Greece is classified according to the rhythm of the dance. They include the *syrtos* or *kalamatianos,* in 7/8 time; the *tsamiko,* in 3/4 time; and the *chasapikos,* in 2/4 time. Most dances are done in a circle or broken-circle formation. Men and women dance together without partners. Generally, a basic step is repeated over and over. The dances of the mountainous regions are composed of jumpy movements, in contrast to the slow, even rhythm of the plains region dances.

Ireland's dances include *jigs, reels,* and *hornpipes.* The jigs and hornpipes are characterized by clog or tap steps, and the reels by shuffles or gliding steps. The dances are for solos, couples, groups, or sets. The distinguishing characteristic of such dances is the intricate and exact footwork. The group dances, such as the round, square, or longway formation dances, are based on simple steps.

Italian dance reflects Asian, Northern European, and African invasions. The dances may be classified as *processional* and *religious* dances, *sword* dances, *chain* dances in closed or open circles, and *couple* dances. The dances are generally simple in form and pattern and are performed in a free and easy manner. Steps are precise in sword dances. Pantomime and flirtation are included in many dances, especially courting dances.

Israeli dance reflects the many cultures Jews have experienced. Many dances have been created; first in the hora style and later encompassing accents and rhythms of the Orient. A group of dances come from the Song of Songs. Others come from the Jews of Yemen, who originally came from the southeast corner of Arabia. These dances are slow, gentle, and gradually accelerating.

Mexican dances are of great variety. Although some are primitive Indian dances, most represent Indian, European, and Spanish combinations, with the European and Spanish influences dominant. Indian dance is related to worship and war. When the Spanish arrived, they attempted to demolish the native culture. Although Christianity was introduced and the Aztec priests driven away, the pagan dance connected with religious ceremonies persisted and is still performed. The *zapateados* are the most popular dances today. Men clasp their hands behind their backs and women hold their skirts off the floor. Footwork is quick, with small steps close to the ground. There is a flirtatious aspect to the dance.

Russian dance is of great variety because widespread intermarriage, great movements of people, and the absence of natural geographical boundaries have characterized the country for a long time. Slavs, Turks, Ugrian tribes, Mongolians, and Tartars have all influenced Russian folk dance. The Western influence is limited to court dances and Polish contacts. The dance patterns include circles, processionals, couple dances, and some figure dances. Russian dances are generally characterized by emotional expressiveness.

Scandinavia includes three distinct racial groups: Nordics, Finns, and Lapps, who make up five different nations: Finland, Denmark, Norway, Sweden, and Iceland. The dances of these countries are relatively similar. Danish dancing is very smooth, with no bounce. Generally, frequent stamps are found at the beginning of dance phrases. The dances are generally squares and quadrilles. Walking, running, galloping, skipping, and doing the polka are commonly part of these dances. Finnish dancing tends to display even more vigor. Many dances involve a polka rhythm, small steps, and a good deal of bounce.

Norwegian dance style is somewhat freer and more spontaneous than that of the Danes. It includes three types of dances: *song* dances, *bygdedans*—or country dances, and the *turdans,* or figure dances. The song dance is the oldest form and involves a closed circle and a repetitive step format. This form has died out. The country dances are the oldest living form with an uninterrupted tradition. The figure dances involve quadrilles, contra, and square formations.

Swedish folk dances include three types: *traditional* dances, *choreographed* dances based on folk elements, and the *singing games*. The singing games are the oldest forms, and young and old persons still do them today. The traditional dances are comprised of revived dances, such as quadrilles, and living dances. The influence of the Polish dance in Sweden is evidenced in the *polska*. It is characterized by etiquette and by elegant movements as well as by many figures, with a slow walking part first and a fast part second.

Scottish dancing may be divided into *highland* dances, *reels*, and *country* dances. The reels are the oldest surviving Scottish social dances and are said to be of Celtic, sixteenth-century origin. The country dances developed in the eighteenth-century. The Scots also had sword dances, ritual dances which were connected to old folk customs, and play party games. Scottish dance steps are precise, light, and quick. The dances tend to be zesty. The body is carried erect and the supporting leg is straight. Toes are pointed at all times. Hand and arm positions are exact; fists are at hips, or arms are curved over the head with the thumb and third finger touching.

Switzerland is inhabited by French, German, Italian, and Romanish peoples. Dances reflect these influences: some distinct, others melded together. Some of the common types of dances are *lander, square, longways, chain* (or *round*) and *allenmande, alewander,* or *allemandler*. Swiss dances tend to be simple with precise movements.

Yugoslavia is really a new country formed from Serbia, Croatia, Bosnia, Herzegovina, Slovenia, Macedonia, and Montenegro. The *kolo* dance is very popular. There are open and closed kolos, parallel line dances, processions, solos, and dances for two or three people. The dances are lively and quick. Dancers tend to be relaxed from head to foot. A basic step is performed, which is accented by an occasional hop, spring, jump, stamp, or clap.

Three styles are prevalent: shaking with tiny jumps, hopping, and stepping, where the body trembles with each step.

American traditional dance includes play party games or singing games, mixers, couple dances, longways or contra dances, round dances, square dances, and circle dances. These dances have developed in the United States during the last 200 years. The square and longways (or contra) dances are the product of America's westward expansion and provide a good opportunity for the study of pioneer life. Round and couple dances are frequently of more recent origin and usually are based on combinations of walking steps, the two-step, and the schottische and polka step. They are often put to popular tunes played in a country style. Such dances are generally easy to learn and often provide for many partner changes. Many mixers with simple walking patterns can ease tension between boys and girls in the third and fourth grades. The square and longways dances are vigorous and easy to learn. They do not involve dance positions that require boys and girls to be paired for long periods of time and seem to appeal to intermediate-school boys.

Because traditional dances represent an art form, they may be a valuable part of the school curriculum devoted to the study of other countries and peoples. When the countries, peoples, and customs of a country are being studied in other subject areas, such dances help make the studies come to life for the student and enrich learning in social studies, language, literature, music, and art.

Additionally, early study of these dances may also become a foundation for a lifelong leisure activity. Many adult recreation groups have been formed to enjoy, perform, and study authentic folk dances.

PRESENTING APPROPRIATE AND SEQUENTIALLY ORDERED SKILLS

Ideally, traditional dances should be presented in logical progressions which are in keeping with children's physical skill levels as well as with the content of their curriculum in social studies, art, music, language, and literature. The required motor skills are discussed below.

Basic Locomotor Movements and Dance Steps

Locomotor movements are those that move the body from one place on the ground to another by means of the feet. The basic locomotor movements most frequently used in traditional dances are the walk, run, jump, and hop. Each of these has been defined earlier in Chapter 7. Dance steps are combinations of basic locomotor movements. They include the gallop, slide, skip, 3/4 run, step-hop, schottische, two-step, polka, waltz, and mazurka. The gallop, slide, and skip have been defined earlier in Chapter 7.

Step-hop. The step-hop is a combination of a walk and a hop, usually performed in a forward direction. The walk is taken forward with a strongly accented movement. This provides the take-off for the hop, which is done in place. The free foot in the hop is bent under the body. When the step is repeated, it begins with the alternate foot. The two movements in the step-hop are done to 2/4 meter musical accompaniment. The walk and hop have the same relative time value. The accent in the step-hop is on the walk.

Schottische. The schottische is a combination of three short running steps and a hop, usually performed in a forward direction. The three running steps are taken forward with an accent on the first run. The hop is done on the foot which takes the third run. The free foot on the hop is bent under the body. When the step is repeated, it begins with the alternate foot. The movements are done to a 4/4 meter musical accompaniment. The runs and hop have the same time value. The accent is on the first run with a secondary accent on the third.

3/4 Run. The 3/4 run is a combination of three runs done to music in 3/4 meter. It is a series of running steps. The first run is accented more than the other two. The 3/4 run is done to the three beats of an accompaniment in 3/4 meter. The three runs have the same relative time value.

Two-step. The two-step is a combination of three walking steps, usually performed in a sideward direction, progress through space being made by body turns. The first walk is taken sideward with the outside edge of the foot leading and the position of the feet open. The second walk brings the feet together into a closed position. The third walk is taken in the same direction as the first, ending in an open position of the feet, which is held for the fourth beat. In a series of two-steps, progression through space is accomplished by turning the body from side to side. Thus, the outside of one foot leads forward on one two-step and the outside of the other on the next. The two-step is done to 2/4 meter accompaniment. The first two walking steps have the same relative timing and the third is twice as long as the first two. The accent is on the first walk, with a secondary accent on the third. The word cues are step-together-step-hold. The rhythm is uneven.

Polka. The polka is a combination of a hop and three springy walking steps. It is usually performed sideward. The hop serves as a preliminary lift for the first walking step. This is taken sideward with the outside edge of the foot leading. The second walk brings the feet together into a closed position. The third walk is taken in the same direction as the first, ending the combination in an open position, which is held for part of the fourth count. The space pattern of the three walking steps is identical to that of the two-step. In a series of polka steps progression through space is accomplished by turning the body from side to side so that the outside of one foot leads forward, then the outside of the other. The polka is done to 2/4 meter accompaniment. The first two walking steps have the same relative timing, the third walking step is usually one and a half times as long as the first two, and the landing of the hop and the take-off into the first walk is half as long. The accent in the polka falls on the first walking step, and the hop is a means of emphasizing this accent. The hop is actually the beginning of the polka.

Waltz. The waltz is a combination of three walking steps, with an accent on the first of the three steps. The first walking step is a relatively long one taken either forward or backward and resulting in an open position of the feet. The second step is short and taken in a sideward direction with the other foot. It results in a second open position of the feet. The third step, taken with the first foot, brings both feet together. The waltz is done to three beats of an accompaniment in 3/4 meter. All three walking steps have the same relative time value, making the intervals in the waltz equal and the timing triple. The accent in the waltz is on the first of the three walking steps.

Mazurka. The mazurka is a combination of two springy walking steps and a hop. The two walking steps are taken forward and the hop is taken after the second walking step and on the same foot. During the hop, the free leg is bent under the body. The mazurka is done to a 3/4 meter accompaniment. The two walking steps and the hop have the same relative time value, making the intervals in the mazurka equal and the timing triple. The accent in the mazurka is on the first walking step, with a characteristic secondary accent on the second of the walking steps.

Suggested Performance Standards for Basic Locomotor Movements and Dance Steps

The following chart relates performance standards to grade level.

CHART 23.1 Suggested performance standards

	Suggested Grade Level		
	1–2	3–4	5–6
BASIC WALK	*		
WALK VARIATIONS			
Changes in direction—in place; backward; sideward (step-together); turning around	*		
Sideward (crossing feet in front or in back)		*	
Sideward (feet crossing alternately in front and in back, grapevine); change facing from forward to backward, sideward, and turning around, while continuing in same direction			*
Changes in level—on tiptoe; with knees half bent; with knees fully bent	*		
Changes in dimension—steps shorter than natural; steps longer than natural	*		
Changes in tempo—steps faster than natural; steps slower than natural	*		
Changes in shape—knees bent up high in front; body bent forward; hands on knees; arms high over head	*		
Legs crossing on every step; legs kicking up in front; arms held in any position; arms swing in any direction		*	
Knees bent up at sides; legs kicking up at sides; both arms swinging parallel or in opposition in any direction			*
With one other—side by side, inside hands joined, walking forward; facing, both hands joined, walking around in a small circle	*		
Side by side, arms linked, walking forward; one behind the other, both facing forward, one hand on shoulder of person in front		*	
Side by side in open social dance position, walking forward; right sides together in social dance position, walking around (turning)			*
With two others—side by side, inside hands joined, walking forward; in a circle, hands joined, walking around circle	*		
Side by side, arms linked, walking forward		*	
With three others—right or left side toward center and right or left hands joined in center, walking around (star formation)		*	
With many others—in a circle, hands joined, walking around circle; in a line with one child leading, hands joined, walking forward	*		

(continued)

CHART 23.1 (*Continued*)

	Suggested Grade Level		
	1–2	3–4	5–6
In a circle, hands joined, walk forward toward the center and backward from the center			*

BASIC RUN   *

RUN VARIATIONS

	1–2	3–4	5–6
Changes in direction—in place, turning around	*		
Backward		*	
Sideward, crossing feet in front or in back; change facing from forward to backward while continuing in same direction			*
Changes in level—crouching low		*	
Changes in dimension—steps shorter than natural; steps longer than natural		*	
Changes in shape—knees bent up high in front; arms extended forward or backward	*		
Legs kicking up in front or back; arms held in any position		*	
Crossing legs on each step; bending knees up at sides; bending body sharply forward or backward			*
Changes in dimension, level, timing, and force—doing several continuous leaps using slower timing, greater elevation from the floor, and longer steps than those used in the run; combining a leap with one or two preparatory runs in a continuous sequence			*
With one other—side by side, inside hands joined, running forward	*		
Facing, both hands joined, running around in a small circle; right or left elbows linked, running around in a circle		*	
Right or left sides together, inside hands on outside hip of partner, running around (turning)			*
With two others—one in front and two in back, or vice versa, all facing forward with hands joined, running forward		*	
Side by side, arms linked, running forward and wheeling in half-circles or circles			*
With many others—in circle, hands joined, running around circle		*	
In circles, hands joined, running around circle and forward and back in circle; in line with one person leading, hands joined, running forward			*

BASIC JUMP   *

JUMP VARIATIONS

	1–2	3–4	5–6
Changes in direction—forward; turning around	*		
Backward; sideward		*	
With half and full turns while in air			*
Changes in level—knees fully bent; knees half bent	*		
Changes in dimension and timing—jumping close to floor; jumping high into the air		*	
Changes in dimension, level, timing, and force—combining a certain number of quick jumps with half that number of slow jumps; combining a fast jump with a slow jump; gradually retarding quick jumps to slower jumps, and vice versa			*
Changes in shape—landing with feet alternately apart and together; swinging arms out and in or feet jumping apart and together	*		
Landing with one foot forward and the other backward, and vice versa; landing with feet alternately apart and crossing; clapping on every other jump; swinging parallel arms from side to side or forward and back		*	
Extending legs sideward while in air; clicking heels together while in air; arms swinging in outward circles or forward and backward			*
With one other—side by side, inside hands joined, jumping forward; facing, both hands joined, jumping around in small circle		*	

(continued)

CHART 23.1 (Continued)

	Suggested Grade Level		
	1–2	3–4	5–6
BASIC HOP	*		
HOP VARIATIONS			
Changes in direction—forward; turning around	*		
Sideward; backward		*	
Changes in shape—changing from one foot to the other after a certain number of hops; with arm on side of hopping foot extended sideward	*		
Lifting free leg forward or sideward, or knee bent up in front; arms folded in front of chest or hands clasped behind back			*
Holding free foot sideward or backward; swinging free leg backward on one hop and forward on the next; folding arms around knee of free leg			*
BASIC GALLOP	*		
GALLOP VARIATIONS			
Changes in shape—clapping thighs as feet gallop; swinging one arm overhead		*	
With one other—side by side, inside hands joined, galloping forward; one in back of the other, both facing forward, both hands joined, galloping forward	*		
With two others—one in front and two in back, or vice versa, all facing forward, galloping forward	*		
Side by side, facing forward, arms linked, galloping forward and wheeling in half-circles or circles		*	
BASIC SLIDE	*		
SLIDE VARIATIONS			
Changes in facing—sliding once with one side forward and then again with the other side forward, continuing in same direction (simple polka)	*		
Changes in shape—extending arms sideward; clapping on each side		*	
With one other—facing, both hands joined, arms extended toward other person or extended sideward, sliding sideward	*		
Side by side, inside hands joined, sliding face to face and back to back (polka with hinge turn)		*	
With many others—in a circle, hands joined, sliding around circle in both directions		*	
BASIC SKIP	*		
SKIP VARIATIONS			
Changes in direction—turning around	*		
Changes in level, dimension, and timing—crouching low; skipping high		*	
Changes in shape—arms folded on chest or behind back; clapping on each skip		*	
With one other—side by side, inside hands joined, skipping forward; side by side, inside hands cross and joined with outside hands, skipping forward; right or left hands joined, skipping in small circles; facing, both hands joined, skipping in small circle	*		
Right or left arms linked, skipping around in small circle		*	
With two or three others—side by side, inside hands joined, skipping forward; in circle, hands joined, skipping around circle; in line, one child leading, hands joined, skipping forward	*		
With many others—in circle, hands joined, skipping around circle in both directions; in line, with one child leading, hands joined, skipping forward		*	

(continued)

CHART 23.1 (*Continued*)

	Suggested Grade Level		
	1–2	3–4	5–6
BASIC STEP-HOP		*	
STEP-HOP VARIATIONS			
Changes in direction—forward; backward; in place; sideward; turning		*	
With one other—side by side, inside hands joined, moving forward or backward; facing, both hands joined, moving in place, turning around, or one moving forward and the other backward		*	
With two others—inside hands joined, going under arch formed by other two persons		*	
With many others—in circle, hands joined, moving around circle in both directions and forward and backward		*	
BASIC SCHOTTISCHE		*	
SCHOTTISCHE VARIATIONS			
Changes in direction—forward and backward; in place; turning		*	
Changes in shape—free leg swings forward and across supporting leg		*	
With one other—side by side, inside hands joined, moving forward; facing, both hands joined, turning around; right or left arms linked, turning around		*	
BASIC ¾ RUN		*	
¾ RUN VARIATIONS			
Changes in direction—forward; in place; backward; turning in place		*	
Changes in shape—arms extended sideward or swung from side to side		*	
With one other—side by side, inside hands joined or arms linked, moving forward		*	
With two others—side by side, inside hands joined or arms linked; with one in front and two in back, or vice versa, facing forward, hands joined around a circle		*	
With many others—in a circle, hands joined, facing toward the center, moving forward and backward; facing around the circle, moving forward; in a line, side by side or one behind the other, hands joined, moving forward		*	
BASIC TWO-STEP			*
TWO-STEP VARIATIONS			
Changes in direction—forward; backward; in place; quarter turns; half turns; sideward; hinge turn			*
With one other—in closed dance position attempt changes in direction forward, backward, in place, quarter turns, half turns; in open social dance position attempt hinge turn			*
BASIC POLKA			*
POLKA VARIATIONS			
Changes in direction—forward; backward; sideward			*
With one other—side by side, with inside hands joined, starting with the outside feet and moving forward in a series of face-to-face, back-to-back turns; facing, with both hands joined, starting with the feet on the same side, one moving forward and the other backward with a series of diagonal or hinge turns; facing, with hands on each other's elbows, turning always in the same direction with quarter turns, forming a square with a polka on each side; facing, in waist-shoulder or closed social dance position, moving in all directions with a series of hinge turns			*

(*continued*)

CHART 23.1 *(Continued)*

	Suggested Grade Level		
	1–2	3–4	5–6
BASIC WALTZ			*
WALTZ VARIATIONS			
Changes in direction—forward; backward; turning			*
Changes in timing—Viennese waltz (faster than normal); peasant waltz (very fast)			*
With one other—facing, in closed social dance or waist-shoulder position, moving forward and backward, continuously backward or continuously forward or turning around			*
BASIC MAZURKA			*
MAZURKA VARIATIONS			
Changes in direction—forward; backward; in place; turning			*
Changes in shape—two running steps may be substituted for the walking steps; arms leading movement may be extended in line of direction or placed on the leading hip while other arm is extended overhead			*
With one other—using basic mazurka, with right or left sides together, inside arms linked, and the other arm extended overhead, turning around; using the sideward-moving mazurka, facing, hands joined away from the line of direction of the step, other hand on hips or extended sideward, starting with the feet on the same side; one in back of the other and facing in the same direction, arms extended sideward and hands joined, starting with the feet on the same side and moving sideward			*
With many others—in a circle, hands joined, moving around the circle with the basic or sideward-moving mazurka			*

Age-Related Dances

The following charts relate various types of dances to the grade levels for which they are appropriate. Records and record sources are listed at the end of this chapter.

CHART 23.2 Dances based on the walk and/or skip for younger children

NAME	SUGGESTED GRADE LEVEL	NATIONALITY	FORMATION	SKILLS	RECORD
Baa Baa Blacksheep	1–2	English	Single circle, all facing center	Walk, stamp, bow	FC 1191 R 700A RCA E-83
Bluebird	1–2	American	Single circle, no partners	Walk and dramatization of bluebirds	FC 1180 RCA 20214
Did You Ever See a Lassie?	1–2	Scottish	Single circle, no partners, hands joined, facing left, extra person	Skip clockwise (CW) with hands joined; imitate one person's actions	FC 1183 RCA 45-5066 RCA 41-6152
Farmer in the Dell	1–2	English-American	Single circle, hands joined, facing the center	Walk CW	FC 1182 RCA 45-5066 RCA 41-6152

(continued)

CHART 23.2 (*Continued*)

NAME	SUGGESTED GRADE LEVEL	NATIONALITY	FORMATION	SKILLS	RECORD
Go Round and Round the Village	1–2	English	Single circle, hands joined, no partners, extras	Walk, skip	FC 1191 RCA EPA 4144
Jolly Is the Miller	2–3	American	Double circle, partners with inside hands joined, facing counterclockwise (CCW), boys on inside	Marching	RCA 45-5067 FC 1192 EA 10, Side 3
London Bridge	1–2	English	File	Walk, arches	RCA 20806 RCA 41-6151
Muffin Man	1–2	English	Single circle, facing center, no partners, extras	Walk	FC 1188 RCA WE 87
Mulberry Bush	1–2	English	Single circle, hands joined, facing center	Walk or skip CCW	WF 2, Side B RCA 45-5065 FC 1183
Oats, Peas, Beans, and Barley Grow	1–2	English	Single circle, hands joined, partners, farmer stands inside	Walk or skip CW, partner choosing	RCA 45-5667 FC 1182 WF 2, Side B
Ring Around the Rosie	1–2	English	Single circle, facing center, hands joined	Walk	FC 1199
Shoo Fly	2–3	American	Mixer, single circle, hands joined, facing center, girl on left of boy	Walk or skip	FC 1102 FC 1185
Sing a Song of Sixpence	1–2	English	Single circle, facing center, hands joined, no partners, extras	Walk forward and backward	FC 1180 RCA 22760 R 700
Thread Follows the Needle	1–2	American	Single line, hands joined, no partners	Walk, turning under an arch	RCA 22760-E87

CHART 23.3 Dances based on the skip, slide, or run for younger children

NAME	SUGGESTED GRADE LEVEL	NATIONALITY	FORMATION	SKILLS	RECORD
Carrousel	2–3	Swedish	Circle, no partners, hands joined	Skip, sideward step, ends with a fast slide	RCA 45-6179 FC 1183
Children's Polka	2–3	German	Single circle, partners	Draw, stamp	FC 1187 RCA 1625
Chimes of Dunkirk	2–3	French	Double circle, partners	Skip CW, turn CW with partner	FC 1187 EA 26, Side 5

(*continued*)

CHART 23.3 (*Continued*)

NAME	SUGGESTED GRADE LEVEL	NATIONALITY	FORMATION	SKILLS	RECORD
				while both hands joined, stamp	RCA 45-6176
Danish Dance of Greeting	2–3	Danish	Single circle, partners, all facing center	Run, bow, curtsy	FC 1187 RCA EPA 4146 R 726
Farmer in the Wheat	1–2	American	Single circle, facing center, farmer stands in center	Skip, walk	RCA 41-6152 RCA 45-5066 FC 1182
Five Little Chickadees	1–2	English	Single circle, facing center, no partners, five in center	Run	FC 1184
Hickory Dickory Dock	1–2	American	Double circle, partners facing	Run with a partner, hands joined, CCW	RCA 22760
How Do You Do My Partner	1–2	Swedish	Double circle, partners facing, boys on the inside	Skip, bow, curtsy	FC 1190 RCA 21685 RCA EPA 4144
Let Your Feet Go Tap, Tap, Tap	2–3	German	Double circle, partners, boys on inside, facing CCW	Skip CCW with partner while inside hands are joined	FC 1184 RCA 45-6182
Looby Loo	1–2	English	Single circle, facing center, hands joined, no partners	Skip, dramatization with various body parts	FC 1184 RCA 20214 R 702
Muffin Man	2–3	English	Single circle	Walk, word dramatization, jumping	FC 1180
Noble Duke of York	2–3	English	Contra or longways, partners	Skip, cast-off	RCA LE 3000
Pease Porridge Hot	2–3	English	Double circle, partners	Skip CCW and CW with a partner while both hands are joined	FC 1190
Rig-a-Jig-Jig	2–3	American	Single circle, facing center, one child in center, no partners	Skip, slide	FC 1199 FD MH-1043 WF 2, Side B
Sally Go Round the Moon	1–2	American	Single circle, facing center, hands joined	Skip	FC 1198 RCA 45-5064
Shoemaker's Dance	1–2	Danish	Double circle, partners facing, boys on inside	Skip with partner, inside hands are joined	FC 1187 RCA LPM 1624 R 750
Ten Little Indians	1–2	American	Single circle, no partners	Skip, simulated Indian dancing	FC 1194 RCA WE87 WF 2, Side B
Black Nag	4–5	English	Longways	Slide	WF 109 FC 1174

(*continued*)

CHART 23.3 (*Continued*)

NAME	SUGGESTED GRADE LEVEL	NATIONALITY	FORMATION	SKILLS	RECORD
Bow Belinda	5–6	American	Contra, partners	Walk, skip, cast-off, do-si-do, elbow swing, employs all figures of "Virginia Reel" except reel	FC 1189 RCA LE 3001
Cshebogar	3–4	Hungarian	Single circle, partners	Slide, skip, draw, turn	FC 1195 RCA EPA 4143 WF 6, Side A
Gustaf's Skoal	3–4	Swedish	Quadrille, partners	Forward and back, couples skip through arches	FC 1196 RCA 45-6170 WF 108
Paw Paw Patch	3–4	American	Contra, partners	Skip, cast-off	FC 1182 WF 111 FD MH 1109

CHART 23.4 Dances based on the step-hop and schottische

NAME	SUGGESTED GRADE LEVEL	NATIONALITY	FORMATION	SKILLS	RECORD
Bleking	3–4	Swedish	Free, couples	Bleking step, step-hop turn	RCA 1626 FC 1188
Crested Hen	3–4	Danish	Open, groups of three	Step-hop, stamp, arches	RCA 45-6176 FC 1159 WF M108
Danish Schottische	3–4	Danish	Double circle, partners	Schottische, step-hop	RCA 1622
Ersko Kolo	5–6	Yugoslavian	Single circle, partners	Schottische, step-hop	FD MA 3020A
Gerakina Syrto	3–4	Greek	No partners	Walk, step-hop	FC 1060
Highland Schottische	4–5	Scottish	Circle, partners, mixer	Schottische, step-hop, linked arm turns, toe touch	RCA 45-6179
Hora	4–5	Israeli	Single circle	One sideward schottische and one step-hop repeated continuously	FC 1110 RCA EPA 4140 FD MH 1052
Korobushka	4–5	Russian	Circle, mixer, partners	Schottische, Hungarian break step	FC 1170 FD MH 1059 I 1022
Rheinlander Schottische	4–5	German	Sets of three	Two schottisches and four step-hops used in a forward and backward space pattern	FD MH 1050

(*continued*)

CHART 23.4 (Continued)

NAME	SUGGESTED GRADE LEVEL	NATIONALITY	FORMATION	SKILLS	RECORD
Road to the Isles	5–6	Scottish	Free, couples	Heel touch and side cross walk schottische, with quick turns	FC 1416 I 1005 FD MH 3003
Rumunsko Kolo	3–4	Yugoslavian	No partners	Schottische	FC MH1010 FC 1402
Seven Jumps	3–4	Danish	Single circle, no partners	Accumulative "jumps" such as lifting knees and kneeling, etc., alternated with circular step-hop	RCA LPM 1623 RCA EPA 4138 WF 4, Side A
Shibolet Bassadet	4–5	Israeli	Circle, no partners	Dancers face in and out of circle, step-hop forward and backward	RCA LPM 1622 RCA EPM 4361 EA 22, Side 1
Weggis	5	Swiss	Couples	Schottische	FD MH 1046 FC 1170 I 1008

CHART 23.5 Dances based on the run and ¾ run

NAME	SUGGESTED GRADE LEVEL	NATIONALITY	FORMATION	SKILLS	RECORD
La Raspa	4	Mexican	Couples	Bleking step, run	FC 1119 EA 26, Side 6 RCA LPM 1623
Mayim	5–6	Israeli	Single circle	Cross grapevine run	FC 1108
Norwegian Mountain March	4–5	Norwegian	Groups of three, open	One person in front and two behind, hands joined, turn under arches, ¾ run	RCA 6173 FC 1177
Troika	5–6	Russian	Groups of three, open	Running, hands joined, one person runs under arch made by other two	WF 105 FD MH1059 FC 1170

CHART 23.6 Dances based on the two-step and polka

NAME	SUGGESTED GRADE LEVEL	NATIONALITY	FORMATION	SKILLS	RECORD
Ace of Diamonds	5	Danish	Double circle, partners	Face-to-face, back-to-back polka, elbow swing	RCA LPM 1622 WF 102 RCA LPM 4137
Cotton-Eyed Joe	6	American	Mixer, round circle, partners	Heel-toe polka, hop, two-step	WF 118 ER FD3 FC 1035
Heel and Toe Polka	5–6	American	Couple, open, partners	Heel-toe followed by a polka in closed position, continuous polka turns	FC 1035 WF 102 M 400
Hopp Mor Anika	4–5	Swedish	Double circle, partners	Walk, skip, polka face-to-face and back-to-back	RCA EPA 4142 RCA LPM 1624
Jessie Polka	5–6	American	Couple or round, free, partners	Two-step or polka	FC 1071 M 6325 ER FD2
Kalvelis	5–6	Lithuanian	Single circle, partners	Polka used around single circle, forward and back, grand right and left and in closed position, linked-arm turns	FC 1051
Lott Ist Tod	5–6	Swedish	Double circle, partners	Slow and quick slides, face-to-face and back-to-back polka	RCA LPM 1622 RCA EPA 4135 EA 22, Side 5
Patty Cake Polka	4	American	Mixer, double circle, partners	Heel-toe, slide, skip, polka	FC 1124 W 4624 FD MH1501
Susan's Gavotte	5	American	Mixer, circle, partners	Walk, slide, step-swing, two-step face-to-face and back-to-back or in closed position	FC 1094 EA 9, Side 2 WF 1, Side A
Tantoli	4	Swedish	Double circle, partners	Heel-toe polka, step-hop turn	FC 1160
Teton Mountain Stomp	5–6	American	Double circle, partners	Two-step, closed and right-and-left reverse social dance positions, side walk, stamp	WD 7615
Weggis	4	Swiss	Free, couples in promenade position	Heel-toe polka, step-hop, schottische	WF M101 FC 1170 FD MH1046

CHART 23.7 Dances based on the waltz and mazurka

NAME	SUGGESTED GRADE LEVEL	NATIONALITY	FORMATION	SKILLS	RECORD
Little Man In A Fix	5–6	Danish	Open, mixer, couples, two couples	Couples turn in a wheel, and women run under arches, fast waltz in closed position, run	RCA 20449 FD MH1054
Rye Waltz	6	American	Open or double circle, boys in center, open dance position	Slide, waltz in closed position	FC 1103
Varsouvianna	5–6	American	Open, partners	Waltz	W 7516 FC 1165
Varsouvienne	5–6	Swedish	Open, partners	Mazurka, waltz	FD MH1023

CHART 23.8 Dances based on the walk for older children

NAME	SUGGESTED GRADE LEVEL	NATIONALITY	FORMATION	SKILLS	RECORD
Darling Nellie Gray	5–6	American	Square	Honor, allemande left, do-si-do, circle four, right-and-left through and back, swing	EA 2, Side 5
Divide the Ring	5–6	American	Square	Honor, grand right and left, promenade, bow, swing, divide the ring and cut off six, do-si-do	RCA 3000
Do-Si-Do and Swing	3–4	American	Square	Honor, circle four, do-si-do, swing	EA 1, Side 4
Double Sashay	5–6	American	Square	Circle left and right, grand right and left, allemande left, promenade, sashay	RCA LE 3001
Duck for the Oyster	5–6	American	Square	Honor, circle left and right, allemande left, grand right and left, promenade, circle four, duck under an arch	RCA LE 3000
Form an Arch	5–6	American	Square	Honor, circle left and right, allemande left, grand right and left, promenade,	RCA LE 3001

(continued)

CHART 23.8 (Continued)

NAME	SUGGESTED GRADE LEVEL	NATIONALITY	FORMATION	SKILLS	RECORD
Girls to the Center	5–6	American	Square	forward and back, pass through arch, swing Circle, grand right and left, promenade, swing, walk to center and back	RCA LE 3000
Glow Worm	4	American	Mixer, circle, partners	Walk	FC E1158 EA 9, Side 3 RCA LPM 1623
Grand March	5	American	Mixer, single lines of boys or girls	Marching in twos, fours, eights	
Greensleeves	4	English	Double circle, two couple sets	Walking backward under arches, four-hand star	WF 106 RCA EPA 4141 EA 13, Side 5
Heads and Sides	3–4	American	Square	Honor, do-si-do, swing, promenade, circle	EA 1, Side 2
Hinky Dinky Parley Vous	6	American	Square	Do-si-do, allemande left, grand right and left, allemande right	FC 1023 RCA LE 3000
Hokey Pokey	3	American	Mixer, single circle	Walk, body part identification	MC 699
Hot Time in the Old Town	5–6	American	Square	Honor, swing, promenade, couples lead right and left	EA 18, Side 3 W 7115
Ladies Chain	5–6	American	Square	Honor, do-si-do, promenade, couples lead right and left, circle, allemande left and right	EA 2, Side 4
Ladies Chain the Mountain	5–6	American	Square	Honor, circle, forward and back, two ladies chain, swing, allemande left, promenade	EA 18, Side 1
Left Hand Lady Pass Under	5–6	American	Square	Honor, do-si-do, promenade, circle, forward and back, couples lead right and left	EA 3, Side 4
Life on the Ocean Wave	5–6	American	Square	Circle, allemande left, grand right and left, right-	RCA LE 3001

(continued)

CHART 23.8 (*Continued*)

NAME	SUGGESTED GRADE LEVEL	NATIONALITY	FORMATION	SKILLS	RECORD
				and-left through, swing	
Miserlou	6	Greek	Line, no partners	Walk, slow touch step, grapevine, two-step forward and back with swinging body turns	RCA 1620 FC 1060 CO 7217F
Nine Pin	5–6	American	Square	Honor, allemande left, grand right and left, swing, promenade, forward and back, circle, do-si-do	EA 18, Side 2
Oh Johnny	5–6	American	Square	Swing, allemande left, do-si-do, promenade	FC 1037 I 1099 M 6525
Oh Susannah	5–6	American	Mixer, single circle, face center, hands joined, girl on boy's right	Walk, grand right and left, do-si-do, promenade, slide	FC 1186 RCA 45-6178 RCA LPM 1623
Red River Valley	5–6	American	Square	Circle, swing, ladies' star, men's star	FC 1053 I 1096 RCA LE 3000
Sicilian Circle	5–6	American	Mixer, couples in square formation	Forward and back, circle, ladies' chain, right-and-left through	W A754A FC 1115 ME 104
Solomon Levy	5–6	American	Square	Swing, allemande left, grand right and left, promenade	M 007-4A
Skip to My Lou	4	American	Single circle	Walk, skip	FC 1192 FD MH1110
Swing at the Wall	5–6	American	Square	Allemande left, grand right and left, promenade, couples separate and divide, swing	RCA LE 3001
Take a Little Peek	5–6	American	Square	Honor, swing, promenade, couples separate and divide	RCA LE 3000
Ten Pretty Girls	5–6	American	Mixer, single circle, partners	Walk, point	WF 113 RCA LPM 1624 RC 1036
Texas Star	5–6	American	Square	Honor, allemande left, grand right and left, forward and back, boys' star	EA 3, Side 3

(*continued*)

CHART 23.8 (*Continued*)

NAME	SUGGESTED GRADE LEVEL	NATIONALITY	FORMATION	SKILLS	RECORD
Two Head Ladies Cross Over	3–4	American	Square	Honor, pass through, forward and back, swing, circle	EA 1, Side 6
Virginia Reel	4–5	American	Longways, partners	Honor, skip, left-and-right elbow swing, two-hand swing, do-si-do, sashay, cast-off, arch, reel	FC 1141 FD MH 1040 RCA 45-6202
Waves of Tory	6	Irish	Longways	Walk, star, promenade, cast-off	WF 102
Wrangler's Two-Step	5–6	American	Round, double circle, partners	Walk, grapevine, balance turn	WD 7621
Yankee Doodle	5–6	American	Square	Star, swing, grand right and left, promenade	EA 2, Side 1

TEACHING DANCES

General Method of Instruction

The direct method of instruction is most often employed to teach dances that require specific formations, steps, positions, figures, and patterns. Some preliminary teaching is necessary for each dance. This may take the form of long-term preparation, where dance steps, positions, and figures are explored, learned, and performed in many variations. It may also take the form of preparation immediately prior to the learning of the dance, at which time a new figure specific to that dance is learned.

Initially children should be in the formation required for the dance. The music should be played often enough to familiarize the children with its character and speed. If they are able, the children should attempt to define parts of the musical pattern. They may attempt to clap the beat of the music.

After listening to the music, the children should see the dance demonstrated by the teacher to the music. Sometimes it is not possible for the teacher to do this alone. Early selection and training of a child partner may provide a solution when a demonstration is required that involves partner interactions.

Such demonstrations provide children with a better understanding of how the various parts of the dance relate to the whole.

Whenever possible, verbal descriptions should accompany the demonstration. Children's attention should be drawn to the part structure of the dance. Verbal cues that signal important dance actions should be shared.

Afterward children should be asked to try the dance with the teacher, without the music. The teacher should continue doing the dance with the class, giving appropriate word cues when there is a change of direction, position, or step.

Next, children should practice with the music. Long practice sessions without music should be avoided. Music helps children feel the pattern and holds their attention. If a variable-speed record player is available, the speed can be decreased while the dance is being learned and then gradually increased. Children often find abrupt changes in speed difficult.

When the dance is composed of many parts, it is often a good strategy to learn the first part, then the second, try both the first and second parts together, learn the third part, then try the first, second, and third parts together, and so on. This is called the "progressive part method" of instruction.

The teacher should continue to use cue words but should also stress listening to the music and particularly to the phrases. Children's attentiveness will increase when they have to depend on their own resources rather than those of the teacher.

A dance should be practiced several times during subsequent class periods so that children learn it well and derive enjoyment from doing it. Attention to style, good posture, formation neatness, and other details is appropriate only after the steps and dance sequences have been mastered.

Since many dances require partner interactions, the teacher should have a prearranged plan to set up partner relationships quickly. Intermediate-grade boys often have ambivalent attitudes toward dance and girls, and intermediate-grade girls are often taller and heavier than intermediate boys. Many potential problems can be eliminated by careful selection of dance content and careful structuring of the class atmosphere. The teacher should not hesitate to make changes in dances that are too difficult or to change positions calling for close proximity of boys and girls if this causes discomfort. The varsouvienne position can be replaced by a two-hand promenade position to eliminate problems due to discrepant height among boys and girls.

Though it is desirable for everyone to choose their own partner, this is not always practical. There is frequently an unequal number of boys and girls in a classroom, and some would always be asked last or would argue over the choice. Effort should be made by the teacher to help the children realize that it is fun to dance with different people, a challenge to adjust to different people's styles, polite to accept a first invitation, and desirable to help other people learn and improve.

Mixers are excellent for deemphasizing partner choices. After a certain sequence in a dance, everyone automatically gets a new partner. If partner selection is allowed, little time should be given for a choice and emphasis should be placed on choosing the nearest boy or girl. One way to facilitate partner selection is to have boys form a circle facing in one direction and girls form a circle facing the opposite direction. All walk to the music and when it stops, everyone stops, turns, and faces their partner. A second effective way of pairing boys and girls is to have all form a large circle with every other person a boy. The girl on the boy's right is his partner.

Teaching Specific Dance Steps

In general, the following procedure will prove successful when teaching a new dance step. Because some steps present unique problems, specific suggestions are made for each step. All the steps of the general format should be incorporated into the teaching of each dance step.

1. Play appropriate music.
2. Clap the rhythm.
3. Step in place with the music.
4. Teacher or other model performs the step to the music while facing the same direction as the children.
5. Children should attempt the step to the music.
6. Verbal description of the step should be given with a demonstration by the teacher. The teacher should face the same direction as the children. No music should be used. Key verbal cues should be introduced.
7. Children should work on the step while the teacher helps those having trouble and employs the verbal cues introduced in 6.
8. Children should work on the step to music while the teacher helps those having trouble and employs the verbal cues introduced in 6.
9. Children should invent and attempt variations in terms of direction, level, and magnitude and in work with one other person and with two other persons to the music.
10. Children should learn a dance that uses the step.
11. Children should invent a dance to the music, using the step.

Walk, run, jump, and hop. Selected records provide suitable accompaniment for the walk, run, jump, and hop. For the walk FC Album 20, No. 1440; EA Album 7, Sides

1, 3, and 4; and EA Album 11 may be used. For the run FC Album 20, No. 1441A and EA Album 7, Side 5 will prove satisfactory. For the jump FK 20-1442B is suitable. For the hop FK 20-1442B and EA 7, Side 5 may be employed.

Gallop. A gallop is most easily learned by imitating others or by moving with another person who can gallop. By joining hands with the learner on the side on which he or she will start the gallop, a teacher, starting with the same foot as the learner, should gallop forward with the learner, lifting the child up on the run. It is difficult to gallop in place or backward. These variations should not be attempted when the gallop is first introduced. Certain records provide suitable accompaniment, for example, FC 20-1442B and EA 7, Side 5.

Slide. A slide is a gallop done sideward. FC 20-1442B provides a suitable recorded accompaniment.

Skip. A skip is best learned through imitation or by moving with another person who can skip. Help children who can skip with one foot but not the other by joining hands with them on the side on which they cannot hop. This will help communicate the lift. It is difficult to skip in place or backward when first learning. These variations should not be attempted when the skip is first being learned. Suggested records include FC 20-1441B and EA 7, Side 6.

Step-Hop. This step is generally performed to an even accompaniment in 2/4 meter.

Count:	1	2	1	2
Cue words:	step	hop	step	hop
Foot pattern:	left	left	right	right

Suggested records include RCA 1957 and FC 21-1445. Teaching progression for the step-hop:

1. Perform the step-hops in place with cue word: *step left, hop left, step right, hop right.*
2. Perform the step-hops forward.
3. Perform the step-hops backward and sideward.

Schottische. This step is generally performed to an even accompaniment in 4/4 meter.

Count:	1	2	3	4
Cue words:	step	step	step	hop
Foot pattern:	left	right	left	left

Suggested records include I 1046A and FC 21-1445. Teaching progression for the schottische:

1. Perform in place. Take three steps on alternate feet and on the fourth count lift the leg and hold. Repeat using the cue words: *step left-right-left, lift right, step right-left-right, lift left.*
2. Perform in place, progressing to hopping on the supporting foot on the fourth count as the leg is lifted and swung slightly forward.
3. Perform the schottische forward, backward, sideward, and in a circle.
4. Perform the schottische using a light run and light spring in the air on the hop.
5. Accent the fourth count with an arm lift to coincide with the hop.
6. Invent variations with partner and two other people.

Polka. This step is done to one equally divided and one unequally divided pulse interval in 2/4 meter.

Count:	and	1	and	2
Cue words:	(hop)	step	close	step
Foot pattern:	(right)	left	right	left
	and	1	and	2
	hop	step	close	step
	(left)	right	left	right

Suggested records include RCA 25-2009 and FC 21-1446.

The hop on the polka is on the last *and* of the measure. It comes on the upbeat. Because of this, the step has a bouncy quality. The polka is easily learned by using the slide in the following manner:

1. Stand in a circle and take eight slides to the right.
2. Turn your back to the center and take eight slides in the same direction.
3. Turn to face the center and take four slides in the same direction.
4. Turn your back to the center and take four slides in the same direction.
5. Turn to face the center and take two slides in the same direction.

6. Turn your back to the center and take two slides in the same direction.
7. Continue turning on every two slides. This is the polka.

Two-Step. The two-step is done to one equally divided and one undivided pulse interval in 2/4 meter.

Count:	1	and	2	and
Cue words:	step	close	step	(hold)
Foot pattern:	left	right	left	
	1	and	2	and
	step	close	step	(hold)
	right	left	right	

Suggested records include WF 7621 and FC 21-1444A. Teaching progression for the two-step:

1. Standing in place, clap the rhythm. Clap, clap, clap, with no clap on the fourth count. The idea of quick-quick-slow, quick-quick-slow should be imparted.
2. Step in place. Left-right-left, hold weight on left; right-left-right, hold weight on right. Continue and then use cue words *quick-quick-slow.*
3. Move forward with the cue words *step-close-step, step-close-step.* Alternate with cue words *quick-quick-slow.*
4. Move to the side, changing direction as lead foot alternates.
5. Move forward four two-steps and backward four two-steps. Continue pattern.
6. Holding hands and facing a partner do 5 with one two-step moving forward and one two-step moving backward.
7. Make a half turn alone. On the first step turn the left shoulder to the left and step with left foot, placing toes toward the left; bring right foot beside the left and step and hold on the left foot.
8. Try various combinations of quarter turns, half turns, and sequences of steps in different directions.

3/4 Run. This step is done to three beats of an accompaniment in 3/4 meter.

Count:	1	2	3	1	2	3
Cue words:	step	step	step	step	step	step
Foot pattern:	right	left	right	left	right	left

Suggested record is M L49. Teaching progression for the 3/4 run:

1. Listen to well-accented music or drumbeats in fast 3/4 meter.
2. Make a hand response to the beats with a downbeat on the first.
3. Run in place to all three beats.
4. Run forward to the accompaniment, keeping in time with the pulse beats.
5. Make a hand response to the accents only.
6. With the tempo slowed, walk in a zigzag line down the floor, three steps to the right beginning with the right foot, then three steps to the left beginning with the left foot. Accent the first step in the new direction and take short steps.
7. Gradually increase the tempo to a run.
8. Practice it forward, decreasing the extent of the diagonal direction.
9. Invent variations alone, with a partner, and in groups of three.

Waltz. This step is done to three beats of an accompaniment in 3/4 meter.

Count:	1	2	3	1	2	3
Cue words:	step	step	close	step	step	close
Foot pattern:	left	right	left	right	left	right

Suggested record is M 649. Teaching progression for the waltz:

1. Clap the three-beat rhythm to the music, accenting the first beat with a louder clap.
2. In place, step on alternate feet, counting 1, 2, 3. Accent the first step of the three-beat measure with a slightly heavier step.
3. Step forward taking a very long step on the first count, a moderate step on the second count, and a small step on the third count. Move about the room with this pattern.
4. Move forward, taking a long first step on the left foot, a short step sideward with the right foot, and bringing the left foot close up to the right foot. The word cues for this would be *forward, side, together.* Step backward on the right foot, step sideward on the left foot, and bring the right foot close up to the left foot. The word cues for this would be *backward, side, together.* This is the box waltz.
5. Move forward four waltz steps, move backward four waltz steps.
6. Turn, using the first long step as the move in a new direction and the second closing step to complete the turn.
7. Facing partner and holding hands, waltz forward, backward, do a box waltz, turn, and repeat.

Mazurka. This step is done to an accompaniment in 3/4 meter.

Count:	1	2	3	1	2	3
Cue words:	step	close	hop	step	close	hop
Foot pattern:	left	right	right	left	right	right

Suggested record is FC 1130. Teaching progression for the mazurka:

1. Clap 1, 2, 3; 1, 2, 3, accenting the first and second counts.
2. Standing in place, step left, right, hold left. Accent counts 1 and 2 with a slightly heavier step.
3. Still in place, step left, right, and hop on right.
4. Move forward. Step left, step right, then hop on right; step left, step right, then hop on right. The same foot always leads as the weight is held on the hopping foot.
5. Lead left, right, hopping, swinging the free leg down for the next lead step.
6. Try the step with a partner.

Other dance steps. A number of other, less common, dance steps are used in traditional dances and are defined here.

Stamp. One foot strikes floor forcefully, but no weight is taken on the stamping foot.

Draw. A step to the side is taken, the free foot is then drawn up close to the supporting foot, and the weight is usually shifted.

Bleking. A hop is taken on the left foot, and the right leg is extended forward with the heel touching the floor. A hop is taken on the right foot, and the left leg is extended forward with the heel touching the floor. Positions of the heels are exchanged in a rhythmic sequence.

Heel and Toe. The heel of one foot is touched to the floor forward, the toe of the same foot is touched to the floor backward. Sometimes the heel of one foot is touched diagonally forward and a slight hop is taken on the other foot. The toe of the same foot is then touched to the floor across the other foot near the instep. A slight hop is taken on the other foot as the change is made.

Step-Swing. A step is taken on the left foot and the right foot is swung across in front of the left; a step is taken on the right foot and the left foot is swung across in front of the right leg. The toe of the swing foot is pointed in the direction of the diagonal swing.

Buzz. With weight kept on one foot, the other foot pushes against the floor as the weight revolves around the pivot foot. A pushing step is taken on each beat of the music. Usually done with a partner.

Grapevine. This is a sideways walking step. The right foot is crossed over in front of the left foot; another step is taken on the left foot; the right foot is brought behind the left foot, then a step is taken on the left foot. Cue words are *right over, left, right back, left*. The step may be done in either direction.

Basic Indian Step. A step is taken on the ball of the left foot, then weight is dropped onto the heel of the left foot. A step is taken onto the ball of the right foot, then weight is dropped onto the heel of the right foot. The knee bend should be exaggerated and the arm on the opposite side swung forward.

Dance Terminology

Dance formations. In a *free* formation, couples or groups of three take a position anywhere in room.

In a *circle* formation, couples or groups form a ring.

1. *Single with no partners*—All dancers stand in a ring facing the center or facing counterclockwise in the circle (Figure 23.1).
2. *Single with a partner*—All dancers stand in a ring. If facing center of circle, girl is on boy's right. If partners face each other, girl's right hand is toward the inside of the circle and boy's left hand is toward the inside (Figure 23.1).
3. *Double*—Couples stand in a ring formation. Boy is inside the circle. Usually, both face counterclockwise if not facing each other (Figure 23.1).
4. *Open*—All persons in the circle join hands except for two, one of these being the leader.

In a *group of two or three* any combination of three people may be in a circle or in free formation. Boy dances with two girls, or vice versa.

In a *longways or contra* formation any number of couples stand in a double line, usually boys on one side, girls on the other, with partners facing. Head of the set is on end nearest the music. Foot of set is at the opposite end (Figure 23.1).

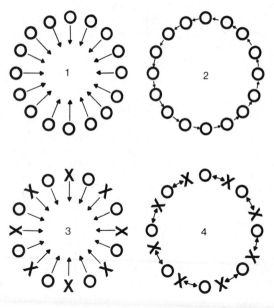

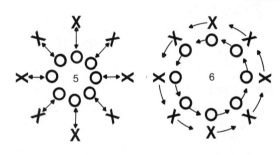

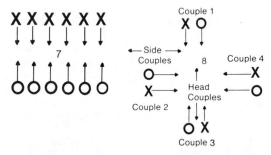

X X X X X X

7

O O O O O O

FIGURE 23.1 Dance formations. Single circle: 1. All facing center, no partners. 2. All facing counterclockwise. 3. By partners, all facing center. Double circle: 5. Partners facing each other. 6. Partners side by side, facing counterclockwise. Other formations: 7. Longways set. 8. Square dance formation.

Couple 1
X O
← Side →
Couples
8
Couple 4
O → ← X
X → Head → O
Couples
Couple 2
O X
Couple 3

In a *square* formation, a set of four couples is arranged in a square. The couple with its back to the music is called couple number 1. The couple to their right is number 2, the couple opposite them is number 3, and the couple on their left is number 4 (Figure 23.1).

In a *quadrille* formation a set of four couples is arranged in a square. The couples facing the music and with their back to the music are the head couples. The other two are side couples.

Directional terms. *Clockwise* refers to the direction in which a clock moves.

Counterclockwise refers to the direction opposite of clockwise; usual direction of movement in a circle.

Dance positions. In the *open* position partners stand side by side with inside hands joined. Girl is usually on the boy's right.

In the *skating or promenade* position partners stand side by side facing same direction. Girl is on boy's right. Hands are held, right in right and left in left, with the left arms above right (Figure 23.2).

In the *Varsouvienne* position partners stand side by side facing forward. Boy stands slightly behind and to the left of the girl. Boy holds girl's right hand in his right, her left hand in his left just above shoulder level (See Figure 23.3).

In the *two-hand* position partners stand face to face and join both hands. May be used

FIGURE 23.2 Skaters' position.

FIGURE 23.3 Varsouvienne position.

in place of closed position or shoulder-waist position.

In the *shoulder-waist* position partners stand face to face; boy puts both hands on girl's sides. Girl puts both hands on boy's shoulders.

In the *closed* position partners stand face to face. Boy puts his right arm around the girl, placing his hand just below her right shoulder blade. Girl puts left hand on boy's right shoulder. The girl's right hand rests lightly in the boy's left palm which is held just below shoulder level. They look over each other's right shoulder.

Position terms. The *inside foot or hand* refers to the foot or hand nearest the partner when side by side.

The *outside foot or hand* refers to the foot or hand farthest from partner when side by side.

Home refers to the original or base position in a set or circle.

Corner refers to the girl on the boy's left or the boy on the girl's right.

Dance figures. There are three *turns:*

1. *Elbow*—Boy and girl hook elbows and walk, skip, or step-hop around each other as directions indicate.
2. *Two-hand*—Right hands and left hands clasped and walk, skip, or step-hop around each other.
3. *Hungarian*—Partners stand with right sides together, right arms on each other's waist, left hand raised above head with elbow bent.

There are three *swings:*

1. *Elbow*—Partners hook elbows and swing around clockwise with either a running or walking step; usually two complete turns.
2. *Two-hand or one-hand*—Holding hands, partners swing around clockwise with either a running or walking step.
3. *Buzz*—In either an elbow, two-hand, or closed turn position, weight is held on one foot, and the other foot pushes against the ground while child pivots on the right foot. Movement is clockwise, and usually two complete turns are made.

In a *promenade* partners walk or dance around the circle or set side by side in a counterclockwise direction.

In a *grand right and left,* in a circle or square formation partners face one another, holding right hands. All boys face counterclockwise and all girls clockwise. All move forward, passing right shoulders, reaching out for the next person's hand. When the hand of the next person is grasped, the other hand should be released and that arm extended to meet the next person. Continue around the circle in the same direction, alternating right and left hands and right and left shoulders. The figure appears as a weaving in and out. Continue until original partners meet.

In an *allemande right* partners face each other, join right hands, and then walk completely around once in a clockwise direction, returning to their original positions.

The *allemande left* is the same as allemande right, only left hands are grasped and the walk is in a counterclockwise direction. May be done with a partner or a corner.

In a *do-si-do* partners face one another, cross arms over chest, and move forward four steps; then take one step to the side and walk backward to their place. May be done with corners.

In a *reel* the head couple goes to the center of a set and does an elbow turn one-and-a-half times around. The girl goes to the first boy in the boy's line and does an elbow swing, boy does same with first girl in girl's line. They both return to the center and do an elbow swing once around with each other. They then return to the third boy and girl respectively and do an elbow swing and go back to the center for an elbow swing. They proceed in like manner to the end of the line.

In a *right-and-left through or pass through* two couples exchange places; both walk forward. They drop hands when they meet the opposite couple, whom they pass through by passing right shoulders. The boy turns the girl around in the new position so that she is on his right.

In a *ladies' chain* girls walk across set and meet the opposite girl, grasp right hands, pass right shoulders, drop hands, and reach out to take left hand of the opposite boy. He turns her around and the ladies repeat the same pattern back across the set, back to their homes.

In a *star* four dancers go to the center of the set, join right hands high in the center, and walk around in a counterclockwise direction. They may reverse direction and reverse hands and go once around in clockwise direction.

RECORDS AND RECORD SOURCES

A number of record companies produce recorded music for traditional dance. Record supply vendors may be written to for listings of available recordings.

Bowmar Records, 622 Rodier Drive, Glendale, California 91201

Burns Record Company, 755 Chickadee Lane, Stratford, Connecticut

Canadian Folk Dance Record Service, Educational Recordings, 605 King Street, West Toronto 2B, Ontario, Canada

Childhood Rhythms, 326 East Forest Park Avenue, Springfield, Massachusetts

Children's Music Center, 5373 West Pico Boulevard, Los Angeles, California 90019

Columbia Records (CO), 1473 Barnum Avenue, Bridgeport, Connecticut

Dance Record Center, 1161 Broad Street, Newark, New Jersey 07114

David McKay, Inc., 750 Third Avenue, New York, New York 10017

Educational Activities, Inc. (EA), P.O. Box 392, Freeport, New York 11520

Educational Dance Recordings, Inc., P.O. Box 6062, Bridgeport, Connecticut

Educational Recordings of America, Inc., Box 6062, Monroe, Connecticut 06468

Educational Record Sales, 157 Chambers Street, New York, New York 10007

Folkcraft Record Company (FC), 1159 Broad Street, Newark, New Jersey 07114

Folk Dancer (FD), Box 201, Flushing, New York

Freda Miller Records for Dance, Department J. Box 383, Northport, New York 11768

Hoctor Educational Records, Inc., Waldwick, New Jersey 07463

Imperial Records (I), 137 North Western Avenue, Los Angeles, California

Instructor Publications, Inc., Dansville, New York 14437

Israeli Music Foundation, 931 Broadway, New York, New York

Kimbo Educational Records (K), P.O. Box 55, Neal, New Jersey 07725

MacGregor Records (M), 729 South Western Avenue, Hollywood, California

Master Record Service, 708 East Garfield, Phoenix, Arizona 85000

Merrback Records Service, P.O. Box 7308, Houston, Texas 77000

Methodist Publishing House (ME), 150 Fifth Avenue, New York, New York

Old Timer Record Company, Inc., 708 East Weldon Avenue, Phoenix, Arizona

Pioneer Records, 2005 Labranch, Houston, Texas

Radio Corporation of America (RCA), Victor Record Division, 1133 Avenue of the Americas, New York, New York 10036

Record Center, 2581 Piedmont Road, N.E., Atlanta, Georgia 36324

Rhythm Record Company, 9203 Nichols Road, Oklahoma City, Oklahoma 73120

Russell Records (R), P.O. Box 3318, Ventura, California 93003

Sets in Order Records, 462 North Robertson Boulevard, Los Angeles, California

Square Dance Square, Box 689, Santa Barbara, California 93100

Western Jubilee Master Record Service, 1210 East Indian School Road, Phoenix, Arizona

Windsor Records (W), 5530 North Rosemead Boulevard, Temple City, California 91780

World of Fun Records, Cokesbury (WF), Regional Service Center, 1600 Queen Anne Road, Teaneck, New Jersey 07666

24

adventure activities

Adventure activities include all pursuits that provide experience related to specific aspects of the natural environment (air, wind, water, hills, rocks, woods, streams, rivers, lakes, ice, snow, caves, and so on). Outdoor activities typically involve elements of adventure, exploration, and travel. Each activity requires specific skills for success, yet there are common elements in all adventure activities that contribute to individual and group development. Adventure activities often included in school programs are initiative games, hiking, camping, canoeing, boating, orienteering, climbing, rappelling, skiing, and biking.

There are many good reasons for including adventure units in elementary-school physical education programs. These advantages apply both to programs that are designed to be completed away from school grounds and to those aspects of adventure skill development that can be taught at the school site.

Active participation regardless of skill level. Children are most often totally involved in adventure activities and can participate successfully because the activities tend to accommodate a wide range of skills.

Success in challenging activities. Not all adventure activities are "challenging," but most do contain some element of challenge. If properly programmed with adequate progressions, all children will experience success, and achieving successful outcomes in these activities is a strong contributor to positive self-concept.

Contact with natural settings. Adventure programs can have aesthetic and even inspirational overtones, especially when they are done in natural settings. Bringing children into contact (in appropriate ways) with our dwindling outdoor spaces has high potential for many positive outcomes.

Development of important skills. The skills associated with outdoor adventure activities are important in the immediate sense because they are valued by children; they are important in the long term because they can be used profitably throughout life.

Experience in a different competitive atmosphere. The competition in outdoor activities is often with nature—Can I climb the hill? Can I navigate the course? Children do not compete against one another. Indeed, they often have to cooperate in order to complete the activity successfully. Criteria can be easily adjusted to ensure success, and activities can be made progressively more challenging to maintain interest and enthusiasm.

Demands for responsible behavior. Outdoor activities often require a higher level of responsible behavior among participants than is typically expected within a gymnasium. Equipment concerns must be addressed as well as safety concerns. Activities often take place in an unfamiliar setting, with cooperation required to complete tasks. This requires responsible behavior among participants, and outdoor activities are often a useful vehicle for teaching such behavior.

TEACHING AND ORGANIZING ADVENTURE ACTIVITIES

The teaching skills necessary in an adventure unit are no different than those required for the many other activities discussed in this text. Careful planning, the development of appropriate skill progressions, success-oriented learning, safe yet challenging activities, and appropriate teacher-student interaction patterns will yield positive results in the adventure areas, just as they will in more traditional activities.

The fact that adventure activities often take place off school grounds means that the managerial aspects of effective teaching need to be emphasized. Adventure activities accomplish little if they are poorly managed. Students must behave in a responsible, consistent manner if the activities are to be successful. Thus, the skills of behavior management (see Chapter 11) are crucial to successful teaching in the adventure area.

Teaching progressions in adventure activities can be arranged in ways similar to other activities (see Chapter 9). Success-oriented learning should be emphasized with small yet meaningful increments in challenge and the skill required to meet the challenge imbedded within the activity. First, the natural environment can be changed—for example, backpacking in a city park as opposed to lands belonging to the U.S. Forest Service. Second, the topographical nature of the setting can be made more difficult—for example, the elevation of the terrain can be increased in climbing activities. Third, the degree of challenge can be directly increased, as in navigating through unknown territory. Fourth, time constraints can be placed on participants—for example, you might require that a group initiative problem be solved in less time. Fifth, an activity can be made more physically demanding—for example, by increasing the height of the beam in the group initiative game.

The skills used in many adventure activities can be taught within regular school programs. Teachers do not need a particular natural setting to teach important skills. Indeed, a strong case can be made for teaching the basics in the more controlled setting of the school. Orienteering courses can be set up on school playgrounds. Climbing and rappelling can be taught in gyms. Many water skills can be taught in pools, if teachers have access to school or community facilities.

Legal Liability

At an advanced level, adventure activities can carry a higher degree of risk than many physical education activities. This is due to the unpredictability of natural elements, the lack of well-defined boundaries, and the inability to anticipate all potential occurrences. With advanced students risks become a concern.

Although legal liability laws differ among states, all require that negligence must be established before legal restitution is made. Negligence is the failure to act as a reasonably prudent person in a given situation. Therefore, teachers need to prepare students adequately for the adventure programs in which they will participate.

The use of waivers to avoid liability has proven ineffective in most cases. Responsibility cannot be signed away on a form. The sponsoring institution and persons in charge cannot release their obligation to act in reasonable and prudent ways. The best way to ensure that the requirements of liability are met is to prepare students adequately for the demands of the tasks they will face and to establish clear, public procedures for safety that are taught and enforced consistently.

Programming

When planning adventure programs, a number of considerations must be taken into account. These are discussed below.

Sequencing skills. Basic skills must be mastered first. The program should consist of combining and expanding upon previously learned skills. For example, fire building and safety should be learned before cooking and survival techniques are introduced. Many basic skills can be learned in regular classes at the school site.

Timing of activities. Timing relates not only to relevant seasonal considerations but also to establishing blocks of time for learning. Adventure activities do not easily fit into typical scheduling patterns. They require flexible blocks of time. Some factors which must be considered in making decisions about time appropriations include the type of activity to be taught, the location, the specific skills to be taught, and class size.

Insurance. Two types of insurance coverage are appropriate for adventure activities. One type should cover the personnel involved, while the other type should cover program participants.

a. Personnel coverage. There are a variety of policies available for educational institutions or agencies and individual staff members. Insurance companies generally recommend that the institution and staff be covered for a minimum of $1,000,000. An insurance agent or attorney can determine the type of policy needed by examining the number of activities, the type of opportunities offered in the program, and the duration and extent of the program.
b. Participant coverage. Although many individuals may be covered by parent or school insurance, a special policy should be available for individuals participating in the program. This policy should cover personal injury and accidental death. No individual should be allowed to participate without adequate coverage.

Medical form. In addition to insurance policies, it is recommended that each participant have a medical form on file. Physicians completing the form should have a clear concept of the activity to be performed by the child. In order for the physician to make specific recommendations regarding the child's ability to participate, the medical forms provided by the school should describe the nature and demands of the activity. Medical forms should have a place for physicians to report individual allergies, medical conditions, and the need for special diets or medications.

Accident reports. In case of any accident or injury, no matter how slight, a staff member should fill out an accident report. Only facts should be reported. Opinions, statements, or suggestions on procedures which could have prevented the accident should not be included. The accident report should include the name of the injured party, the date, the location of the accident, a statement of what occurred prior to the accident, a description of the injury, treatment administered, and a description of the injury, treatment administered, and a description of follow-up care. If possible, the signature of a witness who can verify what happened should be obtained.

Parents' notice. A notice should be sent to parents informing them of the details of the activity. Such a notice should include the date, time, and place for dropping off and picking up the child as well as a specific list of personal items (that is, clothing and equipment) that will be needed by the child. The notice should include a phone number for parents to call in order to inquire about the trip or at which they can leave an emergency message. Such a notice can also serve to promote support for the adventure program. When parents know and approve of a child's learning experiences, they can generate a good deal of support in the community for the program.

Equipment

The equipment and facilities used in adventure activities must be safe. Awareness of equipment safety standards and features prior to purchase is required. Inadequate equipment, poorly selected facilities, inadequate emergency resources, and inappropriate use of materials can cause injury and result in legal action. After safety is considered, most equipment selections are made on the basis of cost-effectiveness. Care is taken to ensure that equipment is selected with the child users' body size and weight, as well as comfort, in mind. Serviceability, durability, appropriateness for the purpose, cost, construction, and composition are other factors that need to be taken into account.

Whether equipment has been purchased, constructed, or rented, it should be checked prior to use. If any piece is questionable in terms of safety, it should not be used. Upon returning from an activity, all equipment should be cleaned and again reexamined. Any defects or potential problems with owned or rented equipment should be recorded and reported. Faulty equipment should not be reused until it has been repaired or replaced. Staff should be knowledgeable about emergency equipment repairs. Equipment repair kits should accompany personnel on an adventure activity.

First Aid

All staff members should be certified in first aid and should be up to date on current first-aid methods and procedures. The primary leader should be knowledgeable in emergency mountaineering medical aid. On trips students might carry a small personal first-aid kit containing bandaids, lip balm, antiseptic cream, moleskin or molefoam, dry matches, a pocket knife, and personal medication. The instructor should have a list of the personal medications needed by each student as well as a record of the times and amount of each dosage or application.

A group first-aid kit should include bandaids, antiseptic cream, adhesive tape, ace and triangular bandages, antihistamine, laxative, constipator, sun screen, water purification tablets, safety pins, and other items appropriate to the location, activity, and season (for example, snake bite kit, molefoam, fire starter unit).

Commercial first-aid kits can be purchased at local wilderness supply shops. These kits are expensive and usually need to be supplemented with items needed in a particular adventure activity. The contents associated with commercially available first-aid kits are usually so compactly packed that they are difficult to supplement. Because of this it is suggested that group first-aid supplies be packaged by the adventure staff leader. A master list of recommended supplies can be preestablished for each adventure trip.

Transportation

Regardless of whether transportation is a group or individual responsibility or whether a short or long trip is planned, a number of factors must be considered. Drivers and vehicles must be properly licensed and insured. Regulations pertaining to passenger safety and vehicle loading capacity must be strictly enforced. Logistics should be clearly outlined prior to the actual trip. Date, time, and place of departure and pick-up, estimated time of arrival and departure to and from the adventure site, map and directions to each stopover area, and the number and names of individuals in each vehicle must all be determined ahead of time. If there are several drivers, a "lead" and "sweep" driver should be appointed. No one should go ahead of the lead driver or fall behind the sweep driver. Whenever possible, it is best to transport an entire group in one vehicle.

Post-Activity Procedures

In administering any adventure activity, follow-up procedures are crucial for creating a safe environment. Equipment should be cleaned and inspected. Damaged equipment should be replaced or reported before storage. Supplies for equipment repair and first-aid kits should be replenished. Accident reports should be given to appropriate administrators. Written reports of the trip describing unusual conditions, attitudes, trip evaluation, assessment of student experiences, and learning and environmental conditions should be completed.

INITIATIVE GAMES

Many adventure activities can be done at the school site. Often these provide a solid foundation from which off-campus adventure programming might develop. A favored point to begin an adventure curriculum is with initiative games, group activities in which members of each group must utilize their combined talents to complete an activity goal or solve an activity problem. Group initiative games are most often designed so that individual members of groups (a) experience the responsibility needed for collective action, (b) gain experience in decision making, and (c) have an opportunity for leadership.

Initiative games present the opportunity for the teacher to emphasize cooperative effort toward a collective goal, the ingredients of group decision making, and the skills necessary to carry out a plan of action. Feedback from the teacher should be directed toward each of these important process-oriented aspects of the initiative experience and not only toward the manner in which the actual goal solution was accomplished.

What follows are group initiative games requiring little or no equipment.*

Trust walk. This introductory experience requires that students be placed in pairs with one blindfold provided for each pair. The blindfolded partner is led through a predetermined path (in woods if possible or through some obstacle course on a playspace). The partners should communicate with each other as they proceed, particularly the "leader" partner who forewarns the other partner about upcoming obstacles and safety considerations. After several minutes of walking, the partners should switch roles. Group discussion can follow with emphasis on safety, responsibility for one another, meaning of trust in a physical experience, and so on.

Human chain. Children are formed into circles. Children place right hands in the center and take the hand of a person on the opposite side of the circle. Then children ex-

tend their left hands into the center of the circle and grasp the hand of another child (other than those whose right hand they are holding). One pair of hands is then separated and the children are told to untangle themselves so that they form a straight line—but this is to be accomplished without breaking hand-holds. Depending on how the original hand-hold combinations occurred, two lines may develop, or one line and one circle, or one line.

Monster. Children are divided into groups (typically five to ten children). The object is to move collectively a predetermined distance (such as 15–25'). The restrictions are that only ⅓ of the total number of legs in the group can be used and only ½ of the total number of hands in the group can be used. All group members must be a part of the monster and all parts of the monster must be connected.

Fog horn. Children are asked to form a channel that winds and bends. One child is blindfolded and placed at the entrance to the channel. Children forming the channel may direct the blindfolded child through the channel (crawling) only by sounding like a fog horn. The goal of the crawling child is to negotiate the channel without touching the sides.

Catch the dragon's tail. This game is best done on a large playspace. Children are formed into lines (eight to twelve children per line). Children are directed to put their arms around the waist of the child in front. This creates a "head" and "tail" of the line. The last child in line tucks a flag into the back of his belt, creating a tail. At a signal the game begins and the goal is for the head of the line to chase its own tail and to pull the tail from the belt of the last child in line. This game requires that children at the back of the line try to get away from children at the front of the line to whom they are attached. The line cannot break. When the flag is captured, children should rearrange themselves in the line so that each experiences the front, center, and rear positions. A variation of this game is to have one dragon attempt to catch the tail of other dragons.

*Sources for initiative games are: K. Rohnke, *Cowtails and Cobras*, Hamilton, Mass., Project Adventure, 1977; and B. Simpson, *Initiative Games*, Butler, Penn., 1978.

The four pointer. Children are divided into groups of seven. The goal of the game is for the group to get across a space that is 30 feet wide. The restriction is that the group may have only four points of contact with the ground and that all the children must be in contact with one another as they cross the space. The following games require some equipment that should be set up prior to the start of the activities.

Electric fence. The equipment needed is one 15′ length of rope that is ½″ in diameter, one log, 4–6″ in diameter, that is 5′ long, and two trees (or poles) that are 8–10′ apart. The rope is tied between the trees at a height of 3′ or more to simulate a fence. The log is left on the ground somewhere nearby. The object of the activity is to get the entire group over the fence without touching it in any way. Should any group member touch the fence or the trees, the entire group has to begin again. Once a group member gets over the fence, that member may not walk back around the trees to help. With larger classes, two to three fences would expedite things and reduce waiting time for children.

Beam. The equipment needed consists of one log, 8″ in diameter, that is 10′ long, two 20′ ropes that are ¼″ in diameter, and two sturdy trees or poles that are 6–9″ apart (several of these setups would expedite the activity for a large class). The log should be securely lashed between the trees so that the bottom of the log is 6′ or more above the ground. The object is to get each member of the group over the log as quickly as possible. No aids can be used and no member can touch the trees to which the log is lashed. Once over the beam, no one can walk around the trees to come back to help.

Maze. The equipment needed consists of 300′ of binder's twine or light rope, a small grove of trees that are fairly close together, and a blindfold for each person. The rope is strung through the trees at waist level to create a maze (zigzag patterns). A small space is left for an exit to the course at one edge of the pattern. Each child is blindfolded. The group is led into a corner of the maze. The goal is to find one's way out as quickly as possible. Once out, a child may remove the blindfold and assist other children with verbal instructions.

Swamp. The equipment needed consists of two 10′-long boards (2″ × 4″) and ten ropes that are 4′ long and ¼″ in diameter. A course is created that is marked by two boundary lines approximately 25′ apart. The boards and rope are placed behind one of the lines. The object is for the group to travel from one boundary line to the other without anyone touching the ground (the swamp). Only the boards and ropes may touch the ground—only the boards will "float" in the swamp. If anyone touches the ground while crossing, the entire group must begin again. Employing several setups will expedite things for larger classes.

Kitten crawl. The equipment needed consists of one rope, 1″ manila that is 68′ long, and two trees, 8–10″ in diameter, set about 12′ apart. The rope is tied securely around one tree and stretched around the other tree, then brought back to the first tree and tied with secure knots. The object is to crawl across the ropes from one tree to the other.

CAMPING

Camping is an adventure activity in which daily activities such as eating, sleeping, cooking, and washing are performed in nontraditional settings. The camping environment is usually an outdoor setting (for example, the school grounds, private and public established campground sites, or backcountry and wilderness areas). The camping experience may take place in the natural environment (land, trees, sky) or may be associated with several artificial or contrived settings (for example, a shelter without electricity, a building without plumbing or cooking facilities, a self-contained traveling unit). The educator who teaches a camping unit must be able to perform daily life activities in natural or contrived settings. Although some individuals enjoy the natural environment, many camping skills can be taught either indoors, out-doors, on school property, or at public and private campgrounds.

In teaching a unit on camping, educators should not assume that the initial experience must always be a "survival" experience, where only minimal resources are available. A camping experience may occur in almost any setting. These settings range from situations in which campers enjoy modern conveniences and where only their cooking is done outside to situations in which campers use the natural environment in order to perform all daily activities. The educator should teach children individual camping skills, eliminating customary conveniences gradually, in keeping with evolving levels of skillfulness.

It is important for the teacher to work toward the development of the following goals:

1. Encourage attitudes and skills which emphasize minimal impact on the natural environment.
2. Design exercises in which children have decision-making responsibilities for the planning, packing, and design of the camping experience.
3. Teach individual skills, such as those pertaining to fire building, cooking, equipment use, and shelter building, prior to providing an overnight experience. There is nothing more uncomfortable for beginners than to learn a new skill under adverse weather conditions.
4. Have children and staff check all equipment prior to use. Clean and properly store all equipment after use.
5. Remind children of safety and first-aid procedures. Explain the reasons for certain safety practices in a camping situation.

Incorporating camping units in a school curriculum will not necessarily significantly increase budget expenses. Most items used to teach camping skills can be made or rented. The school does not need to purchase all equipment. There are several ways equipment and materials may be obtained. For example:

1. Children who participate in the activity may be responsible for providing all personal gear, such as sleeping bags, first-aid kits, and utensils. Educators should give them a list of the equipment needed, along with adequate description criteria.
2. Most outdoor stores welcome the opportunity to visit the school or allow field trips to their shops. These sessions can be set up to allow the sales people to teach various skills while demonstrating equipment.
3. Several outdoor supply stores have equipment discount rental rates for school groups. Checking with the stores in your local area will provide you with specific details.
4. Outdoor supply stores which rent equipment usually have end-of-the-season clearance sales on their rental equipment. Schools can often obtain good buys on such equipment. Just make certain the equipment is safe and in good operating condition prior to using it in the program.

Teaching a camping unit is exciting and challenging. Teaching units can be modified to suit and challenge the skill level of children by changing environmental situations, climatic conditions, and type and amount of equipment used. Camping skills can be important prerequisites to many other types of outdoor recreational pursuits (for example, canoe camping, winter and ski camping, and backpacking).

The following camping skills and activities should be included in a camping unit for children.

Fire building. Practice arranging tinder, kindling, twigs, and different size logs for easiest and most versatile fire frames (either log or criss-cross); practice checking for any brush or burnable materials on the site, as well as for overhanging tree limbs and branches; practice collecting dry twigs under "bush" trees, wood pitch from rotted trees, birch bark from downed birch trees, and dry moss or lichen; practice lighting a match and placing it on fire material located on the ground; practice building fire frames which are for heat (criss-cross), boiling (teepee), baking (reflector), and slow cooking (bean hole).

Cooking. Practice cooking hot dogs, hamburgers, and rolls—these foods are simple to cook and difficult to burn; dip matches in paraffin prior to trip and store them in a watertight container; provide nutritional information on basic foods and the manner in which they are used during camping and give examples of how they can be provided for during trips; discuss advantages and disadvantages of canned, freeze-dried, dehydrated, boxed, and fresh foods; practice maintaining coals to keep a desirable baking temperature, rotating food, and keeping flames away from food.

Pitching tents and shelters. Practice pitching tents away from dead trees with overhanging limbs. Clear ground of sharp or bulky objects. Provide a diagram of the tent. Explain the placement of tent poles and stakes. Keep all loose or odd-shaped edges inside square folds.

Practice selecting sites which are not low spots or in run-off areas. Avoid pitching tents near a water source that may quickly rise during a storm. Avoid pitching tents below steep inclines or loose rocks, under dead trees, or near poisonous plants.

Practice placing stakes and pulling draw strings so as to remove wrinkles and properly balance the tent. Uneven and excessive tension will deform a tent and/or allow for water leaks.

Practice building shelters using natural caves, tarps, ponchos, branches, and logs. Allow students to be creative. Discuss how shelters will protect campers from wind, rain, cold, and harmful bugs and animals.

Sanitation. Dig a small hole at least 200 yards from a water source. Spread a layer of dirt at each use. Cover with rocks when leaving. Burn toilet paper in a fire. Use biodegradable soap. Empty soapy water away from water source.

CANOEING

Canoeing is an adventure activity which allows individuals to participate in outdoor recreation using a mode of travel that makes it possible to explore terrain not always accessible by other modes of transportation. The canoe is a small, shallow water craft which is propelled by one or two individuals using a paddle. *Solo* canoeing is a term used to indicate one paddler in the canoe, while the term *tandem* is used to indicate two paddlers.

Canoeing is a unit which should only be taught to children who demonstrate adequate swimming and water safety skills. As the skill level demanded in canoeing activities increases, so must the individual's swimming and water safety skills. Educators responsible for teaching a canoeing unit should have current certification in water safety procedures and must be aware that teaching and learning may go on in a variety of settings (for example, pools, lakes, rivers, flat or rough water, calm and windy days, slow- and fast-moving currents). Any or all of these conditions may be used, depending on the skill level of the children being taught.

It is important for the teacher to work toward the following goals:

1. Evaluate the swimming and water safety skills of children and establish specific self-rescue procedures to be used in canoeing situations.
2. Teach proper storage, maintenance, and use of equipment.
3. Help children become familiar with canoeing terminology.
4. Design games and activities which emphasize accurate and efficient maneuvering of canoes through and around obstacles.
5. Provide children with the opportunity to "rock" canoes to test the craft's stability in safe situations.
6. Have children wear adequate personal flotation devices.
7. Examine the skills of intermediate canoers prior to allowing them to canoe in fast-moving or white-water situations.

Providing a canoeing unit does not mean that the school need purchase expensive equipment and materials. Several methods exist for financing a program, including children sharing expenses, the school renting equipment, or the school purchasing equipment. If purchasing equipment, several factors pertinent to canoe and paddle construction should be considered: durability, utility, maintenance, and repair procedures. For school programs canoes constructed from ABS Royalex or aluminum are usually recommended because of their durability and low maintenance requirements. Paddles made of hardwoods should be purchased.

The following canoeing skills and activities should be included.

Forward stroke. Practice feathering the blade underwater and returning the paddle horizontally, slightly above the surface of the water and not in the water. Teach steps of "catch, draw, feather, recover."

J-stroke. This stroke is only performed in the stern. Make certain that the side of the paddle which pushed water during the draw sequence also pushes water away from the canoe.

Sweep stroke and inverted sweep stroke. Extend paddle far from canoe. Raise lower hand to a higher position on the paddle shaft.

Jam stroke. After executing the jam stroke to stop the canoe, the paddler may need to scull, or paddle slightly forward to backward, in order to maintain position.

Draw, pry, or push stroke. Bringing paddle in too close to the gunwhales (sides) of the canoe or starting the paddle in too close to the gunwhales of the canoe causes this error.

Sculling. Top arm must be extended outward. Do not let elbow of top arm drop.

Maneuvering craft in tandem and solo. Have the students practice the various strokes and experience the reaction of the craft while paddling solo and tandem. Set up obstacle courses for paddler(s) to steer through.

Changing position. One paddler moves to the center of the canoe, bends low, keeps weight low, and maintains paddle in the water. The other paddler crawls over the center to new canoe position and keeps weight low.

Varying the blade angle. For every action there is an equal and opposite reaction. Have the paddlers angle their blades in the water and note the canoe's reaction (for example, while solo stern paddler is paddling on the left, a forward stroke combined with an angled draw stroke will cause the canoe to go forward and slightly to the right).

Crossbar draw. This is a bow paddler's stroke only. Do not shift grip position. Rotate body at waist and enter paddle on opposite side. Pull toward the canoe.

Loading canoe. Distribute weight evenly in the center of the canoe, with heaviest items on the bottom. Bow slightly lighter than stern except when greater maneuverability is needed in rapids.

ORIENTEERING

Moving from one point to another in unfamiliar or unmarked territory is a part of the adventure activity known as orienteering. Most orienteering activities require the use of a map and compass. Not getting lost in the outdoors while attempting to travel from one point to another can be accomplished by making use of the sun, the stars, compasses, roads, maps, and trail signs. This section focuses predominantly on the use of the map and compass.

It is important for the teacher to work toward the development of the following goals.

1. Keep all skills presentations simple. Establish a map skill sequence and follow it with a compass skill sequence. Finally, provide a combination of both.
2. Use manageable-size topographic maps. Cut the maps to 8½″ × 11″ or 8½″ × 15″. Initially use maps which incorporate very few symbols. Later gradually incorporate greater numbers of symbols as students are ready to deal with them.
3. When helping children read topographic maps, try to relate the features on the topographic maps to two-dimensional pictures or three-dimensional representations. Some children may have difficulty with the abstractions represented by the topographic map.
4. Teach "finding" a bearing after children have mastered walking while following a "given" bearing.
5. Explain and demonstrate the importance of knowing how to use a map and compass in order to travel from one point to another. Explain and demonstrate the importance of pre-planning a hike by first consulting a map.

Advanced orienteering depends not only on the mastery of physical skills and fitness components but also on the mastery of various math and science skills. An orienteering unit with heavy emphasis on map and compass skills readily lends itself to interdisciplinary coordination.

Orienteering skills can be used along with other adventure activities skills to help individuals enjoy the outdoors while on foot, on skis, in canoes, or on snowmobiles.

The following orienteering skills should be included in an orienteering unit for children.

Understanding the N-S-E-W direction concept. Provide examples (for example, when facing the rising sun, the left side of the body is facing north; yet when facing the setting sun, the right side of the body is facing north).

Reading topographic maps. Make use of a diagram that emphasizes certain symbols. Make use of special coloring to help children identify symbols. Ask students to practice locating symbols on maps. Show a cut-out section and demonstrate altitude changes by diagramming sections.

Using N-S-E-W to locate points relative to one another. Use a drawn N-S line crossing an E-W line on the map. Ask students to identify the position of one point relative to another point on the map with regard to the lines. Later use a paper circle with an asterisk in the center. Label the points N, NE, E, SE, S, SW, W, NW. Have students identify relative positions by placing the center of the circle on one location identifying the direction of travel needed to get to the new location. The direction of travel would be a position between a major direction and a secondary direction (N-NE).

Identifying landmarks while walking with a map. Rotate the map until it is oriented in the same way as the environment with regard to the orienteer. Walk with the map, identifying landmarks as you go.

Identifying compass parts. Use a large-scale cardboard compass with a rotating dial. Demonstrate how each part works.

Calculating bearings. Practice facing different directions of travel and orienting compass. Keep compass level to eliminate some inaccuracy in direction.

Walk a bearing. Practice walking a bearing by walking toward sighted landmarks.

Walk a bearing with obstacles. Walk around obstacles by turning at right angles. After each right-angle turn, hold compass so that magnetic needle is aligned with orienting arrow and walk beyond area of obstacle.

Determining paces. Measure off a specific distance. Calculate the number of paces needed to traverse the distance.

Using map scales. Practice using ruler after identifying map scale in order to estimate distances between points.

Determine location using cross-bearings. Sight two permanent and prominent landmarks. Point direction-of-travel arrow to one landmark. Orient the compass and read degrees. Repeat the process for the second landmark. Add 180 degrees to each number. On oriented map find prominent points. Draw lines from landmarks in the direction of travel. Where the two marks cross is the location on the map.

Orienting map and compass to the environment. Line up the side of the base plate with magnetic North lines drawn on the map. Then turn the map with the compass resting on the map until compass is oriented.

CLIMBING AND ROPES

Climbing with and without ropes is part of the adventure activity of rock climbing. There are two kinds of rock climbing: free climbing and direct-aid climbing. Free climbing makes use of both natural and artificial surfaces and may or may not involve the use of ropes. When used, ropes and pitons serve as protective and safety devices. Direct-aid climbing is a part of advanced technical rock climbing. In addition to pitons, other pieces

FIGURE 24.1 Climbing wall located inside an elementary school gymnasium

of equipment such as chocks, various-shaped nuts and bolts, and hammers are used. Other areas of advanced rock climbing involve lead and solo climbs and snow or glacier travel. Because of the type of equipment used and the need for the climber to have advanced knowledge, these areas are not discussed in this chapter.

It is important for the teacher to work toward the development of the following goals.

1. Teach all children to maintain three points of contact during all climbing moves and stress that they should never leap for a hold.
2. Explain the importance of moving in a smooth and rhythmical manner, concentrating on looking ahead.
3. Stress using the legs for climbing. Arms should be used more for balance than for "pulling" the body upward.
4. Emphasize the need for adequate preparation, proper technical execution, and rest, rather than speed.
5. Emphasize safety procedures, reminding the children to check for loose rocks and to guard against insecure holds.
6. Encourage the development of attitudes and skills which emphasize minimal impact on the natural environment.
7. Skill sequences should be developed which reflect progress from
   a. Large handholds and footholds to smaller ones
   b. Gentle to steeper slopes
   c. Indoor to outdoor settings
   d. Lower to higher climbing elevations
   e. Simple to more complex knot usage
   f. Instructor-directed-and-supervised climbs

to climbs in which children assume greater responsibility
   g. Shorter to longer climbing periods

The climbing skills described in this chapter are those that can be taught at the school site. They represent an introduction to climbing skills that might later be extended at a school camp or other natural site. There is much to be said for the greater degree of control a teacher can exert at a school climbing site rather than when utilizing natural terrain. A beginning climbing program might include skills in climbing, belaying, and rappelling. In order to develop such a program, a climbing wall would need to be constructed at the school site. Climbing activities can be started with equipment as simple as climbing ropes and ladder constructions (Andres and Rees, 1979). They can become as complex as the conversion of an exterior wall of a school building to a climbing wall (March and Toft, 1979). However,

FIGURE 24.2 Blocks bolted to wall form the climbing wall

FIGURE 24.3 Beginning rappelling station on gymnasium wall

Safety also involves the anticipation of common problems and the teaching of appropriate responses to the problems. What do I do if I start to fall? What if my clothes get caught in a rope? What if my belay line is too tight? Too slack? These situations should be anticipated and children should be taught how to respond to them. Safety helmets should be worn by all in the climbing unit. Hand care requires the use of leather gloves.

The equipment needed for the climbing/ rappelling unit consists of the following items:

Safety helmets and leather gloves
7/16″ goldline ropes
Locking carabiners
Figure eight descenders
1″ nylon webbing
14″ seat slings for children
5/16″ goldline rope for chest harness (12′ per student)

FIGURE 24.4 Rules posted for rappelling

RAPPELLING RULES

1. **WARNING**

   ANY ACTIVITY INVOLVING MOTION OR HEIGHT CREATES THE POSSIBILITY OF ACCIDENTAL INJURY. THIS EQUIPMENT IS INTENDED FOR USE **ONLY** BY PROPERLY TRAINED AND QUALIFIED PARTICIPANTS UNDER **SUPERVISED CONDITIONS**. USE WITHOUT PROPER SUPERVISION COULD BE **DANGEROUS** AND SHOULD **NOT** BE UNDERTAKEN OR PERMITTED.

   ALWAYS INSPECT FOR LOOSE FITTINGS OR DAMAGE AND TEST STABILITY BEFORE EACH USE.

2. A QUALIFIED INSTRUCTOR MUST BE PRESENT AND YOU MUST HAVE HIS PERMISSION TO USE THE ROPES.

3. DOUBLE CHECK ALL KNOTS AND SEATS. HAVE THE INSTRUCTOR CHECK THEM FOR YOU.

4. ALWAYS HAVE A SAFETY LINE ATTACHED WHEN CLIMBING THE LADDER/WALL OR ON THE PLATFORM.

5. ALWAYS WEAR LEATHER GLOVES, AND GIVE THE FOLLOWING COMMANDS:
   BELAY
   BELAY ON
   RAPPELL
   RAPPELL AWAY

the best solution for most programs would be to use ropes and ladders and to construct an interior climbing wall in the gymnasium.

A climbing wall in a gymnasium should incorporate ropes, a climbing ladder, and a climbing course with platforms at the top from which students can rappel down the wall (Rohnke, 1977). The climbing course is made by bolting different-sized hardwood blocks to the brick or concrete wall of the gymnasium. The blocks are bolted at different angles and different distances to create courses that vary in difficulty. The blocks are typically 3 inches wide, from 2 to 3 inches deep, and 4 inches long.

Safety is, of course, a primary concern in teaching climbing and rappelling. Children must have knowledge of safety rules, a command of the language to be used as signals in the climbing activities, and skills in utilizing the safety equipment. There should be back-up safety systems for each feature in the program.

Standard screw in floor plate with eye
Climbing wall and rappelling tie-ins with back-up systems for all hookups   (Rohnke, 1977)

The following skills and activities would be included in an on-site climbing program for elementary-school physical education.

Climbing skills.   Maintain three bases of support on the wall at all times. Don't hug or cling to the wall. Extend only within comfortable limits when climbing. Keep body weight over the support areas. Climb as much as possible with the legs.

Knots.   Square knot, overhand safety knot, prusik knot, and bowline.

Belaying.   Belaying means to make something fast with a rope (Smith, 1977). In climbing it is the belaying system which secures the climber and acts as the primary safety system. Children learn belay skills and commands. They should never take their hands off the belay line.

Rappelling.   Rappelling is a method of negotiating descent down a steep slope using a rope. The rappeller backs down the climbing wall. Appropriate form is to be perpendicular to the wall, which brings the body parallel to the floor. The rappeller walks down the wall in a series of short hops. Rappellers should always be belayed.

Securing equipment.   Procedures to learn include tying the chest harness; attaching the chest harness to the belay line; tying the seat sling; hooking up the carabiners; securing the figure-eight descender. (See Figures 24.5 and 24.6.)

Knowledge of ropes.   Children should learn to identify different types of rope and their uses in climbing and rappelling.

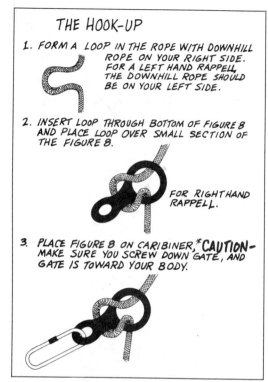

FIGURE 24.5   Clear instructions are important

FIGURE 24.6   Safety is always emphasized

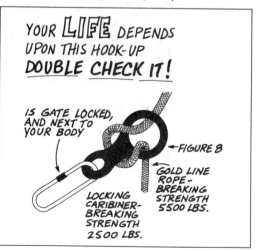

25

special programs
and
events

The regular instructional period of physical education provides the foundation for a sound program. If it is planned well, managed effectively, and taught well within a humane climate, children will grow in their abilities and in their attitudes toward physical education. However, what children will remember about their elementary-school physical education program are the programs and events that were "special," the so-called "frosting on the cake."

IMPORTANCE OF SPECIAL EVENTS

Special programs and events are an important aspect of the total physical education effort. They should not be considered as frills. They provide the traditions that define a program. They breed excitement among children. They convey to children a sense that physical education is important. They often provide the experiences which children remember most vividly. They create a festival climate within schools. They can bring teachers and children together to share an important moment.

This chapter will underscore the importance of special programs and events to the total physical education program and suggest a few activities that can be developed within this area.

The Festival Nature of Competition

Throughout history sport events and tests of physical prowess have been associated with festivals. We know, for example, that the ancient Olympic games were as much a religious festival as they were a series of athletic contests. Festival events are extremely important in the life of a school. They give rise to traditions. They provide for ritual and celebration, characteristics that are often lacking in daily life.

A competition is first of all a coming together, a festival, a celebration. A competition provides a framework within which children can celebrate together and test their skills. The notion of *rivalry* is only one aspect of the meaning of competition and probably not the most important aspect. The terms *compete* and *competence* both derive from the Latin work *competere*. Pursuing excellence (competence) within the rules and limits of a festival (a competition) is the best and most accurate definition of what it means to compete. The experiences shared together within the festival nature of the competition not only provide individual meaning for the child but also contribute a great deal to the way in which the group (the teachers and children of the school) tends to define itself. Festival events help provide a rich climate in which children can grow psychologically and emotionally.

The Scope of Special Programs and Events

Often adults are too limited in what they consider to be special. Adult thinking leads to very elaborate programs. Some of these may be very exciting, useful additions to the physical education program. However, often things that adults view as routine are perceived by children to be very special. Thus, it is important to understand that opportunities abound for the teacher, almost on a daily basis, to create programs and events that are perceived by children to be special.

Obviously, a playday, an all-school track meet, a fitness week, or a major field trip would be viewed by everybody as a special event. These kinds of events often become regular parts of the school calendar and are eagerly anticipated by everybody in the school. They tend to involve all the children and their teachers. They often require a great deal of planning and can be integrated nicely into academic studies in classrooms. Several such events are described later in this chapter.

However, smaller, less obvious events are often of special importance to children. Many of the strategies suggested elsewhere in this text can be considered to be within the special events and programs category. Being able to write your name on a "Top-of-the-Rope club" poster once you have learned to climb a rope to a criterion height is such an event. Being mentioned in a physical education newsletter as a finalist in an intramural volleyball tournament is such a special event. Being selected as a gym aide, to help the physical education teacher with equipment

FIGURE 25.1 Special events tend to involve all the children and their teachers and can be integrated nicely into academic studies.

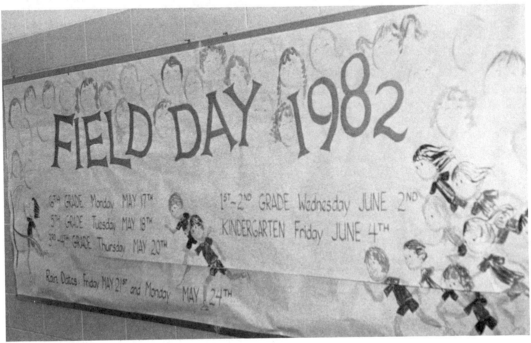

each day, is often a position highly prized by children. Going to the gym or playground on Friday afternoon for a "Friday fitness" session can be special to many children. Demonstrating skills to parents at an open house can be very exciting. Such little "extras" are very important to children's growing sense of themselves as competent, important persons. Each new accomplishment and recognition, no matter how trivial it might seem to an adult, is a building block for a child's sense of identity as a physically educated person. It can also be argued that lifelong attitudes toward participation and competition are no doubt affected by the degree to which children have success experiences in situations which are special in the sense we have described here.

Teachers should look for opportunities to create programs and events in which children can accomplish things that are important. We are not suggesting that trivial events be arranged and trivial performances be recognized. We *are* suggesting that teachers try to understand what is important to children and not be limited by an adult perspective. Being a member of a team that wins the team beanbag toss in a relay playday might not seem important to an adult, but to the child who performs well enough to win and then has that performance recognized, it is important.

EXAMPLES OF SPECIAL PROGRAMS AND EVENTS

Physical Education Newsletter

One good way for a physical educator to communicate with parents is through a periodic newsletter which is sent home with children. The recognition children receive through the newsletter provides a source of support for their efforts in physical education. Newsletters can be typed by school secretaries from copy provided by the teacher. The newsletter can be duplicated on a school machine either through ditto, stencil, or photocopying.

Newsletters should serve several purposes. First, they can inform parents of activities in the physical education program. Second, they can enlist the aid of parents; for example, asking that each parent send in several old golf balls so that a large number can be collected for a beginning golf unit. Third, they can inform parents of special upcoming activities, such as a gymnastics performance at a parents' program. Fourth, they provide an opportunity to recognize children who have accomplished something in physical education.

Extra Gym Sessions

Extra gym sessions can be scheduled for a variety of purposes. They can be fitted into gaps in a schedule, or they can be planned as regular features of a weekly schedule. Extra gym sessions can be used to provide additional instruction for activities within the program. In this case an "open gym" session each week might focus on the unit that is being studied that week in the regular program. Extra gym sessions can be scheduled for children who need a particular kind of activity that is not available in the regular program. An example of this would be a special gym session for young children who have been shown to need developmental work in the perceptual-motor area. Extra gym sessions can focus on certain physical education goals for which there is not sufficient time in the regular program. A good example of this would be a once-a-week "fitness session" in which children come to a gym and go through a series of stations, each of which requires a specific exercise.

Sport or Fitness Week

Each year at the local, state, or national level there is an officially designated week in which the citizens are called to focus on sport or fitness. There is a national sports week each spring in the month of March. Teachers should make these events important within the school, using them in various ways to help to extend the instructional program and to emphasize the importance of sports and fitness to our society.

THE SPORTS PAGE

TOP OF THE ROPE CLUB...We have some new members in the Top of Rope Club. Andy Robinson, Cindy Stasiak, Erin Connor, Tom Gorey.

*

The 5th and 6th graders are having a team hand ball tournament at noon. Here are the players:

DIVISION 1

Quick Shooters
Doug Beck, Tracie Goodall, Brian Farst, Erik Anderson, Denise Ross, Steve Van Straten, Andy Brown,

Hot Shots
Jim Kozelek, Stuart Brody, Steve Calhoun, Sarah Ryan, Buffy Winans, Kevin Furgason, Jenny Larrabee.

Dynamite Defense
David Hunt, Ted Grimm, Scott Olson, Tina Cockrell, Nancy Cohn, Michelle Trammell, Paco Schauweker.

Sharp Shooters
Pat Giller, Danny Moore, Brett Bachus, Amy Tague, Loryn Rosenblum, Tracey Snyder, Rob Jonas

DIVISION 2

Swift 6 + 1
David Brody, Josh Topolosky, Mike Littman, Sue Bonowitz, Karyn Koltun, Doug Lunsford, Larry Beim.

Basket Stuffers
Tom Smith, Lisa Shamhart, Jon Collin, Matt Freeman, Lisa Phillips, Whitney Bennett, David DeVictor,

Super 7
Gary Bell, John Sweney, Tom Early, Kim Bragg, Cathy Culbertson, Robyn Aurnou, Leslie Dollinger.

Dribbling Gang
Andy Kohler, Paul Vollmer, Tonya Hysell, Amy Dressel, Bill Diehl, Peter Jones, Missy Tell.

WINNERS OF DIVISION 1:
Hot Shots
WINNERS OF DIVISION 2:
Dribbling Gang, Basket Stuffers, Swift 6 + 1
WINNERS OF PLAYOFF:
BASKET STUFFERS

VOLLEYBALL

The 5th and 6th graders are learning to play volleyball during their physical education classes. Here are the skills they are learning: Bump, volley, serve and spike. They are also learning some of the rules of the official game. It's lots of fun. We will have a volleyball tournament at noon very soon!

*

A BIG THANKS

to: Steve Calhoun, Cathy Culbertson, Buffy Winans, Scott Olson, Abe Bonowitz, and David DeVictor for being the scorers and timers for all the team handball games. We couldn't do without your help. Good job!

*

Newcomb

The third and fourth graders have learned a new game called Newcomb. It is played with a net and a ball. Two teams play against each other. Some days we take the nets outside and play newcomb at recess, too.

*

ROLLER SKATING...The younger children will be roller skating in physical education classes soon. The school owns some skates, but the children who own skates may bring their own, too. We skate outside. We skate on the dirt baseball field first. That way, if we fall, it doesn't hurt. After we get better, we can skate on the red track. Sometimes we skate through obstacle courses and "cross Country. It is a lot of fun and helps us with our balance.

*

Coming Events

* NCAA Men's Volleyball Championship at O.S.U. May 5th and 6th.
* Team Handball playoffs at Maryland Gym
* Volleyball Tournament at noon at Maryland Gym
* Teacher-Student Volleyball game at noon-- Maryland Gym.
* Spring Track Meets - June, for grades 3,4,5,6.
* Field Day for Grades 1 and 2, in June.

*

Question: Why is tennis a noisy game?
Answer: Because each player raises a racket. (racquet).

Many activities can take place during a sports/fitness week. A special edition of a newsletter could be published. A special activity program could be planned for the week. Each morning the physical educator could use the school public address system to do a short "radio show." The show could emphasize information relevant to the event being celebrated. A good way to make sure the information is attended to is to do it in the form of a daily sports or fitness quiz in which the questions are read over the loudspeaker and the children answer in their rooms.

Bulletin boards in the common areas of the schools could also be decorated to emphasize the events being celebrated.

Sports Show

In many communities each year there are garden shows, travel shows, home shows, or hobby shows. These are events at which many things are brought together to show people new products or new activities. One of the best ways for physical educators to educate children to the "wonderful world of sport" is to do a sport show. In a sport show, equipment for many different sports is brought together for children to view. Posters can be made to emphasize the major features of the sport, the space on which it is played, the formation used, the major skills, how it is scored, and other features. This is expecially useful to teach children about sports they are unlikely to encounter in their own programs or in their local area. Local citizens, local clubs, or nearby colleges/universities can be contacted to gain the necessary equipment. Children can then actually see a lacrosse stick, a wicket used in circket, a slalom ski for water skiing, the ball used in European team handball, a foil used in fencing, a cesta used in jai alai, or a polo mallet.

The gymnasium, or some other suitable space, can be set up with each sport displayed in a particular area. The equipment and posters should be presented in sufficient detail so that children get a good idea of how the game is played and how the equipment is utilized. Children can then "visit" each of the displays, ask questions about the equipment, and perhaps even pick up the equipment to see how it feels.

Gym Helpers

At several points in this text we have emphasized the importance of teachers utilizing children as helpers. Children can help to get equipment out each morning, move equipment for different activities, put equipment away after school, help to score and/or referee contests, and help to teach younger children. Children should be selected on the basis of how responsible they are and according to their interest in physical education. Their own skill abilities are less important, although those most interested will often tend to have good skills.

A regular schedule for gym helpers should be established. This schedule should be cleared with the building principal and the classroom teachers. Gym helpers should be rewarded periodically with special gym time, parties, field trips, or other such events. Not only can gym helpers relieve the physical education teacher or classroom teacher of many of the daily chores associated with the program, but they can also actually extend the program in the sense that their presence and contribution enables the teacher to do more than would be possible without them.

Open Houses and Demonstrations

The support of parents is crucial to the long-term success of a physical education program. Parental support can take many forms, ranging from comments of appreciation to strong backing of a program or a teaching position when cutbacks are threatened due to economic difficulties. Parents learn about the physical education program in two ways. First, they learn about it on a regular basis through their children. If the children enjoy the program, feel good about their participation in it, and talk about it at home, parents will perceive it to be a positive factor in their children's educational experience.

Parents can also learn about the program through open houses and demonstrations. This kind of evening program should be designed to "show and tell" the basics of the program. Two ingredients are important in demonstration programs. First, the children participating should demonstrate that they have acquired meaningful skills. Second, the demonstration should show clearly the manner in which the physical education program is designed to produce those skills. This is the opportunity to show that although children respond to the *fun* components of the activities and the skills, a sound educational design was necessary to produce both the skills and the fun.

We favor demonstration programs in which all children (perhaps at a particular grade level) participate rather than just a subset of the more highly skilled children. The program should allow the parents to see their children accomplish skills; therefore, it ought to be built around skills the children have mastered thoroughly in the program. Also, the program should *inform* the parents about the major emphasis within the program. Programs should be designed to show a limited number of skills and activities completely rather than attempt to sample all the skills and activities within a program, showing each only minimally. It is helpful if the demonstration program has a theme. Often the most useful kind of theme is one that emphasizes the main educational strategies used in the program.

Playdays

Playdays are special events that children often remember fondly. They consist of one-day events that emphasize participation and fun. Often they involve novel kinds of competitions and are described as "Fun Olympics." What follows is a description of a relay playday.*

RELAY PLAYDAY: GENERAL INFORMATION

1. Take one large outdoor space and set up (15) stations around the perimeter. (Sample stations are attached.)

2. Take all the children you can find and divide them into teams (15 or 30) with approximately the same number on each.

3. If 15 teams, all will move from one station to the next in a clockwise direction. If 30 teams, the odd numbered teams move clockwise while the even numbered teams rotate in a counterclockwise direction. In this case, each team will compete in 13 different competitions against 13 different opponents (there are two rest stations).

4. Each station has a station manager (older student or teacher). The manager
   (a) has the first team at that station set up the event at the start of the Play Day.
   (b) explains the event to each team.
   (c) marks the score card for each team
   (d) has the last team at that station put the equipment away at the end of the Play Day.

5. Each team has a team leader (perhaps an older student) who:
   (a) carries the team score card.
   (b) ensures that each student gets to take a turn.

6. Timing for events:
   1 minute—explanation of event
   3 minutes—continuous activity
   2 minutes—score activity and move to next event

7. Teams follow their leader from one station to the next. They *sit* in file to await instructions.

8. All scoring is done by counting the number of children on a team completing the event in the three minutes. In situations where teams are small, each child may have several trials.

9. *Overall* scoring is done by totaling the points awarded for the 13 events. An *alternative* to this procedure in the 30-team event is to simply establish a won-lost record for each team.

---

*Suggested by Thom McKenzie, San Diego State University; used by him at the Parkside School in Canada.

CHART 25.1 Relay playday: events and procedures

EVENT	PROCEDURE	SCORING	EQUIPMENT (TEAM)
1. Ball Kick	A ball is kicked from 5 feet away in an attempt to score between two cones. Continue in file	One point for each score	1 soccer ball 2 cones
2. Bean Bag Toss	Three bean bags are tossed into a hoop from 10 feet away. Continue with each child in file.	One point for each bag landing inside hoop	3 bean bags 1 hoop
3. Soccer Dribble	Students dribble ball with feet around 4 cones and back.	One point for each successful completion	1 soccer ball 4 cones
4. Ball Toss	A volleyball is tossed into a wastebasket from a distance of 5 feet.	One point for each successful attempt	1 volleyball 1 wastebasket
5. Marble Relay	Each student carries a marble in a spoon for a distance of 10 feet and returns	One point for each successful return	2 spoons 6 marbles
6. Rest Station			
7. Tire Roll	Each student rolls a tire 15 feet and returns	One point for each completion	1 small tire
8. Fun Race	A player puts on an old sweater, runs a distance of 10 feet and returns.	One point for each completion	1 large old sweater
9. Bench Hop	Pupils hop over a bench 4 times using their hands to help . . . continue.	One point for each student completing hops	1 bench
10. Obstacle Course		One point for each completion	Tire, bench and so forth
11. Hoop Jump	Each child runs 5 yards, jumps throwing a hoop 3 times and returns.	One point for each completion	2 hoops
12. Bean Bag Walk	With bean bag on head, each student in order walks a distance of 15 feet and returns.	One point for each successful completion	2 bean bags
13. Rest Station			

(continued)

CHART 25.1 (Continued)

EVENT	PROCEDURE	SCORING	EQUIPMENT (TEAM)
14. Obstacle Course		One point for each completion	obstacles
15. Bench Walk	Upright bench. Players from each end meet and attempt to pass without falling off.	One point for each successful pair	1 bench

Source: Thom McKenzie, San Diego State University.

The playday should involve all students and encourage participation. Therefore, awards should be available for all children who participate (if awards are to be presented at all). One method of providing awards for all participants is to have children who attain different levels of skill achievement receive different awards. In this way all are rewarded, yet differential performance is also recognized.

It is seldom possible to arrange for all children in a school to participate at the same time. The personnel demands for such an all-school event require a great deal of planning. The following example of a playday, the Lee Olympics,* divides the school into three participation times, each lasting between 1 hour 15 minutes and 1 hour 30 minutes. This playday is explained through a letter that is sent home to parents, an excellent example of helping to ensure appropriate participation while communicating effectively to parents to secure their support.

The Lee Olympics utilizes eight to ten activities at stations, with children rotating among the stations. Also included in this example is a memo to the classroom teachers in the school describing how classroom activities might be developed to further enhance the playday events.

*Suggested by Dolly Lambdin and Thom McKenzie; used by Ms. Lambdin at the Robert E. Lee Elementary School in Austin, Texas.

FIGURE 25.3   Lee Olympics: Letter to Parents (D. Lambdin and T. McKenzie)

Dear Parents:
Friday, April 25 has been selected for our annual Field Day, the Lee Olympics (in case of rain, April 28). In order to be consistent with the goal of the physical education program at Lee (to help *each* child develop to potential), the Lee Olympics will be organized and conducted in a special manner. Each student will receive a ribbon in each event according to the performance level achieved in that event. This differs substantially from traditional field days where children compete against each other and only the top performers earn a ribbon.

The method we have selected supports our aim of encouraging children to be concerned with their own improvement rather than their standing relative to their peers.

Example: In the rope jump event for 4th grade, level 1 (green ribbon) = 20

(continued)

FIGURE 25.3 (*Continued*)

jumps in a minute; level 2 (red) = 40 jumps; level 3 (white) = 60 jumps; level 4 (yellow) = 80 jumps; level 5 (blue) = 100 jumps. The same format is followed in the other events. Scoring for the event is broken into different levels and all children who score at a similar level receive a ribbon of the same color. In this manner children are competing against a standard rather than each other.

You can help by:

1. Reading this notice and talking with your child about this setup so that you both understand the situation.

2. Demonstrating your understanding of the format when dealing with your child's performance. For example, asking what level your children achieved rather than asking if they won the event and discussing whether the performance was an improvement rather than who they beat in the contest.

Please join us in supporting this exciting event. The schedule for different grades is listed below:

8:15– 8:45	Opening Ceremony
8:45–10:00	2nd and 3rd grades
10:15–11:30	K and 1st grade
12:00– 1:30	4th and 5th grades

During the time period, your children will be participating in eight different events. In six events they will compete and earn ribbons according to their level of performance. The two other events will involve structured play. All events will involve some vigorous physical activity.

Please ensure that your children can participate safely and to the best of their ability by encouraging them to wear running shoes and other clothing in which they can move freely.

FIGURE 25.4 Lee Olympics: Notice to Teachers (D. Lambdin and T. McKenzie)

LEE OLYMPICS
Activities and Competition for Everyone

On April 29 we will have the 2nd annual "Lee Olympics." By looking ahead to that event it should be more meaningful and important to everyone involved. As you know, the Olympic Games involves much more than just a race. It is a social and cultural event where people of many nations come together to share their traditions, history, music, sport, and—in fact—their individual ways of life.

Here are some ways in which the regular classroom subjects might be coordinated with the "Lee Olympics" to make both the classroom and the Olympics more interesting and meaningful for the children.

Geography: Each homeroom might select a country to represent. They might study the dress, industry, crops, sport, and culture of their "chosen country."

Art: The flag of one's chosen country might be painted and displayed.

(*continued*)

FIGURE 25.4 (*Continued*)

	Advertisements, posters, and so on might be drawn up to depict the various events.
English:	Reports and themes might be written to describe the history and tradition of the Olympic games and the events and people that take part.
Math:	This year the events will be measured in meters and centimeters, similar to the actual Olympic games. These could be explained in terms of instruments used to measure them.

Each homeroom teacher will make up an entry list. Events, rules, and entry sheets will be forthcoming.

FIGURE 25.5 Suggested layout for Lee Olympics (D. Lambdin and T. McKenzie).

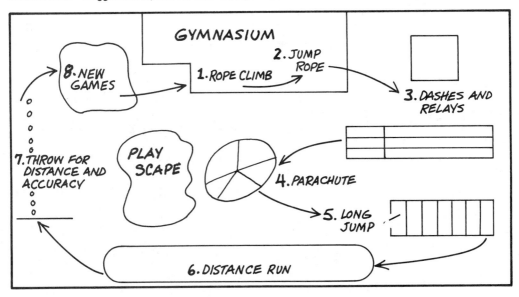

All-School Events

An "all-school event" can be defined loosely as a full school day in which all teachers and children participate in a common event; that is, the school day is given over to the event, which has a theme, but is primarily oriented around physical education activities. An all-school event requires planning and cooperation. The physical educator should take the leadership role and utilize the entire school teaching staff in the preparation. Themes can be local, regional, or national. The event should require preparation by students, too. It might involve making costumes. It often involves studying certain historical, geographical, and cultural traditions that are associated with the theme. The all-school event, though centered around physical education activities, should be used to integrate various kinds of study around the central theme; that is, it should be an integrative experience for the children.

What follows are brief descriptions of two all-school events.* They are offered as exam-

*Suggested by Thom McKenzie, San Diego State; used by him at the Parkside Elementary School in Canada.

ples of the kinds of events that can be planned. Clearly, the theme should be one that has particular meaning to the students and teachers in the school.

Centennial Day was an all-school event used to celebrate the centennial year of Prince Edward Island in Canada. In the morning of the event the teachers and students dressed as people dressed in the year 1873. All the regular classes were conducted as they would have been in 1873; that is, without electric lights, without any audiovisual materials, with few books, and with only basic tools. There were displays of typical activities from 1873, such as making yarn, quilts, and ice cream. Lunch was served as a typical "social event" from the 1873 period. Obviously, students and teachers had prepared for some time to be able to participate effectively in these activities. In the afternoon of Centennial Day a playday was held that utilized events that were popular 100 years ago. These included sack races, tug-of-war events, distance races, and dances of that period.

Another all-school event utilized a somewhat similar format. One day was set aside as "Klondike Day." Teachers and students arrived at school dressed in the fashions of the 1890s. An announcement was made that gold had been discovered in the Klondike (which is in western Canada). It was then announced that the entire school would "trek" across Canada to seek riches in the gold fields. Preparation for this trek had been made in the children's classes, where children had studied the geography of the land to be crossed and the history of the gold rush.

The event itself involved such things as an obstacle course in which the obstacles represented geographical features of the Canadian landscape. This part of the event included a hike around the school grounds (with signs indicating the advance across Canada), climbing, a water obstacle course, a trek through the basement of an adjacent school (in darkness, simulating a cave), and mountain climbing (using a cargo net and ropes). The completion of this "trip" brought the students back to their school, which had been set up to represent a typical Klondike town. Each of the classrooms had chosen to represent a typical Klondike establishment, such as a saloon, a sheriff's office, a restaurant, or a hotel. Students visited the various "establishments" and were served a lunch of typical foods from that era. Later in the afternoon competitions were held, such as log rolling, king of the mountain, arm wrestling, and other activities typical of the frontier in the 1890s.

Clearly, these kinds of all-school events require careful planning and cooperation to succeed. If planning and cooperation are forthcoming, these can be memorable experiences for the teachers and the children.

References

AMERICAN ALLIANCE FOR HEALTH, PHYSICAL EDUCATION, RECREATION AND DANCE. *Adapted Physical Education Guidelines: Theory and Practice for the Seventies and Eighties.* Reston, Va.: AAHPERD, 1976.

_____. *Exercise and Fitness.* Reston, Va.: AAHPERD, 1972.

_____. *Youth Fitness Test Manual.* Reston, Va.: AAHPERD, 1976.

_____. *Children's Dance.* Reston, Va.: AAHPERD, 1973.

_____. *Choosing and Using Phonograph Records for Physical Education, Recreation and Related Activities.* Reston, Va.: AAHPERD, 1977.

_____. *Health Related Physical Fitness Test Manual.* Reston, Va.: AAHPERD, 1980.

AMERICAN NATIONAL RED CROSS. *Adapted Aquatics.* Garden City, N.Y.: Doubleday, 1977.

_____. *Advanced First Aid and Emergency Care,* 2nd ed. Garden City, N.Y.: Doubleday, 1980.

_____. *Methods In Adapted Aquatics: A Manual For the Instructor.* Garden City, N.Y.: Doubleday, 1977.

_____. *Standard First Aid and Personal Safety.* Garden City, N.Y.: Doubleday, 1977.

_____. *Swimming and Water Safety.* Garden City, N.Y.: Doubleday, 1968.

_____. *Swimming and Water Safety Courses Instructor's Manual.* Washington, D.C.: The American National Red Cross, 1968.

_____. *Teaching Johnny To Swim: A Manual for Parents.* Washington, D.C.: The American National Red Cross, 1963.

An Introduction to Physical Fitness. Washington, D.C.: The President's Council on Physical Fitness and Sports, 1973.

ASMUSSEN, E. "Growth in Muscular Strength and Power." In *Physical Activity,* ed. G. L. Rarick. New York: Academic Press, 1973, 60–79.

BARLIN, ANNE AND PAUL BARLIN. *Dance-A-Folk Song.* Los Angeles: Bowmar, 1974.

BARNETT, L. "Current Thinking about Children's Play: Learning to Play or Playing to Learn?" *Quest* 26 (Summer 1976), 5–16.

BARTELS, ROBERT. *Swimming Fundamentals.* Columbus, Ohio: Chas. E. Merrill, 1969.

BEHNKE, A. R. AND J. H. WILMORE. *Evaluation and Regulation of Body Build and Composition.* Englewood Cliffs, N.J.: Prentice-Hall, 1974.

BERLINNER, D. "Impediments to the Study of Teacher Effectiveness." *Journal of Teacher Education* 27 (Spring 1976), 5–13.

_____. "Tempus Educare" in *Research on Teaching,* ed. Peterson and Walberg. Berkeley: McCutchan Publishing, 1979.

BERLYNE, D. "Laughter, Humor and Play." In *Handbook of Social Psychology,* ed. G. Lindzey and E. Aronson. Reading, Mass.: Addison-Wesley, 1969.

BILES, F. "The Physical Education Public Information Project. *Journal of Health, Physical Education and Recreation,* September 1971.

BLEY, EDGAR S. *The Best Singing Games for Children of All Ages.* New York: Sterling, 1957.

BOORMAN, J. *Creative Dance in the First Three*

Grades. Ontario: Longmans Canada, Ltd., 1969.
————. *Creative Dance in Grades 4–6.* Ontario: Longmans Canada, Ltd., 1971.
————. *Dance and Language Experiences with Children.* Ontario: Longmans Canada, Ltd., 1973.
BRUNER, J. *The Process of Education.* Cambridge: Harvard University Press, 1960.
BUCHER, C. *Foundations of Physical Education,* 4th ed. St. Louis, Mo.: C. V. Mosby, 1964.
BURKE, LYNN AND DON SMITH. *The Young Sportsman's Guide to Swimming.* New York: Cornerstone Library, 1963.

CAILLOIS, R. *Man, Play, and Games.* New York: The Free Press of Glencoe, 1961.
CHEFFERS, J. AND V. MANCINI. "Teacher-Student Interaction." In *What's Going on in the Gym,* ed. W. Anderson and G. Barrette. Monograph 1, Motor Skills: Theory Into Practice, 1978.
CHRISTIAN, QUENTIN A. *The Bean Bag Curriculum: A Homemade Approach to Physical Activity for Children.* Wolfe City, Texas: The University Press, 1973.
CLARKE, H. H. *Physical Motor Tests in the Medford Boys' Growth Study.* Englewood Cliffs, N.J.: Prentice-Hall, 1971.
CORBIN, CHARLES B. *Inexpensive Equipment for Games, Play and Physical Activity.* Dubuque, Iowa: Wm. C. Brown, 1972.
————. "Physical Fitness: The Performance of Children." *A Textbook of Motor Development,* ed. C. B. Corbin. Dubuque, Iowa: Wm. C. Brown, 1980.
COUNSILMAN, JAMES E., ed. *Competitive Swimming Manual for Coaches and Swimmers.* Bloomington, Ind.: Counsilman Co., 1977.
————. *The Science of Swimming.* Englewood Cliffs, N.J.: Prentice-Hall, 1968.
CRATTY, BRYANT J. "The Body Image." *Perceptual and Motor Development In Infants and Children.* Englewood Cliffs, N.J.: Prentice-Hall, 1979, 131–148.
————. "The Child In Competitive Sport." *Perceptual and Motor Development In Infants and Children.* Englewood Cliffs, N.J.: Prentice-Hall, 1979, 250–261.
————. ed. *Perceptual and Motor Development In Infants and Children.* Englewood Cliffs, N.J.: Prentice-Hall, 1979.
————. "The Physical Educator and the Clumsy Child." *Issues in Physical Education and Sports,* ed. G. McGlynn. Palo Alto, Calif.: The National Press, 1974.
————. "Social Development." *Perceptual and Motor Development In Infants and Children,* En-

glewood Cliffs, N.J.: Prentice-Hall, 1979, 228–249.
————. *Social Dimensions of Physical Activity.* Englewood Cliffs, N.J.: Prentice-Hall, 1967.
CURETON, K. "Distance Running Performance Tests In Children," *Journal of Physical Education, Recreation and Dance* 53 (1982): 64–66.

DAUER, V. AND PANGRAZI, R. *Dynamic Physical Education for Elementary School Children,* 6th ed. Minneapolis, Minn.: Burgess, 1979.
DESSECKER, W. "The Effects of Audiotaped Intervention on Student Teacher Behaviors." Unpublished doctoral dissertation, Ohio State University, 1975.
DICK, W. AND CAREY, L. *The Systematic Design of Instruction.* Chicago: Scott-Foresman, 1978.
DUKE, D. "Looking at the School as a Rule Governed Organization." *Journal of Research and Development in Education,* Summer 1978, 116–126.

EDGERTON, V. R. "Exercise and the Growth and Development of Muscle Tissue." *Physical Activity,* ed. G. L. Varick. New York: Academic Press, 1973, 1–31.
E'EUGENIO, TERRY. *Building with Tires.* Cambridge, Mass.: Early Childhood Education, 1971.
ELLEFELDT, LOUIS. *Folk Dance.* Dubuque, Iowa: Wm. C. Brown, 1969.
ELLIS, M. J. *Why People Play?* Englewood Cliffs, N.J.: Prentice-Hall, 1973.
————. AND SCHOLTZ, G. J. L. *Activity and Play of Children.* Englewood Cliffs, N.J.: Prentice-Hall, 1978.
ERIKSON, E. *Childhood and Society,* 2nd ed. New York: W. W. Norton, 1963.
EVALUATING PHYSICAL FITNESS. Athletic Institute, Room 805, Merchandise Mart, Chicago, Illinois.

FLENGELMAN, A, ed. *The New Games Book.* San Francisco: Doubleday-Dolphin, 1976.
FROST, J. L. AND B. L. KLEIN. *Children's Play and Playgrounds.* Boston: Allyn and Bacon, 1979.

GAGE, N. *Teacher Effectiveness and Teacher Education.* Palo Alto, Calif.: Pacific Books, 1972.
GALLAHUE, DAVID L. *Developmental Play Equipment for Home and School.* New York: John Wiley, 1975.
GILBERT, CECILE. *International Folk Dance at a Glance.* 2nd ed. Minneapolis, Minn.: Burgess, 1974.

GODFREY, S. *Exercise Testing in Children.* Philadelphia: Saunders, 1974.

GORDON, T. *Teacher Effectiveness Training.* New York: Wyden, 1977.

GREEN, A. *Sociology.* New York: McGraw-Hill, 1956.

GREULICH, N. W., R. I. DORFMAN, H. R. CATCHPOLE, C. I. SOLOMON, AND C. S. CULOTTA. "Somatic and Endocrine Studies of Puberal and Adolescent Boys." *Monographs of the Society for Research in Child Development,* 1942, VII, Serial No. 33, Number 3.

HACKETT, L. AND R. JENSON. *A Guide to Movement Exploration.* San Francisco: Peek Publications, 1966.

HAMILL, P. V., T. A. DRIZD, C. L. JOHNSON, R. B. REED, AND A. F. ROCHE. "National Center for Health Statistics Growth Charts 1976." *National Center for Health Statistics Monthly Vital Statistics Reports* 25 (1976): 1–22.

HARRIS, JANE, ANNE PITTMAN, AND MARLYS WALLER. *Dance a While.* Minneapolis, Minn.: Burgess, 1978.

HERKOWITZ, JACQUELINE. "Social-Psychological Correlates to Motor Development." In *A Textbook of Motor Development,* ed. C. B. Corbin. Dubuque, Iowa: Wm. C. Brown, 1980, 225–243.

HETHERINGTON, C. "Fundamental Education." *The Making of American Physical Education,* ed. A. Weston. New York: Meredith Publishing, 1962.

HEWES, J. J. *Build Your Own Playground.* Boston: Houghton Mifflin Company, 1974.

HOUGH, J. AND J. DUNCAN. *Teaching: Description and Analysis.* Reading, Mass.: Addison-Wesley, 1970.

HUIZINGA, J. *Homo Ludens: A Study of the Play Element in Culture.* Boston: Beacon Press, 1962.

HUNT, S. E. AND E. CAIN. *Games the World Around.* New York: Ronald Press, 1950.

JENSEN, MARY BEE AND CLAYNE R. JENSEN. *Square Dancing.* Provo, Utah: Brigham Young University Press, 1973.

JERNIGAN, SARA STAFF AND C. LYNN VENDIEN. *Playtime—A World Recreation Handbook of Games, Dances, and Songs.* New York: McGraw-Hill, 1972.

JONES, H. E. *Motor Performance and Growth.* Berkeley: University of California Press, 1949.

KADMAN, G., AND T. HODES. *Israeli Folk Dance.* Tel Aviv: Education and Culture Center, 1959.

KRAUS, RICHARD. *Folk Dancing.* New York: Macmillan, 1962.

———. *A Pocket Guide of Folk and Square Dances and Singing Games for the Elementary School.* Englewood Cliffs, N.J.: Prentice-Hall, 1966.

KRITCHEVSKY, S., E. PRESCOTT, AND L. WALLING. *Planning Environments for Young Children— Physical Space.* Washington, D.C.: National Association for the Education of Young Children, 1969.

KROGMAN, N. M. *Child Growth.* Ann Arbor, Mich.: University of Michigan Press, 1972.

KUHN, T. *The Structure of Scientific Revolutions,* 2nd ed. Chicago: University of Chicago Press, 1970.

KULBITSKY, OLGA AND FRANK L. KALTMAN. *Teacher's Dance Handbook Number One, Kindergarten to Sixth Year.* Newark: Bluebird Publishing Company, 1960.

LABAN, R. *Modern Educational Dance,* 2nd ed. Revised by L. Ullman. New York: Frederick A. Praeger, Publishers, 1963.

LARSON, R. L. "Physical Activity and the Growth and Development of Bone and Joint Structures." *Physical Activity,* ed. G. L. Rarick. New York: Academic Press, 1973, 32–59.

LATCHAW, MARJORIE, AND JEAN PYATT. *Folk and Square Dances and Singing Games for Elementary Schools.* Englewood Cliffs, N.J.: Prentice-Hall, 1966.

LAWRENCE, CONNIE C. AND LAYNE C. HACKETT. *Water Learning: A New Adventure.* Palo Alto, Calif.: Peek Publications, 1975.

LAWTHER, J. *The Learning of Physical Skills.* Englewood Cliffs, N.J.: Prentice-Hall, 1968.

LOCKE, L. "From Research and the Discipline to Practice and the Profession: One More Time." Proceedings of NCPEAM/NAPECW Conference, Orlando, Florida, 1977.

———. AND D. LAMBDIN. "Teacher Behavior." In *Personalized Learning in Physical Education.* Reston, Va.: AAHPERD, 1976, 9–33.

LOGSDON, B., K. BARRETT, M. BROER, M. AMMONS, L. HALVERSON, AND M. ROBERTON. *Physical Education for Children: A Focus on the Teaching Process.* Philadelphia: Lea and Febiger, 1977.

LOHMAN, T. G. "Measurement of Body Composition in Children." *Journal of Physical Education, Recreation and Dance* 53 (1982): 67–70.

———. AND M. L. POLLOCK. "Which Caliper? How Much Training?" *Journal of Physical Education, Recreation and Dance* 52 (1981): 27–29.

LONDEREE, BEN R. ed. "Exercise Prescription For the Practitioner." *Journal of Physical Education, Recreation and Dance* 52 (1981): 35–46.

LOWREY, G. H. *Growth and Development of Children.* Chicago: Year Book Medical Publishers, 1978.

LUNDHOLM, JEAN K. AND MARY JO RUGGIERI. *Introduction to Synchronized Swimming.* Minneapolis, Minn.: Burgess, 1976.

MCCLENAGHAN, BRUCE A. AND DAVID L. GALLAHUE. *Fundamental Movement: A Developmental and Remedial Approach.* Philadelphia: Saunders, 1978.

MCGRAW, MYRTLE B. Swimming Behavior of the Human Infant. *Journal of Pediatrics* 15 (1939): 485–490.

MAGER, R. *Measuring Instructional Intent.* Belmont: Fearon Publishers, 1962.

MALINA, R. M. *Growth and Development—The First Twenty Years in Man.* Minneapolis, Minn.: Burgess, 1975.

———. "Environmentally Related Correlates of Motor Development and Performance During Infancy and Childhood." *A Textbook of Motor Development,* ed. C. B. Corbin. Dubuque, Iowa: Wm. C. Brown, 1980, 212–224.

MARTENS, R. *Social Psychology and Physical Activity.* New York: Harper & Row, Pub., 1975.

MARTINEK, T. J. "Aggressive Behavior In Children: New Concerns For the Physical Educator." In *Motor Skills: Theory Into Practice,* 3 (1979): 99–101.

MASON, BERNARD, S. *Dances and Stories of the American Indian.* New York: Ronald Press, 1944.

MAULDON, E. AND J. LAYSON. *Teaching Gymnastics.* London: MacDonald and Evans, Ltd., 1965.

———. AND H. B. REDFERN. *Games Teaching.* London: MacDonald and Evans, Ltd., 1969.

MAYER, J. *Overweight, Causes, Cost and Control.* Englewood Cliffs, N.J.: Prentice-Hall, 1968.

MERRILL, D. *Instructional Design: Readings.* Englewood Cliffs, N.J.: Prentice-Hall, 1971.

METZLER, M. "The Measurement of Academic Learning Time in Physical Education." Unpublished doctoral dissertation, Ohio State University, 1979.

MILLER, D. *Gods and Games.* New York: World Publishing, 1970.

MONSOUR, S., M. C. COHEN, AND P. E. LINDELL. *Rhythm in Music and Dance for Children.* Belmont, Calif.: Wadsworth Publishing Co., 1966.

MOORE, G. "Early Bird Gymnastics Program." *Journal of Health, Physical Education, Recreation, and Dance.* 50 (March 1979).

MORIARTY, PHILLIP E. *The Father and Son Swimming Book.* New York: Harper & Row Pub., 1970.

MORISON, R. *A Movement Approach to Educational Gymnastics.* London: J. M. Dent and Sons, Ltd., 1969.

———. *Educational Gymnastics.* Liverpool: I. M. Marsh College of Physical Education, 1956.

MOSSTON, M. *Teaching Physical Education.* Columbus, Ohio: Merrill Pub., 1966.

MURRAY, JOHN L. *Infaquatics: Teaching Kids To Swim.* West Point, N.Y.: Leisure Press, 1980.

MURRAY, RUTH L. *Dance in Elementary Education.* New York: Harper & Row Pub., 1975.

MYNATT, C. V. AND B. D. KAIMAN. *Folk Dancing for Students and Teachers.* Dubuque, Iowa: Wm. C. Brown, 1968.

NATIONAL RECREATION AND PARKS ASSOCIATION. "Proposed Safety Standard for Public Playground Equipment." Developed for the Consumer Product Safety Commission. Arlington, Va.: National Recreation and Park Association, 1976.

NEALE, R. *In Praise of Play.* New York: Harper & Row, 1969.

NELSON, ESTHER L. *Dancing Games for Children of All Ages.* New York: Sterling, 1973.

NEWMAN, VIRGINIA HUNT. *Teaching an Infant to Swim.* New York: Harcourt Brace Jovanovich, 1967.

———. *Teaching Young Children to Swim and Dive.* New York: Harcourt Brace Jovanovich, 1969.

New York State Physical Fitness Test for Boys and Girls Grades 4–12. Albany, N.Y.: State Education Department, 1966.

NIXON, J. AND L. LOCKE. "Research on Teaching Physical Education." In *Second Handbook of Research on Teaching,* ed. R. Travers. Chicago: Rand-McNally, 1973.

O'RAFFERTY, P. *The Irish Folk Dance Book.* London: Peterson Publications, Ltd., (with music).

ORLICK, T. *The Cooperative Sports and Gamesbook: Challenge With Competition.* New York: Pantheon Books, 1978.

PANGRAZZI, R. "Treating the Obese Child in the Public School Setting." *AAHPERD Research Consortium Symposium Papers* 1 (1978): 58.

PARIZKOVA, J. "Body Composition and Exercise During Growth and Development." *Physical Activity, Human Growth and Development,* ed. G. L. Ranrick. New York: Academic Press, 1973.

PIAGET, J. *Play, Dreams and Imitation in Childhood.* New York: Norton, 1951.

———. *The Moral Judgment of the Child.* New York: Free Press, 1968.

PRESTON, V. *A Handbook for Modern Educational*

Dance. London: MacDonald and Evans, Ltd., 1963.

PRUDDEN, BONNIE. *Your Baby Can Swim*. New York: Reader's Digest Press, 1974.

QUARTERMAN, J. "A Descriptive Analysis of Physical Education Teaching in the Elementary School." Unpublished doctoral dissertation, Ohio State University, 1977.

REIDER, N. "Preanalytic and Psychoanalytic Theories of Play and Games." In *Motivation in Play, Sport and Games*, ed. R. Slovenko and J. Knight, Springfield, Ill.: Chas. C. Thomas, 1967.

RICHARDSON, H. A. *Games for the Elementary School Grades*. Minneapolis: Minn.: Burgess, 1972.

RILEY, M. I. Games and Humanism. *JOPER* 46 (1975).

RINK, J. "Development of an Instrument for the Observation of Content Development in Physical Education." Unpublished doctoral dissertation, Ohio State University, 1979.

ROBERTON, MARY ANN AND LOLAS E. HALVERSON. "The Developing Child—His Changing Movement." *Physical Education for Children: A Focus on the Teaching Process*, ed. B. J. Logsdon. Philadelphia: Lea & Febiger, 1977, 24–67.

ROSENSHINE, B. "Evaluation of Classroom Instruction." *Review of Educational Research* 40 (1970) 61–64.

_____. "Recent Research on Teaching Behaviors and Student Achievement." *Journal of Teacher Education* 27 (Spring 1976).

ROYAL SCOTTISH COUNTRY DANCE SOCIETY, THE. *Twenty-Four Favorite Scottish Country Dances*. London: Peterson Publications, Ltd., (with music).

RUSHALL, B. AND D. SIEDENTOP. *The Development and Control of Behavior in Sport and Physical Education*. Philadelphia: Lea & Febiger, 1972.

RUSSELL, J. *Creative Dance in the Primary School*. London: MacDonald and Evans, Ltd., 1965.

_____. *Creative Movement and Dance for Children*, 2nd ed. London: MacDonald and Evans, Ltd., 1975.

SCHURR, E. *Movement Experiences for Children*, 3rd ed. Englewood Cliffs, N.J.: Prentice-Hall, 1980.

SELTZER, C. C. AND J. MAYER. A Simple Criterion of Obesity. *Postgraduate Medicine* 38 (1965): 101.

SHERRILL, C. "Postures." *Adapted Physical Education and Recreation*. Dubuque, Iowa: Wm. C. Brown, 1976, 77–120.

_____. *Adapted Physical Education and Recreation*. Dubuque, Iowa: Wm. C. Brown, 1981.

SIEDENTOP, D. *Developing Teaching Skills in Physical Education*, 2nd ed. Palo Alto, Calif.: Mayfield Publishing, 1982.

_____. *Physical Education: Introductory Analysis*, 3rd ed. Dubuque, Iowa: Wm. C. Brown, 1980.

_____. "Self Control." In *Personalized Learning in Physical Education*. Reston, Va.: AAHPERD, 1976.

_____, D. BIRDWELL, AND M. METZLER. "A Process Approach to Measuring Teaching Effectiveness in Physical Education." Unpublished paper, Ohio State University, School of Health, Physical Education, and Recreation, 1978.

SIMMONS, K. Physical Growth and Development. *Monographs of the Society for Research in Child Development*, 1944, IX, Serial No. 37, Number 1.

SIMMS, EDNA. *Teach Your Child to Swim*. London: Cox and Wyman, Ltd., 1963.

SINCLAIR, D. *Human Growth After Birth*. London: Oxford University Press, 1978.

SKIDELSKY, R. *English Progressive Schools*. Baltimore: Penguin Books, 1969.

SOCIETY FOR INTERNATIONAL FOLK DANCING. *A Selection of European Folk Dances*, 2 volumes. New York: Pergamon Press, 1964 (with music).

SPENCER, H. *Principles of Psychology*. New York: Appleton, 1873.

STANLEY, S. *Physical Education—A Movement Orientation*. Toronto: McGraw-Hill Co. of Canada Limited, 1969.

STEWART, M. "Teaching Behavior of Physical Education Teachers in the Natural Environment." *College Student Journal* 14 (Spring 1980) 76–82.

STONE, G. "The Play of Little Children." *Quest* 4 (April 1965) 23–31.

STRAUSS, R. AND K. L. DeOREO. *Assessment of Individualized Motor Skills*. Austin, Texas: Texas Education Agency, 1979.

STUART, FRANCES R. AND VIRGINIA L. GIBSON. *Rhythmic Activities: Series III*. Minneapolis, Minn.: Burgess, 1961.

TANNER, J. M. *Education and Physical Growth*. New York: International Universities Press, 1979.

_____. *Fetus into Man: From Conception to Maturity*. Cambridge, Mass.: Harvard University Press, 1978.

Time of Our Lives, The (16 mm., color, sound, 28 minutes). Association Films. Free rental. Reston, Va.: AAHPERD.

TIMMERMANS, CLAIRE. *How To Teach Your Baby To Swim*. New York: Stein and Day, 1975.

TOBITT, JANET. *Red Book of Singing Games and Dances from the Americas*. Evanston, Ill.: Summy-Birchard, n.d.

_____. *Yellow Book of Singing Games and Dances*

from Around the World. Evanston, Ill.: Summy-Birchard, n.d.

TUDDENHAM, R. D. AND M. M. SNYDER. *Physical Growth of California Boys and Girls from Birth to Eighteen Years.* Berkeley: University of California Press, 1954.

VICK, MARIE AND ROSANN MCLAUGHLIN COX. *A Collection of Dances for Children.* Minneapolis, Minn.: Burgess, 1970.

VICKERS, BETTY J. AND WILLIAM J. VINCENT. *Swimming.* Dubuque, Iowa: Wm. C. Brown, 1976.

Vigorous Physical Fitness Activities (16 mm., sound, color and black and white, 13 minutes). President's Council on Physical Fitness, Washington, D.C.

WAKEFIELD, E. E. *Folk Dancing in America.* New York: J. Lowell Pratt, 1966.

WERNER, PETER AND LISA RINI. *Perceptual Motor Development Equipment.* New York: John Wiley, 1976.

WERNER, PETER AND RICHARD SIMMONS. *Inexpensive Physical Education Equipment for Children.* Minneapolis, Minn.: Burgess, 1976.

WESSEL, JANET A., ed. *Planning Individualized Education Programs in Special Education With Examples From I Can.* Northbrook, Ill.: Hubbard Scientific Co., 1977.

WHITING, H. T. A. *Teaching the Persistent Non-Swimmer: A Scientific Approach.* New York: St. Martin's Press, 1970.

WICKSTROM, RALPH L. *Fundamental Motor Patterns.* Philadelphia: Lea & Febiger, 1977.

WILLIAMS, H. G. AND K. DEOREO. "Perceptual-Motor Development." *A Textbook of Motor Development,* ed. C. B. Corbin. Dubuque, Iowa: Wm. C. Brown, 1980, 135–196.

Your Child's Health and Fitness (16 mm., color, filmstrip, 33 and 1/3 r.p.m. record). Washington, D.C.: AAHPERD.

Youth Physical Fitness—A Basic School Program (16 mm., color and black and white, sound, 13 minutes). President's Council on Physical Fitness, Washington, D.C.

Youth Physical Fitness, A Report to the Nation (16 mm., color, sound, 28 minutes). Equitable Life Assurance Company, 1285 Avenue of the Americas, New York, New York 10019. Free loan.

Youth Physical Fitness: Suggestions for School Programs. Washington, D.C.: President's Council on Physical Fitness and Sports, 1973.

ZAICHKOWSKY, L. D., L. B. ZAICHKOWSKY, AND T. J. MARTINEK. *Growth and Development.* St. Louis, Mo.: C. V. Mosby, 1980.

ZOHMAN, L. R. *Beyond Diet: Exercise Your Way to Fitness and Heart Health.* Englewood Cliffs, N.J.: CPC International, 1974.

index